IMPLEMENTATION OF SUSTAINABLE DEVELOPMENT IN THE GLOBAL SOUTH

This open access book hinges on three broad but interlinked elements: sustainable development as a concept, sustainable development in the Global South, and implementation challenges.

The advent of the Sustainable Development Goals and the 2030 Agenda have contributed to the deepening of the concept of sustainable development within global and national policy schemes. The fact that sustainable development is crucial for our very survival is no longer a contested issue; rather, the key concern now is how this can be achieved equitably by reconciling competing priorities and concerns of the Global South and the Global North. While the Global South countries are eager to adopt and integrate the 2030 Agenda in their respective policy frameworks, local contexts are often at odds with the global model of sustainable development.

The book examines national capacities and institutional arrangements in countries in the Global South. It considers the challenges of integrating sustainable development in national policy frameworks. This includes the role, interactions, and inter-dependence of different branches of international law in, inter alia, protecting human rights, promoting access to justice, ensuring environmental justice, guaranteeing social protection, and safeguarding the rule of law for sustainable societies. This book explores the emerging patterns and processes of development projects that have either succeeded or failed, critical reflections on what has been achieved and whose interests the projects served, and the costs and benefits of particular interventions.

Implementation of Sustainable Development in the Global South

Strategies, Innovations and Challenges

Edited by
Sumaiya Khair
Shawkat Alam
and
Muhammad Ekramul Haque

•HART•
OXFORD • LONDON • NEW YORK • NEW DELHI • SYDNEY

HART PUBLISHING

Bloomsbury Publishing Plc

Kemp House, Chawley Park, Cumnor Hill, Oxford, OX2 9PH, UK

1385 Broadway, New York, NY 10018, USA

29 Earlsfort Terrace, Dublin 2, Ireland

HART PUBLISHING, the Hart/Stag logo, BLOOMSBURY and the Diana logo are trademarks of Bloomsbury Publishing Plc

First published in Great Britain 2024

A catalogue record for this book is available from the British Library.

A catalogue record for this book is available from the Library of Congress.

Library of Congress Control Number: 2024944196

ISBN: HB: 978-1-50996-375-1
ePDF: 978-1-50996-377-5
ePub: 978-1-50996-376-8

Typeset by Compuscript Ltd, Shannon

FOREWORD: A PLEA FOR FUNDAMENTAL SHIFTS AND A NEW MODEL OF DEVELOPMENT

It gives me immense pleasure to write the foreword for this important book, *Implementation of Sustainable Development in the Global South: Strategies, Innovations and Challenges*. I commend the volume editors – Professors Sumaiya Khair, Shawkat Alam and Muhammad Ekramul Haque – for conceiving the project and bringing together a range of voices to discuss challenges in realising sustainable development from a Global South perspective and explore solutions to these challenges.

The volume's focus on the Global South is significant. The term 'Global South' has a geographical connotation. But it denotes more than this:[1] there is a Global South in the Global North and vice versa. The term Global South depicts the idea of colonised, excluded or marginalised voices *anywhere* challenging the normalisation of political, economic and cultural hegemony of a few. We can see such Global South voices in the growing calls to reform the unjust international financial architecture, address development finance debt traps, stop dumping of hazardous waste into developing countries, demand changes to intellectual property regimes impacting access to life-saving medicines, share green technologies, abandon neo-colonial policies and practices, and seek compensation for climate change-related loss and damage. Only by making these transformative changes, the Global South will be able to realise sustainable development and in turn assert its rightful place in the world polity.

The timing of this book is also important for several reasons. First, the 2023 Sustainable Development Goals Report points to a grim picture about the lack of progress in realising the Sustainable Development Goals (SDGs) and in turn leave no one behind: 'An assessment of the around 140 targets for which trend data is available shows that about half of these targets are moderately or severely off track; and over 30 per cent have either seen no movement or regressed below the 2015 baseline.'[2] The Covid-19 pandemic and conflicts might have played their part in disrupting the plans to meet the SDGs. However, there are more deep-rooted and systemic reasons for such a dismal report card, such as continued push

[1] See Aude Darnal, '"Global South" is Real. Deal with It' (*World Politics Review*, 28 September 2023), www.worldpoliticsreview.com/global-south-countries-term-brics/, accessed 6 April 2024.

[2] United Nations, *The Sustainable Development Goals Report 2023: Towards a Rescue Plan for People and Planet* (United Nations, 2023) 4.

for accumulated economic growth, business models profiteering from exploitation of people and the planet, lack of meaningful participation of individuals and communities (especially marginalised or vulnerable voices) in decision-making processes, trade and investment regimes aimed to favour the rich, limited financial and technological support, and unfair or unaccountable governance systems.

Second, many developing countries are trapped in an unprecedented debt crisis. The number of developing countries facing high levels of debt – that is, more than 60 per cent of the GDP – has increased from 22 countries in 2011 to 59 countries in 2022.[3] Developing countries spent 'a record $443.5 billion to service their external public and publicly guaranteed debt in 2022'.[4] Consequently, today '3.3 billion people live in countries that spend more on interest payments than on education or health'.[5] The current debt crisis is perhaps reflective of 'a continued adherence to neoliberal ideology in macroeconomic policy making and to the punitive subordination of developing countries in debt distress'.[6]

Third, the world leaders are currently negotiating the Pact for the Future[7] to be adopted at the Summit of the Future in September 2024.[8] This provides a timely opportunity to reinforce the need to find multilateral solutions for a better tomorrow for both present and future generations. Although the UN Secretary General's Policy Briefs offer some glimpses of what fundamental shifts are required,[9] there is a risk that the Pact may end up offering more of the same empty rhetorical vision without a genuine agreement to bring those shifts.

There are many reasons why the goal of securing sustainable development is becoming a mirage for many states and their peoples, especially in the Global South. In my vision report presented to the UN Human Rights Council in September 2023, I argued that states both in the Global North and the Global South should pay greater attention to realising the right to development – not merely economic development, but a holistic vision of development encompassing economic, social, political and cultural facets.[10] Pursuing these four facets of the right to development provides a pathway to realise not only all human rights but also achieve inclusive and sustainable development.

[3] ibid 6–7.

[4] World Bank Group, 'Developing Countries Paid Record $443.5 Billion on Public Debt in 2022' (*World Bank Group*, 13 December 2023), www.worldbank.org/en/news/press-release/2023/12/13/developing-countries-paid-record-443-5-billion-on-public-debt-in-2022, accessed 6 April 2024.

[5] UN Global Crisis Response Group, *A World of Debt: A Growing Burden to Global Prosperity* (July 2023) 4.

[6] See AM Fischer and S Storm, 'The Return of Debt Crisis in Developing Countries: Shifting or Maintaining Dominant Development Paradigms?' (2023) 54 *Development and Change*.

[7] See United Nations, 'Pact for the Future: Zero Draft', www.un.org/en/summit-of-the-future/pact-for-the-future-zero-draft, accessed 6 April 2024.

[8] See United Nations, 'Summit of the Future', www.un.org/en/summit-of-the-future, accessed 6 April 2024.

[9] See United Nations, 'Policy Briefs', www.un.org/en/common-agenda/policy-briefs, accessed 6 April 2024.

[10] S Deva, 'Reinvigorating the Right to Development: A Vision for the Future' (United Nations Human Rights Office of the High Commissioner 2023) A/HRC/54/27.

Equally important are the four overarching principles of the right to development – self-determination, intersectionality, intergenerational equity and fair distribution – which we can derive from the 1986 Declaration on the Right to Development and other related instruments.[11] For example, respecting the principle of intergenerational equity would require taking seriously the human rights of future generations,[12] while the principle of fair distribution would demand addressing inequalities within as well as among states (including through international cooperation).

The world is at a crossroads. We need a new model of development because the current model 'is neither inclusive nor sustainable: it is focused on cumulative economic development, does not ensure the participation of people and ignores the planetary boundaries'.[13] I believe that states, UN agencies, development banks, businesses, civil society organisations and other actors should embrace a model of 'planet-centred participatory development'.[14] This model of development embodies two key departures from existing approaches of development such as sustainable development, development-based human rights and people-centred development. It adopts an ecosystem approach comprising people, biodiversity and the environment. Integrating this approach will require reimagining the goal of 'leaving no one behind' to include not only human beings but also other living beings such as plants and animals. Moreover, all development policies, programmes and projects should be developed through an active, free and meaningful participation of people in an inclusive manner. Adopting such a bottom up approach would mean that development would look very different based on diverse aspirations of different communities.

It is my hope that this volume will stimulate academic discussion and inform policy-making around sustainable development in years to come. Readers in all world regions should enjoy reading various chapters in this volume.

Professor Surya Deva
UN Special Rapporteur on the right to development
3 April 2024

[11] ibid, paras 10–14. The other relevant instruments are the Rio Declaration on Environment and Development, the Vienna Declaration and Programme of Action, the Addis Ababa Action Agenda of the Third International Conference on Financing for Development, the Beijing Declaration and Platform for Action, the 2030 Agenda for Sustainable Development and the Paris Agreement.

[12] See 'Maastricht Principles on the Human Rights of Future Generations' (*Rights of Future Generations – The Principles*, July 2023), www.rightsoffuturegenerations.org/the-principles, accessed 6 April 2024.

[13] Deva (n 10) para 63.

[14] ibid paras 64–68.

PREFACE

Introducing the Vision

In 2015, the United Nations unveiled the Agenda for Sustainable Development 2030, a bold framework aimed at addressing the most pressing global challenges. With its 17 Sustainable Development Goals (SDGs), the agenda calls for unprecedented global solidarity to eradicate poverty, achieve equality, and protect our planet. This commitment to 'leave no one behind' underscores an inclusive approach to development, emphasising the importance of incorporating every individual in the journey toward sustainability.

While the SDGs are universal, their implementation raises significant debates, especially between the Global North and South. The diverse realities of countries in the Global South – marked by varying stages of development, capacities and policy priorities – necessitate a differentiated approach to the SDGs. This book investigates the experiences of these countries, exploring how they navigate the complex landscape of sustainable development amidst myriad challenges.

The Core of the Book

At the heart of this work lies an in-depth exploration into how countries within the Global South navigate the intricate path of sustainable development. It meticulously examines the incorporation of the Sustainable Development Goals (SDGs) into national policies, evaluates the readiness and capabilities of states, and assesses the effectiveness of existing institutional frameworks. Through a critical lens, this book reflects on both the triumphs and setbacks encountered in the realm of sustainable development, offering a comprehensive review of the strategies deployed, the obstacles faced and the valuable lessons learned. It illuminates the lessons learned and best practices identified, exploring the shifting viewpoints and dynamics, the repercussions of sustainable development on global politics, its historical colonial legacies, current debates and its crucial role as a development model for the Global South.

Additionally, this volume undertakes a thorough investigation into how different branches of international law intersect with sustainable development efforts, addressing critical issues like human rights protection, environmental justice and adherence to the rule of law. It examines the intricacies of defending human rights, facilitating access to justice, ensuring environmental fairness, providing social safety nets, and upholding the rule of law as pillars for building sustainable societies. This includes a look at the challenges, infractions, responsibilities, compromises and corrective measures associated with these efforts.

The book encapsulates the emerging patterns and processes of development projects that have either succeeded or failed; critical reflections on what have been achieved and whose interests they served; and costs and benefits of interventions. It examines the economic, environmental and social challenges to sustainable development in the Global South, including the implications for governments and other stakeholders, trade, investment and sustainable development, financing sustainable development, technological innovation, the role and impact of public-private partnerships, strategic interventions and the way forward.

Intended for a wide audience of scholars, researchers, development practitioners, policy planners, NGOs, teachers and students at the national, regional and international levels, practitioners and policymakers, this book aims to enrich the discourse on sustainable development, offering a repository of knowledge and a source of inspiration for future reform agenda.

Sumaiya Khair, *Dhaka, Bangladesh*
Shawkat Alam, *Sydney, NSW, Australia*
Muhammad Ekramul Haque, *Dhaka, Bangladesh*
June 2024

ACKNOWLEDGEMENTS

Our journey in constructing this volume has been enriching and illuminating, made possible by the invaluable contributions of many.

We extend our deepest gratitude to Professor Surya Deva for gracing this book with a thought-provoking foreword, despite his demanding schedule.

To each author who has enriched this volume with their insightful chapters, we offer our heartfelt thanks.

Our sincere appreciation goes to Hart Publishing for their unwavering support and commitment to bringing this work to fruition.

Lastly, we are forever indebted to our families, whose firm support and inspiration have been our guiding light.

This book is a testament to the collective wisdom and collaborative spirit of all those committed to the cause of sustainable development, particularly in the Global South. We hope it serves as a beacon of knowledge, sparking further exploration and action towards a more sustainable and equitable world.

CONTENTS

NOTES ON CONTRIBUTORS

Shawkat Alam, a Professor at Macquarie University, Australia, is renowned for his expertise in International and Environmental Law, with a distinguished scholarship in trade and sustainable development. His research focuses on improving legal, policy, and institutional frameworks in developing economies to support sustainability. His scholarly works, including *International Environmental Law and the Global South* (Cambridge, 2015), alongside contributions to top-tier journals, underscore his scholarship. His leadership has contributed to capacity-building for sustainable development, where his efforts have catalysed widespread community outreach and partnerships.

Christoph Antons is Honorary Professor at the Macquarie Law School, Macquarie University, Sydney, Australia. He is also Senior Fellow at the Center for Development Research (ZEF), University of Bonn; Senior Associate at the Centre for Indonesian Law, Islam and Society (CILIS), University of Melbourne. His latest book publication is *Intellectual Property in South East Asia* (Edward Elgar, 2023, co-editor with Michael Blakeney).

Elena Blanco is an Associate Professor of International Economic Law at the Law School, University of the West of England (Bristol), UK. Her work sits at the intersection of public and private international law and considers the multiple and interconnected injustices of the international legal architecture and the pervasive legacy of colonialism.

Klaus Bosselmann is Professor of Law and Founding Director of the New Zealand Centre for Environmental Law at the University of Auckland. He has done consulting work for the United Nations, the European Union and the governments of Germany and New Zealand. He is the author of 16 books and 150 articles on international environmental law, global governance and ecological law and chair, inter alia, of the Ecological Law and Governance Association, the Earth Trusteeship Initiative and the Global Ecological Integrity Group.

Philippe Cullet is a Professor of International and Environmental Law at SOAS University of London and a Visiting Professor at the National Law University, Delhi. His publications reflect his engagement with international law and policy, the Global South and India. His work focuses on natural resources, development, water and sanitation, climate change, rights of nature and social rights. He is the lead editor of the *Oxford Handbook of Environmental and Natural Resources Law in India* (Oxford University Press, 2024).

Paolo Galizzi is a Clinical Professor of Law and Director of the Sustainable Development Legal Initiative (SDLI) and the Corporate and Social Responsibility Program at the Leitner Center for International Law and Justice at Fordham University School of Law in New York City. Professor Galizzi has been actively engaged in teaching and scholarship and the practical application of international rules in environmental law, climate change law and policy, development, and human rights. He has published extensively in these areas and taught in universities in Italy, the United Kingdom, Ghana and currently in the United States.

Muhammad Ekramul Haque, a Professor of Comparative Constitutional Law at the University of Dhaka, obtained his PhD in Constitutional Law and International Law from Monash University, Australia. He is a Distinguished Senior Research Fellow in the Constitutional Studies Programme at the University of Texas at Austin, USA. He is the State Volume Editor of *Bangladesh*, in the *Encyclopedia of Public International Law in Asia* (Brill, 2021). He co-edited *The Constitutional Law of Bangladesh: Progression and Transformation at its 50th Anniversary* (Springer, 2023).

Jesmul Hasan is a Programme Specialist and the Country Lead for the United Nations Capital Development Fund (UNCDF) in Bangladesh. He has 27 years of experience working in the social development sector, human rights, journalism, and teaching. A lawyer by training, he has a Master's in Public Administration from the Harvard Kennedy School.

Md Rizwanul Islam is a Professor of Law and a member of the Center for Peace Studies, North South University; PhD, Macquarie University; LLM (Intellectual Property & Information Technology Law), National University of Singapore; LLB (Honours), University of Dhaka. He has published extensively on international law, world trade law, and the legal system of Bangladesh.

Stellina Jolly is an Associate Professor at the Faculty of Legal Studies, South Asian University (SAU), India. She is a Visiting Senior Research Associate with the Centre for Emerging Countries in Private International Law at the University of Johannesburg. She is a Fulbright Scholar with the University of San Francisco and a recipient of the International Visitors Leadership Program (IVLP). Her publications include *Indian Private International Law* (Hart, 2021), *Climate Refugees in South Asia: Protection Under International Legal Standards and State Practices in South Asia* (Springer, 2019) and *Private International Law: South Asian States' Practice* (Springer, 2017).

Sumaiya Khair is a Professor of Law at the University of Dhaka, Bangladesh. Her research interests include human rights, access to justice, legal empowerment, refugees, migration, governance, labour standards, child rights and gender issues. She regularly contributes to the Bangladesh State Practice section of the *Asian Yearbook of International Law* (Brill). She is the Editor of the *Dhaka University Law Journal*. She advises Transparency International Bangladesh, an anti-graft organisation, on its policy, programme and fund-raising activities.

Mushtaq H Khan is a Professor of Economics at SOAS University of London and head of the SOAS Anti-Corruption Evidence (SOAS-ACE) Research Partnership Consortium. He pioneered the analysis of political settlements as a framework for the analysis of institutions and policies and has published widely on institutions, governance, anti-corruption, industrial policy and policy implementation. His research countries include Bangladesh, Nepal, India, Pakistan, Sri Lanka, Thailand, Vietnam, Palestine and Tanzania.

Ernie Ko is Associate Professor and Chair of the General Educations Center at National Taiwan University of Arts. He was elected twice (2017–2020, 2020–2023) as a Member of the Membership Accreditation Committee (MAC), Transparency International. He is a co-founder of Rui-Bin Arts and Character Education Camp for underprivileged children in Taiwan since 2012.

Michelle Lim is an Associate Professor at the Yong Pung How School of Law, Singapore Management University, Singapore. Her scholarship occurs at the intersection of biodiversity and sustainable livelihoods. Michelle has experience in South, South-East and Central Asia and East Africa. Michelle was a Fellow of the Global Assessment of the Intergovernmental Science-Policy Platform on Biodiversity and Ecosystem Services (IPBES) and an author of the IPBES-IPCC Co-Sponsored Workshop Report on Biodiversity and Climate Change.

Abdul Paliwala is an Emeritus Professor of Law at Warwick University, United Kingdom. He has previously lectured at Queen's University of Belfast, University of Dar es Salaam and University of Papua New Guinea. He has been involved in Warwick's Law in Development programme since its inception in 1981 and his most recent works on the subject are (edited jointly with Professor Sam Adelman) *The Limits of Law and Development* (Routledge, 2020) and *Beyond Law and Development* (Routledge, 2022).

Mustafizur Rahman is a Distinguished Fellow at the Centre for Policy Dialogue, a leading civil society think tank in Bangladesh. Previously, he had taught at the University of Dhaka, Bangladesh. He has written extensively on the Bangladesh economy, the multilateral trading system and interests of low-income countries, and regional cooperation in southern Asia. His works in these and other areas have been published by Routledge, Springer, Palgrave Macmillan and other reputed publishing houses, as well as in journals at home and abroad. He has been a member of the Panel of Economists for preparing Five Year Plans and Perspective Plans for Bangladesh.

Habib Zafarullah is an adjunct professor at the University of New England, Australia. His areas of academic interest are democratic governance, comparative bureaucracy, public policy and administration, and international development and he has published extensively in these areas. Some of his recent books include *Open Government and Freedom of Information in Asia* (2023), *Handbook of Development Policy* (2021), *Colonial Bureaucracies* (2014), and *Managing Development in a Globalized World* (2012). His works have appeared in international peer-reviewed journals and several edited volumes.

PART I

Introduction

1

Reimagining Routes to Sustainability: Pathways, Obstacles and Innovations in the Global South

SUMAIYA KHAIR, SHAWKAT ALAM
AND MUHAMMAD EKRAMUL HAQUE

I. The Imperative of Sustainable Development

The United Nations Agenda for Sustainable Development 2030 presented the world with an ambitious development framework that seeks to eradicate poverty and hunger, ensure that all people can live a decent life based on equality, safety and security, build strong institutions, and save the planet from the effects of climate change and environmental degradation. Comprised of 17 lofty goals, the 2030 Agenda has brought in a qualitative shift by pledging to 'leave no one behind', which essentially promotes inclusiveness in every aspect of development.

The paramount importance of sustainable development for the continuation of human existence is universally acknowledged. However, the discourse surrounding the methodologies for achieving such development in an equitable manner, especially within the polarised landscape of our contemporary world, presents a complex challenge. This introductory chapter lays the groundwork for a critical examination of sustainable development policies, processes and practices at both national and regional levels, with a particular focus on the experiences of states in the Global South. These states are at the forefront of innovation and strategic planning to address and surmount the vulnerabilities and adversities obstructing their path to sustainable development.

Sustainable development, as a concept, embodies a multifaceted approach to progress, balancing the needs of present and future generations within the limits of the Earth's ecosystem. It is a dynamic process that necessitates adaptability, resilience and a commitment to equity and justice. The Global South, a region often facing the brunt of environmental degradation, socio-economic disparities and political instability, serves as a critical lens through which the challenges and intricacies of implementing sustainable development policies can be examined.

The experiences of these nations reveal a rich tapestry of strategies employed to navigate the obstacles inherent in pursuing sustainability.

This book delves into three interconnected aspects that are critical to understanding and advancing sustainable development: the conceptual framework of sustainable development; its application in the context of the Global South; and the multifarious challenges encountered in its implementation. A critical analysis of these dimensions allows for a comprehensive understanding of the complexities and nuances involved in translating the ideals of sustainable development into tangible outcomes.

First, the integration of sustainable development into national policy frameworks is scrutinised, highlighting the extent to which these policies encapsulate the principles of sustainability. The analysis extends to examining national capacities and institutional arrangements, focusing on preparedness, political leadership, governance, financial resources, coordination, data management, partnerships and stakeholder engagement. This segment also explores the limitations, challenges and opportunities faced by states, especially in the Global South, drawing lessons from good practices.

Second, the interplay and interdependence of various branches of international law in promoting sustainable development are critically assessed. This involves exploring how international legal frameworks contribute to development and investment, protecting human rights, ensuring access to justice, environmental justice, social protection and the rule of law. The challenges of implementation in the Global South, alongside the liabilities, breaches, trade-offs and remedies involved, are thoroughly analysed to understand the legal and ethical dimensions of sustainable development.

Last, the emerging patterns and processes of development projects across the Global South are critically reflected upon. This section evaluates the success and failures of specific interventions, analysing their achievements, the interests they served, and the costs and benefits associated with them. Such critical reflections offer insights into the practical realities of implementing sustainable development initiatives, thus providing valuable lessons for future endeavours.

In sum, this chapter sets the stage for a nuanced exploration of the intricate journey towards sustainable development in the Global South. Through a critical examination of the policies, practices and challenges, the book aims to contribute to the ongoing discourse on sustainable development, offering perspectives and insights that can guide future policy decisions, strategies and actions.

II. Conceptual Framework of Sustainable Development

Sustainable development has emerged as an innovative paradigm aimed at fostering economic growth while safeguarding environmental integrity. The seminal Brundtland Report of 1987, 'Our Common Future', marked a pivotal moment in the evolution of international environmental law towards embracing sustainable development principles.[1] This report articulates sustainable development as the process of meeting current needs without jeopardising the capacity of future generations to satisfy their own needs. Highlighting the critical needs of the global poor and the challenges in addressing these needs sustainably, it outlines a framework for development strategies that both developed and developing nations should pursue. Since its publication, the term 'sustainable development' has gained widespread popularity, resonating with a diverse array of stakeholders including governments, economic forums, aid agencies and development practitioners. 'Our Common Future' aimed to harmonise the pursuit of development with environmental considerations; ensuring that both objectives could coexist sustainably,[2] and proposing that the essence of sustainability lies in ensuring that current development does not impair future generations' ability to meet their needs.[3] Consequently, the discourse around development, both in the Global North and South, has been reframed to emphasise not only ecological considerations but also the broader spectrum of human needs, desires and priorities. This shift has reinforced the concept of development while recasting sustainability in a more human-centric light.[4]

III. The Millennium Development Goals and the Sustainable Development Goals

A. The Millennium Development Goals

In 2000, countries signed up to the Millennium Development Goals (MDGs) following the adoption of the Millennium Declaration at the Millennium Summit of the United Nations. The MDGs broadly focused on social, economic and political rights, human capital and infrastructure. They emphasised the role of developed countries in assisting developing countries to achieve the goals by 2015 and helped forge a global consensus on poverty reduction and human development. With the launch of the MDGs, the world leaders entered into a global commitment to ensure that all people are freed from abject poverty and hardship and that they are assured of a robust future. Based on inspiring framework of eight goals and

[1] P Sands, *Principles of International Environmental Law* 2nd edn (Cambridge University Press, 2003) 10.

[2] W Sachs, 'Environment' in W Sachs (ed), *The Development Dictionary: A Guide to Knowledge as Power* (Zed Books, 2001) 26.

[3] World Commission on Environment and Development, 'Our Common Future' (Oxford University Press, 1987) 8.

[4] LK Caldwell, 'The Concept of Sustainability: A Critical Approach' in J Lemons, L Westra and R Goodland (eds), *Ecological Sustainability and Integrity: Concepts and Approaches* (Kluwer Academic Publishers, 1998) 1, 254.

wide-ranging practical steps, the MDGs helped to lift more than one billion people out of extreme poverty, to make inroads against hunger, to enable more girls to attend school, and to protect the planet by generating new and innovative partnerships and by galvanising public opinion, among other things.[5]

While the MDGs placed people and their well-being at the forefront and reshaped decision-making in developed and developing countries alike, the framework yielded mixed and, in certain cases, uneven results in countries across the world.[6] Although in developing countries the proportion of people living on less than $1.25 a day reportedly dropped from 47 per cent in 1990 to 22 per cent in 2010 and about 700 million fewer people lived in conditions of extreme poverty in 2010 compared to 1990,[7] the results fell short of global expectations, manifest from the continued threats to the environment and bio-diversity, and persisting poverty and inequalities. The achievements of the MDGs varied significantly around the world, as illustrated by the disparate rates of extreme poverty reduction across different regions:

- Southeastern Asia surpassed its extreme poverty reduction target by 16 per cent;
- Southern Asia outperformed its goal by 12.5 per cent;
- Northern Africa barely met the target with a reduction of about 1.2 per cent;
- Sub-Saharan Africa lagged considerably, falling 12.5 per cent short of reaching the extreme poverty reduction goal.[8]

A brief literature review reveals a number of factors that have caused major setbacks in achieving the MDGs. A health professional, for instance, questioned whether the 'world would be better off with or without the MDGs and similar UN-sponsored, time-limited, quantitative development goals?' He on to observe that, the answer to this question should be guided by two key considerations: one, 'whether such goals are interpreted so as to advance the dignity and well-being of the large number of people who live in extreme poverty, and two, whether such goals advance the reputation of the UN and the global development establishment'; he believed that the MDGs were confronted with risks on both fronts.[9] One of the most commonly cited concerns was the process through which the MDGs were developed involved only a few countries, which

[5] VN Guibou, 'Critical Analysis of the Millennium Development Goals (MDGs)' [2017] *SSRN Electronic Journal*.

[6] ibid.

[7] United Nations, *World Economic and Social Survey 2013: Sustainable Development Challenges* (United Nations Publication, 2013) iv.

[8] Borgen Project, 'MDG Failures: Shortcomings of the Millennium Development Goals' (*The Borgen Project*, 19 November 2015), borgenproject.org/mdg-failures/, accessed 6 April 2024.

[9] A Attaran, 'An Immeasurable Crisis? A Criticism of the Millennium Development Goals and Why They Cannot Be Measured' (2005) 2(10) *Policy Forum*. (The Policy Forum is a platform for health policy makers around the world to discuss challenges and opportunities for improving health care in their societies.)

unilaterally decided on the choice of goals with very little involvement of developing countries.[10] Some believed that, given that the MDGs were primarily determined by the OECD countries and international donor agencies, the 'domestication' of these internationalised goals was problematic as they were seemingly detached from the ground realities and rooted in a one-size-fits-all formula with multiple objectives. Indeed, if the goals were to be realistically achieved, efforts ought to have been invested to set them in context first and accordingly internalised in different local/country situations.[11] The unevenness in progress has also been attributed varyingly to disparate socio-economic conditions, conflict and political instability, and limited access to social protection and basic services by people living in poverty. Civil society groups protested the omission of inequality, weak goals on global 'partnership' that lacked quantitative targets, the lack of ambition in the targets,[12] and the failure to emphasise on good governance, transparency, participation and human rights,[13] which together formed the basis of the Millennium Declaration, and all of which were critical for achieving the goals. Critics maintained that the MDGs projected 'a simplistic vision of meeting basic needs for all without recognizing the root causes of poverty embedded in power relations and exacerbated by current economic models of neoliberal globalization that prioritize corporate profit over human rights'.[14]

The gaps left in the wake of the implementation of the MDGs also feature in the UN Report on the MDGs in 2015, which acknowledges that despite the successes of the MDGs, the poorest and the most vulnerable people are being left behind.[15] According to this report, gender inequality persists, gaps exist between the poorest and the richest households and between urban and rural areas, climate change and environmental degradation undermine the progress achieved and the poor suffer the most, conflicts remain the biggest threat to human development, and millions of poor people still live in poverty and hunger without access to basic services.[16]

[10] M Fehling, BD Nelson and S Venkatapuram, 'Limitations of the Millennium Development Goals: A Literature Review' (2013) 8(10) *Global Public Health* 1118.

[11] See ME Villarino, 'Sounding off on the Shortcomings of the Millennium Development Goals' *Devex* (2 October 2014), www.devex.com/news/sounding-off-on-the-shortcomings-of-the-millennium-development-goals-84433, accessed 6 April 2024; Abbyragan, 'Limitations of the MDGs' (*Inclusive Sustainable Development*, 6 November 2017) disabilitydevelopment.com/2017/11/06/limitations-of-the-mdgs/, accessed 6 April 2024.

[12] See S Fukuda-Parr, 'From the Millennium Development Goals to the Sustainable Development Goals: Shifts in Purpose, Concept, and Politics of Global Goal-Setting for Development' in K Conca and GD Dabelko (eds), *Green Planet Blues: Critical Perspectives on Global Environmental Politics* (Routledge, 2016).

[13] United Nations Office of the High Commissioner for Human Rights, *Claiming the Millennium Development Goals: A Human Rights Approach* (United Nations Publications, 2008) vii.

[14] See Fukuda-Parr (n 12).

[15] United Nations, *The Millennium Development Goals Report* (UNDP, 2015) 8.

[16] ibid.

B. The Sustainable Development Goals (SDGs): Continuing the Legacy of the Millennium Development Goals (MDGs)

Acknowledging the gains and gaps of the implementation of the MDGs, the UN had already begun to contemplate the next steps even before the conclusion of the MDGs. To this end, the UN Conference on Sustainable Development in 2012 constituted an inter-governmental working group, which was tasked with the formulation of a set of development goals to succeed the MDGs post 2015.[17] The working group released a draft set of SDGs in 2014, which was subsequently adopted as the Agenda 2030.[18]

The advent of the Agenda 2030 or the Sustainable Development Goals (SDGs) has contributed to deepening the concept of sustainable development within global and national policy schemes. Unlike the MDGs which targeted only developing economies, the SDGs apply to all countries, whether rich, middle-income or poor, and are expected to be implemented by home-grown implementation frameworks. Learning from the MDGs experience, world leaders recognised that there was a need for collective, long-term efforts, harnessed by strong political will, to address the root causes of poverty and inequalities and to efficiently integrate the economic, social, cultural and environmental aspects of sustainable development.

The SDGs represent a significant evolution from their predecessors, the MDGs, in several key aspects. First, the SDGs were formulated through a highly collaborative process that included both middle-income and low-income countries, and were the result of detailed international negotiations. In contrast to the MDGs, the SDGs adopt a more inclusive approach, with specific targets aimed at eliminating discrimination, enhancing the inclusion of persons with disabilities, and addressing the needs of people in vulnerable situations. Furthermore, the SDGs are firmly grounded in human rights principles and standards, emphasising the importance of tackling systemic discrimination and disadvantage. Another distinctive feature is the active engagement of the private sector, recognised for its critical role in bolstering and complementing global development initiatives. Furthermore, the SDGs offer broader opportunities for civil society participation, promoting local action through partnerships.[19]

Seen holistically, the SDGs 'epitomise a rights-based approach to a transformative, integrated and inclusive development paradigm built on economic, social

[17] See JH Knox, 'Human Rights, Environmental Protection, and the Sustainable Development Goals' (2015) 24 *Washington International Law Journal* 517, 518.

[18] See Open Working Group Proposal on Sustainable Development Goals available at 'Open Working Group Proposal for Sustainable Development Goals' (*United Nations Sustainable Development Goals Knowledge Platform*) sustainabledevelopment.un.org/index.php?page=view&type=400&nr=1579&menu=1300, accessed 6 April 2024.

[19] JS Clarke, '7 Reasons the SDGs will be better than the MDGs' *The Guardian* (26 September 2015), www.theguardian.com/global-development-professionals-network/2015/sep/26/7-reasons-sdgs-will-be-better-than-the-mdgs, accessed 6 April 2024.

and environmental pillars'.[20] In fact, the concept was first acknowledged by the International Court of Justice in 1997, when Judge Weeramantry observed that sustainable development is a 'principle with normative value' which constitutes 'a part of modern international law by reason not only of its inescapable logical necessity, but also by reason of its wide and general acceptance by the global community'.[21] Accordingly, the concept has made its way into several international and national legal instruments, highlighting concerns that go beyond simple economic growth to encompass a 'wide range of objectives, including protection of the natural environment, promotion of sustainable economic growth, and achievement of social development'.[22] As such, international law of sustainable development is by no means self-sufficient but cuts across other branches of international law.

C. The North–South Divide on Sustainable Development

The SDGs aim to address the needs of both developed and developing countries, yet discussions on sustainable development implementation are dominated by the differing priorities and concerns of the Global North and South. This division is characterised by philosophical conflicts over environmental protection, assigning responsibility for environmental degradation, and balancing development with environmental conservation. These disagreements have hindered negotiations and compliance with existing environmental treaties.[23] Environmental challenges now span wider geographical and temporal scopes, introducing moral considerations that encompass both current and future generations. The concept of intergenerational equity, which underlies sustainable development, emphasises the need to balance the interests of present and future generations.[24] This principle was highlighted in the Stockholm and Rio Declarations and integrated into various treaties, such as the preamble of the Convention on Biological Diversity, which mentions the conservation and sustainable use of biological diversity for the benefit of future

[20] D Bhattacharya and S Jahan, 'Initial Challenges to SDG Implementation: Regional Trends and Country Experiences' available at 'Global State of the SDGs: Three Layers of Critical Action' (*Southern Voice – Southern Perspectives. Global Debates*, 28 February 2020), southernvoice.org/state-of-the-sdgs/, accessed 6 April 2024.

[21] *Gabčíkovo-Nagymaros Project (Hungary v Slovakia)* (Justice Weeramantry, Separate Opinion) [1997] *ICJ Reports* 228.

[22] I Iqbal and C Pierson, 'A North-South Struggle: Political and Economic Obstacles to Sustainable Development' (2017) 16(2) *Sustainable Development Law and Policy* 16, 17.

[23] See generally R Anand, *International Environmental Justice: A North-South Dimension* (Routledge, 2004); P Birnie and others, *International Law and the Environment* 3rd edn (Oxford University Press, 2009) 2–31; P Sands and others, *Principles of International Environmental Law* (2012) 22–49; DB Hunter, 'International Environmental Law: Sources, Principles, and Innovations' in PG Harris (ed), *Routledge Handbook of Global Environmental Politics* (Routledge, 2010) 124, 124–37.

[24] M Jacobs, 'Sustainable Development as a Contested Concept' in A Dobson (ed), *Fairness and Futurity: Essays on Sustainability and Environmental Justice* (Oxford University Press, 1999) 21, 26.

generations.[25] However, a tension exists between the need to restrict development to protect future interests and the South's desire to achieve the development levels of the North. This conflict is encapsulated in the 'right to development', as recognised by the United Nations Declaration on the Right to Development and the Rio Declaration[26] as an important element in achieving sustainable development. While the Rio Declaration stressed the importance of development, it did not explicitly focus on 'sustainable development'[27] presenting a challenge in harmonising these competing priorities without establishing a hierarchy, but rather seeking interconnectedness.

To bridge this gap, the principle of intragenerational equity has been introduced, acknowledging the link between ecological degradation and underdevelopment. It addresses the inability to safeguard future generations' equity without first resolving current global issues such as poverty, hunger and lack of sanitation. Intragenerational equity, correlating with the 'right to development', is crucial for achieving fairness across generations.[28] The Convention on Biological Diversity asserts the significance of present generations' interests alongside those of the future, stating that 'the economic and social development and poverty eradication are the first and overriding priorities of developing countries'.[29] While consensus on the interplay between intergenerational equity, the right to development, and intragenerational equity has led to their inclusion in treaty preambles and articles, the main challenge remains in their practical application. This underscores the complexity of achieving sustainable development that equitably addresses the needs and rights of both present and future generations across the globe.

The divergent priorities of the North and South significantly influence the global discourse on sustainable development. The North has historically highlighted environmental issues such as ozone depletion and species extinction, while the South has focused on addressing immediate local concerns, including poverty alleviation, food security, access to clean water, and sanitation.[30] This difference in focus underscores a broader debate about responsibility and approaches to global environmental challenges. Although the South has pursued the North to take responsibility for its role in triggering climate change, the North has reluctantly conceded to the principle of common, but differentiated, responsibility, informed only by its superior technical and financial resources, without acknowledging its contributions in furthering these crises.[31]

[25] Convention on Biological Diversity (opened for signature 5 June 1992, entered into force 29 December 1993) 1760 UNTS 79 (CBD Preamble).

[26] UNGA RES 41/128 (1986) Annex UN Doc A/RES/41/128.

[27] D Hunter, J Salzman and D Zaelke, *International Environmental Law and Policy* 3rd edn (Foundation Press, 2007) 480.

[28] A Marong, 'From Rio to Johannesburg: Reflections on the Role of International Legal Norms in Sustainable Development' (2004) 16 *Georgetown International Environmental Law Review* 59.

[29] Convention on Biological Diversity (n 25).

[30] See Anand (n 23) 6; CG Gonzalez, 'Beyond Eco-Imperialism: An Environmental Justice Critique of Free Trade' (2001) 78 *Denver Law Review* 979, 1008–09.

[31] See CG Gonzalez, 'Environmental Justice and International Environmental Law' in S Alam and others (eds), *Routledge Handbook of International Environmental Law* (Routledge, 2013) 77, 91–92.

This backdrop frames the Southern countries' approach to international and regional negotiations on sustainable development, particularly concerning the implementation of the SDGs. The South argues for a differentiated approach to applying the SDGs, taking into account the varied developmental stages, local capacities and policy priorities of Southern nations. It asserts that while the SDG framework is universally applicable and globally relevant, the specifics of implementation must be tailored to fit the unique contexts of different countries. This stance emphasises the need for flexibility and context-specific strategies in the global effort to achieve sustainable development. Referring to the seventh Rio Principle (1992) on common but differentiated responsibilities (CBDR), developing countries have consistently opposed blanket attempts at universalisation of the SDG framework without so much as taking into account practical problems that beset the process of translating the goals into targets in their respective jurisdictions. In fact, they 'unanimously called for both a stand-alone goal on means of implementation as well as its integration across each goal, emphasising that the concept embodies not just financial resources, but also technological development and transfer and capacity building'.[32] In a nutshell, replicating the mode and pathway of development of countries as practiced in the North is not necessarily a viable option for the South.

The origins of the North–South divide can largely be traced back to the colonial era – a period characterised by the exploitation of natural resources and economic dominance by European powers over Asia, Africa and the Americas.[33] During this time, colonial governments implemented policies that prioritised resource extraction for short-term gains, often with little concern for the environmental repercussions.[34] This model of environmental exploitation, which facilitated the growth of the Global North by transferring energy and material from the periphery to the industrial centre, was eventually extended to the Global South, laying the groundwork for the current disparities in resource consumption and environmental degradation.[35] In contemporary discussions, scholars[36] highlight the South's concerns regarding the North's historical and ongoing environmental practices. The South criticises the North for developing its economies without

[32] 'North-South Debate in the UN within Context of Sustainable Development Goals' *Social Watch* (21 March 2014) www.socialwatch.org/node/16369, accessed 6 April 2024.

[33] WE Rees and L Westra, 'When Consumption Does Violence: Can there be Sustainability and Environmental Justice in a Resource Limited World?' in J Agyeman, RD Bullard and B Evans (eds), *Just Sustainabilities: Development in an Unequal World* (MIT Press, 2003) 104.

[34] K Harper and SR Rajan, 'International Environmental Justice: Building the Natural Assets of the World's Poor' (2005) 71 *Political Economy Research Institute University of Massachusetts Amherst: Anthropology Department Faculty Publication Series 2.*

[35] See R Anand, *International Environmental Justice: A North-South Dimension* (Ashgate Publishing, 2004).

[36] See P Orebech and F Bosselman, 'The Linkage between Sustainable Development and Customary Law' in *The Role of Customary Law in Sustainable Development* (Cambridge University Press, 2005) 13; F Soltau (2009) 7–8 *Fairness in International Climate Change Law and Policy* 13; GC Bryner, *From Promises to Performance: Achieving Global Environmental Goals* (WW Norton and Company, 1997) 260–61.

considering environmental impacts and for consuming a disproportionate share of the world's natural resources. Despite this, the North advocates for policies that restrict the South's ability to utilise its natural resources, expand its industrial base, and manage population growth. Such measures, according to the South, not only perpetuate the impoverishment of developing nations but also add to their burdens in environmental protection.

These policies are viewed by the South as attempts by the North to maintain its dominance, echoing past practices of colonial expansionism, financial exploitation and economically driven military interventions. The South contends that the North's approach to environmental policy and resource management serves to reinforce historical inequities rather than address the urgent need for a more equitable distribution of responsibilities and resources.

Colonial encounters have profoundly impacted indigenous civilisations in Asia, Africa, and the Americas, primarily by imposing European notions of nature as a commodity for human exploitation and fostering a global economy that systematically marginalised the Global South.[37] This historical context set the stage for international law to portray native populations as racially and culturally inferior, promoting the idea that dominating nature and industrial development were hallmarks of civilised states.[38] This perspective has been echoed in environmental treaties, which often emphasise the need for development in poorer nations without considering ecological limits or acknowledging how the prevailing economic model exacerbates North–South inequalities and deepens the wealth divide globally.[39] The global economy and international institutions have a significant influence on the economies and ecologies of the Global South.

The necessity to generate foreign exchange for repaying international debts has pushed these nations towards producing export-oriented cash crops, adopting harmful agricultural practices,[40] and permitting the overexploitation of forestry and mineral resources by multinational corporations.[41] Structural adjustment programmes, imposed by the World Bank and the International Monetary Fund (IMF), have led to severe environmental and social consequences, including damage to local environments, disruption of subsistence farming, and

[37] C Gonzalez, 'Bridging the North-South Divide: International Environmental Law in Anthropocene' (2015) 32 *Pace Environmental Law Review* 407.

[38] See A Geisinger, 'Sustainable Development and the Domination of Nature: Spreading the Seed of the Western Ideology of Nature' (1999) 27 *Boston College Environmental Affairs Law Review* 43, 52–58; U Natarajan and K Khoday, 'Locating Nature: Making and Unmaking International Law' (2014) 27 *Leiden Journal International Law* 586–87.

[39] Natarajan and Khoday (ibid) 589.

[40] Rees and Westra (n 33) 105; C Gonzalez, 'The Global Food Crisis: Law, Policy, and the Elusive Quest for Justice' (2010) 13 *Yale Human Rights and Development Law Journal* 465; C Gonzalez, 'Markets, Monocultures, and Malnutrition: Agricultural Trade Policy Through an Environmental Justice Lens' (2006) 14 *Michigan State Journal of International Law* 357.

[41] D McLaren, 'Environmental Space, Equity and the Ecological Debt' in J Agyeman, RD Bullard and B Evans (n 33) 19.

accelerated urbanisation.[42] Trade and the restructuring of rural economies often displaced people from productive landscapes to overcrowded cities, primarily to supply urban industrial regions that are mainly in the North. This dynamic has not only contributed to local environmental decay and urban migration but has also facilitated the impoverishment of these regions. International development models and debt-driven development strategies have further depleted the natural capital of the South, resulting in a net transfer of wealth to the Global North.[43] This process has perpetuated poverty and ecological decline in the Global South, highlighting the enduring legacy of colonial exploitation and the need for a more equitable global economic system.

The geographic construction of 'development' or the more commonly used term 'international development' is yet another area of concern which has been questioned by many scholars and activists. Drawing on different scholarship, Horner[44] describes how the term international development is often associated with actions designed for, and research relating to, poor countries,[45] including foreign aid;[46] more specifically, countries in the Global South, ie Asia, Latin America, Africa and the Pacific.

D. Sustainable Development Challenges for the Global South

The multi-dimensional challenges and vulnerabilities which developing countries face in pursuing sustainable development are many. With the exception of a few countries that have to date achieved economic stability, countries in the South host the poorest and the most vulnerable of the world's population. Indeed, for these countries, the road to achieving sustainable development is long, difficult and, in some instances, downright impossible.[47] UNCTAD's analysis of the Least Developed Countries Report series highlights a range of sustainable development challenges faced by the world's most vulnerable nations. These challenges include volatile economic growth, overdependence on commodity exports, weak productive capacities, and a lack of structural transformation. Furthermore, these

[42] Rees and Westra (n 33) 105 (noting traditional farmers and agricultural workers are often driven from rural areas as their markets are undercut by corporate producers or imports).

[43] ibid 106.

[44] R Horner, 'Towards a New Paradigm of Global Development? Beyond the Limits of International Development' (2020) 44(3) *Progress in Human Geography* 415–36.

[45] See Mönks and others, 'Towards a Renewed Vision of Development Studies' (2017) 8(1) *International Development Policy* 3.

[46] B Currie-Alder, 'The State of Development Studies: Origins, Evolution and Prospects' (2016) 37(1) *Canadian Journal of Development Studies* 7.

[47] See generally United Nations Economic and Social Commission for Asia and the Pacific, *Achieving the Sustainable Development Goals in South Asia: Key Policy Priorities and Implementation Challenges* (United Nations, 2018); UNDP and UNRISD, *Global Trends, Challenges and Opportunities in the Implementation of the sustainable Development Goals* (New York, 2017); UNESCAP, *Asia and the Pacific SDG Progress Report* (Bangkok, 2017).

countries grapple with infrastructure deficits, limited domestic resource mobilisation, insufficient development financing, and poor export competitiveness. They are also highly susceptible to various shocks and disasters, compounded by issues such as gender inequality, rising youth unemployment, significant rural-urban disparities, and inadequate human capacities. UNCTAD emphasises the critical need for improved developmental governance and capacity building in both the public and private sectors to address these interconnected challenges and foster sustainable development.[48]

The above observation sums up the formidable problems that frustrate sustainable development efforts in the Global South. Indeed, countries live and experience their susceptibility from multiple aspects, 'often simultaneously and where one can be, at the same time, cause and consequence of the other'.[49] Indeed, the situation is made more complex by the omnipresent tension between the Global North and the South over their respective roles in advancing environmental protection and economic development. Subject to differing value judgements, 'sustainability and development, collide with each other on the implementation phases by nations, revealing differences of opinions between industrialized and developing nations'.[50] While the North emphasises on the economics of sustainable development, the South feels that now that the developed countries have achieved development, they want to deprive the poorer states of the opportunity to achieve the same, by compelling them to sacrifice development in the name of sustainability. A close look at the Johannesburg Declaration on Sustainable Development[51] reveals the critical role of developed countries in achieving development goals and targets. Article 22 of the Declaration urges 'developed countries that have not done so to make concrete efforts to reach the internationally agreed levels of official development assistance'. Again, Article 24 reiterates that special attention must be paid to the developmental needs of small island developing states and the least developed countries. In practical terms, however, the developed countries in the North have not lived up to these pledges.

IV. Bridging the Divide through Global Partnership

The 2030 Agenda for Sustainable Development, like any international framework, demands concerted efforts from all nations, both developed and developing, to take urgent action towards its goals. These goals, designed to be universal and

[48] UNCTAD, *Forging a Path Beyond Borders: The Global South* (New York, 2010) 7.

[49] United Nations Development Group (Inter-Agency Group of SDGs), *Challenges and Strategies for Sustainable Development in Latin America and the Caribbean* 4.

[50] S Shim, 'The North-South Divide on Sustainable Development and the Recent Developments in the Asian Context' (2018) 6 *Korean Journal of International and Comparative Law* 85.

[51] Adopted at the 17th plenary meeting of the World Summit on Sustainable Development, on 4 September 2002.

interconnected, require a globally equitable, balanced approach to sustainability and emphasise the necessity for a worldwide partnership. This partnership hinges on the collective mobilisation of knowledge, creativity, technological expertise and resources. However, the implementation of the SDGs presents a disproportionate challenge to countries in the Global South. These challenges stem from a range of issues including inadequate resources, limited governmental capacity, weak governance structures, insufficient data availability, infrastructural and resource deficits, low stakeholder engagement, and a lack of the expertise needed for tracking progress effectively.

The ambitious scope of the SDGs, coupled with the short timeframe for achieving them and the uncertainty of continuous funding from international development partners, raises concerns about the feasibility of meeting the targets. Despite the enthusiasm and initiative shown by countries in the Global South to incorporate the Agenda 2030 into their policy frameworks, they face a myriad of practical obstacles. These include 'first generation challenges', or initial hurdles, and 'second generation challenges', which represent mid-term obstacles. While attempts have been made to overcome these challenges, results have been variable, ranging from limited success to unsuccessful outcomes.

Nevertheless, the process of confronting these challenges also presents opportunities for growth and evolution. The pressure to overcome obstacles has inspired many countries in the Global South to craft their future development paths, leveraging the potential for innovation and progress that the 2030 Agenda offers. This dynamic illustrates a complex landscape where the pursuit of sustainable development is marked by both significant challenges and the transformative potential for countries to build on their capacities and aspirations.

V. Critical Reflections, Obstacles to Implementation and Prospects for Advancing SDGs in the Global South

In the pursuit of the SDGs, nations across the Global South stand at a critical juncture, facing numerous challenges that test their resolve, resources and readiness to navigate the path towards sustainability. This journey, set against a backdrop of diverse cultures, landscapes and historical legacies, is both promising and fraught with formidable challenges. The SDGs, with their noble intent to address global issues ranging from eradicating poverty to mitigating climate change, present an ambitious agenda that aims to foster equity, fairness and justice on a global scale. However, the quest for their realisation in the Southern hemisphere is marked by obstacles that disproportionately affect the very nations they seek to benefit.

These nations grapple with issues that underscore the intricate relationship between development and sustainability. Economic growth, while a necessary pursuit for improving living standards, often comes at the expense of environmental degradation. The Brundtland Report of 1987 laid the groundwork for understanding sustainable development to harmonise economic growth with environmental stewardship and social equity. Yet, translating this balanced approach into actionable strategies remains a daunting challenge for countries in the Global South. The transition from the MDGs to the SDGs highlighted a shift towards inclusivity and a broader scope of objectives, but the realisation of these goals continues to be impeded by structural inequalities and resource constraints.

The disparity in progress towards achieving these goals within the Global South is stark. While some regions have made significant strides, others lag far behind, hindered by factors such as conflict, political instability, and limited access to social protection and basic services. This unevenness is not merely a reflection of differing capacities but also a consequence of the historical and ongoing power dynamics that shape the global order. The principle of CBDR emphasises the need for a nuanced approach to implementing the SDGs, considering the diverse realities of countries in the Global South. However, the challenge of operationalising this principle in a manner that is both fair and effective remains.

VI. Respecting Local Contexts

In the discourse on sustainable development, it is imperative to advocate for an approach that moves beyond traditional, uniform frameworks towards one that is inclusive and recognises the diversity of global communities. This evolution is critical not only theoretically but also as a fundamental step towards addressing the complex challenges that our world faces. Emphasising the importance of local contexts underscores the need for strategies that genuinely reflect the needs and realities of diverse populations in achieving the SDGs.

A. Localising Global Ambitions

A significant challenge in applying global initiatives at the local level is adapting broad international agendas to the unique circumstances of various local communities.[52] The SDGs, like to human rights initiatives, represent a global ambition aimed at enhancing justice and sustainability worldwide.[53] However, despite these universal goals, local stakeholders often find themselves on the periphery of the main UN agenda-setting events for the SDGs.[54]

[52] See M Goodale, 'Introduction Locating Rights, Envisioning Law Between the Global and the Local' in M Goodale and S Engle Merry (eds), *The Practice of Human Rights, Tracking Law Between the Global and the Local* (Cambridge University Press, 2007) 1–38; C Taylor, 'Modern Social Imaginaries' (2002) 14(1) *Public Culture* 91, 92.

[53] See S Moyn, *The Last Utopia. Human Rights in History* (Harvard University Press, 2010) 225.

[54] NL Immler and H Sakkers, 'The UN-Sustainable Development Goals Going Local: Learning from Localising Human Rights' (2022) 26(2) *International Journal of Human Rights* 262.

B. Marginalised Voices in Sustainable Development

A key to this journey is the inclusion and amplification of marginalised voices, whose insights offer invaluable contributions to the development dialogue. Integrating these perspectives ensures that strategies are not only equitable but also rooted in the lived experiences of those they intend to serve. Such an approach champions a development model that is responsive and adaptable to specific community needs, highlighting the importance of context-specific solutions.

C. Integrating Diverse Onto-epistemological Approaches

Acknowledging and incorporating the unique onto-epistemological approaches of various communities enriches our collective understanding of sustainable development. These perspectives offer innovative solutions that respect the environmental, social and economic nuances of each community, advocating for development that is tailored rather than generic. This necessitates a flexible, nuanced approach that recognises the distinct challenges and opportunities across different contexts, such as the prioritisation of certain SDGs based on geographical and cultural specifics.

D. Fostering Co-Creation and Participatory Development

The promotion of co-creation and participatory processes is also crucial, ensuring that development is a collaborative effort with local communities at the helm. This method fosters empowerment and alignment with community aspirations and cultural contexts, paving the way for interventions that are more effective and respectful of local dynamics.

E. From Anthropocentrism to Ecocentrism: Rethinking Human–Nature Relations

The dominant anthropocentric viewpoint, which places human needs above environmental concerns, starkly contrasts with the ecocentric perspective that values the inherent worth of all life forms and ecosystems. The Anthropocene is a 'clarion call for change'.[55] Kotzé and Kim contend that current legal frameworks and scientific approaches are ill-equipped to address the complexities of the Anthropocene, highlighting the necessity for a profound reassessment of law's role and relevance in contemporary society.[56] Such a re-evaluation is rooted in the understanding

[55] SH Baker, 'Adaptive Law in the Anthropocene' (2015) 90(2) *Chicago-Kent Law Review* 563, 567.

[56] LJ Kotzé and RE Kim, 'Earth System Law: The Juridical Dimensions of Earth System' (2019) 1 *Earth System Governance* xx, 2.

that our environmental awareness is shaped by the attitudes and values that have historically governed human–nature interactions.

The push towards an ecocentric viewpoint is essential for establishing sustainable human–nature relationships, advocating for policies and practices that protect the Earth's resources and its diverse life. This shift is imperative in the context of environmental emergencies, demanding a critical examination of our development paradigms to embrace ecological sustainability, social fairness, and enduring economic health. It advocates for a unified commitment to stewardship and coexistence, guided by principles that prioritise ecosystem well-being, aiming for a future that is both sustainable and equitable.

F. Towards a Truly Inclusive Sustainable Development

Furthermore, critiques of the implementation of the SDGs often highlight the shortcomings of a universal approach that neglects the varied realities across the globe, particularly in the Global South. This homogenised strategy fails to accommodate the distinct socio-cultural and ecological nuances that characterise different regions. The lack of representation in shaping and implementing the SDGs compromises their effectiveness and risks sidelining vital indigenous knowledge systems essential for sustainable development. Thus, realising the SDGs in a way that genuinely resonates with the diverse global communities necessitates a shift towards greater inclusivity and acknowledgment of local expertise. It calls for redefining development as a cooperative, inclusive endeavour that honours the plethora of worldwide cultures, knowledge bases and environmental conditions. Adopting an inclusive approach ensures that sustainable development transcends beyond a mere ideal, moving towards a universally attainable reality that fosters equity, resilience and sustainability for everyone.

Ensuring economic growth, resource mobilisation and financing for the SDGs in the Global South is a daunting task, exacerbated by deep economic disparities. The ambitious goal of the SDGs to leave no one behind is challenged by the economic divide, which limits access to financial resources, technology and infrastructure. This hinders the ability of these nations to invest in key sectors like education and healthcare, undermining the equity principle of the SDGs amid uneven wealth distribution and opportunity.

G. Colonial Legacy and Economic Disparities

The lingering effects of colonialism, characterised by unequal trade practices and exploitative resource extraction, have played a significant role in creating the current disparities seen in global economic structures. These structures continue to exacerbate inequality through unfair trade agreements and burdensome debt, impeding the economic advancement of countries in the Global South. This, in turn, affects their ability to achieve the SDGs and undermines efforts towards achieving global equity and justice.

H. The Impact of Economic Globalisation and Market Dynamics

Economic globalisation has brought about a skewed distribution of economic benefits, offering significant opportunities for some countries while leaving others to face minimal benefits alongside new risks and threats. Countries in the Global South, with their underdeveloped infrastructure, low industrialisation levels and largely unskilled labour force, find themselves without the means to leverage the opportunities presented by globalisation. This results in their limited participation in and access to global markets. Furthermore, economic globalisation has reshaped state sovereignty, creating a divide between winners and losers. Northern states have emerged as the winners, reaping the benefits from trade liberalisation in manufactured goods and services, and from strengthened protections for investor rights and intellectual property. Conversely, the exclusion of agricultural trade, technology transfer and cross-border human movement from World Trade Organization (WTO) agreements has disadvantaged Southern states. These countries face economic and political upheavals and a diminution of sovereignty, as their scarce resources are increasingly allocated to meet the demands of consumers in the North. This pursuit of foreign currency to service external debt exacerbates poverty and malnutrition among their populations.[57] As globalisation intensifies, the capacity of Southern states to provide essential life necessities – such as food, health services, clothing, housing, clean drinking water, a safe environment, social security and education – dwindles. This decline is occurring amid an increasing concentration of power in the hands of major market forces, chiefly multinational corporations (MNCs), leading to a market dynamic that is more monopolistic than competitive. The influence exerted by the North over key global institutions, including the World Bank, the IMF, and the WTO, grants Northern states privileged access to the wealth, natural resources, inexpensive labour, and vast consumer markets of the South. 'This dynamic has transformed the concept of a 'free' market into a variant of market colonialism, which subjugates peoples and governments under the guise of market forces' neutral operations.'[58] This modern form of economic dominance perpetuates inequalities, limiting the ability

[57] K Sauvant, 'From Economic to Socio-Cultural Emancipation: The Historical Context of the New International Economic Order and the New International Socio-Cultural Order' (1981) 3 *Third World Quarterly* 58; J Collins, 'World Hunger: A Scarcity of Food or a Scarcity of Democracy?' in M Klare and D Thomas (eds), *World Security: Challenges for a New Century* (Wordsworth Publishing, 1994) 356, 358; R Litan, 'The "Globalization" Challenge' (2000) 18 *Brookings Review* 35.

[58] M Chossudovsky, *Global Poverty and New World Economic Order* (1991) 26(44) *Economic and Political Weekly* 2527.

of Southern countries to meet the basic needs of their populations. The marginalisation of the Global South in global decision-making processes exacerbates existing power imbalances and hinders the pursuit of truly cooperative sustainable development. This exclusion raises concerns about the equity of these processes and undermines the global efforts to achieve the SDGs. To bridge these gaps, it is imperative for developed countries to fulfil their promises related to financial support, technology transfer and the practice of fair trade. These commitments are not merely ethical duties but critical steps towards creating an equitable foundation for sustainable development worldwide. Ensuring equitable access to resources, conducting technology transfers in a manner that respects the autonomy of recipient countries, and fostering fair trade practices are essential actions.

I. Rethinking Measures of Success and Development Strategies

Furthermore, moving beyond gross domestic product (GDP) as the sole indicator of success towards more comprehensive metrics that include well-being, environmental sustainability and social equity is vital. The prevailing focus on GDP growth often comes at the expense of the environment and social welfare, highlighting the need for a paradigm shift. Embracing development strategies that value economic, social and environmental goals equally is crucial in order to address the multifaceted challenges of sustainable development effectively. Furthermore, financing sustainable development in the Global South requires a multifaceted approach, utilising diverse funding sources, including domestic revenues, international assistance, debt relief, technology transfer and private sector investments. Strengthening domestic resource mobilisation through improved taxation and anti-corruption measures, and advocating for a fair global financial architecture, are crucial steps towards achieving the SDGs and fostering a more equitable and resilient global economy. This comprehensive and innovative financing approach reflects the complexities of achieving the SDGs, and acknowledges the varied contexts and capacities within the Global South. It underscores the need for a global economic order that is balanced, equitable and conducive to sustainable development for all.

VII. Reinventing Governance for SDG Success

Effective governance is essential for achieving the SDGs, necessitating a comprehensive overhaul of existing structures to enhance coordination, bolster institutional capacities and ensure transparency and accountability. There is a growing acceptance that no single body or category of governance institution can effectively combat environmental change and, instead, what is needed is a multilevel, multiscale governance system.[59] This approach aims to make the ambitious SDGs attainable by rooting solutions in the specific realities of diverse communities through decentralisation, which empowers local levels with decision-making authority, thereby making governance more responsive and ensuring inclusivity.

A. Capacity Building for Sustainable Development

Effective governance also depends on the capabilities of states to achieve the kinds of changes in society that their leaders have sought through state planning, policies and actions.[60] Critical to this endeavour is building the capacity of public officials through targeted training, enhancing their ability to navigate the intricacies of sustainable development. Such capacity-building initiatives are fundamental to effective SDG implementation, enabling officials to formulate and execute relevant policies efficiently. Moreover, the engagement of civil society is pivotal, enriching the governance process with diverse perspectives and fostering a sense of ownership among stakeholders. This inclusivity is achieved by creating platforms for dialogue and ensuring access to information, thereby enhancing transparency and accountability. Additionally, leveraging multi-stakeholder partnerships amplifies the impact of development initiatives, by pooling diverse expertise and resources to innovate solutions that address complex challenges collaboratively. These partnerships exemplify the synergy needed to align efforts with the broad objectives of the SDGs. Goal 16 of the UN SDGs highlights this, representing a restatement of the central importance of good governance as an aspirational goal in the UN system. In its targets, Goal 16 promotes the rule of law at international level (16.3); aims to develop effective, accountable and transparent institutions at all levels (16.6); aims to ensure responsive, inclusive and participatory, representative decision-making at all levels (16.7); and aims to broaden and strengthen the participation of developing countries in the institutions of global governance (16.8). Although Goal 16 places an imperative on better global governance, it also pushes for reform within states' internal modes of governance and, importantly, emphasises that making political reform a priority is imperative in strengthening fragile states.[61] Enhancing governance, especially in the Global South, requires a multifaceted approach that includes strengthening institutional capacities, simplifying administrative processes, and promoting inclusivity in policymaking. Central to achieving resilient and equitable governance is the streamlining of administrative procedures and the development of policies that incorporate a wide range of societal views.

[59] H Leck and D Simon, 'Fostering Multiscalar Collaboration and Cooperation for Effective Governance of Climate Change Adaption' (2013) 50(6) *Urban Studies* 1221, 1223.

[60] D Joshi, B Hughes and T Sisk, 'Improving Governance for the Post-2015 Sustainable Development Goals: Scenario Forecasting the Next 50 Years' (2015) 70 *World Development* 286, 287.

[61] MS Edwards and S Romero, 'Governance and the Sustainable Development Goals: Changing the Game or More of the Same?' (2014) 34(2) *SAIS Review of International Affairs* 146.

B. Transparency and Public Engagement

Transparency and public engagement play critical roles in this process, as they allow for the scrutiny of sustainable development efforts and foster a participatory democracy where people have the right to influence decisions impacting their lives.[62] The involvement of marginalised groups in policy discussions is essential, not only to uphold their rights but also to ensure the successful advocacy and reform needed to improve living standards through the implementation of the SDGs. Building the capacity of various stakeholders is fundamental to the effective achievement of the SDGs. This includes government bodies, civil society organisations and the private sector, and requires a deep comprehension of sustainable development principles beyond mere technical training. Enhancing strategic planning and management abilities, and nurturing a culture of innovation and flexibility, are key aspects of this comprehensive capacity-building approach. It ensures all parties are adequately prepared to actively participate in and monitor the progress of SDG-related initiatives.

To effectively implement the SDGs a comprehensive, multifaceted approach is essential, central to which is enhancing governance, capacity building and fostering inclusive and strategic collaboration. The Rio Declaration sets the goal of establishing a new and equitable global partnership through new levels of cooperation among states, people and key sectors of society.[63] Renewed collaboration for the greater good of humanity and the environment requires a new approach to international relations[64] based on compromise, common interests and long-term perspectives.[65]

This collaboration is vital for pooling collective expertise, resources and knowledge to tackle development challenges, by encouraging multi-stakeholder partnerships that leverage each participant's strengths towards achieving the SDGs. Such partnerships not only generate innovative solutions and optimise resource use but also promote a shared responsibility for sustainable outcomes.

Investing strategically in sectors poised for sustainable impact and conducting thorough evaluations to pinpoint where resources can be most efficiently allocated are crucial. This targeted approach, underpinned by continuous sectoral needs assessment and adaptability, aims to make transformative strides in sustainable development. Moreover, assessing institutions' capacity and readiness to engage with the SDGs helps to identify and address capability gaps and barriers, thus preparing the ground for effective capacity-building initiatives that enhance institutional frameworks and processes for better SDG implementation.

[62] N Arajärvi, 'The Rule of Law in the 2030 Agenda' (2017) *Hague Journal on the Rule of Law* 3.

[63] Principle 5 states: 'All States and all people shall cooperate in the essential task of eradicating poverty as an indispensable requirement for sustainable development, in order to decrease the disparities in standards of living and better meet the needs of the majority of the people of the world.'

[64] K Hossain, 'Sustainable Development: A Normative Framework for Evolving a More Just and Humane International Economic Order' in SR Chowdhury and others (eds), *The Right to Development in International Law* (Martinus Nijhoff, 1992) 259.

[65] P Sands (ed), *Greening International Law* (Earthscan, 1993) 20–33.

C. Policy Frameworks, Social Cohesion, and Reliable Data as Building Blocks for Sustainable Development

Reconceptualising policy frameworks within a rights-based approach that underscores equity and environmental integrity is vital, especially in light of exacerbated inequalities and environmental issues post-pandemic. This requires aligning sectoral policies with the SDGs and overcoming systemic obstacles to ensure policy coherence and integrated approaches that overcome traditional decision-making barriers. Addressing structural injustices and promoting development models centred on inclusivity and global solidarity are paramount, especially for the Global South, to surmount significant SDG challenges through collaborative and solution-oriented efforts. The integration of sustainable development principles into domestic laws and policies necessitates reliable data and insights into the environmental impacts of development activities, in order to balance economic growth with sustainability. However, a re-evaluation of the development model is crucial, given its failure to eradicate poverty and its unsustainable consumption patterns leading to resource depletion and pollution. The economic model's role in driving anthropogenic climate change, culminating in a global climate crisis, underscores the need for a radical rethink towards sustainability.

Furthermore, enhancing social cohesion and trust through dialogue, collaboration and mutual respect among government, civil society and the private sector is fundamental. Empowering marginalised groups in decision-making promotes social justice and equitable development outcomes, contributing to the sustainable advancement of global objectives. Capacity building and knowledge sharing across countries, especially in the Global South, form the foundation for informed decision-making and efficient SDG project execution. Leveraging peer learning networks, workshops and research partnerships accelerates progress by facilitating the exchange of insights, best practices and innovative solutions.

Reliable data and robust monitoring systems are indispensable for tracking SDG progress, guiding interventions and ensuring accountability. Improving data infrastructure and adopting innovative collection methods enhance data reliability, while engaging communities in monitoring ensures development efforts resonate with those most affected. Investing in education and training bolsters the human capital necessary for sustainable development, thus encouraging a learning culture that adapts to evolving SDG implementation challenges.

D. Towards an Integrated Strategy for Advancing the SDGs

Advancing the SDGs demands an integrated strategy that acknowledges the interplay between socio-economic, environmental and governance factors. This strategy should focus on contextualising priorities, integrating policies, mobilising resources, and promoting rights and inclusivity. This strategy recognises the interconnected nature of socio-economic, environmental and governance factors in advancing the SDGs. Central to this strategy is the engagement of a wide array of stakeholders, ranging from government bodies constructing supportive policies and regulations to international organisations setting the frameworks for global cooperation. The integration strategy, however, goes beyond these formal actors to include civil society and the private sector, ensuring a plurality of voices contribute to a participatory process reflective of the needs and entitlements of marginalised communities.

The operationalisation of this strategy involves nuanced alignment of national policies with international goals, with a clear emphasis on tailoring local strategies to unique challenges and opportunities. The implementation must foster a feedback loop that incorporates both local realities and global standards, facilitated by meaningful collaboration.

As this narrative unfolds, it becomes evident that the transformative changes called for by the Global South are not merely aspirational but critical. They demand a reformed international financial architecture, equitable sharing of green technologies, and a departure from neo-colonial practices. In reimagining development, the global community must reconcile the urgency of climate change, environmental, developmental and social crises with the imperative for radical rethinking. This conclusion encapsulates a renewed commitment to recalibration of developmental paradigm that is equitable, sustainable and recognises the standing of the Global South in global governance – forging a future where no one is left behind.

PART II

Sustainable Development as a Changing Discourse

2

Sustainable Development: Contested Notions

KLAUS BOSSELMANN

I. Introduction

The notion of sustainable development can be described as the intersection between economic, environmental and social concerns. International law reflective of sustainable development is an emerging substantive body of legal instruments, norms and treaties, which are supported by distinctive procedural elements.

It is common for sustainable development to be an agreed objective of many international agreements. Contributing to this ever-developing area of law are examples such as the 2015 United Nations' Agenda, 'Transforming Our World: The 2030 Agenda for Sustainable Development'[1] and the UN Secretary-General's 2021 Report locating the 2030 Agenda for Sustainable Development Goals at the core of 'Our Common Agenda'.[2]

However, defining what sustainable development encompasses – what is specifically being referred to when it is discussed – remains obscure.[3] As a point of departure we have to go back to the origins of sustainable development, particularly its articulation in the Brundtland Report published in 1987. Through its evolution – notably at the United Nations Conference on Environment and Development ('Rio Earth Summit') in 1992 – two predominant interpretations of sustainable development can be identified: the anthropocentric or 'weak' form and the ecocentric or 'strong' form of sustainable development. How this interpretation has been conceptualised historically and developed over time in the broader area of international environmental law will be at the centre of this chapter. It aims to

[1] UNGA Res 70/1 (21 October 2015) UN Doc A/Res/70/1.

[2] Report of the Security Council, 'Our Common Agenda' (2021) UN Doc A/75/982.

[3] See, for example, JH Armstrong and S Kamieniecki 'Sustainability Policy Research: A Review and Synthesis' (2019) 47(1) *Policy Studies Journal* 45. In essence, there are contested notions around the importance of ecological sustainability with respect to sustainable development. For details see K Bosselmann, *The Principle of Sustainability: Transforming Law and Governance* 2nd edn (Routledge, 2017) 8–53.

show that the common 'weak' form of sustainable development has dominated the sustainable development discourse, and while this is so, the essence of this concept has not been captured. Significantly, the challenge of adopting and securing the strong definition – ecological sustainability – becomes especially fundamental to prospects for social justice and economic prosperity, when deepening inequalities keep prevailing between the Global North and South due to false promises of a weak definition of sustainable development.[4]

For these reasons, this chapter speaks in favour of conceiving the environmental justice component of sustainable development in ecocentric terms. Aiming for ecological sustainability would give a meaningful direction to the process of bridging the North and South divide by reminding all nations equally, whether coming from the industrialised and the developing world, to protect and preserve the integrity of the Earth System. Such an understanding of sustainable development implies the acceptance – although there is no other alternative but to make the shift or face an increasingly unhospitable planet[5] – that the Earth's integrity is crucial as a supporting basis for our present and future generations, including all forms of life independent from any instrumental values for us humans. This understanding must, however, be accompanied by social justice considerations that the Global North has been largely ignorant of. The bottom line of development in order to become 'sustainable' is the Global North's responsibility for social justice and economic prosperity in the Global South, as, for example, expressed in the principle of common, but differentiated responsibility.[6]

II. Origin and Evolution of the Concept of Sustainable Development

The origin of the concept of sustainable development cannot be exactly pinpointed. Some argue for its use by ancient civilisations wherever there was an attempt at reconciling the needs of development with the protection of the environment. However, in international and national laws, the idea of sustainable development is a recent development. It was the 1987 Brundtland Report that

[4] For an analysis of the North–South divisions, see CG Gonzalez, 'Global Justice in the Anthropocene' in LJ Kotze (ed), *Environmental Law and Governance for the Anthropocene* (Hart, 2017). The author exposes that the deep injustice between the Global South and Global North are the results 'of neoliberal development, industrialization, and economic growth for the benefit of the North to consume a disproportionate share of the planet's resources' (at 219). See also A Malm and A Hornborg, 'The Geology of Mankind? A Critique of the Anthropocene Narrative' (2014) 1(1) *The Anthropocene Review* 62.

[5] For a full debate on the concept of 'planetary boundaries', see J Rockström and others, 'Planetary Boundaries: Exploring the Safe Operating Space for Humanity' (2009) 14(2) *Ecology and Society* 32; W Steffen and others, 'The Trajectory of the Anthropocene: The Great Acceleration' (2015) 2(1) *The Anthropocene Review* 81; FP Saunders, 'Planetary Boundaries: At the Threshold … Again: Sustainable Development Ideas and Politics' (2015) 17 *Environment, Development and Sustainability* 823.

[6] Bosselmann (n 3) 52, 54, 69–70.

brought it to wider public attention as an overarching objective for the world community to strive towards.[7]

The Brundtland Report is commonly recognised as having created the term 'sustainable development'.[8] The report was the outcome of the work of the United Nations World Commission on Environment and Development (WCED), established in 1983 by a resolution. of the General Assembly of the United Nations.[9] The WCED was established against the background of two emerging global themes.[10] The first theme is that development is not a uniform process benefiting all people and nations, but is divided between developed and developing countries. The second emerging global theme is the observation that the planet's resources are finite, requiring careful management.[11]

The origins of the concept of sustainable development go back to the 1970s, notably the release of the Club of Rome report 'Limits to Growth'[12] and the 1972 United Nations Conference on the Human Environment, which resulted in the Stockholm Declaration on the Human Environment.[13] The Club of Rome report forecast that unless countries learned to recognise and respect absolute limits to growth, especially population growth, there would be widespread economic, social and environmental collapse.[14] In a similar vein, Principle 13 of the Stockholm Declaration urged states to 'adopt an integrated and coordinated approach to their development planning so as to ensure that development is compatible with the need to protect and improve environment for the benefit of their population' and Principle 14 promoted rational planning as 'an essential tool for reconciling any conflict between the needs of development and the need to protect and improve the environment'.[15] However, there was a key difference between the Club of Rome report and the Stockholm Declaration. The Club of Rome report saw economic

[7] HC Bugge and C Voigt, 'Introduction' in HC Bugge and C Voigt (eds), *Sustainable Development in International and National Law: What did the Brundtland Report do to Legal Thinking and Legal Development, and Where Can We Go From Here?* (Europa Law Publishing, 2008) vii.

[8] T Kolari, 'The Principle of Common but Differentiated Responsibilities as Contributing to Sustainable Development through Multilateral Environmental Agreements' in Bugge and Voigt (n 7) 256; P Sands and J Peel, *Principles of International Environmental Law* 4th edn (Cambridge University Press, 2018) 252; P Sands, 'International Law in the Field of Sustainable Development: Emerging Legal Principles' in W Lang (ed), *Sustainable Development and International Law* (Graham & Trotman, 1995); C Voigt, *Sustainable Development as a Principle of International Law: Resolving Conflicts between Climate Measures and WTO Law* (Martinus Nijhoff Publishers, 2009) 46.

[9] HC Bugge, '1987–2007: "Our Common Future" Revisited' in Bugge and Voigt (n 7) 1; UNGA Res 38/161 (23 February 1983) UN Doc 38/161.

[10] K Bosselmann, 'The Concept of Sustainable Development' in K Bosselmann, D Grinlinton and P Taylor (eds), *Environmental Law for a Sustainable Society* 2nd edn (New Zealand Centre for Environmental Law Monograph Series: Vol 1 2013) 97.

[11] ibid.

[12] M-C C Segger, 'Sustainable Development in International Law' in Bugge and Voigt (n 7) 93.

[13] *Stockholm Declaration on the Human Environment* (A/Conf/48/14/Rev.I, United Nations 1972), wwwcdn.imo.org/localresources/en/KnowledgeCentre/ConferencesMeetings/Documents/A%20CONF.48%2014%20Rev.1.pdf, accessed 9 May 2024.

[14] Segger (n 12) 93.

[15] Stockholm Declaration (n 13).

growth on a collision course with ecological sustainability, while the Stockholm Declaration aimed to reconcile the two.[16]

The term sustainable development had arisen prior to the Brundtland Report, appearing in the World Conservation Strategy,[17] which was prepared by some of the world's leading non-governmental organisations (NGOs) in 1980.[18] The World Conservation Strategy was commissioned by the United Nations Environment Programme, which also provided financial assistance and contributed to the formulation of the basic themes of the Strategy, together with the World Wildlife Fund.[19] The aim of the Strategy was:[20]

> … to help advance the achievement of sustainable development through the conservation of living resources. The Strategy is intended to stimulate a more focussed approach to living resource conservation and to provide policy guidance on how this can be carried out.

Two years later, in 1982, the United Nations General Assembly adopted the World Charter for Nature.[21] While the World Charter for Nature does not expressly refer to sustainable development, it provides that nature conservation is a prerequisite for all forms of resource use and development.[22] Further, it acknowledges that 'mankind is part of nature and life depends on the uninterrupted functions of natural systems which ensure the supply of energy and nutrients'.[23] Like the World Conservation Strategy, the World Charter for Nature emphasised the non-anthropocentric nature of sustainability, as is reflected in the first four general principles of the World Charter for Nature:[24]

1. Nature shall be respected and its essential processes shall not be impaired.
2. The genetic viability on earth shall not be compromised; the population levels of all life forms, wild and domesticated, must be at least sufficient for their survival, and to this end necessary habitats shall be safeguarded.
3. All areas of the earth, both land and sea, shall be subject to these principles of conservation; special protection shall be given to unique areas, to representative samples of all different types of ecosystems and to the habitats of rare or endangered species.
4. Ecosystems and organisms, as well as the land, marine and atmospheric resources that are utilised by man, shall be managed to achieve and maintain optimum sustainable productivity, but not in such a way as to endanger the integrity of those other ecosystems or species with which they coexist.

[16] Bosselmann (n 3) 25.

[17] International Union for Conservation of Nature and Natural Resources, *World Conservation Strategy: Living Resource Conservation for Sustainable Development* (IUCN-UNEP-WWF 1980).

[18] Bosselmann (n 3) 97.

[19] IUCN (n 17) ii.

[20] ibid iv.

[21] World Charter for Nature, UNGA Res 37/7 (28 October 1982) UN Doc A/Res/37/7.

[22] Bosselmann (n 3) 97.

[23] World Charter for Nature (n 21) preamble.

[24] ibid Arts 1–4.

The Brundtland Report definition of sustainable development therefore arose out of a background of increasing awareness of the disparities between developed and developing countries and the need to resolve these equity issues in an ecologically sustainable manner.[25] It has both social and ecological aspects – social aspects being demonstrated by the recognition that development should meet basic human needs (particularly of the poor) and ecological aspects by providing that human activity (state of technology and social organisation) must occur within environmental limitations.[26]

Hans Christian Bugge has summarised the Brundtland Report in similar but slightly different terms.[27] In his view, the term 'sustainable development' comprises four core elements:[28]

1. Social equity and justice – meeting basic needs for all.
2. Integration of environmental considerations into all aspects of economic and social development.
3. An absolute prohibition on destroying the environment and natural resources on which future generations' life and welfare depends.
4. A long-term view in decision making.

In the same vein, Christina Voigt has expressed the view that even though the Brundtland Report has been criticised for not going far enough and diluting the focus of protection of the environment by including economic and social interests into account, its value cannot be underestimated.[29] It has both shaped a new perception of the Earth and the crisis it faces, and created momentum, at a global level, to embrace the concept of sustainable development.[30]

Since its expression in the Brundtland Report in 1987, the concept of sustainable development has had far reaching implications on a global scale: forming the subject of three Earth Summits (Rio 1992, Johannesburg 2002, Rio+20 2012), being incorporated into a multitude of (hard and soft law) international agreements and being given weight in international and national jurisprudence.[31]

As a direct response to the Brundtland Report, the United Nations convened a conference in Rio de Janeiro – the United Nations Conference on Environment and Development ('Rio Earth Summit')[32] – with the aim of addressing the 'urgent problems of environmental protection and socio-economic development'.[33] By this time, public awareness of the environmental issues the world was facing had reached an extremely high level, and it was becoming clear that the use of

[25] Bosselmann (n 3) 27.
[26] ibid 28.
[27] In 1986–87, Hans Christian Bugge served as personal adviser to Norway's Prime Minister Gro Harlem Brundtland in her capacity as chair of the WCED and as State Secretary in Norway's Ministry for Development Cooperation.
[28] Bugge (n 9) 20.
[29] Bugge and Voigt (n 7) 16.
[30] ibid.
[31] Bugge (n 9) vii, viii.
[32] Segger (n 12) 98.
[33] United Nations, 'Earth Summit+5', www.un.org/esa/earthsummit, accessed 24 November 2022.

traditional strategies for development was not providing adequate results for developing countries.[34] The Rio Earth Summit was attended by 172 governments and 2,400 representatives of NGOs, with 17,000 people attending the parallel NGO forum.[35] It is therefore not surprising that the Summit has been described as a 'scene of high tensions, vigorous debates and extremely active participation from civil society, scientists, business leaders and many others'.[36]

The Rio Declaration did not define the concept of sustainable development. Instead it laid out a series of principles relevant to achieving sustainable development.[37] Principle 2, for example, provides for development to meet the needs of present and future generations.[38] Principle 4 provides for the integration of environmental considerations into all aspects of development, stating that 'in order to achieve sustainable development, environmental protection shall constitute an integral part of the development process and cannot be considered in isolation from it'.[39] Notably, Principle 7 stipulates the duty of states to 'co-operate in a spirit of global partnership to conserve, protect and restore the health and integrity of the Earth's ecosystem'.[40] The duty of states to cooperate to protect and restore the integrity of the Earth's ecosystem has since been repeated in more than 25 international environmental agreements including, for example, the 2015 Paris Agreement.[41] Such steering towards Earth's ecological integrity signals a shift away from Western anthropocentric, utilitarian perceptions and can be interpreted as an overarching objective or *grundnorm* underpinning international environmental law.[42] The Rio Declaration itself, however, offers little guidance for the core meaning of sustainable development. The general legacy of the Rio Earth Summit was one of 'unfinished business'[43] which has not been completed as yet.

III. The Various Interpretations of Sustainable Development

Since sustainable development has come to pervade environmental policy discourse, it is not surprising that its meaning and significance are highly contested.

[34] Segger (n 12) 98.
[35] United Nations, 'Earth Summit', www.un.org/en/conferences/environment/rio1992.
[36] Segger (n 12) 98.
[37] ibid 99.
[38] UNGA, 'Report of the United Nations Conference on Environment and Development by UNGA Res 47/190' (3–14 June 1992) UN Doc A/CONF.151/26/Rev l (Vol I) Principle 2.
[39] ibid Principle 4.
[40] ibid Principle 7.
[41] K Bosselmann, 'The Ever-Increasing Importance of Ecological Integrity in International and National Law' in L Westra and others (eds), *Ecological Integrity, Law and Governance* (Routledge, 2018) 225–32.
[42] R Kim and K Bosselmann, 'Operationalizing Sustainable Development: Ecological Integrity as a *Grundnorm* in International Law' (2015) 24 *RECIEL* 194; K Bosselmann, *Earth Governance: Trusteeship for the Global Commons* (Edward Elgar, 2015) 250–51.
[43] Bosselmann (n 3) 34.

Like the general environmental debate, the debate on sustainable development reflects a wide spectrum of political views.[44]

The debate about the interpretation of the term sustainable development can generally be summarised as the divide between the anthropocentric or 'weak' form of sustainability and the non-anthropocentric/ecocentric or 'strong' form of sustainable development.[45] The divide can be traced to a 'paradigmatic difference': the environment is either everything, that is, the biosphere as a whole including humankind, or alternatively, the environment is the physical surroundings of humans.[46]

In the weak form of sustainable development, the social, economic and environmental/ecological elements of the concept are of equal importance and sustainable development is the common ground where the three elements intersect.[47] Implicit in the weak form of sustainable development is the need for compromise – namely trade-offs in one element to allow improvements in another.[48] The weak form of sustainable development is the prevalent view on the concept, as demonstrated in the soft law documentation arising out of the Rio Earth Summit and Johannesburg Summit.[49]

The strong form of sustainable development sees ecology or the environment as the overriding system within which society forms part, and the economy falling within both the ecological and societal systems.[50] In short, the strong approach to sustainable development encourages economic and social development within the parameters of the biosphere.[51] The strong view of sustainable development was envisaged by the Brundtland Report; it anticipated that the concept of sustainable development did 'imply limits – not absolute limits but limitations imposed by the present state of technology and social organization on environmental resources and by the ability of the biosphere to absorb the effects of human activities'.[52]

Nonetheless, regardless of the difference in view as to the weighting to be given to the social, economic and ecological elements, both the strong and weak interpretations of sustainable development involve the integration of these three elements.[53] Further, it is generally accepted that the dual goal of intragenerational (between the rich and poor) and intergenerational (between the present and the future generations) equity forms part of the concept of sustainable development.[54]

There have been many efforts to break the concept down into more manageable principles and policy goals. A few examples are given below.

[44] Segger (n 12) 100.
[45] ibid 102.
[46] ibid.
[47] ibid 103.
[48] ibid 104.
[49] Bosselmann (n 3) 34.
[50] ibid.
[51] ibid.
[52] Bugge and Voigt (n 7) 8.
[53] Bosselmann (n 3) 104.
[54] ibid 108.

In 2002, the International Law Association produced the New Delhi Declaration of Principles of International Law Relating to Sustainable Development suggesting that there was:[55]

> [a] need to further develop international law in the field of sustainable development, with a view to according due weight to both the developmental and environmental concerns, in order to achieve a balanced and comprehensive international law on sustainable development, as called for in Principle 27 of the Rio Declaration and Chapter 39 of Agenda 21 of the UN Conference on Environment and Development as well as in the various resolutions on legal aspects of sustainable development of the International Law Association.

The New Delhi Declaration identifies seven principles, for which it states 'the application and, where relevant, consolidation and further development of [these] principles … would be instrumental in pursuing the objective of sustainable development in an effective way'.[56] The seven principles identified are:[57]

1. The duty of states to ensure sustainable use of natural resources.[58]
2. The principle of equity and the eradication of poverty.[59]
3. The principle of common but differentiated responsibilities.[60]
4. The principle of the precautionary approach to human health, natural resources and ecosystems.[61]
5. The principle of public participation and access to information and justice.[62]
6. The principle of good governance.[63]
7. The principle of integration and interrelationship, in particular in relation to human rights and social, economic and environment objectives.[64]

[55] International Law Association, 'New Delhi Declaration of Principles of International Law Relating to Sustainable Development' in International Law Association Report of the Seventy-Second Conference (New Delhi, 2002) (International Law Association, New York 2002).

[56] ibid.

[57] ibid.

[58] States are under a duty to manage natural resources, including natural resources within their own territory or jurisdiction, in a rational, sustainable and safe way so as to contribute to the development of their peoples, to the conservation and sustainable use of natural resources, and the protection of the environment.

[59] This principle relates to both intergenerational and intragenerational equity – namely the right of all people (both present and future generations) of fair access and entitlement to the Earth's natural resources.

[60] All states are under a duty to cooperate in the achievement of global sustainable development and the protection of the environment; however, the special needs and interests of developing countries and their ability to respond must be recognised.

[61] A precautionary approach needs to be taken in light of scientific uncertainty, particularly where activities may cause serious long-term or irreversible harm.

[62] Public participation in decision-making and a right to appropriate, comprehensible and timely information.

[63] Responsive, transparent and accountable governments are seen as essential to sustainable development.

[64] The principle of integration reflects the interdependence of social, economic, financial, environmental and human rights aspects of principles and rules of international law relating to sustainable development as well as the interdependence of the needs of current and future generations of humankind.

Philippe Sands has in turn identified 'four elements [that] can be considered to provide the core legal elements of "sustainable development" as used in the Brundtland Report'.[65] These four core elements were identified as:

1. The principle of intergenerational equity.
2. The principle of sustainable use.
3. The principle of equitable use.
4. The principle of integration.[66]

Philippe Sands then goes on to outline seven principles 'having particular relevance in the field of sustainable development',[67] namely:[68]

1. Sovereignty over natural resources and the responsibility not to cause environmental damage.[69]
2. The principle of good neighbourliness and international cooperation.[70]
3. The principle of common but differentiated responsibility.[71]
4. The principle of good governance, including participatory democracy.[72]
5. The principle of preventive action.[73]
6. The precautionary principle.[74]
7. The polluter pays principle.[75]

Others have also suggested a range of concepts and principles of international law for sustainable development.[76] However, the principles of the law of sustainable development do not give an overall direction; they are more like tools in the sustainable development toolbox.

[65] Sands (n 8) 58.

[66] ibid 58–61.

[67] ibid 62.

[68] ibid 62–66.

[69] That states have sovereign rights over their natural resources, but also the obligation not to cause damage to the environment.

[70] Namely the obligation to cooperate, captured in Art 74 of the Charter of the United Nations in relation to social, economic and commercial matters.

[71] This principle has two aspects. The first is the common responsibility of states for the protection of the environment. The second is the need to take into account the differing economic, social and other circumstances particularly as they relate to each state's contribution to the creation of the particular problem and its ability to respond to, prevent, reduce and control that problem.

[72] Reflecting that citizens are entitled to participate in decision making, including access to information and access to remedy and redress.

[73] The obligation to protect the environment (or minimise environmental damage), as an end in itself. The Principle requires action to be taken at an early stage, and if possible, before any damage has occurred.

[74] The need to take steps to protect the environment in the face of scientific uncertainty.

[75] The costs of pollution should be borne by the person or persons responsible for causing the pollution, including the consequential costs.

[76] For example, *Report of the Expert Group Meeting on Identification of Principles of International Law for Sustainable Development, Geneva, Switzerland, 26–28 September 1995* (United Nations, 1996). It identifies 19 principles and concepts of international law for sustainable development in the context of the Rio Declaration, Agenda 21, international treaties and other legal instruments at that time. See also Segger (n 12) 165.

To this end, it is necessary to turn to the United Nations' Sustainable Development Goals of Importance (SDGs). Emerging from the 2012 Rio+20 Summit and adopted in 2015, they provide states with a framework for law and policy development.[77] The 17 goals, while mostly relevant and succinct are, however, not without flaws. They are not legally binding, not well-connected, partially self-contradicting and without an unifying purpose.[78] All this makes them vulnerable to political manoeuvring, manipulation and deviation. Essentially, there is no mutual understanding on how to achieve the goals and, crucially, sustainable development.

One way to make the SDGs more operable is to distinguish between ecological, social and economic goals and organise them in a hierarchical, nested-egg manner: SDGs protecting the biosphere (6, 13, 14, 15) form the basis for achieving social goals (1, 2, 3, 4, 5, 7, 11, 16) to give direction for achieving economic goals (8, 9, 10, 12). The means to guide this process are addressed in SDG 17 (Partnerships for Goals).[79] Even more direction could be provided if the SDGs are viewed as a nested system of goals, targets and indicators with an overarching objective to preserve and restore the integrity of the Earth system.[80] This advanced concept of the SDGs would meet the widely expressed criticism that by 2030 a number of the SDGs may have been achieved, yet the world may have become even more unsustainable than today.[81]

The essence of sustainable development must be the concern for ecological integrity. As expressed by Christina Voigt:[82]

> In establishing the core of sustainable development, ecological thresholds cannot be ignored without rendering the result unsustainable. They provide the nucleus around which clearer meaning and content of sustainable development evolves.

Without this recognition, the implementation of sustainable development will be ineffective:[83]

> … 'sustainable development', as formally characterized, invites an overly anthropocentric and instrumentalist interpretation which in the long run is apt to thwart the very pursuit of those goals that 'sustainability' is said to embody.

[77] United Nations, 'Sustainable Development Goals: Knowledge Platform', sustainabledevelopment.un.org/index.html, accessed 22 May 2024.

[78] Bosselmann (n 3) 37–38.

[79] D Griggs and others, 'An Integrated Framework for Sustainable Development Goals' (2014) 19(4) *Ecology and Society* 49.

[80] Bosselmann (n 3) 20; Rakhyun Kim, Klaus Bosselmann and Volker Mauerhofer, *Planetary Boundaries in Post-2015 Sustainable Development Goals: Safeguarding Ecological Integrity as a Priority Goal and a Grundnorm of International Law* (Planetary Boundaries Initiative, 2013), www.planetaryboundariesinitiative.org/wp-content/uploads/2013/07/The-Kim-Report-September-2013.pdf, accessed 29 November 2022.

[81] J Randers and others, 'Achieving the 17 Sustainable Development Goals Within 9 Planetary Boundaries' *EarthArXiv* (2018), www.eartharxiv.org/xwevb/, accessed 30 November 2022.

[82] Bugge and Voigt (n 7) 5.

[83] G Handl, 'Sustainable Development: General Rules versus Specific Obligations' in W Lang (ed), *Sustainable Development and International Law* (Graham & Trotman, 1995) 38.

This meaning of sustainable development becomes even more apparent when one traces the principle back in history – '[a]lthough the term "sustainable development" has been used only since the 1980s, the underlying idea is probably as old as humanity's struggle with the forces of nature'.[84] The history of sustainable development was also highlighted in the separate opinion of Vice-President Weeramantry in the *Gabčikovo-Nagymaros Project* case.[85]

> Sustainable development is thus not merely a principle of modern international law. It is one of the most ancient of ideas in the human heritage. Fortified by the rich insights that can be gained from millennia of human experience, it has an important part to play in the service of international law.

When the history of sustainable development is traced, it becomes apparent that the legal principle of (ecological) sustainability creates the meaning and essence of sustainable development.[86]

The term 'sustainable development' was first documented in laws governing forest industry management practices in Europe toward the end of the eighteenth century.[87] The laws permitted harvesting of only as much of the forest as would grow again each year, so that the forest as a whole would be maintained.[88] However, others have traced sustainability concepts back as early as around 1350 when continental Europe suffered a major ecological crisis.[89] At that time, townships and local principalities undertook large-scale reforestation and enacted laws based on sustainability – the idea was to only harvest as much wood as would grow again, and to plant trees for the benefit of future generations.[90] This was all reversed with the industrial revolution, bringing with it a resource-intensive and short-term orientation, and changes to legislation to mirror this shift in focus.[91]

The constant theme throughout history in relation to sustainable practices was to live from the yield and not from the substance of the resource.[92] In essence, development and use of resources was to take place without jeopardising ecological integrity.

IV. The Status of Sustainable Development in International Law

A helpful approach to sustainable development is to liken it to the idea of justice. We accept justice as a fundamental principle of society and, although we may not

[84] Bosselmann (n 3) 95.
[85] *Gabčikovo-Nagymaros Project (Hungary v Slovakia)* [1997] ICJ Rep 7 [107]–[108].
[86] Bosselmann (n 3) 5.
[87] Segger (n 12) 92.
[88] ibid.
[89] Bosselmann (n 3) 12.
[90] ibid.
[91] ibid 20.
[92] ibid.

have an agreed definition, we know when it is not there or when we are moving towards it. The same is true for sustainability. The ethical impetus behind both is widely accepted as central for building a just, sustainable society.[93]

Not only is the core meaning of sustainable development the subject of much debate, so too is its legal status in international law. Some argue that sustainable development is a new customary principle of international law, which is in the process of being established as binding on all but a few persistently objecting states. Others suggest that it is a general principle of international law,[94] and others consider that given its broad and vague nature it has no status at all.[95]

Sustainable development has been recognised in international jurisprudence. Examples of this include the *Gabčikovo-Nagymaros Project*[96] and the *Pulp Mills* case[97] – both decisions of the International Court of Justice – and the award of the Permanent Court of Arbitration in the *Iron Rhine (Belgium v The Netherlands)* case.[98]

The decision of the International Court of Justice in *Gabčikovo-Nagymaros Project* was the first time sustainable development was given express recognition in international jurisprudence.[99] The case involved a dispute over the construction of a number of dams along the Danube River. Hungary and Czechoslovakia had entered into a treaty agreeing to build and jointly operate these dams; however, after a short period of construction, Hungary suspended work on the project in 1989. Hungary did so on the basis of the potential for significant environmental harm to the ecological river system and its biological diversity and to the water supply for Budapest. Nonetheless Czechoslovakia, and, after 1993, Slovakia, proceeded with constructing one of the dams (the Gabčikovo power plant), which required the diversion of approximately 80 per cent of the shared water into a bypass canal on Slovak territory. In 1992 Hungary purported to terminate the 1977 treaty. When Slovakia disagreed, the matter was referred to the International Court of Justice.[100]

While the Court did not address whether the project was sustainable, the Court did require the parties to look afresh at the environmental consequences of the project and to find a satisfactory solution that took account of the objectives of the 1977 Treaty, as well as the norms of international environmental law and the principles of the law of international watercourses.[101]

[93] ibid 96.

[94] Voigt (n 8) 145–86.

[95] G Winter, 'A Fundament and Two Pillars: The Concept of Sustainable Development 20 Years after the Brundtland Report' in Bugge and Voigt (n 7) 25; M McCloskey, 'The Emperor Has No Clothes: The Conundrum of Sustainable Development' (1999) 9 *Duke Environmental Law & Policy Forum* 153.

[96] *Gabčikovo-Nagymaros Project* (n 85).

[97] *Pulp Mills on the River Uruguay (Argentina v Uruguay)* [2010] ICJ Rep 14.

[98] *Iron Rhine (Belgium v The Netherlands)* 24 May 2005, pca-cpa.org/en/cases/1, accessed 25 November 2022.

[99] Voigt (n 8) 172.

[100] Summary of the facts provided in Voigt (n 8) 173.

[101] *Gabčikovo-Nagymaros Project* (n 85) [140]–[141].

In terms of sustainable development, the majority decision commented:[102]

> Throughout the ages, mankind has, for economic and other reasons, constantly interfered with nature. In the past, this was often done without consideration of the effects upon the environment. Owing to new scientific insights and to a growing awareness of the risks for mankind – for present and future generations – of pursuit of such interventions of unconsidered and unabated pace, new norms and standards have been developed, set forth in a great number of instruments during the last two decades. Such new norms have to be taken into consideration, and such new standards given proper weight, not only when States contemplate new activities, but also when continuing with activities begun in the past. This need to reconcile economic development with protection of the environment is aptly expressed in the concept of sustainable development.

While the majority decision did not go so far as to acknowledge sustainable development as a legal principle, Vice-President Weeramantry was prepared take the matter of the status of sustainable development further. In his separately issued opinion, he stated that sustainable development was 'more than a mere concept … a principle with normative value which is crucial to the determination of this case'.[103]

In the *Iron Rhine* case,[104] the Permanent Court of Arbitration also acknowledged the status of sustainable development as an emerging principle in international law. The dispute concerned the reactivation of the historic Iron Rhine railway that ran from Belgium to Germany, crossing the territory of the Netherlands. Rights of transit through the Netherlands had been conferred to Belgium in the 1939 Treaty of Separation. The route had effectively been out of use during the 1990s and the Netherlands had in the meantime designated a number of nature reserves on either side of the route. In 2001, Belgium undertook an Environmental Impact Assessment, intending temporary use of the route with the prospect of full reactivation. Belgium and the Netherlands however disagreed on the use of the route and the allocation of costs for the environmental measures required by the Netherlands.[105]

At para 59 of the award, the Tribunal commented:[106]

> Importantly, these emerging principles [making reference to conservation, management, notions of prevention and of sustainable development, and protection for future generations] now integrate environmental protection into the development process. Environmental law and the law on development stand not as alternatives but as mutually reinforcing, integral concepts, which require that where development may cause significant harm to the environment there is a duty to prevent, or at least mitigate, such harm … This duty, in the opinion of the Tribunal, has now become a principle of general international law.

[102] ibid [140].
[103] ibid [85] (Vice-President Weeramantry).
[104] *Iron Rhine* (n 98).
[105] Summary of the facts provided in Voigt (n 8) 175.
[106] *Iron Rhine* (n 98) [59].

The Tribunal referred to the decision of the International Court of Justice in the *Gabčikovo-Nagymaros Project* case and came to the opinion that sustainable development was as relevant in determining the application of the Treaty in the present case, as it was in *Gabčikovo-Nagymaros Project*.

In *Pulp Mills*, a decision of the International Court of Justice, there was a recognisable progression in the terminology surrounding sustainable development from the *Gabčikovo-Nagymaros Project*. In this case, Argentina argued that Uruguay had violated the Statute of the River Urugay in constructing two pulp mills on the banks of the river which had caused damage to both the environment of the river and its coastal zone.[107] In a separate opinion, Judge Cançado Trindade stated that sustainable development evolved to a 'general principle of International Environmental Law'.[108] While not going this far, the majority did use terminology beyond that of the majority in *Gabčikovo-Nagymaros Project*.[109] Here, the majority stated that the object of Article 27 of the Statute of the River Uruguay, which is what Argentina claimed Uruguay had breached, was 'consistent with the objective of sustainable development'.[110] Further, the court read sustainable development into the meaning of Article 27, meaning its implementation must be consistent with this objective.[111] Sustainable development in *Pulp Mills* was recognised as more than a concept, it was considered an objective that state conduct, here as defined by Article 27, had to be consistent with.[112]

Sustainable Development has been referred to in many key treaties, including the 1992 United Nations Framework Convention on Climate Change, the 1992 United Nations Convention on Biological Diversity, and the 1994 United Nations Convention to Combat Desertification. In these and other state-negotiated agreements sustainable development still lacks a clear direction needed for its operationality, and in this context it is helpful to consider the Earth Charter which was drafted in direct response to the 1992 Earth Summit failing to reach consensus on a sustainable development treaty.

The Earth Charter, adopted in 2000, had no input from states. Rather, numerous civil society groups created it as a global, cross-cultural, cross-religious ethical framework for achieving sustainable development.[113] It adopts an ecocentric approach to sustainable development based on 'respect and care for the community of life' (main principle 1). Its second main principle defines ecological integrity as the core of sustainability. For example, sub-principle 5 provides for the 'protect[ion] and [restoration of] the integrity of Earth's ecological systems, with special concern for biological diversity and the natural processes that sustain

[107] *Pulp Mills* (n 97).
[108] ibid [177].
[109] Bosselmann (n 3) 86.
[110] *Pulp Mills* (n 97) [177].
[111] Bosselmann (n 3) 86.
[112] ibid.
[113] Earth Charter Initiative, 'What is the Earth Charter?', earthcharter.org/about-the-earth-charter/, accessed 22 May 2024.

life'. And sub-principle 7, in turn, provides for the '[adoption of] patterns of production, consumption, and reproduction that safeguard Earth's regenerative capacities, human rights, and community wellbeing'.[114]

V. Conclusion

Sustainable development has created a body of substantive law at the intersection of international economic, environmental and social law. Key to understanding what this encompasses is the conceptual understanding of sustainable development, which underpins this body of law. In order to achieve this, the main focus of this chapter has been to trace the development, evolution and application of the term 'sustainable development' in international environmental law and jurisprudence.

It is clear that sustainable development is an emerging fundamental legal principle of increasing importance. Starting with the definition of the term in the 1987 Brundtland Report, the term has received increasing acceptance. However, the generally accepted interpretation of the term, at least at state-level, is the weak and more politically palatable form of sustainable development – according equal weight to the social, economic and environmental/ecological elements of the concept.

While there has been much debate over the content or core of sustainable development, when tracing back through the history of the concept, the core essence of sustainable development becomes clear: ecological sustainability. Without this core meaning, and without the biosphere forming the parameter within which social and economic development must take place, sustainable development will be ineffective.

The challenge posed by the adoption of a strong form of sustainable development is not insubstantial and will require changes to how we live and operate. Subsequently, this shift in conception will promise to transform the relationship between the Global North and Global South from disparity to equal members of a community of states committed to the same goal of preserving Earth's integrity. However, the choice of whether to adopt the strong form of sustainability will, undoubtedly, soon be out of our hands. As the authors of the Brundtland Report pointed out 35 years ago:[115]

> We are not forecasting the future; we are serving a notice – urgent notice based on the latest and best scientific evidence – that the time has come to take the decision needed to secure the resources to sustain this and coming generations.

[114] ibid.
[115] Bugge and Voigt (n 7) 1–2.

3

Sustainable Development Principles and the Global South in the Context of Planetary Change

MICHELLE LIM

I. Introduction

> The principle of sustainable development is thus a part of modern international law by reason not only of its inescapable logical necessity, but also by reason of its wide and general acceptance by the global community.
>
> Vice-President Weeramantry, Separate Opinion, *Gabčíkovo-Nagymaros Project (Hungary v Slovkia)*, 1997 ICJ Rep 7 (25 September), p 95.

Many scholars and students of environmental law readily recite the paragraph above in support of arguments as to the legal status of sustainable development. Importantly, particularly in the context of this volume, Justice Weeramantry's separate opinion is also a fundamental contribution to underscoring sustainable development discourse as being of, and for, the Global South – with, of course, implications for the Global North.

For Weeramantry, the 'inescapable logical necessity' of sustainable development stems from the need to harmonise 'developmental and environmental concepts'.[1] As will be discussed, core principles of sustainable development also include inter- as well as intragenerational equity. In other words, sustainable development means ensuring that activities of current generations do not jeopardise the ecological foundation that both present and future generations rely on for continued well-being. At the same time, intra-generational equity is equally important in recognition not only of historical contributions to planetary scale disruption but also of the unequal distribution of the benefits and burdens across geographical as well as temporal scales.

[1] *Gabčíkovo-Nagymaros Project (Hungary v Slovakia)* (Justice Weeramantry, Separate Opinion) [1997] ICJ Rep 7, 87.

Sustainable development and the Global South are therefore inextricably interconnected. These concepts are intertwined in consideration of issues of power, geopolitics and equality. Most notably, unsustainable consumption levels of the Global North are made possible by the continued extraction of the labour and resources of the Global South. This occurs on unequal terms between the North and South, resulting not only in global inequality but also planetary scale ecological breakdown evidenced, for example, across global climate and biodiversity.[2] As a consequence, how we frame sustainable development and the Global South impacts on the governance of, relationships to and narratives about continued human well-being and the natural world.

However, 'sustainable development' and the 'Global South' are both characterised as much by their widespread usage as their definitional ambiguity. As a concept that has normative and policy weight, sustainable development is also shrouded in *legal* uncertainty. Despite decades of academic commentary and debate, alongside consideration in multiple judicial fora[3] (including the ICJ[4]), discussion continues around the legal status of sustainable development. What is undisputed is that the concept has legal, normative and policy influence.[5]

A similar lack of preciseness characterises notions of a 'Global South'. The term has connotations of Earth's southern hemisphere yet many attempts to describe the term emphasise that 'the South' is not a geographical designation. Nevertheless, while the territory of a number of 'Southern' states is located predominantly if not entirely North of the equator, discussion of a global 'South' is often the starting point for considering levels of economic disparity between regions of the world. Yet, it is unclear whether states 'graduate' from being a country of the Global South once they attain a certain level of economic development or whether the South has a deeper meaning, of connection to particular ideals due to shared historical and contemporary solidarities. Indeed, there is increasing engagement with whether notions of a global 'South' extend beyond the state to embody a movement united by shared motivations to address inequalities across but also within national borders.

This chapter engages with the continuing usefulness (or otherwise) of both 'sustainable development' and the 'Global South'. This is not about whether global issues should be determined only by economically and politically powerful states. On the contrary, the central question of this chapter is how 'sustainable development' and the 'Global South' should be defined in the context of global

[2] J Hickel and others, 'Imperialist Appropriation in the World Economy: Drain from the Global South Through Unequal Exchange, 1990–2015' (2022) 73 *Global Environmental Change* 102467, 102468.

[3] United States – *Import Provisions of Certain Shrimp and Shrimp Products*, WT/DS58/AB/R, WTO Appellate Body Report, 12 October 1998.

[4] *Gabčíkovo-Nagymaros Project (Hungary v Slovakia)*, Judgment ICJ Reports (1997); *Case Concerning Pulp Mills on the River Uruguay*, Judgment ICJ Reports (2010).

[5] D French, 'Sustainable Development' in M Fitzmaurice, D Ong and P Merkouris (eds), *Research Handbook on International Environmental Law* (Edward Elgar, 2010).

environmental change so that the inextricable issues of human well-being and ecological integrity can be addressed equitably and in a way that sustains the functions of the Earth system. It is therefore to interrogation of sustainable development and its legal status, as well as evolving understandings of the 'South', that this chapter turns.

The chapter first engages with existing definitions and sub-principles of sustainable development. Next, the chapter examines whether sustainable development can be considered either a principle of customary law or a general principle of international law. The chapter then explores evolving understandings of the Global South and what implementation of sustainable development means and could mean in the context of an increasingly hyperconnected and neo-liberalised world.

II. What is Sustainable Development?

The most frequently cited definition of sustainable development comes from the Brundtland Report. The Report states:

> Sustainable development is development that meets the needs of the present without compromising the ability of future generations to meet their own needs.[6]

The flexibility and scope of the concept has added to its broad appeal. These same characteristics make the precise definition, implementation and legal characterisation of the norm particularly challenging. Key components have nevertheless emerged.

Sands and Peel identify four recurring elements: (i) inter-generational equity; (ii) sustainable use; (iii) equitable use and intra-generational equity; and (iv) integration of environmental considerations.[7] These broadly reflect the International Law Association's (ILA's) seven principles on Sustainable Development.[8] Principle 1 of the ILA's principles concerns sustainable use for current and future generations. In addition, a precautionary approach (Principle 4) is included as a further principle to avoid human activities that cause irreversible harm to human health, natural resources and ecosystems. Inter-generational equity also features in Principle 2: equity and poverty eradication. Equity here encompasses both intra- and inter-generational equity. Integration is the focus of ILA Principle 7. The ILA Principles however extend this more broadly across the social, economic and environmental pillars rather than just the integration of environmental considerations in Sands and Peel's framing. In addition, the ILA Principles dedicate

[6] World Commission on Environment and Development (WCED), 'Our Common Future' (Oxford University Press, 1987).

[7] P Sands, *Principles of International Environmental Law* 2nd edn (Cambridge University Press, 2003); P Sands and J Peel, *Principles of International Environmental Law* 3rd edn (Cambridge University Press, 2012) 207.

[8] ILA New Delhi Principles on Sustainable Development (2002).

three principles to issues of governance. These include common but differentiated responsibilities (Principle 3); public participation (Principle 5); and good governance (Principle 6).

Schrijver views sustainable development law as being derived from international economic law, international environmental law and international human rights law.[9] He therefore sees sustainable development as encompassing: (i) rule of law in international economic relations;[10] (ii) the duty to cooperate for sustainable development;[11] and (iii) respect for human rights.[12] Schrijver argues that international economic law has progressed from an international law of co-existence to one of cooperation. At the same time, he cites Principle 7 of the Rio Declaration which calls for cooperation to 'conserve, respect and restore the health and integrity of the Earth's ecosystem' as well as the Declaration's preamble, which emphasises new and equitable partnership, to highlight that cooperation refers increasingly to the protection of the vital functions of the Earth.[13] Thus, Schrijver views the content of Sustainable Development as being founded on integration of international law across economic, environmental and human rights pillars and attributes a duty of cooperation to achieve this integration.

Meanwhile, French draws out four key principles which he sees as the legal minimum encompassed in Sustainable Development. Integration is again a key principle as is the duty to cooperate. The other two principles include sustainable use; and the principle of equity and the right to sustainable development.[14] French considers but leaves out precaution as a core principle, arguing that precaution only applies to discrete areas of international law.

While there is scant jurisprudence to confirm the precise content of sustainable development, and while different emphases are articulated in the literature, I suggest that four key principles can be distilled. These are: (1) integration; (2) inter-generational equity; (3) intragenerational equity; and (4) governance imperatives such as the duty to cooperate, common but differentiated responsibilities, and public participation. Each of these are discussed further below.

A. Integration

Despite ambiguity surrounding the precise content of sustainable development alluded to above, integration is front and centre of all attempts to define it. For example, Schrijver describes integration as the most innovative of all sustainable

[9] N Schijver, *The Evolution of Sustainable Development in International Law: Inception, Meaning and Status* (Hague Academy of International Law, Martinus Nijhoff Publishers, 2008) 162.
[10] ibid 163–64.
[11] ibid 164–65.
[12] ibid 167–71.
[13] ibid 166–67.
[14] French (n 5) 58.

development principles,[15] while Jodoin calls it the 'most essential' of all seven ILA principles.[16] For Voight, integration is the context within which all other components of sustainable development (eg the precautionary principle, polluter pays and common but differentiated responsibilities) take effect;[17] and McGoldrick emphasises that it is from its integrationist nature that sustainable development derives its fundamental importance.[18] Meanwhile, Schacherer's recent work cites extensive literature which continues to confirm integration as central to operationalising sustainable development.[19] Similarly, French explains that without integration sustainable development cannot achieve proper and full implementation.[20]

There is thus little argument that integration is at the core of sustainable development. Schacherer draws attention to the 'shall' and the word 'integral' in Principle 4 of the Rio Declaration. Principle 4 states:

> in order to achieve sustainable development, environmental protection shall constitute an integral part of the development process and cannot be considered in isolation from it.

She goes on to explain that 'shall' indicates the imperative of integrating environmental concerns, while 'integral' hints at other sectors also being important.[21]

Nevertheless, it is the need to take into account multiple, often conflicting, societal goals that creates the conundrum and lack of determinacy around sustainable development in the first place. Kent therefore points to the requirement to design laws and policies that achieve a 'balance' across multiple sectors and considerations as being the key challenge for implementing the principle of integration.[22] As alluded to above, while it is possible to concurrently achieve economic, social and environmental objectives, in many cases this involves addressing intractable trade-offs.

Integration often refers to the consideration of each of the three pillars of sustainable development across jurisdictions and sectors. The three pillars are made up of the environment, society and the economy. Voight describes the equal

[15] Schrijver (n 9) 203.

[16] S Jodoin, 'The principle of integration and interrelationship in relations to human rights and social, economic and environmental objectives' (2005) CISDL Legal Working Paper commissioned by Foreign Affairs Canada; J Ellis, 'Sustainable development and fragmentation in international society' in D French (ed), *Global Justice and Sustainable Development* (Martinus Nijhoff, 2010) 57; A Kent, 'Implementing the Principle of Policy Integration: Institutional Interplay and the Role of International Organizations' (2014) 14 *International Environmental Agreements* 203, 204.

[17] C Voight, *Sustainable Development as a Principle of International Law – Resolving Conflicts Between Climate Measures and WTO Law* (Martinus Nijhoff Publishers, 2009) 38.

[18] D McGoldrick 'Sustainable Development and Human Rights: An Integrated Approach' (1996) 45 *ICLQ* 796, 818.

[19] S Schacherer, 'Sustainable Development in the International Legal Order' in S Schacherer, *Sustainable Development in EU Foreign Investment Law* (Brill Nijhoff, 2021) 28. See in particular footnote 48 of that chapter.

[20] French (n 5) 59.

[21] Schacherer (n 19) 28.

[22] Kent (n 16) 204.

treatment of each of the three pillars as an 'illusory goal' and insisting that each pillar has the same importance 'could prove to be the major obstacle to sustainable development'.[23] But which goal to prioritise? Across the literature there is a clear difference in emphasis. Kent defines integration as an implication that:

> economic laws should not be designed solely for the purpose of maximizing financial profits, but also with the object of improving human well-being, and addressing social and environmental concerns.[24]

On the other hand, Kim and Bosselmann stress that ecological integrity needs to be at the core, not only of sustainable development, but of international law as a whole. In contrast to Kent, who concedes that economic laws should not be designed *solely* (my emphasis) for delivering and *maximising* financial profit, Kim and Bosselmann underscore the importance of centring the integrity of the Earth's fundamental natural life support systems.[25]

B. Other Sustainable Development Principles

i. Inter-generational Equity

Inter-generational equity has always been central to the concept of sustainable development. Recalling the most widely used definition of sustainable development cited above, the 'ability of future generations to meet their own needs' lies at the core of understandings of sustainable development itself. Meanwhile, Schacherer highlights the emergence of this principle even prior to that of the sustainable development agenda, noting its incorporation, for example, in the preamble of the 1946 International Convention on the Regulation of Whaling.[26]

Inter-generational equity can be characterised as a commitment to the aspiration that economic development should not jeopardise the well-being nor the ecological foundations of future generations. In the principle, we see also components of rationale and sustainable use of components of the planet 'in a way which would not preclude lasting development and conditions of life on the planet for future generations'.[27] Development of this scholarship, which encompasses other principles linked to sustainable development such as sustainable use, precaution and prevention, is highly indebted to the work of Brown Weiss.[28]

[23] Voight (n 17) 41.

[24] Kent (n 16) 203.

[25] R Kim and K Bosselmann, 'Operationalizing Sustainable Development: Ecological Integrity as a Grundnorm of International Law' (2015) 24 *Review of European, Comparative & International Environmental Law* 194.

[26] Schacherer (n 19) 32.

[27] F Francioni, 'Revisiting Sustainable Development in Light of General Principles of International Environmental Law' in *Reflections on the Constitutionalisation of International Economic Law* (Brill Nijhoff, 2014) 473, 475.

[28] See, for example, EB Weiss, 'In fairness to future generations: international law, common patrimony, and intergenerational equity' (Hotei Publishing, 1988); EB Weiss, 'Our rights and obligations

ii. Intragenerational Equity and Respect for Human Rights

Sustainable development concerns, of course, not just future generations. The economic, social and cultural, civil and political rights of current generations are also embedded within the concept and are characterised in terms of intra-generational equity. Considered in light of the principle of integration, fundamental labour principles including the freedom of association, elimination of forced labour, the abolition of child labour, and the elimination of all forms of discrimination have also been characterised as specific rights connected to sustainable development.[29]

While inter-generational equity looks to the future, intra-generational equity concerns not only the present generation but also past inequities that have contributed to current living standards. The emergence of this in a legal sense can be seen around what Schacherer identifies as 'the more concrete principle of common but differentiated responsibilities (CBDR)'.[30] Drawing on Rio Declaration Principles such as 5, 6, 7 and 11, CBDR acknowledges the greater contribution of the Global North to planetary degradation; and therefore, in turn, greater responsibility to carry the burden of ameliorating such harm. This principle is particularly prominent within the climate regime of the United Nations Framework Convention on Climate Change (UNFCCC) and Paris Agreement but also applies across a range of other multilateral environmental agreements.[31] The UNFCCC, for example, emphasises differing contributions and impacts of climate change in its preamble, principles[32] and commitments.[33] The starkest legal application of CBDR is arguably in the annex approach of the UNFCCC's Kyoto Protocol.[34] Though abandoning the annex approach, the Paris Agreement, the successor instrument to the Kyoto Protocol, retains an emphasis on CBDR.[35]

iii. Governance Imperatives

Across all discussions of sustainable development and what it entails is also the emergence of a range of interrelated governance imperatives such as the duty to cooperate, public participation and of good governance itself.[36] Schrijver goes as

to future generations for the environment' (1990) 84 *American Journal of International Law* 198; EB Weiss, 'The Plantetary Trust: Conservation and Intergenerational Equity' (1983) 11 *Ecology LQ* 495.

[29] See, for example, Schacherer (n 19) 34. Nevertheless, Novitz warns that the inclusion of sustainable development terminology in trade agreements has not, of itself, advanced fundamental worker protections; T Novitz, 'Labour standards and trade: Need we choose between "human rights" and "sustainable development"?' (2018) *Labour Standards in International Economic Law* 113.

[30] Schacherer (n 19) 33.

[31] ibid.

[32] UNFCCC, Art 3(1), (3), (4).

[33] UNFCCC, Art 4.

[34] P Castro, 'Common But Differentiated Responsibilities Beyond the Nation State: How Is Differential Treatment Addressed in Transnational Climate Governance Initiatives?' (2016) 5 *Transnational Environmental Law* 379.

[35] See, for example, Paris Agreement, Art 2(2), Art 4(3).

[36] See, for example, Schacherer (n 19) 34–36.

far as to state that the principle of good governance has 'acquired a central place in the development debate' and is 'widely viewed' as fundamental to sustainable development and its implementation.[37] It is also worth noting that of the seven principles of the International Law Association's New Delhi Declaration of Principles of International Law Relating to Sustainable Development (2002), two focus explicitly on governance: Principle 5 on public participation and Principle 6 on 'The principle of good governance'.[38] Principle 5 of the ILA Declaration echoes Principle 10 of the Rio Declaration which emphasises the imperative not only of access to information but also to 'judicial and administrative proceedings, including redress and remedy'.[39] Meanwhile, the 'good governance' principle of the ILA Declaration focuses on:

- democratic and transparent decision-making and financial accountability;
- corruption;
- respect of due process, rule of law and human rights; and
- public procurement based on the WTO code.[40]

As will be discussed later in this chapter, while not discounting the importance of such principles, there needs to be an awareness of how the narratives of 'good governance' and the perceived lack thereof in the Global South have been used by the Global North to perpetuate assumptions that the economic plight of the Global South as its own doing. In other words, placing the blame on the South while diverting attention away from the continued appropriation of Southern labour and resources.[41]

This section has started to engage with what 'sustainable development' means. Ultimately, the integration of environment and developmental priorities sits at the core of this concept. Intertwined with this is the need for concern for equity between current as well as future generations when making decisions about what actions would be consistent with sustainable development. Governance concerns often go hand-in-hand with discussions of sustainable development, particularly as it concerns implementation. The importance of sustainable development's sub-principles, particularly as they relate to continued flourishing of Southern societies and environments will be examined in sections IV and V. Focus will be on what equity means for current and future generations of Southern countries and societies and also what this in turn requires of the Global North with the essence of CBDR in mind.

[37] Schrijver (n 9) 200–01.

[38] International Law Association, 'New Delhi Declaration of Principles of International Law Relating to Sustainable Development' 2002) in *International Law Association Report of the Seventy-Second Conference* (New Delhi 2002) (International Law Association, 2002).

[39] UNGA, 'Report of the United Nations Conference on Environment and Development by UNGA Res 47/190' (3–14 June 1992) UN Doc A/CONF.151/26/Rev l (Vol I) Principle 10.

[40] ILA Declaration, Principle 6.

[41] J Hickel, D Sullivan and H Zoomkawala, 'Plunder in the Post-Colonial Era: Quantifying Drain from the Global South through Unequal Exchange, 1960–2018' (2021) 26 *New Political Economy* 1030, 1031.

First, though, the encompassing nature of sustainable development has challenged attempts to characterise its legal nature. Section III therefore explores the concept's legal status and its implications.

III. What is the Legal Status of Sustainable Development?

Sustainable development as a legal principle suffers as much as it benefits from its ambiguity. Goepel points out, for example, that while the lack of conceptual clarity of the term creates not only interpretation but also implementation challenges; the flip side is that such characteristics may help ensure its acceptability from many different local and global perspectives, from many cultures and regions.[42] Its broad scope means that it has been adopted in multiple international and national legal and policy instruments[43] as the term can be interpreted generally to suit a range of different purposes. At the same time, operationalising sustainable development and reconciling and coordinating legal regimes across social, economic and environmental spheres presents significant challenges.

Despite significant academic discourse and jurisprudence surrounding sustainable development and its potential customary law status,[44] it remains unclear whether the term constitutes a binding principle[45] of international law or instead merely an objective[46] or a concept.[47] This stems from the definitional ambiguity of sustainable development[48] with competing interpretations of the norm a key hurdle to determining its legal status. Uncertainty surrounding the legal status and definition of sustainable development should not, however, be taken as lack of legal influence.[49] With its incorporation in a large number of international and

[42] M Goepel, 'Formulating Future Just Policies: Applying the Delhi Sustainable Development Law Principles' (2010) 58 *The Indian Economic Journal* 3.

[43] See Voight (n 17) which provides a list of the range and number of instruments that have included sustainable development.

[44] V Barral, 'Sustainable Development in International Law: Nature and Operation of an Evolutive Legal Norm' (2012) 23 *European Journal of International Law*; MCC Segger, 'Significant Developments in Sustainable Development Law and Governance: A Proposal' (2004) United Nations Natural Resources Forum; V Lowe, 'Sustainable Development and Unsustainable Arguments' in A Boyle and D Freestone (eds), *International Law and Sustainable Development: Past Achievements and Future Challenges* (Oxford University Press, 1999); *Case Concerning Pulp Mills on the River Uruguay*, Judgment ICJ Reports (2010); *Gabčíkovo-Nagymaros Project (Hungary v Slovakia)*, Judgment ICJ Reports (1997).

[45] Weeramantry, *Gabčíkovo-Nagymaros; Iron Rhine Case.*

[46] *WTO Shrimp-Turtle* case.

[47] *Gabčíkovo-Nagymaros Project (Hungary/Slovakia)*, Judgment, ICJ Reports (1997) 7, 78. In the *Gabčíkovo-Nagymaros* case, the ICJ invoked sustainable development as an international legal concept that refers to the 'need to reconcile economic development with protection of the environment'.

[48] E Scotford, *Environmental Principles and the Evolution of Environmental Law* (Hart Publishing, 2017) 94.

[49] French (n 5) 54.

national instruments[50] across a range of sectors it is clear that sustainable development has some normative value even if the extent of its normative function and precise content are less clear.[51]

If sustainable development is an established principle of international law, whether as customary law or as a general principle of international law, it is binding on states regardless of any treaty obligations.[52] However, despite being first considered almost 30 years ago by the International Court of Justice (ICJ),[53] and with 21 years having passed since the formulation of the 2002 International Law Association (ILA) Delhi Principles,[54] the legal status of sustainable development remains unclear.

Though some trace the genesis of sustainable development to traditional practices dating back millennia,[55] it is in more recent times that sustainable development has gained prominence in international law – in the Westphalian sense. Sustainable development has been described as 'the dominant global environmental policy' since the 1980s[56] and more than half a century has passed since the emergence of the term within international discourse.[57]

Sustainable development forms a ubiquitous framing of global governance issues and has been incorporated in a range of international law and policy instruments. Yet, there remains no absolute judicial or scholarly consensus as to what exactly sustainable development principles encompass.

There is no disputing that sustainable development is at the very least a globally recognised aspiration that has gained traction within international and domestic courts and legislatures. Contemporary international law cases are increasingly being addressed by reference to sustainable development. This is true not only of courts of general jurisdiction such as the ICJ, but also the dispute settlement bodies of the World Trade Organization (WTO).[58] In *Gabčíkovo*, the ICJ recognised sustainable development as an international legal concept that refers to the

[50] Incorporation in such a large number of international and national instruments (see, for example, Voight (n 17) 21): 'Gradual growing commitment of international community sustainable development' includes 'Examples of amendments by the 1997 Treaty of Amsterdam, the EC Treaty and the 1992 Maastricht Treaty on the European Union'. Article 2 of the Treaty Establishing the European Union 'mentions the achievement of sustainable development as a fundamental objective of the European Union', suggesting that sustainable development has some sort of normative status.

[51] French (n 5) 54.

[52] Voight (n 17).

[53] *Gabčíkovo-Nagymaros Project (Hungary v Slovakia)* (Judgment) [1997] ICJ Rep, 7, 78.

[54] Delhi Principles 2002.

[55] Justice Weeramantry for example claims that sustainable development is 'one of the most ancient ideas in the human heritage'. See *Gabčíkovo-Nagymaros Project (Hungary v Slovakia)* (Separate Opinion – Judge Weeramantry) [1997] ICJ Rep 7, 12.

[56] JS Dryzek, 'Paradigms and Discourses' in D Bodansky, J Brunnée and E Hey (eds), *The Oxford Handbook of International Environmental Law* (Oxford University Press, 2007) 45, 56–58.

[57] Measured as the time since the conclusion of the *Stockholm Declaration* in 1972. *Declaration of the United Nations Conference on the Human Environment* (Stockholm) 16 June 1972, A/CONF.151/26 (Vol I).

[58] T Stephens, 'Sustainability Discourses in International Courts: What Place for Global Justice?' in D French (ed), *Global Justice and Sustainable Development* (Martinus Nijhoff, 2010).

'need to reconcile economic development with protection of the environment'.[59] Though the court emphasised that new norms and standards should be given proper weight,[60] they did not extend this to conferring on sustainable development the weight of a customary law principle or a general principle of international law.

Given the ambiguity surrounding the legal status of sustainable development, this section examines whether the concept can be considered a binding principle of international law either by meeting customary law requirements or as a general principle of international law.

A. Is Sustainable Development a Customary Law Norm?

International custom is an important source of law defined in the ICJ Statute.[61] If sustainable development were to assume customary status it would need to meet both the requirements of state practice and *opnio juris*. This would require not only 'constant and uniform usage'[62] by states but also that states act in such a manner because they believe they have a legal obligation to apply the norm of sustainable development.

Early commentary was hesitant to recognise that sustainable development had any customary status. Prior to *Gabčíkovo*, Bodansky argued that though the concept provided an underlying idea of integrated decision-making, it did not meet state practice requirements to be a binding principle of law.[63] In the aftermath of *Gabčíkovo*, Akhtar-Khavari and Rothwell concluded that the concept failed to reach the status of customary law as there was no consensus on its definition or how to give it practical effect.[64] Such sentiment was echoed by Lowe who argued that the term did not possess a 'fundamentally norm-creating character'[65] and lacked specific substance to guide determination of the legality of a state's action.[66]

The *ILA New Delhi Declaration*[67] moved beyond characterising sustainable development as a mere concept framing it as a global objective to which all human

[59] *Gabčíkovo-Nagymaros Project (Hungary v Slovakia)* (Judgment) [1997] ICJ Rep, 7, 78.

[60] *Gabčíkovo-Nagymaros Project (Hungary v Slovakia)* (Merits) (1997) ICJ Rep 88, para 140.

[61] Statute of the International Court of Justice, Art 38(1)(b).

[62] *Asylum Case Columbia v Peru* ICJ Reports 1950, 266. The International Law Commission indicates that state practice may take the following into account as examples of 'constant and uniform usage': treaties, decision of international and national courts, national legislation, diplomatic correspondence, opinions of national legal advisers .... etc. 'Ways and Means of Making the Evidence of Customary International Law More Readily Available' Report of the International Law Commission (1950) II YBILC, 368–72.

[63] D Bodansky, 'Customary (and Not So Customary) International Environmental Law' (1995) 3 *Indiana Journal of Global Legal Studies* 105.

[64] A Akhtar-Khavari and DR Rothwell, 'The ICJ and the Danube Dam Case: A Missed Opportunity for International Environmental Law?' (1998) 22 *Melbourne University Law Review* 507, 522.

[65] *North Sea Continental Shelf (Germany v Netherlands and Denmark)* 1969 ICJ Rep 3.

[66] Lowe (n 44) 25.

[67] International Law Association (ILA) New Delhi Declaration of Principles of International Law Relating to Sustainable Development, 2 April 2002 (70th Conference of the International Law Association, held in New Delhi, India, 2–6 April 2002).

activities must strive. At the same time, in the *Shrimp-Turtle Case*,[68] the Appellate Body of the WTO indicated that sustainable development must 'add colour, texture and shading to interpretation of agreements annexed to the World Trade Organization Agreement'.[69] Much of this hinged, however, on the inclusion of sustainable development as an objective in the Preamble of the WTO Agreement.[70] The Appellate Body did not classify sustainable development as a broader principle of international law. The decision did suggest, however, that due to its inclusion in the WTO Agreement, sustainable development has normative influence over annexed agreements. Similarly, Lydgate argues that even if sustainable development is deemed a WTO principle this is to be distinguished from WTO rules which are more binding in nature. This echoes the discussion of integration above. In the WTO context, Lydgate points to the 'balancing' role of sustainable development, which calls upon a weighing up for social, environmental and economic objectives when any of these inevitably clash.[71]

In rejecting sustainable development as a binding customary legal norm Lowe stressed that frequent use of a term is by no means evidence of a general practice.[72] Twenty years on, sustainable development has been incorporated into countless legal and policy instruments at the international and domestic level. This begs the question, at what point does sustainable development move beyond the status of a concept or a goal of the international community to that of a binding legal principle?

As highlighted at the start of this chapter, for Vice-President Weeramantry of the ICJ, that point was achieved more than 25 years ago. In *Gabčíkovo*, Judge Weeramantry declared in a separate opinion that sustainable development was a principle of law with normative force.[73] Citing numerous sources which included the term sustainable development, Weeramantry concluded that, in his opinion, the required degree of recognition among states as to the obligatory nature of the practice was sufficient to give sustainable development the status of a customary law norm.[74]

More recently, in the *Iron Rhine Arbitration*[75] the Tribunal recounts Principle 4 of the Rio Declaration which states that 'environmental protection shall constitute an integral part of the development process'. The Tribunal then declares that:

[68] *Appellate Body Report, United States – Import Prohibition of Certain Shrimp and Shrimp Products*, WTO Doc WT/DS58/AB/R (12 October 1998) [12] ('*Shrimp-Turtle Case*').

[69] ibid [153].

[70] Marrakesh Agreement Establishing the World Trade Organization ('WTO Agreement), Done at Marrakesh, 15 April 1994.

[71] EB Lydgate, 'Sustainable development in the WTO: from mutual supportiveness to balancing' (2012) 11 *World Trade Review* 621, 625, 637–38.

[72] Lowe (n 44) 24.

[73] *Gabčíkovo-Nagymaros* (n 59) (Separate Opinion Judge Weeramantry) 88.

[74] ibid 104.

[75] *Iron Rhine Arbitration (Belgium v Netherlands)*, Award of the Arbitral Tribunal, Permanent Court of Arbitration 2005, para 59.

> environmental law and the law on development stand not as alternatives but as mutually reinforcing, integral concepts, which require where that where development may cause significant harm to the environment there is a duty to prevent, or at least mitigate such harm. This duty, in the opinion of the Tribunal, has now become a principle of general international law.[76]

Barral indicates that this statement suggests that the Tribunal, by the wording above, accepts the customary law status of sustainable development.[77] Upon a closer reading, however, one could argue that the duty in question is not a duty, or in other words a customary law obligation, to implement sustainable development. Rather, it is a recognition of the duty of the closely linked precautionary principle. Further, it is unclear whether the 'duty' in question is that of international custom[78] or a general principle[79] in the distinct sources of law listed in the ICJ Statute.

To date, it remains unclear whether sustainable development has crystalised as a customary law norm. It is to the question of sustainable development as a general principle, the third source of law of the ICJ Statute, that this chapter now turns.

B. Is Sustainable Development a General Principle?

Voight[80] and French[81] have both argued that, rather than constituting a customary law norm, the legal significance of sustainable development is best characterised as a 'general principle of law'[82] as set out in Article 38(1)(c) of the ICJ Statute. If sustainable development is recognised as a general principle it would be unencumbered with demonstrating state practice and *opinio juris* to demonstrate international custom.[83]

As part of the argument that sustainable development is a general principle rather than a customary law norm, Voight highlights that lawyers do not have a suitable methodology to produce reliable empirical evidence of the existence of near-universal state practice. She therefore urges conceptualisation of sustainable development as a general principle through examination of the legal nature of the norm.[84]

Voight distinguishes general principles from custom by highlighting that states become bound by general principles through their participation in the development of the norm while avoiding the 'troublesome customary law element of

[76] ibid.
[77] Barral (n 44) 387.
[78] United Nations, *Statute of the International Court of Justice*, 18 April 1946 (ICJ Statute) Art 38(1)(b).
[79] ibid Art 38(1)(c).
[80] Voight (n 17) 145–88.
[81] French (n 5) 56.
[82] United Nations, *Statute of the International Court of Justice*, 18 April 1946 ('ICJ Statute').
[83] ICJ Statute, Art 38(1)(b).
[84] Voight (n 17) 147.

universal state practice'.[85] Voight describes general principles are also described as being 'inherently broad and open-textured' and leave room for further continuous development.[86] Similarly, Scotford describes environmental principles as a 'new kind of high-level transnational legal norm'. Principles enable expression of the goals of the community, which are made concrete only within particular legal contexts. While appreciating the importance of principles, Scotford also acknowledges that they are inherently doctrinally challenging.[87]

In the context of sustainable development, Voight stresses the importance of recognising the advantage of its breadth[88] and in maintaining the distinction between a legal rule and a principle. A rule would require definition of complete and precise content while a principle assumes a level of indeterminacy.[89]

More than 30 years ago, Handl observed that sustainable development was a notion around which legally significant expectations had begun to crystalise.[90] Decades later, Voight highlighted the multiple references to sustainable development in numerous international and national instruments as evidence of acceptance of sustainable development as a normative concept.[91] Though the flexibility of sustainable development has frustrated efforts to entrench it as a binding norm, this flexibility has meant that sustainability as a discourse has retained ongoing relevance.[92] At the same time, French emphasises that questions surrounding the exact legal status of sustainable development should not be used to discount its legal influence.[93] He points out that while ambiguity remains around the precise legal status of sustainable development, the idea that sustainable development has some form of substantive legal status continues to garner significant attention.[94] Schacherer is even more direct, calling the continued debate of the precise legal status of sustainable development 'tedious' when it is clear that the concept has normative effects.[95] As an aspirational objective, Schacherer argues, sustainable development plays an important facilitating role in the integration of environmental and developmental through collective action.[96] Nevertheless, French warns that the scope of agreed understanding of sustainable development must be tempered by an awareness of the extent to which universal consensus exists on what is encompassed in 'sustainable development'.[97]

[85] ibid 149, 160.
[86] ibid 152.
[87] Scotford (n 18) 3 and 6.
[88] Voight (n 17) 163.
[89] ibid 165.
[90] G Handl, 'Environmental Security and Global Change: The Challenge to International Law' (1990) 1 *Yearbook of International Environmental Law* 3, 25.
[91] Voight (n 17) 145–46.
[92] JS Dryzek, 'Paradigms and Discourses' in D Bodansky, J Brunnée and E Hey (eds), *The Oxford Handbook of International Environmental Law* (Oxford University Press, 2007) 45, 56 ('sustainable development is a discourse, not a concept').
[93] French (n 5) 55.
[94] ibid 58.
[95] Schacherer (n 19) 38.
[96] ibid 39.
[97] French (n 5) 51–52.

The discussion above highlights that sustainable development carries legal weight – even as its exact legal status continues to be debated. States have an obligation to take into account twin goals of environment and human well-being, both for current and for future generations. This is reinforced in domestic laws across multiple jurisdictions. Particularly in international law, sustainable development does not prescribe the exact action or inaction that is required. Such ambiguity provides an opportunity to explore what sustainable development means in context. It is to the context of the 'Global South' that this discussion turns.

IV. What Even is the 'Global South' in a Multi-polar Hyper-connected World?

What is the 'Global South'? What should it mean and what could it mean amidst interconnected global geopolitical and environmental change? This section first engages with current and evolving understandings of the Global South. It then considers whether and how the Global South needs to be reconceptualised, taking into account the increasingly globalised nature of economies and societies and the emergence of transnational non-state actors. This sets the scene for considering (in section V) the possibilities for contemporary implementation of sustainable development in the Global South.

A. What is the Global South?

In 1980, the Independent Commission on International Development Issues released the report *North-South: A Programme for Survival*.[98] The report, also known as 'the Brandt Report' in recognition of the Chair of the Commission, former German Chancellor Willy Brandt, emphasised economic disparities between regions of the world. The report's 'Brandt Line', also emerged as 'one of the most recognisable and influential ways of visualising world politics'.[99]

The Brandt Line divides the world into the Global North (countries characterised by economic prosperity) and the Global South (countries that are less industrialised). Rather than the strict hemispheric division across the equator that the terms 'Global North' and 'Global South' suggest, the Brandt Line differentiated a global *economic* North and South at about 30°N.

When drawn on the world map, the Brandt Line crosses between North and Central America, then continues in a largely horizontal manner north of the

[98] W Brandt, *North-South: A Programme for Survival; Report of the Independent Commission on International Development Issues* (MIT, 1980).

[99] N Lees, 'The Brandt Line after Forty Years: The More North-South Relations Change, the More they Stay the Same?' (2021) 47 *Review of International Studies* 85.

African continent. The line then snakes slightly further north as it moves towards the east – denoting India and China as part of the Global South and the entirety of the USSR (as it then was) as part of the Global North. The line dips abruptly south where Chinese territory meets its eastern-most border with the former USSR. This designation thus includes Japan as part of the Global North before moving much further south to encircle Australia and New Zealand as part of the North. Notably, the Brandt Line therefore designated, at that point in time, South Korea, Singapore and all of the Gulf States as part of the Global South.[100]

The concessions and qualifications of the Brandt Line highlight that notions of Global Norths and Souths are not determined by hemispheric locations. Indeed, a lot of the Global 'South' is located north of the equator, whether in whole or in part. What then does the political shorthand of North and South stand for?

Like 'sustainable development', a precise definition of the 'Global South' has proved elusive. Nevertheless, the term has gained prominence as other terms have become unpalatable,[101] in particular, language which distinguishes between 'First' and 'Third' Worlds. Though the ranking of 'Worlds' was not originally meant to invoke hierarchy between countries,[102] in contemporary usage the juxtaposition of 'First' and 'Third' world denotes a magnitude of superiority of those who are 'First' without acknowledging the past and continued extractivism of colonialism.[103] In addition, though often forgotten in contemporary usage, the terms 'First' and 'Second' World were used to characterise a geopolitical division between the capitalist economies of the United States, much of Europe and aligned countries including Japan, Australia and New Zealand; and the communist countries of the then USSR and its Eastern European satellites. In other words, 'First World' originally denoted countries that were aligned with the 'West'. Those aligned with the former USSR were known as the 'Second World'. The 'Third World' in its original conception was of 'ex-colonial, newly independent and non-aligned states'.[104]

A shift from 'First' and 'Third' World to 'North-South' reflects not only the more than three decades since the fall of the USSR it also avoids the implications of characterising countries in a way that conjures imagery of a podium finish. Mohanty describes the Global North as being broadly understood by reference to the political economies of Western Europe and North America and countries that

[100] Brandt (n 98).

[101] M Mohanty, 'Inequality from the Perspective of the Global South' in M Juergensmeyer and others (eds), *The Oxford Handbook of Global Studies* 214–15; AG Mahler, 'Beyond the Color Curtain – The Metonymic Color Politics of the Tricontinental and the (New) Global South' in K Bystrom and JR Slaughter (eds), *The Global South Atlantic* (Fordham University Press, 2017) 100.

[102] MW Solarz, 'Third World': the 60th Anniversary of a Concept that Changed History' (2012) 33 *Third World Quarterly* 1561.

[103] M Silver, 'Memo to People of Earth: "Third World" is an Offensive Term!' *NPR* (8 January 2021), www.npr.org/sections/goatsandsoda/2021/01/08/954820328/memo-to-people-of-earth-third-world-is-an-offensive-term, accessed 31 March 2024.

[104] P Worsely, *The Three Worlds: Culture and World Development* (London, 1984) 309 in discussion of P Worsely, *The Third World* (London, 1964) cited in BR Tomlinson, 'What Was the Third World?' (2003) 38(2) *Journal of Contemporary History* 307.

share characteristics of 'relatively higher per capita income, free market economy, and liberal democratic polity'.[105] In turn, a key characteristic of countries of the Global South is that they were previously colonised (by and large by the Global North). Haug describes the South in terms of structural disadvantage and notes that indicators of countries of lower incomes are also reflected in interrelated issues of lower levels of education and health outcomes. For Mahler, the North-South descriptor also alludes to a shift from East-West colonisation and post-Cold War tensions to one of disparate beneficiaries of capital flows between the North and the South.[106] Hickel illustrates the significant unequal exchange of embodied labour and natural resources from the South to the North. This in turn results in inequitable and uneven development and ecological breakdown.[107] A further manifestation of this, as highlighted in the introduction to this chapter, is illustrated in disruptions in the Earth system – a key example being the continued and historical contributions of the Global North to climate change, with its impacts already severely felt by Southern countries.

It is critical that the South is recognised as far more than a collective of economic 'have nots'. Simone, for example, notes how the concept of 'the South' has facilitated 'solidarity, cooperation, and interchange among nations and societies that have found themselves marginalised in the predominant geopolitical and geocultural arrangements'.[108] Indeed, it is an undercurrent of 'challenging Western hegemony'[109] and an ongoing 'transnational struggle for racial justice'[110] that binds the South. Yet, the motivation for such solidarity has evolved from a context of post-World War II independence to continued decolonisation efforts in an increasingly neoliberal world.[111] Indeed, Golub suggests that capitalist globalisation and associated diverging development trajectories across the South have resulted in the dilution of Southern solidarities rooted in an anti-colonial quest for emancipation.[112]

Lees highlights how the 1955 Bandung Conference emerged from a common anti-colonial stance of newly independent African and Asian nations. This movement found solidarity amongst Latin American states dissatisfied with increasing marginalisation. From this emerged the United Nations Conference on Trade and Development (UNCTAD) and then the Group of 77 (G77)[113] which aimed to create a 'new and just economic order'.[114] Founded in 1964, the G77 became the

[105] Mohanty (n 101) 216.
[106] Mahler (n 101) 100.
[107] Hickel and others (n 2) 102467.
[108] AM Simone, 'Cities of the Global South' (2020) 46 *Annual Reviews of Sociology* 603, 606.
[109] ibid 605.
[110] Mahler (n 101) 101.
[111] Mohanty (n 101) 214–15; Lees (n 99) 86; ibid 100.
[112] PS Golub, 'From the New International Economic Order to the G20: how the 'Global South' is Restructuring World Capitalism from within' (2013) 34 *Third World Quarterly* 1000.
[113] Lees (n 99) 86.
[114] 'Joint Declaration of the 77'.

Global South's primary organ for setting out and arguing for common economic interests and political positions.[115] In the words of Julius Nyerere, then President of the United Republic of Tanzania, at the Fourth Ministerial Meeting of the G77 in Arusha, Tanzania in 1979, the shared interest of the G77 was to 'complete the liberation of Third World countries from external domination'.[116] Southern countries negotiating as a bloc in the United Nations system has enabled the Global South to put developing country concerns on the international agenda. Nevertheless, attempts to engender more systematic transfer of wealth and power has arguably remained elusive.[117]

The active undermining, by a number of developed countries and the United States in particular, of the New International Economic Order (NIEO), is an apt illustration of concerted neo-colonial and neoliberal undermining of attempts to institutionalise global wealth redistribution. Golub explains that the NIEO stems from discussions at the 1955 Bandung Conference. Then in May 1974, the *Declaration on the Establishment of a New International Economic Order* was adopted by the United Nations General Assembly. The Declaration sought to establish binding rules and the international institutional frameworks that would address North-South inequalities and centre Global South interests. The Declaration also called for the reform of Bretton Woods Institutions and the International Monetary Fund. However, the NIEO was seen by dominant powers of the West as a challenge to the existing order and the extractive benefits accrued to the North. As a result, in 1979 the US Federal Reserve raised interest rates to reclaim monetary control. This had a profound negative economic impact on Latin American countries in the late-1970s to early-1980s. Similarly, the actions and inactions of the US and European countries amidst the 1997–1998 Asian Financial Crisis, by refusing to come to the assistance of allied countries, enabled the existing western hegemony to pressure East Asia to conform to the US-anchored neoliberal regime. Alongside earlier stagnation in Latin American this also underscored the continued structural power of the United States, which due to its position in the world economy was able to shape international frameworks in service of US interests. All of this occurred amidst the global rise of neoliberalism and nationalistic and economic divergence within Southern states.[118]

Today, the G77 is comprised of 124 countries and remains focused on South-South cooperation. Its membership includes some of the world's wealthiest countries: Brunei Darussalam, Singapore, the United Arab Emirates and founding member Saudi Arabia. Meanwhile, Costa Rica, Chile and Columbia, founding members of the G77 have joined the Organisation for Economic Cooperation

[115] Lees (n 99) 86; K Sauvant, 'Early Days of the Group of 77, www.un.org/en/chronicle/article/early-days-group-77.

[116] Julius K Nyerere Address, 4th Meeting of the Group of 77, Arusha, Tanzania (February, 1979) cited in Sauvant (n 115).

[117] Lees (n 99) 86.

[118] Golub (n 112) 1002–07.

and Development (OECD) – a group of countries that is largely characterised as high-income countries, while remaining part of the G77. This therefore begs the question posed in the next sub-section:

B. Does it Still Make Sense to Speak of a 'Global South'?

In response to the question posed by the heading to this section, the short answer is 'yes'. This chapter presents two reasons for answering in the affirmative. The first is based on the fact of continued relative inequality; the second is the remaining potency of continued explorations of the importance of Global South solidarity – alongside the reimagination of the South that such explorations compel.

Lees points out that there is limited 'consensus about whether the Global South still exists as an economic and political reality'.[119] Teasing apart economic and political realities is an important task when considering the prospects of Global South framings. It is to these two distinct, yet interrelated, issues of economics and of political solidarities that the discussion now turns.

Economically, countries of the South have largely seen significant economic growth in the last few decades following the independence waves of the 1950s to 1970s. Indeed, as discussed in section IV.A, the new century has born witness to the economic rise of a number of Asian nations alongside oil-producing states. This contrasts sharply with the economic decline of the United Kingdom – particularly poignant given the colonisation of the British empire of earlier centuries. Can it be said therefore that the G77 has achieved its purpose? Have we witnessed a reversal of the fortunes of the North and South? Unfortunately, no.

Systematic evaluation of relative inequality between North and South demonstrates that little has changed in four decades. While the Global South as a whole has become more significant in the world economy – there is no indication that countries have become more satisfied with where they sit within the global economic rankings. The relative ranking of incomes has experienced limited change and shifts in the order of economic rankings has been most significant between Southern states.[120] As Lees highlights, absolute income inequality between the North and South has in fact increased, with current trajectories pointing to a sustained rise in such inequality. At the same time, in the context of the BRICS countries (Brazil, Russia, India, China and South Africa), he also points out that it is unclear whether there is continued commitment to the Global South amongst those who have experienced notable economic growth.[121]

Even despite the continued disparate economic realities of North and South the political weight of the term is perhaps an even more critical point of

[119] Lees (n 99) 93.
[120] ibid 86.
[121] ibid 87.

exploration. Mohanty notes that the last 30 years of neoliberal globalisation has resulted in the popularisation of terms such as 'emerging economies' or 'emerging markets'.[122] This occurs alongside growing global homogenisation, particularly in urban landscapes.[123] Mohanty stresses that Southern countries are, of course, far more than markets and economies. Reducing the South as such, disregards Southern lives, histories and civilisations.[124] It is heartening, therefore, to not only see broad ongoing efforts to 'sustain the Global South as a salient discursive construct in struggles for global justice'[125] but also the expansion of the concept from a geographical demarcation to one which explores spaces within and between countries that are adversely impacted by globalised neoliberalism.[126] Mahler, for example, points to how the 'Global South' as a framing has evolved to embody 'the mutual recognition amongst the world's poor of their shared condition at the margins of global capitalism'. Mahler therefore draws attention to the political action and imagination that such solidarity enlivens across contemporary social movements.[127] Mahler cites Prasad who sees the South as 'a world of protest, a whirlwind of creative activity'. Such creativity, Prasad argues results from the systematic emergence of communities objecting to the privatisation and commodification of the commons alongside the denigration of human dignity and rights all under the guise and promise of 'modernity'.[128] It is here, again, that we see convergence with the evolving definitions of the South and the core principles of sustainable development: that is, the need to integrate the environment and human well-being in considerations of economic development and for equity between current and future generations. Recognising a broader understanding of the South beyond merely a state-based approach (and their arguably diverging positions as economic trajectories differ within the South) therefore allows societies, non-state actors and individuals to draw on sustainable development and its sub-principles in claims to a fairer and more sustainable world.

Therefore, while Lees highlights a common southern position that appears to exist, and continue to exist, in the United Nations General Assembly,[129] Simone, on the other hand, speaks of a Global South that has 'largely been fractured into a multiplicity of domains and histories'. This, he argues, 'opens up spaces for the reiteration of many Souths'.[130] This is critical when considering not only what the 'Global South' means but also what 'sustainable development' means in the

[122] Mohanty (n 101) 214–15.
[123] Simone (n 108).
[124] Mohanty (n 101) 214–15.
[125] Simone (n 108) 605.
[126] Mahler (n 101) 100; Simone (108) 604.
[127] Mahler (ibid) 100.
[128] V Prashad, 'Dream History of the Global South' (2012) 4 *Interface: A Journal for and about Social Movements* 43 in Mahler (n 101) 100.
[129] Lees (n 99) 105.
[130] Simone (n 108) 603.

context of a hyperconnected transnational, multi-polar present and future. It is to these current and emerging realities that I now turn.

C. The 'Global South' in a Hyperconnected World

The evolving and continued relevance of a 'Global South' is influenced by the hyperconnected nature of the world in which we now live. Both Mahler[131] and Simone[132] highlight the deterritorialised nature of the South of today. This refers, at once, to the transnational (more-than-state-based) connections alluded to above but also to the need to be cognisant of 'Souths' within 'Northern' states. In other words, historical notions of a world categorised by 'Northern' and 'Southern' countries has expanded to recognise politically and economically marginalised groups and areas within economically developed countries. At the same time, many developing countries are home to a growing middle class and/or a small group of elites whose economic conditions are similar to the societies in the Global North. In the case of 'Souths' within 'Northern' states, Mahler, for example, with African-American resistance in mind, refers to 'oppressed peoples located inside the geopolitical boundaries of imperial centres'.[133] Such marginalisation can also be observed in the deliberate dispossession and disenfranchisement of Indigenous peoples in 'settler' countries such as Australia. It is also evident in countries and societies that experience high levels of economic inequality. Poor and working-class whites in capitalist America an example that comes easily to mind – while recognising the disproportionate economic marginalisation of Hispanic, African-American and Indigenous communities in that country. Shining light on multiple 'Souths' therefore recognises that indicators such as per capita GDP grossly conceal the realities of life for many particularly in highly unequal societies.

Furthermore, the discussion of transnational links above refers not only to international connections but importantly also to the cross-scale realities of global issues. The term therefore recognises the range of global actors and the multiple public and private sectors that these actors represent and operate within. It is in this context of the intertwined aspects of hyperconnected transnationalism that Mahler highlights how contemporary capitalist globalisation alongside instantaneous transfer of information across international boundaries and the unprecedented movement of goods and people has enabled grassroot alliances which bypass notions of the 'nation-state'.[134] Meanwhile, Simone points to the accelerated intensity of material and financial flows which redefine the boundaries

[131] AG Mahler, *From the Tricontinental to the Global South: Race, Radicalism, and Transnational Solidarity* (Duke University Press, 2018) 6.
[132] Simone (n 108) 606.
[133] Mahler (n 131) 102.
[134] Mahler (n 101) 99.

within which societies operate as a result of multi-scale interactions of capital, expertise and legal arrangements.[135] From this, what also emerges is transnational forms of racial violence,[136] where the labour of the racialised other is commodified; and the lands, far from the offices of the North are paradoxically characterised as uncivilised barren wastelands. Yet, somehow, faraway economic interests compete to extract from places deemed economically and culturally 'empty' – thereby justifying such extraction.[137] In other words, the perpetuation of what Hickel terms the logic of colonisation. Here, the Global South is 'integrated' into the US–Europe centred global economy on unequal terms resulting in the appropriation by the West of labour and resources from developing countries. Meanwhile, economically and geopolitically powerful countries maintain the narrative that the economic success of high-income countries is the result not of this extraction but of good governance, strong institutions and free markets. The corollary of such a narrative is that the underdevelopment of the South is due to corruption, red-tape and inefficiency.[138]

Meanwhile, urbanisation in the South hurries to convert fertile farming, foraging and grazing lands into landscapes that mirror the cities of the North.[139] As such, the remaining potency of the concept of the South needs to thwart powerful pressures of homogenisation that come from the allure of capitalist globalisation. This includes contemporary infrastructural development across southern urban spaces which respond to local needs.[140] A seeming contradiction is that while large areas of the South engage in 'development' premised on the trajectories of the North, the global intersecting sustainability crises have also resulted in attention on the South for visions of what a more sustainable planet might look like.[141]

The rise in economic prosperity of oil rich countries alongside rapid economic development, particularly in Asia, as well as economic growth across most of what was previously designated as an underdeveloped 'South' brings about legitimate questions about the continued relevance of the Global South. It also enables reckoning with the objectives of Global South countries and what indicators are used to illustrate whether the objectives of Global South countries have been met. Put another way, is the objective of the Global South to contort itself so that it resembles the Global North not only in terms of development indicators such as GDP but also the societal and lifestyle shifts that result from 'development' that mirrors Northern models?

[135] Simone (n 108) 606.
[136] Mahler (n 131).
[137] ibid.
[138] Hickel, Sullivan and Zoomkawala (n 41) 1030.
[139] Simone (n 108) 604.
[140] ibid 606.
[141] ibid.

Imagination of what 'development' is, could be and should be in the Global South has been captured by Global North imaginaries and interests that result in development models that mirror the Global North. The issue, however, is where the spoils of such 'development' are often held by a select few that are subscribed to Northern ways and often linked to Northern networks of capital and global extraction. Kotze and Adelman argue that '[t]he idea of development was promoted by the West as a means to save benighted and feckless developing countries from themselves'.[142]

They go on to state that the fundamental problem of sustainable development derives from its untethered commitment to Western developmentalism offers only a slightly modified version of dominant capitalist economic development instead of offering any form of alternative development.[143]

In the current neo-colonial hyperconnected world, perhaps more than ever, there is the need for frameworks and ideologies that draw on historical practices that allow continued relationships with the natural world for many generations to come. At the same time, there needs to be substantive and procedural equality and equity in the sharing of wealth (broadly defined and encompassing forms of capital beyond economic wealth).[144] This in turn finds support in sustainable development's sub-principles of inter- and intra-generational equity.

At the same time, further questions arise around the desirability of emulating development trajectories of the North. This is not to be misunderstood as a call, in any way whatsoever, for a continuously underdeveloped South. Rather, it is an urging for the South to think through whose interests Northern development models serve. It is a call not only to governments, elites but also importantly to citizenry to consider what forms of development best serve communities as a whole – now and into the future.

Armillas-Tiseyra and Mahler explain that retaining (and reimagining) the Global South as a conceptual framework provides the opportunity to shift the scale at which North-South and South-South comparative analysis occurs. The emergence and continued importance of the term, they argue, is due to, and not in spite of its conceptual indeterminacy.[145] Conceptual indeterminacy but also geographical inequities bring to mind the framework of sustainable development. The remainder of this chapter interrogates whether sustainable development does and can bring about such aspirations in the context of continuously evolving notions of a 'Global South'.

[142] LJ Kotzé and S Adelman, 'Environmental Law and the Unsustainability of Sustainable Development: A Tale of Disenchantment and of Hope' (2023) 34 *Law and Critique* 227, 231.

[143] ibid 234.

[144] A Sen, *Commodities and Capabilities* (Oxford University Press, 1999); A Sen, *Development as Freedom* (Oxford University Press, 1999).

[145] M Armillas-Tiseyra and AG Mahler, 'Introduction: New Critical Directions in Global South Studies' (2021) 58 *Comparative Literature Studies* 465.

V. Sustainable Development for the Global South in the Anthropocene

The discussion above hints not only at a range of similarities between the Global South and sustainable development, but also multiple points of interconnection between the two terms. These two concepts are characterised not only by the indeterminacy of their definition. I also set out above the need for evolved understandings of both terms if either is to retain usefulness and relevance in light of present and future realities. Further, sustainable development and the Global South share common concerns of equity across pasts, presents and futures. These concerns in the hyperconnected present and future address not only point to shared solidarities to address continued colonialism. Both sustainable development and the understandings of the Global South also provide a platform with which to address similarly extractive systems of neoliberal capitalism.

Mohanty highlights how contemporary globalisation replicates the economic exploitation and cultural subjugation of the colonial era.[146] Historical colonial extraction and exploitation is continued by consumption pressures of the Global North. This is intertwined with contemporary 'development' models in the South that seem far too eager to replicate the economic models of the North.

In this section, I bring together discussion of the four components of sustainable development: principles of integration; inter-generational equity; intragenerational equity; and governance imperatives. In doing so, I consider how sustainable development might evolve to centre Southern understandings – where 'the South' is understood as disparities not only between but within nation states and where transnational realities of multiple actors and sectors need to be considered in a hyperconnected world of accelerating global change.

A. Integration

Section II discussed the centrality of integration to sustainable development. The section also highlighted the challenges of addressing inescapable trade-offs across the three 'pillars' of sustainable development. While the prioritisation of economic interests exemplifies the current status quo, doing so will not bring about sustainable development, and certainly will not do so in the Global South. Indeed, as highlighted above, this prioritisation of the dominant neoliberal capitalist model is at the core of global inequities and unsustainability. The Intergovernmental Science-Policy Platform on Biodiversity and Ecosystem Services' (IPBES Values Assessment) concludes, for example, that it is the elevation of the economic values of nature that has led to current rates of unprecedented global extinctions.[147]

[146] Mohanty (n 101) 255.
[147] IPBES Values Assessment 2022.

Meanwhile, particularly in the context of the Global South, prioritising ecological integrity alone, without considering human dignity and human needs across the globe cannot be justified. Instead, the twin goals of environment and society need to be pursued simultaneously. This echoes the key finding of the IPBES-IPCC Joint Workshop Report on Biodiversity and Climate Change.[148] The report stresses that not only must biodiversity and climate be addressed simultaneously, but so too must human well-being.

B. Inter- and Intragenerational Equity

Leach and others coin the term 'equitable-sustainability' in recognition of the dynamic interactions and inextricable connections between human and natural systems.[149] The authors draw attention to linkages and feedbacks between biophysical systems (eg climate, biodiversity, freshwater and nitrogen cycles) and of the well-being of human societies. For example, environmental shocks can often exacerbate economic, social and spatial inequities. This can force the poorest and most vulnerable to act in unsustainable ways. The end result is a vortex of increased human and environmental degradation and vulnerability.[150]

It is clear, that in the pursuit of sustainable development the social and environmental pillars (and their varied interactions) need to be prioritised. Considering evolving understandings of the transnational nature of the Global South it is critical that the distribution of benefits and burdens is considered not only across time and space but also across and within social groups.[151] In other words, the intra- and inter-generational equity sub-principles of sustainable development.

Despite this, and despite the clear increase of individuals, groups, nations, religions and cultures across the world laying claims to equity dignity across multiple scales; recent decades have borne witness to growing social and economic inequality.[152] This has not only occurred alongside unprecedented global environmental change. Global scale ecological shifts can also be attributed to unequal exchange between North and South. Northern consumption is sustained by continued extraction of labour and resource primarily from the South, while waste and ecological degradation is also largely borne by the South. As discussed above, climate change presents a clear example where countries in the South, particularly

[148] H O Pörtner and others, 'IPBES-IPCC Co-Sponsored Workshop Biodiversity and Climate Change Workshop Report' (2021), www.ipbes.net/events/ipbes-ipcc-co-sponsored-workshop-biodiversity-and-climate-change, accessed 28 May 2024.

[149] M Leach and others, 'Equity and Sustainability in the Anthropocene: A Social–Ecological Systems Perspective on their Intertwined Futures' (2018) 1 *Global Sustainability* e13.

[150] M Lim, 'Securing Equitable and Sustainable Futures in the Anthropocene – What Role and Challenges for Environmental Law?' in M Lim (ed), *Charting Environmental Law Futures in the Anthropocene*, Vol 245 (Springer, 2019).

[151] ibid.

[152] Mohanty (n 101) 211.

those which have contributed least to global emissions, are facing far greater and more imminent impacts of global heating.

C. Governance

As highlighted in earlier sections, sustainable development calls for the consideration of current and future generations while also taking into account historical contributions to the manifestation of the present. The chapter has also drawn attention to the growing literature that re-envisages a Global South characterised by transnational solidarities beyond the nation state. Desirable Southern futures, and indeed Northern ones as well, in our hyperconnected world, require understandings of sustainable development as the integration of intertwined equitable-sustainability. Implementing procedural and institutional components of sustainable development (eg public participation, good governance, transparency) is important. Nevertheless, solidarities with and across the Global South also require significant reckoning with the underlying structural issues that stem from continued unequal exchange in the flows of labour and resources and result in unsustainable exploitation of societies and ecologies.

VI. Conclusion

The overarching question posed in this chapter is how 'sustainable development' and the 'Global South' should be defined in the context of global environmental change so that the inextricable issue of human well-being and ecological integrity can be addressed equitably and in a way that sustains the functions of the Earth system. While both the 'Global South' and 'sustainable development' remain important and useful concepts, such usefulness is dependent on continuing to engage with and reimagine the contours and realities of the term in an era of rapid and unprecedented planetary scale environmental and social change. Engagement with the 'Global South' as a framing concept requires the acknowledgement of multiple Souths within and between countries. It calls for a shift in a purely nation-state approach and for new and varied solidarities in the face of the environmental destruction and inequity brought about by rampant neoliberal capitalism. Similarly, sustainable development and its sub-principle of integration must appreciate the interlinked feedbacks across inseparable and co-evolving social-ecological systems while engaging deeply with what equity between current and future generations requires.

4

Contextualising Sustainable Development: Local Interpretations of the Global Framework

ELENA BLANCO

I. Introduction

The chapter begins with a critical re-description of the construction of the idea of development as a project of control and its iteration against the global first, and, lately, the local. The argument presented is that the hegemonic, colonial and extractivist undertones of development were never successfully addressed by its evolution into *sustainable* development, and that while the 'turn to the local' could, potentially, enable a departure from development's hegemonic origins, and allow pluriversal conceptions and practices of life on Earth,[1] such a 'local' will need to be carefully constructed. The local, to become 'the local we want'[2] would need to be anchored in plural normativities[3] and embrace the many places, practices and fractures of living and world making that may unfold in an ever changing, non-lineal pluriverse.[4]

The chapter proceeds as follows: section II briefly introduces the evolution of the development as an international law project of the decolonisation era and critiques its conceptual frame and prioritisation of interests of the Global North. This critique extends to its evolution into sustainable development and to later versions including the Sustainable Development Goals (SDGs) and the

[1] A Kothari and others (eds), *Pluriverse: A Post-Development Dictionary* (Tullika Books, 2019).

[2] 'The local we want' is a paraphrase of the GA Resolution 'The Future We Want', A/RES/66/288 *The Future We Want*; GA Resolution stating 'Our Common Vision' at Rio+20, sustainabledevelopment.un.org/futurewewant.html, United Nations Conference on Sustainable Development in Rio de Janeiro from 20 to 22 June 2012.

[3] BZ Tamanaha, *Legal Pluralism Explained: History, Theory, Consequences* (Oxford University Press, 2021).

[4] A Escobar, *Designs for the Pluriverse: Radical Interdependence, Autonomy, and the Making of Worlds* (Duke University Press, 2018); W Mignolo, *The Darker Side of Western Modernity: Global Futures, Decolonial Options* (Duke University Press, 2011).

2030 Agenda.[5] Section III discusses the turn to the local under the auspices of the SDGs and 2030 Agenda. The local is considered both theoretically and practically though a variety of projects implementing the 2030 Agenda. Section IV introduces the local-Other as an alternative version to the local of the SDGs. The chapter concludes that although the turn to the local encourages the participation of a variety of actors, mostly at the city level, this participation is often reduced to the implementation phase of the projects. It argues that to harness the potential promised by the 'turn to the local', a cultural dimension must be introduced as a component of the SDGs.[6] Encouraging intercultural dialogue[7] and engaging with the variety of transition discourses and a decolonial formulation of the local as a 'local-Other' offers the opportunity to humbly draft some suggestions for opening up the variety of options for operationalising alternatives to the SDGs and the global-colonial legacy they, consciously or unconsciously, contain.

II. Development as a Postcolonial Programme of Control

The contemporary notion of development as a global plan for economic growth is often tracked back to the aftermath of World War II when the new world order was inaugurated by US president, Harry Truman: 'We must embark on a bold new program for making the benefits of our scientific advances and industrial progress available for the improvement and growth of underdeveloped areas … The old imperialism – exploitation for foreign profit – has no place in our plans.'[8] It appeared from Truman's words that the era of old imperialism was nominally abandoned but, unfortunately, not for a liberatory programme of national sovereignty and free political and economic choices by newly independent states as many had hoped; instead, it was repackaged as a programme of control which replicated old interest and power structures.[9] This new framework of neo-colonial

[5] 'Future We Want' (Outcome document … Sustainable Development Knowledge Platform), sustainabledevelopment.un.org/futurewewant.html, accessed 25 July 2023.

[6] NL Immler and H Sakkers, 'The UN-Sustainable Development Goals Going Local: Learning From Localising Human Rights' (2022) 26(2) *International Journal of Human Rights* 262. Discussed in section IV of this chapter.

[7] See J-M Barreto, 'Decolonial Strategies and Dialogue in the Human Rights Field: A Manifesto' (2012) 3 *Transnational Legal Theory* 1.

[8] President Harry S Truman inaugural address on 20 January 1949. The address can be found in S Pahuja, *Decolonising International Law: Development, Economic Growth and the Politics of Universality* (Cambridge University Press, 2011) 263–69. 'Forward' in A Kothari and others (eds), *Pluriverse: A Post-Development Dictionary* (Tullika Books, 2019) xi.

[9] K Nkrumah, *Neo-Colonialism: The Last Stage of Imperialism* (International Publishers, 1965) 239–354; along the same lines AL Stoler, *Duress: Imperial Durabilities in our Times* (Duke University Press, 2016); A Anghie, *Imperialism, Sovereignty and the Making of International Law* (Cambridge University Press, 2004); W Mignolo, *The Darker Side of Western Modernity: Global Futures, Decolonial Options* (Duke University Press, 2011).

control would extend its grip and agenda progressively to newly independent countries, crashing any dreams of change and hope. Setting aside the historiography of Truman's intentions,[10] the end of World War II signified very different things to different countries, and these differences would, in turn, meet within the 'space' of international law where conflicting interests were cast and recast in various ways though the heuristic of 'development'.[11] Imperial and colonial ties were cut, either voluntarily or forcibly, while the West, through a carefully planned and executed 'international law project'[12] reframed its relationship to the newly independent countries through what was then a new paradigm: development.[13]

As the geopolitical programme of the post-colonial era[14] development suggested an emancipatory potential that remained at all times heavily mediated by international law and its agencies through an extensive programme of infrastructure building, loans, foreign investment protection, and economic interventions that thinly disguised the deeper political interventions at stake.[15] Decolonisation was, after all, '[s]imultaneously an emancipatory awakening of peoples [and] a heteronomous process of imperial restructuring'.[16] Newly independent countries initially welcomed the promise of equality it embodied – even though it was nothing more than a promise, which would never materialise at the end of an arduous path of 'becoming'.[17] Sovereignty and statehood[18] were the prizes newly independent states aspired to, but only those countries developing in certain ways, and following the parameters of statehood established by European modernity would be welcomed into the civilised family of international law.[19] Postcolonial states

[10] For an enlightening discussion see L Eslava and S Pahuja, 'The State and International Law: A Reading from the Global South' (2020) 11(1) (Special Issue) *Humanity: An International Journal of Human Rights, Humanitarianism and Development* 118, 145–46.

[11] ibid 117–20.

[12] ibid.

[13] See S Pahuja, 'Corporations, Universalism and the Domestication of Race in International Law' in D Bell (eds), *Empire, Race and Global Justice* (Cambridge University Press, 2018); K Nkrumah, *Neo-Colonialism: The Last Stage of Imperialism* (International Publishers, 1965) 239–354; D Fieldhouse, *The West and the Third World: Trade, Colonialism, Dependence and Development* (Wiley, Blackwell Publishing, 1999) 254–86.

[14] L Eslava, 'The Developmental State: Independence, Dependency and the History of the South' in J von Bernstorff and P Dann (eds), *The Battle for International Law in the Decolonization Era* (Oxford University Press, 2019) 72.

[15] S Pahuja, 'Technologies of Empire: IMF Conditionality and the Reinscription of the North/South Divide' (2000) 13(4) *Leiden Journal of International Law* 749. A Escobar, *Encountering Development: The Making and Unmaking of the Third World* 2nd edn (Princeton University Press, 2011).

[16] G Wilder, *Freedom Time: Negritude, Decolonization, and the Future of the World* (Duke University Press, 2014) 241. See also A Getachew, *Worldmaking after Empire: The Rise and Fall of Self-Determination* (Princeton University Press, 2019); Eslava (n 14).

[17] S Pahuja, 'Laws of Encounter: A Jurisdictional Account of International Law' (2013) 1 *London Review of International Law* 65.

[18] A Anghie, *Imperialism, Sovereignty and the Making of International Law* (Cambridge University Press, 2005).

[19] L Eslava and S Pahuja, 'The State and International Law: A Reading from the Global South' (2020) 11 (Special Issue) *Humanity: An International Journal of Human Rights, Humanitarianism and Development* 118.

were constantly trying to 'catch up' with the colonial masters through development projects that perpetuated the hierarchies of the colonial era.[20] Eurocentric ideals of modernisation, democracy, rule of law and socio-economic parameters enabled the re-enactment of the extractive and appropriative practices of coloniality to be adapted to the changing times.[21] And it was through development, and its technical interventions of modernisation, capitalist accumulation and economic growth, that the 'freely' agreed access to resources in newly independent sovereign states was secured in the post-colonial world.[22]

Imperial practices of extraction enabled by the international development institutions[23] accelerated irreparable ecological decline.[24] Injustice, as Pahuja observes, 'gripped the global South with similar violence to that of the first colonisations'.[25] International law played a crucial role in this violent process of appropriation, as it did in the first colonisation, through its continuous process of world-making actualisation.[26] This actualisation enabled the articulation of tensions between newly independent countries generally 'less developed' and the established colonial and neo-colonial powers[27] through a variety of projects – like development – and global visions and agendas, amongst them sustainable development. Sustainable development is defined as development as development that meets the needs of the current generation without compromising the ability of future generation to meets their own needs.[28] As a global vision it was soon labelled as the third phase of colonisation by countries in the Global South, which considered it just a switch of 'the white man's burden' to the protection of the environment – a protection that extended to protection against the 'savages' and that involved taking control of their rights and resources.[29]

[20] S Parashar and M Schulz, 'Colonial Legacies, Postcolonial "Selfhood" and the (Un)doing of Africa' (2021) 42(5) *Third World Quarterly* 867.

[21] Eslava and Pahuja (n 19).

[22] P Dann and J von Bernstorff, 'The Battle for International Law in the Decolonization Era: An Introduction' in J Von Bernstorff and P Dann (eds), *The Battle for International Law: South-North Perspectives on the Decolonization Era* (Oxford University Press, 2019).

[23] J Stiglitz, *Making Globalization Work* (Allen Lane, 2006); JE Stiglitz and K Tsuda, 'Democratizing the World Bank' (2007) 13(2) *Brown Journal of World Affairs* 79; S Pedersen, *The Guardians* (Oxford University Press, 2015); P Sharma, *Robert McNamara's Other War: The World Bank and International Development* (University of Pennsylvania Press 2017). For a critical review of this period see R Peet, *Unholy Trinity: The IMF, World Bank and WTO* 2nd edn (Bloomsbury, 2009).

[24] I Mies and V Shiva, *Ecofeminism* (Zed Books, 2014) 264–65.

[25] S Pahuja, 'Decolonization and the eventfulness of international law' (2020) 11 (Special Issue) *Humanity: An International Journal of Human Rights, Humanitarianism and Development* 1.

[26] ibid 118–38, 145–46; Eslava and Pahuja (n 19) 28–30.

[27] Eslava and Pahuja (n 19) 30.

[28] Sustainable development entered the mainstream of development studies and international law with the publication of the World Commission on Environment and Development Brundtland Report entitled 'Our Common Future' in 1987; sustainabledevelopment.un.org/content/documents/5987our-common-future.pdf. The evolution of sustainable development is well known and is discussed in other chapters in this book.

[29] M Langan, *Neo-Colonialism and the Poverty of 'Development' in Africa* (Springer Link, 2018) 177–205; R Nelson, 'Environmental Colonialism: "Saving" Africa from Africans' (2003) 8(1) *Independent Review* 65; B Büscher and R Fletcher, 'Conservation by Accumulation' (2014) 19(1) *New Political Economy* 1.

It was also, and rightly so, considered a step back from the hard won battles of post-independence: the principle of sovereignty over natural resources[30] and the New International Economic Order (NIEO).[31] Development, now 'sustainable', continued to be defined globally, technocratically and under the Global North's agenda through successive global visions of markedly colonial inspiration.[32]

III. 'The Future We Want' and 'Other Possible Futures' in the Sustainable Development Agenda: The Turn to the Local

In 2015 Ban-Ki Moo, at the UN Sustainable Development Summit, launched Agenda 2030 to the world: 'We can say to all the people around the world, the 2030 Agenda is for you, is for everyone, everywhere. Claim it, demand that commitments be made, and promises kept. Be part of this global call to action'.[33] The transformative potential of Agenda 2030, and its call to action to 'everyone' included more democratic and participatory channels for a variety of stakeholders.[34] Transformation, it was hoped, would take place through a better articulation between the global vision and local action.[35]

[30] UNGA RES 1803 (XVII) (14 December 1962) Permanent sovereignty over natural resources. See for a classical, if slightly outdated discussion, see N Schrijver, *Sovereignty over Natural Resources: Balancing Rights and Duties* (Cambridge University Press, 1997).

[31] UN RES 3201 (1 May 1974) UN Doc A/RES/3201(S-VI). On the set of proposals that constituted the NIEO see JN Bhagwati (ed), *The New International Economic Order: The North-South Debate* (MIT, 1977). See also P Dann and J von Bernstorff, 'The Battle for International Law in the Decolonization Era: An Introduction' in J von Bernstorff and P Dann (eds), *The Battle for International Law: South-North Perspectives on the Decolonization Era* (Oxford University Press, 2019).

[32] Langan (n 29); D Le Blanc and others, 'Development Cooperation in the Light of Sustainable Development and the SDGs: Preliminary Explorations of the Issues' (2012) Rio+ 20 Working Papers, 1.

[33] Martin, 'Highlights of the UN Sustainable Development Summit' (United Nations Sustainable Development, 30 September 2015), www.un.org/sustainabledevelopment/blog/2015/09/highlights-of-the-un-sustainable-development-summit, accessed 1 April 2024. Cited in NL Immler and Hans Sakkers, 'Transforming our world: the 2030 Agenda for Sustainable Development', sdgs.un.org/2030agenda, accessed 25 July 2023. A Orford, 'Constituting Order' in J Crawford and M Koskenniemi (eds), *The Cambridge Companion to International Law* (Cambridge University Press, 2012).

[34] SDG Principles 10, 20, 21, 22, 'Transforming Our World: The 2030 Agenda for Sustainable Development' (Department of Economic and Social Affairs), sdgs.un.org/2030agenda, accessed 25 July 2023.

[35] A Appadurai, 'Grassroots Globalization and the Research Imagination'(2000) 12(1) *Public Culture* 17. Cited by Immler and Sakkers (n 6). The debate about the localisation of human rights has an ample literature that cannot be explored in this chapter but see M Goodale, 'Introduction: Locating Rights, Envisioning Law Between the Global and the Local' in M Goodale and SE Merry (eds), *The Practice of Human Rights, Tracking Law Between the Global and the Local* (Cambridge University Press, 2007).

A. The 'Future We Want' and the One-World-World[36]

The unitary paradigm that informs the sustainable development agenda, as discussed earlier in this chapter, is often perceived by the Global South as a continuation of colonial practices and interests reconfigured by the Global North through the development project.[37] Beyond the policies, projects and more or less forced economic interventions in the Global South there is another dimension to the development project and its interventions – the rejection of all other visions, cultures and ways of world making.[38] The Global North's hegemonic paradigm of economic growth and accumulation rests within the onto-epistemology of what John Law calls the One-World-World (OWW).[39] The OWW has its origins in European modernity and the colonisation of the New World, and was later expanded and imposed by colonial, imperial and neo-colonial practices. It expresses itself by a set of global projects, visions and values deemed universal, incontrovertible and unchallengeable.[40] It represents, in Escobar's terms, 'the hegemonic oppression and domination of the global North, the unitary rules that dismiss all other practices of world making, all other cultures, all other choices'.[41] The OWW operates by creating what it calls global visions, global values and global projects conceived and articulated by global institutions like the United Nations and its agencies, and serving the interests, mostly, of the Global North. In Law's conception, the OWW presents itself as a 'one box universe'. In this box, and depending on how liberal a particular society is, there is space for variants of the same values, or even for different values if these can be mediated, assimilated or understood through the epistemology of the OWW-box-universe.[42] If they cannot be mediated, the different cultures, values, beliefs or practices will be dismissed as worthless or, simply, non-existent[43] and condemned to an ontological abyss.[44] There is no possibility of

[36] J Law, 'What's Wrong with a One-World World?' (2015) 16(1) *Journal of Social Theory* 126.

[37] For an overview of SDG critique see F Sultana, 'An (Other) Geographical Critique of Development and SDGs' (2018) 8(2) *Dialogues in Human Geography* 186. For critique on SDG indicators see S Mair and others, 'A Critical Review of the Role of Indicators in Implementing the Sustainable Development Goals' in W Leal Filho (ed), *Handbook of Sustainability Science* (Springer, 2017).

[38] A Quijano, 'Coloniality and Modernity/Rationality' (2007) 21 *Cultural Studies* 168.

[39] Law (n 36). In this chapter this is referred to as onto-epistemology because, as Law explains and is briefly discussed in this text, the OWW is conceptualised not just as a matter of beliefs (epistemology) but also as a matter of ontology, or of 'what if's'.

[40] E Said, *Culture and Imperialism* (Knopf Doubleday Publishing Group, 1993); D Chakrabarty, *Provincializing Europe: Postcolonial Thought and Historical Difference* (Princeton University Press, 2008); GK Bhambra, 'Postcolonial and Decolonial Dialogues' (2014) 17(2) *Postcolonial Studies* 115.

[41] A Escobar, 'Thinking-feeling with the Earth: Territorial Struggles and the Ontological Dimension of the Epistemologies of the South' (2016) 11 *Revista de Antropologıa Iberoamericana* 11.

[42] See C Taylor, 'The Politics of Recognition' in A Guttman (ed), *Multiculturalism* (Princeton University Press, 1992).

[43] The OWW is thematically linked to abyssal thinking, see B de Sousa Santos, 'Beyond Abyssal Thinking: From Global Lines to Ecologies of Knowledges' (2007) 30 REV63.

[44] The production of non-existing realities by abyssal thinking leads to what Santos calls the 'sociology of absences' a concept recurring throughout his work, ibid and B de Souza Santos, *Epistemologies of the South. Justice against Epistemicide* (Routledge, 2016), esp ch 6.

acknowledgement or recognition of divergent or 'un-common'[45] views – there is only one world, one 'we'. Liberal politics may try to include and respect other views or beliefs through processes of intercultural dialogue[46] but this inclusion is always within the 'one box' and does not extend to the acknowledgement or acceptance of the existence of other worlds – other 'boxes' – of other realities.[47] This is important, as Law explains, because if we accept that there are other *reals* we are in the terrain of ontology and we must accept the existence of a 'fractiverse' (instead of a universe)[48] or a pluriverse.[49] In the fractiverse there is no 'we' and there are no 'overarching' beliefs or 'global agendas' – there is no global. Differences in beliefs, or in multiple and diverse realities, cannot and do not need to be mediated though participatory channels – differences just coexist with and alongside multiple realities.[50]

The 2030 Agenda for sustainable development is firmly anchored in that OWW, and that world is the world of coloniality and extractivism and development through growth. A world where the 'local' is articulated as a territorial or political variation of the only version of the world that is accepted and acceptable. Local communities, municipalities, indigenous communities and other minority groups[51] may be invited to participate in the implementation of *global* goals according to the aphorism 'Think Global, Act Local'. In some cases, and depending on how well any of these groups fits within the OWW parameters for a particular design or vision, local groups may be invited to participate in the discussions about options; for example the Bristol initiative included a variety of local stakeholders.[52] If the 2030 Agenda is part of the OWW, its potential for real change will be limited by its self-imposed onto-epistemological borders. This section will turn now to explore how the turn to the local has been articulated so far as part of the implementation of the SDGs before considering how other possible constructions of the local can open possibilities for pluriversal realties, or at least engagements with other world conceptions.

B. The Local as a Geographic Demarcation of the OWW

The first version of the local is a version that fits firmly within the OWW paradigm. In the UN-sponsored hub 'Local 2030, Localising the SDGs', local action is framed

[45] The word 'un-common' and the 'un-commons' is borrowed from H Verran, 'The Politics of Working Cosmologies Together While Keeping Them Separate' in M Blaser and M de la Cadena (eds), *A World of Many Worlds* (Duke University Press, 2018).

[46] See JM Barreto, 'Decolonial Strategies and Dialogue in the Human Rights Field: A Manifesto' (2012) 3 *Transnational Legal Theory* 1.

[47] J Law, 'What's Wrong with a One-World World', Center for the Humanities, Wesleyan University (*Heterogeneities.net*, 2011).

[48] Law uses the terminology of the 'fractiverse' to illustrate the fractures and divergences between the different worlds instead of the more common decolonial term 'pluriverse'. This chapter will not discuss the differences between both and, outside's Law's discussion, the word pluriverse is used in this chapter.

[49] Escobar (n 4).

[50] Law (n 36).

[51] These are not the same but their distinction goes beyond the scope of this chapter.

[52] Discussed in Immler and Sakkers (n 6).

as an enabling institutional arrangement for the implementation of the SDGs within a territorial, multi-stakeholder inclusive approach. The idea behind this approach is explained as aiming to foster participation by a variety of stakeholders,

> by enabling dialogues between core and peripheries, among members of civil society and the private sector. The approach also improves how local institutions relate and interact with each other, especially by incorporating their specific knowledge and practical know-how within policymaking. This allows for an inclusive response to development challenges in a given territory.[53]

The local, in this conception, is mostly a geographic variation of the OWW global agenda. The initiatives in the Local2030 platform are mostly designed and managed by think-tanks, governments and development organisations from the Global North and are due to be implemented in cities and regional units in the Global North and the Global South.[54] The eight thematic hubs in the Local 2030Agenda host a combination of projects and initiatives in the Global North and the Global South. The 'Local Sweden Hub',[55] Malmo Local Ocean Hub[56] and Liverpool 2030 hub[57] are sited in the Global North and consist of municipal and city level participatory initiatives where the local is interpreted as a territorial marker. The projects based in the Global South – the 'Parana Hub',[58] Sahel Hub,[59] Hawaii Green Growth Hub[60] or 'Como Vamos Hub'[61] are still examples of the OWW global vision of development through growth, green economy, poverty eradication and participation at the local level, all measured through globally set indicators.[62] For example in the 'Como Vamos Hub'

[53] 'Local 2030' (Localizing the SDGs), www.local2030.org/library/tools/territorial, accessed 23 May 2024.

[54] For example, 'Operationalizing the Urban NEXUS Towards resource-efficient and integrated cities and metropolitan region' was an initiative led by the German Development Cooperation under the lead of the Federal Ministry for Economic Cooperation and Development with case studies in Dar es Salaam, Nashik, Vancouver, Hannover, Tianjin, Durban, Lille and Medellin. See Cities and Infrastructure Transition in China, https://transition-china.org/cities/, accessed 19 July 2023.

[55] 'Local 2030-Sweden Hub'. The purpose of the hub is twofold, geographically it will be a platform to gather Swedish experiences of local implementation of the 2030 Agenda. Thematically, the hub will improve inter-regional and North–South collaboration and highlight local challenges and local solutions in adapting the SDGs to local governance and urban settings.

[56] The 'Malmo Local Ocean Hub' is mentioned at www.local2030.org/local2030hubs.

[57] D Connor, '2030hub' (*2030hub*, 5 October 2023), the2030hub.com/, accessed 19 July 2023.

[58] 'Conselho Estadual de Desenvolvimento Econômico Social', www.boaspraticasods.pr.gov.br/, accessed 19 July 2023.

[59] 'Our Programs' (SOS SAHEL), sossahel.ngo/our-programs/, accessed 19 July 2023. Hosted by SOS SAHEL. It focuses on the local-level promotion of climate resilience, evergreen agriculture and sustainable livelihoods for agricultural out-grower communities. SOS SAHEL is an African-born grassroots organisation with over 40 years of experience. Food security and nutrition of rural communities in Sub-Saharan Africa lie at the heart of its actions.

[60] 'A Leading Hub for Sustainability & Island-Led Solutions' (Hawai'i Green Growth UN Local 2030 Hub), www.hawaiigreengrowth.org/, accessed 19 July 2023.

[61] 'Como Vamos' is a network comprised of 35 Colombian municipalities – representing 20 million people. The network supports SDG monitoring and sharing of best practices on monitoring. 'Proyectos' (Red de Ciudades Cómo Vamos), redcomovamos.org/proyectos/, accessed 21 August 2023.

[62] For a critique of Western type indicators to measure the SDGs, see G Burford, P Tamás and MK Harder, 'Can We Improve Indicator Design for Complex Sustainable Development Goals?' (2016) 8 *Sustainability* 861.

a network of Colombian cities created for the implementation and monitoring of the SDGs, action is focused, at the city level, on measuring indicators of progress toward attaining the SDGs.[63] Other projects, for example, the 'Hawaii Green Growth Local2030' hub, which seeks to develop 'local solutions to global sustainability challenges, building on island culture and values, and indigenous knowledge'[64] include an impressive variety of local participants, including indigenous groups, who participate and contribute in discussions on policies and priorities, although the overall aim of the scheme is a commitment to the green economy and green growth which are to be implemented through public private partnerships.[65] Local diversity is welcomed, but managed and mediated through the global growth agenda, and local and indigenous values like mālama (stewardship) are put at the service of the global vision of green growth and green economy.[66] These initiatives that localise the global development agenda are not necessarily reproachable. Indeed, it is the global agenda and the funding it often attracts, that enables the provision of basic public services and local level engagement with objectives that are valuable and worthwhile for many communities and groups. The limitations and potential problems with this approach lie on three related but not inter-dependent concerns. First, there are problems related to translation of visions and goals from the global to the local; second, there are problems of inclusion and/or marginalisation of certain communities and other minority stakeholders; and, finally, the limitations imposed by the OWW conception constitute a lost opportunity to engage with pluriversal realities.

One of the problems with local implementation of global initiatives is the difficulty of translating global agendas into diverse local communities' settings.[67] The SDGs, much like human rights, is a global agenda that aspires, in principle, to make the world a better place.[68] Despite the global aspirations in terms of improving justice and sustainability, local actors are not really included in the main SDGs UN agenda-setting events,[69] and when they are, their involvement is mostly around implementation or monitoring.[70] While some examples of localisation of the 2030 Agenda have been successful in cities in the global North (Utrecht,

[63] 'Proyectos' (n 61).

[64] 'A Leading Hub' (n 60).

[65] ibid.

[66] www.hawaiigreengrowth.org/malama/.

[67] See Immler and Sakkers (n 6) where the authors engage in a useful discussion of Goodale's work on the tensions between the global and local in the context of human rights; M Goodale, 'Introduction – Locating Rights, Envisioning Law Between the Global and the Local' in M Goodale and SE Merry (eds), *The Practice of Human Rights: Tracking Law Between the Global and the Local* (Cambridge University Press, 2007); C Taylor, 'Modern Social Imaginaries' (2002) 14(1) *Public Culture* 91, 92.

[68] See S Moyn, *The Last Utopia: Human Rights in History* (Harvard University Press, 2010) 225, 1.

[69] Immler and Sakkers (n 6).

[70] For a culture, value driven or bottom-up approach to SDGs, see G Burford and others, 'Bringing the "Missing Pillar" into Sustainable Development Goals: Towards Intersubjective Values-Based Indicators' (2013) 5 *Sustainability* 3035–59.

Baltimore, Bristol, New York)[71] these have remained, in the main, implementation of multi-stakeholder initiatives.[72] When the projects move to locations in the Global South local communities are perceived often as beneficiaries of the projects, not partners.[73] Despite a plethora of guidelines and toolkits (created by the Global North) to increase participation[74] there is very little engagement with cultural difference[75] and there is frequently little sense of ownership of projects by local communities, who feel disengaged, misunderstood or misrepresented by top-down and technocratic approaches to implementation by external organisations.[76] The risk of misrepresentation of communities views and values is even higher when local communities lack formal education and are considered unable to understand or participate in political choices.[77] This marginalisation and exclusion of local communities and/or other minority stakeholders takes place not only in respect of global/local projects within the context of Agenda 2030, but in a wide range of settings including marginalisation at the hands of other local groups and local elites.[78]

Within the setup of epistemic neo-coloniality, the domination and consequent marginalisation of local communities and other minority stakeholders is almost unavoidable. Local marginalised stakeholders' views are persistently misunderstood, ignored or misrepresented as they are filtered through the sieve and measuring bar of Western knowledge.[79] Unless a complete overhaul of values, indicators and knowledge takes place through a process of carefully crafted intercultural dialogue[80] the SDGs will remain an interventionist and oppressive instrument of advancing the Global North's interests.[81]

[71] Immler and Sakkers (n 6).

[72] ibid.

[73] SJ Caballero Paz, 'Inclusion of Local Actors in Sustainable Development Projects: Evaluation of Co-Management in Sustainable Development Projects Based in the Bolivian Amazonia' (kungliga tekniska högskolan, 2018), www.diva-portal.org/smash/get/diva2:1277241/FULLTEXT01.pdf, accessed 19 July 2023.

[74] ibid.

[75] Burford (n 70).

[76] R Chowdhury, 'Misrepresentation of Marginalized Groups: A Critique of Epistemic Neocolonialism' (2023) 186 *Journal of Business Ethics* 553.

[77] ibid.

[78] R Chowdhury, 'Critical Essay: (In)Sensitive Violence, Development, and the Smell of the Soil: Strategic Decision-making of What?' (2021) 74(1) *Human Relations* 131.

[79] Chowdhury (n 76). Chowdhury discusses, in particular, the misunderstanding and marginalisation of victims in the wake of the Rana Plaza disaster.

[80] J Pascual, 'Cultural Rights, Local Cultural Policies and Sustainable Development: Constructing a Coherent Narrative' (2018) 22 *Journal of Law, Social Justice and Sustainable Development* 41, 45.

[81] For example, inclusion of indigenous knowledge and tribal understanding of stewardship for protection of forest and rivers and biodiversity. See P Greenfield, 'Trust Our Expertise or Face Catastrophe, Amazon Peoples Warn on Environment' *The Guardian* (28 January 2020). www.theguardian.com/environment/2020/jan/28/trust-our-expertise-or-face-catastrophe-amazon-peoples-warn-on-environment-aoe, accessed 1 April 2024.

IV. Is Another Future Possible?[82] The Local-Other, Transition Discourses and Pluriversal Worlds and the SDGs

As the preceding sections explained, the developmental discourse is semantically and ontologically constrained within the epistemology of neoliberal globalisation and the unnegotiable idea of economic growth.[83] As such, the concept of development, and its sequel, sustainable development, are firmly contained by the parameters of capitalist modernity.[84] Within this conception, 'the local' is not a real 'other' to globalisation as it cannot escape it. Against the proposed 'Future We Want' there are alternative global visions that challenge the embedding of sustainable development within the global capitalist project of appropriation, unbridled growth and ecological destruction.[85] The local, within these visions, is offered as a variety of futures enmeshed into different cultures and world-making practices.[86]

In the context of implementation of the SDGs it is possible to have a different reading of the local, unfolding against the global, that considers the engagement with the local/s as part of an encounter with the Other.[87] Looking at engagements with the local through theories of the Other allows us to articulate the potential of a 'localising' agenda of the SDGs and its potential for inclusivity, cultural differences and the recognition of local choices. Othering, established firmly through the colonial encounter, operates through a perpetual dynamic of difference[88] – a difference that is constructed upon the inferiority of the Other.[89] This representation of the Other is firmly imbued by coloniality and is palpable as an underlying

[82] The slogan comes from opposition to the document proposed by the UN negotiators for the Conference on Sustainable Development (Rio+20), 'The Future We Want'. It entrenches many of the documents drawn up on the basis of the work accomplished by more than 20 Thematic Groups at the 'Thematic Social Forum, Capitalist Crisis, Social and Environmental Justice', which was called to prepare the Rio+20 Peoples' Summit and was held in Porto Alegre; www.rio20.net/wp-content/uploads/2012/02/Another-Future-is-Possible_english_web.pdf, 'Another Future Is Possible', accessed 29 May 2024.

[83] Even though studies have shown that to achieve the SDGs the global economy will have to grow by a factor of 12. See Sachs' 'Fortress, Globalism, and Solidarity' pathways, which represent three distinct ways of confronting socio-ecological catastrophe, in JD Sachs and others, 'Six Transformations to Achieve the Sustainable Development Goals' (2018) 2 *Nature Sustainability* 805.

[84] A Escobar, *Pluriversal Politics: The Real and the Possible* (Duke University Press, 2020).

[85] An alternative global vision entitled *Another Future Is Possible!* This collation of alternative views comes from opposition to the document proposed by the UN negotiators for the Conference on Sustainable Development (Rio+20), 'The Future We Want'. It entrenches many of the documents drawn up on the basis of the work accomplished by more than 20 Thematic Groups at the 'Thematic Social Forum, Capitalist Crisis, Social and Environmental Justice', which was called to prepare the Rio+20 Peoples' Summit and was held in Porto Alegre.

[86] Escobar (n 41).

[87] B Santos, *Epistemologies of the South: Justice against Epistemicide* (Paradigm Publishers, 2014).

[88] EW Said, *Orientalism* (Penguin, 2003); Chakrabarty (n 40).

[89] ibid, also RM Dainotto, *Europe (In Theory)* (Duke University Press, 2007).

ethos in many development projects and their local implementation. Our interpretation of the local suggests that 'the local', like the colonised, is often a 'local-Other' portrayed as 'indigenous', small, native and underdeveloped.[90] The local implementation of global visions produces frequently an inferior and marginalised local-Other who much as the indigenous in the New World is acknowledged in its suffering, but needs to be converted, transformed and guided – excluded from debates and choices by epistemic neo-coloniality.[91] In this version of the local and of what it represents, the 'local-Other' (to globalisation) is conceptualised as an inferior, subjugated-other, a subaltern[92] who does not count as a full person or (or place) and becomes the recipient of top-down actions which produce further marginalisation.[93] Many sustainable development programmes and initiatives fall, by design or by accident, into this category.[94] In these projects, choices are made in the centres of power of the Global North and its universal agencies, by the 'we's' who proclaim to know the future that everybody wants. The local, in those programmes, is reduced to the local execution of a preordained hegemonic design.[95]

Within this rather bleak panorama of exclusion and neocoloniality it is possible, however, to recast the historiography of the Other from below.[96] In this alternative conception, the Other is given agency and is recast as the one who *chooses* to remain outside, to resist, to defy the globalising matrix of the OWW.[97] In this context, the local, recast as a 'local-Other', exemplifies the potential of 'what the world's spaces contain'[98] and by engaging outside the colonial, now recast as the global, we are made aware of the many alliances and connections made between situated heterogeneous entities.[99]

[90] Chakrabarty (n 40); B de Sousa Santos, 'Beyond Abyssal Thinking: From Global Lines to Ecologies of Knowledges' (2007).

[91] GC Spivak, *A Critique of Postcolonial Reason: Toward a History of the Vanishing Present* (Harvard University Press, 1999); A Gramsci, *Selections from the Prison Notebooks* (Lawrence and Wishart, 1971); H Mussell, 'The Silenced and Unsought Beneficiary: Investigating Epistemic Injustice in the Fiduciary' (2021) 31 *Business Ethics Quarterly* 549; G Liguori, 'Conceptions of Subalternity in Gramsci' in M McNally (ed), *Antonio Gramsci: Critical Explorations in Contemporary Political Thought* (Palgrave Macmillan, 2015).

[92] In post-colonial terms subaltern is a space of difference, a space where there is no access or a very limited one, to the cultural hegemonic imperial space. GC Spivak, *A Critique of Postcolonial Reason: Toward a History of the Vanishing Present* (Harvard University Press, 1999).

[93] ibid.

[94] Burford and others (n 70); G Burford, P Tamás and MK Harder, 'Can We Improve Indicator Design for Complex Sustainable Development Goals?' (2016) 8 *Sustainability* 861.

[95] P Nirmal and D Rocheleau, 'Decolonizing Degrowth in the Post-Development Convergence: Questions, Experiences, and Proposals from Two Indigenous Territories' (2019) 2 *Environment and Planning E: Nature and Space* 465.

[96] B de Sousa Santos and C Rodríguez-Garavito, 'Law, Politics and the Subaltern in Counterhegemonic Globalisation' in B de Sousa Santos and C Rodríguez-Garavito (eds), *Law and Globalization from Below. Towards a Cosmopolitan Legality* (Cambridge University Press, 2009).

[97] Escobar (n 4).

[98] D Harvey, 'Notes towards a Theory of Uneven Geographical Development' in D Harvey (ed), *Spaces of Global Capitalism: A Theory of Uneven Geographical Development* (Verso, 2009).

[99] W Mignolo, *Local Histories/Global Designs* (Princeton University Press, 2000).

This local, conceptualised against the global, offers also the promise of proximity, of place.[100] Place, in Escobar's work, is understood not just as a territorial space but as a living experience that is inclusive of history, culture, environment and social life.[101] The revindication of place in this context allows the formation of identities outside the global and the subordinating dynamic of difference operating in the construction of the inferior and subordinated Other.[102] The local, transformed into a local-Other, is able to choose alternative paths of development (within or outside the global parameters of the SDGs and their global design) or development including exiting modernisation and capitalism.[103] The local-Other offers the potential for resistance to the homogenous global, transforming the negative connotations of othering into an opportunity to engage, exist and 'feel otherwise'.[104] This local-Other can only operate in a fractiverse or pluriverse where multiple local-Other-worlds are allowed to be imagined, practised, built and rebuilt in a variety of ways that may encompass different versions of thinking-feeling with the Earth[105] through multiple indigenous, non-indigenous, communal and situated practices.

In Escobar's words, what is at stake in engaging with the Other as a gateway to diversity outside colonial one-ness is 'a re-articulation of belonging – a new discursive horizon of meaning – that enables the creation of an unprecedented political imaginary in terms of difference, autonomy, and cultural rights'.[106] In this conception or, more accurately, in the multiple conceptions of local-Others, the paradigm proposed by the SDGs is thus reversed: there is not a single, overarching global vision and multiple, but ultimately homogenous local actions; instead, the point of departure is the multiplicity of local thoughts, feelings and practices.[107] Thinking and feeling locally means engaging with the milliard entities that co-create the varied experiences that together constitute the co-existing realities

[100] There is an ample literature on 'place' which draws on a variety of disciplines. For the purposes of this chapter we briefly borrow Escobar's understanding of place in the context of a social theory of alterity and based largely in ethnographic accounts and critical social theory. cf A Escobar, *Territories of Difference: Place, Movements, Life, Redes* (Duke University Press, 2008).

[101] ibid.

[102] A Escobar, 'Culture Sits in Places: Reflections on Globalism and Subaltern Strategies of Localization' (2001) *Political Geography* 20.

[103] GA Collier and EL Quaratiello, *Basta! Land and the Zapatista Rebellion in Chiapas* 3rd edn (Food First Books, 2005); C Bauhardt, 'Solutions to the Crisis? The Green New Deal, Degrowth, and the Solidarity Economy: Alternatives to the Capitalist Growth Economy from an Ecofeminist Economics Perspective' (2014) 102 *Ecological Economics* 60.

[104] Escobar (n 100); Collier (n 103). P Nirmal, 'Being and knowing differently in living worlds: Rooted networks and relational webs in indigenous geographies' in *The Palgrave Handbook of Gender and Development* (Palgrave Macmillan, 2016) 232.

[105] A Escobar, 'Thinking-feeling with the Earth: Territorial Struggles and the Ontological Dimension of the Epistemologies of the South' (2016) 11 *Revista de Antropologıa Iberoamericana* 11; A Escobar, 'Other Worlds Are (Already) Possible: Self-Organization, Complexity and Post Capitalist Cultures' in Savyasaachi and R Kumar (eds), *Social Movements: Transformative Shifts and Turning Points* (Routledge, 2014).

[106] Escobar (n 100) 215.

[107] Escobar (n 105).

of the pluriverse.[108] The *global*, in this conception, is non-existent, reality is – in Maturana's words – 'the presence of our experience. I saw it, I heard it, I touched it'.[109] Under this new paradigm that could be expressed as '*act local, think plural*', local thoughts, feelings and actions do not need to be mediated in their multiplicity to create a unitary global; instead, the various 'locals' coexist as un-commons, as pluriversal, autonomous yet correlational realities.[110] In the words of the Ejército Zapatista de liberación nacional: 'In the world of the powerful there is room only for the big and their helpers. In the world we want, everybody fits. The world we want is a world in which many worlds fit.'[111] The local is, or can be, in itself, plural, and as such, capable of imagining new ways of being that reject the current path of ongoing devastation, seemingly without end in sight, brought about by predatory global capitalism and its generalised mode of expulsion.[112]

The local, recast as the local-Other to the global project of development encompasses any of the many 'transition discourses'[113] including degrowth,[114] *buen vivir*,[115] indigenous cosmologies, *ubuntu*, commoning,[116] solidarity economy, food and energy sovereignty, ecofeminism and post-development.[117,118] This local-Other does not appeal to universals, instead it sees itself as a 'constellation of local meanings that are mutually intelligible'.[119] In Escobar's words, the local-Other seeks to challenge the 'civilizational model' of globalised development.[120]

V. Conclusion

The sustainable development agenda forms part of the epistemology of the Global North. There have been no alternatives to economic growth as the measure of

[108] Escobar (n 84).

[109] H Maturana, 'Metadesign: Part II' in A Kothari and others (eds), *Pluriverse: A Post-development Dictionary* (Tullika Books, 2019).

[110] De la Cadena and Blaser (eds) (n 45).

[111] Fourth Declaration of the Lacandón Jungle, 1996; a translation in other words of 'epistemic pluralism'; F Demaria and A Kothari, 'The Post-Development Dictionary Agenda: Paths to the Pluriverse' (2017) 38(12) *Third World Quarterly* 2588.

[112] Nirmal and Rocheleau offer an inspiring overview of practices and transition discourses on reconnection to territory and its living elements through degrowth and post-development options. P Nirmal and D Rocheleau (n 95) 465–92. S Sassen, *Expulsions: Brutality and Complexity in the Global Economy* (Harvard University Press, 2014).

[113] Demaria and Kothari (n 111).

[114] Nirmal and Rocheleau (n 95).

[115] B Thomson, 'Pachakuti: indigenous perspectives, buen vivir, sumaq kawsay and degrowth' (2011) 54(4) *Development* 448.

[116] D Bollier, *Think like a Commoner: A Short Introduction to the Life of the Commons* (New Society Publishers, 2014).

[117] De la Cadena and Blaser (n 45) for alternative cosmovision.

[118] See Demaria and Kothari (n 111) 2.

[119] Escobar (n 105).

[120] ibid 26.

development and progress within the neo-colonial globalised paradigm of the OWW. There is only one destructive voice, which articulates itself though a logic of appropriation, extraction and accumulation – which discards and eradicates everything outside its remit of neoliberal predation. In this version of abyssal thinking there is no 'local', there is no 'other'.[121] There is only a disenfranchised, marginalised and silenced recipient, often hidden under the label of 'stakeholderism'.[122] The territorially diverse 'localised' project of sustainable development, unfortunately, does little to advance the *local as an epistemic place of difference*, but it is the acknowledgement of difference – either within the parameters of the OWW as cultural difference[123] or, outside its parameters, as pluriversal realities – that can effect the change and aspirations contained within the SDGs. Local communities, local-Others, indigenous peoples and those inhabiting worlds-otherwise, with their varied experiences and entanglements should be allowed to choose diverse ways of being, even if those choices mean that those worlds, will, at times, collide.[124] Development as a global project must be abandoned and, instead, different paths of development and alternatives to development must enable cultural differences and choices to be articulated, especially the voices of those silenced by the epistemicide of coloniality.[125] The forum for such dialogue needs to be de-centred and decolonised itself[126] as a plural reality of other-local spaces that offer an alternative world-making experience.[127]

Rethinking development and the local requires a considerable shift in thinking. First, it requires an acknowledgment that the 'we' so visibly spelled out in the sustainable development goals does not exist – that it is just part of the epistemology of the North.[128] Second, since there is no 'we', there are no universal theories – everything is possible and it is 'up for grabs'. Third, intercultural dialogue or the inclusion of 'culture' in the sustainable development discourse requires a move of the locus of enunciation from the Global North to the multiplicity of points in the Global South.[129] This move, which has been suggested in the context of human

[121] See WD Mignolo, 'The Geopolitics of Knowledge and the Colonial Difference' (2002) 101 *South Atlantic Quarterly* 57. See generally Chakrabarty (n 40).

[122] Chowdhury (n 78).

[123] Burford and others (n 62).

[124] Escobar (n 97).

[125] A Quijano, 'Coloniality of Power and Eurocentrism in Latin America' (2000) 15 *International Sociology* 215.

[126] FB Mills, 'Conclusion: Toward a Transmodern Pluriverse' in *Enrique Dussel's Ethics of Liberation* (Palgrave Macmillan, 2018).

[127] JM Barreto, 'Decolonial Strategies and Dialogue in the Human Rights Field' (2012) 3(1) *Transnational Legal Theory* 3–5, 10–16; Mignolo (n 121).

[128] JM Barreto, 'Epistemologies of the South and Human Rights: Santos and the Quest for Global and Cognitive Justice' (2014) 21(2) *Indiana Journal of Global Legal Studies* 394, 404. Also Chowdhury (n 76); Chowdhury (n 78).

[129] See B De Sousa Santos, De la Mano de Alicia, lo Social y lo Político en la Postmodernidad (Consuelo Bernal and Mauricio Garcia Villegas trans, Siglo del Hombre Editores, 1998) 345 Also B de Sousa Santos, 'Human Rights as an Emancipatory Script? Cultural and Political Conditions' in *Another Knowledge* (n 5) 3, 4.

rights, 'goes beyond the deconstructive gesture of bringing the margins to the center. It is a labor of erasing or multiplying the center, so that there is no center anymore or so that centers emerge everywhere'.[130] It is only within the inclusive atmosphere of the 'infinite experiences of the world' in which a 'plurality of heterogeneous knowledges' inhabit or converge that the pluriverse, the local (s), the alternatives are possible.[131] Achieving the dialogue that secures the co-existence of knowledges is not an easy task. It requires departing from the ontology of disconnection[132] that has been imposed by the global north to a transitional space, which accepts other knowledges, including, indigenous, ancestral and alternative ways of living together – the un-commons.[133]

[130] Barreto (n 128) 408.
[131] Escobar (n 97).
[132] Escobar (n 105).
[133] Barreto (n 128).

5

Promises and Perils of Economic Development

PHILIPPE CULLET

I. Introduction

Development has been framed around the pursuit of growth.[1] In a context where colonisation had left most colonised countries extremely poor and often poorer than they were before colonisation, the central policy prescription for newly independent countries became to 'develop' as fast as possible. It is in this context that the world became structured into 'developed' and 'developing' countries – a division that has endured under different terms over the decades.[2] This division led to development policy being framed around the idea that the ideal is what 'developed' countries have achieved and 'developing' countries are trying to catch up.

This framing has worked out for some countries but it has failed many other countries. This is reflected in the vast gap in human development index scores between countries with very high human development and the 46 least developed countries, small-island developing states and more generally the majority of small developing countries.[3] The failure of development affects developing countries first but there is also a broader failure, which affects even those countries with the highest development indicators.

This crisis was first highlighted in the early 1970s when the idea that there were 'limits' to growth was popularised.[4] This logically coincided with the rapid growth of an environmental consciousness of the dangers that unchecked use of natural resources was causing to the world. In the meantime, the understanding that (economic) development is going to cause catastrophic environmental upheaval is well recognised in mainstream policy, with the global climate crisis being at

[1] G Rist, 'Is "Development" a Panacea? How to Think beyond Obsolete Categories' (2010) 30(3–4) *Canadian Journal of Development Studies* 345.

[2] For an account of the way in which countries are currently classified see, for example, United Nations, 'World Economic Situation and Prospects' (2023) 115.

[3] United Nations Development Programme, *Human Development Report 2021/2022* (UNDP, 2022).

[4] DH Meadows and others, *The Limits to Growth* (Universe Books, 1972).

the centre of the news cycle on a regular basis.[5] Yet, neither destructive droughts, heatwaves nor floods have managed to shake belief in development as the solution to the world's problems and development is still seen as a marker of 'progress'.[6]

If mainstream policy-making is yet to reflect the failure of 70 years of 'development' to foster the well-being and the basic realisation of the human rights of all human beings, increasing inequalities, the global climate crisis and the Covid-19 pandemic have all contributed to an increasing awareness that the way forward must be a new path. This is not confined to the margins, and the 2020 Human Development Report recognised that '[b]usiness as usual simply will not work'.[7] This does not yet mean that economic development is no longer at the centre of policy attention but, at least, it is now recognised that 'economic growth is more means than end'.[8]

In this broader context where economic growth has been seen as the answer to all the problems faced by individuals and countries, it is an immense challenge to question what has seemed to be the most central part of every government's policy for decades. This sometimes seems to pit the Global North and Gobal South against each other, with the latter justifiably arguing that a simple brake on economic growth will spell further catastrophes for their own populations. However, there are other answers that do not lead to the conundrum of restricting developing countries' options where basic human rights for all have not yet been realised. The solution lies in a multi-pronged strategy that moves away from the current model of development. This involves redistribution from North to South and from rich to poor within every country – something that has never sufficiently happened. At a broader level, this involves moving away from sustainable development that has failed to prioritise the environment and people over economy.

This chapter starts by engaging with (sustainable) development and the emphasis on economic growth that has been the marker of success for decades. It examines policy developments around sustainable development and the progressive push for an alternative framing. The next section then moves on to focus on issues of inequality and redistribution. A much more determined focus on both would go a long way towards addressing not only the massive poverty that still affects most of the world, but also impoverishment caused though the process of development. The third section then moves on to consider ways to frame a new paradigm to displace (economic) development as the main measure of well-being. The limitation of the lack of an effective rights framework in sustainable development calls for a different approach. In this context, the evolving discourse on rights of nature constitute one of the ways in which a clear priority can be given

[5] R Kunelius and A Roosvall, 'Media and the Climate Crisis' (2021) 3(1) *Nordic Journal of Media Studies* 1.

[6] UNGA Res 77/212 (15 December 2022) UN Doc A/RES/77/212.

[7] United Nations Development Programme, *Human Development Report 2020 – The Next Frontier – Human Development and the Anthropocene* (UNDP, 2020) 9.

[8] ibid 6.

to the environment, moving away from the balance and integration that has been at the centre of the sustainable development discourse since the late 1980s. This may be linked to pre-existing (human) environmental rights as eco-human rights to ensure that the complementary strengths of the two framings can be made to work together.

II. (Sustainable) Development: Failure to Effectively Address the Primacy of Economic Goals

The focus of development on economic growth has come under increasing scrutiny over time. This is what led to the framing of the concept of 'sustainable development', as a way to address some of the critiques. The early policy framing of sustainable development in the 1992 Rio Declaration centred around the idea of integrating development and environment.[9] This constituted a major change compared to the emphasis on economic growth that had been the hallmark of previous decades. At the same time, even in this early version, there was no implied challenge to the idea of development per se or to the idea that economic growth would be the main vehicle for progress.[10] This was the original compromise from which the notion did not recover.[11]

One of the promises of sustainable development was the focus on poverty reduction. As such, this was not new, since 'development' had been seeking to lift countries and people out of poverty.[12] The underlying rationale was that poverty is a static baseline and that development is a positive move forward. In this view, development can only be seen as something positive.

The focus on extreme poverty eradication has remained a constant priority over decades, even though this ideal has not yet been achieved. This is still reflected in the Sustainable Development Goals (SDGs) whose Goal 1 is the eradication of absolute poverty.[13] Yet, even in 2015, poverty remained primarily framed in economic terms, though other dimensions were also taken into account. The framing of poverty through a dollar figure is problematic in multiple ways. It reflects an account of poverty eradication as linked to economic growth and thus seems to fail to take into account the fact sustainable development was premised in the first place on displacing the importance given to economic growth in view of its

[9] UNGA 'Report of the United Nations Conference on Environment and Development by UNGA Res 47/190' (3–14 June 1992) UN Doc A/CONF.151/26/Rev l (Vol I) Principle 2.

[10] A Bernier, 'La face cachée des sommets de la Terre' (2022) 819 *Monde diplomatique* 1, 23.

[11] JE Viñuales, 'Sustainable Development' in L Rajamani and J Peel (eds), *Oxford Handbook of International Environmental Law* (Oxford University Press, 2021) 285.

[12] JH Adler, 'Development Theory and the Bank's Development Strategy – A Review' (1977) 14(4) *Finance and Development* 31.

[13] Sustainable Development Goals and Targets, UNGA Res 70/1 (21 October 2015) Goal 1 UN Doc A/Res/70/1.

negative environmental and social side-effects. This is a perspective that seems to endure even though crises like the Covid-19 pandemic are known to have thrown hundreds of millions of people back in poverty. Yet, the UN General Assembly was still calling in 2022 for a New International Economic Order premised on the idea that international trade is 'an engine for development and sustained economic growth, as well as the eradication of poverty'.[14] More generally, it is now well-understood that poverty is 'multidimensional' and must be addressed in its multiple forms.[15]

Another disturbing dimension is that development can also lead to impoverishment, which is the antithesis of poverty eradication.[16] This is, for instance, the case of forced displacement linked to development interventions such as large dams or mining. The idea that displacement may be a cost for some people for the greater benefit of society and that the displaced people should be grateful for their displacement that will allow them to enjoy 'the fruits of science and technology for better health and have a higher quality of lifestyle' is generally not palatable any more.[17] At the same time, the recognition that some people suffer in the name of betterment and progress puts in question the legitimacy of the idea of development. Further, this provides a reminder that the yardstick should not be aggregate economic growth but rather, the impacts of development on the poorest and most marginalised. In other words, the benefits of developmental activities should first of all go to the poorest – something that often fails to happen.[18]

Overall, it is unclear that there was ever any strong will to challenge the pre-eminence of economic growth in international policy-making. In fact, starting at the 1972 Stockholm Conference, member states agreed 'not to invoke environmental concerns as a pretext for discriminatory trade policies or for reduced access to markets'.[19] There are thus some intrinsic contradictions in the framing of environmental policy over the past 50 years.

The lack of prioritisation eventually led to pragmatic ways of addressing the 'integration' of environment, society and development. In principle, environmental and social impact assessment is the main tool that is used to balance the competing interests of infrastructure, environment and people.[20] This is a compromise because it is not undertaken until relatively late in the project cycle, by which time

[14] UNGA Res 77/174(14 December 2022) UN Doc A/RES/77/174.

[15] See UNDP and OPHI, *Global Multidimensional Poverty Index 2023* (United Nations Development Programme (UNDP) and Oxford Poverty and Human Development Initiative (OPHI), 2023).

[16] U Ramanathan, 'Rethinking Poverty: A Socio-Legal Enquiry' (2019) 15 *Socio-Legal Review* 84, 92.

[17] *Narmada Bachao Andolan v Union of India* (2000) 10 SCC 664, [241].

[18] DT Greenwood and RPF Holt, 'Growth, Inequality and Negative Trickle Down' (2010) 44(2) *Journal of Economic Issues* 403.

[19] Report of the United Nations Conference on the Human Environment (5–16 June 1972) UN Doc A/CONF48/14/Rev1 (1972).

[20] N Craik, 'The Assessment of Environmental Impact' in E Lees and JE Viñuales (eds), *The Oxford Handbook of Comparative Environmental Law* (Oxford University Press, 2019) 876.

vested interests have been built around taking the project forward. At worst, partly constructed projects may be allowed to be completed regardless of their consequences because of the amount of time and money already invested in them.[21]

More broadly, the attempt to reconcile the different dimensions of sustainable development has not succeeded in addressing their competing nature. This has led to a situation where (economic) development generally prevails.[22] This is well illustrated in the case of the international trade and intellectual property regimes. The proposed reform of the World Trade Organization (WTO) has been pending for more than two decades and with it, any hope for strengthening social and environmental protection measures remains on hold.[23] At the same time, dozens of bilateral agreements adopted since the beginning of the century have further tightened existing investment, trade and intellectual property rules at the expense of the environment and people.[24] The limited progress that can be identified has been generally by way of transparency measures, such as procedural guarantees, a number of which have been adopted as non-binding measures, such as in the case of mining.[25]

Even assuming that sustainable development could achieve the balance and integration on which it was initially premised, policy instruments progressively moved away from this framework. This is well illustrated by the introduction of the concept of green economy at the 2012 Rio+20 summit.[26] This would have displaced integration and balance in favour of prioritising the economy, or as put by Dasgupta watering 'down the developmental dimensions of sustainable development'.[27] In 2015, the SDGs constituted a sort of mainstreaming of environmental concerns in development policy. Yet, the environmental content of SDGs is relatively minor. In addition, while there is a goal that specifically calls for 'sustained' growth,[28] there is no similar prioritisation of the environment. In fact, the first mention of the environment simply calls for decoupling 'economic growth from environmental degradation'.[29]

[21] *Antarsingh Patel v UoI* Appeal No 26/2012 (National Green Tribunal, New Delhi (Principal Bench), Judgment, 9 August 2012) [20].

[22] Viñuales (n 11) 300.

[23] For an account of the difficult and limited progress with regard to environmental aspects, for example, R Tarasofsky and A Palmer, 'The WTO in Crisis: Lessons Learned from the Doha Negotiations on the Environment' (2006) 82(5) *International Affairs* 899.

[24] S Alam, 'Natural Resource Protection in Regional and Bilateral Investment Agreements – In Search of an Equitable Balance for Promoting Sustainable Development' in S Alam, JH Bhuiyan and J Razzaque (eds), *International Natural Resources Law, Investment and Sustainability* (Routledge, 2017) 108.

[25] Extractive Industries Transparency Initiative (EITI), 'The EITI Standard 2019'.

[26] UNEP, *Towards a Green Economy: Pathways to Sustainable Development and Poverty Eradication – A Synthesis for Policy Makers* (UNEP, 2011).

[27] C Dasgupta, 'Reflections on the Relationship between the "Green Economy" and Sustainable Development' in UNCTAD, The Road to Rio+20 – For a Development-led Green Economy (UN, 2011) 33, 35.

[28] Sustainable Development Goals and Targets (n 13) Goal 8.

[29] Sustainable Development Goals and Targets (n 13) Goal 8.4.

Over time, the potential of sustainable development to give effective prioritisation to the environment and society has been questioned.[30] In response, alternative concepts, such as degrowth or ecological democracy have been proposed.[31] Degrowth emphasises the problem with the prominence given to economic growth without actually calling for negative economic growth. The central point is to highlight the need to move away from a framing that gives priority to economic growth as the main vehicle for eradicating poverty and addressing environmental harm. In other words, it is a shift from a quantitative to a qualitative understanding of well-being.[32] The call for a focus on qualitative well-being is in keeping with the progressive understanding that development is more than economic growth – as reflected in the human development index – or that poverty must be looked at in its multidimensional aspects, rather than mostly in its economic dimension.

Degrowth is often seen as a diversion from the imperative of economic poverty eradication. Yet, the actual questions are elsewhere. The first is the need for a reduction of consumption in the Global North. The second is the essential need for resource redistribution among and within countries. This would go a long way towards addressing the overall breaching of planetary boundaries while ensuring the vast majority of the world's population sees its standard of living improve dramatically.[33] One of the starting points for a new future is to share existing resources, rather than compete while contributing to destroying the bases of humankind's life on Earth.

III. Development and the Global South: Failure to Ensure Substantive Equality

The focus of (sustainable) development policy on poverty alleviation has been one of the main sources of its legitimacy. This worked as a consensus building exercise for decades, to the extent that it could be shown that absolute poverty was consistently decreasing. The Covid-19 pandemic shattered this certitude with the massive increase in poverty that accompanied it.[34]

Even without the pandemic, it was already apparent that decades of 'extreme' poverty reduction measures had not had the desired results. First, the limited goal

[30] N Eisenmenger and others, 'The Sustainable Development Goals Prioritize Economic Growth over Sustainable Resource Use: A Critical Reflection on the SDGs from a Socio-Ecological Perspective' (2020) 15 *Sustainability Science* 1101.

[31] A Kothari, F Demaria and A Acosta, 'Buen Vivir, Degrowth and Ecological Swaraj: Alternatives to Sustainable Development and the Green Economy' (2014) 57 *Development* 362.

[32] V Liegey, 'Éloge de la décroissance' (2021) 811 *Monde diplomatique* 20.

[33] J Hickel, 'Is it Possible to Achieve a Good Life for All Within Planetary Boundaries?' (2019) 40(1) *Third World Quarterly* 18.

[34] DG Mahler and others, 'Updated Estimates of the Impact of COVID-19 on Global Poverty: Turning the Corner on the Pandemic in 2021?' *Work Bank Data Blog* (24 June 2021), blogs.worldbank.org/opendata/updated-estimates-impact-covid-19-global-poverty-turning-corner-pandemic-2021.

of eradication of extreme poverty was only envisaged by 2030 and the likelihood of reaching this landmark was already doubted on the basis of long-term trends.[35] Second, the mainstream measure of absolute poverty at $2.15 is very low and eradicating it does not necessarily imply that everyone will enjoy the realisation of the basic content of all their rights. An increase of the poverty line to $5 would have led, for instance, to a finding that poverty rates had hardly changed between the end of the Cold War and the mid-2010s.[36]

Further, there is no universal goal to eradicate poverty itself, with SDGs only seeking to reduce by half the number of people living in poverty.[37] This puts into question the very focus on poverty eradication as the right lens of approach. Indeed, poverty is not only yet to be eradicated but also, over the past few decades, inequalities have increased overall.[38] This is problematic, even from an economic point of view since inequality is no longer understood as beneficial for growth.[39]

In policy terms, there is concern about inequality between people, as well as inequality between states. The former was not formally part of the framing of sustainable development policy until 2015 when SDG 10 foregrounded inequality as a major issue.[40] Yet, SDG 10 lacks in ambition. For instance, its first target only seeks to ensure that the income growth of the bottom 40 per cent of the population should be higher than the national average.[41] This approach is equivalent to seeking a reduction in income inequality, as measured by the share of the bottom 40 per cent of the population in national income.[42] The problem is that this fails to address overall income inequality and is framed in such a way that the target can be realised while income inequality increases overall. It also fails to address the fact that inequality increases are created mostly at the top end of the income scale.[43]

Inequality has remained on the policy agenda in the aftermath of the Covid-19 pandemic.[44] At the same time, the latest UN General Assembly resolution on a New International Economic Order only mentions inequality in the preamble and it still affirms that growth is what needs to be looked after since 'persistently

[35] D Woodward, '*Incrementum ad Absurdum*: Global Growth, Inequality and Poverty Eradication in a Carbon-Constrained World' (2015) 4 *World Economic Review* 43.

[36] P Edward and A Sumner, 'Global Inequality and Global Poverty Since the Cold War: How Robust is the Optimistic Narrative?' Global Challenges Working Paper Series No 1, University of Bergen (2016).

[37] Sustainable Development Goals and Targets (n 13) Goal 1.2.

[38] United Nations Development Programme, *Human Development Report 2019* (UNDP, 2019) 111.

[39] O Galor, 'Inequality, Human Capital Formation and the Process of Development' Working Paper 17058, National Bureau of Economic Research (2011) 1, reminding readers that 'the Classical viewpoint … underlined the beneficial effects of inequality for the growth process'.

[40] Sustainable Development Goals and Targets (n 13) Goal 10.

[41] Sustainable Development Goals and Targets (n 13) Goal 10.1.

[42] E Anderson, 'Equality as a Global Goal' (2016) 30(2) *Ethics and International Affairs* 189, 193.

[43] R van der Hoeven, 'Can the SDGs Stem Rising Income Inequality in the World?' in PAG van Bergeijk and R van der Hoeven (eds), *Sustainable Development Goals and Income Inequality* (Edward Elgar, 2017) 208.

[44] UNGA Res 76/175 (16 December 2021) UN Doc A/RES/76/175.

high levels of inequality pose a challenge to robust growth and sustainable development'.[45]

The second level is inequality between states. This conversation starts from the idea that international law is fair because it recognises the sovereign equality of states. This formal equality is understood as satisfying the demands of equity. The limitations of this framing have been obvious for a long time. Decolonisation was the trigger for a progressive but limited understanding that 'preferential' measures would need to be adopted to address actual inequalities between states, as soon as it became apparent that legal equality was not going to necessarily ensure substantive equality.[46] This was first done mostly in the context of international economic law where the legitimacy of differential treatment for developing countries was established.[47]

This early framing is what has allowed a growing number of differential measures in the law of sustainable development, in particular since the 1980s. One of the ironies is that the recognition that formal equality as an insufficient basis for fair and legitimate law and policy-making was already enshrined in the 1992 Rio Declaration through its Principle 7.[48] Yet, it took until 2015 for inequality to be officially recognised as a framing concern concerning sustainable development.

The need for measures to foster substantive equality rather than formal equality were and remain controversial.[49] Thus, in the aftermath of the setting up of the WTO in 1995, formal equality became again the expected framing principle for trade relations. Overall, the special and differential treatment measures that had been added in the previous decades remained in place but the Uruguay Round was marked by 'increasing pressure exerted by developed countries for reciprocal obligations and concessions from developing countries'.[50] In the end, developing countries ended up focusing on preserving what existed rather than pushing for further enhancement.[51]

This is despite the fact that the developed/developing country categorisation remains a crucial marker of inequality and differential treatment in favour of countries with low human development is still a priority. This is not entirely

[45] UNGA Res 77/174 (14 December 2022) UN Doc A/RES/77/174.

[46] P Slinn, 'Implementation of International Obligations Towards Developing States: Equality or Preferential Treatment?' in WE Butler (ed), *Control over Compliance with International Law* (Nijhoff, 1991) 165.

[47] NK Kale, 'The Principle of Preferential Treatment in the Law of GATT: Toward Achieving the Objective of an Equitable World Trading System' (1987/88) 18 *California Western International Law Journal* 291.

[48] UNGA, 'Report of the United Nations Conference on Environment and Development by UNGA Res 47/190' (3–14 June 1992) UN Doc A/CONF.151/26/Rev l (Vol I) Principle 7.

[49] cf S Pahuja, *Decolonising International Law – Development, Economic Growth, and the Politics of Universality* (Cambridge University Press, 2011) 46.

[50] H Youssef, 'Special and Differential Treatment for Developing Countries in the WTO' Working Paper, South Centre (1999) 15.

[51] J Whalley, 'Special and Differential Treatment in the Millennium Round' CSGR Working Paper No 30/99, University of Warwick (1999) 11.

unacknowledged, as witnessed in the various climate finance pledges made since the beginning of the century.[52] Yet, the extent to which this contributes to addressing inequality is unclear. In the case of the $100 billion per year pledge made in 2009, the lack of clarity on what would count makes it difficult to even assess. An OECD estimate for 2020 puts finance provide and mobilised at $83.3 billion.[53] The same figure is estimated by Oxfam to have a real value of only $21 to $24.5 billion.[54] In addition, a very small percentage of climate finance is allocated as grants.[55]

Another crucial element is that the pendulum has swung away from large multilateral deals. Two distinct examples exemplify this. The first is the Paris Agreement, which formally remains a multilateral deal. Yet, the reformulation of the principle of differential treatment with the addition of 'in the light of different national circumstances' is what led to the 'nationally determined contributions' where each state decides on its own level of ambition.[56] This has led to the current situation where aggregate pledges are insufficient in terms of the objectives of the Paris Agreement.[57] The second example is the move away from multilateral deals in international economic law. In this case, the emphasis on bilateral deals has ensured that countries with low human development are much less able to rely on the strength that multilateral bargaining can bring. As a result, their sovereignty has been repeatedly restricted in ways that do not foster substantive equality but rather the interests of countries with high levels of human development. This is, for instance, the case of international investment agreements that tend to favour foreign investors over host states.[58]

Overall, even where inequality is recognised as a problem, effective measures are not necessarily taken to address it, because of competing understandings of equality and equity. Where equity is equated with formal equality, substantive inequality may not raise equity concerns. In the real world where resources are limited and infinite economic growth is impossible, inequality calls for framing the response in terms of redistribution. There has never been a consensus over redistribution because it mobilises concepts, such as distributive justice. Thus, the principle of 'common but differentiated responsibilities' is framed in Principle 7

[52] J Timmons Roberts and others, 'Rebooting a Failed Promise of Climate Finance' (2021) 11 *Nature Climate Change* 180.

[53] OECD, *Aggregate trends of Climate Finance Provided and Mobilised by Developed Countries in 2013–2020* (OECD, 2022).

[54] OXFAM, *Finance Shadow Report 2023 – Assessing the Delivery of the $100 Billion Commitment* (OXFAM, 2023).

[55] A Goswami and AA Rao, *Beyond Climate Finance – Climate Ambition in the Global South Requires Financial System Reforms* (Centre for Science and Environment, 2023).

[56] United Nations Framework Convention on Climate Change (adopted 12 December 2015, entered into force 4 November 2016) 3156 UNTS 79 (Paris Agreement) Art 2.2, 4.2.

[57] UNGA Res 77/165 (14 December 2022) UN Doc A/RES/77/165, para 7.

[58] M Chi, 'Reforming International Investment Treaties for an Equitable Natural Resource-Related Investment Governance Regime' in ML Fremuth, J Griebel and R Heinsch (eds), *Natural Resources and International Law – Developments and Challenges* (Nomos/Hart, 2021) 291.

of the 1992 Rio Declaration in such a way that it does not entail an enforceable duty of redistribution.[59] This is not because such a formulation is impossible – in fact, an earlier version of the principle sought to emphasise the responsibility of developed countries and singled out their duties to provide the resources and technologies.[60]

The arguments for distributive justice are well-rehearsed.[61] Yet, over the past couple of decades, the discourse has shifted away from this basic structural issue towards highlighting the changing status of new Global South resource-rich countries. This reflects a changing reality that needs to be addressed, such as through more individualised differentiation. At the same time, even if the likes of Brazil, China, India and South Africa have become leading economic powers, this does not stop India from having the highest child wasting rate,[62] hence confirming that, at least to a certain extent, calls for North–South redistribution remain fundamentally valid.

IV. Beyond Development: The Promise of a Rights Framework Prioritising Nature and People

The optimism that characterised the Agenda for Sustainable Development in the second half of the 2010s has now given way to severe concerns that half of the goals are 'moderately or severely off track' and 30 per cent have 'seen no movement or regressed below the 2015 baseline'.[63] There is thus a crisis of confidence in the ability of the development model that has been at the centre of international policy-making for decades to achieve even the limited goals set in 2015.

The answer to the current crisis requires, however, much more radical rethinking. The post-pandemic economic crisis is a symptom of a much bigger crisis of an economic development model that has failed to eradicate poverty after decades of failed promises. Further, the current economic model is unsustainable because its consumption-based framing leads to natural resources exhaustion and massive pollution. In addition, development is the root cause of anthropogenic climate change, which has led to the global climate crisis threatening human life on Earth as it exists today. The combination of these different factors calls for a new approach.

[59] The US sought to make this clear, with its statement that principle 7 cannot be interpreted as creating any obligation or liability for the North. See Report of the UN Conference on Environment and Development (Rio de Janeiro, 3–14 June 1992), UN Doc A/CONF.151/26 (Vol IV) (1992).

[60] Principles on General Rights and Obligations – China and Pakistan – Draft Decision, Preparatory Committee for the UN Conference on Environment and Development, 4th session, UN Doc A/CONF.151/PC/WG.III/L.20/Rev.l (1992).

[61] P Cullet, *Differential Treatment in International Environmental Law* (Ashgate, 2003).

[62] K von Grebmer and others, *Global Hunger Index: Food Systems Transformation and Local Governance* (Bonn/Dublin, Welthungerlife/Concern Worldwide, 2022) 10.

[63] Report of the Secretary-General (special edition) 'Progress Towards the Sustainable Development Goals: Towards a Rescue Plan for People and Planet' (2023), UN Doc A/78/80-E/2023/64, para 4.

The first priority is to frame policy in terms of priorities, rather than the amorphous idea of balance and integration of sustainable development that has allowed for economic growth to dominate.[64] Nature needs to come first, followed by people and the economy. In other words, it is necessary to call into question the premise of human development framed in 1990 by the UNDP as an opposition between people and trees.[65] Today, in what we know as the Anthropocene, even the UNDP advocates that 'the apposition of people and nature needs to be re-examined'.[66]

In other words, there is now a mainstream recognition from within the discourse of development that nature and humankind are interdependent. This will be insufficient to ensure sustainability, as long as the ideology of sustainable or human development prevails. Putting nature first is then a way to reflect the need to ensure that policy-makers remember at every step that human well-being depends on a healthy environment.

This new emphasis and prioritisation requires a different framing from sustainable development, which has been consensual in part because of its lack of specificity. There exist different ways to move forward. One of the lacunae of the existing policy framing is the lack of reliance on a rights discourse. This has the potential to make a crucial difference for the most marginalised, and is indeed one of the central premises of human rights, which often remain one of the few safeguards that people can hope to mobilise against the state, in countries where they operate. This missing link has in fact been taken up in recent years with the proposal to adopt a convention on the right to development.[67] This could strengthen the amorphous right recognised in the 1996 UN General Assembly resolution.[68] At the same time, even if it were adopted, it is a question of too little too late. At this juncture, new thinking is needed to address the various crises caused by development, and this cannot be achieved through this same framework.

One of the discourses that has attracted increasing attention in recent years is rights of nature. This is used, first, to emphasise the need for an ecocentric perspective to environmental protection to counter or rebalance the anthropocentric frameworks that have marked environmental policy over the past 50-odd years. The second key element is to frame nature protection in terms of rights, in part in reaction to the often limited implementation and enforcement of environmental protection standards.

Some of the literature on rights of nature implies that the main contribution of the new language is its ecocentric perspective. This comes in part from an understanding of rights of nature as having emerged in the context of a 1972 article about

[64] UNGA Res 70/1 (2015) UN Doc A/RES/70/1, para 2.

[65] United Nations Development Programme, *Human Development Report 1990* (Oxford University Press, 1990) 62.

[66] United Nations Development Programme, *Human Development Report 2021/2022* (UNDP, 2022) 22.

[67] UN Human Rights Council, 'Revised Draft Convention on the Right to Development', UN Doc A/HRC/WG.2/23/2 (2022).

[68] UNGA Res 41/128 (4 December 1986) UN Doc A/RES/41/128.

whether trees should have standing.[69] This is one of the elements that make rights of nature potentially controversial as reflecting a pure conservationist perspective, which may be opposed to people's needs and rights. Yet, this early mooring has been overtaken more recently through the implementation of a number of rights of nature regimes. These include broad recognition of rights of all nature, as in the case of Ecuador where the protection is framed at the constitutional level.[70] Other examples include protection of specific elements of nature, such rivers, animals or a sea.[71]

The development of these existing regimes is sometimes led by indigenous peoples who have lived in the environment to be protected.[72] The resulting regimes are strongly informed by the lived experience of people who depend on these environments. As a result, rather than reflecting an opposition between the natural and human environment, they tend to integrate both, but in a manner that gives priority to nature. This has been the case both in the Global North and Global South where one of the central contribution of rights of nature regimes is to give nature-dependent people more control over their surrounding environment.[73] The extent to which this will be transformative in practice is yet to be ascertained but, for example, the change of perspective implied in a legal regime that moves from absolute sovereign control to a distinct entity being the human face of the river, constituted of one government representative and one indigenous representative, as in the case of the Whanganui River in New Zealand, is significant.[74]

One of the elements that transpires through rights of nature is the need to rethink the place of property rights, in particular land rights. This is crucial insofar as the dependence of economic development on natural resources is directly linked to access, usually mediated through property rights, as in the case of water rights linked to land rights.[75] A rejection of the model of property rights brings in itself a completely different perspective to the relationship between nature, society and economy since it removes a link that often contributes to giving primacy to exploitation driven by profit. This was, for instance, a central part of the discussions between the Crown and the Maori concerning the Whanganui river, as the latter did not want control to be framed in terms of property rights.[76]

[69] CD Stone, 'Should Trees Have Standing? Toward Legal Rights for Natural Objects' (1972) 45 *Southern California Law Review* 450.

[70] Constitution of the Republic of Ecuador, 2008.

[71] Te Awa Tupua (Whanganui River Claims Settlement) Act, 2017 (New Zealand); *Narayan Dutt Bhatt v Union of India* [2018] SCC OnLine Utt 645 (Uttarakhand High Court, India); Ley 19/2022 de 30 de septiembre, para el reconocimiento de personalidad jurídica a la laguna del Mar Menor y su Cuenca (Spain).

[72] D Takacs, 'We Are the River' (2021/2) *University of Illinois Law Review* 545, 555.

[73] T Collins and S Esterling, 'Fluid Personality: Indigenous Rights and the Te Awa Tupua (Whanganui River Claims Settlement) Act 2017 in Aotearoa New Zealand' (2019) 20 *Melbourne Journal of International Law* 1; P Wesche, 'Rights of Nature in Practice: A Case Study on the Impacts of the Colombian Atrato River Decision' (2021) 33 *Journal of Environmental Law* 531.

[74] Te Awa Tupua (Whanganui River Claims Settlement) Act, 2017, s 18.

[75] TG Puthucherril, 'Riparianism in Indian Water Jurisprudence' in R Iyer (ed), *Water and the Laws in India* (Sage, 2009) 99.

[76] D Takacs, 'Standing for Rivers, Mountains – and Trees – in the Anthropocene' (2022) 95 *Southern California Law* Review 1469, 1496.

Overall, rights of nature are particularly important because they put forward a clear prioritisation for the environment. At the same time, this is not a perspective detached from human societies but one that understands society within the context of the environment in which it lives and on which it depends. In this context, the economy becomes subsidiary to both nature and society.

Rights of nature are also not entirely detached from the rights language more generally. They constitute both an ecocentric counter and an additional dimension to existing (anthropocentric) environmental rights. In the diverse contexts where rights of nature reflect indigenous perspectives in particular, there is no opposition but rather synergies between ecocentric and anthropocentric perspectives. A link can thus be drawn with the right to a clean environment.[77] This is an appropriate comparison to the extent that it highlights the priority that needs to be accorded to nature, in the same way that human rights highlight the priority that needs to be given to each individual.

In practice, rights of nature can come to reinforce the rights language and benefit from its growing acceptability. On the one hand, the widely recognised right to a clean environment at the national and regional level has eventually been given formal, though non-binding, recognition in 2022 through a UN General Assembly resolution.[78] On the other hand, rights of nature that are not constrained by the limitations of international human rights can contribute to broadening the relevance of the rights language related to the environment. This is, for instance, the case with regard to the usual framing of human rights as individual rights. This limits the relevance of rights discourses since environmental issues often cannot be reduced to individual concerns. Existing rights of nature regimes confirm the need for a broader perspective and are frequently framed around existing community management and protection norms of the concerned environment. As a result, the rights and obligations linked to the environment may be conceived as collective in nature. In other words, there is ample scope for building on synergies between (human) environmental rights and rights of nature, which can be framed, for instance, in terms of eco-human rights.[79]

In terms of scale, debates over rights of nature have until now often focused on relatively specific environments, in line with the fact that the push for a legal framework tends to come from people who depend on this environment or live in it. At the same time, there is no scale limitation and in fact, there are increasing debates about rights of nature applied to parts of nature as big as the seas.[80] This reflects two crucial elements. First, rights of nature tend to be framed at the

[77] LJ Kotzé and S Adelman, 'Environmental Law and the Unsustainability of Sustainable Development: A Tale of Disenchantment and of Hope' (2023) 34 *Law and Critique* 227.

[78] UNGA Res 76/300 (28 July 2022) UN Doc A/RES/76/300.

[79] P Cullet, 'Confronting Inequality Beyond Sustainable Development – The Case for Eco-human Rights and Differentiation' (2022) 31(1) *Review of European, Comparative & International Environmental Law* 7.

[80] H Harden-Davies and others, 'Rights of Nature: Perspectives for Global Ocean Stewardship' (2020) 122 *Marine Policy* 104059.

local level and in that sense offer a distinct take on law and policy-making, since environmental and sustainable development policies have often been largely top-down. Second, rights of nature are not limited to a local context and can be applied in multi-scalar contexts. This is, for instance, true in the case of rivers, which may, as in the case of the Ganga, cross through various sub-national entities and be also transboundary at the same time.[81] This is also true of an area of land protected through rights of nature whose protection has local to global impacts, such as in the case of forests and their relevance to tackling the climate crisis or addressing the sixth mass extinction of biodiversity.[82]

The increasingly broad take-up of rights of nature in different parts of the world and in different contexts reflects a wider understanding that new thinking is needed. The attraction that rights of nature in this context is that they offer a way to rethink the different parameters that make up human civilisation without excluding any aspect. The real contribution that they make is not so much the ecocentric turn but rather the re-ordering of priorities within a context where society, livelihoods and economy are not excluded but are made subsidiary to the environment on which we depend for our survival. It is easier to identify these links at a local level and therefore it makes sense that such policy-making would have a marked bottom-up framing. At the same time, in the context of the global climate crisis whose impacts are increasingly evident at many levels, the relevance of rights of nature goes far beyond local environments, as in the case of transboundary rivers or forests, whose protection have positive impacts on the global environment.

V. Conclusion

The development model based on economic growth as a source of prosperity and increased well-being for all has been unsuccessful, in particular for the least well-off. Further, the idea that economic growth is the only real marker of successful welfare policies has failed, not only because poverty is far from being eradicated, but also because inequality has increased significantly in the past decades.

Different attempts have been made over time to address some of the perceived shortcomings of development framed mostly around economic growth. One of the major adjustments was the introduction of the concept of sustainable development. Initially, it reflected the realisation that economic growth's dependence on natural resources and economic growth's impact on the environment could not be sustained in the long term. Progressively, a broader understanding that included the links between society and economic growth led to framing sustainable development as centred around the three pillars of economy, society and environment, the latter remaining in practice the lesser partner.

[81] For the judgment of the Uttarakhand High Court, see *Mohd. Salim v State of Uttarakhand* [2017] SCC OnLine Utt 367.

[82] New Zealand, Te Urewera Act 2014.

The severe economic crisis of the late 2000s, and the crisis linked to the Covid-19 pandemic, have led to a realisation that a constant harping back to economic growth in times of crisis is not solving the issues arising. On the one hand, the Covid-19 pandemic led to a massive surge in poverty around the world. On the other hand, every attempt to address poverty through untrammelled economic growth causes further environmental harm and more specifically contributes to aggravating the global climate crisis.

At this juncture, policy-making must be radically rethought. A majority of countries of the Global South have not seen their relative position in terms of human development improve significantly over the past few decades. Further, hundreds of millions of people have seen their standards of living stagnate and for many, the push for development has been equated with impoverishment.

The lack of a rights framing in development policy is in part to blame for the present situation. The attempt to remedy this through a convention on the right to development arrives far too late. At this juncture, it is crucial to rethink the bases for thinking about improvements in welfare and well-being based on the principles of environmental protection, social justice and economic equity.

This must be through new conceptual tools. Rights of nature, together with existing (human) environmental rights can provide an answer to the current crises. They provide stronger bases for ensuring that nature, as well as the situation of the most marginalised, is effectively prioritised.

PART III

Institutional, Policy and Legal Framework for Sustainable Development

6

Environmental Constitutionalism for Sustainable Development in the Global South

MUHAMMAD EKRAMUL HAQUE*

I. Introduction

Environmental constitutionalism goes hand in hand with sustainable development principles, emerging as a flourishing concept in the Global South. As it becomes pertinent to deal with environmental protection through an intersectional lens, the incorporation of such ideals into constitutional provisions strengthens the groundwork for climate justice and environmental constitutionalism. In juxtaposition to the idea through which states used to put economic growth ahead of environmental protection,[1] countries in the South have come to see the need to incorporate environmental rights in their respective constitutions. The inclusion of provisions relating to the protection of the environment in the constitutions of the Global South countries from traditional legal structures signifies a paradigm shift,[2] acknowledging the intrinsic link between a robust environmental ethos and the goals presented by sustainable development.

Constitutionalism, encompassing principles defining and limiting government powers[3] through universally accepted legitimate constitutions,[4] establishes a framework to hold the state accountable to human rights and constitutional values.[5] Numerous nations have gradually adopted the notion of environmental

* I gratefully acknowledge the research assistance provided by Ishraque Labib (PhD Candidate, University of Dhaka) and Zaid Ekram (University of Dhaka) in writing this chapter.

[1] W Beckerman, 'Economic Growth and the Environment: Whose Growth? Whose Environment?' (1992) 20 *World Development* 481.

[2] K Bosselmann, 'Global Environmental Constitutionalism: Mapping the Terrain' (2015) 21 *Widener Law Review* 177.

[3] RS Kay, 'American Constitutionalism' in L Alexander (ed), *Constitutionalism: Philosophical Foundations* (Cambridge University Press, 2001) 16.

[4] LJ Kotzé, 'Arguing Global Environmental Constitutionalism' (2012) 1 *Transnational Environmental Law* 204.

[5] ibid 206.

constitutionalism, where it can be seen that environmental protection is incorporated into their respective constitutions.[6] This acknowledgement, through incorporation into their constitutions, elevates the importance of environmental protection to one of the highest concerns of the states, while at the same time creating a scenario conducive to the safeguarding of the environment through a constitutional framework.[7] These acts, done by many countries, have been lauded by the international community along with extensive recognition.[8] This change is in line with the UN's Sustainable Development Goals (SDGs), which aim to create a more just and sustainable society by 2030. Through the simultaneous cognition of sustainable development practices and safeguarding the environment,[9] environmental constitution enables the realisation of the goals enshrined in the SDGs.[10]

Purposeful channelling of environmental constitutionalism towards implementing and complementing the SDGs is analysed in this chapter. This chapter posits that in order to utilise the full potential of environmental constitutionalism, it is pertinent to adopt a synergistic approach that capitalises simultaneously on both 'Big-C' and 'small-c' elements, along with addressing the obstacles in implementing these constitutional provisions in actual practice. The chapter wraps up by underscoring the critical significance of environmental constitutionalism in the Global South's pursuit of the SDGs.

II. The Global South and Environmental Constitutionalism

Regrettably, the Global South is inadequately represented in the field of comparative constitutional law, regardless of its substantial contribution to constitutional debates and significant representation as a demographic group.[11] This gap is particularly pronounced given the recent emergence of environmental constitutionalism in these regions, signalling a transformative shift in legal perspectives. Despite there being significant movement in these countries towards incorporating

[6] ibid 208.

[7] LJ Kotzé, 'Six Constitutional Elements for Implementing Environmental Constitutionalism in the Anthropocene' in E Daly and JR May (eds), *Implementing Environmental Constitutionalism: Current Global Challenges* (Cambridge University Press, 2018) 18.

[8] LK Weis, 'Environmental Constitutionalism: Aspiration or Transformation?' (2018) 16 *International Journal of Constitutional Law* 837.

[9] JR May and E Daly, *Global Environmental Constitutionalism* (Cambridge University Press, 2015) 33.

[10] R Mwanza, 'The Relationship between the Principle of Sustainable Development and the Human Right to a Clean and Healthy Environment in Kenya's Legal Context: An Appraisal' (2020) 22 *Environmental Law Review* 185.

[11] P Dann, 'The Southern Turn in Comparative Constitutional Law: An Introduction' in P Dann, M Riegner and M Bönnemann (eds), *The Global South and Comparative Constitutional Law* (Oxford University Press, USA, 2020) 1.

constitutional provisions for the protection of the environment, they rarely come up in discussion in regional and international forums when it comes to speaking about comparative constitutional law. While the world hurtles through the concept of environmental protection, the Global South is still plagued with inherited titles such as 'Third World' which sheds light onto the inherently disadvantaged economic sphere of Global South countries.[12] The term 'sustainability' is often defined as 'the capacity to endure'.[13] It is the ability to preserve something over a period of time.[14] The Agenda 2030 for Sustainable Development, passed and adopted by a whopping 193 nations in 2015, set out 17 United Nations Sustainable Development Goals (SDGs).[15] The SDGs set forth a very comprehensive entailments to address a multitude of areas such as environmental, social and economic challenges, which need to be addressed on a truly global scale to have the most impact. While the Global South fends off challenges on multiple fronts, environmental constitutionalism provides a guiding beacon to help them navigate the waters of the implementation of SDGs.

III. Synergy of 'Big-C' and 'small-c' Constitutionalism in Achieving SDG Goals

Constitutionalism, with its possibilities, has the potential to fulfil the maxim that humanity can achieve triumphs greater than the sum of its parts.[16] 'Big-C' constitutionalism pertains to a nation's formal, inviolable constitution that functions as the preeminent legal document, delineating governmental frameworks, essential tenets and individual liberties.[17] Conversely, 'small-c' constitutionalism comprises a more extensive corpus of constitutional law that originates from various sources, such as treaties, conventions and judicial decisions.[18] It includes practices, interpretations and implicit regulations, which inevitably shape a country's constitutional landscape. It functions as the most conspicuous embodiment and substantiation of the values and guiding principles of a given social order.[19] In her analysis of the

[12] ibid 5.
[13] M Thompson, 'Climate, Imagination, Kant, and Situational Awareness' (2011) 7 *Journal of Global Ethics* 137.
[14] J Mensah, 'Sustainable Development: Meaning, History, Principles, Pillars, and Implications for Human Action: Literature Review' (2019) 5 *Cogent Social Sciences* 2.
[15] S Bernstein, 'The United Nations and the Governance of Sustainable Development Goals' in N Kanie and F Biermann (eds), *Governing through Goals: Sustainable Development Goals as Governance Innovation* (MIT Press, 2017) 213.
[16] R Albert, 'The Cult of Constitutionalism' (2012) 39 *Florida State University Law Review* 382.
[17] T Khaitan, 'Political Parties in Constitutional Theory' (2019) 73 *Current Legal Problems* 89.
[18] A Chilton and M Versteeg, 'Small-c Constitutional Rights' (2022) 20 *International Journal of Constitutional Law* 141.
[19] LJ Kotzé, 'Six Constitutional Elements for Implementing Environmental Constitutionalism in the Anthropocene' in E Daly and JR May (eds), *Implementing Environmental Constitutionalism: Current Global Challenges* (Cambridge University Press, 2018) 18.

relationship between human rights and environmental conservation, Shelton lays forth three primary legal frameworks.[20] Environmental protection is a prerequisite for establishing the recognition of several other human rights.[21] Furthermore, procedural safeguards, including rights to access to information and participation in decision-making, would serve to advance environmental protection. This brings us to the third point: the 'human rights catalogue' should incorporate the right to the environment.

The development of small-c constitution expands the scope of Big-C constitution, allowing the holistic constitutional framework to move forward organically, reflecting the needs of generations preceding the one which the constitutions were originally written for. Often, after enough small-c jurisprudence has developed surrounding a certain issue it morphs into Big-C constitution – this is what aids the text of the constitution to adapt to changing circumstances in society, and to be better fit to act as a comprehensive constitutional text through the test of time. In the case of environmental protection, giant leaps are continually made in terms of scientific discoveries, information, perspectives of the international community, and consensus among scientists and scholars; these develop alongside small-c constitution, which helps to solidify and strengthen Big-C constitution, as when the small-c components morph into Big-C components, they are already honed and structured. Small-c constitution is technically tasked with bridging this gap between state-of-the-art needs and the Big-C constitution; this includes connecting and interpreting existing constitutional provisions to new developments, taking heed of new scientific developments, and adapting to the needs of future generations. For example, one of these bridges can be observed in Bangladesh, where after having considerable developments in the field of environmental constitutionalism through judicial activism, the constitution was then lauded with a very new provision which sought to establish, quite concretely, environmental protection. Following many cases with respect to environmental protection, and multiple attempts at grouping this with the right to life and other fundamental rights and freedoms, once the jurisprudence surrounding the small-c concept of environmental protection gained enough traction, it morphed into a Big-C component: a constitutional provision, namely Article 18A (new article inserted in 2011) of the Constitution of the People's Republic of Bangladesh. This was the very first explicit mention of environmental protection in the constitution, with specific mentions of the terms 'to protect' and 'to preserve', including the notion of sustainable development, and 'future citizens' which included the internationally growing concept of intergenerational equity and justice. This was a very apt example of how when there is a culmination of small-c developments, this opens the door to a new amalgamated constitutional provision.

[20] D Shelton, 'Human Rights, Environmental Rights, and the Right to Environment' (1991) 28 *Stanford Journal of International Law* 103.

[21] ibid.

IV. Justiciability of Environmental Constitutionalism

It has long been the case that many nations in the Global South have put economic growth ahead of environmental protection. In the absence of an explicit provision for environmental constitutionalism within their constitution, the approach taken to address environmental concerns was predominantly through state policies, without substantial constitutional safeguards. In this context, a transformative shift is underway, recognising the direct justiciability of environmental matters as fundamental rights or through interpretative means.

A. Non-Justiciable Provisions

In some Global South countries, environmental conservation is outlined as a state policy within the constitution, rendering it non-justiciable in that country's courts. Article 48A of the Constitution of India,[22] and Article 18A of the Constitution of Bangladesh,[23] are two such examples; the former is subject to restrictions imposed by Article 37, while the latter is subject to restrictions imposed by Article 8(2).[24] Just because these provisions have been characterised as non-justiciable does not mean that they are absent or silent in the purview of obligating the state to perform in accordance with them.[25] It is incumbent on the state to make sure that these principles are adhered to the fullest when making policies and laws.[26] Despite the prescription of non-justiciability, the courts are playing a vital role in environmental litigation. A broader interpretation of the right to life is sought in court even when particular clauses are not justiciable;[27] this allows for legal recourse

[22] Article 48A of the Indian Constitution is as follows:

> Protection and improvement of environment and safeguarding of forests and wild life. – The State shall endeavour to protect and improve the environment and to safeguard the forests and wild life of the country.

[23] Article 18A of the Constitution of Bangladesh states:

> The State shall endeavour to protect and improve the environment and to preserve and safeguard the natural resources, bio-diversity, wetlands, forests and wild life for the present and future citizens.

[24] Part II of the Constitution of Bangladesh and Part IV of the Constitution of India contain chapters devoted to Fundamental and Directive Principles of State Policy, respectively.

[25] ME Haque, 'Constitutional Protection of Economic and Social Human Rights' in R Chowdhury and R Hoque (eds), *A History of the Constitution of Bangladesh: The Founding, Development, and Way Ahead* (Taylor and Francis, 2023) 186.

[26] M Guruswamy and B Aspatwar, 'Access to Justice in India: The Jurisprudence (and Self-Perception) of the Supreme Court' in DB Maldonado (ed), *Constitutionalism of the Global South: The Activist Tribunals of India, South Africa, and Colombia* (Cambridge University Press, 2013) 337.

[27] ME Haque, 'Economic, Social and Cultural Rights: Transformation of Non-Justiciable Constitutional Principles to Justiciable Rights in Bangladesh' in MR Islam and M Ekramul (eds), *The Constitutional Law of Bangladesh: Progression and Transformation at its 50th Anniversary* (Springer Nature, 2023).

for environmental issues, but however widens the ambit for the enforcement of the right to life instead of directly incorporating the right to environment as an enforceable provision.

i. Bangladesh

In the midst of the Constituent Assembly deliberations in Bangladesh, former Prime Minister Tajuddin Ahmad argued against the enforcement of the Fundamental Principles of State Policy (FPSP) by the judiciary.[28] His point of view was not that these principles would never be put into practice; instead, he highlighted how the framers intended for the state to automatically and steadily uphold the FPSP over time.[29] It is quite apparent from Dr Kamal Hossain's remarks as the chairman of the Constitution Drafting Committee that the Constituent Assembly relied on constitutive intention, with his emphasis on the responsibility upon the elected representatives chosen by the people to realise the full potential of these fundamental principles. Therefore, critics, including opposition and neutral members, cannot assert that the Constitution lacks provisions for realising these principles, provided they place trust in the people and their elected representatives.[30] As originalists subscribe to a strict interpretation of the Constitution,[31] from an originalist standpoint it can easily be argued that the mechanisms for implementing FPSP are likely to be found within the constitutional framework itself. The underlying notion was that the state would not necessarily act in a way that goes against its own constitutional values.

In a similar vein, Badrul Haidar Chowdhury CJ agreed that the government should exert every effort to realise the FPSP.[32] Despite the lack of legal enforceability, Naimuddin Ahmed J made the perceptive observation in the obiter of the case *Kudrat-E-Elahi Panir vs Bangladesh* that although the FPSPs are not yet subject to positive justiciability, they can be subject to negative enforcement.[33] Article 7(2) of the Bangladesh Constitution sets forth the strongest weapon for the negative enforcement of FPSP, through the proclaiming of any law incongruent with the Constitution as null and void.[34] The *Kudrat-E-Elahi* case is an apt example of

[28] *Bangladesh Constituent Assembly Debates (Gono Parishader Bitarka, Sarkari Biboroni)* 386.

[29] Haque (n 25) 187.

[30] *Bangladesh Constituent Assembly Debates* (n 28) 421.

[31] LG Simon, 'The Authority of the Framers of the Constitution: Can Originalist Interpretation Be Justified?' (1985) 73 *California Law Review* 1496.

[32] He stated:

> Though the directive Principles are not enforceable by any Court, the principles therein laid down are nevertheless fundamental in the [g]overnance of the country and it shall be the duty of the State to apply these principles in making laws … This alone shows that the directive principles cannot be flouted by the executive. The endeavour of the Government must be to realize these aims and not to whittle them down (*Anwar Hossain Chowdhury vs Bangladesh* (1989) 41 DLR (AD) 165).

[33] *Kudrat-E-Elahi Panir v Bangladesh* [1991] 20 CLC (HCD).

[34] Article 7(2) of the Constitution of Bangladesh is as follows:

> This Constitution is, as the solemn expression of the will of the people, the supreme law of the Republic, and if any other law is inconsistent with this Constitution that other law shall, to the extent of the inconsistency, be void.

the utilisation of Article 7(2) to expand the horizon of negative enforcement. It showed how, despite the bar on positive enforcement, the legal interpretations of the FPSP breathe life into negative enforcement. This cohesion not only regulates harmony between constitutional provisions but also paves the way for the proper negative enforcement of economic, social and cultural (ESC) rights. Current judicial trends in Bangladesh are hinting towards endorsing the enforceability of ESC rights by treating them as a part of the FPSP. In *K M Safiullah vs Bangladesh*, the High Court Division (HCD) of the Supreme Court of Bangladesh took the step of positively implementing the FPSP in order to successfully conserve Suhrawardy Udyan.[35] This is an interesting judicial interpretation which enables the court to positively enforce the FPSP. Nevertheless, given the deviation from an established legal principle that the FPSP is not positively enforceable, the court had to provide justification for the positive enforcement of the FPSP, which, unfortunately, was not articulated in this instance.

ii. *India*

Dr BR Ambedkar, who presided over India's constitution-drafting committee, admitted that the Directive Principles of State Policy (DPSP) could not be enforced. Nevertheless, he emphasised that there may still be repercussions for violation of the DPSP.[36] The Indian constitution does not contain any provision similar to Bangladesh's Article 7(2). The absence of a constitutional clause in the Indian constitution akin to Article 7(2) may hinder the direct negative enforcement of ESC rights highlighted by the DPSP; however, this opens an aspect of comparative constitutional law wherein the Bangladesh constitution empowers its apex court to make void any law inconsistent with the constitution, thereby opening the door to negative enforcement, whereas the Indian constitution does not take this step.[37] In *S P Gupta vs Union of India*, the Supreme Court of India stated that the judiciary must actively promote social justice and become a tool of the economic and social revolution.[38] The Indian Supreme Court, in the *Minerva Mills* case, remarked that the socio-economic rights encapsulated in the Directive Principles are inherently integral to human rights, comparable in significance to the Fundamental Rights.[39]

[35] *K M Safiullah v Bangladesh* [2010] 18 BLT (Special Issue) 1.

[36] Dr Ambedkar stated the following in the Constituent Assembly of India (Constituent Assembly Debates, vol VII, 41):

> If it is said that the Directive Principles have no legal force … I am prepared to admit it. But I am not prepared to admit it that they have no sort of binding force at all. Nor am I prepared to conceive that they are useless because they have no binding force in law … The Draft Constitution as framed only provides a [piece of] machinery for the government of the country … But whoever captures power will not be free to do what he likes with it. In the exercise of it, he will have to respect these instruments of instructions which are called Directive Principles.

[37] ME Haque, 'Justiciability of Economic, Social and Cultural Rights under International Human Rights Law' (2022) 32 *Dhaka University Law Journal* 52.

[38] *S P Gupta v Union of India* [1981] 1 SCC 87, [27].

[39] *Minerva Mills Ltd v Union of India* [1980] 3 SCC 625, [107].

Despite the bar to enforce the DPSP, the Court acknowledges and fulfils its responsibility towards the DPSP and does apply them in its decisions. Often the judiciary takes the leniency to intertwine the DPSP with fundamental rights, utilising the right to life to enforce socio-economic rights like the right to food, shelter, health and others, these actions are what give shape to the jurisprudence surrounding the enforcement of the DPSP.[40] In cases where the executive is clearly neglecting their duties, the Court exercises liberty to take a proactive stance. For example, in cases like *Central Inland Water v Brojo Nath*[41] and *Ratlam v Shri Vardhichand*[42] it can be seen that the Court not only compelled other organs of the state to abide by the DPSP but also ventured to prevent actions which ran contrary to the principles set out in the DPSP. In instances such as *State of Himachal Pradesh v a Parent of a Student of Medical College*,[43] the Court asserts its authority to require the legislative or executive branches to fulfil their constitutional duties in implementing the DPSP. Through cases like *Maneka Gandhi v Union of India*,[44] and *Francis Coralie Mullin v Union Territory of Delhi*,[45] the Court expanded the protection of the right to life in Article 21 to encompass various provisions from the DPSP. Notably, in the *Bandhua Mukti Morcha* case, the court issued directives related to labour rights, through aligning them with the principles set out in the DPSP, evidencing a trajectory of Indian courts actively enforcing DPSP, with emphasis on the lens of the right of life. This has left a positive mark on the standard of justiciability and jurisprudence of the DPSP.[46]

B. Justiciable Provisions

It can now be seen that countries in the Global South are incorporating textual provisions in their constitutions, making them justiciable and providing a robust ground for environmental conservation within the periphery of Big-C constitutional law. The right to a healthy environment is specifically recognised in Article 79 of Colombia's 1991 Constitution.[47] In line with this, the safeguarding of the environment and the advancement of intergenerational environmental justice are also

[40] BA Gebeye, 'The Potentials of Directive Principles of State Policy for the Judicial Enforcement of Socio-Economic Rights: A Comparative Study of Ethiopia and India' (2016) 10 *Vienna Journal on International Constitutional Law* 54.

[41] *Central Inland Water v Brojo Nath* [1986] AIR 1571.

[42] *Ratlam v Shri Vardhichand* [1980] AIR 1622.

[43] *State of Himachal Pradesh v a Parent of a Student of Medical College* [1985] AIR 910.

[44] *Maneka Gandhi v Union of India* [1978] AIR 597.

[45] *Francis Coralie Mullin v Union Territory of Delhi* [1981] AIR 746.

[46] *Bandhua Mukti Morcha v Union of India and Others* [1984] AIR 802.

[47] Article 79 of the Constitution of Colombia says:

> Every individual has the right to enjoy a healthy environment. An Act shall guarantee the community's participation in the decisions that may affect it. It is the duty of the State to protect the diversity and integrity of the environment, to conserve the areas of special ecological importance, and to foster education for the achievement of these ends.

emphasised in the constitutions of other Global South countries. For instance, the provision for a balanced environment is enshrined in Article 225 of the Brazilian Constitution, which obliges both the government and the community to safeguard the environment for the benefit of current and future generations.[48] Section 24 of the Constitution of South Africa guarantees the right to a healthy environment for all individuals and requires its preservation for both the current and future generations. Legislative measures adopted in tandem with economic and social progress serve to accomplish this by preventing pollution, encouraging conservation, and ensuring sustainable development. According to Article 42 of the Kenyan Constitution, it is everyone's right to live in a healthy and clean environment. It requires the execution of environmental commitments under Article 70 as well as the implementation of legislative measures to protect current and future generations, as outlined in Article 69.[49] These provisions are now justiciable, meaning they can be legally enforced in the respective countries' courts.

V. Adjudication of Environmental Constitutionalism

Judicial adjudication exists in countries which have recognised as either justiciable or non-justiciable constitutional provisions regarding the environment, to some degree or in some form or the other. Pursuing a legal recourse becomes a right when the right to a healthy environment is infringed for a person or community. The number of environmental courts and tribunals is growing rapidly in nations in the Global South. Bangladesh has established environmental courts,[50] India has institutionalised the National Green Tribunal that adjudicates environmental disputes,[51] Kenya has Environment and Land Courts with equivalent authority to the High Court,[52] and a separate Environment Tribunal. On the other hand, environmental courts are non-existent in Brazil, South Africa and Colombia. It is worth mentioning that aggrieved persons can seek judicial recourse for such infractions under a number

[48] Article 225 of the Brazilian Constitution is delineated as:

> All have the right to an ecologically balanced environment, which is an asset of common use and essential to a healthy quality of life, and both the Government and the community shall have the duty to defend and preserve it for present and future generations.

[49] Article 42 of the Constitution of Kenya is as follows:

> Every person has the right to a clean and healthy environment, which includes the right—
>
> (a) to have the environment protected for the benefit of present and future generations through legislative and other measures, particularly those contemplated in Article 69; and
> (b) to have obligations relating to the environment fulfilled under Article 70.

[50] A Hasanat, 'Environmental Courts in Enforcement: The Role of Law in Environmental Justice in Bangladesh' (2021) 21 *Australian Journal of Asian Law* 85.

[51] GN Gill, 'Mapping the Power Struggles of the National Green Tribunal of India: The Rise and Fall?' (2020) 7 *Asian Journal of Law and Society* 85.

[52] CB Soyapi, 'Environmental Protection in Kenya's Environment and Land Court' (2019) 31 *Journal of Environmental Law* 151.

of constitutional regimes across the world. For instance, Article 22 of the Kenyan Constitution,[53] Articles 32[54] and 226 of the Indian Constitution,[55] Article 102 of the Constitution of Bangladesh,[56] item LXIX of Article 5 of the Brazilian Constitution,[57]

[53] Article 22 of Kenyan Constitution is described as:

(1) Every person has the right to institute court proceedings claiming that a right or fundamental freedom in the Bill of Rights has been denied, violated or infringed, or is threatened.
(2) In addition to a person acting in their own interest, court proceedings under clause (1) may be instituted by—

 (a) a person acting on behalf of another person who cannot act in their own name;
 (b) a person acting as a member of, or in the interest of, a group or class of persons;
 (c) a person acting in the public interest; or
 (d) an association acting in the interest of one or more of its members.

[54] Article 32(1) of the Indian Constitution states:

The right to move the Supreme Court by appropriate proceedings for the enforcement of the rights conferred by this Part is guaranteed.

[55] Article 226 of the Constitution of India is as follows:

Power of High Courts to issue certain writs.—

(1) Notwithstanding anything in article 32, every High Court shall have power, throughout the territories in relation to which it exercises jurisdiction, to issue to any person or authority, including in appropriate cases, any Government, within those territories directions, orders or writs, including writs in the nature of habeas corpus, mandamus, prohibition, quo warranto and certiorari, or any of them, for the enforcement of any of the rights conferred by Part III and for any other purpose.

[56] Article 102 of the Constitution of Bangladesh is as follows:

(1) The High Court Division on the application of any person aggrieved, may give such directions or orders to any person or authority, including any person performing any function in connection with the affairs of the Republic, as may be appropriate for the enforcement of any of the fundamental rights conferred by Part III of this Constitution.
(2) The High Court Division may, if satisfied that no other equally efficacious remedy is provided by law—

 (a) on the application of any person aggrieved, make an order—

  (i) directing a person performing any functions in connection with the affairs of the Republic or of a local authority, to refrain from doing that which he is not permitted by law to do or to do that which he is required by law to do; or
  (ii) declaring that any act done or proceeding taken by a person performing functions in connection with the affairs of the Republic or of a local authority, has been done or taken without lawful authority and is of no legal effect; or

 (b) on the application of any person, make an order—

  (i) directing that a person in custody be brought before it so that it may satisfy itself that he is not being held in custody without lawful authority or in an unlawful manner; or
  (ii) requiring a person holding or purporting to hold a public office to show under what authority he claims to hold that office.

[57] Item LXIX of Article 5 of the Brazilian Constitution is as follows:

a writ of mandamus shall be issued to protect a clear and perfect right, not covered by *habeas corpus* or *habeas data*, whenever the party responsible for the illegal actions or abuse of power is a public official or an agent of a corporate legal entity exercising duties of the Government; ....

and section 38 of the South African Constitution[58] allow individuals to approach the courts in their respective countries to enforce environmental rights. Some of the Global South courts, including those in India, Bangladesh, Colombia and Brazil, have moved beyond the traditional requirement of proving personal injury for locus standi in environmental cases and enabled individuals concerned about environmental rights for marginalised communities to move such cases in court. The Colombian Constitution itself directly allows any person to come before the court for infringement of fundamental constitutional rights.[59]

The concept of a healthy environment encompasses both individual and collective aspects in Kenya. The individual dimension entails the obligation of states and individuals to collaborate to address environmental issues, whereas the collective dimension imposes restitution as a right for victims or prospective victims of environmentally destructive activities.[60] Article 70(1) of the Kenyan Constitution allows individuals to seek redress in court if their right to a clean and healthy environment, recognised under Article 42, 'is likely to be, denied, violated, infringed, or threatened'.

South Africa's Constitutional Court, in *Ferreira v Levin*, overturned the practice of requiring actual personal injury for environmental standing, emphasising a liberal interpretation, especially in public concern matters like environmental preservation.[61] *Mazibuko v City of Johannesburg* expanded standing, allowing groups and individuals to contest environmental infractions without direct personal injury.[62] The Phiri people contested a water policy despite no total water outage, recognising collective interest in water access. The court acknowledged standing based on collective interest, acknowledging the multiplicative impact of environmental damage on communities and the right to initiate environmental cases without direct personal injury proof.[63]

[58] Section 38 of the South African Constitution states:

> Anyone listed in this section has the right to approach a competent court, alleging that a right in the Bill of Rights has been infringed or threatened, and the court may grant appropriate relief, including a declaration of rights. The persons who may approach a court are—
>
> (a) anyone acting in their own interest;
> (b) anyone acting on behalf of another person who cannot act in their own name;
> (c) anyone acting as a member of, or in the interest of, a group or class of persons;
> (d) anyone acting in the public interest; and
> (e) an association acting in the interest of its members.

[59] Article 86 of the Colombian Constitution is as follows:

> Every individual may claim legal protection before the judge, at any time or place, through a preferential and summary proceeding, for himself/herself or by whoever acts in his/her name, the immediate protection of his/her fundamental constitutional rights when the individual fears the latter may be jeopardized or threatened by the action or omission of any public authority.

[60] MK Mbondenyi and O Ambani, *New Constitutional Law of Kenya: Principles, Government and Human Rights* (Lawafrica Publishing, 2013) 186.

[61] *Ferreira v Levin* [1995] ZACC 13.

[62] *Mazibuko v City of Johannesburg* [2009] ZACC 28.

[63] ibid per O'Regan J [165].

In *S P Gupta v India*, the Indian Supreme Court recognised the limitations faced by the impoverished and disadvantaged in seeking legal remedies, relaxing *locus standi* principles.[64] Bhagwati J highlighted that public-spirited individuals could file petitions on behalf of those unable to approach the court under Articles 226 and 32. In *People's Union for Democratic Rights v India*, the Court extended this concept, allowing third parties to directly petition the court when fundamental rights were violated, emphasising equal access to the rule of law.[65] The Supreme Court of India has taken on the role of environmental protector through public interest litigation (PIL) due to a combination of factors, including ineffective administrative enforcement, a lack of clarity in environmental regulations, and multiple forms of corruption, including corruption in politics for personal benefit.[66]

Bangladesh initially expanded *locus standi* to include any citizen when the matter affects the state through *Kazi Mukhlesur Rahman v Bangladesh*, drawing on comparative constitutional law.[67] *Dr Mohiuddin Farooque v Bangladesh* formalised standing in public interest environmental litigation, adopting a liberal stance and invoking aspirational constitutionalism.[68] Both these cases together have been pioneered the environmental protection jurisprudence landscape of Bangladesh, through enunciating the periphery of locus standi to include any person aggrieved, setting precedents as to public interest litigation, and paving the road for environmental activism through formal environmental constitutionalism. In Bangladesh, Naima Haidar J has designated PIL as a forum for the enforcement of fundamental rights and matters of public significance, in addition to ensuring the proper performance of constitutional duties and functions.[69]

VI. Evaluating Governmental Action and Inaction

In order to fully comprehend the entire periphery of impact that constitutional provisions have in granting courts the authority to assess government actions in regard to climate change in the Global South, it is necessary to revisit the way in which these legal structures and principles coincide with a larger body of constitutional principles. Courts in the Global South often find themselves at the helm of the fight against climate change, showing a fervour towards intervening in situations where the other two governmental wings, the legislative

[64] *S P Gupta v India* [1982] AIR SC 149.
[65] *People's Union for Democratic Rights v India* [1982] AIR 1473.
[66] GN Gil, 'Human Rights and the Environment in India: Access through Public Interest Litigation' (2012) 24 *Environmental Law Review* 201.
[67] *Kazi Mukhlesur Rahman v Bangladesh* [1974] 3 CLC 1181 (AD).
[68] *Dr Mohiuddin Farooque v Bangladesh* [1997] 17 BLD (AD) 1.
[69] *Human Rights and Peace for Bangladesh v Bangladesh* [2024] 24 BLC 1 [9].

and the executive, have indubitably been lethargic.[70] In order to make such actions actionable and justiciable, despite the apparently non-enforced or seemingly irrelevant provisions of textual guarantees of life, liberty, dignity, health and environmental quality, courts tend to include within their ambit the establishment of climate justice. This takes the limelight when the courts sustain the practice of adhering to interpretive conventions. Equitable remedy authority is regularly employed by the Court, consequently establishing mechanisms including the guardianship of ecosystems, which in turn enunciates a proper check and balance scenario for the government.[71]

The base formulated by constitutional underpinnings in the Global South act as pillars for the court to analyse governmental actions in response to climate change, for example the FAP-20 case in Bangladesh which was inevitably pioneering the field of both public interest litigation and climate justice in Bangladesh. It did very well in portraying the imminent requirement to protect basic rights, within the ambit of which falls the right to an environment free from pollution, while the pertinence of furthering economic progress and environmental protection simultaneously, in more of an equilibrium, came into the limelight. The fact that the court opined that such was the duty of the government, in line with the relevant constitutional provisions, shows how the constitution eventually paves the way for climate justice, as employed by the courts in the Global South. While at the same time, the fact that the executive branch of the government felt the heat after the court verdict, yet was roused from its usual lethargy back to a more responsible and proactive role, enunciated a beautifully pleasant display of the doctrine of separation of powers, evident from their eventual implementation of the court's directives to reformulate the flood action plan. The reformulated plan displayed characteristics of higher levels of sensitivity towards environmental control, reflecting perfectly the drive behind the court action in the first place. Similarly, the EarthLife case in South Africa was also an example of evaluating government actions in relation to climate change, when the court ventured as far as comprehensively evaluating the Thabametsi Power Project's influence on the environment surrounding the project.[72] Where the state had to take into account the climate change effects of coal-fired power stations, this brought on a invigorated era of discourse in South Africa in relation to climate justice and the fight against climate change.[73]

In *Human Rights and Peace for Bangladesh*,[74] the High Court Division (HCD) granted rivers legal personality and proclaimed them to be a public

[70] JR May and E Daly, 'Global Climate Constitutionalism and Justice in the Courts' in J Jaria-Manzano and S Borràs (eds), *Research Handbook on Global Climate Constitutionalism* (Edward Elgar, 2019).

[71] ibid.

[72] *EarthLife Africa Johannesburg v Minister of Environmental Affairs* [2017] ZAGPPHC 58.

[73] M Murcott, *The Practical Significance of Transformative Environmental Constitutionalism* (Brill, 2022) 180.

[74] *Human Rights and Peace for Bangladesh v Bangladesh* (HCD, 3 February 2019).

trust,[75] committed to the government on behalf of the general people, employing the concept of constitutional protection of the environment in multiple folds. Additionally, the case acknowledged the polluters pay principle and the precautionary principle. When the HCD set forth to enunciate the public trust doctrine, it utilised comparative constitutional law, through borrowing and transplanting analyses from English, American, and Indian case laws. Simultaneously, reference has been made to the Constitutions of Ecuador, the State of Montana and the State of Pennsylvania for recognising public trust doctrine. Article 21(1), coupled with Article 8(2), places a distinct onus on the state, compelling it to preserve public assets.[76] This now stands as a settled law in Bangladeshi constitutional jurisprudence. Likewise, judicial intervention was necessitated in the Atrato River case in Colombia due to the worsening degradation of the river caused due to executive inaction.[77] To safeguard the river and assure its continued existence, the courts granted it legal personality in recognition of the gravity of the environmental issues at hand. In light of these events, it is clear that the two arms of government must work together in protecting the environment. Although the executive has the authority to formulate policies and enforce regulations, its apparent lethargy frequently requires the intervention and supervision of the judiciary to safeguard environmental constitutionalism, hence beckoning forth seemingly revolutionary advances in judicial activism which would not have been necessary had there been prescriptive frameworks governing and policing the matter.

VII. Implementation of International Law in Constitutional Jurisprudence and Environmental Constitutionalism in Achieving the SDGs: Example of Bangladesh

In an effort to safeguard the environment and biodiversity, the government of Bangladesh has ratified a large number of international agreements and expressed its support for Multilateral Environmental Agreements.[78] Article 25

[75] The doctrine of public trust is a legal principle affirming that specific natural resources, such as air, water, and coastlines, are held in trust by the government for the collective benefit of the public. This doctrine imposes a governmental obligation to safeguard and oversee these resources for the well-being of both current and future generations.

[76] S Alam and SMA Naznin, 'Environmental Constitutionalism in Bangladesh: From Recognition to Practice in the Twenty-First Century' in MR Islam and ME Haque (eds), *The Constitutional Law of Bangladesh: Progression and Transformation at its 50th Anniversary* (Springer Nature, 2023) 260.

[77] *Center for Social Justice Studies v Presidency of the Republic*, Constitutional Court of Colombia, Judgment T-622/16.

[78] See 'Forest Department', bforest.gov.bd/site/page/b81a2e19-f10f-480c-9a88-b5e572197f39/International-conventions, accessed 9 March 2024.

of the Constitution enunciates respect for international law as a base for its international relations.[79] In the domain of international law within the framework of the Constitution of Bangladesh, an inclination towards a dualist perspective is discernible, shaped by historical elements and interpretations of existing legal norms.[80] Article 149 emphasises the continuity of laws, including the common law tradition, but debates persist on the recognition of international treaties as domestic law. However, judicial decisions affirm the dualist stance, restricting the direct application of treaties by the executive and the judiciary without implementing domestic legislation. In *Bangladesh v Somboon Asavaham*,[81] the AD stated that in cases where municipal law exists regarding an international subject, it is the court's responsibility to interpret the municipal law as per the literal interpretation. The periphery of the use of international law has been elucidated by the Supreme Court of Bangladesh in several instances. In *Bangladesh vs Sheikh Hasina*,[82] the AD held that Bangladeshi courts will not enforce international law even if ratified by the state unless these are incorporated in municipal laws. In *BNWLA v Bangladesh*,[83] the HCD observed:

> It has now been settled by several decisions of this subcontinent that when there is a gap in the municipal law in addressing any issue, the courts may take recourse to international conventions and protocols on that issue for the purpose of formulating effective directives and guidelines to be followed by all concerned until the national legislature enacts laws in this regard.[84]

In *H M Ershad vs Bangladesh*,[85] the AD of the Supreme Court of Bangladesh interpreted Article 25 and held that in the absence of any specific national law

[79] Article 25 of the Constitution of Bangladesh is as follows:

> The State shall base its international relations on the principles of respect for national sovereignty and equality, non interference in the internal affairs of other countries, peaceful settlement of international disputes, and respect for international law and the principles enunciated in the United Nations Charter, and on the basis of those principles shall –
>
> (a) strive for the renunciation of the use of force in international relations and for general and complete disarmament;
> (b) uphold the right of every people freely to determine and build up its own social, economic and political system by ways and means of its own free choice; and
> (c) support oppressed peoples throughout the world waging a just struggle against imperialism, colonialism or racialism.

[80] ME Haque, 'Constitutional Status of International Law in Bangladesh' in the Bangladesh section in *Encyclopedia of Public International Law in Asia* (Brill, 2021) vol 3; ME Haque, 'Application of International Law in the Supreme court of Bangladesh' in the Bangladesh section in *Encyclopedia of Public International Law in Asia* (Brill, 2021) vol 3; Kr Ahmed, 'The Constitution of Bangladesh and International Law' in R Hoque and R Chowdhury (eds), *A History of the Constitution of Bangladesh: The Founding, Development, and Way Ahead* (Taylor & Francis, 2023) 47.

[81] *Bangladesh v Somboon Asavaham* [1980] 32 DLR (AD) 194.

[82] *Bangladesh v Sheikh Hasina* [2008] 28 BLD (AD) 163.

[83] *BNWLA v Bangladesh* [2001] 40 CLC (HCD).

[84] ibid [20].

[85] *H M Ershad v Bangladesh* [2001] 21 BLD (AD).

provision, the court may apply international law in domestic jurisdiction. BB Roy Chowdhury J observed:

> Although universal human rights norms, whether given in the UDHR or in the Covenants, are not directly enforceable in national courts, they are enforceable by domestic courts if such norms are incorporated into the domestic law. However, national courts should not ignore the international obligations which a country undertakes. National courts should draw upon the principles incorporated in the international instruments if the domestic laws are ambiguous or absent. Where the domestic laws are clear, but inconsistent with the international obligations of the state concerned, the national courts will be obliged to respect national law …[86]

On top of that, in the cases of *Shipra Chowdhury*[87] and *Professor Nurul Islam*,[88] the Supreme Court has leaned on non-binding soft instruments as though they had persuasive force. In Bangladesh, therefore, international law and domestic law are inextricably linked, notwithstanding the absence of a specific constitutional provision to that effect.[89]

Article 18A of the Constitution of the People's Republic of Bangladesh is the first explicit mention of environmental protection in the Constitution, and this stands as a cornerstone of its regime in Bangladesh serving as both a beacon and framework for protection and preservation. The inclusion of the terms 'to protect' and 'to preserve' includes in the periphery of the article the notion of sustainable development, while the term 'future citizens' pertains to the internationally evolving jurisprudence of intergenerational equity and justice. The Appellate Division of the Supreme Court of Bangladesh in a recent case of *Grameenphone Ltd. and Others v Bangladesh Telecommunication Regulatory Commission and Others* affirmed the constitutional obligation of the state under Article 18A 'to protect and improve the environment and to preserve and safeguard the natural resources' and observed that Article 18A 'makes it clear that the state is the legal owner of the natural resources as a trustee of the people and although it is empowered to distribute the same, the process of distribution must be guided by the Constitutional principles including the doctrine of equality and larger public good'.[90]

In *Dr Mohiuddin Farooque vs Bangladesh (1996)*, the AD of the Supreme Court of Bangladesh defined the right to a habitable and secure environment as an essential aspect of the right to life.[91] The Court observed:

> … articles 31 and 32 of our Constitution protect right to life as a fundamental right. It encompasses within its ambit, the protection and preservation of environment,

[86] ibid [3].
[87] *Dr Shipra Chowdhury v Bangladesh* [2009] 29 BLD (HCD) 183, 186 [24].
[88] *Professor Nurul Islam v Bangladesh* [2000] 20 BLD (HCD) 377, 386 [9].
[89] Ahmed (n 80) 56.
[90] *Grameenphone Ltd and Others v Bangladesh Telecommunication Regulatory Commission and others* (10.01.2023 – BDAD): LEX/BDAD/0013/2023 [para 33].
[91] *Dr Mohiuddin Farooque vs Bangladesh* [1997] 17 BLD (AD) 1.

> ecological balance free from pollution of air and water, sanitation without which life can hardly be enjoyed. Any act or omission contrary thereto will be violative of the said right to life.[92]

In *Dr Mohiuddin Farooque*,[93] the right to life was once again used to uphold the right to a healthy environment.[94] The HCD of the Supreme Court of Bangladesh issued an ad-interim injunction in *Sharif N Ambia vs Bangladesh (2006)*,[95] regarding the construction of a 10-story market, due to its possibility of causing environmental hazard. In 2009, the Human Rights and Peace for Bangladesh filed a writ petition seeking an order to protect four rivers from encroachment; in response, a bench of the HCD issued a series of nine directives, which included surveying the river boundary zone and evicting intruders.[96] The HCD issued directives specifying the necessary timeframe and actions to be taken in order to expel the intruders. Therefore, the highest courts in both India and Bangladesh have provided broad interpretations of the right to life, even while there are legislative restrictions on actively implementing the DPSP or the FPSP. Hence, the enforcement of FPSP has been prompted by this, leading to the right to a healthy environment being implicitly implemented on several occasions.

Demonstrating the application of public trust doctrine in the *Shah Abdul Hannan* case,[97] the Court pondered the state's function as a custodian of the public trust, emphasising the protection of natural and mineral resources. This decision borrowed from the Indian theory of public trust, and the Supreme Court ruled that the role of the state is similar to that of a public trust trustee, vested in safeguarding the public interest. In a more assertive stance observed in *Faridul Alam vs Bangladesh*,[98] the court not only endorsed the doctrine but went further, instructing the government to safeguard the environmentally sensitive zones of Cox's Bazar Sea beach. This dynamic judicial engagement reaffirms an evolving interpretation of the state's responsibilities in safeguarding public resources. By providing a legal framework that requires the prudent management of vital natural resources, the public trust doctrine contributes significantly to the advancement of sustainable

[92] ibid [96].
[93] *Dr Mohiuddin Farooque v Bangladesh* [1998] 48 DLR (HCD) 338.
[94] The Court observed:

> [The] right to life is not only limited to the protection of life and limbs but extends to the protection of health and strength of workers, their means of livelihood, enjoyment of pollution-free water and air, bare necessaries of life, facilities for education, development of children, maternity benefit, free movement, maintenance and improvement of public health by creating and sustaining conditions congenial to good health and ensuring the quality of life consistent with human dignity.

Dr Mohiuddin Farooque vs Bangladesh [1998] 48 DLR (HCD) 442 [17].
[95] *Sharif N Ambia vs Bangladesh* [2006] 58 DLR (AD) 253.
[96] 'HC Seeks Names, Addresses of *Buriganga* Encroachers' *The Business Standard* (12 October 2020), www.tbsnews.net/bangladesh/court/hc-seeks-names-addresses-buriganga-encroachers-144274, accessed 9 March 2024.
[97] *Shah Abdul Hannan v Bangladesh* [2011] 16 BLC 386.
[98] *Faridul Alam v Bangladesh* [2010] 18 BLT 323.

development. This doctrine imparts on the government a responsibility to exercise prudent management and safeguard specific resources, including ecological zones and water bodies, which are considered public trust assets. This legal principle serves as a powerful tool for environmental conservation, ensuring the preservation of biodiversity, ecosystems, and vital resources. In *BELA v Bangladesh*, the use of saline water for shrimp aquaculture on agricultural and forest lands was deemed unlawful by the HCD.[99] In another writ petition, the Court has ordered the Department of Environment to establish a committee to safeguard the natural environment, biodiversity, carp-like mother fish, and dolphins inhabiting the Halda River.[100] In *Bangladesh v Mushfaqur Rahman*,[101] Syed Mahmud Hossain CJ observed:

> In order to successfully confront the twenty-first century environmental challenges that include managing the current and mitigating the future impacts of climate change; conserving natural resources and biodiversity and preventing pollution, and to ensure environmental justice, it is incumbent upon the state to develop, implement and enforce environmental laws and upon Judiciary to see that all parties concerned follow the laws and no one transgresses the same.[102]

Similarly, in *Rana Surong vs Bangladesh*,[103] Hasan Foez Siddique J observed:

> The principle adopted is that ecology and environment are not objects of ownership but are nature's gift intended to be preserved in trust for future generations. The main motto of social life is to live in harmony with nature. Ongoing environmental degradation that is going must now come to a stop …[104]

It is clear from the above discourse that the balance between the constitutionalism between the Big-C and small-c in Bangladesh precedes a pattern, displaying a clear path to the realisation of SDGs and pioneering the entitlement to the protection of the environment in the country.

VIII. Obstacles in Ensuring Environmental Constitutionalism

The prevalence of environmental legislation poses a direct obligation on all organs of the state to ensure the proper implementation of the provisions of those laws.[105]

[99] Staff Correspondent, 'HC Asks Govt to Save Agri-Farm, Forest Lands' *The Daily Star* (2 February 2012), www.thedailystar.net/news-detail-220894, accessed 21 February 2024.
[100] TBS Report, 'HC: Form Committee to Protect Halda River Biodiversity, Dolphins' *The Business Standard* (19 May 2020), www.tbsnews.net/bangladesh/court/hc-form-committee-protect-halda-river-biodiversity-dolphins-83302, accessed 24 February 2024.
[101] *Bangladesh v Mushfaqur Rahman* [2020] 72 DLR (AD) 211.
[102] ibid [38].
[103] *Rana Surong v Bangladesh* [2020] 72 DLR (AD) 153.
[104] ibid [12].
[105] A Hasanat, 'Legal Aid in Environmental Litigation: How to Promote Sustainable Development in Bangladesh' [2024] SSRN Electronic Journal 6.

However, a dichotomy arises between economic growth and environmental protection, where Global South governments often tend to veer on the side of economic growth, stilting existing legal obligations.[106] In response to this inaction, judges in the Global South have assumed a more proactive stance on environmental concerns. However, environmental constitutionalism is not always upheld by courts in the Global South – a phenomenon that can be explained by a web of interrelated causes. The lack of sufficient financial and human resources is a major obstacle to the creation of effective environmental regulating agencies and courts.[107] They are severely hindered in their ability to tackle and enforce environmental laws due to this constraint. Constant political uncertainty and instability breed an environment devoid of policy consistency and the courts are inclined to exercise caution when deciding how to play a role in environmental protection when the political climate is unstable.[108] Even courts which display the most progressive actions at times veer away from establishing the prowess of environmental constitutionalism, as seen in *Bangladesh v BAPA*.[109] In Appellate Division of the Supreme Court of Bangladesh the argument of state necessity and public interest prevailed over the argument of environmental preservation in regards to the construction of the Speaker and Deputy Speaker's residence. Rather, the Court observed:

> The residences are not meant for an individual person, but for the Speaker and the Deputy Speaker who uphold a unique position under the Constitution and in the said way the impugned project is being implemented for the public interest being the same is a state necessity.[110]

Article 18A does not go out of the picture as FPSP, even when dealing with unique constitutional provisions. The framers of the constitution of Bangladesh anticipated that the government would refrain from taking any action 'against' the FPSP. It is not difficult to deduce the present state of executive branch operations and the execution of their environmental policies if the proactive judiciary holds this view.

Courts are understandably reluctant to give environmental concerns priority when confronted with apparently 'more urgent and compelling social concerns', such as poverty, healthcare and education.[111] This is evident from a recent decision of the Indian Supreme Court, wherein Indira Banerjee J remarked that industrial establishments, sustaining the livelihoods of numerous employees

[106] ibid.

[107] K Georgieva, V Gaspar and C Pazarbasioglu, 'Poor and Vulnerable Countries Need Support to Adapt to Climate Change' (IMF, 3 March 2022), www.imf.org/en/Blogs/Articles/2022/03/23/blog032322-poor-and-vulnerable-countris-need-support-to-adapt-to-climate-change, accessed 10 March 2024.

[108] CG Gonzalez, 'Environmental Justice, Human Rights, and the Global South' (2015) 13 *Santa Clara Journal of International Law* 170.

[109] *Bangladesh v BAPA* [2023] 75 DLR (AD) 417.

[110] ibid [26].

[111] S Talukdar, 'Introduction' in S Talukdar and VE de Aquino (eds), *Judicial Responses to Climate Change in the Global South: A Jurisdictional and Thematic Review* (Springer Nature, 2023) 1.

and bolstering the nation's economy, ought not to be compelled into closure solely due to the absence of pre-existing environmental clearance.[112] The Court observed:

> The manufacturing units of the Appellants appoint about 8,000 employees and have a huge annual turnover. An establishment contributing to the economy of the country and providing livelihood ought not to be closed down only on the ground of the technical irregularity of not obtaining prior Environmental Clearance irrespective of whether or not the unit actually causes pollution.[113]

In the Global South, environmental constitutionalism encounters numerous constraints that impede its efficient execution and enforcement. The implementation of judicially unenforceable constitutional principles in nations such as Bangladesh and India presents a notable obstacle. There is a discrepancy between constitutional demands and actual execution since the executive branch fails to adequately execute these principles, despite the fact that they are integral to government. Environmental legislations of Bangladesh allow the executive branch to exert vast power without holding them to account for their inactions.[114] The lack of executive, legislative and judicial action by government agencies is clear even in India.[115] This lack of action renders environmental constitutionalism almost ineffective since even after judicial activism occurs the executive proves lethargic in carrying out actions under those principles in tackling urgent environmental concerns.[116] Consequently, this creates a hesitant tendency inside the judiciary to scrutinise the feasibility of their intervention, further choking the realisation of environmental constitutionalism. Informal pressure from industries benefitting from high levels of pollution results in a lot of unwanted advance for the economic growth part of the dichotomy. In the most serious circumstances these industries bring their fire and fury when progressive environmental policies are proposed, citing economic and financial reasons. When the court is left to struggle between the pressures of environmental protection and economic growth, with the added obstacle of informal pressure from influential polluters, the decision-making process becomes haphazard. On top of all that, a lack of environmental awareness, along the lines of both international law obligations and national law, amongst the general public, ensues a veil of ignorance, letting pollution and environmental degradation hide behind the façade of economic growth. The consequential lack

[112] K Rajagopal, 'Environment or Other Rights: Supreme Court Differs in 4 Days' *The Hindu* (29 March 2022), www.thehindu.com/news/national/environment-or-other-rights-supreme-court-differs-in-4-days/article65271269.ece, accessed 10 March 2024.

[113] *Pahwa Plastics Pvt Ltd v Dastag NGO* [2022] SCC 362 [56].

[114] MG Sarwar, 'Making a Case for Environmental Rule of Law in Bangladesh' *The Daily Star* (8 June 2021), www.thedailystar.net/law-our-rights/news/making-case-environmental-rule-law-bangladesh-2106989, accessed 22 March 2024.

[115] M Niyati, 'Judicial Activism for Environment Protection in India' (2015) 4 *International Research Journal of Social Sciences* 11.

[116] N Rühs and A Jones, 'The Implementation of Earth Jurisprudence through Substantive Constitutional Rights of Nature' (2016) 8 *Sustainability* 174.

of public support further reduces the tendency of the court to vie for progressive environmental protection.

One may wonder why Global Southern judges are using their judicial activism to push the right to the environment to the margins,[117] since, in reality, the Northern Hemisphere does not typically need the similar sort of environmental constitutionalism for the protection of the environment.[118] In order to deal with this question, we are required to look through a contextual lens.[119] Comparatively, the North has a robust legal framework with a keen eye towards environmental democracy,[120] coupled with a strong rule of law,[121] and a distinct separation of powers.[122] While on the other hand, Southern judiciaries pick up the pace that their legislatives and holistic government do not, unlike Northern constituencies, hence they play a major role in the development of the jurisprudence surrounding environmental constitutionalism, quite evident in landmark judgments such as Amazon deforestation, river pollution and the protection of disproportionately affected vulnerable communities. When looking at this from a comparative constitutional law point of view, the differences between the North and the South become more vivid and the legal struggles of the latter become more pronounced. Thick comparison, rather than superficial thin analysis, is required with an emphasis on the implications of these contextual differences.[123]

An additional challenge arises from the inadequate execution of judicial decisions on environmental issues. In practice, environmental constitutionalism fails due to the scarcity of effective implementation mechanisms, notwithstanding decisions by the courts concerning environmental matters.[124] The stark difference between judicial decisions and their eventual implementation, or lack thereof, eats away at the apparent credibility of judicial decisions, and subsequently erodes the effect of environmental constitutionalism, since litigation alone cannot shoulder the burden of all forms of environmental protection.[125] Even though the judiciary does take responsibility and move forward with progressive interpretations of constitutional provisions enumerating newer environmental protection

[117] DB Maldonado, 'Introduction: Toward a Constitutionalism of the Global South' in DB Maldonado (ed), *Constitutionalism of the Global South: The Activist Tribunals of India, South Africa, and Colombia* (Cambridge University Press, 2013) 21.

[118] CG Gonzalez, 'Bridging the North-South Divide' (2015) 32 *Pace Environmental Law Review* 409.

[119] J Blake, 'Achieving Justice in Global Environmental Protection' (2011) 8 *Environmental Science* 16.

[120] M Mason, *Environmental Democracy: A Contextual Approach* (Routledge, 1999) 212.

[121] See 'WJP Rule of Law Index 2023 Global Press Release' *World Justice Project* (25 October 2023), worldjusticeproject.org/news/wjp-rule-law-index-2023-global-press-release, accessed 22 February 2024.

[122] D Bilchitz and D Landau, 'The Evolution of the Separation of Powers in the Global South and Global North' in D Bilchitz and D Landau (eds), *The Evolution of the Separation of Powers: Between the Global North and the Global South* (Edward Elgar, 2018) 19.

[123] R Hirschl, 'From Comparative Constitutional Law to Comparative Constitutional Studies' (2013) 11 *International Journal of Constitutional Law* 9.

[124] May and Daly (n 9).

[125] Murcott (n 73) 172.

jurisprudence, more often than not these courts lack the inherent specialised expertise to advise on specific frameworks and comprehensive guidelines for the implementation of said frameworks. Relying exclusively on judicial decisions restricts the efficacy of environmental conservation endeavours, particularly in situations involving scientific expertise, such as the Turag River in Bangladesh. Enhancing the quality of environmental guidelines and bolstering the preservation of natural resources could be accomplished through collaboration with specialists and scientists. The public trust doctrine, which enunciates particular natural resources as public trusts, is hurt because of the lack of explicit directives as to the exact responsibilities of the trustees. Hence, even though rivers are recognised as public trusts, the consequences of the lack of duty are not known, nor are the details of such duties of the trustee. In the Global South, due to neoliberal version of capitalism which focuses more on individual rights rather than collective rights, a privileged few exploit nature to their advantage, leading to environmental damage.[126] The present predominance of anthropocentric rather than ecocentric priorities, compounded by the absence of environmental rule of law, makes matters worse.[127] The aforementioned factors pose substantial challenges in pursuing environmental constitutionalism in the Global South.

IX. Conclusion

Environmental constitutionalism has the proven potential to bring together constitutional provisions, judicial activism and SDGs, culminating in a pronounced shift towards holistic sustainability. One of the pivots in this path is the connection between formal and informal constitutionalism, with the Big-C establishing a framework and the small-c empowering stakeholders – within both, the written text of the constitution receives life. Although this harmony can be seen, it is pertinent to simultaneously pay heed to the obstacles entrenched on this path. Effective implementation of environmental constitutionalism requires first and foremost the capacity enhancement of Southern judiciaries and the establishment of legislative frameworks for public involvement and access to environmental information. South-South collaboration and information exchange can also help the Global South achieve environmental sustainability.

Environmental constitutionalism offers the Global South a persuasive and implementable structure to strive to successfully implement sustainable

[126] GM Cuadros, 'Environmental Rights, Responsibility and Care: A New Constitutional Paradigm' in J Jaria-Manzano and S Borràs (eds), *Research Handbook on Global Climate Constitutionalism* (Edward Elgar, 2019).

[127] JRM Leite and P de Araujo Ayala, 'Global Environmental Constitutionalism as a Constitutionalism of the Earth' in J Jaria-Manzano and S Borràs (eds), *Research Handbook on Global Climate Constitutionalism* (Edward Elgar, 2019).

development goals. Boyd considers this to be a transformative move towards the protection of the environment.[128] Successfully harmonising formal and informal constitutionalism, empowering stakeholders and bringing about international cooperation, are ways that the South can pioneer the field of sustainable development and maintain the emerging jurisprudence of intergenerational equity and justice. This is not merely an option; it is an incumbent responsibility surrounding one of the most pertinent areas of action in present times.

[128] DR Boyd, *The Environmental Rights Revolution: A Global Study of Constitutions, Human Rights, and the Environment* (University of British Columbia Press, 2012) 3.

7

Promoting Sustainable Development in the Global South: Governance Challenges for Valuing Ecosystem Services

HABIB ZAFARULLAH AND SHAWKAT ALAM

I. Introduction

'Sustainable development' is a contemporary concept that has become prominent since the release of the Brundtland Report, 'Our Common Future' in 1987. While emphasising that humanity can sustain development by meeting current needs without jeopardising future generations' ability, the report cautioned that achieving that goal would necessitate balancing present and future priorities.[1] This balancing out makes sustainable development both a dynamic and predictable phenomenon. However, the concept has been criticised for apparent contradictions and uncertainties, especially in reconciling resource conservation imperatives with economic development goals and means. Due to conceptual ambiguity, its goal and objective are understood differently, with numerous approaches used to combine the goals of social progress, environmental protection and economic growth.[2]

Nevertheless, despite its initial conceptual ambiguity and systemic complexities, sustainable development as a concept and practice has evolved, seeking to reconcile differences and integrating the plethora of concerns relevant to a *common-wealth* and human welfare. To effectively achieve the Sustainable Development Goals (SDGs), a comprehensive approach is essential. This approach should embrace all dimensions of sustainability, including social, economic, political, ethical, environmental and psychological aspects, with a strong emphasis

[1] GH Brundtland, 'Our Common Future: Report of the World Commission on Environment and Development' (1987), www.un-documents.net/ocf-ov.htm, accessed 26 October 2023.

[2] SM Lélé, 'Sustainable Development: A Critical Review' (1991) 19 *World Development* 607; D Worster, 'The Shaky Ground of Sustainability' in W Sachs (ed), *Global Ecology: A New Arena of Political Conflict* (Bloomsbury, 1993).

on intergenerational equity. These principles should serve as the foundation for shaping norms, laws, policies and strategies, ensuring a unified global effort to combat challenges like poverty, hunger, inequality, disease, environmental degradation, and other barriers to a high standard of living. A well-structured action plan is crucial, backed by a robust set of laws, policies and regulations dedicated to sustainable development. Whenever possible, these guidelines should derive from international agreements and be adapted to unique circumstances, either through legal or statutory adjustments.

Historically, the distinction between the Global North and South has been pronounced; it is rooted in a multitude of factors, including economic disparities, colonial legacies, technological advancements, and cultural distinctions. Despite globalisation and various international cooperation initiatives, the prospects of closing this gap and fostering global convergence remain distant, both now in the foreseeable future.

However, this challenging backdrop impels developing nations to be proactive and ambitious in their efforts to induce meaningful societal transformations. These nations have a responsibility, not just to the international community but, more crucially, to their citizens, to improve living standards, infrastructural facilities, educational access, healthcare provisions and more. A pivotal approach for these nations would be intertwining the SDGs into their governance structures. Since the Covid-19 pandemic gripped the planet, progress towards attaining the SDGs has declined; indeed, in some countries, there have been reversals.[3] Beyond the challenges posed by the pandemic, the Global South faces significant implementation setbacks. Political indifference, governance challenges, inadequate bureaucratic support, misalignment with international treaties, and a disconnect between policy intentions and their actual execution are primary contributors to these delays.

The purpose of this chapter is to explore the specific governance challenges that face developing countries in implementing sustainable development objectives through policy and law. This chapter will first examine the integration of sustainable development into domestic policies in poor nations, followed by a discussion on current trends in sustainability accounting. Subsequently, the chapter will analyse the effectiveness of existing governance systems in achieving these objectives. It is vital that environmental and sustainable development are no longer made randomly in a disjointed way; instead, as this chapter will advocate, more integrated approaches requiring a high degree of cohesion, coordination and collaboration are needed. This would enable decision-makers to execute more informed policies that incorporate environmental accounting and quantify the benefits associated with ecosystem services into the decision-making process.

This chapter will examine the necessity of going beyond the mere formulation of framework policies and providing guidance on essential objectives and

[3] JD Sachs and others, *Sustainable Development Report 2022: From Crisis to Sustainable Development – The SDGs as Roadmap to 2030 and Beyond* (Cambridge University Press, 2022) vii.

priorities for implementing sustainable development at a national level. The next challenge for developing countries is ensuring that there is sufficient integration, both vertically and horizontally, to drive policy-making and arrive at informed decisions. Not only will cross-institutional bodies such as taskforces play an increasingly important role, but this must also be supported by enabling multiple stakeholders to create a polycentric governance environment. For environmental accounting and environmental accounting and reporting (EAR) practice, this requires greater engagement with industry, community and stakeholders to ensure that high-quality inputs and considerations are captured early in the policy design process and backed with an independent judiciary with sufficient expertise in EAR and sustainability accounting to interrogate decision-making with effectiveness.

II. Integration of Sustainable Development into Policy: The Competing Priorities Faced by Decision-makers in the Global South

Sustainable development has progressed far beyond the stage of being merely a collection of ideas, concepts, policy goals or benchmarks. It is widely conceded that, in tandem with good governance, the SDGs offer a solution to global problems affecting humanity and the natural environment.[4] Several principles and propositions emanating from international agreements and protocols have or are being built into relevant national policies, strategies and instruments to put them into practice along with distinctive procedural elements. These constitute the legal and operating framework of sustainable development and cover both laws and policies.[5]

Despite the array of policies on sustainable development themes – ranging from poverty reduction, human development, and environmental conservation

[4] N Schrijver and F Weiss (eds), *International Law and Sustainable Development: Principles and Practice* (Martinus Nijhoff, 2004).

[5] See 'Report of the United Nations Conference on the Human Environment' (5–16 June 1972) UN Doc A/CONF.48/14/Rev.1; 'Report of the UN Water Conference on Clean Water and Sanitation' (14–25 March 1977) UN Doc E/CONF.70/29; See also the 1979 World Climate Conference on global warming causing the 'greenhouse' effect; the 1982 UN Convention on the Law of the Sea related to marine pollution; the 1977 UN Conference on Desertification and the follow-up Convention of 1994; the 1993 World Conference on Human Rights for promoting and safeguarding the rights of women, children and indigenous peoples; the World Conference on Women held in 1975, 1980, 1985 and 1995 that acknowledged women's rights and privileges in society; the 1997 UN Framework Convention on Climate Change and, last but not least, the Kyoto Protocol of 2002, which legally obligated developed nations to reduce emissions of greenhouse gases. All these events and agreements have had wide ramifications for sustainable development. However, Agenda 21 of 1992, the 1995 World Summit for Social Development and the World Summit on Sustainable Development held the same year, the United Nations Millennium Summit of 2000, the Rio+20 Summit and the more recent 2030 Agenda for Sustainable Development outlined in 2015 directly contributed to serve as the fundamental footings of sustainable development emerging as a concept and a practice in the Global South.

to climate change, universal education, health access, gender equality and human rights – many nations continue to exhibit a deficiency in formulating and implementing a sustainable development policy or strategy. However, only a small number of countries have sustainable development strategies, and many of those are outdated.[6] Since institutions, capacities and sustainable development priorities vary by country, each must create and implement its own strategy.[7] This must occur to enable governments to respond to the specific sustainable development needs and considerations that impact the community. Human rights, justice, social and political inclusion, and effective governance form part of a broader agenda. For sustainable development strategies to truly succeed, they need a robust foundation. Decisive actions from determined political leadership should complement this foundation – all set against a backdrop of accountability and transparency.

Implementing sustainable development projects requires intricate policy integration and painstaking policy coordination. Integration fails when nations prioritise one policy sector over another. For instance, developing countries may need to consider promoting high emissions intensity, export-orientated industries to promote employment opportunities and wealth creation. Even within the environmental sphere, priorities may differ – some focusing on climate change, biodiversity, air quality or recycling, and others preferring natural resources management, environmental health or disaster management in the environmental sphere. The social dimension of sustainable development is centred on health, quality of life, environmentally friendly consumption, education and interpersonal relations.[8] Sustainable development's success hinges on maintaining a balance across sectors. The proficiency of administrators in crafting a conducive political and regulatory landscape, coupled with their capacity to establish robust institutional frameworks for intersectoral interactions, will be pivotal in determining the efficacy of development initiatives.

III. Shifts in Contemporary Sustainable Development Policy Practice: Ecosystem Services and Sustainability Accounting

Ecosystems and sustainable development share a profound and intricate relationship. A thriving and balanced ecosystem is not just an environmental asset but a

[6] See UN (2023) *National Reports by Topic: National Sustainable Development Strategies (NSDS)*, sustainabledevelopment.un.org/topics/nsds/nationalreports, accessed 27 September 2023. This website has since migrated to a new platform, sdgs.un.org/.

[7] UN Department of Economic and Social Affairs, 'Guidance in Preparing a National Sustainable Development Strategy: Managing Sustainable Development in a New Millennium' (2002) DESA/DSD/PC2/BP13.

[8] OECD, 'Good Practices in the National Sustainable Development Strategies of OECD Countries' (2006).

cornerstone for human survival, prosperity and overall well-being. Every aspect of human life – from the air we breathe, the food we consume, to the water we drink – relies on the health and equilibrium of these ecosystems.

The term 'ecosystem services' encompasses the vast array of tangible and intangible benefits humans derive from the environment. Beyond the obvious material gains such as food, water and raw materials, ecosystems enrich human life in subtler ways too. The astounding biological diversity of our planet offers a wealth of non-material advantages. For instance, diverse ecosystems have historically inspired knowledge structures, influenced cultural narratives, and shaped societal interactions.[9] Negative ecosystem changes cause human suffering and economic deficits that must be thwarted through sound ecosystem service management (ESM) whose goal is 'to achieve a more sustainable resource use, contributing to the well-being of every individual, now and in the future by providing an equitable, adequate, and reliable flow of essential ecosystem services to meet the needs of a burgeoning world population'.[10] The ESM regulatory framework should be guided by prevalent cultural values and people's rights. These must be rooted in decision-making processes that consider the full scope of potential benefits to the public without compromising environmental standards.[11]

Strategies for sustainable development should incorporate the potential effects on ecosystems and the benefits derived from ecosystem services. Policies should be formulated to prevent adverse impacts on society, the economy and the environment. Moreover, the execution of these policies should be complemented with robust review, monitoring and reporting mechanisms. Such measures will facilitate the collection of valuable data and insights, which will further guide and refine future policy decisions. The advantages of protecting ecosystem services far outweigh their costs, so policy responses should be evaluated from various angles, including those of law, technology, institutions, economics and even the psychology of policy-makers. To make such policies work, expertise in and evaluation of ecosystem services and their benefits to human health and well-being are essential.[12] Human well-being, ecosystems and ecosystem services all have trade-offs and synergies, and it is crucial to understand these relationships before making any decisions.[13]

[9] R Hassan, RJ Scholes and N Ash (eds), *Ecosystems and Human Well-Being: Current State and Trends* Vol 1 (Island Press, 2005) 14.

[10] S Jacobs, N Dendoncker and H Keune (eds), *Ecosystem Services: Global Issues, Local Practices* (Elsevier, 2014).

[11] KMA Chan and others, 'Where are Cultural and Social in Ecosystem Services? A Framework for Constructive Engagement' (2012) 62 *BioScience* 744; P Kareiva and others (eds), *Natural Capital: Theory & Practice of Mapping Ecosystem Services* (Oxford University Press, 2001).

[12] LH Goulder and D Kennedy, 'Interpreting and Estimating the Value of Ecosystem Services' in P Kareiva and others (eds), *Natural Capital: Theory & Practice of Mapping Ecosystem Services* (Oxford University Press, 2001).

[13] K Chopra and others (eds), *Ecosystems and Human Well-Being: Policy Responses* Vol 3 (Island Press, 2005).

Sustainable or environmental accounting and reporting (EAR) and impact assessment are pivotal in modern policy formation and decision-making. They comprehensively view an organisation's environmental footprint, and guide more informed, ecologically aligned decisions. These tools promote transparency, thus enabling stakeholders to understand environmental implications and pushing entities towards sustainable practices. By highlighting potential risks and inefficiencies, EAR spurs innovation and compliance with global standards, ensuring organisations not only meet regulatory requirements but also gain a competitive edge in international markets. As the nexus between sustainability and actionable insights, EAR and impact assessments are crucial for aligning economic growth with environmental responsibility. This process help 'achieve the complex balance between the human well-being and the natural well-being – the symmetry between humans and the environment'.[14] It is necessary to make significant changes to institutional structures and practices to achieve sustainable development.

Thus, EAR is essential for supporting ecosystems, developing climate change adaptation and mitigation strategies, and choosing response instruments. The underlying reason for a rational EAR system is to help adjust existing policies or introduce new ones, if necessary. Frequently, environmental policies are reversed if found to be non-compliant with international standards. Strategic policy implementation using the ecosystem approach necessitates the incorporation of cutting-edge scientific knowledge and innovative management techniques. Both macro- and micro-level policies support the solution of environmental problems. These may include institutionalising environmental entrepreneurship centred on market inputs and adopting methods for assessing externalities and incorporating them into strategic operations.[15]

However, accounting and reporting are no longer restricted to ecosystem and environmental issues. They now embrace all constituents of sustainable development to improve the quality of decision-making for policy development and effectively deliver economic, social and environmental services. In sustainable development, environmental and social accounting and reporting are complementary and focused on accountability structures within the gamut of governance. Together, termed as 'sustainability accounting', it covers actions directly affecting society and the ecosystem and assesses the economic performance of development institutions. In addition to the government and independent agencies carrying out the task, citizens and other stakeholders also participate in the process. This takes the form of 'social accountability' – a concept developed to increase government openness and transparency by giving citizens information and voice and multiple channels for participatory monitoring and policy advocacy. Malena and McNeil suggest that 'social accountability mechanisms can contribute to better policy, program design, more development resources, more equitable and efficient

[14] M-G Baldarelli, M Del Baldo and N Nesheva-Kiosseva (eds), *Environmental Accounting and Reporting: Theory and Practice* (Springer, 2017).

[15] M Fitzmaurice, *Contemporary Issues in International Environmental Law* (Edward Elgar, 2009).

public spending, and great and more sustainable development outcomes'.[16] Social accountability assessments undertaken by government agencies with multiple stakeholder collaboration can serve a useful purpose in improving the quality and effectiveness of policy and strategy building in sustainable development. Informed by such assessments, the policy-making process is more likely to produce rational, outcome-driven sustainable development initiatives.

In developing nations, assessing social and environmental benefits is crucial, especially given their emphasis on poverty reduction. By measuring these benefits, policy-makers can make more holistic decisions that align with long-term goals, ensuring economic advancements do not come at unsustainable social or environmental costs. While it is widely acknowledged that economic progress frequently has beneficial social consequences, tools like EAR and sustainable accounting enable leaders in the Global South to analyse and maximise advantages. This ensures that the impact is generational – steering clear from favouring just short-term or niche interests.

Developing countries, despite the pressing need to enhance environmental accounting and appraise ecosystem services, confront significant obstacles in its effective deployment. A crucial aspect of precise EAR is the availability of high-quality environmental and spatial data. However, these nations often grapple with the challenge of producing or accessing granular datasets essential for accurate local predictions. Such limitations inadvertently pave the way for potentially flawed policy designs. Even the most well-meaning decision-makers are left navigating mindlessly, unable to pre-empt risks or harness prospective socio-environmental advantages of their initiatives. Further complicating the situation is the lack of robust governance structures supporting EAR, making its challenges even more insurmountable. Addressing these governance hurdles is vital and presents its own set of distinct challenges.

IV. Effective Governance and Implementation of Sustainable Development Objectives

Effective governance and strong institutional capacity are imperative for implementing sustainable development goals. This is evident in Goal 16 of the UNSDG's which states: 'Goal 16 of the Sustainable Development Goals is dedicated to the promotion of peaceful and inclusive societies for sustainable development, the provision of access to justice for all, and building effective, accountable institutions at all levels.'[17] Generally, governance in the context of sustainable development

[16] M McNeil and C Malena (eds), *Demanding Good Governance: Lessons from Social Accountability Initiatives in Africa* (World Bank, 2010).

[17] 'Sustainable Development Goals: 17 Goals to Transform Our World' (United Nations, May 2018), www.un.org/en/exhibits/page/sdgs-17-goals-transform-world, accessed 26 October 2023.

refers to processes of socio-political governance oriented towards attaining sustainable development. This encompasses public debate, political decision-making, policy implementation, and interactions among public authorities, private business and civil society.[18]

Strong governance is vital for sustainability. According to the European Commission, good governance consists of openness and participation, accountability, effective coherence, efficiency and sensitivity to greater context.[19] For sustainability, governance also includes internalising external costs, ensuring the integration of policy considerations, evaluating options and dealing with trade-offs. A challenge with developing such governance regimes is establishing them so that at all levels of government there is a reasonable coherence of vision and commitment, where trust and accountability are evident, and where institutions have sufficient capacity for coordination and redirection.[20]

Although Goal 16 places an imperative on better global governance, it also pushes for reform within states' internal modes of governance and, importantly, emphasises that making political reform a priority is imperative in strengthening fragile states.[21] At their core, governance structures determine objectives, influence motivations, set standards, allocate resources, monitor compliance, impose penalties, initiate consultation and collaboration, or reduce conflict and resolve disputes. The most significant challenge is to ensure that multi-player governance regimes embody capacity for sustainability-oriented coordination, direction and redirection. Finding ways to ensure that all actors – business organisations, civil society, groups and citizens and formal governments – engage coherently and efficiently in the pursuit of sustainability demands much higher aims and underlines the crucial role of informal institutions.[22]

Due to the all-encompassing nature of sustainable governance in its interactions with economic, social and environmental spheres, governments must facilitate adjustments needed to orient social development along more sustainable lines.[23] Therefore, governance for sustainable development must focus on three main issues. First, the identification and management of critical threats to sustainability. Second, the integration of sustainability into general practices of governance. Third, the organisation of collective reflection and decision with respect to reconciling social priorities and orienting the overall development trajectory. Here, the emphasis is less on the totality of socio-political governance and instead focuses on the reform of that totality considering sustainable development.[24]

[18] J Meadowcroft, 'Who is in Charge Here? Governance for Sustainable Development in a Complex World' (2007) 9 *Journal of Environmental Policy and Planning* 299, 301.

[19] ibid 299.

[20] ibid 302.

[21] MS Edwards and S Romero, 'Governance and the Sustainable Development Goals: Changing the Game or More of the Same?' (2014) 34 *SAIS Review of International Affairs* 140, 146.

[22] R Kemp and S Parto, 'Governance for Sustainable Development: Moving from Theory to Practice' (2005) 8 *International Journal of Sustainable Development* 12, 17.

[23] Meadowcroft (n 18) 301.

[24] ibid.

There is a growing acceptance that no single body nor category of governance institution can effectively combat environmental change and, instead, what is needed is a multilevel, multiscale governance system.[25] Governance in the context of environmental policy is 'bound up in a messy and unpredictable set of interactions in which unintended consequences are inevitable'.[26] There are five key factors contributing to this. First, governing branches find issues in addressing problems through different jurisdictions, both horizontally between adjoining entities or vertically among different levels of authority, as each may have different capacities in terms of resources and priorities. Second, environmental change can be approached from different angles, including as a security, environmental or economic issue, each with profoundly different implications for policy reform. Third, different policies have different interpretations of the causes, severity and urgency of addressing environmental change and how this should be done, for example, through treaties, conventions, associated ratified legislation, sub-national and non-state actors, unilaterally or multilaterally, market measures or environmental activism, or fiscal measures such as tax investment incentives, quotas and fines.[27] Fourth, substantial differences exist in priorities and policies among these governance institutions, reflecting the prevailing political affiliations of the respective bodies as well as situational variables such as social diversity, rural or urban populations and wealth distribution. Finally, the pace of globalisation and the associated increases in human mobility, trade and associated transformations of environmental resources cause significant challenges for coordinating policies and their enforcement among static political entities, not designed for these circumstances.[28]

Joshi, Hughes and Sisk suggest that the most effective concept of governance is a dynamic and inextricably interconnected process of governing inputs, outputs and contexts.[29] Their research suggests that three fundamental governance transitions have historically characterised the development of modern states; achieving greater domestic security, building more robust state capacity, and increasing inclusion. Okwechime suggests that good governance should manifest in a genuine respect for the people, a commitment to providing a voice for all, transparency and effectiveness in decision-making, encouraging people to become involved, a commitment to a collaborative process, taking responsibility to monitor and evaluate the outcome of government developmental policies and programmes, and an openness to learning from poor decisions.[30]

[25] H Leck and D Simon, 'Fostering Multiscalar Collaboration and Cooperation for Effective Governance of Climate Change Adaption' (2013) 50 *Urban Studies* 1221, 1223.

[26] ibid.

[27] ibid 1224.

[28] ibid 1225.

[29] D Joshi, B Hughes and T Sisk, 'Improving Governance for the Post-2015 Sustainable Development Goals: Scenario Forecasting the Next 50 Years' (2015) 70 *World Development* 286, 287.

[30] C Okwechime, 'Interfacing Effective Communication, Good Governance and Sustainable Development in Nigeria' (2015) 2 *GSTF Journal on Media & Communications* 21, 36.

Importantly, going without plural centres of power would be detrimental. To strip out the functional differentiation between economic, legal and political spheres and discourses; to move back from specialisation and differentiation of labour and knowledge; and to do away with fragmented jurisdictions and the multitude of self and co-regulating processes would prevent the proper functioning of key legal principles. Therefore, effective governance must manage the diffusion of power and work to reap its benefits. Such functional specialisation and democratisation open the door for multiple routes of intervention to encourage the turn towards sustainable development.[31] To achieve this, governments must steer society within the context of distributed power. Meadowcroft[32] suggests this can be achieved in the following ways. First, governments must act from the understanding that they are just one component of the overall process of societal governance. Thus, government actions are oriented to increase the likelihood that the entire governance system will evolve in the desired direction, with the government acting as an enabler. Second, by exploiting interactions among actors to gain knowledge about interests, perspectives and capacities. Third, by establishing long-term objectives and adjusting goals as developments arise. Fourth, by supporting the extension of co-governance networks around specific issues. Fifth, by ensuring the development of carried institutions to track trends, evaluate existing policy initiatives, and audit their performance. Sixth, supporting a vibrant public sphere to accommodate continuous discussion of social choices and critically reflecting on the development path and policy approaches. Finally, by encouraging the growth of 'ecological citizenship' among actors. By promoting forms of citizenship that think critically about social/environmental interactions, engage practically with collective problems, and assume responsibility for conduct in private and public life, the government can strengthen the foundation for the transition towards sustainable development.

When working in a context of diffused power, governments must shift power balances in ways that encourage adjustments conducive to sustainable development.[33] Techniques used to pursue this include the following. First, adjusting legal rights and responsibilities to make some avenues of development easier or harder to pursue. For example, industries must identify hazardous substances through disclosure statements or by requiring companies to make such information public so that the balance is tipped slightly in favour of groups campaigning against toxic releases. Second, by creating new institutional actors and encouraging the establishment of new actors who can promote change. This may help to free bodies from bureaucratic routines, increase public confidence, and hedge against changed political priorities. Third, governments can establish new economic centres of power and intervene to strengthen economic actors whose activities point toward

[31] Meadowcroft (n 18) 308.
[32] ibid 209.
[33] ibid 310.

desired social ends. For example, governments can encourage green businesses (for example renewable energy and organic farming). Finally, governments can encourage inter-organisational collaboration by encouraging new patterns of interaction in a collaborative, solution-oriented framework and creating organisational allies to strengthen resources championing sustainable development.[34]

Overall, governance for sustainability needs governance structures and practices that can foster, guide and coordinate positive work by a host of actors on a vast complex of issues through webs of interconnection and across multiple levels and scales, with sensitivity to their contexts and respect for uncertainties.[35]

At a higher level, the 2030 Sustainable Development Agenda will be difficult to implement unless a robust, sustainable development governance structure encompassing inclusive decision-making, coordination, participation, collaboration and networking, alongside transparency and accountability, is in place at the country level. Synergism between all the elements of governance in producing positive outcomes would be unavoidable. However, since sustainability is a dynamic phenomenon, it cannot remain entrapped or constrained by fixed structures and rules. As the demands of the triple bottom line[36] constantly change, sustainability initiatives must adapt accordingly, and so should the rules of governance.

A 'framework for public action' within an inclusive policy environment is essential to realise the SDGs in the Global South.[37] The policy-making space needs widening to enable the participation of and inputs from multiple stakeholders in policy development and execution. Development policies require multi-dimensional, multi-stakeholder and right-sized sequences.[38] Institutional practices in government embedding an inclusive orientation will positively spin on social interaction. The greater the spectrum of engagement, the more credible, legitimate and acceptable policies will be, both in society and beyond.[39] The policy process will then take on an inclusive perspective and be more equity-weighed. Only inclusive policy-making (information based, evidence driven and citizen centred) can be attentive to the wide range of perspectives and demands created by the policy environment.[40]

The corollary to inclusive policy-making is participation for its effectiveness in producing desired outcomes, legitimising policies and improving the quality

[34] ibid 312.

[35] Kemp and Parto (n 22) 20.

[36] Triple bottom line approaches seek to achieve environmental, social and economic outcomes holistically. See W Norman and C MacDonald, 'Getting to the Bottom of "Triple Bottom Line"' (2004) 14 *Business Ethics Quarterly* 243.

[37] UNESCO, 'Analytical Framework for Inclusive Policy Design: Of Why, What and How' (20 October 2015), en.unesco.org/inclusivepolicylab/sites/default/files/2022-03/IPL_framework1.pdf, accessed 26 October 2023.

[38] H Silver, *Framing Social Inclusion Policies: Background Paper* (World Bank, 2012).

[39] UNDP, 'Human Development Report 2002: Deepening Democracy in a Fragmented World' (2002), hdr.undp.org/content/human-development-report-2002.

[40] H Zafarullah and AS Huque, *Managing Development in a Globalized World: Progress, Processes, Institutions* (CRC Press, 2012).

of decision-making. By involving citizens, public and private stakeholders, and development partners at multiple levels, a more inclusive and transformative agenda can be created for sustainable development. Participation would enable a wide range of actors playing pivotal roles in mobilising resources, providing solutions and innovations, shifting production and consumption patterns and lifestyles, advocating for change, and monitoring those responsible and holding them accountable for anticipated results. That way, participation would enhance democratic governance, strengthen social capital, generate long-term outcomes, ensure efficiency, and sustain economic growth.[41] Initiatives and choices can then be made with the greater good in mind.

Sustainable development calls for proactive coordination between organisations, multi-stakeholder collaboration, partnerships and networking to advance projects in a unified and coherent fashion, maximise synergies between and among several components of the SDGs, and limit trade-offs. In such moves, coordination (vertical, horizontal or lateral, procedural or substantive, and internal or external) would result in harmonious relationships depending on the kind of goals pursued, the individuals and organisations involved, and the process and techniques used. In sustainable development, multilevel interests are at play across public and private sectors influenced by local, national and international demands. Because of social, political, economic and spatio-temporal complexities, solving specific coordination challenges based on a commitment to building the grounds for 'negotiated consent, resource sharing, and concerted action' can be constraining[42] and, therefore, proper coordination plans and negotiating methods must be in place.

In a hierarchical system, the coordination process often risks becoming mired in red tape and cumbersome bureaucratic procedures. Such systems can stifle innovation and responsiveness, leading to inefficiencies and delays in decision-making. Conversely, in a decentralised democratic setup, the dynamics shift towards collaborative engagement. Here, various stakeholders collaborate to co-create solutions, leveraging their unique perspectives and expertise. This collaborative approach not only reshapes the operational context in which entities function but also cultivates innovative methodologies to address both strategic and operational challenges. By encouraging open dialogue and shared responsibility, a decentralised democratic environment can efficiently navigate complexities, making it more agile and adaptive to evolving needs and circumstances.[43] *Agenda 2030* focuses on the importance of partnerships and collaboration and the need to build networks at local, national and global levels. The core idea behind partnerships and

[41] OECD, *Governance as an SDG Accelerator: Country Experience and Tools* (2019); UNDESA, 'Principles of Effective Governance for Sustainable Development' (2018) E/2018/44-E/C.16/2018/8; E Swyngedouw and others (eds) *Participatory Governance in Multi-level Context. Concepts and Experience* (Leske & Budrich, 2002).

[42] E Swyngedouw and others (eds), *Participatory Governance in Multi-level Context. Concepts and Experience* (Leske & Budrich, 2002) 39.

[43] WJM Kickert, E-H Klijn and JFM Koppenjan (eds), *Managing Complex Networks* (Sage, 1997).

collaboration is to create values across the entire sustainable development process. Collaboration and partnerships can generate additional strength or intrinsic value toward achieving the SDGs.[44]

Networking is also a powerful tool for fostering and deepening collaboration and partnerships through which inclusive policy-making is enhanced. It is 'a form of organizational alliance in which relevant policy actors are linked together as co-producers where they are more likely to identify and share common interests'.[45] Sustainable development initiatives and outcomes, and the resolution of societal problems more generally, are aided by networking. Apart from collaboration, it presupposes interdependence, mutual adjustments and consensus among autonomous stakeholders, each pursuing specific interests but engaged in reaching compromises when contributing to policy-making.[46] The United Nations maintains action-oriented networks to advance intertwined sustainable development themes.[47] The Sustainable Development Solutions Network (SDSN) collaborates with relevant stakeholders at local, national and international levels to determine and propagate the best strategies for achieving sustainable development.[48]

V. Reality on the Ground: Governance across the Global South

Regrettably, the slow progress toward achieving the SDGs in the Global South is directly attributable to the weakness of the various components of governance. The World Bank's Worldwide Governance Indicators provide a comparative perspective of the state of governance in the Asia-Pacific, African, Middle Eastern and Latin American regions between 2015 (when the SDGs commenced) and 2021 (the year for which data is available). These regions perform poorly on various governance indicators, well below the global average scores, ranging from over 73 to 87.6.[49] However, countries in East Asia and the Pacific and Latin America and the Caribbean are performing better than the rest of this Global South group (see Table 7.1).

[44] D Stibbe and others, *Maximising the Impact of Partnerships for the SDGs: A Practical Guide to Partnership Value Creation* (The Partnering Initiative, 2019).

[45] J Kim, 'Networks, Network Governance, and Networked Networks' (2006) 11 *International Review of Public Administration* 22.

[46] G Bouckaert, BG Peters and K Verhoest, *The Coordination of Public Sector Organizations: Shifting Patterns of Public Management* (Palgrave Macmillan, 2010); J Koppenjan and E-H Klijn, *Managing Uncertainties in Networks* (Routledge, 2004); P Valkama, SJ Bailey and A-V Anttiroiko, *Organizational Innovation in Public Services: Forms and Governance* (Palgrave Macmillan, 2013).

[47] UN, 'Action Networks for the SDGs', sustainabledevelopment.un.org/partnerships/actionnetworks, accessed 26 October 2023.

[48] SDSN, 'SDSN Networks in Action 2022' (2022), resources.unsdsn.org/2022-sdsn-networks-in-action-report, accessed 26 October 2023.

[49] See World Bank, 'Worldwide Governance Indicators' (2023), info.worldbank.org/governance/wgi/Home/Reports, accessed 27 September 2023.

Table 7.1 Worldwide Governance Indicators & Performance of Different Regions in the Global South in 2021

Indicator	Region	Percentile Rank
Voice & Accountability	East Asia & The Pacific	55.35
	Latin America & the Caribbean	58.52
	Middle East & North Africa	23.74
	South Asia	36.47
	Sub-Saharan Africa	32.94
Political Stability	East Asia & The Pacific	66.32
	Latin America & the Caribbean	56.96
	Middle East & North Africa	28.21
	South Asia	33.31
	Sub-Saharan Africa	30.46
Government Effectiveness	East Asia & The Pacific	57.46
	Latin America & the Caribbean	50.10
	Middle East & North Africa	42.35
	South Asia	43.03
	Sub-Saharan Africa	26.66
Regulatory Quality	East Asia & The Pacific	54.04
	Latin America & the Caribbean	52.58
	Middle East & North Africa	42.17
	South Asia	30.89
	Sub-Saharan Africa	27.23
Rule of Law	East Asia & The Pacific	59.71
	Latin America & the Caribbean	49.04
	Middle East & North Africa	42.08
	South Asia	39.84
	Sub-Saharan Africa	29.08
Control of Corruption	East Asia & The Pacific	58.28
	Latin America & the Caribbean	49.80
	Middle East & North Africa	39.84
	South Asia	38.82
	Sub-Saharan Africa	32.28

Source: info.worldbank.org/governance/wgi/Home/Reports.

The Bertelsmann Stiftung Governance Index gives a moderate score to Latin America and the Caribbean, moderate to weak for the Middle East and North Africa, moderate to failed (>3.0) for Sub-Saharan Africa, and moderate to weak for Asia (including South Asia). The average quality of governance is deficient in terms of consensus-building, steering capability, resource efficiency and cooperation. In countries where the trend of populism is high, all aspects of governance suffer mainly because of weak leadership and poor steering capabilities.[50] On a 0–9 score continuum, in terms of citizen participation and its influence on policy-making, Africa scores reasonably low (0.29), while Latin America (0.56) and Asia/Pacific (0.43) indicate a moderate to low score.[51] Technology can play a critical role in advancing open government that, in turn, can contribute to implementing the SDGs. However, most countries of the Global South are not yet network-ready and, because they are unable to take full advantage of digital technologies due to structural limitations and regulatory constraints, leveraging economic and social benefits tend to be difficult.[52] They cannot move the SDGs forward due to low levels of trust and a lack of commitment toward inclusion, participation, collaboration and co-production.

There remain several potential causes of poor integration. When rules are inconsistent due to overlaps and interplays, it can have unfavourable effects on enforcement, incentive systems, and the clarity and feasibility of planning.[53] The intersectoral dimension of public administration and public policy is crucial for addressing these complicated legal and policy issues. For policy integration to have a positive impact on sustainable development outcomes, policy-makers and administrators need to find ways to connect the governance-related conceptual disjunctions and implement horizontal policies for which multiple organisations are responsible by adopting coordination arrangements that are both adaptive and reflective.[54] The success of Agenda 2030 hinges on harmonising sustainable development outcomes through cohesive planning, execution and accountability. By ensuring that institutions are inclusive and accountable, seamlessly merging voice, design and delivery, comprehensive, integrated results can be achieved. This approach paves the way for policy-making that is inherently more democratic. It has been reported that in many countries, government agencies tasked with enacting and implementing climate change policies lack the authority, technical capability, or legal mandate to facilitate inter-institutional coordination.[55]

[50] Bartelsmann Stiftung, 'The Transformation Index' (2022), bti-project.org/en/?&d=G&cb=00000, accessed 7 November 2022.

[51] V-Dem Institute, 'Democracy Report 2022 – Autocratization Changing Nature?' (2022) 10, v-dem.net/media/publications/dr_2022.pdf, accessed 4 June 2024.

[52] Portulans Institute, 'The Network Readiness Index 2021' (Portulans Institute, 2021).

[53] T Bolognesi and S Nahrath, 'Environmental Governance Dynamics: Some Micro Foundations of Macro Failures' (2020) 170(3) *Ecological Economics*.

[54] A Molenveld and others, 'Images of Coordination: How Implementing Organizations Perceive Coordination Arrangements' (2020) 80 *Public Administration Review* 9.

[55] UNDP, 'Institutional and Coordination Mechanisms: Guidance Note on Facilitating Integration and Coherence for SDG Implementation' (2017).

Thus, sound policy management for sustainable development must be complemented by proper legal coordination between law makers and law implementers. From the standpoint of law, the legal roles of the executive, legislature, judiciary and bureaucracy in environmental protection and development come into play. Proper judicial and administrative procedures would help facilitate legal redress and provide remedial measures against unlawful actions affecting the environment and development. Individuals and institutions with a recognised legal interest and citizens whose legal rights are infringed must be protected. It is imperative that public and private entities at all levels of government, both nationally and locally, maintain accountability for their activities in accordance with their obligations.[56]

Also, international legal instruments, especially those relating to climate change and environmental control and monitoring, need to be adapted to suit local conditions and incorporated into national strategies. Legal loopholes should be closed as much as possible to facilitate close coordination among key stakeholders for the SDGs to be effectively implemented. Vertical coherence could be achieved through partnerships with non-governmental actors, such as dynamic civil society groups with local expertise. To elevate this partnership beyond a merely informal arrangement, a functional legal framework would be required.[57] The international covenants and protocols need to be revisited often and national policies that impede implementation of the SDGs should be overturned or amended, and recent breakthroughs that enhance them should be ramped up quickly.[58]

VI. Fostering Policy Coherence and Improving Accountability

Sustainable development involves a complex interplay of various institutions, including public authorities, private enterprises and civil society. Achieving sustainable development requires effective coordination and collaboration among these actors. This is particularly relevant in developing country contexts with limited access to funding arrangements, which require targeted assistance and strong policy coherence to create new incentives for change and implement sustainable development projects in areas that can achieve the most impact. In recent years, these countries have taken proactive initiatives to promote policy coherence by adopting sound policy frameworks, such as National Adaptation Plans (NDPs) and Nationally Determined Contributions (NDCs) under the Paris Agreement. These provide high-level statements from national governments that

[56] UNDESA, 'International Law: Decisions of the GA and CSD' (1997), www.un.org/esa/sustdev/sdissues/intl_law/law_decisions.htm#19th, accessed 24 May 2024.

[57] UNDP, 'Institutional and Coordination Mechanisms: Guidance Note on Facilitating Integration and Coherence for SDG Implementation' (2017).

[58] UN, 'The Future is Now: Science for Achieving Sustainable Development' (2019).

can guide policy directions and priorities for decision-makers at national and sub-national governments.

On a policy level, one of the more significant challenges is ensuring that these high-level statements are mainstreamed and addressed in sub-national decision-making mechanisms and that governance structures are in place to capture complex issues that do not neatly fit within the responsibilities of one departmental agency or portfolio. The increasing sectoral specialisation of the modern state limits the scope of actions that different actors can take to address sustainability issues. Sustainable development problems often transcend administrative divisions, territorial jurisdictions and the traditional division between the economic and political domains.

To illustrate this issue, developing countries face significant difficulty in building a highly skilled, scalable workforce that can implement sustainable development projects, given the complexity of addressing this issue in a coordinated way. There are several reasons why developing countries continue to face barriers in creating a skilled workforce, each highly specific to individual country's circumstances. But overarching issues include long-term migration patterns towards developed countries (or 'brain drain')[59] and poor credit ratings that prevent project proponents from undertaking sustainable development projects in the first place.[60] Improving workforce coordination and creating a skilled workforce base is one solution to address this issue, but it requires both short and long-term policies across several different government departments and agencies to be actioned. This includes improving the mobility of the existing workforce through steps such as mutual recognition of vocational training or formalisation of existing experience[61] to long-term policy action such as improving education and vocational training opportunities for young workers and improving the visibility and transferability of workers' hard and soft skills so that they can effectively participate in the labour market.[62] Targeted support that improves the attractiveness of developing country economies to potential employees, such as providing transport options, housing or healthcare,[63] further underscores the cross-institutional and complex nature of the measures needed to address barriers to effective sustainable development implementation.

[59] See JH Aarhus and TG Jakobsen, 'Rewards of Reforms: Can Economic Freedom and Reforms in Developing Countries Reduce the Brain Drain?' (2019) 22(4) *International Area Studies Review* 327; F Docquier, O Lohest and A Marfouk, 'Brain Drain in Developing Countries' (2007) 21(2) *The World Bank Economic Review* 193.

[60] OECD, 'Bottlenecks to Access Sustainable Development Goals Finance for Developing Countries' (2023), www.oecd.org/g20/oecd-g20-bottlenecks-sdg-finance-developing-countries.pdf, accessed 26 October 2023.

[61] SK Misra, 'Skill Development: A Way to Create Skilled Workforce for Strong and Sustainable Growth' (11 October 2016), ssrn.com/abstract=2883735, accessed 26 October 2023.

[62] D Lam and A Elsayed, 'Barriers to Labour Market Efficiency in Low-Income Countries' in D Lam and A Elsayed (eds), *Labour Markets in Low-Income Countries: Challenges and Opportunities* (Oxford Academic, 2021).

[63] ibid.

Improving policy coherence and coordination amongst several government departments and actors requires the next step beyond establishing a framework that outlines a high-level direction to be achieved at a national level. In this respect, transparency and accountability is critical. Governments must have a strong incentive to ensure that they take responsibility for issues that do not neatly fit into their portfolio responsibilities and are encouraged to act and create cross-departmental agencies, taskforces and action committees that are responsible for and can report on complex policy issues and address the barriers towards effective sustainable development implementation. Improving cross-institutional collaboration must also occur on both horizontal and vertical scales, that is, between government agencies and different levels of government from the sub-national to the national. Whilst national governments can take the lead in establishing policy leadership and direction on contentious issues, genuine engagement with local government is vital to inform the substantive content of sustainable development policy and allow decision-makers to identify specific barriers towards effective implementation.

With specific reference to sustainability accounting and EAR, improving coherence and coordination is required at all steps of the policy-making process. Having a cross-institutional body which is responsible for complex sustainable development implementation problems allows it to address information gaps, interrogate and oversee the collection of data and other inputs required to make policy, and to collaborate with local agencies to ensure that data and information flows remain relevant and fit for purpose. Vertical integration also allows agencies to improve their capacity to gain datasets and obtain inputs with sufficient granularity to make ecosystem services assessments valuable.

VII. Creating Polycentric Governance and Dispersing Centres of Power

Decision-makers and government are made up of people who make mistakes. However, creating a polycentric form of governance that actively engages multiple stakeholders to test, challenge and improve policy-making creates an environment that can improve the delivery of sustainable development policy and its outcomes. Whilst actively engaging community and external feedback adds to the complexity of the policy-making process, this reduces the downstream costs associated with policy failure or the need to undertake further supplementary action to address the policy issue. Fostering genuine engagement and participation is also vital for policy-making post-implementation, where feedback from the community, industry or non-government organisations can provide valuable insight for further improvement and evaluating program effectiveness.

Dispersing centres of power also requires an independent judiciary that can uphold the rule of law and create certainty in executive or legislative decision-making. Not only does an independent judiciary improve the accountability and transparency of government and help address issues such as corruption, but an effective judiciary can also act as a conduit in implementing the latest developments in international environmental law into domestic contexts. Further, this creates a regulatory regime that is more predictable and creates a system where conflicting interests can be managed. Nevertheless, to ensure that a judiciary remains effective and interrogates decisions based on EAR and environmental accounting, specialised courts that are staffed with jurists with sufficient knowledge in EAR practices are required. Developing supporting practices such as shared technical assessments between project proponents and complainants also presents good practice by reducing unnecessary litigation on highly technical issues, which adds cost burden and reduces access to justice opportunities for community groups.

VIII. Conclusion

From its inception to current practices, sustainable development has been shaped by numerous global agreements and protocols. Various strategies, laws and policies have been devised and executed at international, regional and national levels to balance social, economic and environmental needs. Implementing sustainable development, particularly in the Global South, is challenging due to its multifaceted nature, demanding collaboration across public and private sectors on local to global scales. Unlike economic growth, which focuses on converting natural capital to human capital and emphasises market efficiency, sustainable development aims to improve the quality of life without harming the environment.

Sustainable development's overarching goal is a future marked by economic prosperity, the absence of extreme poverty, resilient communities and no human-induced environmental degradation. This framework integrates economic, social and environmental goals over time. Practically, regions and countries craft and execute policies that balance these goals, employing governance principles and using scientific and ethical methods for inclusive development. Modern policy practices embrace principles of Environmental Accounting and Reporting (EAR) and sustainability accounting.

As highlighted in this chapter, beyond technical limitations, there is a governance challenge. Effective EAR requires robust governance structures capable of addressing intricate policy issues. Without such structures, achieving evidence-based policy-making, particularly in resource-constrained developing nations, becomes challenging. Owing to the cross-border nature of sustainable development challenges, it is vital for all nations, both developed and developing, to collaborate on solutions, such as environmental and climate change policies. For developed nations, this also presents a chance to tap into emerging markets and potential economic benefits.

Successful policy outcomes hinge on integrating the sustainable development process and the efficacy of relevant institutions in overcoming political, economic and legal hurdles. Collaboration across various sectors, stakeholder engagement and adherence to good governance principles are essential for legitimising development results. Hence, Goal 16 of the 2030 Agenda is pivotal for realising sustainable development objectives efficiently.

Beyond merely formulating policies, the real test for developing countries lies in achieving seamless integration in policy-making and making informed choices. Cross-institutional entities, such as task forces, will be vital. It is also crucial to foster a multi-stakeholder governance environment. For EAR and sustainability accounting, this means enhanced industry, community and stakeholder engagement during the policy formation stage, supplemented by a judiciary proficient in EAR and sustainability accounting which is able to review decisions effectively.

8

Promises Unkept: From Words to Actions to Ensure Implementation and Compliance with Agenda 2030 and the SDGs

PAOLO GALIZZI*

I. Introduction

For at least the past 75 years, since the creation of the post-World War II order, one of the main goals of the international community has been to create a more equal world where inequalities are reduced and will be eventually eliminated, and every human being can live lives of dignity and fulfilment. Indeed, after World War II, an international architecture was set up to ensure, *inter alia*, economic development and equity between, within, and amongst nations.[1] Working through international organisations like the United Nations and its agencies and programmes and other international bodies of global cooperation,[2] international leaders have over the years made political commitments, countless pledges and created programmes to help achieve the overall objective of building a world that accommodates all in peace and prosperity.[3] However, these 'commitments' have hardly been a resounding global success and some have entirely failed to hit their pre-established goals and objectives. Arguably, the world today is as unequal as it was in 1945, or maybe even more so.[4]

* The author would like to thank his research assistants at Fordham Law School, Eric Aguda, Noah Ephraem Adamtey, Gnim Bazim, Mateo Camacho, Chukwuemeka Obinna Ginikawa and Georgette Hesse for their help with this chapter. The author is particularly grateful to his colleague, Jeanmarie Fenrich, for revising an earlier draft of this chapter. Errors and omissions are entirely the author's.

[1] See, for example, UN Charter, Art 1; United Nations, 'United Nations Charter: Preamble', www.un.org/en/about-us/un-charter/preamble, accessed 28 October 2022. Also see the World Bank Group, the IMF and other major international organisations.

[2] See, for example, World Bank Group and OECD.

[3] See, for example, Stockholm Declaration of 1972, Rio Declaration of 1992, United Nations Millennium Declaration of 2000, etc.

[4] United Nations Development Programme (UNDP), 'Human Development Report: Uncertain Times, Unsettled Lives: Shaping our Future in a Transforming World' (2022), hdr.undp.org/content/human-development-report-2021-22, accessed 15 December 2023.

At the beginning of the New Millennium, the international community gathered in New York to propose an ambitious set of objectives to create a more equal planet and set out a concrete set of deliverables that have become known as the Millennium Development Goals (MDGs).[5] The MDGs, launched with great fanfare and strong political support, are, however, a prime example of such global 'commitments' that arguably have achieved very limited success.[6] For example, Millennium Development Goal #1 sought to eradicate extreme poverty and hunger globally by 2015. This goal, while having had a substantial amount of success in the aggregate, was not universally achieved. Success was found only in some regions of the world, such as the Far East, Southeast Asia and Eastern Europe. A poorer record of achievement was found in Africa, for example – the only continent that failed to even halve its extreme poverty by 2015.[7] A similar picture of mixed success can be painted for the other MDGs.[8]

Various analyses and reasons have been advanced to explain why many developing nations failed to achieve the MDGs and the mixed records among countries in implementing them. They include low-income earnings, infrastructural deficiencies, weak institutions and unstable governments. It has also been argued that the shortfall of the MDGs is to be blamed on their structure rather than extrinsic reasons.[9] The MDGs were shaped by western models, technologies and financial structures,[10] which might have been incompatible with the realities of the developing nations. Although developing countries participated in designing the MDGs, the extent of their influence in crafting them was limited and the Global South's perspectives and needs were arguably not the driving force in the process.[11]

In September 2015, world leaders gathered again in New York at the United Nations headquarters, to renew their commitment to creating a more equal world and adopted the 2030 Agenda for Sustainable Development with 17 Sustainable

[5] The specific MDGs were: (1) eradicate extreme poverty and hunger; (2) achieve universal primary education; (3) promote gender equality and empower women; (4) reduce child mortality; (5) improve maternal health; (6) combat HIV/AIDS, malaria, and other diseases; (7) ensure environmental sustainability; and (8) develop a global partnership for development. These goals were intended to be achieved by the year 2015, and they were replaced by the Sustainable Development Goals (SDGs) in 2015; United Nations, 'Millennium Development Goals and Beyond 2015', www.un.org/millenniumgoals/, accessed 15 December 2023.

[6] M Darrow, 'The Millennium Development Goals: Milestones or Millstones? Human Rights Priorities for the Post-2015 Development Agenda' (2012) 15 *Yale Human Rights and Development Law Journal* 55.

[7] M Loewe, 'African Developments: Sub-Saharan Africa, too, Could Achieve the Millennium Development Goals' (2010) German Development Institute, Briefing paper 15/2010, www.idos-research.de/uploads/media/BP_15.2010.pdf, accessed 30 October 2023.

[8] 'Confident That Despite Uneven Progress, Setbacks, Millennium Development Goals Can Still Be Achieved by 2015, Leaders Adopt "Action Agenda" on Way Forward' (Meetings Coverage and Press Releases, 22 September 2010), press.un.org/en/2010/ga10993.doc.htm, accessed 29 March 2024.

[9] M Fehling, BD Nelson and S Venkatapuram, 'Limitations of the Millennium Development Goals: A Literature Review' (2013) 8 *Global Public Health* 1109.

[10] ibid.

[11] ibid.

Development Goals (SDGs).[12] Acknowledging that the MDGs fell short in many areas, the Agenda 2030 provides a sort of recommitment 'to the full realization of all the Millennium Development Goals' and states that the new agenda 'builds on the Millennium Development Goals and seeks to complete what they did not achieve, particularly in reaching the most vulnerable'.[13] The overall objective of the SDGs is to meet the targets the MDGs failed to achieve and to tackle sustainable development challenges through 17 goals and 169 targets.[14]

Much has been written on the SDGs and Agenda 2030.[15] For example, according to the UN, the SDGs 'provide a shared blueprint for peace and prosperity for people and the planet, now and into the future'.[16] Some scholars consider the SDGs as 'the most important frame of the global development agenda until 2030'[17] and praise the ambition to tackle major development (eg economic growth and responsible production), humanitarian (eg poverty, hunger and disease injustice), and environmental challenges (eg climate change and biosphere integrity) in the same plan[18] with the primary purpose that 'no one will be left behind'.[19] Others have expressed less optimism about the possibility of the success of the SDGs, going as far as describing the SDGs as a mixture of 'business as usual' and the MDGs rebooted and a negotiated wish list.[20]

To avoid the failures of the MDGs and more generally the unkept promises made to create a more equal world over the past 75 years, the implementation of the SDGs must move from mere pledges by nations to sustainable implementation that treats all states as equal and yet recognises the financial inequities between the Global North and South and the differences in their contribution to global problems and capability to tackle global issues.

This chapter will focus on the critical question of implementation of the SDGs. First, it will review existing implementation and compliance mechanisms within environmental and human rights treaties and assess their possible adaptation to ensure the realisation of the SDGs and Agenda 2030. In particular, the chapter will focus on lessons learned within the Montreal Protocol regime to address ozone depletion, whose financial and compliance mechanisms were created to ensure a fair and equal participation between developed and developing countries. The chapter will conclude with a discussion of the way forward and a discussion of

[12] UNGA Res 70/1 (25 September 2015) UN Doc A/RES/70/1.

[13] ibid.

[14] United Nations, 'The 17 Goals' (Department of Economic and Social Affairs – Sustainable Development, 2015), sdgs.un.org/goals, accessed 20 December 2023.

[15] I Kaul, I Grunberg and MA Stern, *Providing Global Public Goods: Managing Globalization* (Oxford University Press, 2003); JD Sachs, *The Age of Sustainable Development* (Columbia University Press, 2015); UNGA Res 70/1 (n 12).

[16] UNGA Res 70/1 (n 12).

[17] JA van Zanten and R van Tulder, 'Multinational Enterprises and the Sustainable Development Goals: An Institutional Approach to Corporate Engagement' (2018) 1 *Journal of International Business Policy* 208, 209.

[18] ibid 208–33.

[19] UNGA Res 70/1 (n 12).

[20] R Horton, 'Offline: Why the Sustainable Development Goals Will Fail' (2014) 383 *The Lancet* 2196.

possible mechanisms/tools to improve the implementation of the SDGs, with a focus on the existing implementation system within the High-Level Political Forum. It will propose a fuller participation and ownership of countries from the Global South and more robust binding mechanisms. The chapter argues that the SDGs could achieve greater universal success by adopting and adapting many of the implementation mechanisms seen under past, successful treaties.[21]

II. Implementation in Selected International Treaty Regimes: Lessons for the SDGs within Human Rights and Environmental Treaties?

Agenda 2030 is halfway into its lifespan, and there are already clear indications of poor compliance, especially by countries in the Global South. If the present tide is to be reversed to guarantee an expedited ascent towards Agenda 2030 and the full implementation of the SDGs, there is a need for the adoption of proven implementation mechanisms that are workable by and in the Global South. Challenges in compliance with international commitment are not a new problem and certainly not one limited to Agenda 2030.[22] This section will focus on reviewing the existing compliance mechanisms under major international Human Rights and Environmental Treaties that might be useful in meeting the goals set out in the SDGs.

A. Compliance Mechanisms under Human Rights Treaties

Since the establishment of the United Nations, the international human rights architecture has grown into a rather complex net of commitments to ensure the fulfilment of basic human rights for all. The Universal Declaration on Human Rights, adopted in 1948 was followed by the adoption of several other treaties focusing on civil and political rights[23] as well as economic social and cultural rights.[24] More specialised treaties have been adopted over the years on issues as

[21] This chapter does not explore the longer term critical issue of reducing and eliminating existing imbalanced donor-recipient relationships. In the longer term and to achieve true sustainability, it is imperative for the Global South to bolster its own economic independence to reduce donor dependency and further strengthen regional cooperation between and within Global South countries and regions. It is also imperative for the Global North to be held accountable and fully pay for its historic responsibilities in creating the current unsustainable path in full accordance with the principle of common but differentiated responsibility.

[22] RO Keohane and JS Nye, *Power and Interdependence: World Politics in Transition* (Scott Foresman, 1977).

[23] International Covenant on Civil and Political Rights (adopted 16 December 1966, entered into force 23 March 1976) 999 UNTS 171 (ICCPR).

[24] International Covenant on Economic, Social and Cultural Rights (adopted 16 December 1966, entered into force 3 January 1976) 993 UNTS 14531 (ICESCR).

diverse as the prohibition of racial discrimination, the prohibition of torture, and the prohibition of gender-based discrimination etc.[25]

All human rights treaties include mechanisms for the implementation of their substantive obligations. Each treaty sets up a monitoring body, which is usually a committee composed of independent experts, to ensure constant oversight of its implementation. Each treaty further provides for tools to ensure compliance. Such mechanisms can be largely divided into: (a) reporting; (b) general comments; (c) inter-state complaints; (d) individual complaints; (e) other mechanisms (such as inquiries and urgent appeals).[26]

i. Self-reporting Mechanisms

A common compliance mechanism under the international human rights regime is self-reporting by contracting parties on their own record in meeting the obligations set out under a given treaty regime. Almost all human rights treaties mandate states to submit reports to treaty monitoring bodies. Treaties such as the Convention Against Torture (CAT), the International Covenant on the Elimination of Racial Discrimination (ICERD), or the International Covenant on Civil and Political Rights (ICCPR) all include mandatory reporting by member states to update the respective committees on the measures they are undertaking to progress the goals of the treaty and reporting the results of those efforts.[27] Further, in virtually all treaty regimes, the monitoring committee engages in a sort of back and forth where it reviews each state's submissions and identifies specific areas that need improvement in each particular state – providing constant, vital, state-specific feedback. Over time, the self-reporting mechanism has proven to be an effective mechanism, given that there has been a correlation between mandatory reporting and the successful implementation of treaties.[28] The success of the self-reporting mechanism can be partly attributed to the alternative or shadow

[25] These treaties include the International Convention on the Elimination of All Forms of Racial Discrimination (ICERD), the Convention on the Rights of the Child (CRC), the Convention on the Rights of Persons with Disabilities (CRPD), the Convention against Torture and Other Cruel, Inhuman or Degrading Treatment or Punishment (CAT), the Convention on the Elimination of All Forms of Discrimination against Women (CEDAW), the International Convention on the Protection of the Rights of All Migrant Workers and Members of Their Families (ICRMW), and the International Convention for the Protection of All Persons from Enforced Disappearance (ICPPED).

[26] United Nations Human Rights Office of the High Commissioner, 'Complaints procedures under the human rights treaties' (United Nations), www.ohchr.org/en/treaty-bodies/human-rights-bodies-complaints-procedures/complaints-procedures-under-human-rights-treaties, accessed 27 December 2023.

[27] See, for example, the Convention Against Torture and Other Cruel, Inhuman or Degrading Treatment or Punishment 1984, Art 19; the International Covenant on Civil and Political Rights 1966, Arts 40–41; the Convention on the Rights of Persons with Disability 2006, Art 35; the Convention on the Elimination of All Forms of Discrimination 1979, Art 18.

[28] CD Creamer and BA Simmons, 'Do Self-Reporting Regimes Matter? Evidence from the Convention Against Torture' (2015) 63 *International Studies Quarterly* 1051. The UPR was introduced on 15 March 2006 by UNGA Res 60/251.

reporting by non-governmental organisations. These NGO reports highlight issues not raised by governments and point out where governments may be providing misleading information.[29]

Recognising the value of reporting as a tool to improve compliance with human rights treaties, in 2006 the UN created a universal reporting system on human rights compliance when it reformed the Charter-based system for the promotion of human rights: the newly created Human Rights Council (HRC) requires all member states of the UN to submit to a Universal Periodic Review (UPR) of their human rights commitments.[30] The UPR enables the Human Rights Council to facilitate peer review among states based on their own submitted reports, records submitted by stakeholders and the UN's own records.[31]

However, the effectiveness of reporting mechanisms in international human rights regimes is often undermined by the inaccurate, incomplete or total absence of reporting by some states, particularly developing states. Although the failure of some states to submit reports is attributable to lack of political will, most developing states lack the financial ability to conduct a thorough review of their internal progress regarding their obligations in international treaties, effectively limiting their ability to effectively self-report, which in turn has the effect of making it harder to track their progress and ultimately meet whatever agreed upon objective has been set out on a global scale – leading to the Global South lagging behind in meeting international treaty obligations.[32]

The SDGs also have a similar reporting mechanism. Unsurprisingly, the SDG reporting system faces the same problems as under the human rights treaties. Information from the 2021 World Development Report: Data for Better Lives Countries by the World Bank indicates that there is clear data deficit in SDG reporting by countries.[33] A recent report by the Partnership in Statistics for Development in the 21st Century (PARIS21) found even highly developed countries are still not able to report more than 40–50 per cent of the SDG indicators.[34] The Global South has also struggled with reporting due to financial constraints. The overall

[29] 'Shadow Reporting to UN Treaty Bodies' (International Women's Rights Action Watch), hrlibrary.umn.edu/iwraw/reports.html, accessed 20 December 2023.

[30] UPR (n 28).

[31] United Nations Human Rights Council, 'Universal Periodic Review', www.ohchr.org/en/hr-bodies/upr/upr-main, accessed 20 December 2023.

[32] C Buamah, 'Legal Pluralism and the Implementation of International Human Rights Law in Africa: The Case of the Convention of the Rights of Rights Law in Africa: The Case of the Convention of the Rights of Persons with Disability (CRPD) in Ghana' (SJD Dissertation, Fordham University, 2018) 11.

[33] L Kitzmueller, B Stacy and DG Mahler, 'Are We There Yet? Many Countries Don't Report Progress on All SDGs According to the World Bank's New Statistical Performance Indicators' (*World Bank blogs*, 10 August 2021) blogs.worldbank.org/opendata/are-we-there-yet-many-countries-dont-report-progress-all-sdgs-according-world-banks-new, accessed 21 December 2023.

[34] International Institute for Sustainable Development, 'Are We Serious About Achieving the SDGs? A Statistician's Perspective' (IISD, 11 January 2020), sdg.iisd.org/commentary/guest-articles/are-we-serious-about-achieving-the-sdgs-a-statisticians-perspective/, accessed 21 December 2023.

amount of funding for data and statistics remains low. Between 2015 and 2020, donors and governments fell short of required investments in survey and administrative data systems by $2.7 billion. This shortfall affected time-use surveys in particular, with barely 1 per cent of the required funding allocated.[35] According to the 2018 edition of the Partner Report on Support to Statistics (PRESS), issued annually by the Secretariat of PARIS21, a large share of global support to statistics continues to come from a very small number of providers. The top five providers of development cooperation in statistics are the World Bank, the UN Population Fund (UNFPA), Eurostat, the International Monetary Fund (IMF) and the UN Children's Fund (UNICEF). This lack of funding has led to inadequate reporting in many countries in the Global South.[36]

ii. Domestication of Rights

Another often used implementation mechanism in international human rights treaties[37] is the commitment by contracting parties to domesticate the rights created under those treaties through enabling legislation.[38] The parties are then obligated to file periodic reports with treaty bodies on the steps taken to reform their respective domestic laws as well as steps taken to protect convention rights.[39] This also allows for contracting states to conduct legislative audits and reforms to bring their local laws into compliance with relevant international laws. However, it has been observed that there are poor levels of compliance with this mechanism due to financial constraints, lack of political will, institutional weaknesses and corruption. However, for many African countries, high levels of poverty forms the

[35] KJ Baptista and S Badiee, 'A Sharp Decline in Funding for Gender Data Puts SDG 5 at Risk: Charting a Way Forward – Data2X' (*Data2X*, 8 December 2022), data2x.org/sharp-decline-in-funding-for-gender-data-sdg5-at-risk/, accessed 21 December 2023.

[36] ibid.

[37] The United Nations Human Rights Office of the High Commissioner has identified 18 core international human rights treaties – nine being conventions and the other nine being optional protocols to some of the said conventions. United Nations, 'Human Rights Instruments (Human Rights Office of the High Commissioner) www.ohchr.org/en/instruments-listings, accessed 20 December 2023.

[38] See, for example, the Convention against Torture and Other Cruel, Inhuman or Degrading Treatment or Punishment 1987, Art 2(1); the Convention on the Elimination of All Forms of Discrimination against Women 1979, Art 2(b); the Convention on the Rights of Persons with Disabilities 2008, Art 4(1)(a); the Convention on the Rights of the Child 1990, Art 4; etc. United Nations, 'Human Rights Instruments (Human Rights Office of the High Commissioner), www.ohchr.org/en/instruments-listings, accessed 20 December 2023.

[39] The International Covenant on Civil and Political Rights (ICCPR)1966, Arts 40–41; the International Covenant on Economic, Social and Cultural Rights 1966, Part IV; The Convention on the Elimination of All Forms of Discrimination Against Women 1979, Part V; the Convention Against Torture and Other Cruel, Inhuman or Degrading Treatment or Punishment 1984, Part II; the Convention on the Rights of the Child 1989, Part II; the International Convention on Protection of the Rights of All Migrant Workers and Members of Their Families 1990, Part VII; the Convention on the Rights of Persons with Disability 2006, Arts 34–35; the International Convention for the Protection of All Persons from Enforced Disappearance 2010, Part II.

major reason for their non-compliance. These countries are inclined to focus their limited resources on other pressing matters in sectors such as health and education, rather than on expensive legislative reforms.[40]

iii. Other Mechanisms

Other interesting mechanisms found in human rights treaties that might be useful to the implementation of the SDGs include General Comments[41] issued by the relevant treaty implementing bodies to guide states in understanding their commitments. Guidance to states on understanding the SDGs and tools for their implementation might be useful too.

Human rights treaties also provide for inter-state and individual complaints subject to various criteria. Such tools could also be applied in the context of the SDGs, even though one can hardly see the political will to do so (even in the human rights context, states are reluctant to accept such mechanisms). With a few exceptions, current state practice suggests that states consider their political and economic relations as more important than concerns over human rights protection in other states.[42] This contributes to why states are reluctant to use the complaint mechanisms under international human rights instruments.

There is no denying that the compliance mechanisms under the international human rights instruments, as discussed above, have so far made significant impact across the globe even though significant acts of abuses still exist around the world. However, the ambitious nature of Agenda 2030 and the SDGs vis-à-vis the challenges facing the Global South casts substantial doubts on the effectiveness of adopting or relying solely on human rights compliance mechanisms towards achieving SDGs in the Global South. For the South to achieve its targets under Agenda 2030 and the SDGs, it needs measures that go beyond regular reporting and the other mechanisms discussed above, as well as addressing the inequity of capabilities and resources among countries from the Global South and Global North. Luckily, this last issue has already been addressed, and arguably with some success, in at least one international environmental law regime.

[40] Buamah (n 32) 112–23. Buamah further notes other factors undermining compliance in the Global South to include Westernization of International Law, Poor Political Leadership, Poverty and Legal Pluralism.

[41] 'Utilizing International Human Rights Mechanisms' (*SDG Accountability Portal*, 4 April 2019), www.sdgaccountability.org/working-with-formal-processes/utilizing-international-human-rights-mechanisms/, accessed 27 December 2023.

[42] S Leckie, 'The Inter-State Complaint Procedure in International Human Rights Law: Hopeful Prospects or Wishful Thinking?' (1988) 10 *Human Rights Quarterly* 249.

B. Compliance Mechanisms under Environmental Treaties: Lessons from the Montreal Protocol on the Depletion of the Ozone Layer

Useful lessons for the implementation of the SDGs may also be drawn from environmental treaties and in particular from the successful regime found under the Montreal Protocol on the Depletion of the Ozone Layer. Since 1972 and the Stockholm Conference on the Human Environment,[43] the protection of the environment has been at the centre of the international agenda. The need for countries to undertake their developmental agenda in a sustainable way without polluting the air, water and oceans, and guaranteeing the well-being of people around the world, has become an issue of central importance and several international agreements have been adopted with the goal of improving the health of our planet.[44]

Indeed, both the MDGs and the SDGs focus on the protection of the environment and improving sustainability. MDG 77 focuses on the need to 'ensure environmental sustainability'[45] and several SDGs focus on environmental issues: SDG 6 (clean water and sanitation), SDG 7 (affordable and clean energy), SDG 13 (climate action), SDG 14 (life below water) and SDG 15 (life on land).

Compliance with environmental treaties and more generally with the environmental agenda at the global level has also been a challenge. In fact, the state of our planet's health, notwithstanding all the commitment to improve it, continues to deteriorate.[46] However, there is arguably a positive exception in this negative story: the issue of ozone depletion. The successful tackling of ozone depletion cannot be attributed to a single factor, but if an overarching reason is needed, it is the unprecedented level of cooperation and commitment shown by the international community under the Montreal Protocol.[47]

[43] United Nations, 'United Nations Conference on the Human Environment, Stockholm 1972' (United Nations, 1 May 2009), www.un.org/en/conferences/environment/stockholm1972, accessed 20 December 2023.

[44] The Montreal Protocol (adopted 1 January 1989, 1522 UNTS 3, 26 ILM 1541, 1550); the Basel Convention on the Control of Transboundary Movements of Hazardous Wastes and Their Disposal (adopted 5 May 1992, 1673 UNTS 126); the Convention on Biological Diversity (adopted 29 December 1993, UNGA A/RES/64/203); and the United Nations Framework Convention on Climate Change (adopted 21 March 1994 A/RES/48/189).

[45] Department of Economic and Social Affairs, United Nations and United Nations Office for ECOSOC Support and Coordination, *Achieving Sustainable Development and Promoting Development Cooperation: Dialogues at the Economic and Social Council* (United Nations Publications, 2008).

[46] UN Environment, 'Global Environment Outlook 6: Healthy Planet, Healthy People' (UN Environment Programme, 4 March 2019), www.unenvironment.org/resources/global-environment-outlook-6, accessed 21 December 2023.

[47] I Rae, 'Saving the ozone layer: why the Montreal Protocol worked' (*The Conversation*, 9 September 2012), theconversation.com/saving-the-ozone-layer-why-the-montreal-protocol-worked-9249, accessed 20 December 2023.

As discussed, implementation has been a central issue in the design of environmental treaties and one excellent and successful example of this effort can be found in the Montreal Protocol[48] – arguably a model that might be inspiring similar measures to successfully implement the SDGs.

With emerging evidence that the Global South is lagging behind in Agenda 2030 and the SDGs, the need to rethink implementation strategies that are workable for achieving the said targets in the South has become imperative.

Like in human rights treaties, the environmental treaties set up bodies to review compliance and adopt regular reporting by member states to such designated treaty bodies. For example, under Articles 4 and 12 of the United Nations Framework Convention on Climate Change (UNFCCC), the contracting parties are required to file with the Secretariat established thereunder, regular reports on levels of anthropogenic emissions and greenhouse gases not covered by the Montreal Protocol.[49] These reports are based on self-imposed commitments communicated by the parties to the Secretariat. Even though the UNFCCC clearly identified the developed world and other emerging countries as the major emitters of greenhouse gas, this reporting approach to compliance had loose ends as no consequences were levied for non-compliance. The UNFCCC was ineffective, a situation that necessitated the adoption of two Protocols thereunder – the Kyoto Protocol and the Paris Agreement – to ensure better control of greenhouse gases. These Protocols also adopt regular reporting by members as a compliance mechanism. Under Articles 7 and 8 of the Kyoto Protocol, members are obligated to report, among other things, steps taken to implement the Protocol.[50] This time around, the reports are critically examined by a committee of experts with the aim of, *inter alia*, identifying compliance bottlenecks and steps that may be taken to circumvent them. There exist similar reporting conditions under Article 13(4) and 13(7)(a) of the Paris Agreement requiring members to file with the Secretariat biennial reports (together with updates) and national inventory reports on greenhouse gases.[51] Despite the levying of these reporting obligations under the foregoing environmental treaties, the evidence thus far, points to a poor compliance culture.[52]

[48] UN Environment, 'About Montreal Protocol' (Ozonaction), www.unep.org/ozonaction/who-we-are/about-montreal-protocol, accessed 20 December 2023.

[49] United Nations Climate Change, 'What is the United Nations Framework Convention on Climate Change?' (UN), unfccc.int/process-and-meetings/what-is-the-united-nations-framework-convention-on-climate-change, accessed 21 December 2023.

[50] United Nations Climate Change, 'What is the Kyoto Protocol?' (United Nations), unfccc.int/kyoto_protocol, accessed 20 December 2023.

[51] United Nations Climate Change, 'The Paris Agreement' (United Nations), unfccc.int/process-and-meetings/the-paris-agreement, accessed 20 December 2023.

[52] Some examples of evidence that may point to a poor compliance culture with respect to reporting obligations under environmental treaties include parties failing to submit required reports or submitting them late, parties submitting incomplete or unreliable reports, parties failing to provide sufficient information in their reports to allow for a proper assessment of their progress in meeting their commitments under the treaty, and parties not responding to requests for clarification or additional information on their reports.

Another compliance feature of the international environmental treaties is capacity-building through technical and financial support. This is evident in the Framework Convention and its accompanying Protocols. The Framework Convention enjoins parties to, inter alia, exchange relevant scientific, technical and technological information and for support to be extended by developed to developing countries in the building of capacities and capabilities in those relevant fields.[53] Upon request, the Conference of Parties/Meeting of the Parties may extend to developing countries technical and financial assistance needed to implement treaty objectives.[54] In addition, developed countries are enjoined to extend financial assistance to developing countries to help them discharge their obligations under the Convention.[55] The foregoing financial and technical mechanisms under the UNFCCC have substantially been adopted under both the Kyoto Protocol and Paris Agreement.[56] As may be observed, the financial obligations are tilted against developed and emerging economies who, no doubt, are super emitters of greenhouse gases. Such an arrangement was put in place to enable the Global South, in particular, to adapt and mitigate the effects of global warming while discharging their obligations under the relevant treaties. The continuous failures by developed countries in honouring commitments under the respective treaties will necessarily lead to the Global South's inability to discharge obligations under the foregoing instruments in the areas of, for example, sustainable mining and agriculture.

III. The Montreal Protocol: A Success Story in Tackling Ozone Depletion?

The Montreal Protocol to the Vienna Convention for the Protection of the Ozone Layer was adopted as a timely response to the need for countries around the world to take action to reverse the depletion of the ozone layer. The Montreal Protocol has been lauded as one of the most successful treaties.[57] This success can be attributed to the unprecedented level of cooperation and commitment shown by the international community.[58] The Protocol has successfully contributed to the healing of the Antarctic ozone hole, which is expected to fully recover by the 2060s. It has also had many positive environmental impacts, including reducing the risk of damage to crops and other vegetation, protecting ecosystems and reducing greenhouse gas

[53] United Nations Framework Convention on Climate Change (adopted 9 May 1992, entered into force 21 March 1994) 1771 UNTS 107 (Framework Convention) Art 4(1)(g) and (h), 5.

[54] ibid Art 12(7).

[55] ibid Art 11(5).

[56] Kyoto Protocol to the United Nations Framework Convention on Climate Change (adopted 11 December 1997, entered into force 16 February 2005) 2303 UNTS 162 ('Kyoto Protocol'), Art 11.

[57] United Nations Environment Programme, 'The Montreal Protocol' (United Nations), www.unep.org/ozonaction/who-we-are/about-montreal-protocol, accessed 20 December 2023.

[58] Rae (n 47).

emissions through the use of alternatives to ozone-depleting substances.[59] Aside from the control measures provided under the Protocol, it relied heavily on the then-nascent principle of Common But Differentiated Responsibilities (CBDR),[60] and a compliance procedure that allowed countries to meet their commitments with a mix of carrot and stick measures.[61]

The Protocol identifies two factors that determine parties' treaty obligations in the ozone regime – first, the level of depleting substances emitted by a party, and second, the economic, technological and scientific capacity capabilities of parties to reduce proscribed emissions.[62] Considering the international response to ozone depletion that was required and the developing world's goals of development, a compromise had to be reached. Indeed, the Montreal Protocol recognised the peculiar economic and technical circumstances of the Global South, and this largely informed the compliance mechanisms thereunder.

Comparisons between the implementation regime under the Montreal Protocol and the SDGs may be criticised because, unlike the SDGs, the Montreal Protocol dealt with tackling a discrete substance with perfect market alternatives while the SDGs cover a much broader set of issues. However, both the SDGs and the Montreal Protocol require unyielding international cooperation and an equitable regime to succeed. The Montreal Protocol built mechanisms that recognised the inequities existing between states which was instrumental in garnering cooperation. The SDGs may benefit from these mechanisms to achieve a successful implementation.

A major reason for the success of the Montreal Protocol can be attributed to the control measures adopted by the Protocol.[63] Unlike many other treaties, the Protocol provided a clear and specific phase-out schedule consisting of percentage reductions in consumption and production by specified years.[64] The Protocol also detailed the procedure to calculate control levels.[65] This also helps states to easily measure their consumption levels, hence making compliance easy for the parties. The Protocol recognises the different depleting potentials of the various ozone-depleting substances. Each substance is assigned its own ozone-depleting potential, making it easy for state parties to monitor their consumption levels.

At the time of adoption, the parties adopted the unique approach of not stating the effect of non-compliance by a party. Article 8 of the original Montreal

[59] United Nations Environment Programme, 'Assessment for Decision Makers: Scientific Assessment of Ozone Depletion: 2014' (World Meteorological Organization, September 2014), ozone.unep.org/sites/default/files/2019-05/ADM_2014OzoneAssessment_Final.pdf, accessed 20 December 2023.

[60] MJ Bortscheller, 'Equitable But Ineffective: How the Principle of Common but Differentiated Responsibilities Hobbles the Global Fight against Climate Change' (2010) *Sustainable Development Law & Policy* 49, 65–68.

[61] ibid.

[62] ibid.

[63] UN Environment (n 48).

[64] The Montreal Protocol on Substances that Deplete the Ozone Layer (adopted 16 September 1987, entered into force 1 January 1989) 1522 UNTS 3 ('Montreal Protocol'), Art 2.

[65] ibid Art 3.

Protocol simply said that: 'The Parties, at their first meeting, shall consider and approve procedures and institutional mechanisms for determining non-compliance with the provisions of this Protocol and for treatment of Parties found to be in non-compliance'.[66] In 1992, after there had been available data on state party compliance, the parties agreed on a full structure for non-compliance. The non-compliance procedure has been regarded as the most effective under any treaty.[67] It revolves around the Protocol's Implementation Committee, which comprises two member states from each of the United Nation's five geographical regions. The committee relies mainly on data reports presented to the Secretariat to determine non-compliance. This helps track parties who have not submitted reports and those who have reported data showing breach of the control schedules. Where there is no justification for such non-compliance, the secretariat requests that the party draw up an action plan for its return to compliance. Although measures that might be in respect of non-compliance with the Protocol include issuing formal cautions and the suspension of specific rights and privileges under the Protocol, such as those dealing with finance and trade. The aim is not to punish the state but to assist it to return to compliance.

The international community took a landmark step in the development of the CBDR when it finally addressed the issues of financing and technology transfer necessary for compliance to be realistically feasible for much of the developing world.[68] One of the implementation mechanisms under the Montreal Protocol is the provision of technical assistance, especially to developing countries. The preamble to the Protocol recognises the need to develop relevant scientific knowledge to form the basis for actions towards restoring the ozone layer, taking into account technical considerations. Accordingly, Article 6 stipulates that the control measures set out under Article 2 shall be assessed 'on the basis of available scientific, environmental, technical and economic information'.[69] Often developing countries are less able to access technology and scientific and technical advancements. Therefore, without the necessary assistance, they were not going to be in the position to discharge their obligations under the Protocol. This distinction and call for aid are furthered in Articles 9 and 10 of the Montreal Protocol which state, inter alia, that the 'Parties shall cooperate' in promoting 'research, development

[66] ibid Art 8.

[67] S Jolly and A Trivedi, 'Principle of CBDR-RC: Its Interpretation and Implementation through NDCS in the Context of Sustainable Development' (2020) 11 *Washington Journal of Environmental Law and Policy* 309.

[68] Second Meeting of the Parties to the Montreal Protocol on Substances that Deplete the Ozone Layer, London, UK, June 27–29, 1990, Report of the Second Meeting of the Parties to the Montreal Protocol on Substances that Deplete the Ozone Layer, annexes I–III (June 29, 1990); Adoption of Adjustments and Amendments by the Fourth Meeting of the Parties to the Montreal Protocol on Substances that Deplete the Ozone Layer, Nov 23–25, 1992, 32 ILM 874; Ninth Meeting of the Parties to the Montreal Protocol on Substances that Deplete the Ozone Layer, Montreal, Canada, Sept 15–17, 1997, Report of the Ninth Meeting of the Parties to the Montreal Protocol on Substances that Deplete the Ozone Layer, dec. IX/15 (Sept 25, 1997).

[69] Emphasis added.

and exchange of information' and 'technical assistance to facilitate participation in and implementation of this Protocol'. To forestall this, Article 10(1) expressly provided for the parties to take into account the particular needs of developing countries and cooperate in promoting technical assistance to facilitate participation in and implementation of the Protocol. Furthermore, the Montreal Protocol specifies that the Secretariat for the Montreal Protocol will also serve as a facilitator for the exchange of information and technical assistance when a party to the Protocol requests such assistance, thus facilitating the flow of information and assistance in relation to implementing and complying with the Montreal Protocol. The Secretariat, upon receipt of such requests, notifies all Parties to facilitate the provision of such assistance.[70] To this end, compliance on the part of developing countries is substantially enabled because the scientific and technical knowledge needed to implement the Protocol, though not locally available, may be accessed from the developed countries through the Secretariat.

Second, another implementation mechanism under the Montreal Protocol is the provision of financial resources and instruments by the developed world to developing countries. As at the date of ratifying the Protocol, available technology largely appropriated controlled substances. Compliance with the Protocol required a necessary transition from technologies that relied on controlled substances to those based on environmentally safe alternative substances. This was certainly going to come at a cost that could tolerably be borne by the developed countries but was to be a challenge to the developing countries. The way around this challenge was to ensure that the financial burdens to be assumed by the developing countries in implementing the Protocol was ameliorated. Accordingly, Article 5(2) provides for developed countries to facilitate access to alternative technologies and substances that are environmentally safe to developing countries and to assist in the expeditious use of such alternatives.[71] The assumption of the costs associated with the said facilitation and assistance by developed countries was, arguably, a good motivation for developed countries to transition to safe substances and technologies. The prospects of implementation in the Global South were deepened when developed countries further undertook to provide developing countries with subsidies, aid, credits, guarantees and insurance packages to enable the acquisition and use of alternative technology and substitute products. In effect, the Protocol does a frank assessment of the poverty situation of the developing world and duly accounts for the same in the foregoing compliance mechanisms. Relatedly, the Montreal Protocol has established a central fund, known as the Multilateral Fund, to help developing countries comply with the treaty by helping ease some of the financial burdens that they have to carry in relation to the implementation of the treaty.

Third, the Montreal Protocol recognised the need not to subject all members to the same compliance standards thereby subjecting developing countries to much

[70] Montreal Protocol (n 65), Art 12(d).
[71] ibid Art 5(2).

lower timelines. For instance, even though Article 2 mandates parties to, seven months after ratification, reduce their consumption levels of controlled substances to their 1986 levels, Article 5 made an exception for developing countries by delaying their compliance through the stipulation that developing countries with emissions of controlled substances lower than 0.3 kg per capita on the date of entry into force of the Protocol or within 10 years of that date are 'entitled to delay its compliance with the control measures' by 10 years subject to certain conditions.[72] In hindsight, this exception was reasonable in view of the successes chalked under the Montreal Protocol. The present mechanism under review drives home the need to tailor treaty-compliance standards to the abilities and capacities of participating members without unduly burdening developing countries economically or developmentally.

A fourth implementation mechanism under the Montreal Protocol is the equality that underpins decision-making by the Parties. There is no denying that developed countries bear much more responsibility – especially financial and technology transfer – under the Protocol. If what prevails at some global institutions like the World Bank[73] is anything to go by, one would have thought the developed countries will insist on having greater say by way of votes in the decision-making process. On the contrary, however, the decision-making process under the Protocol is underpinned by equality of membership – each member having one vote. For example, under Article 11 of the Protocol, provision for meetings of the parties is made.[74] The Article mandates parties to, in their first meeting, adopt by consensus procedures to regulate subsequent meetings and the financial scheme under the Protocol.[75] Power is not concentrated in any particular block or blocks. The Parties are mandated to formulate strategies for the implementation of the Protocol, and review progress of implementation, among others. Such equality of participation engenders ownership of decisions made at meetings and deepens member-commitment towards implementing those decisions.

Closely related to equality at decision-making is the resolve of the promoters of the Protocol not to cloud its terms with western standards. It has been argued, for example, that African countries are performing poorly at implementing human rights treaties partly because some of their terms are western-centric.[76] The Montreal Protocol sought to avoid this trap by allowing member-perspectives to inform its implementation standards. Under Article 3, for example, each member was to determine its own calculated levels of production, imports, exports and

[72] ibid Art 5.

[73] The World Bank has 189 members and an Executive Board of 25 members. The five largest shareholders are entitled to appoint an Executive Director and the remaining Executive Directors are elected by the members. See the World Bank, 'Organization', www.worldbank.org/en/about/leadership#:~:text=The%20World%20Bank%20is%20like,finance%20or%20ministers%20of%20development, accessed 20 December 2023.

[74] Montreal Protocol (n 65), Art 11.

[75] ibid Arts 13(2), 2(4) (setting out a non-discriminatory formula for voting to make exceptions to party-obligations).

[76] Buamah (n 33).

consumption of controlled substances as provided for by Article 5.[77] Such autonomy in contributing to the setting of standards helps to yield implementable outcomes because the resulting standards are self-impositions which are likely to be based on local realities.

Finally, the Protocol provides an effective mix of reporting and expert reviews that engender compliance. For example, Article 7 requires each party to report to the Secretariat the production, importation, and exportation of controlled substances as of 1986, and thereafter, annually.[78] The Secretariat is enjoined under Article 12 of the Protocol to receive and circulate among other members the reported information and data received.[79] This enables the necessary transparency needed to identify compliant members and those who fall short of the expectations of the Protocol. In addition, such reports are presented to and analysed by expert panels constituted by the Parties under Article 6.[80] The analyses are done on the basis of available scientific, environmental, technical and economic information and the outcomes are communicated to members. Lessons from the human rights front suggest that the process of circulating reports among members and peer reviewing each other enhances compliance.

To sum up, mechanisms for the successful implementation of the SDGs should include instruments similar in design and structure to those found in the Montreal Protocol: mechanism to ensure compliance control and compliance assistance, fully structured on the basis of the principle of common but differentiated responsibility and with an equal footing for all members in the decision-making process at all levels.

IV. Existing Strategies to Implement SDGs

The main existing strategies to implement the SDGs may be grouped into two: financial support to developing countries and the review and reporting mechanism.[81] The Agenda recognised that due to financial inequalities, the developing countries will require some financial support to fulfil their SDG commitments. For instance, the 2014 World Investment Report estimated that USD$5 trillion to USD$7 trillion per year, between 2015 and 2030 would be necessary to globally achieve the SDGs, where USD$3.3 trillion to USD$4.5 trillion per year would be dedicated to developing countries, mainly for basic infrastructure,

[77] Montreal Protocol (n 65) Arts 3, 5.
[78] ibid Art 7.
[79] ibid Art 12.
[80] ibid Art 6.
[81] Addis Ababa Action Agenda of the Third International Conference on Financing for Development (the Addis Ababa Action Agenda) The final text of the outcome document adopted at the Third International Conference on Financing for Development (Addis Ababa, Ethiopia, 13–16 July 2015) and endorsed by the General Assembly in its resolution 69/313 of 27 July 2015.

food security, climate change policies, health and education.[82] Post Covid-19, the annual financing gap for the Global South to achieve the SDGs has actually grown to over US$4 trillion (up from US$2.5 trillion in 2014), according to the United Nations.[83]

Importantly, the agenda also recognised that the SDGs' success will require a commitment by countries and will rely on countries' own sustainable development policies, plans and programmes, and will be led by countries. The SDGs would, therefore, only serve as a compass for aligning countries' plans with their global commitments.

Nationally owned and country-led sustainable development strategies require resource mobilisation and financing strategies. All stakeholders: governments, civil society, the private sector, and others, are expected to contribute to the realisation of the new agenda. A revitalised global partnership is needed to support national efforts. Multi-stakeholder partnerships have been recognised as an important component of strategies that seek to mobilise all stakeholders around the new agenda.

To ensure compliance with SDG commitments, the Agenda adopted a system to monitor at both national and global levels. The UN introduced the indicators for the SDGs. Each target has indicators which track countries' progress in reaching the targets. The indicators provide the framework for measuring progress towards achieving the targets. At the national level, governments will develop their national indicators to assist in monitoring progress made on the goals and targets. The follow-up and review process will be informed by an annual SDG Progress Report to be prepared by the Secretary-General. Countries are then encouraged to present their Voluntary National Reports to the High-Level Political Forum for review. The SDGs' monitoring mechanism has enjoyed some limited success. However, it has been plagued by inadequate reporting due to the limited financial and technical capabilities of many countries' statistical organisations and units. As such, the lack of data may be a major issue in the progress of assessing the performance of SDGs.[84]

At the global level, the 17 Sustainable Development Goals (SDGs) and 169 targets of the new agenda will be monitored and reviewed using a set of global indicators.[85] The global indicator framework for Sustainable Development Goals was developed by the Inter-Agency and Expert Group on SDG Indicators

[82] UNCTAD, *World Investment Report 2014: Investigating the SDGs* (United Nations Publication, 2014).

[83] UNCTAD, 'SDG investment is growing, but too slowly: The investment gap is now $4 trillion, up from $2.5 in 2015' (United Nations, 14 September 2023), unctad.org/system/files/official-document/diaemisc2023d6_en.pdf, accessed 21 December 2023.

[84] M Nilashi and others, 'Critical Data Challenges in Measuring the Performance of Sustainable Development Goals: Solutions and the Role of Big-Data Analytics' (2023) 5(3) *Harvard Data Science Review*.

[85] UNGA A/RES/70/1 'Transforming our world: the 2030 Agenda for Sustainable Development' (25 September 2015).

(IAEG-SDGs) and agreed upon at the 48th session of the United Nations Statistical Commission held in March 2017.[86] NGOs, CSOs and the private sector also play an important role in SDGs implementation directly via the implementation of their projects and in holding governments accountable.

The annual meetings of the High-level Political Forum on sustainable development play a central role in reviewing progress toward the SDGs at the global level. The means of implementation of the SDGs is monitored and reviewed as outlined in the Addis Ababa Action Agenda to ensure that financial resources are effectively mobilised to support the new sustainable development agenda.[87]

V. The High-Level Political Forum

The enforcement of the SDGs has been a state-led enterprise. States have adopted voluntary national reviews as a means of measuring and informing the UN of their efforts to achieve the SDGs targets. However, the High-level Political Forum on Sustainable Development (HLPF) is at the heart of the United Nations sustainable development governance. The HLPF was established by the UN member states in 2012 at the Rio + 20 UN Conference on Sustainable Development as a universal, intergovernmental high-level political forum,[88] and in 2013 adopted the resolution on the HLPF's mandate.[89] In 2014/15, in the context of the negotiations of the Sustainable Development Goals (SDGs) and the 2030 Agenda on Sustainable Development they assigned the HLPF with a central role in overseeing follow-up and review at the global level.[90] The High-Level Political Forum (HLPF) was formally established through UN General Assembly Resolution A/67/290 in July 2013.[91] The HLPF, meeting every four years under the auspices of the General Assembly at the level of Heads of State and Government, is tasked with the primary focus on reviewing their commitments regarding the implementation of the agenda on a 'voluntary basis'. Moreover, there is a provision to ensure that UN bodies are enabled to work collaboratively with member states, as well as a reference to providing a 'platform for partnerships, including through the participation of major groups and other stakeholders'.[92] Paragraph 8 of UNGA Resolution 67/290 states that the forum, meeting under the auspices of ECOSOC for a period

[86] Department of Economic and Social Affairs, 'Global indicator framework for the Sustainable Development Goals and targets of the 2030 Agenda for Sustainable Development' (United Nations), unstats.un.org/sdgs/indicators/indicators-list/, accessed 29 December 2023.

[87] UNGA Res 69/313 (27 July 2015) UN Doc, A/RES/69/313.

[88] UNGA Res 64/236 (27 July 2012) UN Doc A/RES/66/288.

[89] UNGA Res 66/288 (9 July 2013) UN Doc A/RES/67/290.

[90] UNGA Res 70/1 (n 13).

[91] See n 89 above.

[92] EM Lockwood, 'Disability Rights Monitoring: Focus on the Sustainable Development Goals' in MH Rioux and others (eds), *Handbook of Disability: Critical Thought and Social Change in a Globalizing World* (Springer, 2022).

of eight days, will conduct regular reviews on the follow-up and implementation of the SDGs. In particular, the forum's reviews:

> a. Shall be voluntary, and will include developed and developing countries, and relevant United Nations entities; b. Shall be State-led, involving ministerial and other relevant high-level participants; c. Shall provide a platform for partnerships, including through the participation of major groups and other relevant stakeholders; d. Shall replace the national voluntary presentations held in the context of the annual ministerial-level substantive reviews of the Economic and Social Council, building upon the relevant provisions of General Assembly resolution 61/16 as well as experiences and lessons learned in this context ...[93]

While the primary function is to enable dialogue between member states, there is a clear recognition of the need for wider engagement with all relevant stakeholders in this Agenda. According to the resolution, para 15 states that:

> while retaining the intergovernmental character of the forum, the representatives of the major groups and other relevant stakeholders shall be allowed: a. To attend all official meetings of the forum; b. To have access to all official information and documents; c. To intervene in official meetings; d. To submit documents and present written and oral contributions; e. To make recommendations; f. To organize side events and round tables, in cooperation with Member States and the Secretariat.[94]

An early study commissioned by the UN Department of Economic and Social Affairs (DESA)[95] pictures the HLPF as the 'dedicated home for sustainable development in the UN system' and suggests it should be an 'orchestrator, building links to intermediaries' within the UN system as well as other international organisations, (public-)private networks, and stakeholder initiatives in the broader sustainable development governance architecture.

A. HLPF Weaknesses

The HLPF has a high degree of legitimacy and can be considered a focal actor due to its universal membership and its connections to both the UN's Economic and Social Council (ECOSOC) and the UN General Assembly (UNGA). However, the HLPF has many weaknesses. Some have argued that the HLPF could become another 'talk shop'.[96] As a voluntary, non-binding forum, the HLPF does not have

[93] CIVICUS, 'How to Engage With the High Level Political Forum' action4sd.org/wp-content/uploads/2016/07/HLPF.UserGuide.pdf, accessed 29 December 2023.

[94] UNGA Res 61/16 (9 January 2007) UN Doc A/RES/61/16.

[95] S Bernstein, 'The Role and Place of the High-Level Political Forum in Strengthening the Global Institutional Framework for Sustainable Development' (Department of Economic and Social Affairs, September 2013), sdgs.un.org/documents/role-and-place-high-level-political-19959, accessed 21 December 2023.

[96] J Espey, K Walęcik and M Kühner, 'Follow-up and Review of the SDGs: Fulfilling Our Commitments' (2015) *Sustainable Development Solutions Network*.

the power to enforce the implementation of the SDGs or to hold governments accountable for their progress. This can limit its effectiveness in promoting the implementation of the SDGs and in supporting the efforts of Member States to achieve sustainable development. Relying on the voluntary participation of Member States and other stakeholders means that the HLPF may not have full representation from all countries or sectors. This can limit the inclusivity and diversity of the discussions and exchanges that take place at the forum. And because the HLPF relies on member states to report on their progress on the SDGs, and these national reviews are expected to serve as a basis for the regular reviews by the HLPF, this can make it difficult for the HLPF to accurately assess progress and identify areas where further action is needed if the data, they are provided is not reliable or comparable.

The HLPF also operates with limited resources, which can impact its ability to carry out its mandate effectively. For example, the HLPF may not have sufficient funding or staffing to support its annual meetings and other events or to conduct in-depth reviews and assessments of progress on the SDGs.

Others have drawn similarities between the HLPF and its predecessor, the Commission for Sustainable Development (CSD), and claim that the HLPF, just like the CSD, could be an empty institution intentionally designed by member states to be without capacity, producing no outputs in terms of regulatory policy-making or policy implementation.[97]

B. Suggestions for Improvement

Before Rio + 20, experts had suggested upgrading the CSD to a Sustainable Development Council (modelled after the Human Rights Council); and afterward, there was hope that the HLPF could become an 'apex body' that reviews implementation, takes decisions, and delivers political guidance, thereby ultimately steering the UN system's efforts on the 2030 Agenda and SDGs.[98] However member states could not agree on a stronger institutional setup with such elaborate oversight powers and responsibilities. There have been calls by NGOs[99] and scholars[100] for a stronger HLPF that goes beyond simple interplay management and orchestration by a more structural change that establishes hierarchical orders among institutions and actors in global governance. These calls should finally

[97] RS Dimitrov, 'Empty Institutions in Global Environmental Politics' (2019) 22 *International Studies Review* 626.

[98] IISD, 'Daily Report for 26 June 2015' (29 June 2015), https://enb.iisd.org/events/hlpf-2015/daily-report-26-june-2015, accessed 21 December 2023.

[99] Forus, 'The review of the HLPF as an opportunity to strengthen multi-stakeholder participation & improve SDG implementation', www.forus-international.org/en/pdf-detail/75816-the-review-of-the-hlpf-as-an-opportunity-to-strengthen-multi-stakeholder-participation-improve-sdg-implementation, accessed 20 December 2023.

[100] RE Kim and others, 'Hierarchization' in F Biermann and RE Kim (eds), *Architectures of Earth System Governance: Institutional Complexity and Structural Transformation* (Cambridge University Press, 2020).

be heeded: a strong permanent Sustainable Development Council with strong enforcement mechanisms and well-resourced is the *conditio sine qua non* if the international community is at least serious in trying to achieve the SDGs.

Although the HLPF serves as an 'orchestrator', it falls under the auspices of the ECOSOC.[101] Thus, those member states that hold the ECOSOC Presidency and the ECOSOC Bureau decide on the program of the forum. The 2013 resolution on the HLPF grants comprehensive participation rights to the 'Major Groups and other Stakeholders' (MGS), which consists inter alia of representatives from civil society organisations, academia or the private sector.[102] The 2030 Agenda calls on these non-state actors to support the implementation of the SDGs and their follow-up and review during the HLPF.[103] Hence, they may be seen as potential intermediaries and target actors.

Member states agreed that the HLPF would have a central role in overseeing a network of follow-up and review processes at the global level.[104] Accordingly, the HLPF features thematic and SDG reviews as well as all Voluntary National Reviews (VNRs). In a broader sense, the forum should be a platform 'for regular dialogue and stocktaking and agenda-setting'.[105] In this context, there are other mandated deliverables like discussing challenges for countries in special situations, considering new and emerging issues, enhancing integration of the three dimensions of sustainable development, or providing a platform for partnerships as part of the forum's 'action-oriented agenda'.[106] As for the outcome, member states agreed that the HLPF should 'provide political leadership, guidance and recommendations'.[107] For this, member states negotiate and adopt a declaration. The forum meets annually for eight days in July under the auspices of ECOSOC and, in addition, every four years for up to two days in September at the level of heads of state and government under the auspices of the UNGA. Every four years, a political declaration is adopted by heads of state and government when the HLPF meets under the auspices of the UNGA in September, the so-called SDG Summit. The next such meetings will take place respectively in July and September 2023.[108]

C. Mandatory National Reviews

The HLPF should mandate all member states to submit periodic reports to the body instead of relying on the voluntary participation of Member States. As part of its follow-up and review mechanisms, the 2030 Agenda for Sustainable Development encourages member states to 'conduct regular and inclusive reviews of progress at

[101] Bernstein (n 96).
[102] UNGA Res 66/288 (9 July 2013) UN Doc A/RES/67/290.
[103] UNGA Res 70/1 (n 13).
[104] ibid para 82.
[105] UNGA Res 66/288 (n 103).
[106] ibid para 2.
[107] ibid para 2.
[108] United Nations, 'High-level Political Forum 2023', hlpf.un.org/2023, accessed 20 December 2023.

the national and sub-national levels, which are country-led and country-driven'.[109] Presented every year at the HLPF during its three-day ministerial segment in July, these reviews are supposed to be voluntary, state-led, undertaken by both developed and developing countries, and provide a platform for partnerships, including through the participation of major groups and other relevant stakeholders.[110] The Voluntary Nation Review (VNR) is a process through which countries assess and present national progress made in implementing the 2030 Agenda, including achieving its 17 SDGs and the pledge to leave no one behind. VNRs provide a snapshot of where a country stands in the implementation of the Sustainable Development Goals, to help accelerate progress through experience sharing, peer learning, identifying gaps and good practices, and mobilising partnerships. VNRs are a soft accountability and progress-monitoring mechanism of the 2030 Agenda.[111] VNRs provide the opportunity for countries to share their individual experiences, including successes, challenges and lessons learned, to accelerate SDG implementation.

These national reviews are expected to serve as a basis for regular reviews by the HLPF, meeting under the auspices of ECOSOC. VNRs typically consist of the following broad phases: initial preparation and organisation; preparation of the VNR report; presentation at the HLPF; and follow-up after the HLPF.[112] Stakeholder engagement may occur throughout all of these phases. The main guidance for countries preparing for VNRs is the updated UN Secretary-General's voluntary common reporting guidelines, which provide a framework for common elements for the reviews.[113] While there is no frequency for reporting mandated for VNRs, the UN Secretary-General has recommended that all countries conduct at least two VNRs during the 15-year period of the SDGs.[114] By the end of July 2018, more than half of all UN Member States had presented VNRs at the HLPF.[115]

VNRs aim to facilitate the sharing of experiences, including successes, challenges and lessons learned, with a view to accelerating the implementation of the 2030 Agenda.[116] The VNRs also seek to strengthen policies and institutions of governments and to mobilise multi-stakeholder support and partnerships for the

[109] UNGA Res 70/1 (n 13) para 79.

[110] ibid para 84.

[111] United Nations Human Rights Office of the High Commissioner, 'OHCHR and the 2030 Agenda for Sustainable Development' (United Nations), www.ohchr.org/en/sdgs, accessed 20 December 2023.

[112] UN DSD and UN DESA, 'Handbook for the Preparation of Voluntary National Reviews' (2018) 9, archive.unescwa.org/sites/www.unescwa.org/files/page_attachments/handbook-preparation-voluntary-national-reviews-2018-en_0.pdf, accessed 21 December 2023.

[113] United Nations, 'Voluntary common reporting guidelines for voluntary national reviews at the high-level political forum for sustainable development (HLPF)' sustainabledevelopment.un.org/content/documents/17346Updated_Voluntary_Guidelines.pdf, accessed 20 December 2023.

[114] Report of the Secretary-General, 'Critical milestones towards coherent, efficient and inclusive follow-up and review at the global level' (2016) UN Doc A/70/684.

[115] *Human Rights and the 2030 Agenda for Sustainable Development: Lessons Learned and Next Steps* (Danish Institute for Human Rights, 2018) 18.

[116] United Nations Department of Economic and Social Affairs, 'Handbook for the Preparedness of Voluntary National Reviews' (United Nations, 2024), hlpf.un.org/sites/default/files/vnrs/hand-book/VNR%20Handbook%202024%20EN%2B_0.pdf, accessed 21 December 2023.

implementation of the Sustainable Development Goals. Member states have shown great interest in the VNR process; 22 countries presented VNRs in the first year (2016) of implementation, while 43 countries presented in 2017 and 47 presented in 2018.[117] The process has also generated interest on the part of stakeholders – some are contributing to the preparation of VNRs, while others are commenting on the reports. A growing debate has emerged on this new process and on ways to improve its effectiveness. Speaking at the 2021 HLPF, Amina J Mohammed, UN Deputy Secretary-General, stated that '177 countries having presented at least one VNR to date, they are a testament to the enduring commitment of national governments to implement the 2030 Agenda and achieve our global goals'.[118] She further added that

> the VNRs are not simply a report or a presentation at the HLPF. They are a national process of in-depth review and consultation on the implementation of the 2030 Agenda … Ultimately, VNRs create space for governments and their partners to identify what is needed to keep the promise of the SDGs.

VNRs are a key tool for accountability for the SDGs at both the national and global level. As the main mechanism for tracking progress on the SDGs at the national level and reporting on it at the global level, VNRs provide an important opportunity for countries to be answerable to their citizens in relation to their implementation of the SDGs, especially for members of civil society who have limited space to participate in SDG accountability processes at a national level.

VNR reports are expected to show what steps a country has taken to implement the 2030 Agenda and provide an assessment of the results on the ground including successes, challenges, gaps in implementation, possible solutions and emerging issues. As a tool for accountability, the VNR process can strengthen national ownership of the SDGs, promote transparency, inclusiveness and participation in reporting on the SDGs, and support more effective implementation of the 2030 Agenda. Given the 2030 Agenda's voluntary nature, VNRs may be seen as a norm-building process in which individual countries' best practices may persuade others to follow suit and set standards for the international community.

D. Fact-Finding Independent Committees on Each SDG

The HLPF relies on member states to report on their progress on the SDGs, and these national reviews are expected to serve as a basis for the regular reviews by the HLPF, which can make it difficult for the HLPF to accurately assess progress and identify areas where further action is needed if the data they are provided

[117] Department of Economic and Social Affairs, 'Voluntary National Review Reports – what do they report?' (United Nations, July 2018), sdgtoolkit.org/wp-content/uploads/2018/10/Voluntary-National-Review-Reports--2018.pdf, accessed 20 December 2023.

[118] United Nations Human Rights Office of the High Commissioner, 'Voluntary National Reviews' (United Nations, 2021), www.ohchr.org/en/sdgs/voluntary-national-reviews, accessed 29 December 2023.

is not reliable or comparable.[119] This means that the HLPF should establish and use committees and sub-committees of experts for fact-finding purposes and the making of recommendations to the UNGA. The HLPF can also enjoin parties to exchange relevant scientific, technical, and technological information, and enjoin developed countries to extend support to developing countries in the building of capacities and capabilities in those relevant fields. Like with the Framework Convention, the HLPF should upon request, extend to developing countries technical and financial assistance needed to implement objectives. And in addition, developed countries are enjoined to extend financial assistance to developing countries to help them discharge their obligations under the Convention.

E. Finances

The HLPF operates with limited resources, which can impact its ability to carry out its mandate effectively. For example, the HLPF may not have sufficient funding or staffing to support its annual meetings and other events or to conduct in-depth reviews and assessments of progress on the SDGs. So, like with the Montreal Protocol, the HLPF and member states should establish a central fund to help developing countries comply with SDGs by helping ease some of the financial burdens that they must carry in relation to the achievements of the SDGs. The HLPF can create an independent committee made of members from developed and developing countries tasked to oversee the fund. The Fund should be jointly administered by the World Bank, the United Nations Development Programme, and the United Nations, with the Bank handling the project financing arrangements. The committee will receive donations from developed countries and other donor countries or bodies and develop guidelines to distribute the funds equitably. For instance, the funds could be available to eligible countries that have made progress in meeting their targets and submitted reports for review. Possible challenges to the central fund may include a lack of incentive for developed countries to contribute to the achievement of the goals by developing countries. In this regard, donors may be allowed to donate to specific goals or targets, like climate, gender, poverty or other goals and targets.

VI. Conclusion

At the time of writing in 2023, 2030 is not too distant in the future and, at the current pace of implementation of the SDGs, it is easy to predict that failure may be the key word again when assessing the realisation of the commitments states

[119] High-Level Political Forum on Sustainable Development, 'Voluntary National Reviews' (United Nations), hlpf.un.org/vnrs, accessed 29 December 2023.

made in 2015 to create a more equal world. Seven years are left to truly to take on the central issue of implementation and turn the tide. Indeed the 2023 High-Level Political Forum is meant to focus on 'Accelerating the recovery from the coronavirus disease (COVID19) and the full implementation of the 2030 Agenda for Sustainable Development at all levels'.[120]

If this is to happen, the current architecture for implementation must truly be enhanced and reinforced. The focus, in particular, should be an architecture centred on the full participation of the Global South, with the transformation of the High-Level Political Forum into a fully fledged permanent Sustainable Development Council. Member states should be mandated to submit periodic reports; expert committees and sub-committees should be established for fact-finding and making recommendations; the exchange of relevant information and support for developing countries should be encouraged; and a central fund should be established to help ease financial burdens on developing countries in achieving the SDGs. If the world is to become more equal, the voice of the Global South must be at the centre of implementation efforts. The expertise and knowledge base in the Global South must drive the implementation of Agenda 2030. The Global North must not only provide the needed resources and support but must truly and fully embrace a spirit of true cooperation and partnership with the Global South. Equality and equity should not be mere rhetorical words written in declarations and legally binding treaties: they should be core commitments in implementing efforts and centred throughout the efforts to ensure a fairer world for all. Also, the Global South must adopt collaborative endeavours that aim to address common developmental challenges by sharing resources, best practices and expertise.

[120] United Nations, 'High-level Political Forum on Sustainable Development' (2023), hlpf.un.org/2023, accessed 20 December 2023.

9

The Regulation of Agricultural Knowledge, Seed Policies and the UN Sustainable Development Goal of 'Zero Hunger'

CHRISTOPH ANTONS

I. The Discourses on Sustainable Development, Sustainable Agriculture and Food Systems

In 1987, the World Commission on Environment and Development (WCED) in its report 'Our Common Future', commonly known as the Brundtland Report,[1] put the concept of sustainable development onto the policy agenda of international organisations and nation states. Although it is now regarded as representing mainstream thinking about the relationship between environment and development,[2] the report's attempt to move to a new development paradigm by integrating environmental, economic and social considerations has fostered many different interpretations of the concept of sustainable development.[3] Susan Baker has contrasted the different policy approaches in a graph that moves from mere pollution control to ideal models with weak and strong forms of sustainable development in the middle, and from governance models informed by anthropocentric to ecocentric philosophies.[4] There is a similar diversity of interpretations regarding the more recent Sustainable Development Goals (SDGs), conceptualised at the Rio+20 United Nations Conference in 2012.[5] Researchers writing from an African or Asian perspective, for example, have spoken of a 'discourse' of SDGs.[6] It has

[1] The WCED was chaired by then Norwegian Prime Minister Gro Harlem Brundtland.
[2] S Baker, *Sustainable Development* 2nd edn (Routledge, 2015) 7.
[3] S Hsu, 'Framework for understanding sustainable development' in S Hsu (ed), *Routledge Handbook of Sustainable Development in Asia* (Routledge, 2018) 21–22.
[4] Baker (n 2) 38–39.
[5] 'Sustainable Development Goals' (*Sustainable Development Goals Knowledge Platform*), sustainabledevelopment.un.org/topics/sustainabledevelopmentgoals, accessed 4 September 2023.
[6] T Halvorsen and J Higgins, 'Growth or Solidarity? The Discourse of the SDGs' in M Ramutsindela and D Mickler (eds), *Africa and the Sustainable Development Goals* (Springer, 2020) 13; Hsu (n 3).

been criticised that 'growth' remains a keyword in this SDG discourse[7] and that 'attempts to reconcile environmental protection with economic growth through green growth do not fundamentally shift the tenets of the capitalist economy'.[8] Such authors also stress the importance of understanding the context in which the SDGs are implemented in Africa and Asia.[9] While advocates of pollution control and weak sustainable development approaches continue to seek solutions in human ingenuity, trade and technology, strongly ecocentric policy models emphasise to varying degrees the need to transition from what is often regarded as the current obsession with growth to alternative economic models.[10] As Baker points out,[11] both pollution control and what she terms the 'ideal model' ultimately reject the mainstream conceptualisations of (weak or strong) sustainable development as either going too far or not far enough in promoting alternatives to the traditional growth-oriented development model.

There are similar debates and divergences of opinion with regards to agricultural policy. The term 'food security' has been used in United Nations discourses since the mid-1970s but was soon criticised for putting too much emphasis on the supply side and thereby neglecting the question of access.[12] Although the concept has evolved over the years and continues to be widely used, it has not been subject to a discussion about 'where food should be produced, how, by whom, under what conditions, for whose benefit, and under whose control'.[13] The concept has remained open to 'productivist' interpretations such as 'sustainable intensification', which does not problematise the use of genetically modified organisms (GMOs), chemical fertilisers and similar forms of input.[14] This has in recent years been countered by a 'food sovereignty' discourse, popularised initially by the international farmers' organisation La Via Campesina[15] and its

[7] Halvorsen and Higgins (ibid) 15.

[8] M Ramutsindela and D Mickler, 'Global Goals and African Development' in Ramutsindela and Mickler (n 6) 6.

[9] ibid 8; Hsu (n 3) 21.

[10] Baker (n 2) 40–44. Ecocentric policy approaches in legislation are few and far between. The Constitution of Ecuador of 2008 referring to 'rights of nature' is mentioned as an example as well as legislation in New Zealand granting rights to land and water, see F Medlock and R White, 'Ecocide, Ecocentrism and Social Obligation' (2022) 3 *Erasmus Law Review* 6. For these and further examples, see also S De Vido, 'A Quest for an Eco-centric Approach to International Law: the COVID-19 Pandemic as Game Changer' (2021) 3 *Jus Cogens* 107.

[11] Baker (ibid) 44.

[12] N McKeon, *Food Security Governance: Empowering Communities, Regulating Corporations* (Routledge, 2015) 73–74.

[13] ibid 76.

[14] ibid 72. See also J Blesh and others, 'Development Pathways towards "Zero Hunger"' (2019) 118 *World Development* 2.

[15] For the influential role of La Via Campesina in the adoption of the United Nations Declaration on the Rights of Peasants and other People Working in Rural Areas (UNDROP), see P Claeys and M Edelman, 'The United Nations Declaration on the Rights of Peasants and Other People Working in Rural Areas' (2020) 47(1) *Journal of Peasant Studies* 1.

many affiliates in different countries.[16] Localising food systems, including their knowledge base and control mechanisms, is at the heart of the food sovereignty movement. This means it is opposed to a globalised food system emphasising international trade and intellectual property rights in agricultural technologies and input, which monopolise such technologies and prevent broader access.[17] Further, in academic discourses, holistic food systems or food regimes analysis has been developed, which integrates approaches from ecology, agricultural and environmental sciences with nutrition, public health and political economy and policy science.[18]

The SDG 2 of 'zero hunger' in its targets has addressed many of the criticisms directed at the earlier Millennium Development Goals[19] by linking environmental concerns to public health and socio-economic factors.[20] Nevertheless, critics have again identified a 'productionist' bias, which continues to identify scarcity as the root cause of food insecurity.[21] It displays internal contradictions which are said to result from a 'goal-led, top-down formulation process'.[22] Others see problems with the framing of SDG 2, but conclude that it also opens 'the possibility of shifting the conversation in a more holistic direction'.[23]

Agricultural knowledge occupies a key position in such discourses, because it has become subjected to intellectual property rights, and opposition to the patenting and monopolisation of seeds and other agricultural input material is a key argument of the food sovereignty movement, which after all developed in the 1990s in opposition to the agenda of the newly formed World Trade Organization (WTO) and the increasing role of corporations and private interests in a globalised food system.[24] The remainder of this chapter will show how these

[16] In Indonesia, an alliance of individual farmers, farmer and human rights organisations launched a partially successful challenge in the Indonesian Constitutional Court in 2012/13 against restrictive provisions of Law No 12 of 1992 on the Plant Cultivation System. However, while a revision in 2019 acknowledged the implications of the decision, the new Law on the Sustainable Agricultural System also brought new and different restrictions. In India, a movement for seed freedom (seed satyagraha) in the state of Karnataka and mass demonstrations by farmers preceded the adoption of the WTO TRIPS Agreement and triggered the debate about farmers' rights in the country, which subsequently were included in the Protection of Plant Varieties and Farmers' Rights Act of 2001; see C Antons and A Sreedevi Babu, 'Plant Variety Protection and Farmers' Rights in India and Indonesia' in E Derclaye (ed), *Research Handbook on Empirical Studies in Intellectual Property Law* (Edward Elgar, 2023) 74. Specifically on the developments in Indonesia see also C Antons, YT Winarto and AF Prihandiani, 'Farmer-plant-breeders and the Law on Java, Indonesia' (2020) 52(4) *Critical Asian Studies* 589; and C Antons, YT Winarto, AF Prihandiani and S Uli, 'Farmers as Researchers: Government Regulation of Farmers' Local Knowledge in Indonesia' in M Blakeney and KHM Siddique (eds), *Local Knowledge, Intellectual Property and Agricultural Innovation* (Springer Nature, 2020) 117.

[17] For a summary of the food sovereignty movement, see McKeon (n 12) 77–81.

[18] See Blesh and others (n 14).

[19] J Battersby, '*MDGs* to SDGs – New Goals, Same Gaps: The Continued Absence of Urban Food Security in the Post-2015 Global Development Agenda' (2017) 36(1) *African Geographical Review* 115.

[20] Blesh and others (n 14) 2.

[21] Battersby (n 19) 122.

[22] ibid 124.

[23] Blesh and others (n 14) 10.

[24] McKeon (n 12) 80.

different knowledge discourses are visible in international treaties, policy discussions around free trade agreements, and national and regional laws in Indonesia and its neighbours within the Association of Southeast Asian Nations (ASEAN). Both international agreements as well as national laws aiming at incentivising plant breeding and standardising seed supply attempt to occupy a middle ground and seek to promote agribusiness interests at the same time as attempting to safeguard the interests of agricultural smallholders and Indigenous Peoples. As the chapter will demonstrate, the attempts remain lopsided, with strong intellectual property rights for the industry, and vaguely defined equitable benefits and compensation mechanisms for those various 'communities' that are supposed to play a key role in sustainable agriculture. Community focused sustainable agriculture stresses locality and limited needs for non-local and expensive input, whereas seed and intellectual property policies modelled after international standards promote higher yields and standardisation of input material and production techniques at the national level. This is visible, for example in seed testing procedures and the requirement in seed certification laws to produce 'superior seeds'.[25]

II. Agricultural Knowledge in International Law

In international legal frameworks, agricultural knowledge sits at the intersection of intellectual property, environmental and human rights law. Multiple international law regimes are involved in governing agricultural knowledge, including treaties administered by the World Intellectual Property Organization (WIPO), the World Trade Organization (WTO) and the United Nations Environment Programme (UNEP), as well as non-binding UN resolutions. While there are conflicting values and priorities due to the different objectives and approaches of these legal frameworks, the extent of such clashes and the necessity to harmonise different legal regimes has remained controversial. The Convention on Biological Diversity (CBD) does not discourage intellectual property rights,[26] but asks parties to collaborate 'to ensure that such rights are supportive of and do not run counter to' the objectives of the CBD.[27] As will be discussed below, proposals from countries in the Global South such as India to harmonise the apparent contradictions between the two regimes[28] did not find support of the industrialised countries.[29] Because of similar differences in view, discussions at WIPO about protection of 'traditional knowledge' promoted in the CBD have only made relatively modest

[25] Antons, Winarto and Prihandiani, 'Farmer-plant-breeders' (n 16).

[26] Convention on Biological Diversity, Art 16(2).

[27] ibid Art 16(5).

[28] M Kruger, 'Harmonizing TRIPS and the CBD: A Proposal from India' (2001) *Minnesota Journal of International Law* 197.

[29] C Antons, 'Biodiversity, Intangible Cultural Heritage and Intellectual Property' in C McManis and B Ong (eds), *The Routledge Handbook on Biodiversity and the Law* (Routledge, 2018) 313.

progress. The clearest opposition to intellectual property rights is to be found in the United Nations Declaration on the rights of peasants and other people working in rural areas, but it is a non-binding declaration.

A. The UPOV Convention and the WTO TRIPS Agreement

Intellectual property rights related to plants were pioneered in the United States with the Plant Patent Act of 1930,[30] followed by plant variety rights legislation in European countries such as the Netherlands and Germany in the 1940s and 1950s.[31] It was also in Europe that the International Convention for the Protection of New Varieties of Plants, known under its French acronym as the UPOV Convention was concluded. It was first ratified by Germany, the Netherlands and the United Kingdom, followed by other mostly European countries in the first three decades of the convention.[32]

Few countries from the Global South joined during this period and expansion outside of Europe was equally slow.[33] The Convention was revised in 1972, 1978 and 1991 and its current members are bound by either the 1978 or 1991 version.[34] Like other intellectual property conventions, the UPOV Convention softens the strong exclusive rights granted to breeders of new, distinct, uniform and stable varieties[35] with limitations on the scope of protection due to public interest considerations and considerations of competing interests. These limitations are the breeder's exemption to use protected subject matter, the seed-saving exception exempting farmers using farm-saved seed for replanting from liability, an exhaustion of rights rule, and a compulsory licence provision.[36] Again, as in other intellectual property conventions, the balance between exclusive rights and limitations has been modified in revision conferences, most importantly in the 1991 revision of the UPOV Convention. The 1991 revision eliminated the previous ban on dual protection under plant breeders' rights and patent law, which had prevented the United States from ratifying UPOV because of its traditional preference for plant patents.[37] It extended protection to varieties 'essentially derived' from a protected variety,

[30] K Aoki, *Seed Wars: Controversies and Cases on Plant Genetic Resources and Intellectual Property* (Carolina Academic Press, 2008) 30; MD Janis, HH Jervis and R Peet, *Intellectual Property Law of Plants* (Oxford University Press, 2014) 184–85.

[31] Janis, Jervis and Peet (ibid) 70.

[32] C Antons, 'Intellectual Property in Plant Material and Free Trade Agreements in Asia' in K-C Liu and J Chaisse (eds), *The Future of Asian Trade Deals and IP* (Hart, 2019) 233.

[33] ibid 234.

[34] See the list of members on the UPOV website, www.upov.int/edocs/pubdocs/en/upov_pub_423.pdf, accessed 20 December 2022.

[35] UPOV (1991), Art 5. As per Janis, Jervis and Peet (n 30) 74–75, the terminology has slightly changed from UPOV (1961) and (1978) to UPOV (1991).

[36] For details see ibid 84–87.

[37] ibid 71.

thereby expanding the rights of first-generation breeders.[38] Finally, it included an explicit, but narrowed seed-saving exception,[39] making the exception optional and allowed 'within reasonable limits and subject to the safeguarding of the legitimate interests of the breeder'.[40] As Janis, Jervis and Peet point out,[41] this enables countries to consider a variety of factors in their legislations, including the type of the variety, size of holding, crop area or value, and the amount of the harvested crop.

Countries in the Global South typically had large smallholder farming sectors, few if any private seed companies, and agricultural research dominated by public sector institutions. As a result of such profiles, their reluctance to join UPOV and provide private intellectual property rights for commercial breeders was perfectly justified. They had to rethink their policies, however, after the conclusion of the WTO Agreement on Trade-related Intellectual Property Rights (TRIPS) in 1994. Although plant variety rights are not specifically covered in this agreement, they have gained in popularity via the back door of a provision in the part on patents, which was introduced to allow WTO members to exclude certain material from patent protection.[42] Article 27(1) TRIPS required from WTO member to offer patent protection 'for any inventions' and 'in all fields of technology' that meet the general patentability requirements of novelty, inventive step and industrial applicability. Further subsections specified possible exclusions with the so-called 'biotechnology clause' of Article 27(3)b allowing WTO member states to exclude from patentability 'plants and animals other than micro-organisms, and essentially biological processes for the production of plants or animals other than non-biological and micro-biological processes'. The provision continued, however, to require that 'Members shall provide for the protection of plant varieties either by patents or by an effective *sui generis* system or by any combination thereof'. Thus, the TRIPS Agreement required a plant variety protection system, but allowed countries the freedom to design it with the only further condition that it had to be 'effective'.

This meant a substantial amount of freedom to design such laws at a time when few countries outside of Europe were bound by the requirements of the UPOV Convention. However, the opportunity to come up with creative solutions was largely not taken up. Instead, the majority of countries in the Global South designed laws based on the UPOV model and confined themselves to limited modifications to this model.[43] Lack of time and expertise in designing alternatives, fear of trading partners' criticisms of laws as not being effective, but in some cases also own

[38] J Sanderson, 'Essential Derivation, Law and the Limits of Science' (2006) 24 *Law in Context* 34.

[39] Prior to UPOV (1991), the seed-saving exception had been inferred from the limitation of infringing acts done for commercial purposes, see Janis, Jervis and Peet (n 30) 86; Aoki (n 30) 65, fn 24.

[40] UPOV (1991), Art 15(2).

[41] Janis, Jervis and Peet (n 30) 86–87.

[42] Antons, 'Intellectual Property in Plant Material' (n 32) 235.

[43] CM Correa, *TRIPS-Related Patent Flexibilities and Food Security: Options for Developing Countries* (Quaker United Nations Office (QUNO) and International Centre for Trade and Sustainable Development (ICTSD), 2012); R Kanniah and C Antons, 'Plant Variety Protection and Traditional Agricultural Knowledge in Southeast Asia' (2012) 13 *Australian Journal of Asian Law* 12; R Kanniah and C Antons, 'The Regulation of Innovation in Agriculture and Sustainable Development in India and Southeast Asia' in C Antons (ed), *Routledge Handbook of Asian Law* (Routledge, 2017) 294.

ambitions in biotech and agricultural industries are all possible reasons to explain this relative lack of creativity.[44] The model character of the UPOV Convention subsequently triggered a significant expansion in membership, in particular among countries of the Global South. While Japan, Israel and South Africa were the only UPOV members from Asia and Africa prior to the TRIPS Agreement, among its 78 members are now 15 from Asia, six from Africa and 15 from Latin America and the Caribbean.[45] This trend towards UPOV membership is likely to continue as requirements to join UPOV or adhere to UPOV standards are frequently included in bilateral Free Trade and Economic Partnership Agreements, particularly those concluded by the United States, Japan, the European Union and the countries of the European Free Trade Association (EFTA).[46] The Comprehensive and Progressive Agreement for Trans-Pacific Partnership (CPTPP) now also requires several countries to join UPOV, upgrade from UPOV (1978) to UPOV (1991), or adopt standards in conformity with UPOV.[47] Some countries in Asia have further agreed in free trade agreements with the United States to extend patent protection to plant material or to endeavour to do so.[48]

B. Traditional Knowledge in the Convention on Biological Diversity and the WIPO IGC

Around the same time as the UPOV Convention revision of 1991 and the WTO TRIPS Agreement of 1994 expanded the intellectual property protection for commercial and scientific plant breeding, the Convention on Biological Diversity (CBD) of 1992 in its Article 8j promoted the 'traditional knowledge' (TK) of 'indigenous and local communities' and its role in biodiversity conservation. It has been noted that this recognition signalled a significant shift in wider environmental discourses from discriminative attitudes towards such communities in comparison with colonial policies and early post-World War II development planning.[49] However, the CBD also stresses the sovereign rights of states in the exploitation of their resources (Article 3), and their 'authority to determine access to genetic resources' (Article 15(1)). Analysts have referred to such compromises between the international embrace of local stewardship of environmental principles and national sovereignty in the interest of development as a 'somewhat confusing hybrid'.[50]

[44] Antons, 'Intellectual Property in Plant Material' (n 32) 236–37.
[45] See the list of UPOV members (n 34).
[46] Antons, 'Intellectual Property in Plant Material' (n 32).
[47] ibid 246.
[48] C Antons, 'Article 27(3)(b) TRIPS and Plant Variety Protection in Developing Countries' in Hanns Ullrich and others (eds), *TRIPS plus 20: From Trade Rules to Market Principles* (Springer, 2016) 394.
[49] C Antons, 'Biodiversity, Intangible Cultural Heritage and Intellectual Property' in McManis and Ong (n 29) 313.
[50] Y Ariffin, 'Developmental and Environmental Policies: Past Trends, Present Issues, Future Prospects' in P de Senarclens and A Kazancigil (eds), *Regulating Globalization: Critical Approaches to Global Governance* (United Nations University Press, 2007) 216.

The CBD triggered a long standing and still unresolved debate about the role of intellectual property rights, which were supposed to be 'supportive of and not run counter to' the objectives of the CBD, and about harmonisation of the CBD with the intellectual property treaties administered by the WTO and WIPO.[51] The CBD envisaged a quid-pro-quo system and a compromise between biodiversity-rich resource providing countries, which were geographically located predominantly in the Global South, and technologically advanced users of such resources, with the strongest of those coming from the Global North. Resource providers were asked to 'endeavour to create conditions to facilitate access to genetic resources for environmentally sound uses' (Article 15(2)) on 'mutually agreed terms' (Article 15(4),[52] while users should involve resource providers in scientific research projects (Article 15(6) and provide access to and transfer of relevant technology (Article 16). Resource providers were envisaged to control access, which had to be on mutually agreed terms (Article 15(4)) and with prior informed consent of the resource provider (Article 15(5), leading to fair and equitable sharing of 'the results of research and development and the benefits arising from the commercial and other utilization of genetic resources' (Article 15(7)). A similar quid-pro-quo is envisaged for the transfer of technology which makes use of genetic resources provided by the contracting developing country party to the Convention (Article 16(3)). While WIPO has celebrated the success of some benefit-sharing arrangements,[53] in other cases users have simply shunned countries where benefit-sharing obligations were regarded as too stringent.[54] In any case, different models of access and benefit sharing are now seriously threatened and could be made obsolete by the dematerialisation of resources and digital sequencing information, which is discussed below.

While policy makers in resource providing countries hoped for technology transfer and income from a country's wealth of genetic resources, the 'indigenous and local communities' promoted in Article 8j to custodians of biodiversity could certainly hope for some trickle-down effects and application of the access and benefit sharing (ABS) and prior informed consent (PIC) goals to their TK and cultural expressions. This was subsequently made much more explicit in the Nagoya Protocol on Access to Genetic Resources and the Fair and Equitable Sharing of

[51] B Ong, 'Biodiversity and the Law: Mapping the International Legal Terrain' in McManis and Ong (n 29) 5, 9.

[52] This obligation somewhat limits the flexibility of the resource provider. I would like to thank the editors for pointing this out to me.

[53] Such as the commercialisation of the hoodia plant in South Africa, see 'Leveraging Economic Growth through Benefit Sharing' (ip-advantage), www.wipo.int/ipadvantage/en/details.jsp?id=2594, accessed 6 September 2023.

[54] As, for example, in the Philippines, see C Antons, '*Sui Generis* Protection for Plant Varieties and Traditional Knowledge in Biodiversity and Agriculture: The International Framework and National Approaches in the Philippines and India' (2010) 6 *Indian Journal of Law and Technology* 119, discussing Joint Administrative Order No 1 of 2005 and noting that until 2009, no access application had been processed under its bioprospecting guidelines.

Benefits Arising from their Utilization. The Nagoya Protocol was added to the CBD in 2010 and came into force in 2014, a few years after the adoption of the United Nations Declaration on the Rights of Indigenous Peoples (UNDRIP). UNDRIP is recognised in the preamble of the Nagoya Protocol and in provisions, which seek to ensure that the benefits collected by resource providing countries are passed on to indigenous and local communities (Article 5(2)) and that their PIC is obtained and mutually agreed terms are established (Articles 6(2), 7). Indigenous customary laws, community protocols and procedures are also promoted (Article 12(1)). Benefits are defined in an Annex to the Nagoya Protocol as monetary and non-monetary and they may include joint ownership of intellectual property rights.

Countries have implemented these objectives over the years in many different forms, for example as part of legislation on Indigenous Peoples' rights[55] and wildlife conservation and protection laws as in the Philippines,[56] biodiversity acts as in South Africa,[57] or in specific TK laws as in Kenya.[58] Overall, however, the results thus far are regarded as disappointing.[59] Among the reasons are (a) the difficulties to clearly identify the right holders and beneficiaries of newly introduced governance models,[60] in particular in countries in which the concept of 'Indigenous Peoples' is not easily accepted or interpreted differently[61] or where the community focus of Article 8j CBD is not applicable at all, because TK is distributed widely in mainstream society and becomes a form of national heritage, as, for example, with traditional forms of medicines in countries such as China, India, Thailand and Indonesia;[62] (b) the paternalistic attitudes of many

[55] R Andersen, 'The International Treaty on Plant Genetic Resources for Food and Agriculture: Toward the Realization of Farmers' Rights as a Means of Protecting and Enhancing Crop Genetic Diversity' in McManis and Ong (n 29) 144.

[56] C Antons, 'The International Debate about Traditional Knowledge and Approaches in the Asia-Pacific Region' in C Antons (ed), *Traditional Knowledge, Traditional Cultural Expressions and Intellectual Property Law in the Asia-Pacific Region* (Kluwer Law International, 2009) 60.

[57] R Wynberg, 'One Step Forward, Two Steps Back? Implementing Access and Benefit-sharing Legislation in South Africa' in McManis and Ong (n 29) 198.

[58] J Harrington, H Deacon and P Munyi, 'Sovereignty and Development: Law and the Politics of Traditional Knowledge in Kenya' (2021) 13(1) *Critical African Studies* 95; CK Mwangi, 'Traditional Knowledge and the Inclusive Subordination of African Customary Law in Kenya: Lessons from Personal Law' (2022) 66(1) *Journal of African Law* 47.

[59] Antons, 'Biodiversity' (n 29); G Dutfield, 'If We Have Never Been Modern, They Have Never Been Traditional: 'Traditional Knowledge', Biodiversity and the Flawed ABS Paradigm' in McManis and Ong (n 29) 276.

[60] C Antons, 'The Role of Traditional Knowledge and Access to Genetic Resources in Biodiversity Conservation in Southeast Asia' (2010) 19 *Biodiversity and Conservation* 1189; C McManis and Y Terán, 'Trends and Scenarios in the Legal Protection of Traditional Knowledge' in T Wong and G Dutfield (eds), *Intellectual Property and Human Development: Current Trends and Future Scenarios* (Cambridge University Press, 2011) 155; Dutfield (n 59) 248.

[61] Antons, 'The International Debate' (n 56) 51–52; P Drahos and S Frankel, 'Indigenous Peoples' Innovation and Intellectual Property: The Issues' in P Drahos and S Frankel (eds), *Indigenous Peoples' Innovation: Intellectual Property Pathways to Development* (ANU E Press, 2012) 10.

[62] C Antons, 'Epistemic Communities and the "People without History": The Contribution of Intellectual Property Law to the "Safeguarding" of Intangible Cultural Heritage' in I Calboli and S Ragavan (eds), *Diversity in Intellectual Property: Identities, Interests, and Intersections* (Cambridge University Press, 2015) 457–58.

governments vis-à-vis TK holding communities, which assume an important symbolic role in the envisaged exchange relationship between knowledge users and providers, but often leave empty-handed or are referred to vaguely defined compensation schemes;[63] and (c) the reduction of the debate to the exchange value and industrial potential of the genetic resources.[64] As often with such schemes, it is important to bear in mind that they operate in a development context, which is not a 'neutral background'.[65]

A particularly serious threat to developmentalist visions of a trade in genetic resources has emerged in recent years with the de-materialisation of these resources, made possible by synthetic biology and the use of DNA sequence information. This in turn makes it possible to bypass access and benefit-sharing obligations and has the potential to make Material Transfer Agreements obsolete.[66] This issue attracted considerable attention at COP15, which was the UN biodiversity summit in Montreal in December 2022. The summit succeeded in producing the Kunming-Montreal Global Biodiversity Framework (GBF), which includes four long-term goals and 23 action-oriented global targets.[67] Benefit sharing from the utilisation of genetic resources and related digital sequence information and traditional knowledge is covered in Goal C, foreseeing a substantial increase of shared benefits by 2050, and in Target 13, obliging governments to take effective legal, policy, administrative and capacity-building measures to achieve a significant increase of such benefits by 2030. To implement these goals and targets, the summit agreed on the establishment of a multilateral benefit-sharing mechanism.[68] Details will be worked out by an ad-hoc open-ended working group, which in an annex to the decision is provided with issues for further consideration. Parties, other governments, indigenous people, local communities and relevant organisations are invited to submit views on these issues, while the Executive Secretary is requested to compile various reports, including one on lessons learned from other international funding mechanisms, such as the Benefit-Sharing Fund of the International Treaty on Plant Genetic Resources for Food and Agriculture. Vice versa, it is expected that the decisions on this matter at COP15 will have ripple effects on these other treaties and frameworks.[69]

[63] Antons, 'The Role of Traditional Knowledge' (n 60) 1201; Antons, 'Biodiversity' (n 29) 322; Dutfield (n 59) 285.

[64] Dutfield (n 59) 286–87.

[65] MR Dove, 'Use of Global Legal Mechanisms to Conserve Local Biogenetic Resources: Problems and Prospects' in MR Dove, PE Sajise and AA Doolittle (eds), *Conserving Nature in Culture: Case Studies from Southeast Asia* (Yale University Southeast Asia Studies 2005) 302.

[66] MA Bagley, 'De-Materializing Genetic Resources: Synthetic Biology, Intellectual Property and the ABS Bypass' in McManis and Ong (n 29) 219, 227.

[67] Convention on Biological Diversity, www.cbd.int/conferences/2021-2022/cop-15/documents, accessed 3 January 2023.

[68] UNEP Draft Decision Submitted by the President (18 December 2022) UN Doc CBD/COP/15/L/30.

[69] Carbon Brief Staff, 'COP15: Key Outcomes Agreed at the UN Biodiversity Conference in Montreal' (*Carbon Brief*, 20 December 2022), www.carbonbrief.org/cop15-key-outcomes-agreed-at-the-un-biodiversity-conference-in-montreal/, accessed 3 January 2023.

Many of the GBF goals and targets urge respect for indigenous and local communities, their traditional knowledge and rights over their territories.[70] Sustainable agriculture is equally supported in targets which urge a reduction of 'the overall risk from pesticides and highly hazardous chemicals by at least half including through integrated pest management, based on science, taking into account food security and livelihoods';[71] and the sustainable management of areas under agriculture, aquaculture, fisheries and forestry, including through 'a substantial increase of the application of biodiversity friendly practices, such as sustainable intensification, agroecological and other innovative approaches contributing to the resilience and long-term efficiency and productivity of these production systems and to food security'.[72]

Not long after the CBD had established and promoted the concept of TK, the World Intellectual Property Organization (WIPO) entered the debate in 1998 with work in its newly created Global Issues Division on 'expressions of folklore',[73] 'indigenous knowledge' and genetic resources. The terminology subsequently changed when the WIPO Intergovernmental Committee on Intellectual Property and Genetic Resources, Traditional Knowledge and Folklore (IGC) was established in 2000. The IGC's work has been criticised, among other reasons, for failing to appreciate that TK does not fit the intellectual property framework; for the lack of consensus on the purpose of the negotiations at the outset of the negotiations; and that it was established as a practical solution to overcome a stalemate during a Diplomatic Conference related to another treaty, the Patent Law Treaty.[74] The IGC has been engaged in text-based negotiations with the objective of reaching agreement on a text of an international legal instrument or instruments for the protection of genetic resources, TK and traditional cultural expressions since 2009. Although progress has been slow in finding agreement on basic concepts and such issues as the circle of beneficiaries,[75] the WIPO General Assembly decided in 2022 to convene no later than in 2024 a Diplomatic Conference to conclude an International Legal Instrument Relating to Intellectual Property, Genetic Resources and Traditional Knowledge Associated with Genetic Resources.[76] The Diplomatic Conference in May 2024 adopted with some modifications a Basic

[70] See Goal C and Targets 1, 3, 5, 9, 19, 21 and 22.

[71] See Target 7.

[72] See Target 10.

[73] As far as 'expressions of folklore' were concerned, WIPO re-entered a debate in which it had been very active before, often jointly with UNESCO, see C Antons, 'Intellectual Property Rights in Indigenous Cultural Heritage: Basic Concepts and Continuing Controversies' in CB Graber, K Kuprecht and JC Lai (eds), *International Trade in Indigenous Cultural Heritage: Legal and Policy Issues* (Edward Elgar, 2012) 146.

[74] NP de Carvalho, 'Sisyphus Redivivus? The Work of WIPO on Genetic Resources and Traditional Knowledge' in McManis and Ong (n 29) 338, 340, 344–47.

[75] Antons, 'Intellectual Property Rights' (n 73) 172–74.

[76] WIPO, 'Assemblies of the Member States of WIPO: List of Decisions' (World Intellectual Property Organization, 2022).

Proposal prepared by the Secretariat.[77] The new WIPO Treaty on Intellectual Property, Genetic Resources and Associated Traditional Knowledge[78] includes a disclosure requirement in the patent laws of contracting parties, if inventions are based on genetic resources. The applicants in such cases have to disclose the country of origin or, if not known, the source of the genetic resources and, where there is associated TK, the Indigenous Peoples or local community that provided it or, in the alternative for both cases, provide information about the source of the material.[79] Where none of this information is available, a declaration to that effect can be made.[80] A requirement in the Basic Proposal that the claimed invention should be 'materially/directly' based on genetic resources was dropped in favour of a definition that the genetic resources or associated traditional knowledge 'must have been necessary for the claimed invention' and the claimed invention dependent on the specific properties of the genetic resources and/or the associated traditional knowledge. The treaty sets the bar for sanctions in cases of violations fairly high. Except in cases of fraudulent conduct or intent, applicants must be given an opportunity to rectify the failure to disclose the information.[81] Further, except in cases of the notoriously difficult to prove fraudulent intent, 'no Contracting Party shall revoke, invalidate or render unenforceable the conferred patent rights solely on the basis of an applicant's failure to disclose the information'.[82] Some countries, which have already introduced disclosure requirements and sanctioned non-compliance with a revocation of the patent under less stringent requirements,[83] will have to amend their laws upon ratification and entry into force of the treaty.

While the new treaty provides a result of the deliberations related to genetic resources and associated TK, text-based negotiations on draft articles related to TK and traditional cultural expressions respectively as well as stocktaking of further progress with regards to genetic resources will continue at the upcoming IGC meetings.[84] Writing in 2018, former Director of the WIPO Intellectual Property and Competition Policy Division Nuno Pires de Carvalho expressed scepticism, however, that a treaty on a *sui generis* intellectual property (IP) regime for TK could be concluded, enter into force, or become applicable.[85]

[77] Diplomatic Conference to Conclude an International Legal Instrument Relating to Intellectual Property, Genetic Resources and Traditional Knowledge Associated with Genetic Resources, 'Basic Proposal for an International Legal Instrument Relating to Intellectual Property, Genetic Resources and Traditional Knowledge Associated with Genetic Resources' (WIPO, 2023) ('Basic Proposal').

[78] WIPO Treaty on Intellectual Property, Genetic Resources and Associated Traditional Knowledge (WIPO, 2024).

[79] See Arts 3.1 and 3.2.

[80] Arts 3.3.

[81] Art 5.2 and 5.2(*bis*).

[82] Art 5.3 and 5.4.

[83] See, for example, Patents Act 1970 s 64(1)(p) (India); Law No 13 of 2016 on Patents, Art 132 (Indonesia).

[84] See the IGC's mandate for 2024 and 2025, www.wipo.int/export/sites/www/tk/en/igc/docs/igc-mandate-2024-2025.pdf, accessed 11 June 2024.

[85] Carvalho (n 74) 347.

C. The International Treaty on Plant Genetic Resources for Food and Agriculture and the UN Declarations on the Rights of Indigenous Peoples (UNDRIP) and on the Rights of Peasants and Other People Working in Rural Areas (UNDROP)

In harmony with the CBD,[86] but specifically for the conservation and sustainable use of plant genetic resources for food and agriculture and the fair and equitable sharing of benefits arising from their use, the International Treaty on Plant Genetic Resources for Food and Agriculture (ITPGRFA) was concluded in 2001 under the auspices of the Food and Agriculture Organization of the United Nations (FAO). It entered into force in 2004. As of May 2022, it had 149 contracting parties.[87] The conclusion of this treaty was the culmination of earlier discussions in FAO, which had produced non-binding resolutions in 1989 and 1991 as Annexes to the International Undertaking on Plant Genetic Resources of 1983. These resolutions introduced the concept of farmers' rights and confirmed the sovereignty of states over their plant genetic resources as concessions to countries from the Global South, who in return had to give up their long-standing opposition to intellectual property rights in agriculture and agree to an interpretation that plant breeders' rights were not incompatible with the International Undertaking.[88] Although not focused on agriculture, the CBD subsequently extended the circle of intellectual property rights for biotechnology also to patents (Article 16(2) CBD).[89] The ITPGRFA continues the promotion of farmers' rights of the earlier FAO resolutions. The treaty recognises the contributions of 'local and indigenous communities and farmers' to the conservation and development of plant genetic resources (Article 9.1) and it obliges parties to take measures for the protection of relevant traditional knowledge (Article 9.2(a)), enable equitable participation in benefit-sharing (Article 9.2(b)), and allow for participation, at the national level, in relevant decision-making processes (Article 9.2(c)). Article 9.3 confirms the traditional farmers' privilege to 'save, use, exchange and sell farm-saved seed/propagating material'. The confirmation is, however, 'subject to national law and as appropriate'. The other farmers' rights are also required from contracting parties only 'as appropriate, and subject to national legislation'.[90] To remove any doubts about the prerogative in this regard, Article 9.2 confirms that 'the responsibility for realizing Farmers' Rights … rests with national governments'. Accordingly, the ITPGRFA has been criticised for its weak language

[86] See the ITPGRFA, Art 1.

[87] 'Contracting Parties' (Food and Agriculture Organization of the United Nations), www.fao.org/plant-treaty/countries/membership/en/, accessed 6 January 2023.

[88] Ariffin (n 50) 218–19; Andersen (n 55) 136–39.

[89] I would like to thank the editors for pointing out this further shift regarding the strength of the available intellectual property rights.

[90] Antons, 'The International Debate' (n 56) 44–45.

related to farmers' rights.[91] The Multilateral System of Access and Benefit-Sharing introduced by the treaty has also not produced the desired results.[92] Analysts have pointed out that the benefit-sharing fund has been operating solely on the basis of donor country voluntary contributions rather than the envisaged user-based payments, prompting unsuccessful reform efforts between 2013 and 2019.[93] There are no mechanisms ensuring that royalties reach the farming population.[94] Finally, the limiting effect of the treaty on the acquisition of intellectual property rights related to material received from the Multilateral System may not work where such resources have been modified.[95]

While this survey leaves a rather gloomy picture of the international legal framework regarding biodiversity and plant genetic resources as not very effective,[96] commentators have seen 'rays of hope'[97] in developments at the UN Human Rights Council, which led to the adoption in 2018 by the UN General Assembly of the United Nations Declaration on the Rights of Peasants and other People Working in Rural Areas (UNDROP).[98] It follows the earlier UN Declaration on the Rights of Indigenous Peoples of 2007 (UNDRIP), which also included a few provisions of relevance in this context. Article 24(1) UNDRIP guarantees rights to traditional medicines and health practices, including conservation of medicinal plants, animals and minerals. Article 31(1) guarantees Indigenous Peoples' rights to 'maintain, control, protect and develop their cultural heritage, traditional knowledge and traditional cultural expressions, as well as the manifestations of their sciences, technologies and cultures', which include human and genetic resources, seeds, medicines and knowledge of the properties of fauna and flora.[99]

UNDRIP and the other treaties for the protection of biodiversity discussed earlier were referred to in the Preamble of UNDROP, concluded 11 years later. UNDROP also makes reference to the agreed development goals and the 2030 Agenda for Sustainable Development. UNDROP defines the subjects of the

[91] R Beck, 'Farmers' Rights and Open Source Licensing' (2010) 1(2) *Arizona Journal of Environmental Law & Policy* 167–218; quoted in Janis, Jervis and Peet (n 30) 499. See also Andersen (n 55) 144, who finds hardly any examples of direct monetary benefit sharing between resource providers and recipients as a result of country specific legislation, and, at 146, few examples of legislation on farmers' participation in decision-making.

[92] Beck (ibid) 192; Janis, Jervis and Peet (n 30) 499.

[93] E Tsioumani, *Fair and Equitable Benefit-Sharing in Agriculture: Reinventing Agrarian Justice* (Routledge, 2020), 164; See also Bagley (n 66) 230.

[94] Janis, Jervis and Peet (n 30) 499; Andersen (n 55) 144; Beck (n 91) 193–94.

[95] Janis, Jervis and Peet (n 30), noting that Art 12.3(d) bans intellectual property rights on biological resources 'in the form received from the Multilateral System'; Antons, 'The International Debate' (n 56) 45; M Blakeney, 'Bioprospecting and Biopiracy' in B Ong (ed), *Intellectual Property and Biological Resources* (Marshall Cavendish, 2004) 417.

[96] Tsioumani (n 93) 167.

[97] ibid.

[98] UNGA RES 39/12 (21 January 2019) UNGA Doc A/RES/73/165; For a detailed analysis of the development of this Declaration see Claeys and Edelman (n 15).

[99] Antons, 'The International Debate' (n 56) 46–47.

declaration widely. It applies not just to small-scale and artisan farmers, but also to other people engaged in 'crop planting, livestock raising, pastoralism, fishing, forestry, hunting or gathering' and even to handicrafts related to agriculture or related occupations (Article 1.1 and 1.2). It applies further to 'indigenous peoples and local communities working on the land, transhumant, nomadic and semi-nomadic communities, and the landless' (Article 1.3) as well as to hired, migrant and seasonal workers (Article 1.4). TK is referred to in the context of such peoples' contribution to climate change adaptation and mitigation (Article 18.3), in the context of the right to seeds (Article 19.1 and 19.2), state promotion and protection of TK (Article 20), and freedom of cultural development (Article 26). Article 19.1 repeats the farmers' rights guarantees of the ITPGRFA of TK protection, benefit sharing, participation in decision-making and protection of the traditional seed-saving privilege. Quality seeds shall be available in sufficient quantity at an affordable price (Article 19.4), peasants shall be allowed to rely on their own or locally available seeds and decide on the crops and species they wish to grow (Article 19.5), and the needs of peasants and other people working in rural areas shall be included in research and development undertaking and priority setting (Article 19.7). Importantly for regulation, states 'shall ensure that seed policies, plant variety protection and other intellectual property laws, certification schemes and seed marketing laws respect and take into account the rights, needs and realities of peasants and other people working in rural areas' (Article 19.8). Certification schemes and seed marketing laws and policies are mentioned here next to intellectual property, because they often have a similar restrictive effect on the knowledge and practices of small-scale farmers.[100] The seeming 'paradox' that such rules originally intended to protect plant health[101] and farmers from the distribution of bad seeds,[102] contributed to removing the basis for plant health in the future[103] and began to show similarities with intellectual property laws,[104] can be explained with seed policies intended for the development of a private seed breeding and marketing industry.[105] In countries of the Global South, such considerations have to be seen in the developmentalist context of seed policies, which aim at building a national seed industry able to compete in an open market with international competitors.[106] The final section of this chapter will show how such considerations influence the law-making in this field in Indonesia in the context of the Association of Southeast Asian Nations (ASEAN) and as an example for many

[100] Kanniah and Antons, 'The Regulation of Innovation' (n 43) 290–92; Andersen (n 55) 148. Antons and others (n 16); Antons, Winarto and Prihandiani, 'Farmer-plant-breeders' (n 16).

[101] Andersen (n 55).

[102] 'India's New Seed Bill' (*Grain*, 12 July 2005), grain.org/article/entries/457-india-s-new-seed-bill%23_ftn10, accessed 9 January 2023.

[103] Andersen (n 55) 148.

[104] Antons, Winarto and Prihandiani, 'Farmer-plant-breeders' (n 16).

[105] J Kloppenburg, 'Repurposing the Master's Tools: The Open Source Seed Initiative and the Struggle for Seed Sovereignty' (2014) 41(6) *Journal of Peasant Studies* 1225.

[106] 'India's New Seed Bill' (n 104).

countries in the Global South, which try to promote the interests of an emerging seed industry while simultaneously protecting farmers and agrobiodiversity.

III. Intellectual Property, Seed Policies and Farmers' Rights in Indonesia and its ASEAN Neighbours

With a share of agriculture, forestry and fishing of 13.3 per cent of GDP,[107] Indonesia occupies a middle ground in Southeast Asia between wealthy small and predominantly food importing countries such as Singapore and Brunei,[108] and regional least developed economies such as Cambodia and Myanmar.[109] The economic pecking order of the ASEAN countries and their interest in promoting technology and/or biodiversity respectively is to some extent reflected in the membership of countries in and support for intellectual property and biodiversity related treaties and UN declarations respectively. While all ASEAN countries are members of the CBD and the WTO TRIPS Agreement and voted in favour of UNDRIP, Brunei, Singapore and Thailand are absent from the Nagoya Protocol.[110] Brunei, Singapore and Vietnam are not parties to the ITPGRFA, which Thailand has only signed but not yet ratified,[111] and Singapore has abstained from voting on UNDROP.[112] Finally, Singapore and Vietnam are currently the only ASEAN members of UPOV,[113] although this membership may soon expand significantly, supported in some cases by obligations from bilateral and regional free trade agreements.[114] According to the UPOV website, Brunei Darussalam, Malaysia, Myanmar and the Philippines have initiated the procedure for acceding to the UPOV Convention, while Cambodia, Indonesia, Lao PDR and Thailand are in contact with the Office of the Union for assistance in the development of laws based on the UPOV Convention.[115]

[107] The World Bank, 'Agriculture, Forestry, and Fishing, Value Added (% of GDP)' (The World Bank). data.worldbank.org/indicator/NV.AGR.TOTL.ZS, accessed 10 January 2023.

[108] ibid (Agriculture, forestry and fishing contributed 0% to the GDP of Singapore and 1.3% to the GDP of Brunei Darussalam in 2021).

[109] ibid (Agriculture, forestry and fishing contributed 22.8% to the GDP of Cambodia and 23.4% to the GDP of Myanmar in 2021).

[110] Biosafety Unit, 'Parties to the Nagoya Protocol', www.cbd.int/abs/nagoya-protocol/signatories, accessed 10 January 2023.

[111] 'Contracting Parties' (Food and Agriculture Organization of the United Nations), www.fao.org/plant-treaty/countries/membership/en/, accessed 10 January 2023.

[112] 'United Nations Declaration on the Rights of Peasants and Other People Working in Rural Areas: Resolution / Adopted by the General Assembly' (*United Nations Digital Library System*, 17 December 2018), digitallibrary.un.org/record/1656160?ln=en, accessed 10 January 2023.

[113] List of members (n 34).

[114] C Antons and M Blakeney, 'Intellectual Property, Farmers' Rights and Agriculture in the ASEAN Countries' in C Antons and M Blakeney (eds), *Intellectual Property in South East Asia* (Edward Elgar, 2023) 343–44.

[115] Status in Relation to the International Union for the Protection of New Varieties of Plants (UPOV, 2024).

Acceding to UPOV or complying with UPOV standards will require amendments to the current plant variety protection laws in particular in the four older ASEAN members and middle-income economies Malaysia, Thailand, Indonesia and the Philippines. All four have experimented with *sui generis* elements in their plant variety acts,[116] which were otherwise drafted largely based on the UPOV model. Modifications from UPOV standards relate to the extent of the traditional seed-saving privilege, the introduction of two-tier systems of protection for 'new' and 'local' varieties, and the establishment of Plant Variety Protection or Gene Trust Funds, as in Thailand and the Philippines.[117] Some of these laws are said to have been influenced and inspired by the Indian Protection of Plant Varieties and Farmers' Rights Act (PPVFR Act) of 2001.[118] This legislation continues to be regarded as a model how to create legal space for farmers' rights,[119] although commentators have found that farmers' varieties applied for and registered in India were concentrated on rice[120] and benefit-sharing mechanisms did not work.[121] Drawing conclusions from a case study in Kerala, India, Blakeney and others[122] report that all farmers' varieties from Kerala were registered under the PPVFR Act by the M. S. Swaminathan Research Foundation to preserve biodiversity and promote sustainable agriculture, but that there is no evidence of attempts to seek benefit-sharing in relation to the use of such farmers' varieties in the development of new varieties. As for the registration of farmers and local community varieties in Malaysia, Kanniah[123] finds only a single registration. The experiences with plant variety protection funds also have not been encouraging. Writing in 2016, Gagné and Ratnasatien[124] found only 'modest income' for the Plant Variety Protection Fund of Thailand, while Lertdhamtewe and Jefferson concluded a few years later that 'the extent to which disbursements from the Plant Varieties Protection Fund have actually benefitted farmers is unclear'.[125]

[116] Antons and Blakeney (n 114) 331–41; C Antons, 'Intellectual Property in Plant Material in the ASEAN Countries' (2022) 28(2) *Southwestern Journal of International Law* 534.

[117] Antons and Blakeney (n 114).

[118] For the Malaysian legislation see Ida Madieha bt Abdul Ghani Azmi, 'The Protection of Plant Varieties in Malaysia' (2004) 7(6) *Journal of World Intellectual Property* 889.

[119] See, for example, Andersen (n 55) 149.

[120] K Peschard, 'Farmers' Rights and Food Sovereignty: Critical Insights from India' (2014) 41(6) *Journal of Peasant Studies* 1093.

[121] K Peschard, 'Seed Wars and Farmers' Rights: Comparative Perspectives from Brazil and India' (2017) 44(1) *Journal of Peasant Studies* 154.

[122] M Blakeney and others, 'Agricultural Innovation and the Protection of Traditional Rice Varieties: Kerala a Case Study' (2020) 3 *Frontiers in Sustainable Food Systems* 8.

[123] R Kanniah, 'Implementation of the Plant Variety Protection Laws of Indonesia, Malaysia and the Philippines: Trends and Future Prospects' in K Adhikari and DJ Jefferson (eds), *Intellectual Property, Law and Plant Protection* (Routledge, 2020) 81.

[124] G Gagné and C Ratanasatien, 'Commentary on Thailand's Plant Variety Protection Act' in M Halewood (ed), *Farmers' Crop Varieties and Farmers' Rights: Challenges in Taxonomy and Law* (Routledge, 2016) 315.

[125] P Lertdhamtewe and DJ Jefferson, 'A Fresh Look at the Protection of "Domestic" and "Wild" Plant Varieties in Thailand' in Adhikari and Jefferson (n 123) 159.

Article 7 of Indonesia's Law No 29 of 2000 on Plant Variety Protection stipulates that local plant varieties 'owned by the community are controlled by the state'. There is no second-tier registration system for farmer varieties, as in India or Malaysia. The government explanation of the aims of the law makes it clear that its purpose is to foster the use of Indonesia's natural wealth for the creation of 'superior varieties' to support the development of the agricultural sector and national development in general and to achieve an integrated development of agribusiness and seed industry, which is supposed to join the ongoing efforts of government research bodies.[126] As a consequence, the implementing Government Regulation No 13 of 2004 on the Naming, Registration and Use of an Initial Variety for the Making of Essentially Derived Varieties regards local varieties as input material for improved varieties. It puts government authorities in charge of registering the local varieties and concluding agreements with potential users. Such agreements 'may' include compensation to the variety-owning community (Article 9(4)). If compensation is included, it is to be used at the discretion of the authorities for broadly worded purposes such as raising the prosperity of the community, conservation of the variety, and conservation efforts related to genetic resources in the locality of the variety (Article 10(1)). Regarding the important seed-saving privilege, Article 10(1) of Law No 29/2000 allows for the use of a part of the harvest for non-commercial purposes. What this means is outlined in the explanatory memorandum to the provision, which clarifies that it concerns 'the activities of individuals and small farmers in particular for their own needs' and does not allow further distribution to accommodate the needs of a group of people.

While intellectual property rights related to plant varieties are certainly a matter of concern for Indonesian farmers,[127] a more immediate and pressing concern has been the government's seed certification and standardisation requirements, which have made it difficult for farmers to release and exchange their cultivars. These led to the prosecution of farmers under a previous law for releasing and dealing with farm-saved seeds.[128] Following a constitutional challenge brought by NGOs and individual farmers, the Indonesian Constitutional Court declared two key provisions of the previous law unconstitutional.[129] In 2019, this law was replaced with Law No 22 of 2019 on the Sustainable Agricultural Cultivation System. The new law codifies exemptions for small farmers, mandated by the Constitutional Court, from licensing requirements for search and collection of genetic resources and from requirements that results of their plant breeding must be officially released by the government. In both cases, however, new reporting requirements to central

[126] See Antons and Sreedevi Babu (n 16).

[127] S Ghimire and others, 'Plant Variety Protection Law and Farmers' Rights to Save, Exchange and Breed Seeds: The Case of Indonesia' (2021) 16(9) *Journal of Intellectual Property Law and Practice* 1013.

[128] For these prosecutions under Law No 12 of 1992 on the Plant Cultivation System, see F Utomo, *Bersemi Dalam Tekanan Global: Kriminalisasi Petani, Inisiatif Benih Lokal dan Uji Materi UU No. 12/1992 tentang Sistem Budidaya Tanaman* (Jakarta, Yayasan FIELD Indonesia, 2013).

[129] Mahkamah Konstitusi, Decision No 99/PUU-X/2012 of 9 July 2013, 123–29.

and regional governments have been introduced. The new law also restricts the geographical space, in which small farmers are allowed to disseminate their informal varieties to just one regency or city.[130] A certain ambiguity stems finally from the fact that the new law, as is often the case in Indonesia, leaves all implementing regulations for the former law in force, as long as they are not in conflict with the new law.[131] There is no sunset clause requiring the review and update of such regulations. This also leaves in force the Regulation of the Minister of Agriculture No 38 of 2019 on the Release of Plant Varieties, which still refers to Law No 12 of 1992, although it was issued less than three months before this law was replaced by the new law. Article 64 of this Ministerial Regulation requires small farmer varieties to be named and registered with the authorities; requirements which are no longer mentioned in the subsequent Law No 22 of 2019.[132]

IV. Conclusion

The SDG 'zero hunger' and its targets has linked environmental, public health and socio-economic concerns and thereby created possibilities for more holistic discussions. Sustainable agriculture also plays an important role in many of the goals and targets of the Kunming-Montreal GBF adopted at COP15 in 2022. Nevertheless, critics have urged to remain wary of 'productionist' arguments, visible in discourses on scarcity and sustainable intensification. Equally important is, however, that conflicts between policy goals remain unresolved, which allow, on the one hand, the temporary monopolisation of seeds and other agricultural input material under intellectual property rights, while, on the other hand, seeking to promote the aims and targets of the CBD and the Nagoya Protocol. While discussions about the harmonisation of these policy goals have made little progress, intellectual property rights in agriculture have expanded dramatically since the conclusion of the WTO TRIPS Agreement in the early 1990s, as is visible in the continuing growth of UPOV. The governments of countries in the Global South on average have not resisted these trends and given up their initial

[130] On Law No 22 of 2019, see Antons, Winarto and Prihandiani, 'Farmer-plant-breeders' (n 16) 602–03.

[131] Law No 22 of 2019, Art 129.

[132] Noteworthy in Indonesia is also the government promotion of food estates on what Indonesians refer to as the 'outer islands' – the comparatively sparsely populated islands outside of Java and Bali. The government has initiated controversial large-scale estate developments in Central Kalimanatan, North Sumatra and West Papua, see DF Rahman, 'Explainer: All you need to know about the govt's food estates' *The Jakarta Post* (30 September 2020). Analysts have pointed out that they rely on support from the army, encroach on forests and the habitat of minorities and are swiftly becoming the next agricultural frontier, see L Ginting and O Pye, 'Resisting Agribusiness Development: The Merauke Integrated Food and Energy Estate in West Papua, Indonesia' (2013) 6(1) *ASEAS – Austrian Journal of Southeast Asian Studies* 160; HN Jong, 'Indonesia's militarized agriculture raises social, environmental red flags' (*Mongabay*, 27 October 2020), news.mongabay.com/2020/10/indonesia-militarized-agriculture-food-estate-kalimantan-sumatra/, accessed 6 September 2023.

resistance to intellectual property rights in agriculture.[133] They have introduced laws that combine strong intellectual property protection and seed certification standards for breeders and agribusinesses with weak and difficult to implement support measures for indigenous and local farmers such as discretionary forms of compensation. Multilateral and national funds to collect and distribute funds from access and benefit sharing remain a focus, although the results with them so far have been disappointing. Analysts express hope in a developing 'international law from below',[134] which is based on the more holistic approaches of food sovereignty and food systems analysis. Indeed, transnational movements such as La Via Campesina have played an important role in the adoption of UNDROP.[135] Such movements, however, are made up of NGOs mainly operating at the national level and dependent on the political space granted by national governments, which can be restrained by hegemonic discourses about development. Still, lobbying at sympathetic international organisations like the UN Human Rights Commission and FAO as well as public interest litigation and activism at national level for the time being may remain the best options to shift the focus of governments from exploitative and harmful agricultural practices to truly sustainable forms of agriculture.

[133] The very significant expansion of UPOV membership, discussed above under section II.A, is of course the best indicator of this trend. Those countries in the Global South, which are not yet members of UPOV, are under considerable pressure to accede to the Convention and many have promised to do so or to apply UPOV standards in regional or bilateral Free Trade Agreements, see for the examples of Malaysia, Indonesia and the Philippines, Antons, 'Intellectual Property in Plant Material' (n 116). For these and further countries in Asia and South America, see Antons, 'Intellectual Property in Plant Material' (n 32) 248–50. Some countries in Asia, South and Central America have even promised to offer patent protection for plant-related inventions besides plant variety protection or to 'endeavour' to do so, see Antons, 'Intellectual Property in Plant Material' (n 32) 246–48. These developments continue the paradigm shift regarding the international framework for intellectual property in agriculture, which began with the re-interpretation of the FAO International Undertaking for plant genetic resources, the subsequent inclusion of intellectual property rights in the CBD, as discussed in section II.B and the biotechnology clause of Art 27(3)(b) TRIPS, discussed in section II.A.

[134] Tsioumani (n 93), quoting B Rajagopal, *International Law from Below: Development, Social Movements and Third World Resistance* (Cambridge University Press, 2013).

[135] Claeys and Edelman (n 15).

10

Climate Change Induced Forced Displacement: Perils, Protection and Possibilities

SUMAIYA KHAIR

I. Introduction

People move for a variety of reasons. While some move voluntarily in search of better opportunities, for others the act of leaving home and heading for unfamiliar destinations is more often a matter of compulsion than choice. These movements may take place either within the country or across national borders. While forced movements may stem from social, economic and political factors, fear and/or deprivation are pivotal to such movements. Some of the traditional push factors attributed to forced movements include poverty, unemployment, conflicts, persecution, discrimination, exclusion and human rights abuse. Climate change, or rather its impact, is increasingly seen as contributing to this phenomenon, as people are often compelled to migrate in their attempts to cope with changes in the climate.[1] The changes can result from both the slow onset of weather events or rapid onset impacts.

The Framework Convention on Climate Change (UNFCCC) defines climate change as 'a change of climate which is attributed directly or indirectly to human activity that alters the composition of the global atmosphere and which is in addition to natural climate variability observed over comparable time periods' (Article 1). Climate change is typically manifested in rise in temperature (commonly referred

[1] There are divergent views on whether climatic and environmental changes do indeed induce human mobility. Myers and Kent (N Myers and J Kent, 'Environmental Exodus: An Emergent Crisis in the Global Arena' (Climate Institute, 1995)), for example, believe that millions of people are likely to be forcibly displaced as a result of environmental factors, whereas Black (R Black, *Refugees, Environment and Development* (Routledge, 1998); R Black, 'Environmental Refugees: Myth or Reality?' (2001) UNHCR Working Papers 34, 1–19) maintains that environmental factors alone do not account for forced migration but that it is linked to political and economic factors. This chapter does not seek to test either of these two views. It only attempts to examine the vulnerabilities and risks experienced by people who have been displaced as a result of climatic and environmental calamities.

to as global warming), rising sea levels resulting from melting of glaciers, salinity, storm surges, changes in rainfall patterns, frequent floods, desertification, droughts and tornadoes. All environmental and climate changes are interconnected and interdependent. Unpredictable weather patterns also lead to intense natural disasters, to the extent that nine out of every 10 natural disasters today are said to be climate-related.[2] As such, 'environmental change' and 'climate change' often have the same connotation.

Although not all regions and not all peoples will experience the impact of climate change equally, globally and nationally climate change poses a threat to the socio-economic advancement of people, their security, survival and livelihoods. While it is fairly easy to follow the direct impacts of climate change, its secondary implications, such as human displacement, are not so clear. The first UN intergovernmental assessment report on climate change predicted that climate change would impact human migration as millions would be displaced due to shoreline erosion, coastal flooding and severe drought.[3] Climate displacement depends on particular characteristics of the climate crisis and the region where they occur. The Intergovernmental Panel on Climate Change (IPCC) Working Group II Sixth Assessment Report (2022)[4] observes that extreme climate and weather conditions are triggering displacement in all regions, particularly where climate hazards correspond to high vulnerability and low adaptive capacity. It is difficult to distinguish between forced and voluntary movements in situations where the onset of climate and environmental changes is slow as opposed to sudden onset of calamities. Zetter[5] explains that in slow-onset climate and environment scenarios, human movement might initially be voluntary, both internally and cross-border, but subsequently become forced due to permanent depletion of resources, for example, water or grazing land, or due to prolonged inundations, which render livelihoods impossible. Again, the nature of the movement can be temporary or permanent. Extreme hazards usually cause temporary displacement, whereas annual flooding, such as in Bangladesh, renders thousands of people permanently displaced.

The consequences of climate change are most likely to affect developing countries in the Global South, like Africa, the Asian mega deltas and small islands – the citizens of which are heavily reliant on natural resources and systems for their basic livelihoods.[6] It is estimated that by 2050, as many as 216 million people are likely to

[2] 'Opening Remarks by Sir John Holmes, USG for Humanitarian Affairs and ERC at the DIHAD 2008 Conference', reliefweb.int/report/world/opening-remarks-sir-john-holmes-usg-humanitarian-affairs-and-erc-dihad-2008-conference, accessed 14 May 2022.

[3] WMO and UNEP, 'Climate Change: The 1990 and 1992 IPCC Assessments' (Intergovernmental Panel on Climate Change, 1992) 103.

[4] 'AR6 Climate Change 2022: Impacts, Adaptation and Vulnerability – IPCC' (IPCC), www.ipcc.ch/report/sixth-assessment-report-working-group-ii, accessed 22 June 2022.

[5] R Zetter, 'Protecting Environmentally Displaced People. Developing the Capacity of Legal and Normative Frameworks' (Refugee Studies Centre, University of Oxford, 2011) 14.

[6] UNFCC, *Climate Change: Impacts, Vulnerabilities and Adaptation in Developing Countries* (UNFCC, 2007) 18–26.

move within their own countries due to slow-onset climate change impacts, which will affect the poorest and most vulnerable regions and threaten to reverse development gains.[7] According to IDMC's Global Report on Internal Displacement (GRID), disasters played a key role in inducing large-scale internal displacements globally, with 23.7 million recorded in 2021.[8] Weather-related displacement, which accounted for 94 per cent of the total, resulted from preemptive evacuations in the face of cyclones and floods which affected densely populated areas of Asia and the Pacific region. China, the Philippines and India recorded their highest figures in five years at six million, 5.7 million and 4.9 million, respectively. In South Asia, extreme weather conditions, accompanied by rapid economic growth and urbanisation, are instigating human movements.[9] Therefore, internal displacement alone accounts for a large number of the climate displaced.

There is no specific legally binding international instrument safeguarding the climate displaced, whether internal or external. The lack of adequate legal protection exposes them to human rights abuse and insecurity. Drawing on the Global South experience, this chapter expounds on the risks and vulnerabilities that the climate-displaced face and their coping mechanisms, examines the international legal framework and gaps in protection, and concludes by suggesting possible ways forward.

II. Forced Displacement: Risks and Vulnerabilities

Existing literature on forced human movements uses the terms 'forced movement', 'forced migration' and 'forced displacement' interchangeably. Movements are 'forced' by life-threatening circumstances (induced by the threat or impact of hazardous events), or 'obligatory' following the directives of officials acting in the public interest, such as orders to evacuate in anticipation of or after a disaster.[10] Notwithstanding the different terminology, forced movements, whether in the sense of displacement or migration, implicitly signifies the involuntary nature of the passage, which has serious consequences for human rights and security.

The consequences of forced displacement are profound and involve human suffering which includes, but is not limited to, the loss of homes, lands and

[7] V Clement and others, 'Acting on Internal Climate Migration. Groundswell Part 2' (World Bank, Washington, DC, 2021) xxii, openknowledge.worldbank.org/handle/10986/36248, accessed 2 June 2022.

[8] 'All-Time High of Nearly 60 Million People Internally Displaced Worldwide' (IDMC – Internal Displacement Monitoring Centre, 19 May 2022), www.internal-displacement.org/news/all-time-high-of-nearly-60-million-people-internally-displaced-worldwide/, accessed 22 June 2022.

[9] J Podesta, 'The Climate Crisis, Migration, and Refugees' (*Brookings*, 25 July 2019), www.brookings.edu/articles/the-climate-crisis-migration-and-refugees/, accessed 11 March 2022.

[10] IDMC, 'Positioned for Action. Displacement in the Sendai Framework for Disaster Risk Reduction' (2017) Briefing Paper (16 February) 4, www.researchgate.net/publication/319185810_Positioned_for_action_Displacement_in_the_Sendai_Framework_for_disaster_risk_reduction, accessed 26 October 2022.

livelihoods, and the weakening of family structures and social networks, all of which impede the capacity and ability of displaced populations to lead a decent and normal life. The problems that plague the forced displaced are multi-dimensional.[11] Researchers contend that forced displacement causes 'massive loss not only of commodities such as the home, income, land or other forms of property, but also of less tangible symbolic goods, such as cultural heritage, friendship and a sense of belonging to a particular place',[12] and the 'pernicious effects on individuals, families and communities' are wide-ranging which include 'impoverishment, social isolation, exclusion from health, welfare and education provision, the breakdown of social relationships and support structures, and the undermining of authority structures and social roles'.[13]

The risks and vulnerabilities experienced by the forced displaced hinge on several factors, for instance, the reasons for their displacement, the location they are forced to move to, the mode of movement, and their legal status. Although risks and vulnerability interact and go hand in hand, risks heighten vulnerabilities in particular contexts. The nature and magnitude of the risks and vulnerability vary according to the age, gender and other characteristics of the displaced people and are likely to be different at different stages of the displacement cycle.[14]

When displacement becomes inevitable, the affected populations have little choice in how they move and where they move to, their immediate priority being reaching a place of safety. The destination for the forced displaced is primarily a matter of collective choice, informed by considerations such as proximity, ease of travel and other perceived advantages. The journey itself can be arduous and fraught with risks of exploitation and abuse, particularly when it is undertaken through irregular channels, by traversing rough landscapes, and by dodging border control. Desperate, the forced displaced often fall prey to human smuggling networks, which facilitate passage across borders in exchange for some form of payment.[15] Evidence shows that smuggled individuals are at a heightened risk of violence and exploitation, deprivation of freedom, and unpaid work.[16] Women and girls are at particular risk as they are easy targets of human trafficking syndicates, which are quick to capitalise on the uncertainties

[11] See R Sabates-Wheeler, 'Mapping differential vulnerabilities and rights: "opening" access to social protection for forcibly displaced populations' (2019) 7(38) *Comparative Migration Studies* 1; E Alobo and S Obaji, 'Internal Displacement in Nigeria and the Case for Human Rights Protection for Displaced Persons' (2016) 51 *Journal of Law, Policy and Globalization* 26; E Mooney, 'The Concept of Internal Displacement and the Case for Internally Displaced Persons as a Category of Concern' (2005) 24(3) *Refugee Survey Quarterly* 9.

[12] S Castles and others, 'Developing DFID's Policy Approach to Refugees and Internally Displaced Persons, Volume 1: Consultancy Report and Policy Recommendations' (Refugees Studies Centre, University of Oxford, February 2005) 29.

[13] ibid.

[14] Sabates-Wheeler (n 11).

[15] United Nations, *Global Study on Smuggling of Migrants 2018* (United Nations, 2018) 9, www.unodc.org/documents/data-and-analysis/glosom/GLOSOM_2018_web_small.pdf.

[16] ibid 9.

and insecurities of forced displacement. Single or unaccompanied women and girls and women heads of households are found to experience higher degrees of sexual and gender-based violence.[17]

The internally displaced similarly encounter many risks as they 'transit through and [sic] settle (temporarily or permanently) in marginal, hazard-prone areas, with limited ability to access locally available resources and services, little knowledge of the local hazard context, and skillsets and capacities' to cope with the challenges of relocation.[18] In Bangladesh, for example, victims of cyclones, flooding and river bank erosion make their way from rural areas to the urban slums where they not only have limited access to resources and services, but where they are also exposed to different urban hazards.[19] Thus, while they may have effectively moved out of harm's way in the places of origin, in reality, they are confronted with new risks and vulnerabilities in the chosen destinations. As noted by Black and others, 'people are as likely to migrate into places of environmental vulnerability as away from them'.[20]

The breakdown of the social and family structures following displacement compels the displaced to depend on others for basic needs, such as, food, water, sanitation and shelter. Access to health, sanitation, education, social security, medical services and employment is also constrained. Housed in make-shift settings in sub-standard conditions, the forced displaced experience food insecurity, malnutrition and various health hazards, including psycho-social trauma.[21] Possessing very little bargaining power, they experience systematic discrimination and socio-cultural marginalisation, making integration difficult. In most cases, the areas of relocation, whether rural or urban, lack the infrastructure to house such large populations for indefinite periods. Regrettably, 'protracted displacement translates into long-lasting, acute exposure to additional hazards, as well as a progressive erosion of the displaced persons' resilience, [leading to] more frequent and more intense impacts'.[22] Protracted situations also 'set the scene for profound social and cultural changes, and these may entail political radicalization'.[23]

Displaced children constitute a particularly vulnerable group as they experience a higher risk of violence, abuse and exploitation, particularly when they travel alone, without family or kin.[24] Separated from their families during displacement,

[17] UNODC, *Global Report on Trafficking in Persons 2018* (United Nations, 2018) 9, www.unodc.org/e4j/data/_university_uni_/global_report_on_trafficking_in_persons_2018.html, accessed 7 July 2022.

[18] L Guadagno, 'Moving from One Risk to Another: Dynamics of Hazard Exposure and Disaster Vulnerability for Displaced Persons, Migrants and Other People on the Move' (2021).

[19] See KE McNamara and others, 'Insecure Hope: The Challenges Faced by Urban Slum Dwellers in Bhola Slum, Bangladesh' (2016) 5(1) *Migration and Development* 1, 19.

[20] R Black and others, 'Migration as Adaptation' (2011) *Nature* 478, 447–49.

[21] E Mooney, 'The Concept of Internal Displacement and the Case for Internally Displaced Persons as a Category of Concern' (2005) 24(3) *Refugee Survey Quarterly* 9, 17.

[22] Guadagno (n 18) 3.

[23] A Christensen and N Harold, *Forced Displacement. The Development Challenge* (The World Bank Group, 2009) 10.

[24] UNICEF, *Harrowing Journeys: Children and Youth on the Move across the Mediterranean Sea, at Risk of Trafficking and Exploitation* (UNICEF, 2017) 31–32.

unaccompanied children lead precarious lives in the destination areas. Even when they are in the company of their families, they are exposed to contextual, physical, psycho-social risks and vulnerabilities. Indeed, boys and girls tend to experience different risks. Girls are particularly prone to sexual exploitation and gender-based violence.[25] Temporary shelters in camps offer little or no protection from sexual violence, as seen in Haiti.[26] In Somalia, there have been incidents where girls have been sexually assaulted when foraging for firewood and water.[27] In Afghanistan and Yemen, girls are married off at a very early age to offset the insecurities.[28] Boys, on the other hand, are found joining armed groups in exchange for food, as in South Sudan.[29] Others work in hazardous occupations in the informal sector. Deprived of developmental opportunities, displaced children have to fend for themselves and face an uncertain future.

Where forced displacement occurs beyond national borders, the vulnerabilities increase manifold. Compelled to relocate to unfamiliar environments and often devoid of knowledge of the local language, customs and culture, the forced displaced face difficulties on multiple fronts. Clustered in temporary camps, their movement is restricted, their access to resources is limited, and they experience hostility, discrimination and xenophobia in the host community. During emergency movements, people are often unable to bring along important documents to prove their identity. This renders their status irregular, which, in turn, deprives them of legal protection. Lacking political representation, they are unsure of what rights they have and where to go for help. They are largely unable to comprehend local administrative processes, which are usually lengthy, convoluted and non-transparent. Their vulnerability is compounded

> through increasing barriers to international migration, including its criminalization, migration policies based on deterrence, border restrictions, restrictions on migrants' access to labour markets and a lack of safe, accessible and regular migration pathways for work, education, family unity and humanitarian needs.[30]

[25] IDMC, *Women and Girls in Internal Displacement* (IDMC, March 2020) 14.

[26] CH Logie and others, '"Life under the Tent is Not Safe, Especially for Young Women". Understanding intersectional violence among internally displaced youth in Leogane, Haiti' (2017) 10 *Global Health Action* 3.

[27] T Hassan, '"Here, Rape Is Normal"' (*Human Rights Watch*, 2 August 2023), www.hrw.org/report/2014/02/13/here-rape-normal/five-point-plan-curtail-sexual-violence-somalia, accessed 7 July 2022.

[28] S Hall and others, 'Challenges of IDP Protection: Research Study on the Protection of Internally Displaced Persons in Afghanistan' (2012); J Freccero and A Taylor, 'Child Marriage in Humanitarian Crises: Girls and Parents Speak out on Risk and Protective Factors, Decision-Making, and Solutions' (Human Rights Center at the University of California, Berkeley; Information and Research Center King Hussein Foundation, Plan International UK; Save the Children, 2021) 18; K Hunersen and others, 'Child Marriage in Yemen: A Mixed Methods Study in Ongoing Conflict and Displacement' (2021) 34(4) *Journal of Refugee Studies* 4551, 4562.

[29] S Bray-Watkins, *Situation of IDP Children: War Child UK's Recommendations for Consideration and Inclusion in General Assembly Report* (War Child, 2019).

[30] UNGA Res 35/20 (23 April 2018) UN Doc A/HRC/38/21.

While the impact of forced displacement is multi-dimensional and far-reaching, the consequences faced by host territories are no less. The presence of large numbers of people in any territory, whether in-country or across borders, creates increased demand for resources. Hard-pressed to start an altogether new existence, the displaced often cut down trees to use the wood for shelter and cooking and clear space for cultivating crops, which in turn, leads to deforestation and land degradation.[31]

All things considered, climate calamities induce loss and deprivation in the material, psycho-social and cultural sense and expose the forced displaced to innumerable risks and vulnerabilities in the short, medium and long terms.

III. Adaptation as a Coping Strategy

The intensity of extreme and multi-dimensional weather conditions is expected to cause serious strain on the socio-economic development, poverty reduction and security initiatives in the coming years. Adaptation in such situations is fundamental to the survival of climate-displaced populations. Communities, many of which are already struggling against poverty, will need to change their livelihoods, use alternative technologies, and find new ways of managing scarce resources.[32] Climate adaptation measures, preferably community-led, if implemented properly, can help reduce forced displacement and minimise its negative impacts. For example, early warning systems are effective in alerting communities about impending disasters, allowing for timely evacuation and reducing the risk of displacement. Climate-resilient infrastructure such as flood defences and storm and earthquake-resistant housing, and land use regulations to prevent the construction of settlements and infrastructure in high risk areas, potentially reduce the likelihood of people becoming homeless. Diversification of livelihoods equips communities to draw on alternative sources of income at times of disasters. Climate-resilient and drought-resistant agricultural practices and sustainable management of water, forests and fisheries can ensure food security and help deal with resource scarcity. The preservation and restoration of ecosystems, such as mangroves and wetlands, can mitigate the impact of sea-level rise and coastal erosion, and reduce the need for relocation.

While conventional narratives on the effects of climate change on human displacement primarily showcase the negative aspects of forced migration, evidence shows that human movements can also offer opportunities. Undoubtedly, 'people's ability to move, whether spontaneously or in an assisted manner, and whether

[31] I Ruiz and C Vargas-Silva, 'The Consequences of Forced Migration for Host Communities in Africa' (2017) 25 *Revue d'économie du développement* 135, 150.

[32] Food and Agriculture Organization of the United Nations, *The State of the World's Land and Water Resources for Food and Agriculture 2021 – Systems at Breaking Point: Main Report* (Food & Agriculture Org, 2022) 256–327.

more proactively or reactively, is a key component of their resilience – of their capacity to get out of harm's way and keep accessing resources and opportunities needed to cope with and recover from disasters'.[33] The act of moving seemingly has an 'intrinsic risk management value, allowing people a trade-off between the (present or future, well known) impacts they are (or will likely be) suffering in their places of origin and the (potential, less certain) ones they might face elsewhere'.[34] The UK government's Foresight report, which examines the likely movement of people within and outside their countries in the years between 2011 and 2060 due to global environmental change, recognises that 'migration in the face of global environmental change may not be just part of the "problem" but can also be part of the solution. In particular, planned and facilitated approaches to human migration can ease people out of situations of vulnerability'.[35] In fact, 'those who are unable or unwilling to relocate' might encounter greater risks.[36]

A study[37] on the link between climate/weather change and farmer migration in Bihar, India, reveals that migration has typically been a livelihood or survival strategy under adverse and extreme climate conditions. Although farmers moved either to diversify income sources or ensure smooth consumption, migration served as an adaptation strategy. The research found that migrating households had a comparative advantage over non-migrating households in terms of adaptive capacity; for example, they were more capable of adopting knowledge, capital and resource-intensive adaptation strategies due to remittances received from migrating household members. Therefore, migration enables households that are highly dependent on agriculture and natural resources, and consequently, vulnerable to climate-change impacts, to supplement incomes through remittances, investments and diversification of livelihoods.[38] This can have a multiplier effect on host communities. For example, in western Tanzania, researchers found that as a result of the refugee influx, some sections of the host communities experienced an increase in the size of the market for agricultural products, cheap and abundant labour, reduced prices for food products received as part of humanitarian assistance and sold by the refugees, and the transition of small rural settlements into busy market towns.[39] A World Bank report describes how

[33] Guadagno (n 18) 1.

[34] ibid.

[35] *Migration and Global Environmental Change: Future Challenges and Opportunities* (Final Project Report) (The Government Office for Science, 2011) 10.

[36] Black and others (n 20) 447.

[37] CK Jha and others, 'Migration as Adaptation Strategy to Cope with Climate Change. A Study of Farmers' Migration in Rural India' (2018) 10(1) *International Journal of Climate Change Strategies and Management* 121, 134–35.

[38] WN Adger and others, 'Migration, Remittances, Livelihood Trajectories, and Social Resilience' (2002) 31(4) *Ambio* 358.

[39] S Lakhani, *Forced Displacement: Moving from Managing Risk to Facilitating Opportunity* (World Bank Publications, 2013) 8; See also J-F Maystadt and P Verwimp, 'Winners and Losers Among A Refugee-hosting Population' (2009) CORE Discussion Paper 2009/34, 5–7.

> an inflow of forcibly displaced persons (whether refugees or IDPs) increases both the aggregate demand for goods and services and the labor supply in some segments of the job market. The increase in demand is typically driven by the consumption patterns of the forcibly displaced, humanitarian aid, and remittances. Depending on the structure of the economy, it may also create new jobs.[40]

Countries running microcredit schemes are often instrumental in helping displaced populations find paid work. This approach is particularly useful in protracted situations, and when the aid assistance begins to shrink. Forced displacement can have positive outcomes not only for those who move, but also for those who stay behind. For example, while rural-urban migrants benefit from higher incomes and more stable jobs as opposed to those who stay back in the rural areas, this can help narrow the rural-urban gap, and enhance household resilience to climate change impacts.[41] In many instances, the displaced have demonstrated their capability to adopt self-motivated coping strategies to start a new life, and even to flourish in their new environments.[42]

IV. Protecting the Forced Displaced

Forced climate displacement implicates both human rights and human security concerns. The 1972 Stockholm Declaration recognises the interdependence of human rights and the environment (Principle 1). In 1990, the Special Rapporteur on Human Rights and the Environment noted that 'drought and desertification cause massive displacement of peoples, social insecurity and widespread living conditions at a level not commensurate with human dignity',[43] and stated that 'such [displaced] persons have the right to life, the right to health, food and shelter, and the right not to be sent to any location where their lives or security are endangered'.[44] In 2009, the Office of the High Commissioner for Human Rights (OHCHR) released a report on the relationship between climate change and human rights and observed that climate change affected the right to life, adequate food, water, health, adequate housing, and self-determination[45] – rights that are integral to ensuring adequate condition of life for the displaced. Acknowledging that the effects of climate change exacerbate existing vulnerabilities, particularly of

[40] X Devictor, *Forcibly Displaced: Toward a Development Approach Supporting Refugees, the Internally Displaced, and Their Hosts* (World Bank Publications, 2017) 66.

[41] F Gemenne and others, 'Forced displacement related to the impacts of climate change and disasters', Reference Paper for the 70th Anniversary of the 1951 Refugee Convention (The Hugo Observatory, University of Liège (Belgium), 2021) 13.

[42] S Dryden-Peterson, '"I Find Myself as Someone Who is in the Forest": Urban Refugees as Agents of Social Change in Kampala, Uganda' (2006) 19(3) *Journal of Refugee Studies* 381.

[43] FZ Ksentini, 'Final Report Submitted to the UN Sub Commission on Prevention of Discrimination and Protection of Minorities' (United Nations Economic and Social Council, 1994) 46.

[44] ibid para 154, 40.

[45] UNHRC Res 7/23 (15 January 2009) UN Doc 1/HRC/10/61.

women, children, the elderly and persons with disabilities,[46] the report reiterates that, under international human rights law, states are obliged to comply with the principles of equality and non-discrimination when addressing the needs of these special groups.[47]

The UN Commission on Human Security emphasises that human security involves the protection of fundamental freedoms which also means protection of people from serious threats and situations.[48] In the context of climate change, therefore, human (in)security would signify the erosion of state capacity to protect its people from climatic shocks, which undermine livelihoods, divest people of their cultural and individual identities and compel them to migrate in search of a better life. Indeed, those who are already socially and economically marginalised, with little or no access to assets, will progressively experience human insecurity as the climate changes.[49] Judged from this perspective, human (in)insecurity may manifest in

> the relative presence/absence (or increase/decrease) of contingencies that threaten physical and psychosocial harms affecting human dignity, livelihoods, safety, survival, and health & well-being in the contexts (political, economic, socio-cultural, and ecological) within which processes of human development take place.[50]

When discussing displacement protection, it is essential to distinguish between cross-border displacement and internal displacement. It is often argued that international refugee law is most pertinent to address risks and vulnerabilities of cross-border displaced populations generally, and climate refugees in particular. However, the grounds of persecution based on which individuals may be accorded refugee status under the 1951 Refugee Convention do not apply to the circumstances faced by the majority of climate-displaced people. Even if they cross borders, they are only granted humanitarian assistance including temporary protection. When people are displaced from one place to another in search of stability, safety and security due to compelling reasons within their countries of origin they are referred to as 'internally displaced persons' (IDPs). In addition to armed conflicts and generalised violence, internal displacement results from environmental and climatic changes and disasters.

Although forced climate displacement features prominently on the global protection agenda, there is no specific international law instrument on the subject. Notwithstanding the drivers of displacement and irrespective of whether forced migration occurs within or beyond national borders, the fact remains that in the absence of effective legal protection, these movements can compromise the human rights and security of the forced displaced.

[46] ibid 15–18.

[47] ibid 15.

[48] Commission on Human Security, *Human Security Now: Protecting and Empowering People* (Commission on Human Security, 2003) 4.

[49] WN Adger and JM Pulhin, 'Human Security' in CB Field and others (eds), *Climate Change 2014: Impacts, Adaptation, and Vulnerability* (Cambridge University Press, 2014) 759.

[50] J Busumtwi-Sam, 'Contextualizing Human Security: A "Deprivation–vulnerability" Approach' (2008) 27(1) *Policy and Society* 15, 19.

A. Climate Displacement in International Law

In the absence of a dedicated international legal instrument protecting the climate displaced, recourse may be had to the broader international human rights law, which safeguards the rights of all people and provisions of which are equally applicable to the climate displaced. The right to life predominates the overall protection landscape, followed by other rights that directly or indirectly contribute to the enjoyment of the right to life, such as civil, political, economic, social and cultural rights – which also extend to people affected by climate change. Hence, the forced displaced, like all others, are entitled to fundamental human rights as envisaged in the 1948 Universal Declaration of Human Rights (UDHR), and are entitled to dignified treatment regardless of 'the political, jurisdictional, or international status of the country or territory to which a person belongs'.[51] The 1951 Refugee Convention would also apply subject to specific needs, risks and vulnerabilities of the forced displaced, for example, the right not to be returned to a country where their life or freedom would be at risk (Article 33).

Similarly, provisions of the International Covenant on Civil and Political Rights 1966 proclaiming rights to 'life' (Article 6), protection from 'torture, cruel, inhuman, or degrading treatment or punishment' (Article 7), 'freedom of movement' (Article 12) and 'an effective remedy for those whose rights are violated' (Article 13) apply to the forced displaced. The rights to 'an adequate standard of living, including housing' (Article 11), 'the highest attainable standard of physical and mental health' (Article 12), and 'take part in cultural life and to enjoy the benefits of scientific progress and its applications' (Article 15) coined by the International Covenant on Economic, Social and Cultural Rights 1966 are also relevant for the forced displaced.

The Convention on the Elimination of All Forms of Discrimination against Women (CEDAW) 1979 does not explicitly mention climate displacement, but its provisions have implications for addressing specific challenges faced by climate-displaced women. For example, Article 3 mandates equality between men and women in all aspects of public and political life. In the context of climate displacement, this includes that women's voices are heard in decision-making processes related to adaptation, resilience and displacement. Again, Article 11 seeks equal employment opportunities for men and women and the right to safe and healthy working conditions. It is therefore crucial to ensure that climate-displaced women have access to livelihood opportunities without discrimination and that they can work safely, without the risk of violence. Article 14 underpins the importance of ensuring rural women's access to resources, which is vital for the well-being of climate-displaced women.

The Convention on the Rights of the Child (CRC) 1989 has provisions that are relevant for climate-displaced children. Article 3 emphasises that the child's

[51] UDHR, Art 2.

best interests should be pivotal in all actions and decisions involving children. As such, the best interests of climate-displaced children should be of paramount importance in decisions affecting their safety, well-being and protection. The CRC recognises a child's inherent right to life, survival and development (Article 6); alternative care for children who are deprived of family environment (Article 20); highest attainable standard of health (Article 24) and standard of living adequate for their physical, mental, spiritual, moral and social development (Article 27), which includes access to basic necessities, such as food, shelter and clothing; quality education (Article 28); and protection from violence and exploitation (Article 37) including in temporary shelters and camps.

In 2015, the first-ever universal, legally binding international agreement on climate change was negotiated and signed. Recognising several issues pertaining to the impact of climate change, including forced migration and violation of human rights, the Paris Agreement states:

> Acknowledging that climate change is a common concern of humankind, Parties should, when taking action to address climate change, respect, promote and consider their respective obligations on human rights, the right to health, the rights of indigenous peoples, local communities, migrants, children, persons with disabilities and people in vulnerable situations and the right to development, as well as gender equality, empowerment of women and intergenerational equity.[52]

Unfortunately, this recognition alone is not helpful as the '[a]greement lacks the depth to create a regulatory framework that promotes the defense of the rights' of the climate displaced.[53]

In its first ruling on a complaint by an individual seeking asylum from the effects of climate change, the UN Human Rights Committee stated that the return of individuals to countries where they face climate change-induced conditions would constitute a threat to life and may trigger *non-refoulement* obligations of receiving states.[54] Although the full impact of this development is yet to be felt, this decision has certainly 'created a legal opening for climate change displacement where life-threatening conditions exist',[55] whereby states could consider 'wider structural reforms that would enable people to move in advance of harm – by harnessing migration as a form of adaptation – and allow them to apply for protection if they are at risk of being displaced'.[56] By so doing, states would not

[52] Paris Agreement, 'Preamble' (adopted 12 December 2015, entered into force 4 November 2016) 195 UNTS 7.

[53] SL Arenilla and CH Rada, 'Climate Change and Forced Migration' (2020) 11 *Migraciones Internacionales* 1, 2.

[54] UNHRC, 'Views adopted by the Committee under article 5 (4) of the Optional Protocol, concerning communication No. 2728/2016' (2020) UN Doc CCPR/C/127/D/2728/2016.

[55] R McCarney and J Kent, 'Forced Displacement and Climate Change: Time for Global Governance' (World Refugee & Migration Council, 5 January 2021), wrmcouncil.org/news/analysis/forced-displacement-and-climate-change-time-for-global-governance/, accessed 15 November 2023.

[56] J McAdam, 'Protecting People Displaced by the Impacts of Climate Change: The UN Human Rights Committee and the Principle of *Non-refoulement*' (2020) 114(4) *American Journal of International Law* 708, 725.

only be complying with obligations under various international legal frameworks, but could also strengthen displacement governance.[57]

B. Soft-Law Instruments

The lack of a dedicated international instrument protecting the climate displaced within and beyond national borders has been compensated by the emergence of several 'soft-law' instruments with specific provisions related to this issue. These are briefly discussed here.

Recognising that desertification and drought affect sustainable development combined with, amongst others, poverty, lack of food security, human displacement and demographic dynamics,[58] the United Nations Convention to Combat Desertification (UNCCD) 1994 encourages states parties to take into consideration the particular socio-economic conditions and other variables that lead to internal, regional and international migrations.[59]

The 1998 Guiding Principles on Internal Displacement (GPID) come closest to being a comprehensive protection instrument for the forced displaced, but only within national borders. It applies to 'persons or groups of persons who have been forced or obliged to flee or leave their homes or habitual places of residence, in particular as a result of or in order to avoid the effects of … natural or human-made disasters, and who have not crossed an internationally recognized State border'.[60] Consistent with international human rights law, the GPID 'identify rights and guarantees relevant to the protection of persons from forced displacement and to their protection and assistance during displacement as well as during return or resettlement and reintegration'.[61] It embodies 30 concrete Principles which ensure protection against displacement (Principles 5 to 9), protection during displacement (Principles 10 to 23), a framework for humanitarian assistance (Principles 24 to 27), and protection during voluntary return and local integration in locations from which people have been displaced and resettlement in another part of the country (Principles 28 to 30). The Principles also offer protections against arbitrary displacement (Principle 6) and minimum guarantees should displacement occur (Principle 7[3]). The GPID emphasise non-discrimination in the treatment of IDPs (Principles 1, 2[1]), but concedes that certain categories of IDPs, such as children (especially unaccompanied minors), women (especially those who are pregnant), mothers with young children, female heads of households, persons with disabilities, and the elderly merit special attention given their special needs (Principle 2[2]).

[57] ibid.
[58] United Nations Convention to Combat Desertification (UNCCD) 1994, Preamble.
[59] ibid Art 3(e).
[60] 'Guiding Principles on Internal Displacement, Scope and Purpose', Clause 2, www.icrc.org/en/doc/resources/documents/article/other/57jpgl.htm, accessed 15 January 2023.
[61] ibid.

The Nansen Principles on Climate Change and Displacement 2011 call for a 'coherent and consistent approach at the international level ... to meet the protection needs of people displaced externally'.[62] Although not strictly soft law, these principles recommend a broad range of policy measures 'to guide responses to some urgent and complex challenges raised by displacement in the context of climate change and other environmental hazards',[63] and as such, help to place the issue of climate displacement on the international agenda.

Launched in 2012, the Nansen Initiative[64] seeks a consensus amongst states on how to protect and assist disaster and climate change-induced cross-border displaced populations by drawing on the practical experiences of governments in this context. The Initiative builds on para 14(f) of the 2010 UNFCC Cancun Agreements on climate change adaptation that calls on states to adopt '[m]easures to enhance the understanding, coordination and cooperation with regard to climate change induced displacement, migration and planned relocation, where appropriate, at the national, regional and international levels'.[65]

The 2013 Peninsula Principles on Climate Displacement within States[66] provide a comprehensive normative framework, within which climate displacement and the rights of climate-displaced persons can be addressed (Principle 1, scope and purpose). The Principles maintain that climate-displaced persons have the right to remain in their homes (Principle 6[a]) and that states should, in all circumstances, comply with their obligations under international law in terms of preventing and avoiding conditions that might lead to climate displacement (Principle 5).

The Agenda for the Protection of Cross-Border Displaced Persons in the Context of Disasters and Climate Change 2015[67] essentially consolidates the outcomes of the various intergovernmental consultations and meetings convened regionally by the Nansen Initiative to produce a coherent framework that addresses the protection needs of cross-border displaced people, identifies key strategies to reduce their vulnerability to disasters and build resilience against disaster displacement, and facilitates migration out of risky zones. It also prescribes priority actions for the future.

The Global Compact for Safe, Orderly and Regular Migration (GCM) 2018[68] offers measures to address and reduce vulnerabilities in migration, 'which may arise from the circumstances in which they travel or the conditions they face in countries

[62] Nansen Principles on Climate Change and Displacement 2011, Principle 9.

[63] ibid, Preamble.

[64] The Nansen Initiative, 'Agenda for the Protection of Cross-Border Displaced Persons in the Context of Disasters and Climate Change: Volume I' (2015).

[65] UNFCCC *Report of the Conference of the Parties* on its sixteenth session, held in Cancun from 29 November – 10 December 2010, Addendum Part Two: Action taken by the Conference of the Parties at its sixteenth session 'Decision 1/CP.16 The Cancun Agreements: Outcome of the work of the Ad Hoc Working Group on Long-term Cooperative Action under the Convention' UN Doc FCCC/CP/2010/7/Add.1 (15 March 2011), 4, unfccc.int/resource/docs/2010/cop16/eng/07a01.pdf#page=4.

[66] Peninsula Principles on Climate Displacement within States (2013).

[67] 'Agenda for the Protection of Cross-Border Displaced Persons in the Context of Disasters and Climate Change – Volume II' (*Disaster Displacement*, 13 October 2018), disasterdisplacement.org/resource/nipa-vol2/, accessed 12 December 2023.

[68] Global Compact for Safe, Orderly and Regular Migration (Final Draft, 13 July 2018) UN Doc A/RES/73/195.

of origin, transit and destination, by assisting them and protecting their human rights, in accordance with [sic] obligations under international law' (Objective 7). These measures aim at, inter alia, strengthening transnational responses to the smuggling of migrants (Objective 9), preventing, combatting and eradicating trafficking in persons in the context of international migration (Objective 10), discouraging the practice of detention during immigration except only as a last resort (Objective 13), and ensuring that all migrants, regardless of their migration status, have access to basic services (Objective 15). The Compact commits to 'empower migrants and diasporas to catalyse their development contributions, and to harness the benefits of migration as a source of sustainable development' (Objective 19).

The Sendai Framework for Disaster Risk Reduction (SFDRR) 2015–2030[69] identifies actions for strengthening the resilience of populations affected by disasters and recognises that 'migrants contribute to the resilience of communities and societies, and their knowledge, skills and capacities can be useful in the design and implementation of disaster risk reduction'.[70] It asks governments to 'empower local authorities, as appropriate, through regulatory and financial means to work and coordinate with … migrants in disaster risk management at the local level'.[71]

The 2030 Agenda for Sustainable Development[72] recognises for the first time the contribution of migration to sustainable development. SDG target 10.7 specifically urges states to 'facilitate orderly, safe, and responsible migration and mobility of people, including through implementation of planned and well-managed migration policies'.[73] A quick scrutiny of the SDGs reveals that 11 out of 17 goals have targets and indicators that are relevant to migration, including the Agenda's core principle to 'leave no one behind'.[74]

These various instruments promote a rights-based approach to climate displacement so that even in the worst-case scenario, the displaced shall be entitled to the fundamental human rights guaranteed under international law. International law urges states to 'respect, protect and fulfil human rights'[75] – obligations which they owe all persons within their jurisdiction, including the forced displaced. To ensure compliance by the states in this regard, international law has several systems and procedures in place, such as states parties reporting to relevant international committees, shadow reporting by non-governmental organisations (NGOs), reporting by Special Rapporteurs, and where applicable, individual complaints mechanisms.

[69] Sendai Framework for Disaster Risk Reduction 2015–2030 (adopted 18 March 2015, at the Third UN World Conference on Disaster Risk Reduction in Sendai, Japan), UN Doc A/RES/69/283.

[70] ibid para 36(a)(vi).

[71] ibid para 27(h).

[72] 'Transforming Our World: The 2030 Agenda for Sustainable Development' (Department of Economic and Social Affairs), sdgs.un.org/2030agenda, accessed 31 December 2023.

[73] SLOGA Platform and Povod Institute, 'Forced Migration at the Intersection of Development Cooperation and Refugee Admissions in Europe – Policy Brief (2020) 4.

[74] ibid.

[75] OHCHR and Inter-Parliamentary Union, *Human Rights Handbook for Parliamentarians No 26* (The Inter-Parliamentary Union and the United Nations Office of the High Commissioner for Human Rights, 2016) 19.

V. Impediments to International Protection

Vulnerabilities of the forced displaced essentially derive from weak human rights protection. Although many of the international/soft law instruments offer the climate displaced legal protection, the reality on the ground is not encouraging. The treatment by states and border agencies of cross-border forced displaced populations in terms of reception, resettlement and protection often fail to meet the minimum standards prescribed by international law. This precludes the forced displaced from three key important protection mechanisms, and which taken together represent the international minimum standards. These are (i) non-refoulement (protecting against return to their country of origin); (ii) preventing future displacement; and (iii) facilitating safe, orderly and regular migration in the context of disasters and climate change.[76] Of course, components (ii) and (iii) apply equally to IDPs.

While international law has made some progress in recognising climate displacement, without a dedicated legal framework, clear definitions and enforcement mechanisms, the protection of the climate displaced remains inadequate. The protection measures might be compromised owing to several factors. For example, in the case of cross-border displacement, there is an absence of definitional clarity.[77] Although some believe that the inclusion of the cross-border climate-displaced in the 1951 Refugee Convention could potentially mitigate the protection gaps, the UN High Commissioner for Refugees (UNHCR) contend that environmental factors are not grounds, in and of themselves, for granting refugee status under international refugee law.[78] In other words, the inclusion of the climate displaced in the Refugee Convention would necessitate a renegotiation of the Convention, which, in turn, would undermine the international refugee protection regime.[79] There is no explicit provision in international law that articulates whether and in what circumstances the climate displaced shall be admitted to another country, what rights, entitlements and standards of treatment they would be entitled to during their stay, and under what conditions they may be sent back to their countries of origin.[80]

Soft-law instruments often use ambiguous language. The lack of legal precision can pose challenges in establishing clear and coherent standards for addressing a complex phenomenon like forced displacement. These ambiguities often manifest in insensitive policy decisions and shabby treatment of displaced populations in host locations. The absence of dedicated grievance redress mechanisms tailored to

[76] AY Noorda, *Climate Change, Disasters and People on the Move. Providing Protection under International Law* (Brill Nijhof, 2022) 18, 20.

[77] R Cohen and M Bradley, 'Disasters and Displacement: Gaps in Protection' (2010) 1 *Journal of International Humanitarian Legal Studies* 6.

[78] UNHCR, 'Climate change, natural disasters and human displacement: a UNHCR perspective' (2009).

[79] V Kolmannskog and L Trebbi, 'Climate change, natural disasters and displacement: a multi-track approach to filling the protection gaps' (2010) 92(879) *International Review of the Red Cross* 713, 720.

[80] Nansen Initiative (n 64) 8.

meet the needs of the climate victims is yet another problem, without which they have to rely on systems and procedures that cater to general human rights violations, and which might not necessarily offer them the desired relief.

Compliance with international law is largely voluntary, making it difficult to hold states accountable for deficits in prevention and protection. Without sanctions or consequences for non-compliance, states may have little incentive to prioritise the implementation of climate displacement instruments. Political will and the financial / institutional capacity of a state are fundamental to effective enforcement of obligations under international law. One of the ways in which the political will of a state can be assessed is by seeing whether it has ratified the relevant treaties. However, if the political leadership is indifferent to or unwilling to enforce international law obligations, protection measures are unlikely to succeed even if the concerned state has ratified the treaties. It is not uncommon for Global South countries to endorse international treaties more to secure global patronage than to ensure proper execution. When a state is neither party to an international instrument, nor does it have a domestic normative framework to protect the climate displaced, the situation gets complicated as, in the absence of a concrete reference point, the state cannot be held accountable for deficiencies in protection. Besides, the issue of state sovereignty can pose significant challenges to addressing forced displacement. Many states are averse to international interference in their domestic affairs, particularly with regard to border control and immigration. This essentially obstructs the establishment of legal obligations of protecting the climate displaced.

A study of the protection landscape of Kenya, Bangladesh, Ghana and Vietnam from the perspective of environmentally displaced populations reveals that:

- migration and displacement are highly sensitive issues which are marginalised in the political discourse;
- policies to tackle internal migration and displacement are poorly developed and largely reactive;
- state fragility impedes the political commitment to develop effective human rights protection;
- political commitment to human rights is developing but as yet protection frameworks are weak;
- signature and ratification of international treaties have not, as yet, generated strong domestic human rights regimes;
- civil society plays a patchy role in human rights protection, limited by lack of funding, poor coordination and weak state institutions.[81]

States devoid of necessary resources, whether human, financial or institutional, are largely unable to prevent displacement and fully implement existing

[81] R Zetter, 'Protecting Environmentally Displaced People: Developing the Capacity of Legal and Normative Frameworks' (Refugee Studies Centre, University of Oxford, 2011) 6–7.

protection mechanisms, even though they may have the desired level of political will. These states have to invariably depend on international aid, which might not be readily available unless they can mobilise external funding in the name of climate finance, which again has not proved easy. Developed states committed at the 15th Conference of Parties (COP15) of the UNFCCC in Copenhagen in 2009 to mobilise US$100 billion per year by 2020 for climate action in developing countries. This goal was formalised at COP16 in Cancun, and reiterated subsequently at COP21 in Paris, and extended to 2025. In addition, under the Paris Agreement, developed country parties are supposed to provide financial resources to assist developing country parties concerning both mitigation and adaptation in continuation of their existing obligations under the Convention (Article 9.1). Statistics[82] reveal that in 2020, the initial target year of the US$100 billion goal, the total climate finance mobilised and provided by developed countries for developing countries amounted to US$83.3 billion, which is US$16.7 billion short of the goal. Between 2013 and 2020, the Global North collectively provided US$532 billion against a pledge of US$800 billion. According to the IPCC, developing countries alone will need US$127 billion per year by 2030 and US$295 billion per year by 2050 to adapt to climate change; funds for adaptation have only reached US$23 billion to US$46 billion from 2017 to 2018, accounting for only 4 to 8 per cent of tracked climate finance.[83] Therefore, the prospect of securing funds from the Global North countries for infrastructure development, social services and disaster preparedness to address climate displacement continues to remain bleak.

There is a dearth of climate displacement related data. Getting an accurate account of forced displacement can be a daunting task given associated political and technical considerations that influence the availability and quality of data; consequently, commonly cited numbers are often no better than educated guesses.[84] Having credible data is important for a number of reasons: it could help build consensus amongst key stakeholders on informed interventions and for developing evidence-based strategies, policies and plans of action;[85] it could be used to develop early warning systems; it could help governments allocate necessary resources and target interventions in vulnerable spots; and it could raise awareness of local communities and engage them in planning and executing resilience and adaptation strategies.

Finally, deficits in displacement governance present serious challenges. The lack of monitoring, evaluation, transparency and accountability in prevention

[82] OECD, *Climate Finance and the USD 100 Billion Goal Aggregate Trends of Climate Finance Provided and Mobilised by Developed Countries in 2013–2020* (OECD Publishing, 2022) 5.

[83] S Boehm and C Schumer, '10 Big Findings from the 2023 IPCC Report on Climate Change' (World Resources Institute, 2023), www.wri.org/insights/2023-ipcc-ar6-synthesis-report-climate-change-findings, accessed 12 April 2023.

[84] World Bank (n 40) 2.

[85] UNDP and UNHCR, *Facing the Challenges of Forced displacement in Central America and Mexico* (UNDP and UNHCR, 2021) 55.

and protection mechanisms creates scope for corruption, which, in turn, 'prevents assistance from reaching the people who need it most and instead facilitates collusive forces to capitalise on human plight'.[86] Without good governance, there is the risk of misallocation or misappropriation of resources allocated for climate displacement interventions. Research[87] conducted by Transparency International Bangladesh, the country chapter of the anti-graft organisation Transparency International, reveals that aid distribution is sometimes influenced by political patronage, which leads to prioritising certain communities over others, leaving the climate displaced out of intervention efforts. This situation is exacerbated by inefficient government processes, bureaucratic obstacles, lack of coordination between relevant government agencies and unclear responsibilities. Lack of capacity in terms of monitoring and reporting, using technology, having technical knowledge and expertise, and engaging trained personnel in emergency response, can compromise early warnings, evacuations, relief distribution and overall disaster management. Indeed, weak governance erodes public trust in government institutions, leading to non-cooperation with displacement efforts.

Governance is pivotal to determining policy responses to climate displacement. As part of climate governance, many countries in the Global South, for example, Bangladesh, Maldives, Nepal, Kiribati, Costa Rica, Kenya and Brazil have developed policies to address climate change impacts. The effectiveness of these initiatives can vary, and the actual outcome would depend on local contexts and implementation mechanisms. As Warner argues, 'efficacy of governance plays a critical role in whether migrants will return, or whether they will stay away indefinitely'.[88] The timing of displacement interventions is also vital. For example, 'even if people could technically return to hazard-affected areas, they may not choose to return if rehabilitation does not take place soon enough to be in sync with life cycle or other developments (such as employment, or services like schooling for children)'.[89] McAdam observes that governance of climate displacement 'suffers from significant fragmentation, both vertically – with actors at the international, regional, and local levels – and horizontally – with the phenomenon addressed in part or, more rarely, as a whole' by relevant policies and institutions. She believes that this potentially stems from an inadequate understanding of migration versus protection and the factors which hinder its regulation. She adds that since climate displacement 'cuts across several areas of international governance – migration and asylum, the environment, development, human rights, and humanitarian aid and assistance',

[86] S Khair, 'Corruption in Humanitarian Assistance: Challenges and Opportunities' in A Singh (ed), *Disaster Law: Emerging Thresholds* (Routledge, 2018) 207.

[87] See Transparency International Bangladesh (TIB), 'Integrity Watch in Flood 2019 Preparedness and Relief Operations' (TIB, 2019); TIB, 'Cyclone Roanu: Challenges of Good Governance in Disaster Management and Way Forward' (TIB, 2017); TIB, 'Governance Challenges in Disaster Response and Way Forward: Cyclone Amphan and Recent Experiences' (TIB, 2020).

[88] K Warner, 'Assessing Institutional and Governance Needs Related to Environmental Change and Human Migration' (German Marshall Funds of the United States, Washington, 2009) 2.

[89] ibid 3.

and because there is a 'plethora of existing, [and] potential, governance mechanisms, processes, and institutions, no coherent multilateral governance framework exists for this purpose'. It is therefore 'important that responses at the global level do not overlook local knowledge bases for adaptation and resilience, and the cultural and livelihood needs of displaced communities',[90] and unless policies are carefully planned and implemented at the local, national and international levels, displacement would increase.

VI. Possible Ways Forward

There is no denying that forced climate displacement, particularly in protracted situations, poses a development challenge and functions as a barrier to the attainment of sustainable development. The various risks and vulnerabilities experienced by the forced displaced have serious implications for not only human rights and human security but also many of the development goals envisaged in the 2030 Agenda. Climate migrants get left behind in the development process as they lack choices, opportunities and capacity to earn a stable income.

There is a need for a shared understanding of the terminology that is used to depict the forced displaced for better protection. State responsibility to protect the climate displaced might benefit from an 'evolutionary interpretation of the principle of non-refoulement' and the recognition that the climate displaced face 'real and imminent risk' to their right to life.[91] A human-rights-based approach to climate displacement could potentially function as a normative benchmark based on which states may develop protection mechanisms. Ratification of relevant human rights treaties by states alone, while necessary, cannot necessarily ensure the protection of the climate displaced, unless it is accompanied by national strategic law and policy frameworks outlining concrete actions for the displaced. Irrespective of the context in which forced displacement occurs, the primary concern must be to ensure effective access to human rights by all those whose rights have been infringed in the process. Since displacement affects different categories of people in different ways, tailored assistance and protection are required to best protect their rights and ensure their safety.[92] It is time governments clarified the rights of the climate displaced and fixed the responsibilities of both countries of origin and destination in the treatment of the climate displaced, in the short, medium and long terms. In advocating for protection, it is equally

[90] J McAdam, *Climate Change, Forced Migration, and International Law* (Oxford University Press, 2012) 212, 213–14.

[91] Arenilla and Rada (n 53) 12.

[92] H Afsour and others, 'Internal Displacement as a Development Challenge', *Research Briefing Paper*, UNSG High Level Panel on Internal Displacement, Refugee Law Initiative, August 2020, 3, www.un.org/internal-displacement-panel/sites/www.un.org.internal-displacement-panel/files/idrp_hlp_submission_ws3_development_challenge.pdf, accessed 12 February 2023.

important to flag the concept of safe and orderly return of the forced displaced, without which protection initiatives would be piecemeal.

The lack of transparency and good governance can significantly hinder climate displacement. Governments must prioritise good governance practices, transparency and accountability at all stages of forced displacement interventions. Monitoring and reporting are integral to the effective governance of climate displacement. They provide the tools and mechanisms to evaluate and improve the implementation of protection measures. The engagement of civil society, the promotion of open data and information flow, and the strengthening of anti-corruption measures could help mitigate the risks and enhance the effectiveness of displacement interventions. Capacity constraints may be addressed by a combination of domestic reforms and external assistance. Strengthening governance, improving transparency and accountability, investing in education and training, enhancing technical know-how, and improving access to technological innovations are some steps that can help mitigate displacement challenges.

Seeking sustainable solutions to forced climate displacement is of paramount importance. Affected states would require dedicated resources to find context-specific and realistic solutions to the problem. Community-led, home-grown adaptation measures are more likely to yield sustainable solutions, rather than borrowed initiatives. It is essential to ensure that adaptation is done in ways which protect the human rights of the displaced people. Indeed, the impact of forced displacement can be better understood if the phenomenon is not regarded as stemming solely from environmental/climate problems, but as part of the existing social, economic or cultural challenges, which require systematic and multi-dimensional reforms. It is equally important to address the development aspect of forced displacement as legal mechanisms alone cannot fully address the matter. A multi-pronged, context-specific approach involving diplomatic interventions, humanitarian assistance and sustainable development strategies is more likely to succeed than stand-alone strategies. To this end, states need to scale up efforts and allocate sufficient resources to collect, collate and make available evidence-based data through open source systems (but after ensuring proper data protection) that may be used to inform smart policy responses to forced displacement.

Since countries with weak economies, primarily in the Global South, are less likely to have the resources to protect the climate displaced in concrete ways, the international community needs to provide technical and/or financial support to help them better manage climate displacement. In this context, one can only reiterate the significance of the principle of common but differentiated responsibilities, so that the onus of protecting the climate displaced does not only rest on the affected states. Climate displacement must be seen as a global phenomenon and as such, international cooperation must address not only the humanitarian aspect of forced displacement but also the broader development objectives and long-term solutions. There is an urgent need for strategic and clearly-framed protection measures for the climate displaced, who, through no fault of theirs, bear the harshest brunt of the adverse effects of climate change.

PART IV

Implementation of Sustainable Development: Challenges and Prospects for the Global South

11

Trade and Sustainable Development in the Global South: The Role of Special and Differential Treatment in Achieving SDGs

SHAWKAT ALAM

I. Introduction

In the context of the Global South, a rule-based trading system is vital for sustainable development. Such a system can provide a framework that balances economic growth with environmental and social concerns. The Sustainable Development Goals (SDGs) serve as a benchmark for evaluating the effectiveness of these trade practices. Understanding and addressing the nuances of this system are critical for the successful implementation of sustainable development in the Global South.

International trade, characterised by the exchange of goods and services across international borders, has the capacity to significantly reduce poverty, create jobs and promote economic growth. However, its potential can only be fully realised when trade practices are fair and equitable, and do not sacrifice environmental integrity or social well-being. The issue is further complicated by the fact that developing countries cannot pursue the potential benefits that trade liberalisation offers because of existing inequalities in the global trading system. To benefit from trade, developing countries, and more particularly their impoverished citizens, need access to the global market.[1] However, the existing trade regime, driven by both policy and practice, perpetuates inequalities, thereby expanding the economic chasm between the most affluent and the most impoverished nations.

In 2000, the Millennium Declaration set 2015 as the target for the realisation of the Millennium Development Goals (MDGs) – a set of concrete quantifiable objectives for the global reduction of extreme poverty. The issues of trade,

[1] O Omoju and O Adesanya, 'Does Trade Promote Growth in Developing Countries? Empirical Evidence from Nigeria' (2012) 1(3) *International Journal of Development and Sustainability* 743, 747.

environmental sustainability, health, and human rights were at the epicentre of the MDGs. In particular, the eighth goal of the MDGs was concerned with developing a global partnership for development. Its targets are specifically related to trade, including the further development of 'an open trading and financial system that is rule-based, predictable and non-discriminatory' and the provision of tariff- and quota-free access for least developed country exports. The MDGs have since been replaced by the SDGs, which aim to reduce poverty, ensure food security, promote health and gender equality, foster economic growth, reduce inequalities, encourage sustainable practices, support climate action and strengthen global partnerships. SDG 1 (No Poverty) benefits from trade as it opens up markets and increases incomes, thus reducing poverty. SDG 2 (Zero Hunger) is supported through the international trade of agricultural products, aiding food security while balancing the needs of local farmers. For SDG 3 (Good Health and Well-being), trade facilitates access to affordable healthcare products and technologies. SDG 10 (Reduced Inequalities) is addressed by designing trade policies that actively reduce economic disparities, especially between developed and developing nations. In supporting SDG 12 (Responsible Consumption and Production), trade encourages the transfer and use of sustainable practices and technologies. SDG 13 (Climate Action) benefits from trade policies that promote the exchange of renewable energy and environmentally friendly goods. Lastly, SDG 17 (Partnerships for the Goals) is underscored by the collaborative nature of international trade, fostering global partnerships that are essential for sustainable development. In all these aspects, the emphasis is on creating a fair and equitable trading system that acknowledges and addresses the unique challenges faced by the Global South. However, it is important that these trade rules are fair and considerate of the unique challenges faced by developing countries. Unfortunately, market access continues to be a significant barrier for developing countries. Even though one of the objectives of the Doha Round of trade negotiations was to establish a 'development agenda' in relation to trade, this has yet to be concluded.[2]

The implementation of sustainable trade practices poses a unique set of challenges, especially for the Global South. The Global South, encompassing lower-income regions in Asia, Africa, Latin America and the Caribbean, faces a unique predicament. These countries often grapple with weak environmental and labour regulations and are heavily dependent on the export of primary commodities, which are prone to price volatility. The inconsistent role and impact of global trade across these regions highlight the need for a more sustainable and inclusive approach. One of the major hurdles in achieving sustainable trade is the uneven level of development among countries. The longstanding tensions between the North and South regarding responsibilities and power in the global economic order have further complicated these efforts. Despite international recognition of trade as a

[2] MDG Gap Task Force, *Delivering on the Global Partnership for Achieving the Millennium Development Goals* (United Nations, 2008) 17, www.refworld.org/pdfid/4a54bbf1d.pdf, accessed 30 January 2024.

crucial engine for inclusive economic growth and poverty reduction, as seen in the 2030 Agenda for Sustainable Development, actual progress has been slow. Market access remains a significant barrier for developing countries, and while tariff barriers have decreased, non-tariff measures restricting trade have risen. This unequal distribution of trade benefits risks exacerbating existing inequalities and fuelling social unrest. International development models and debt-financed development have furthered the depletion of natural capital, *viz* the world's stock of natural resources and ecosystem services that provide public goods, in the Global South. Furthermore, such development has also contributed to a net transfer of wealth to the Global North, while simultaneously furthering poverty and ecological decline in the Global South.[3] International trade and sustainable development are deeply intertwined with complex legal, environmental and economic dynamics.

II. Special and Differential Treatment Provisions in International Trade: Bridging Trade and Sustainable Development in the Global South

Addressing the concerns of the Global South, ensuring fair participation in international negotiations, and balancing environmental protections with trade regulations are crucial for a sustainable and equitable global trading system. The challenge lies in crafting policies and frameworks that recognise and accommodate the diverse needs and capacities of all nations, especially those in the Global South, in the pursuit of sustainable development.

Special and Differential Treatment (SDT) provisions within the international trade system serve as a vital link between trade policies and the sustainable development of developing countries, particularly those in the Global South. Integral to World Trade Organization (WTO) agreements, these provisions acknowledge the disparities in economic and developmental statuses among member countries. They offer benefits like extended timeframes for implementing agreements and commitments, increased trading opportunities, and mandatory protection of developing countries' trade interests by all WTO members. By offering these flexibilities, SDT provisions help in integrating developing countries into the global economy, ensuring that economic growth is accompanied by environmental sustainability and social inclusiveness. The ultimate objective of SDT provisions is to enable all countries, regardless of their development status, to enjoy the benefits of free trade within a sustainable development framework. This encompasses not only economic growth but also broader aspects of development, such as social

[3] W Rees and L Westra, *When Consumption Does Violence: Can There be Sustainability and Environmental Justice in a Resource-Limited World?* (Routledge, 2003) 106; T Juniper, 'Presentation to the World Trade Organization Symposium' in K Conca and G Dabelko (eds), *Green Planet Blues: Environmental Politics from Stockholm to Johannesburg* 3rd edn (Westview Press, 2004) 190, 191, 193.

well-being and environmental sustainability. Through mechanisms like market access, technology transfer and capacity building, SDT provisions are pivotal in promoting higher living standards in the Global South, ensuring that economic advancements are environmentally sustainable and socially inclusive.

This chapter delves into the theoretical foundations of SDT provisions within the international trading system, underscoring their critical role in forging a more equitable global trade regime. It highlights how SDT provisions are integral in fostering sustainable development in developing countries. The effective implementation of these provisions is vital for the comprehensive engagement of the Global South in international trade, ensuring that the global economy is characterised by fairness, justice and a commitment to sustainable development. By offering benefits like extended implementation timeframes, increased trading opportunities, and mandatory protection of developing countries' trade interests, SDT provisions facilitate the integration of these countries into the global economy in an environmentally sustainable and socially inclusive manner. Following this theoretical examination, the chapter will explore the negotiation history of the Trade-Related Aspects of Intellectual Property Rights (TRIPS) Agreement. It will focus on the specific SDT measures that were incorporated for the benefit of Least Developed Countries (LDCs). This exploration aims to provide a comprehensive understanding of how these measures were negotiated and the impact they are intended to have in balancing intellectual property rights with the developmental needs of LDCs in the realm of global trade.

III. The Rationale for Special and Differential Treatment within the Trade Framework

While the inclusion of SDT provisions within WTO Agreements has been the subject of extensive negotiation, their existence is buttressed by the theoretical underpinnings of free trade and the recognition of SDT provisions as legal instruments in multilateral trade agreements.[4] SDT provisions find theoretical justification in a number of ways, including as a means of furthering the social and economic development of developing countries,[5] and a means of achieving distributive justice.[6] Most important, however, is the justification of SDT provisions on the basis that

[4] N Sutrisno, 'Substantive Justice Formulated, Implemented, and Enforced as Formal and Procedural Justice: A Lesson from WTO Special and Differential Treatment Provisions for Developing Countries' (2010) 13 *Journal of Gender, Race and Justice* 671, 672.

[5] See, for example, Marrakesh Agreement establishing the World Trade Organization, opened for signature 15 April 1994, 1867 UNTS 3 (entered into force 1 January 1995), annex 1A ('General Agreement on Tariffs and Trade 1994'), Art XXXVI(1)(e).

[6] J Paul, 'Do International Trade Institutions Contribute to Economic Growth and Development?' (2003) 44 *Virginia Journal of International Law* 285, 320; C Thomas, 'Poverty Reduction, Trade, and Rights' (2003) 18 *American University International Law Review* 1403.

through liberalising trade, the WTO is concerned with achieving greater freedom and equality between states.[7] The foundational goals of the WTO are rooted in Ricardo's theory of trade liberalisation. This theory argues that by removing trade barriers, countries can leverage their comparative advantages through specialisation, harness economies of scale, and reduce inefficiencies. The expected outcome is that all nations benefit from free trade, evidenced by improvements in standards of living, production, employment and incomes. Despite the growing complexity of international trade, these basic principles, identified by economists at the dawn of the global economy, remain relevant.[8]

Attempts to promote greater equality in trade initially involved notions of non-discrimination and reciprocity, which were embodied within the rules of Most-Favoured-Nation treatment and National Treatment, requiring non-discrimination in trade between country members.[9] The SDT is an exception to the most-favoured nation (MFN) principle which requires equal treatment towards all WTO members[10] and was a deviation from the principle of reciprocity for developing countries.[11] The Preamble of the Marrakesh Agreement[12] states that one of the objectives of the SDT, is to 'ensure that developing countries, and especially the least-developed among them, secure a share in the growth of the world trade commensurate with their needs'.[13] Similarly, in the Doha Round of Negotiations, it was stated that SDT for developing countries 'shall be an integral part of all elements of negotiations'.[14]

The GATT 1994 has acknowledged this aim by codifying the exception to the MFN treatment obligation under Art I:1 by incorporating the 1979 GATT Decision on Differential and More Favourable Treatment, Reciprocity and Fuller Participation of Developing Countries,[15] commonly referred to as the 'Enabling Clause'. Paragraph 1 of the Enabling Clause allows Members to 'accord differential and more favourable treatment to developing countries, without according such treatment to other Members'.[16] Furthermore, under paragraph 2 of the Enabling Clause, members may provide differential treatment to developing members in terms of preferential tariffs through the Generalised System of Preferences (GSP)

[7] Sutrisno (n 4) 672; Note, 'Developing Countries and Multilateral Trade Agreements: Law and the Promise of Development' (1995) 108 *Harvard Law Review* 1715, 1718.

[8] PR Krugman and M Obstfeld, *International Economics: Theory and Policy* 8th edn (Pearson Addison-Wesley, 2009) 23.

[9] General Agreement on Tariffs and Trade 1994 (n 5), Arts I(1), III(1)–(2) and (4).

[10] ibid Art I(1).

[11] V Hedge and J Wouters, 'Special and Differential Treatment under the World Trade Organization: A Legal Typology' (2020) 227 *Leuven Centre for Global Governance Studies* 1, 7.

[12] Marrakesh Agreement (n 5) Preamble.

[13] P Conconi and C Perroni, 'Special and Differential Treatment of Developing Countries in the WTO' (2015) 14(1) *World Trade Review* 67.

[14] ibid.

[15] Differential and More Favourable Treatment, Reciprocity and Fuller Participation of Developing Countries, GATT BISD, 26th Supp, 203, GATT Doc L/4903 (1979) (Multilateral Trade Negotiations Decision, adopted on 28 November 1979) ('Enabling Clause').

[16] ibid.

for non-tariff measures, trade agreements entered into with developing members, and any other measures that aim to promote developing countries in world trade.[17] The GSP programmes provide duty-free treatment to the importation of goods originating in developing countries,[18] and this must be imposed on a non-discriminatory basis.[19] Over the years, developed countries have included various conditions, such as compliance with labour standards, in their GSP programmes, and developing countries must meet these conditions in order to be granted preferential tariff treatment.[20] This practice is referred to as 'negative conditionality' whereby failure to comply would result in the withdrawal of trade preferences.[21] By contrast, since 1994 the European Communities (EC) have operated a GSP scheme of 'positive conditionality', where certain developing countries were provided with *additional* tariff preferences if they complied with specific environmental and labour standards.[22]

A. Special and Differential Treatment in GATT 1994: Enabling Clause, Market Access and Rule-Related Measures

The two major dimensions of SDT are market access and rule-related measures. Market access measures include preferential access for developing countries to developed country markets, complemented by non-reciprocity in trade negotiations. Rule-related measures are those that relate to exemptions such as longer transitionary periods or implementation periods; and the supply of technical assistance by developed countries. Technical assistance helps developing and least-developed countries in the facilitation, implementation, administration, operation and furthering of WTO commitments and objectives.[23]

Today more than two-thirds of 164 WTO members classify as developing and 36 members represent least-developed countries, hence their development concerns must be adequately taken into account in global trade rules. Overall, the provisions can be seen as fundamental to achieving equality, fairness and integration. There are a total of 183 SDT provisions contained across the WTO agreements which reflect the importance of increasing trading opportunities, safeguarding interests of developing country members, flexibility of commitments and action including extending the timeline to successfully reduce the burden on developing countries to compete with more advanced developed countries,

[17] Hedge and Wouters (n 11) 5.
[18] ibid 8.
[19] Preferential or Free Entry of Exports of Manufactures and Semi-Manufactures of Developing Countries to the Developing Countries, the United Nations Conference on Trade and Development Resolution 21(II) (26 March 1968).
[20] M McKenzie, 'Case Note, European Communities – Conditions for the Granting of Tariff Preferences to Developing Countries' (2004) 6(1) *Melbourne Journal of International Law* 481, 482.
[21] ibid.
[22] ibid.
[23] Conconi and Perroni (n 13) 71–72.

technical assistance, and provisions relating to LDC members.[24] For instance, the SPS Agreement provides that in the preparation of sanitary or phytosanitary measures, members must take into account the special needs of developing country members.[25] Practically speaking, this enables developing countries to adopt alternative measures, such as local methods for pest eradication, to reduce sanitary or phytosanitary risk which can still accord to the member's appropriate level of protection. Where an importing member still requires a developing country to adopt the measure and this requires substantial technical investment, the SPS Agreement enables the importing member to provide technical assistance to the developing country in order to meet the importing member's appropriate level of protection.[26]

Despite the overarching comprehensiveness of SDT provisions, the challenge of its effectiveness stems from its implementation and relevance. Uncertainty in the legal status of the provisions is a result of a matrix of legally enforceable obligations and best-endeavour clauses.[27] The relevance of SDT is also scrutinised due to the evolving needs of developing country members. Three areas of concern have emerged regarding SDT: (a) the commitment to preferential market access is much less important presently due to nominal tariff rates being extremely low and the growth of regional trade agreements; (b) the fundamental premises of SDT are increasingly questioned, namely as economic theories and critiques oppose that less liberal trade policies are optimal; and (c) the commitments and rules aimed to support developing countries are flawed due to institutional constraints and lack of consideration given to implementation.[28] The most widely utilised and extensive SDT provisions include Part IV and Article XVIII of the GATT 1994, along with the Enabling Clause. These provisions are essential to creating fair opportunities for developing and least-developed countries. However, an in-depth analysis indicates that for these provisions to manifest tangible benefits and effectiveness, further development and refinement are required.

i. Quantitative Restrictions: Quotas under Article XVIII of the GATT 1994

Quantitative restrictions, such as import quotas, can have significant impacts on developing countries. These restrictions limit the quantity of certain goods that can

[24] J Bacchus and I Manak, 'The Development Dimension: What to Do about Differential Treatment in Trade' Policy Analysis No 887, CATO Institute (13 April 2020) 1.

[25] Agreement on the Application of Sanitary and Phytosanitary Measures (adopted 15 April 1994, entered into force 1 January 1995) 1867 UNTS 493 (SPSS) ('SPS Agreement'), Art 10.

[26] ibid Art 9.

[27] FAH Wibowo, 'Improving the Effectiveness of the Special and Differential Treatment of the World Trade Organization' (Victoria University of Wellington, Research Paper, 2018) 6, openaccess.wgtn.ac.nz/articles/thesis/Improving_the_effectiveness_of_the_special_and_differential_treatment_of_the_World_Trade_Organization/17009855, accessed 1 February 2024.

[28] M Pangestu, 'Special and Differential Treatment in the Millennium: Special for Whom and How Different?' (2000) 23(9) *Journal of International Trade Law and Policy* 1285, 1290–91.

be imported, potentially stifling the growth of industries in developing countries that rely on exporting these goods. This can lead to reduced income, unemployment and slowed economic growth. Furthermore, these restrictions can limit the variety and quantity of goods available to consumers in the developing country, potentially leading to higher prices and reduced consumer welfare. However, it is important to note that quantitative restrictions can also be used as a tool to protect nascent industries in developing countries from overwhelming competition, allowing them to grow and become competitive. Thus, the impact of quantitative restrictions on developing countries is multifaceted and depends on specific circumstances. The preamble to Article XVIII of the GATT 1994 is designed to facilitate the economic growth and development of countries with lower living standards and those in the early stages of development.[29] Article XVIII of the GATT 1994 is structured into three distinct sections, with Section A permitting members to modify or withdraw concessions specified in the relevant Schedules of this Agreement, for the purpose of fostering the growth of a domestic industry,[30] whereas Section B authorises the implementation of quantitative restrictions to safeguard the balance of payments. Meanwhile, Section C allows for the enactment of measures that might be inconsistent with other GATT provisions if they are deemed necessary for the promotion and establishment of a specific industry. This could include practices such as the application of quotas or the setting of discriminatory minimum price requirements.[31]

Article XXVII, sections A and C, within the GATT 1994, provide developing countries with substantial authority to shield their nascent domestic industries. However, the rigorous demands for compensation and the overly stringent conditions have led to a notable lack of utilisation of these provisions. The contentious debate regarding the efficacy of these measures is further highlighted by their limited implementation history. Notably, Article XVIII:A has not been invoked in over half a century. In a similar vein, Article XVIII:C has seen minimal effectiveness, evidenced by its unsuccessful application in the few instances it has been raised since the establishment of the WTO.[32] The limited application of these provisions can also be ascribed to the interpretation of the Dispute Settlement Understanding (DSU) within the WTO, which is frequently characterised as stringent. This has been attributed to WTO adjudicating bodies often taking a textualist approach when interpreting key provisions, but as a consequence, this makes WTO decisions often divorced from the context, object and purpose of the provision, thus why development has often been relegated as a side issue.[33] This

[29] General Agreement on Tariffs and Trade 1994 (n 5), Art XVIII (1).
[30] ibid Art XVIII: A (7).
[31] ibid Art XVIII: C (13).
[32] N Hart, 'Special and Differential Treatment at the World Trade Organisation: A case of Limited Results and Misconstrued Arguments?' (2018) 2 *Western Australian Student Law Review* 1, 4, classic.austlii.edu.au/au/journals/WAStuLawRw/2018/1.html#fn84, accessed 1 February 2024.
[33] P Mavrodis, 'No Outsourcing of Law? WTO Law as Practiced by WTO Courts' (2008) 102(3) *American Journal of International Law* 421, 470.

interpretation has been a contributing factor to the restrained use of such measures in international trade contexts. In the case of India-Quantitative Restrictions[34] the WTO's ruling on India's financial position as 'adequate' negated the necessity for import restrictions. This decision exemplifies the Appellate Body's hesitancy to interpret Article XVIII: B broadly, consequently limiting its impact. Such a stance arguably tilts the balance in favour of developed countries, as it restricts the flexibility intended for developing nations under this provision.[35]

ii. Tariffs and Custom Duties: The Enabling Clause

Under the 1979 GATT Decision on Differential and More Favourable Treatment, Reciprocity and Fuller Participation of Developing Countries[36] commonly referred to as the 'Enabling Clause', the obligations of Most Favoured Nation (MFN) treatment are waived to allow for the establishment of permitted tariff preferences. This significant provision, detailed in para 2(c), also enables developing countries to form preferential trade agreements that are exempt from the stringent criteria set forth in GATT Article XXIV for regional free-trade agreements. The Enabling Clause allows preferential tariff treatment to be established on products that originate in developing countries in accordance with the Generalised System of Trade Preferences (GSP) Scheme.[37] The provision also allows for horizontal agreements between least-developed countries to minimise or eliminate trade barriers. The Appellate Body in *EC – Tariff Preferences* (2004)[38] confirmed the operation of the Enabling Clause as an exception to Article I:1 of the GATT 1994. The success of the GSP has deepened trade preferences for developing and least-developed countries; for example, the EU Everything But Arms initiative and the US African Growth and Opportunities Act, which grants duty and quota-free access for all goods exported by least-developed countries have allowed for significant expansion and growth.[39] However, the effectiveness of this scheme, as outlined in the Enabling Clause, is constrained by several factors, including inadequate policy design, restrictive interpretive criteria, inherent discrimination, and the interpretations made by the Appellate Body. These challenges underscore the necessity for further development and refinement of the Enabling Clause to enhance its utility and effectiveness in addressing the needs of developing countries within the global trade framework.

[34] Panel Report, India – Quantitative Restrictions on Imports of Agricultural, Textile and Industrial Products, WT/DS90/R (6 April 1999) 46–50.

[35] Hart (n 32).

[36] Differential and More Favourable Treatment Reciprocity and Fuller Participation of Developing Countries, L/4903 (28 November 1979) ('Enabling Clause').

[37] World Trade Organization, 'Special and Differential Treatment Provisions' (WTO, 2024), www.wto.org/english/tratop_e/devel_e/dev_special_differential_provisions_e.htm, accessed 1 February 2024.

[38] Appellate Body Report, EC – Tariff Preferences, WTO Doc WT/DS246/AB/R (7 April 2004).

[39] A Keck and P Low, 'Special and Differential Treatment in the WTO: Why, When and How? (WTO, May 2004) 12 www.wto.org/english/res_e/reser_e/ersd200403_e.htm, accessed 1 February 2024.

B. The Developmental Consequences of Weakening SDT in a Shifting Global Trade Context

Developing and least-developed countries are significantly concerned with the diminishing effect of the Enabling Clause as overall multilateral reductions of tariff rates are now like or equal to preferential tariff rates, hence lessening their effectiveness in achieving WTO objectives.[40] Contrasting to regular WTO tariff commitments, they are not 'bound' under WTO agreements which can create instability and uncertainty if changed quickly.[41] The increase of regional trade agreements that provide deeper and more secure preferences, such as NAFTA and MERCOSUR, are also making the preferences provided under the GSP less effective and essential.[42] Considering the power of developed countries, GSP schemes are often manipulated by applying complicated and restrictive rules of origin to decrease indirect groups of beneficiaries.

The current system of granting differential tariff treatment tends to favour developed countries. These countries often grant preferences to least-developed countries or focus on specific regions, creating more favourable conditions for their economies. This approach is evident in the preference given to countries like those in sub-Saharan Africa, while simultaneously restricting nations such as India and China, often to further political or economic agendas that do not align with the objectives of the WTO.[43] The Appellate Body, in *EC – Tariff Preference*[44] stated that to comply with the principle of 'non-discriminatory' treatment, countries offering tariff preferences must ensure equal treatment for all similarly situated beneficiaries of a Generalised Scheme of Preferences. However, this has been broadly interpreted to suit the interests of developed nations. For instance, they might grant preferences to Sub-Saharan Africa, deeming these countries not 'similarly situated' to China, thus exempting themselves from extending benefits to China. Developed countries, therefore, set strict conditions for tariff preferences, favouring developing countries that align with their own economic and political agendas. The analysis above concludes that the positive effects that the Enabling Clause and GSP can create in the current global economy are diminishing. Reform and development are needed to establish preferential treatment conditions that produce evidenced-based outcomes that are fair and non-discriminatory, in order for developing and least-developed countries to see real benefits. Several commentators have criticised SDT provisions on the basis that they merely constitute 'protectionist trade policies', and that these are 'inefficient tools for industrial

[40] World Trade Organization, 'Some Issues Raised' (WTO, 2024), https://www.wto.org/english/thewto_e/whatis_e/tif_e/dev4_e.htm, accessed 1 February 2024.

[41] ibid.

[42] C Michalopoulos, 'Trade and Development in the GATT and WTO: The Role of Special and Differential Treatment for Developing Countries' (2000) Working Paper, World Trade Organization (28 February) 24.

[43] B Hoekman, C Michalopoulos and LA Winters, 'Special and Differential Treatment of Developing Countries in the WTO: Moving Forward After Cancún' (2004) 27(4) *World Economy* 481, 485.

[44] Appellate Body Report, EC – Tariff Preferences, WTO Doc WT/DS246/AB/R (7 April 2004).

development'.[45] It is contended that such measures merely function to prolong the full participation of developing countries in the multilateral trading system, which is hindering their economic development and the achievement of ultimate trade equality.[46]

There is also a broader debate about whether SDT provisions are simply a superficial solution to the deeper systemic challenges faced by developing nations in global trade, suggesting that the rules-based order primarily advantages developed countries over those in the Global South. The argument that SDT provisions are merely a way to placate developing countries into participating in the global trade system is contentious. This issue is further complicated by the significant growth of South–South trade, which has become one of the quickest expanding trade patterns worldwide, increasing from 10.8 per cent of global trade in 1995 to 25 per cent in 2020, indicating a rapid and ongoing growth trend.[47] This growth is occurring despite 70 per cent of tariffs faced by developing country exporters being applied by other developing countries,[48] and views that there has been a lack of solidarity between developing country partners to promote greater trade among other developing country states.[49] These emerging facts on the ground demonstrate that a rules-based trade order do not present a *fait accompli* that developing countries are locked into inequality due to the structural impediments. Each developing country has varying degrees of exposure to developed countries and therefore has varying reliance on SDT provisions to obtain more equitable outcomes.

IV. Intellectual Property Rights in the Global Trade Framework: Special and Differential Treatment as a Compromise in North–South Negotiations

Prior to the creation of the WTO, intellectual property was primarily regulated through a collection of treaties, including the Paris Convention on Industrial

[45] J Stiglitz and A Charlton, *Fair Trade for All* (Oxford University Press, 2005) 88; S Panitchapakdi and P Sutherland, 'The Future of the WTO: Addressing Institutional Challenges in the New Millennium' Consultative Board Report World Trade Organization (2004).

[46] Panitchapakdi and Sutherland (ibid) 24 (as cited in A Brennan, 'The Special and Differential Treatment Mechanism and the WTO: Cultivating Trade Inequality for Developing Countries' (2011) 14 *Trinity College Law Review* 143, 150); A Hold and BC Mercurio, 'Transitioning to Intellectual Property: How can the WTO Integrate Least-Developed Countries into TRIPS?' (October 2012) NCCR Working Paper No 2012/37, 23, www.wti.org/media/filer_public/2f/05/2f051554-f2fa-4018-8c63-c4fbd0eb4841/hold_mercurio_transitioning_to_intellectual_property.pdf, accessed 1 February 2024.

[47] UNCTAD, *Trade and Development Report 2022* (United Nations, 2023) 118, unctad.org/system/files/official-document/tdr2022_en.pdf, accessed 1 February 2024.

[48] Department of Foreign Affairs and Trade, *South-South Trade: Winning from Liberalisation* (Australian Government, 2004), www.dfat.gov.au/sites/default/files/south_south_trade.pdf, accessed 1 February 2024.

[49] J Scott, 'The International Politics of South-South Trade' (2016) 22 *Global Governance* 427.

Property[50] and the Berne Convention on Literary and Artistic Works.[51] These were administered by the World Intellectual Property Organization (WIPO) under the auspices of the United Nations. Furthermore, the protection of intellectual property was recognised as a general exception to free trade under Article XX(d) of the GATT.[52] Nevertheless, concern was expressed by developed countries from the late 1970s that 'the treaty system administered by WIPO failed to adequately protect the interests of their technology-based and expressive industries'.[53] It was the view of developed countries that 'the WIPO system did not provide adequate mechanisms for enforcing obligations'.[54] Such concerns, among others, led to the Uruguay Round trade negotiations, during which developed countries pushed for the development of the TRIPS Agreement in order to 'incorporat[e] intellectual property rights into the larger international trade framework'.[55] In view of the concerns of developed countries, 'the Agreement was designed to fill a perceived gap in the GATT 1947 legal system'.[56]

The inclusion of substantive intellectual property rights standards within the multilateral trade system going beyond limiting restrictive and anti-competitive uses of intellectual property was opposed by developing countries during early Uruguay Round negotiations.[57] As a result, the negotiations 'pitted least-developed countries against developed countries',[58] with developed countries seeking a 'comprehensive agreement to be embodied within the WTO system'[59] and LDCs preferring to rely on the pre-existing treaties administered by the WIPO. For example, India emphasised that the imposition of intellectual property principles and standards 'should be carefully tested against the needs of developing countries'.[60] It was further argued that the 'monopolistic and restrictive character' of the intellectual property system 'had special implications for developing countries' and that 'the freedom of Member states to attune their intellectual property protection system to their own needs and conditions' ought to be maintained.[61] It is clear that developing

[50] Paris Convention for the Protection of Industrial Property (opened for signature 14 July 1967, 828 UNTS 305, entered into force 26 April 1970).

[51] Berne Convention for the Protection of Literary and Artistic Works (opened for signature 24 July 1971, entered into force 15 December 1972) 1161 UNTS 3.

[52] General Agreement on Tariffs and Trade 1994 (n 5), Art XX(d).

[53] UNCTAD-ICTSD, *Resource Book on TRIPS and Development* (Cambridge University Press, 2005) 3; D Fox, 'Technology Transfer and the TRIPS Agreement: Are Developed Countries Meeting their End of the Bargain?' 10 *Hastings Science and Technology Law Journal* 1, 6.

[54] UNCTAD-ICTSD (ibid) 3.

[55] Fox (n 53) 7.

[56] UNCTAD-ICTSD (n 53) 3.

[57] ibid; F Abbott, 'Protecting First World Assets in the Third World: Intellectual Property Negotiations in the GATT Multilateral Framework' (1989) 22 *Vanderbilt Journal of Transnational Law* 689.

[58] Fox (n 53) 7.

[59] OJ Agutu, 'Least Developed Countries and the TRIPS Agreement: Arguments for a Shift to Voluntary Compliance' (2012) 20 *African Journal of International and Comparative Law* 423, 423.

[60] Meeting of Negotiating Group of 12–14 July 1989, GATT Doc MTN.GNG/NG11/14 (12 September 1989) (Note by the Secretariat) 4 [5].

[61] ibid.

countries were 'conscious of their underdeveloped structures and their need for more flexibility' in opposing the inclusion of intellectual property within the trade framework.[62]

Intellectual property rights have limited utility within national boundaries if something can be imitated or copied abroad. In an era where intellectual property provides an important source of wealth generation, intellectual property rights have critical significance as a means of controlling this source of wealth, especially for developed countries that already have global dominance of intellectual capital. The resulting TRIPS Agreement[63] saw developed countries being largely successful in having their intellectual property norms expressed globally through that Agreement, including protection afforded to patents, copyrights, trademarks, industrial designs and trade secrets under the WTO framework.[64] For example, the TRIPS Agreement 'significantly increased the level and expanded the scope of patent protection'.[65] The Agreement requires patent owners to be conferred exclusive rights,[66] for a period of no less than 20 years from the filing of the patent,[67] and requires enforcement procedures to be put in place to 'permit effective action against any act of infringement of intellectual property rights',[68] including patents. In order to be compliant with the TRIPS Agreement, member countries are therefore required to 'amend their legislations to bring them into compliance',[69] which is no mean feat for LDCs that have limited intellectual property protections and reduced institutional and financial capacities.

The success of developed countries in having their intellectual property norms espoused by the TRIPS Agreement was achieved, in part, by way of compromise which saw LDCs being provided with special and differential treatment through 'deferred implementation provisions and promises of technology transfer'.[70] As such, the TRIPS Agreement can be said to be 'microcosmic of the larger "bargained-for" exchange reached during the Uruguay Round'.[71]

[62] Agutu (n 59) 423.

[63] Formally known as the Agreement on Trade-Related Aspects of Intellectual Property Rights, the TRIPS Agreement is a comprehensive international agreement administered by the WTO, www.wto.org/english/docs_e/legal_e/27-trips_01_e.htm; Marrakesh Agreement establishing the World Trade Organization, opened for signature 15 April 1994, 1867 UNTS 3 (entered into force 1 January 1995) annex 1C ('Agreement on Trade-Related Aspects of Intellectual Property Rights').

[64] D Gervais, 'Intellectual Property, Trade & Development: The State of Play' (2005) 74 *Fordham Law Review* 505, 508; C Zhou, 'Can Intellectual Property Rights Within Climate Technology Transfer Work for the UNFCCC and the Paris Agreement' (2018) 19 *International Environmental Agreements: Politics, Law and Economics* 107, 114.

[65] W Zhuang, *Intellectual Property Rights and Climate Change: Interpreting the TRIPS Agreement for Environmentally Sound Technologies* (Cambridge University Press, 2017) 113.

[66] TRIPS Agreement (n 63), Art 28.

[67] ibid Art 33.

[68] ibid Art 41.

[69] Agutu (n 59) 431.

[70] Fox (n 53) 7–8.

[71] J Reichman and D Lange, 'Bargaining Around the TRIPS Agreement: The Case for Ongoing Public-Private Initiatives to Facilitate Worldwide Intellectual Property Transactions' (1998) 9 *Duke Journal of Comparative and International Law* 11, 17 (as cited in Fox (n 53) 8).

However, while other compromises under the multilateral trade framework generally take the form of 'mutually liberalizing "concessions" which benefit both parties', the setting up of minimum intellectual property standards by the TRIPS Agreement largely resulted in 'gains to developed countries and losses to developing ones'.[72] The absence of developing country concerns into the TRIPS Agreement was compounded by the fact that LDCs were not adequately represented during the Uruguay Round negotiations, which led to their needs and priorities not being 'actively articulated'.[73] Thus, the minimum standard protections for intellectual property rights, when isolated, limit access to new and emerging technologies that are needed for developing countries as new forms of economic growth[74] and continue to act as a knowledge blockade and technological protectionism.[75]

A. SDT Provisions within the TRIPS Agreement

While the TRIPS Agreement largely reflects the success of developed countries in incorporating the protection of intellectual property rights within the WTO framework,[76] it nevertheless attempts to balance this protection through provisions related to LDCs and by recognising developmental public policy objectives.[77] For example, the Preamble to the Agreement acknowledges the need to 'promote effective and adequate protection of intellectual property rights', noting they are 'private rights'.[78] However, it also recognises the special needs of LDCs by requiring that they are afforded 'maximum flexibility' in implementing the minimum standards of intellectual property protection required by the Agreement for areas such as copyright, trademark and patent protection.[79] This has been achieved, in part, through extensions of the deadline for LDCs to transition more smoothly into compliance with the Agreement and develop a 'sound and viable technological base'.[80] The machinations of this additional transition period are specifically addressed within Article 66; however, the Preamble's iteration is notable for its recognition that '*maximum*' flexibility ought to be afforded.[81] Additionally, the TRIPS Agreement notes within its objectives in Article 7 that 'intellectual property rights should contribute to the promotion of technological innovation and to the transfer and dissemination of technology'. The Article goes further in noting that

[72] Michalopoulos (n 42) 11.
[73] Agutu (n 59) 429.
[74] TK Giunta and LH Shang, 'Ownership of Information in a Global Economy' (1994) 27 *George Washington Journal of International Law and Economics* 327, 348.
[75] E Su, 'The Winners and the Losers: The TRIPS Agreement and Its Effects on Developing Countries' (2000) 23 *Houston Journal of International Law* 69, 171.
[76] UNCTAD-ICTSD (n 47) 3 and Fox (n 53) 9–10.
[77] TRIPS Agreement (n 63), Preamble para 5 and art 7.
[78] ibid Preamble para 4.
[79] ibid Preamble para 6.
[80] ibid; Zhuang (n 65) 68.
[81] UNCTAD-ICTSD (n 47) 11; Preamble para 6 of the TRIPS Agreement (n 63) (emphasis added).

such transfers should be conducted in a manner 'conducive to social and economic welfare',[82] thereby reflecting the developmental benefits to be gained from effective technology transfer.

The implementation of the minimum standard provisions in the TRIPS Agreement for developing countries impose significant administrative costs and transfer of wealth from developing to developed countries, which hold the significant share of intellectual property. According to Subramanian, the resulting loss to imitative or copying industries for India could equate to US$1.3 billion, US$237 million for the Philippines and US$189 million for Thailand.[83] In recognition of this cost burden, transitional arrangements were included within Part VI of the Agreement, affording differential treatment to developing country members. The provisions contained within Article 66 are specifically targeted towards LDCs. Firstly, Article 66.1 allows LDCs to delay implementation of the Agreement for 10 years in recognition of their 'special needs and requirements', including the 'need for flexibility'.[84] The provision further recognises the 'economic, financial and administrative constraints' impacting the ability of LDCs to implement the Agreement. Additionally, Article 66.2 of the TRIPS Agreement requires developed countries to 'provide incentives to enterprises and institutions in their territories to promote and encourage technology transfer to least-developed country Members'.[85]

The general transition period contained within Article 66.1 provided LDCs with flexibility in compliance with the Agreement's provisions, other than provisions on national treatment and Most Favoured Nation, for a period of 10 years from the date of application of the Agreement, namely one year following entry into force of the WTO Agreement.[86] However, the provision also provides that 'the Council for TRIPS shall, upon a duly motivated request by a least-developed country Member, accord extensions of this period'.[87]

Such extensions have occurred on a number of occasions in the past, with the Council for TRIPS granting extensions to 1 July 2013,[88] to 1 July 2021,[89] and most recently to 1 July 2034.[90] In its decision to extend the transition period, the Council for TRIPS recognised the

> special needs and requirements of least developed country Members, the economic, financial and administrative constraints that they continue to face, and their need

[82] TRIPS Agreement (n 63), Art 7.

[83] A Capling, *Australia and the Global Trade System: from Havana to Seattle* (Oakleigh, 2001) 200.

[84] TRIPS Agreement (n 63), Art 66.2.

[85] ibid.

[86] ibid Art 66.1.

[87] ibid.

[88] Extension of the Transition Period under Article 66.1 for Least-Developed Country Members, WTO Doc IP/C/40 (30 November 2005).

[89] Extension of the Transition Period under Article 66.1 for Least Developed Country Members, WTO Doc IP/C/64 (12 June 2013) (Decision of the Council for TRIPS of 11 June 2013).

[90] Extension of the Transition Period under Article 66.1 for Least Developed Country Members, WTO Doc IP/C/88 (29 June 2021) (Decision of the Council for TRIPS of 29 June 2021).

> for flexibility to create a viable technological base, particularly due to the long-term social and economic impacts of the COVID-19 pandemic on least developed country Members.[91]

Importantly, the existence of such SDT provisions will only benefit LDCs through effective technical and financial cooperation.[92] Mounting dissatisfaction with the outcomes of SDT under the WTO Agreements, including the TRIPS Agreement, led developing countries to request their review during the Doha Round of multilateral trade negotiations. The resulting Doha Ministerial Decision on Implementation-Related Issues and Concerns states that parties are:

> [d]etermined to take concrete action to address issues and concerns that have been raised by many developing-country Members regarding the implementation of some WTO Agreements and Decisions, including the difficulties and resource constraints that have been encountered in the implementation of obligations in various areas.[93]

However, LDCs contend that these implementation concerns are yet to be adequately addressed. The following sections analyse such concerns with reference to the underlying SDT aims of Article 66.1 of the TRIPS Agreement in order to ascertain whether such concerns are warranted.

B. Challenges for LDCs in Implementing the TRIPS Agreement: Evaluating the Impact and Effectiveness of Article 66.1

The TRIPS Agreement is notable for expanding the 'geographical reach' of intellectual property protections through its imposition of mandatory obligations on all Member countries.[94] Many LDCs had never previously recognised intellectual property rights within their domestic legal systems, or at least had not done so to the same degree and in such a formalised manner.[95] Therefore, effective implementation and enforcement of the TRIPS Agreement by LDCs was always going to be a significant administrative and financial burden.[96] In recognition of this, Article 66.1 was inserted into the TRIPS Agreement to allow LDCs to delay implementation of the Agreement in recognition of their 'special needs and requirements'.[97] Notably, Article 66.1 allows for the transitional period to be extended by the Council for TRIPS which was reaffirmed in the most recent extension of the deadline to 1 July 2034. However, recent concerns highlighted

[91] ibid.
[92] ibid.
[93] Implementation-Related Issues and Concerns, WTO Doc WT/MIN(01)/17 (20 November 2001) (Decision of 14 November 2001) Preamble para 3.
[94] G Dinwoodie and R Dreyfuss, *A Neofederalist Vision of TRIPS: The Resilience of the International Intellectual Property Regime* (Oxford University Press, 2012) 21.
[95] Hold and Mercurio (n 46) 3.
[96] Fox (n 53) 10.
[97] TRIPS Agreement (n 63), Art 66.1.

by the LDC Group regarding the difficulties experienced in complying with the TRIPS Agreement raise questions as to the assumptions made regarding the correlation between intellectual property protection and development and the effectiveness of arbitrary transition periods, which can function to undermine SDT aims. These issues will be explored, first through a critique of the relationship between intellectual property and development and then through an examination of WTO Trade Policy Reviews, which provide valuable insights into the challenges faced by LDCs in complying with the TRIPS Agreement. In doing so, this chapter argues that Article 66.1 does not presently function to provide LDCs with adequate special and differential treatment. This is due to a combination of the minimum intellectual property standards of intellectual property protection and enforcement and arbitrary transition periods that require LDCs to comply with the TRIPS Agreement on a certain date or upon graduation from their LDC status, even if they still do not have the implementation capacity to do so.

C. Challenges in Protecting Intellectual Property Rights and Developmental Implications

Attention to the relationship between intellectual property and development has risen significantly in the last decade, particularly in light of the global diffusion of intellectual property norms that have entered 'even some of the world's smallest and most technologically undeveloped countries'.[98] However, views as to the effects of introducing strengthened levels of intellectual property protection within LDCs vary significantly.

While some argue that the introduction and development of intellectual property laws and institutions may provide beneficial developmental impacts and that they are 'preconditions of long-term economic growth',[99] it is generally accepted that the impacts 'in one particular social context may vary dramatically from … another'.[100] These variations may be a result of differing administrative and technical capacity constraints; however they may also be due to more cultural conceptions as to 'how access to and use of knowledge and different types of intangible resources should be regulated'.[101] As such, a more nuanced approach that takes into account the 'industry-specific and country-specific factors' is required in any consideration of the impacts of intellectual property on development.[102] This approach necessarily requires that the social realities of a specific country are engaged with.[103]

[98] M Forsyth and S Farran, *Weaving Intellectual Property Policy in Small Island Developing States* (Intersentia, 2015) 17.
[99] UNCTAD-ICTSD (n 53) 15.
[100] Forsyth and Farran (n 98) 6.
[101] ibid.
[102] UNCTAD-ICTSD (n 53) 15.
[103] Forsyth and Farran (n 98) 6.

In particular, it is becoming increasingly recognised that the introduction of strong intellectual property protection in countries under certain development thresholds such as LDCs 'is unlikely to generate any positive impacts'.[104] As noted by Netanel, 'there appears to be a consensus among leading mainstream development economists that uniformly strong levels of IP are highly detrimental to developing countries'.[105] The reason for the detrimental effect is largely because such strengthening requires increased enforcement, which in turn involves mobilising 'already scarce resources' in order to protect what are generally private commercial interests when such resources need to be leveraged for 'other competing, and more immediate, public policy priorities'.[106] Resourcing burdens, when coupled with the general lack of sufficient political cohesion and weak governance structures characteristic of LDCs, make implementing and enforcing clear national intellectual property policies particularly challenging and undermine the facilitation of development and economic independence.[107]

By imposing minimum standards of intellectual property protection, the TRIPS Agreement limits the flexibility of LDCs to 'tailor their own national [intellectual property] system to their specific needs' and reveals that the SDT aims of Article 66.1 are undermined.[108] In this way, developing country members are precluded from taking the same developmental paths as their developed country counterparts such as Japan and the United States, which benefited from periods of weak intellectual property protection 'so as to achieve their present levels of technological capability'.[109] Indeed, it can be argued that standardising the protection of intellectual property rights perpetuates a false presumption that each country has adequate infrastructure to protect such rights.[110]

V. Examining Implementation Challenges for LDCs

The difficulties faced by LDCs in complying with the TRIPS Agreement were recently highlighted by Chad on behalf of the LDC Group in its Communication made to the Council for TRIPS on 1 October 2020.[111] In this Communication,

[104] D Gervais, '(Re)implementing the Agreement on Trade-Related Aspects of Intellectual Property Rights to Foster Innovation' (2009) 2 *Journal of World Intellectual Property* 324, 350.

[105] N Netanel, *The Development Agenda: Global Intellectual Property and Developing Countries* (Oxford University Press, 2009) 5.

[106] C Correa, 'The Push for Stronger Enforcement Rules: Implications for Developing Countries in ICTSD (ed), *The Global Debate on the Enforcement of Intellectual Property Rights and Developing Countries* (Issue Paper No 22, February 2009) x, 31.

[107] Forsyth and Farran (n 98) 13, 16.

[108] Zhuang (n 65) 72.

[109] ibid.

[110] Michalopoulos (n 42) 8.

[111] Extension of the Transition Period under TRIPS Article 66.1 for Least Developed Country Members, WTO Doc IP/C/W/668 (1 October 2020) (Communication from Chad on Behalf of the LDC Group).

the LDC Group requested that the transition period under Article 66.1 be further extended beyond the present expiration date.[112] The Communication, alongside the decision to extend the transition period, highlights that LDCs continue to face 'serious economic, financial and administrative constraints and are still struggling with various challenges to uplift the socio-economic conditions with very little capacities'.[113] The members emphasise that compliance would require that resources be diverted from much-needed areas, particularly in light of the Covid-19 pandemic which has exacerbated socio-economic pressures.[114] While the eventual strengthening of intellectual property regimes by LDCs in accordance with the TRIPS Agreement will contribute to their development and see them be able to participate more fully in international trade, there is growing consensus that the impact of intellectual property rights is likely to vary on a case-by-case basis.[115] Indeed, a study by Lall found that 'countries at different levels of industrial and technological development face very different economic costs and benefits' from strengthened intellectual property regimes.[116] These conclusions emphasise the need for SDT measures such as those contained within Article 66 to remain in place, as such measures provide the flexibility required to ensure all countries will be able to engage more fully in international trade and realise the benefits of this engagement.

VI. Insights from WTO Trade Policy Reviews

All WTO members are subject to periodic review under the Trade Policy Review Mechanism which aims to 'contribute to improved adherence by all Members to rules, disciplines and commitments made' under WTO Agreements.[117] The reports prepared following such reviews are instructive for present purposes as they are intended to undertake assessments in consideration of the 'wider economic and developmental needs, policies and objectives' of the countries.[118]

Notably, several reports prepared for LDCs recognise that 'structural constraints and vulnerabilities' are present within LDCs, which impact upon economic growth and cause their economies and financial systems to be 'vulnerable to shocks'.[119]

[112] ibid para 14.
[113] ibid para 11.
[114] ibid.
[115] UNCTAD-ICTSD (n 53) 15.
[116] S Lall, 'Indicators of the Relative Importance of IPRs in Developing Countries' (2003) 32 *Research Policy* 1657, 1657.
[117] Marrakesh Agreement establishing the World Trade Organization, opened for signature 15 April 1994, 1867 UNTS 3 (entered into force 1 January 1995) annex 3 ('Trade Policy Review Mechanism') para A(i).
[118] ibid para A(ii).
[119] Cambodia Trade Policy Review, WTO Doc WT/TPR/S/364/Rev2 (27 March 2018) (Report by the Secretariat) 6 [2]; Lao Trade Policy Review, WTO Doc WT/TPR/S/394/Rev1 (2 June 2020) (Report by the Secretariat) 6 [1].

Such shocks include high exposure to natural disasters, global pandemics and socio-political problems, which contribute to the developmental challenges faced by LDCs.[120] The socio-political problems faced include poverty alleviation and political instability, which remain significant challenges and contribute to the difficulties faced by LDCs in implementing and enforcing intellectual property laws.[121] For example, the report prepared for Nepal notes that Nepal suffers from an 'inadequate legal framework to protect intellectual property rights' and even where laws and institutions are in place, 'there is little data on enforcement'.[122] Even where gains are made, LDCs' vulnerability to shocks often functions to undermine such progress. For example, while Myanmar's per capita GDP has grown in recent years, this growth rate was significantly impacted, and is now expected to decline, due to the Covid-19 pandemic.[123]

Similarly, while Bangladesh notes that its Government 'has taken initiatives to amend and introduce new laws in accordance with the TRIPS Agreement',[124] the WTO Trade Policy Review reveals that the 'effective enforcement of existing legislation' continues to be impeded by institutional constraints, among others.[125] Despite the adoption of intellectual property policies and 'seemingly improved' enforcement mechanisms, the WTO remains concerned as to the country's 'limited resources and weak coordination' in the area of intellectual property enforcement.[126] This is of particular concern when noting that Bangladesh is expected to graduate from its LDC status in 2024.[127]

A. Adopting a Development-Centric Approach to TRIPS Compliance

The transitional time provided to LDCs within Article 66.1 constitutes an important SDT measure within the TRIPS Agreement. It is intended to not only allow LDCs more time to comply with the Agreement but also to assist LDCs in developing their domestic laws and policies 'to ensure that the eventual implementation of the TRIPS Agreement will promote rather than undermine their social, economic

[120] Solomon Islands Trade Policy Review, WTO Doc WT/TPR/S/349/Rev1 (6 March 2017) (Report by the Secretariat) 5 [1]; Haiti Trade Policy Review, WTO Doc WT/TPR/S/327Rev1 (25 February 2016) (Report by the Secretariat) 6 [1].

[121] Nepal Trade Policy Review, WTO Doc WT/TPR/S/381/Rev1 (27 February 2019) (Report by the Secretariat) 6 [2], [6].

[122] ibid 24 [2.18]; 6 [6].

[123] Myanmar Trade Policy Review, WTO Doc WT/TPR/S/405 (21 December 2020) (Report by the Secretariat) 7 [1].

[124] Bangladesh Trade Policy Review, WTO Doc WT/TPR/G/385 (6 February 2019) (Report by Bangladesh) 12 [3.19].

[125] Bangladesh Trade Policy Review, WTO Doc WT/TPR/S/385/Rev.1 (21 May 2019) (Report by the Secretariat) 10 [16].

[126] ibid 87 [3.165].

[127] ibid 30 [2.25].

and environmental wellbeing'.[128] In this way, the continued insistence that all country Members achieve uniform levels of intellectual property protection within limited time frames does not adequately take into account 'the context of overall development priorities' which necessarily differ between countries in response to the particular challenges faced.[129] Thus, the intersection of intellectual property and development needs to be approached with regard to the 'social realities' faced by LDCs as essential in comprehending their special and differential needs and how the imposition of new laws and institutions may impact them.[130]

Revising and modernising the principles of SDT is indisputably needed. To remain relevant and appreciative of new trade realities, provisions must be more targeted, operational and effective. This need is represented by the number of proposals to the WTO reflecting such issues. In 2018, a reform proposal by the United States claimed that current SDT is outdated and not reflective of the true dichotomy of the global economy.[131] In 2018, the European Union released a concept paper on WTO reform inclusive of SDT suggestions.[132] In 2019, Norway submitted a communication advocating for constructive advancements which was endorsed by another seven developed countries.[133] Overarchingly the proposals reflect the need to reform aspects such as country qualification, allowable exemptions and flexibility of rules.

VII. Conclusion

This chapter delved into the intricate dynamics between trade, sustainable development and the crucial role of SDT for the Global South. The nexus between trade and sustainable development has garnered substantial attention in contemporary economic discourse, particularly given the overarching framework of the SDGs. Liberalised trade, often lauded as a cornerstone for economic growth and poverty alleviation, is increasingly viewed through the prism of its contribution to sustainable development. In this context, the role of SDT provisions emerges as a linchpin for facilitating the integration of developing countries, especially those in the Global South, into the global trade system. These provisions, rooted in the principle of equity, acknowledge the varied capacities and developmental stages of countries, thereby necessitating differential obligations to level the playing field.

[128] M Azam, *Intellectual Property and Public Health in the Developing World* (Open Book Publishers, 2016) 242.
[129] Michalopoulos (n 42) 3.
[130] Forsyth and Farran (n 98) 6.
[131] Bacchus and Manak (n 24) 1.
[132] ibid 8.
[133] ibid.

However, a critical assessment of the implementation of SDT in the global trade regime reveals a landscape marred by inconsistencies and inadequacies. Despite the longstanding presence of SDT provisions, empirical evidence and narratives from the Global South suggest that the benefits reaped by these countries have been minimal. This situation is exacerbated by the complexities inherent in their diverse resource endowments, institutional capacities and legal frameworks. The WTO thus faces a formidable challenge in reconciling the practical application of SDT with its overarching objectives. The inadequacy of the current system, marked by weak binding authorities, limited access to provisions, and the exploitation of GSP schemes by developed nations, underlines a pressing need for reform.

The TRIPS Agreement, an integral component of the WTO framework, serves as a case study for examining the implications of SDT provisions. The Agreement's expansion of intellectual property rights to a global scale has disproportionately burdened many LDCs that previously did not recognise such rights domestically. Article 66.1 of the TRIPS Agreement, which allows LDCs to defer the implementation of the Agreement, ostensibly acknowledges these challenges. Yet, the effectiveness of this provision in providing meaningful SDT remains questionable, especially in light of the recent concerns raised by LDCs about the practical difficulties in complying with the TRIPS Agreement. These concerns bring to the fore the assumptions underlying the relationship between intellectual property protection and development and highlight the ineffectiveness of arbitrary transition periods, which may inadvertently undermine the aims of SDT.

The 2030 Agenda for Sustainable Development recognises international trade as a catalyst for inclusive economic growth and poverty reduction. SDT provisions are indispensable in this context, but their current underutilisation, attributed to constraints in legal character and construction, demands urgent attention. A paradigm shift focusing on distinct terms of obligations, implementation and technical assistance is imperative to ensure the economic growth, development and competitiveness of developing and least developed countries in the global economy.

Looking ahead, the principles of SDT require substantial revision and modernisation to remain relevant and responsive to new trade realities. Provisions must be more targeted, operational and effective to address the nuances of the evolving global economic landscape. This need for reform is underscored by various proposals submitted to the WTO, reflecting the urgency to recalibrate SDT provisions. For instance, in 2018, the United States proposed a reform,[134] highlighting that current SDT provisions were outdated and not reflective of the true dichotomy of the global economy. Similarly, the European Union's concept paper[135] on WTO reform and Norway's communication, supported by several developed countries, advocate for constructive advancements in SDT provisions, particularly regarding country qualification, allowable exemptions and the flexibility of rules.

[134] ibid 46.

[135] European Council, 'WTO Modernisation, Introduction to Future EU Proposals' Concept Paper (28 June 2018) 6.

The inefficacy of the current SDT framework within the WTO has far-reaching implications for the development trajectories and market access of developing and LDCs. This inadequacy is partly attributable to the non-binding nature of many SDT provisions, which are often phrased as 'best endeavour clauses' rather than mandatory obligations.[136] Consequently, developed members face no legal repercussions for non-compliance, undermining the enforceability and effectiveness of these provisions. This issue is further compounded by the 'one size fits all' approach, which fails to accommodate the varying developmental stages and needs of different countries.

To address these shortcomings, a comprehensive overhaul of SDT provisions is essential. Reforms must ensure that these provisions are not only legally binding but also tailored to the specific developmental needs of each country. This approach would facilitate a more equitable and inclusive global trading system, enabling developing countries and LDCs to harness the full potential of liberalised trade. Moreover, the reformed framework should encourage the gradual integration of these countries into the global economy, allowing them to progressively build the necessary institutional and legal capacities.

In conclusion, this chapter highlights the importance of SDT provisions as essential tools for narrowing the divide between global trade practices and sustainable development, especially for nations in the Global South. The present difficulties and shortcomings in applying these provisions call for a unified push for significant changes. These reforms should seek to ensure that SDT provisions are practical, tailored to the specific circumstances of each country, and consistent with their individual development objectives. Only through such targeted and effective implementation can the international trading system achieve its objective of fostering equitable growth and sustainable development across all nations.

[136] Wibowo (n 27) 16.

12

An Anatomy of Self-Damage and a Quest for Rules and Policies for Promoting Sustainable Investment to the Global South

MD RIZWANUL ISLAM*

I. Introduction

The presence of foreign investors in many sectors which were in the past reserved for governmental entities is commonplace. Increasingly foreign investors are often providers of social services such as education, health, water, electricity and garbage collection as commodities and make many social services tradable opportunities. Concomitant with the expansion of the breadth and diversity of foreign investment, there is an increasing number of foreign investment protection treaties either in the form of investment treaties or chapters in trade agreements. Most analysts are aware that the number of investment treaties protecting foreign investment has risen sharply; while as of July 1996, there were 1,010 bilateral investment treaties (BITs),[1] as of January 2023, there were around 3,000 BITs or analogous treaties with a foreign investment protection mechanism.[2]

In the aspirational part of the treaties, hortatory promises have been made and the developmental role of investment has been touted. However, more often than not, in the dispute settlement stage the protection of the proprietary interest of the investors has been on the forefront. This chapter argues that many of the BITs include provisions which may be labelled as inflicting self-damage on the host least developed countries (LDCs) and small developing countries. The differential

* The author thanks Professor James Thuo Gathii for his insightful comments on a section of a draft version of this chapter. He also gratefully acknowledges the able research assistance of Fateha Tun Noor and Sayere Nazabi Sayem. All errors are, of course, the author's alone.

[1] 'Recent Actions Regarding Treaties to Which the United States is Not a Party' (1996) 35 *International Legal Materials* 1130.

[2] UNCTAD Investment Policy Hub, investmentpolicy.unctad.org/, accessed 8 January 2023.

attitude of the developed economies to the LDCs and developing countries would be evident from the disparity of rights and obligations in the treaty provisions. This chapter argues that ongoing reform initiatives by the United Nations Commission on International Trade Law (UNCITRAL) Working Group III and the International Centre for Settlement of Investment Disputes (ICSID) only address some cosmetic reforms, such as having a more coherent set of precedents,[3] reducing the time and cost of the investor-state dispute settlement (ISDS) regime, and increasing the transparency in the ISDS regime – which would hardly make any improvement for the Global South[4] and might in effect, reinforce or entrench the challenges that they face.[5] This is likely to happen as the arbitrators would resort to the tools at their disposal, that is, the existing investment agreement and the vast body of jurisprudence developed by arbitral bodies formed pursuant to these agreements. Thus, any cosmetic reform without any meaningful overhaul of the root causes of the difficulties confronting the Global South would only send a misleading signal that the long overdue reform was taking place, when that would hardly be the case.

This chapter also analyses some municipal precedents to demonstrate how public interest may be subservient to parochial, private interests in the Global South. While this reference to local precedents may be unconventional, they may be important in the sense that they are under-explored in the existing literature. Even if these decisions are explored, those from the Global North are explored more, and generally the decisions from the Global South are explored when they form part of the issue before an international tribunal. The analysis of precedents of the Global South may thus be more revealing of the potential problems lurking around the national governance mechanism, which militates against the national interest. This would vividly show how a section of the local elite may be oblivious to the public interest or coalesce with foreign interests with no regard for national interest. These precedents imply that some of the challenges of promoting sustainable investment in the Global South are attributable to the lack of accountability of policy-makers in these countries. To this

[3] The interpretations can be so incoherent that one commentator has observed that '[a] most fertile area for finding differing interpretations of the same provision, or of ones that are the same or closely similar in different treaties, is in judgments, awards, and decisions of international tribunals relating to bilateral investment treaties'; see RK Gardiner, *Treaty Interpretation* 2nd edn (Oxford University Press, 2015) 486. For a comprehensive discourse on seeking more coherence in the investment arbitration regime, see G Zarra, 'The Issue of Incoherence in Investment Arbitration: Is there Need for a Systemic Reform?' (2018) 17 *Chinese Journal of International Law* 137.

[4] The term here refers to least developed countries and small developing countries. It is recognised that some of the points discussed in this chapter may not apply to large developing countries such as India, China, Brazil and South Africa, due to their economic size and increasing influence.

[5] For a thorough review of the discourse on reform, see JT Gathii, 'Reform and Retrenchment in International Investment Law' Keynote Remarks prepared for the Santander Roundtable Discussions on International Economic Law, co-hosted by Kenyatta University School of Law (Nairobi); Riara Law School (Nairobi); and the International Investment Law Center, at University of Cologne, 13 January 2021. For an anatomy of the relation between investment agreements and 2030 Sustainable Development Agenda, see L Johnson, L Sachs and N Lobel, 'Aligning Investment Treaties with Sustainable Development Goals' (2019) 58 *Columbia Journal of Transnational Law* 58.

extent, there has to be greater accountability of the negotiators or public officials who negotiate investment treaties or contracts with foreign investors. This, of course, is part of a broader and more complex issue of good governance.[6] This chapter acknowledges that the harms that foreign investment may inflict on the Global South are manifold and its analysis does not capture the full gamut of such harms. This chapter does not claim that all local investments are good and foreign ones are bad, it only seeks to highlight some of the perennial challenges, such as the access of host states and non-state actors in ISDS, the somewhat limited scope of bringing claims against foreign investors in ISDS, and the internal constraints stemming from bad governance or outright corruption in some parts of the Global South. It also seeks to make some observations to address these challenges.

II. What is Sustainable Investment?

When the question of sustainability is at issue, traditionally, the focus has been on environmental sustainability. However, there is no dogmatic formula for environmental sustainability followed in this chapter.[7] It does not adopt any formal, official definition of sustainable investment. This chapter adopts a different, artificially constructed notion of sustainability, in that foreign investment contributes to the overall economic development. It considers foreign investment sustainable as long as it does not reduce the overall economic welfare (broadly-defined) of the host state. It does not follow the traditional environment-centric notion of sustainability, as one state representative has remarked that often there is an unfortunate tendency to solely focus on the environment disregarding the social and economic equity aspects which is a burning reality.[8] In a world where increasingly the impact of the climate change is felt by many, such a focus is understandable but that is a global challenge, not unique to the Global South and beyond the scope of this chapter. This chapter also deems that the principle of non-regression from environmental protection as contained in the domestic law can more or less sufficiently allay the concern of environmental sustainability[9] and as historical polluters, the Global North needs to take the lion's share of countering the challenge of environmental sustainability.

[6] See below n 45 and the accompanying text.

[7] For a scholarly account of the genesis and interpretation of the term sustainable development, see V Barral, 'Sustainable Development in International Law: Nature and Operation of an Evolutive Legal Norm' (2012) 23 *European Journal of International Law* 377.

[8] 'CSD reveals unchanged positions on agriculture, trade, and sustainable development' *Bridges Weekly Newsletter* 4:4 (International Centre for Trade and Sustainable Development, May 2000).

[9] For a thorough review of the principle, see AD Mitchell and J Munro, 'An International Law Principle of Non-regression from Environmental Protections' (2023) 72 *International and Comparative Law Quarterly* 35.

III. The Riddle of the Drive for BITs and ISDS

There are many concerns about the ad hoc nature of the investment arbitration bodies and the propensity towards investor-friendliness of those bodies. Scholarly works have demonstrated that in order to be perceived as an investor-friendly state, a developing state or LDC may opt for a BIT with a binding arbitration mechanism. However, in collective terms, developing states and LDCs would be much better off with a regime in which they would not have to allow foreign investors the right to sue states in arbitral bodies.[10] Of course, one LDC or a small developing state may not have enough clout to influence the behaviour of foreign investors, but in collective terms this would not appear to be the case. The success of the less developed economies in the United Nations General Assembly in adopting Resolution no 1803 (XVII) of 14 December 1962, widely known as the Permanent Sovereignty over Natural Resources (PSNR), would exemplify this.[11]

While one may seek to dismiss the PSNR as an initiative of a bygone era, it has to be borne in mind that the Resolution was widely accepted by most of the developed and developing states. It is also generally accepted as the embodiment of customary international law on foreign investment. For example, in the *Topco/Calastine Case*, it was observed that the 1962 Resolution was an embodiment of the customary international law on foreign investment.[12] Thus, it would be argued that in coming years, the less developed economies would be better off abandoning the bilateral route of signing investment treaties.

In historical terms, the creation of an international investment claim forum was mainly the prerogative of victorious states, taking action over vanquished states when the former states were aggrieved by the action of the latter group of host states on the nationals of victorious states.[13] Host states consented to the jurisdiction of international juridical bodies following war or rebellion for capture, destruction of property, or inability to collect debts remaining due during an armed conflict.[14] Thus, these were acceptances of jurisdiction for past acts of the host states. The implication of this was quite significant, in that it did not in any

[10] AT Guzman, 'Why LDCs Sign Treaties That Hurt Them: Explaining the Popularity of Bilateral Investment Treaties' (1998) 38 *Virginia Journal of International Law* 639.

[11] Resolution no 1803 (XVII): 87 states voted in favour, 2 against, and 12 abstained.

[12] *Texaco Overseas Petroleum Company v California Asiatic Oil Company and the Government of the Libyan Arab Republic* (1978) 17 ILM 3.

[13] DJ Bederman, 'The United Nations Compensation Commission and the Tradition of International Claims Settlement' (1994) 27 *New York University Journal of International Law and Politics* 1, 3. This partially explains why countries such as Brazil, India and South Africa have not joined the International Centre for Settlement of Investment Disputes. For a detailed exposition of the nexus between the history of foreign investor protection and the contemporary international regime on foreign investment, see A Kaushal, 'Revisiting History: How the Past Matters for the Present Backlash against the Foreign Investment Regime' (2009) 50 *Harvard International Law Journal* 491.

[14] J Pauwelyn, 'Rational Design or Accidental Evolution? The Emergence of International Investment Law' in Z Douglas, J Pauwelyn and JE Viñuales (eds), *The Foundations of International Investment Law: Bringing Theory into Practice* (Oxford University Press, 2014) 11, 36.

way curtail or reign in the regulatory freedom of the host states. One can argue about the evolution of international law and point to the emergence of individual rights in the form of human rights. However, the point here is that investor rights were never touted as rights for the sake of investors alone, they were promoted as tools for promoting economic development. And while the investors have achieved rights in the form of directly bringing a legal claim before an international arbitral tribunal, those who are affected by the investors have hardly any corresponding access to international tribunals.

This should be all the more clear when the backlash against the ISDS regime by many of the traditional proponents of the mechanism, such as Canada, Europe and the USA, is observed. There is strong resistance to having an ISDS mechanism in the Transatlantic Trade and Partnership between the EU and the USA and the EU–Canada Comprehensive Economic and Trade Agreement.[15] Similarly, Australia has been reluctant to embrace ISDS in recent investment treaties. There is also the same double standard with regard to the principal architect of the contemporary investment protection regime, the USA, where Congress has passed laws designed to limit the scope of the ISDS regime.[16]

IV. The Absence of the Right of the Local Community or Indigenous People

Unlike a cross-border exchange of goods and services, foreign investment involves a much more direct and deeper engagement with the local community. A big investment project may involve the compulsory acquisition of land of the local community. However, the absence of the right of the local community or Indigenous People is conspicuous in international investment agreements.[17] Arguably, often the rights and interest of the three key actors – the host state, foreign investor and the local or indigenous community – may not coincide, and to assume that the host state would be the bastion of the interests of all interest groups within the host states could often be problematic.[18] At most, the affected local community could be able to submit an *amicus curiae* brief,[19] the value of

[15] A Orford, *International Law and the Politics of History* (Cambridge University Press, 2021) 46.

[16] WW Park, *Arbitration of International Business Disputes Studies in Law and Practice* 2nd edn (Oxford University Press, 2012) 701–06. See also HH Koh, *The Trump Administration and International Law* (Oxford University Press, 2019) 54–61.

[17] NM Perrone, 'The "Invisible" Local Communities: Foreign Investor Obligations, Inclusiveness, and the International Investment Regime' (2019) 113 *AJIL Unbound* 16. The existing international principal instruments dealing with corporate social responsibility – the UN Global Compact and the UN Guiding Principles on Business and Human Rights – if followed by investors, could help to ensure that the investment does not inflict any undue harm to the local community. However, though well-meaning, they do not have any real bite for any deviation by foreign investors; see J Ho, 'The Creation of Elusive Investor responsibility' (2019) 113 *AJIL Unbound* 10, 10.

[18] ibid.

[19] ibid.

which would in practice be left at the discretion of the arbitral tribunal in question. In the first place, they would be reliant on the diplomatic protection of the host states. The disparity of the international investment legal regime is stark here in that the community in whose land the investment is made and who is directly affected by it is relegated to the status of bystander, and the investor has a direct right to sue in a foreign arbitral tribunal. There is a somewhat remote, though not impossible, possibility of bringing human rights violation claims in regional human rights courts such as the African Court of Human Rights, the European Court of Human Rights and the Inter-American Court of Human Rights.[20] As remote as it is, to make things further limited, there is no such supra-national body for the largest continent, Asia. The traditional supra-national courts such as the International Court of Justice (ICJ) would not be the proper forum as only states have *locus standi* there.[21]

The scant regard paid by the investment arbitral tribunal to the interests of the local communities may be typified by *Bear Creek Mining v Peru*,[22] in which the claimant Canadian investor alleged that Peru failed to afford the claimant's investment in Peru the protections set out in the Free Trade Agreement between Canada and Peru. In essence, the claimant alleged that the permit they obtained to mine silver ore in 2007 by a determination of 'public necessity' by the Peruvian government, which the latter revoked after about three and a half years to quench the opposition of the local community, was an expropriation of their right. In essence, the majority of arbitrators accepted the claim.

However, in his partial dissent, Philippe Sands explained what more was expected to happen in this case and what, in his view, led to the collapse of the project. According to him, the project's death was largely due to the failure of the investor to obtain a social licence, that is, mutual trust between the investor and the community that was to be affected.[23] The tribunal pointed out that the project involved an area in which several Indigenous communities lived and that Peru was a signatory to the Indigenous and Tribal Peoples Convention, 1989[24] which was applicable in this case. The tribunal referred to *Urabser v Argentina*[25] and also pointed out the inclusive nature of Article 42(1) of the ICSID Convention and also that of the Canada – Peru FTA, which clearly stipulated that the domestic law of the state parties as well as all international law may be applicable.[26]

[20] ibid.

[21] One may contend that host state and non-state domestic actors may pursue domestic courts and tribunals to seek remedies against foreign investors. However, when the foreign investor has access to ISDS, that domestic access can hardly be meaningful. See below n 72 and the accompanying text; cf CN Brower, *Judging Iran: Judging Iran: A Memoir of The Hague, The White House, and Life on the Front Line of International Justice* (Disruption Books, 2023) arguing (*passim*) that sometimes foreign investors may be left at the mercy of despotic governments with no regard to investor protection.

[22] ICSID Case No ARB/14/21, award of 30 November 2017.

[23] Partial dissenting opinion of Philippe Sands, paras 5–6.

[24] Indigenous and Tribal Peoples Convention, 1989 (ILO Convention 169).

[25] ICSID Case No ARB/07/26, award of 8 December 2016.

[26] CSID Case No ARB/14/21, partial dissenting opinion of Philippe Sands (n 23), paras 10–11.

The majority dismissed the argument that this Convention imposed any obligation on the investor. Only the minority opinion held that it was applicable to the investors as well. The dissenting opinion emphatically observed that, just as international law confers rights on foreign investors 'local communities of indigenous and tribal peoples' also have rights under international law, and these are not lesser rights.[27] This sort of recognition would be of little value if such rights cannot be legally enforced.

In *Copper Mesa v Ecuador*,[28] Copper Mesa, which was involved in an open pit mining project in Ecuador, filed a claim for compensation due to the withdrawal of the concession. This had been withdrawn by the government based on fierce protest from the local community. The PCA arbitrators scathingly noted that the investor company had 'irrevocably, a malign reputation for intimidation, threats, deception, mendacity and violence amongst members of the local communities in the Junín area. It was a place from which there could be no easy return'.[29] Despite this, the claimant's claim was upheld; the tribunal felt that the consolation for the respondent was that the claimant's contribution to its own injury meant that the tribunal reduced the amount of compensation by 30 per cent.[30] This clearly demonstrates very scant regard to the plight of the local community, which was in the view of the tribunal had been subject to, inter alia, threats, deception and violence.

V. The Primacy of Investor Rights

In *Joseph Houben v Burundi*,[31] in 2005, Houben, a Belgian national, acquired around 14 hectares of land in Burundi for developing real estate. In 2007, Houben signed a sales contract with the US Embassy relating to this land, with the option to buy. However, at that time, Mr Houben was informed that back in 2002, the Public Prosecutor had obtained a prohibition on selling this land and so the US Embassy walked away from the contract. Some persons representing themselves as commission agents sold some parcels of the land. Houben claimed that Burundi had violated its obligations under the Agreement between the Belgium-Luxembourg Economic Union and the Republic of Burundi for the Promotion and Protection of Investments,[32] in that it did not follow the obligations to accord fair and equitable treatment (FET). This is because the Burundian authorities took contradictory positions with regard to the ownership of the land and also because the state did not try to prevent the squatters from getting hold of the land or try to

[27] ibid para 36 (emphasis added).
[28] PCA Case No 2012-02, Award (15 March 2016).
[29] ibid para 4.265.
[30] ibid para 6.102.
[31] *Joseph Houben v Burundi* ARB/13/7, Award of 12 January 2016.
[32] Signed 13 April 1989, entered into force 12 September 1993.

expel them from the land. The defence of Burundi that trying to expel the people from the land would have violated their human rights could not sway the tribunal.

However, when it came to an investor's human rights, the reading of another tribunal went in the diametrically opposite direction in *Al-Warraq v Indonesia*,[33] Al-Warraq, a Saudi investor, claimed that Indonesia expropriated his investment. The claimant was the shareholder of First Gulf Asia Holdings (FGAH) Limited a Bahamian company, through which he acquired shares in three banks, merging to form Bank Century (BC). When BC faced liquidity, it received a 'bailout' from Bank Indonesia (BI). BI lodged a complaint against the claimant for banking irregularities and eventually following a trial *in absentia* a judgment against the claimant followed and his assets were confiscated. Relying on the jurisdictional clause of the Agreement on Promotion, Protection and Guarantee of Investments among Member States of the Organization of the Islamic Conference,[34] the claimant argued, inter alia, that his FET treatment guaranteed by Article 14 of the International Covenant on Civil and Political Rights (ICCPR) was violated by the respondent as he was denied a fair trial. He argued that this occurred by conducting a trial in absentia, by disregarding the presumption of innocence until proven guilty, and he was not able to appoint legal counsel and/or appeal his sentence. The tribunal upheld his claim of the FET violation.[35] While the human rights defence could not sway the arbitral tribunal in *Houben*, the claim of human rights violation of the investor could persuade the arbitral tribunal in *Al-Warraq*.[36]

VI. Limited Locus Standi for the Host States

A noticeable feature of many (though not all) investment agreements is that while they allow investors to sue the host state in supra-national bodies, a corresponding right for the host state within the realm of ISDS can hardly be seen. Indeed, the Report of the Executive Directors of the International Bank for Reconstruction and Development accompanying the ICSID Convention asserted the objective of striking a balance between the rights of investors and host states. It proclaimed:

> While the broad objective of the Convention is to encourage a larger flow of private international investment, the provisions of the Convention maintain a careful balance

[33] *Al-Warraq v Indonesia*, Final award, IIC 718 (2014), 15 December 2014, Ad Hoc Tribunal (UNCITRAL).

[34] Entered into force 23 September 1986.

[35] *Al-Warraq* (n 33) para 621. It observed that 'the Claimant was not properly notified of the criminal charges against him, he was tried and convicted *in absentia* and the sentence was not properly notified to the Claimant. The Claimant was not able to appoint legal counsel and was not able to appeal his sentence. The Tribunal concludes, therefore, that the Claimant did not receive fair and equitable treatment as enshrined in the ICCPR for the above reasons – and not for any other pleaded by the Claimant. Accordingly, the Claimant's fair and equitable treatment claim is upheld.'

[36] It should be noted here that on various grounds, the tribunal did not hold in favour of his claim for compensation from Indonesia.

> between the interests of investors and those of host States. Moreover, the Convention permits the institution of proceedings by host States as well as by investors and the Executive Directors have constantly had in mind that the provisions of the Convention should be equally adapted to the requirements of both cases.[37]

However, the subsequent development of ICSID belies the above assertion. One may contend that these BITs are for the protection of investors, and as they are the outcome of negotiation between sovereign states, they would focus on the liability of states. However, as the treaties are signed to protect the right of investors, an absence of a direct mechanism for ensuring their liabilities is questionable. In practice, the general option for the host states is to opt for a counter-claim, but that presupposes that there is already a legal claim brought against the host state. Even within the limited option, there are cases where the arbitrators have followed a more limited literal reading of the treaties in question and have read them not to include any provision for counter-claim.[38]

Simply including the option of bringing counter-claims would have at best a modest value as the investor-right-centric treaties would not change. The ICJ has succinctly summarised the rare use, if not virtual disuse of the diplomatic protection by pointing out that 'the role of diplomatic protection somewhat faded, as in practice recourse is only made to it in rare cases where treaty régimes do not exist or have proved inoperative'.[39] Thus, for the sake of argument, assuming that reverting back to nineteenth and early twentieth century position of net capital importing countries' insistence on complete reliance on the domestic law as the mechanism for the protection of foreign investor rights may no longer be tenable, the special regime for protecting foreign investors with an automatic right to bring a legal claim against the host states should be re-thought.

As a general rule, often international law takes a more permissive approach when it comes to the protection of human life than to the protection of property rights. For example, most commentators tend to broadly agree that the use of force in foreign territories to protect nationals may be permissible in exceptionally grave circumstances but few of serious pedigree tend to argue the existence of any such right for the protection of the property of nationals located overseas. The argument here is not that the insistence on diplomatic protection may be apt for the protection of the interest of nationals; however, if it is tenable for many other areas, even in a comparable area such as international trade, the case for an exception for investment protection regime solely or pre-dominantly giving access only to foreign investors may be re-thought. It is also pertinent to note that since the

[37] Executive Director of the International Bank for Reconstruction and Development, *Report on the Convention on the Settlement of Investment Disputes between States and Nationals of Other States*, icsidfiles.worldbank.org/icsid/ICSID/StaticFiles/basicdoc/partB-section03.htm, para 13.

[38] *Rusoro Minining v Venezuela*, ICSID Case No. ARB(AF)/12/5, Award of 22 August 2016, pp 134–37.

[39] *Ahmadou Sadio Diallo (Republic of Guinea v Democratic Republic of the Congo), Preliminary Objections, Judgment* (2007) ICJ Reports 582, para 88.

advent of the International Military Tribunal at Nuremberg holding individuals liable for international crimes, the practice of a bygone era, in which non-state actors were almost exclusively answerable only to the municipal legal mechanism, no longer applies.[40] If access to justice for foreign investors is laudable, there would appear to be an equally plausible case for the same to apply to the host states and local communities.[41]

Scholarly works rightly point out that the limited scope of the host states to bring claims against investors only applies to the treaty-based ISDS, as states can and do avail of the option of bringing investment claims on the basis of contractual arbitration clauses.[42] However, this is only partially true as these arbitration clauses are fewer than the arbitration clauses in the treaty-based ISDS regime. A related argument also runs that states have sovereign rights, which entitle them to regulate investor conduct. However, but for investment treaty-based rights, investors would have no comparable right to ensure somewhat equality of rights.[43] This seeming truism is only a façade, as this chapter has already demonstrated that the exercise of the so-called unbridled sovereign rights is much narrower than they may seem and they are always susceptible to challenges by the investors.[44]

VII. The Inner Problem within Some States of the Global South

However, the problem with investment agreements or contracts is only partially attributable to the factors emanating from the Global North. In many cases, it is the inherent challenges of lack of a responsible government protecting the public interest in the Global South that are also capable of hurting their own interests. As Metz puts it, '[i]n many parts of the world, the state is a mechanism by which the group that controls it extracts as many resources as possible, whether money, concessions, government jobs, natural resources or pure power'.[45] Thus, any international agreement is only one part of the story which may make an investment unsustainable. An authoritarian, majoritarian, or even democratically elected government may become hostage to the interest of special interest groups over that of the local communities. This may be exemplified by examining case studies from a country in the Global South, Bangladesh. One can argue that cases from a

[40] Ho (n 17) 10.

[41] JS Kern, 'Investor Responsibility as Familiar Frontier' (2019) 113 *AJIL Unbound* 28, 31.

[42] C Braumann and A Reinisch, *Investment Court Systems* (Max Planck Encyclopedia of International Procedural Law, September 2018).

[43] ibid.

[44] For a nuanced treatment of this phenomenon, see V Korzun, 'The Right to Regulate in Investor-State Arbitration: Slicing and Dicing Regulatory Carve-outs' (2017) 50 *Vanderbilt Journal of Transnational Law* 355.

[45] MA Thomas, *Govern Like Us* (Columbia University Press, 2015) 5.

single jurisdiction cannot be representative of the global situation. Of course, such a critique is not implausible but cases of this nature still warrant more attention. As already pointed out, they rarely feature in the literature on international investment law.

In *Engineer Mahmudul-ul Islam and others v Government of the People's Republic of Bangladesh and others*,[46] the government accepted a proposal to set up container terminals in Chittagong Port on a Build Operate and Own (BOO) basis for a joint venture company (JVC) consisting of a Bangladeshi company named Orient Maritime Ltd, and a foreign company named SSA Netherlands. Filing a public interest writ petition, the petitioner, Islam, challenged the approval in the High Court Division (HCD) of the Supreme Court of Bangladesh, alleging that it was given arbitrarily without any public tender process, defying regular practice in Bangladesh. It also posited that building the terminal might jeopardise the operations of the nearby Chittagong Port. The petition also argued that the permission was fraudulently obtained in the name of the JVC consisting of Bangladeshi and US companies, but as per the articles of association, at the relevant time, the JVC which received the government's approval consisted of a Bangladeshi and Dutch company which was not even in existence. That is to say, in fact, only one Bangladeshi company was involved at that stage and there was not really any JVC.

The HCD held that public officials are expected to act in compliance with the law, taking into account the public interest.[47] It also held that as the government officials had acted without analysing the project profile and financial benefit and cost of the proposed container terminals, they acted improperly.[48] Any property or right belonging to the state could not be divested without holding competitive bids. Referring to the prevalent practice of the 'Swiss challenge',[49] the HCD suggested that it could use that mechanism to assess alternative bids.[50] The HCD concluded that awarding any government right or privilege without organising any public advertisement meant a denial of equal opportunity to other interested parties and was in breach of several provisions of the Constitution of Bangladesh.[51]

Rather alarmingly, the Board of Investment (currently renamed as the Bangladesh Investment Development Authority), the highest public body for approving any significant foreign investment proposal, along with top-ranked bureaucrats, failed to appreciate the fictitious nature of one of the shareholders of the JVC.[52] It is also surprising that several other proposals from other foreign

[46] Writ Petition No 4692 of 2000 (2003) 23 BLD (HCD) 80.
[47] ibid para 18.
[48] ibid paras 21–22.
[49] Swiss challenge refers to a special mechanism of bidding for public projects by which an authority receiving any unsolicited bid for any public infrastructure project would publish the bid and invite interested third parties to match or better the existing one.
[50] Petition No 4692 (n 46) para 24.
[51] ibid para 36.
[52] MR Islam, ILDC 3097 (BD 2002) (OUP reference).

investors did not receive sufficient attention.[53] And if there had been a genuine foreign shareholder company involved in this project, as the government had accepted the project proposal, potentially there could have been a plausible claim for expropriation of investor rights.[54] Despite the apparent disregard for domestic laws and practice, the public authorities approved the proposal through private negotiations, and hence, the foreign investor's claim could have prevailed.[55] Thus, this case shows the lack of care which is palpable from the absence of any effort to use the 'Swiss challenge' system[56] which the Court has appeared to suggest should be the norm in Bangladesh in approving a large investment project which could have harmed the public interest.

The second example of public authorities' sloppy approach at best and lack of accountability at worst, to government's commercial dealings is *Omer Ali v Government of Bangladesh* (2022).[57] In this case, the petitioner, the proprietor of an Indenting and Export-Import firm, participated in a tender floated by the Bangladesh Inland Water Transport Corporation (BIWTC) for purchasing and installing fog lights and other related spare parts for public ferries. The firm's bid was successful and upon complying with the legal procedure, the petitioner signed a contract with BIWTC and installed the fog lights and related devices.[58] However, during the winter season it transpired that the fog lights were not performing and the BIWTC asked the relevant bank to encash the bank guarantee provided by the supplier firm.[59] The petitioner filed a writ petition before the HCD challenging this action of the BIWTC.[60]

[53] ibid.

[54] This type of potential is implicit in the following observations of where even expenditures incurred in re-investment regarding a proposed thermal power station intended to supply power to the Ceylon Electricity Board electrical transmission grid on a Build-Own-Transfer (BOT) basis was sought to be recovered by the investor. Though the majority rejected the claim, regard should be had to the following observation in the concurring individual opinion of David Suratgar: 'If private foreign investors are to be encouraged to pursue transparency in seeking such BOT opportunities the international community must address the lessons of this case. Expenditure incurred by successful bidders do indeed produce "economic value" as specified by Article 1 of the US-Sri Lanka BIT and the protection mechanism developed under the aegis of the World Bank in the form of the ICSID Convention should be available to those who are encouraged to embark on such expensive exercises'. *Mihaly International Corporation v Sri Lanka*, Award, ICSID Case No ARB/00/2, (2002) 6 ICSID Rep 310 (2002) 41 ILM 867, para 10 of the concurrent individual opinion.

[55] Under the existing treaty practice it is even common to protect the right of a proposed investment, and the screening process of a proposed investment by the host state may itself give rise to a claim based on fair and equitable standard or most-favoured nation treatment etc. For a detailed exposition on this issue, see T Voon and D Merriman, 'Incoming: How International Investment Law Constrains Foreign Investment Screening' (2022) *Journal of World Investment and Trade* 1.

[56] It is a mechanism by which a public authority receiving any unsolicited bid for any public infrastructure project would publish the bid, and thereby invite all interested third parties to match or better the one that it had already received.

[57] *Omer Ali v Government of Bangladesh* (2022) 30 BLT (HCD) 377, LEX/BDHC/0156/2020.

[58] ibid paras 3–4.

[59] ibid para 3.

[60] ibid.

Four public officials had travelled to the USA to conduct the pre-shipment inspection of the fog lights to be installed and used in public ferries. However, only one of the four officials had the requisite technical knowledge to assess the quality of the lights.[61] Even more intriguingly, the public officials spent only a few hours conducting their examination on a six-day trip.[62] The HCD found that the officials had visited the Statue of Liberty, Liberty Island, Ellis Island, the Memorial Museum and similar places. They, in effect, had not spent even half a day in relation to the actual purpose of their US visit. Instead, the majority of their time had been spent visiting places which had no connection whatsoever to the professed purpose of the travel.[63] While on paper, the initial expenses of the travel were borne by the supplier, as per the terms of the contract, the entire expenses were eventually borne by the government.[64] It would seem that a foreign pre-shipment inspection (PSI) company could render the same service at a substantially lower cost. In fact, it is difficult to envisage how such a professional PSI company could serve any worse.

Even before the final installation, the fog lights were tested in June, during summer in Bangladesh, when naturally there would not be any fog in the rivers of Bangladesh. Thus, while this is not a case of foreign investment, it clearly shows the lack of care of public officials when performing their duties and their wasteful expenditure of public money, bordering on outright corruption. And this may serve as an example of the scant regard that public officials of a state in the Global South have for the waste of public resources. Of course, this is a public procurement and does not have any nexus to foreign investment. It may on first sight, appear as the HCD noted, as an 'innocuous' matter.[65] However, arguably, it is perceptible that this type of scant regard for public interest may be reflected in negotiating investment treaties and contracts. And in potential investment arbitrations, the same attitude is likely to mean a lack of interest in defending the interest of host states and local communities, or perhaps more appositely vested interests getting priority over national interests. Thus, while this second case is merely a commercial transaction involving the procurement by the government, this may, when juxtaposed with the first case analysed in this section of the chapter, offer some clue as to how little attention public interest may receive when negotiating international investment treaties or contracts. Due to the extreme scarcity of the publicly available record on negotiation for investment agreements and contracts, more direct evidence is difficult to obtain and thus they may serve as a valid proxy.[66] Countering these endemic deficiencies in governance in the Global South is a herculean task. However, ensuring greater transparency with investment

[61] ibid para 8.
[62] ibid para 10.
[63] ibid.
[64] ibid paras 12–13.
[65] ibid para 7.
[66] See also n 72 and the accompanying text.

treaties and contract negotiations, dispute settlement and associated matters may be a good beginning. That would allow interested members of the public and civil society some opportunity of knowing what is going on and hopefully foster some semblance of accountability.

VIII. What May the Global South Do?

As it is now more or less settled a question that there is none or only very fragile connection between investment treaty and attracting investment,[67] let alone sustainable investment, the Global South needs to be very circumspect in signing investment treaties following the pattern of the last couple of decades. And the Global South needs to have a paradigm shift on focusing on the quality of foreign investment and abandon its dogmatic faith in the value of the quantity of foreign investment. Perhaps in the most ideal scenario for the Southern states, they would seek a radical overhaul of the existing regime of international investment law which has been branded in scholarly work, as the current one does not allow the Global South to protect the public interest. This is because 'by using private and public power, acting in tandem, by using low order sources of international law, a regime has been created to ensure the modern multinational corporation, the conveyor of foreign investment, is insulated from developing states'.[68]

In view of the existing asymmetries in the investment treaty regimes, there are several things that the Southern states may do. As most treaties are negotiated rights, there may be scope for them to renegotiate treaty provisions that curtail the regulatory autonomy of the host states. In very recent memory, there is at least one radical example of an extensive treaty being completely superseded by a new one – the North American Free Trade Agreement (NFATA), which was superseded by the United States-Mexico-Canada Agreement (USMCA) from 1 July 2020. In future negotiations of treaties, the Global South would seem to be much better off taking the multilateral route where their collective clout should stave off the pressure to accept obligations that may not be in their interest. A parallel may be drawn where almost invariably, Southern states conceded much more in their bilateral treaties than what they offered under the global regime.[69] There should be an explicit recognition that state actions in exercise of its so-called

[67] M Hallward-Driemeier, 'Do Bilateral Investment Treaties Attract Foreign Direct Investment? Only a Bit … and They Could Bite' (2023) (World Bank Working Paper No 3121). See also M Irandoust, 'A Survey of Recent Developments in the Literature of FDI-Led Growth Hypothesis' (2010) 11 *Journal of World Investment & Trade* 275.

[68] J Linarelli, ME Salomon and M Sornarajah, *The Misery of International Law: Confrontations with Injustice in the Global Economy* (Oxford University Press, 2018) 147.

[69] MR Islam, *Economic Integration in South Asia: Charting a Legal Roadmap* (Marinus Nijhoff Publishers, 2012) 104–05.

police powers are not tantamount to indirect expropriation.[70] A professed goal of foreign investment has been to enhance the local skill base, and to ensure this there should be explicit provisions in the investment agreements that foreign investors will appoint and train local people.[71] There has to be much more emphasis on ensuring that foreign investment is not tainted by fraud or corruption on the part of investors and such illegal activities should disentitle them to invoke the jurisdiction of international tribunals.[72] There should be more explicit recognition of the host state's inherent right to act in public interest and they should be incorporated as *rights* of the host states, not as defences to investor's claim for violation of rights. This is important as when they are framed as rights, it is only plausible to expect that the international arbitral bodies would be more deferential to these rights.[73]

IX. Conclusion

It is deplorable that even when the world is beset with perennial issues, such as the Covid-19 pandemic and climate change, the issue of investor protection is sometimes at the centre stage of the global debate. The post-Covid-19 world should harness the perception of common vulnerabilities of humankind. The sacrosanct treatment that the right of investors has sometimes received should not continue to be the norm in the future. The transparency of the ISDS mechanism is not by any means enough. The call for transparency should embrace much more. International investment agreements and major investment contracts need to be signed with as much transparency as possible. Without addressing the Global South's systemic

[70] H Mann, 'Reconceptualizing International Investment Law: Its Role in Sustainable Development' (2013) 17 *Lewis and Clark Law Review* 521, 538.

[71] ibid.

[72] ibid 541. In relatively few cases this has happened, see for example, *World Duty Free Company v Republic of Kenya*, ICSID Case No ARB/00/7, Award of 4 October 2006, (2007) 46 ILM 339, para 146. However, regard should also be had to the case of *Niko Resources (Bangladesh) Limited v Bangladesh Petroleum Exploration & Production Company Limited ('Bapex') and Bangladesh Oil Gas and Mineral Corporation ('Petrobangla')*, Decision on the corruption claim, ICSID Case No ARB/10/11, ICSID Case No ARB/10/18, award of 25th February 2019, brushing aside the charge of Bangladesh that the applicant Niko was involved in corruption. This is despite the fact that the ICSID tribunal did so despite the proven fact of the 'gift' of a vehicle to the State Minister of Energy of respondent Bangladesh and the payment of travel expenses for him, and for these Niko was convicted of corruption. The ICSID tribunal reasoned that it was because the Crown was unable to prove that any influence was obtained as a result of providing the benefits to the Minister. To accept the analogy of the ICSID would mean holding that as long as corrupt acts succeed in yielding tangible outcomes, they are not corrupt. It should be noted here that US authorities also implied that the action of Niko was corrupt by stating: 'While we have determined that prosecution is not necessary at this time in light of Niko's guilty plea in Canada, this letter should not be taken as an indication that *we do not have concerns about Niko's compliance with FCPA*', at para 377 (emphasis added). It may be mentioned that more than a decade after the blowout, the ICSID tribunal is yet to conclude on the liability of Niko.

[73] Mann (n 70) 540.

issues, efforts at UNCITRAL and ICSID revolving around cosmetic changes will not make any meaningful contribution to the Global South.

Under the existing regime, it would be fair to say that foreign investors have greater rights than nationals of host states. And the existing ISDS regime has not been proven to be adequately successful in ensuring the corresponding accountability of the investors.[74] Whether there is a need for a completely new frontier, or whether some radical overhaul of the current regime could ensure a fair balance may be a somewhat open question. There has to be some breathing space for the domestic regulatory autonomy of the host states. An investment regime conferring rights on investors who are only subjects of municipal law with scant duties being imposed on them is something that needs some serious re-thinking. Unless international investment law takes a full account of the interest of the neglected 'others', it is difficult to see how the Global South may meaningfully benefit from it. And without concerted effort from the Global South improvement is likely to remain elusive in the foreseeable future.

[74] See above n 72 and the accompanying text.

13

Beyond Good Intentions: Corruption Challenges in Taiwan's Foreign Aid

ERNIE KO AND SUMAIYA KHAIR

I. Introduction

Aid can take various forms, each serving distinct purposes in the context of international development. These include bilateral aid;[1] multilateral aid;[2] technical assistance;[3] project aid;[4] and debt relief/waivers.[5] Foreign aid, also known as Official Development Assistance (ODA), refers to the financial or in-kind assistance provided by one country to another with the primary aim of promoting economic development and reducing poverty in the recipient country. It is primarily the 'transfer of resources/wealth from developed nations or international financial institutions (IFIs) to less developed countries, … either through bilateral or multilateral source to promote economic growth and development of

[1] Provided directly from one government to another to address specific needs or projects in the recipient country. See OECD, *Glossary of Key Terms in Evaluation and Results Based Management*, 2020, www.oecd.org/dac/evaluation/glossaryofkeytermsinevaluationandresultsbasedmanagement.htm.

[2] Provided by multiple countries through international organisations, for example World Bank, UN agencies for tackling global issues or fund projects that benefit multiple countries. See 'Net Official Development Assistance and Official Aid Received (Current US$)' *World Bank Open Data* (2021), data.worldbank.org/indicator/DT.ODA.ALLD.CD, accessed 30 March 2024.

[3] This is non-financial aid involving the transfer of skills, knowledge, or expertise to strengthen institutional capacity and promote sustainable development. See United Nations, 'About' (UN E-Government Knowledge Base), publicadministration.un.org/egovkb/en-us/About/UNeGovKB-KnowledgeBase/Technical-Assistance, accessed 30 March 2024.

[4] Provided for specific projects or programmes to address targeted issues such as infrastructure development, education or healthcare. See World Bank, 'Project Financing' (2021), www.worldbank.org/en/what-we-do/brief/project-financing.

[5] This involves the reduction or cancellation of a country's debt obligations to help alleviate financial burdens and create fiscal space for development. See International Monetary Fund, 'Debt Relief under the Heavily Indebted Poor Countries (HIPC) Initiative', www.imf.org/en/About/Factsheets/Sheets/2023/Debt-relief-under-the-heavily-indebted-poor-countries-initiative-HIPC, accessed 5 June 2024.

the recipient countries'.[6] All such transfers between the donor and recipient country are driven by various motivations, such as, humanitarian concerns, Christian missionary, geopolitics, postcolonial complex and trade/business. This motivation-based theory is widely acknowledged by the international community, and after World War II such assistance came to be known as 'foreign aid'.[7] Since the 1990s, the term 'international cooperation' has made its way into the aid jargon to signify equal footing between the aid giver and the taker.[8] ODA often comes with concessional terms, meaning that the terms are more favourable than those available in the market. This includes low-interest loans, grants or other financial instruments designed to support the recipient country without imposing an undue financial burden. Foreign aid can be provided through multilateral channels, where multiple countries contribute to a fund managed by an international organisation (eg the World Bank), or through bilateral agreements directly between two countries.

The economic rationales behind foreign aid may be many. For instance, aid is often provided to stimulate, albeit slowly, economic growth[9] in recipient countries, fostering stability, reducing poverty, and promoting sustainable development; it supports investments in education, healthcare[10] and infrastructure, contributing to the development of human capital and enhancing productivity; it may be used to enhance trade capacities and market access, fostering economic integration and competitiveness;[11] it contributes to the provision of global public goods, such as health security, environmental protection and peacekeeping;[12] it can also be used as a tool for conflict prevention by addressing the root causes, promoting good governance, and supporting peace-building efforts.[13]

Indeed, debates and discussions surround the effectiveness, transparency and potential challenges associated with foreign aid. Critics often raise concerns about issues such as corruption, conditionality and the long-term impact of aid programmes. Conversely, proponents argue that well-designed aid initiatives have

[6] DA Mustafa, A-H A Kilishi and SB Akanbi, 'Corruption and Foreign Aid Nexus in the African Continent: An Empirical Analysis for Nigeria' (2015) 6 *Journal of Economics and Sustainable Development* 98, 100.

[7] E Ko, 'International Trend on Foreign Aid and Taiwan Model' (2003) 4 *Yu Da Journal* 127, 129; T-C Lin and J Y-C Lin, 'Taiwan's Foreign Aid in Transition: From ODA to Civil Society Approaches' (2007) 18(4) *Japanese Journal of Political Science* 469.

[8] See M Edwards, 'International Development NGOS: Agents of Foreign Aid or Vehicles for International Cooperation?' (1999) 28 *Nonprofit and Voluntary Sector Quarterly* 25; Lin and Lin (n 7); C-W Tseng and others, 'An Empirical Evaluation of Taiwan's Foreign Aid Projects: Case Study of a Food Security Development Project in Haiti (2011–2013)" (2021) 60(3) *Issues and Studies* 115.

[9] MA Clemens and others, 'Counting Chickens When They Hatch: Timing and the Effects of Aid on Growth' (2011) 122 *The Economic Journal* 590.

[10] AS Rajkumar and V Swaroop, 'Public Spending and Outcomes: Does Governance Matter?' (2008) 86 *Journal of Development Economics* 96.

[11] OECD and World Trade Organization, *Aid for Trade in Action* (OECD Publishing, 2013) 81.

[12] I Kaul and others, *Global Public Goods: International Cooperation in the 21st Century* (Oxford University Press, 1999).

[13] P Collier and A Hoeffler, 'AID, Policy and Peace: Reducing the Risks of Civil Conflict' (2002) 13 *Defence and Peace Economics* 439.

the potential to address global inequalities and promote sustainable development. The nexus between corruption and foreign aid in developing economies is an enduring concern that has deep historical roots. While foreign aid catalyses positive change by supporting development initiatives and addressing development challenges outlined in the Sustainable Development Goals (SDGs), corruption undermines equitable aid distribution manifesting in diversion of funds, mismanagement of resources, and erosion of public trust. The achievement of SDGs therefore requires transparent and accountable governance structures. Countries with robust anti-corruption measures and good governance practices are more likely to utilise foreign aid efficiently, fostering sustainable development outcomes.[14]

Corruption in foreign aid signifies the irregularities and unethical practices which compromise the intended outcomes of aid initiatives. Whether siphoning funds away from development projects or distorting aid distribution based on personal or political interests, corruption erodes the integrity of aid delivery systems. As nations struggle with the complexities of economic development and poverty reduction, the misallocation, diversion and misuse of aid funds significantly obstruct the achievement of sustainable development outcomes, hindering the positive impact that foreign aid is meant to have on recipient nations. It also raises questions about the efficacy of aid delivery mechanisms and the overall integrity of development processes.

This chapter aims to provide an understanding of the link between corruption and foreign aid by exploring its forms and patterns, and the profound impact it has on development outcomes in recipient countries. In examining the relationship between foreign aid and corruption, the chapter draws on Taiwan's foreign aid policy and practice to showcase the impact of foreign aid on corruption in recipient countries. Taiwan's foreign aid has been facing enormous criticism from both home and abroad for its apparent lack of transparency and accountability.[15] Foreign aid from Taiwan is believed to escalate corruption in the aid-recipient countries, which predominantly consist of southern nations. The chapter underpins the significance of good governance for preventing corruption related to foreign aid.

[14] P Bardhan, 'Corruption and Development: A Review of Issues' (1997) 35(3) *Journal of Economic Literature* 1320; P Mauro, 'The Effects of Corruption on Growth, Investment, and Government Expenditure: A Cross-Country Analysis' in KA Elliott (ed), *Corruption and the Global Economy* (Institute for International Economics, 1997); United Nations Development Programme, 'Goal 16: Promote Peaceful and Inclusive Societies for Sustainable Development, Provide Access to Justice for All and Build Effective, Accountable and Inclusive Institutions at All Levels' (United Nations Department of Economic and Social Affairs), sdgs.un.org/goals/goal16, accessed 30 March 2024.

[15] 'Why is Taiwan Losing its Friends?' *The Economist* (28 March 2023), www.economist.com/the-economist-explains/2023/03/28/why-is-taiwan-losing-its-friends, accessed 12 October 2023; E Ko, 'How Does Recipients' Corruption Taint the International Image of Taiwan's Foreign Aid?' *Taiwan Insight* (24 April 2023), taiwaninsight.org/2023/04/24/how-does-recipients-corruption-taint-the-international-image-of-taiwans-foreign-aid/, accessed 12 October 2023; Legislative Yuan 2019, www.ly.gov.tw/Pages/Detail.aspx?nodeid=45831&pid=223832, accessed 12 October 2023.

II. Forms and Mechanisms of Corruption Related to Foreign Aid

There is no single universally applicable definition of corruption due to its diverse causes, forms and impacts.[16] A common definition of public corruption is the misuse of public office for private gain. Put simply, corruption is the illegal and immoral use of authority by public officials, kickbacks in public procurement, and bribery and embezzlement of public funds.[17] Corruption can also arise 'because bad policies or inefficient institutions are put in place to collect bribes from individuals seeking to get around them'.[18]

'The causes of corruption are always contextual, rooted in a country's policies, bureaucratic traditions, political development, and social history.'[19] Corruption is believed to predominate in contexts where public officials enjoy unfettered discretion, where governmental activities lack accountability and transparency, and where the private sector and civil society institutions are weak and ineffective.[20] Indeed, weak governance alone does not cause corruption – other factors work in combination to contribute to corruption, such as imperatives and incentives that encourage someone to engage in corrupt transactions. This includes low salaries for public officials, cultural norms that encourage favouritism and patronisation, and political pressure. Another aspect may be limited risks of exposure and punishment, for example, lack of policing, detection and prosecution, weak internal controls such as financial management, auditing, and human resource systems, and a tightly controlled media and civil society.[21]

Like any other sector, corruption related to foreign aid is a multifaceted challenge, manifesting through various forms and mechanisms that compromise the integrity of aid processes.[22] Some of the distinct facets of corruption that permeate the foreign aid realm are briefly discussed here.

[16] *Anti-Corruption Handbook for Development Practitioners* (Ministry of Foreign Affairs of Finland, 2012) 19. Also see BA Gebeye, 'Corruption and Human Rights: Exploring the Relationships' (2012) Working Paper 705, papers.ssrn.com/sol3/papers.cfm?abstract_id=2075766, accessed 30 March 2024.

[17] J Svensson, 'Eight Questions about Corruption' (2005) 19 *Journal of Economic Perspectives* 19.

[18] S Djankov and others, 'The New Comparative Economic' (2003) 117(1) *Journal of Comparative Economics* 1.

[19] The World Bank, *Helping Countries Combat Corruption: The Role of the World Bank* (September 1997), documents1.worldbank.org/curated/en/799831538245192753/pdf/Helping-Countries-Combat-Corruption-The-Role-of-the-World-Bank.pdf, accessed 5 June 2024.

[20] A Doig and S Riley, 'Corruption and Anti-Corruption Strategies: Issues and Case Studies from Developing Countries' in SJ Kpundeh and I Hors (eds), *Corruption & Integrity Improvement Initiatives in Developing Countries* (United Nations, 1998).

[21] CMI, 'Basic guide to anti-corruption', www.u4.no/topics/anti-corruption-basics/basic, accessed 17 June 2024.

[22] See A Salifu and others, 'Corruption and International Aid' in A Farazmand (ed), *Global Encyclopedia of Public Administration, Public Policy, and Governance* (Springer Nature, 2018).

A. Embezzlement and Misappropriation of Funds

A prevalent form of corruption related to foreign aid involves the misappropriation and embezzlement of funds intended for development projects. This occurs when individuals entrusted with the management of aid finances divert these resources for personal gain, circumventing their intended use in poverty reduction, healthcare, education and other vital sectors.

B. Bribery and Kickbacks

Bribery and kickbacks represent insidious mechanisms through which corruption infiltrates foreign aid. Individuals involved in aid distribution may demand or offer illicit payments to influence the allocation of funds or secure contracts. These practices distort the fair and equitable distribution of aid, compromising its impact on targeted development goals.

C. Nepotism and Favouritism

Nepotism and favouritism introduce personal and familial biases into the allocation of aid resources. Individuals in positions of power may prioritise friends or family members, rather than allocating aid based on merit or the genuine needs of the population. Such practices undermine the principles of fairness and inclusivity in aid distribution.

D. Fraudulent Practices in Aid Projects

Corruption often infiltrates aid projects through fraudulent practices, including the submission of false invoices, inflated costs and misrepresentation of project outcomes. By engaging in fraudulent activities, individuals can siphon off aid funds, leading to the subversion of the intended developmental impact of aid initiatives.

E. Political Interference and Influence on Aid Distribution

Political interference constitutes a critical mechanism through which corruption affects aid distribution. Politically motivated decisions may influence the allocation of aid, favouring regions or groups aligned with those in power. This compromises the impartiality of aid distribution, hindering its effectiveness in addressing the diverse needs of the population.

In essence, these forms and mechanisms of corruption in foreign aid underscore the urgency of robust anti-corruption measures. By understanding the nuanced ways in which corruption manifests, stakeholders in the aid ecosystem can develop targeted strategies to mitigate these challenges and ensure that aid serves its intended purpose of fostering sustainable development and improving the lives of those in need.

III. Good Governance in Foreign Aid

Corruption hits at the very core of good governance. It fosters an environment characterised by uncertainty, unpredictability, declining moral values and disrespect for key institutions of accountability and the rule of law. These deficits negatively impact good governance and encourage corruption. In 1992, the World Bank defined governance as 'the manner in which power is exercised in the management of a country's economic and social resources for development'.[23] The Bank's understanding of 'sound development management thus extends beyond building the capacity of public sector management to encouraging the formation of the rules and institutions which provide a predictable and transparent framework for the conduct of public and private business and to promoting accountability for economic and financial performance'.[24] However, the World Bank does not perceive governance only in terms of rules and institutions; it prefers to extend the notion to the key actors within the system, such as the politicians and bureaucrats and how they exercise their power and authority to influence the institutions and manage the resources available for growth and sustainable development. Some examples of good governance practices in the context of foreign aid include proactive publication of detailed information about aid activities, enabling greater transparency and accountability in aid allocation;[25] participatory budgeting processes involving local communities in decision-making regarding aid fund allocation, and ensuring that projects align with community needs and priorities;[26] adoption of well-defined legal and regulatory frameworks for transparent and accountable aid management;[27] social

[23] World Bank, *Governance and Development* (World Bank Publications, 1992) 3.

[24] ibid.

[25] Launched in Accra in 2008, the International Aid Transparency Initiative (IATI) is a major initiative to improve aid effectiveness by ensuring transparency, accountability and coordination in international foreign assistance. Transparency and accountability of development assistance, as underpinned by the Accra Agenda for Action, also lie at the core of the Paris Declaration on Aid Effectiveness. See International Aid Transparency Initiative, 'About IATI' (undated), www.aidtransparency.net/about, accessed 2 January 2024.

[26] United Nations, 'CEPA strategy guidance note on participatory budgeting' (January 2022), www.oidp.net/docs/repo/doc1198.pdf, accessed 5 June 2024.

[27] UNDP, 'Transparency and accountability in international assistance: The case of Lebanon' (2021), www.undp.org/lebanon/blog/transparency-and-accountability-international-assistance-case-

accountability measures engaging civil society organisations in monitoring and evaluating the use of aid funds, thus fostering transparency and accountability.[28]

Governance can be good and bad. For some, good governance is the sum total of policies and procedures, some equated it with efficiency, while others wonder if the concept is universally applicable or confined to local contexts only. While organisations like the International Monetary Fund (IMF) and the World Bank, when explaining good governance, emphasise government with the capacity to formulate sound policies, tackle corruption and ensure the rule of law and the efficiency and accountability of the public sector,[29] scholars tend to delve deeper. Johnston defines good governance as 'legitimate, accountable, and effective ways of obtaining and using public power and resources in the pursuit of widely accepted social goals'.[30] He believes that good governance signifies far more than the power of the state and that the rule of law, transparency, and accountability are outcomes of democratising processes steered not only by strong and committed leadership but also by the participation of groups and interests in society – 'processes that are most effective when sustained and restrained by legitimate, effective institutions'.[31] Rothstein argues that good governance relates to concepts of state capacity, quality of government, and the government's interactions with various sections of the private sector.[32] According to Rose-Ackerman, good governance refers to 'all kinds of institutional structures that promote both good substantive outcomes and public legitimacy'.[33]

In the context of aid, since the launch of the Millennium Development Goals (MDGs) in 2000, leaders, scholars and aid practitioners have questioned the limited impact of foreign aid in developing countries. Arguably, large amounts of aid delivered over long periods of time, create incentives for both governments and donors to undermine good governance and the quality of state institutions, which in turn lead to aid ineffectiveness.[34] Many believed that one of the major obstacles to aid effectiveness was weak institutional governance in those countries. The debates over the aid–governance relationship underpins the significance of good governance in the development process, further evidenced by the inclusion

lebanon#:~:text=This%20entails%3A%201)%20transparent%20and,community%20complaint%20mechanisms%3B%20and%203), accessed 5 June 2024.

[28] Social Accountability. An Introduction to the Concept and Emerging Practice, Social Development Papers, Paper No 76, 2004, documents1.worldbank.org/curated/en/327691468779445304/pdf/310420PAPER0So1ity0SDP0Civic0no1076.pdf, accessed 5 June 2024.

[29] See en.wikipedia.org/wiki/Good_governance; D Kaufmann, A Kraay and P Zoido-Lobaton, 'Governance Matters' (1999) World Bank Institute Policy Research Working Paper 2196, 1, papers.ssrn.com/sol3/papers.cfm?abstract_id=188568, accessed 2 January 2024.

[30] M Johnston, 'Good Governance: Rule of Law, Transparency, and Accountability' (United Nations Public Administration Network, 2006) 2.

[31] ibid 1.

[32] B Rothstein, 'Good Governance' in D Levi-Faur (ed), *Oxford Handbook of Governance* (Oxford University Press, 2012) 143–44.

[33] S Rose-Ackerman, 'What Does "Governance" Mean?' (2016) 30(1) *Governance* 23, 23.

[34] D Bräutigam, *Aid Dependence and Governance* (EGDI, 2000) 1.

of major governance indicators such as transparency and accountability in the general and specific sectors of the SDGs.[35]

Good governance in the context of foreign aid is vital for the effectiveness, impact and integrity of aid initiatives in recipient economies. Some of the key components of good governance in foreign aid and its transformative potential are discussed below.

A. Transparency

At the heart of good governance is transparency, ensuring that information related to aid allocation, utilisation and outcomes is accessible and comprehensible. Good governance emphasises transparency in decision-making and financial transactions. Transparent processes make it easier for concerned stakeholders, including citizens and donor agencies, to trace the flow of foreign aid funds, scrutinise and understand how aid resources are managed and disbursed, and ensure that they are used for their intended purposes. This openness reduces the risk of corruption, enhances trust and facilitates the alignment of aid with genuine development needs.

B. Accountability

Accountability is a cornerstone of good governance, holding both the providers and recipients of aid responsible for their actions. Donor agencies should be accountable for the effective and ethical use of aid funds, while recipient nations must ensure that aid is utilised for its intended purposes. Robust accountability mechanisms, including audits, monitoring and evaluations, and reporting requirements create a culture of responsibility, help hold individuals and institutions responsible for their actions or inactions, discourage corrupt practices, and promote the achievement of development objectives.

C. Participatory Decision-making

Incorporating the voices of local communities and civil society organisations in decision-making processes is fundamental to good governance in foreign aid. Participatory approaches ensure that aid strategies align with the genuine needs and aspirations of the people. By involving the beneficiaries in the planning, implementation and evaluation of aid projects, the likelihood of success and sustainability is significantly increased. When citizens are involved in the planning

[35] H Chang, *Impact of Foreign Aid on Governance: A Latin American Perspective* (Masters Thesis, KDI School of Public Policy and Management, 2015) 3.

and monitoring of aid projects, there is greater oversight, which reduces the likelihood of corruption. Informed and engaged citizens can act as watchdogs, ensuring that aid is distributed fairly and used efficiently.

D. Rule of Law

Adherence to the rule of law is indispensable for good governance in foreign aid. This entails the establishment and enforcement of legal frameworks that govern the allocation, management and utilisation of aid resources. A strong legal foundation safeguards against corruption, ensures the protection of human rights, and provides a framework for resolving disputes, thus fostering an environment conducive to sustainable development. When there are clear and enforceable laws governing the use of foreign aid, individuals engaging in corrupt activities can be prosecuted, which reinforces the notion that corruption will not go unpunished.

E. Institutional Capacity Building

Good governance requires the development of robust institutions with the capacity to effectively manage and implement aid programmes. Strengthening institutional frameworks in recipient nations enables them to absorb aid efficiently, enhances policy coherence, and builds resilience against corrupt practices. Capacity-building initiatives contribute to the long-term success and sustainability of aid interventions. Strong institutions are better equipped to manage and oversee foreign aid initiatives, which reduces the risk of corruption. This includes training personnel, improving administrative processes, practising due diligence by establishing internal controls, undertaking periodic risk assessments to identify potential vulnerabilities, and designing safeguards and corruption prevention measures accordingly.

F. Ethical Leadership

Ethical leadership is a critical element of good governance. Leaders who uphold integrity, accountability and a commitment to the public good set the tone for ethical conduct within institutions. Ethical leadership is particularly crucial in the foreign aid context, where the responsible use of funds and commitment to development goals are paramount. Ethical leadership at all levels of government and institutions helps to prioritise integrity and create a culture that discourages corrupt practices and mismanagement of foreign aid.

Good governance in foreign aid is not a one-size-fits-all concept, but rather a dynamic and context-specific approach that evolves in response to the unique challenges and opportunities within each developing economy. Irrespective of the varying connotations, the inherent message is clear – strong institutions and accountable management of resources are fundamental to good governance, and that applies equally to the control and management of foreign aid.

IV. Does Foreign Aid Fuel or Reduce Corruption?

Perceptions about whether foreign aid facilitates or reduces corruption are somewhat mixed. There are arguments on both sides of the debate regarding whether foreign aid fuels or reduces corruption. Some experts suggest that foreign aid triggers corruption.[36] They argue that countries with weak governance structures might encounter challenges in managing foreign aid due to weak accountability measures, and inadequate transparency and oversight. It is not uncommon for governments to consume a large part of the ODA to further their own interests. When aid money is controlled by the bureaucracy, often only a limited amount is allocated to development projects. Besides, the sudden influx of aid, if not managed properly, can result in the misallocation of resources and economic distortions, potentially creating an environment conducive to corruption. Moreover, foreign aid can create opportunities for rent-seeking behaviour, where individuals or groups try to extract economic benefits without contributing to productivity. Rent-seeking can take place by way of, inter alia, embezzlement of foreign funds by public officials for personal gain, elite capture of aid funds to the exclusion of vulnerable or marginalised groups, capture of market access by influential business groups preventing fair competition over economic benefits, distribution of aid resources based on political allegiance, and misallocation of aid to serve the interests of vested groups.

Donors often attach conditions to aid, requiring recipient countries to implement reforms and adhere to certain standards. It is argued that while aid conditionality can promote reforms and anti-corruption measures, it may sometimes lead to unintended consequences.[37] For example, stringent conditions may put pressure on governments to achieve short-term goals, potentially fostering corrupt practices to meet immediate demands. It is contended that aid dependence can discourage public officials from engaging in efforts to reform weak and corrupt governments. Moreover, aid-dependent countries are exposed to the

[36] See S Asongu and J Nnanna, 'Foreign Aid, Instability and Governance in Africa' [2015] *International Review of Applied Economics* 5; M Busse and S Gröning, 'Does Foreign Aid Improve Governance?' (2009) 104 *Economics Letters* 76; DA Bräutigam and S Knack, 'Foreign Aid, Institutions, and Governance in Sub-Saharan Africa' (2004) 52 *Economic Development and Cultural Change* 255, 277; Bräutigam (n 34); V Finckenstein, 'How International Aid Can Do More Harm Than Good: The Case of Lebanon' (*Medium*, 26 February 2021), lseideas.medium.com/how-international-aid-can-do-more-harm-than-good-the-case-of-lebanon-6134c274a232> accessed 1 January 2024; Chang (n 35) 19.

[37] B Cooksey, 'Can Aid Agencies Really Help Combat Corruption' (2002) 2(1) *Forum on Crime and Society* 45, 49.

inherent weaknesses of the aid system, which can impede the performance of public officials and counter the development of the states.

Others believe that foreign aid reduces corruption in recipient countries.[38] Aid programmes designed to address poverty and social development can potentially lessen corruption. As people's economic conditions improve, the incentive and tolerance for corrupt practices may decline. Foreign aid is often geared to strengthen institutions and governance structures so that they become more capable of managing and utilising resources effectively. Improved institutional capacity may create an environment less susceptible to corrupt practices. Besides, international aid often operates within a global governance framework, including anti-corruption standards. Aid-recipient countries are required to align with these standards by adopting anti-corruption policies and practices to maintain their credibility to secure international assistance. While aid conditionality may induce corruption, it can also help reduce corruption. Conditionality can encourage recipient countries to implement reforms, improve governance and tackle corruption.

The relationship between foreign aid and corruption is complex and varies based on several factors, including the context of the recipient country, the design of aid programmes, and the effectiveness of governance structures. While aid can create opportunities for corruption, it also has the potential to be a powerful tool for promoting good governance, reducing poverty and fostering sustainable development. The effectiveness of aid in mitigating corruption depends on the alignment of donor intentions, recipient country commitment, and the adaptability of aid programmes to the unique challenges of each context.

V. Taiwan's Foreign Aid Practice: The ODA-for-Recognition Model

This section draws on the aid practice of Taiwan as a case study to demonstrate how well-intentioned aid assistance can be diverted to serve corrupt purposes. Taiwan's aid policy and practice suggest that for the country 'the political and economic motives [seemingly] carry more weight than the moral and humanitarian ones'.[39] For the first two decades after World War II, Taiwan predominantly depended on

[38] MR Mohamed and others, 'Effect of Foreign Aid on Corruption: Evidence from Sub-Saharan African countries' (2015) 42(1) *International Journal of Social Economics* 47, 61; K Okada and S Samreth, 'The Effect of Foreign Aid on Corruption: A Quantile Regression Approach' (2012) 115 *Economics Letters* 240; J Tavares, 'Does Foreign Aid Corrupt' (2003) 79(1) *Economics Letters* 99, 104; G Dijkstra, 'Aid and Good Governance: Examining Aggregate Unintended Effects of Aid' (2018) 68 *Evaluation and Program Planning* 225, 231; RM Quazi and A Alam, 'Foreign Aid and Quality of Governance in Developing Countries: An Econometric Case Study of South Asia and East Asia' (2015) 8(9) *International Business Research* 21.

[39] G Chan, 'Taiwan as an Emerging Foreign Aid Donor: Developments, Problems, and Prospects' (1997) 70(1) *Pacific Affairs* 37, 40.

the USA for foreign and military aid. The 'Vanguard Project' was instrumental in converting Taiwan from a recipient country to a donor country in 1960. With financial support from the USA, Taiwan implemented the Vanguard aid project by dispatching agriculture experts to newly independent states in Africa and Latin America to consolidate their political support amid the bipolar struggles during the Cold War. The Vanguard Project enabled Taiwan to develop 'a sustainable aid mentality' by utilising its expertise to achieve both farming and diplomatic goals.[40]

Taiwan faced a severe diplomatic challenge when it was expelled from the United Nations General Assembly in 1971 under UN Resolution 2758, which meant that China exclusively figured in both the UN General Assembly and the Security Council. This proved to be another turning point which compelled Taiwan to add direct grants and loans to existing technical assistance to its diplomatic allies to secure a *de jure* sovereign state status. Both Taiwan and China have historically used foreign aid to pursue political motives and to shape their foreign policy. Following Taiwan's expulsion from the United Nations, 'diplomatic and aid-giving competition with China became more intense' and its 'struggles to gain supporters [were] reflected in foreign aid strategies'.[41] According to Weaver-Lee, 'the competition with the People's Republic of China (PRC) for diplomatic allies subsequently took on even greater urgency for Taipei's foreign policy, and many official relationships developed and withered alongside the level of economic aid'.[42]

Weaver-Lee's update on Taiwan's ODA policy reveals that since 1988, when Taiwan's Ministry of Economic Affairs (MOEA) established the International Economic Cooperation Development Fund (IECDF) – subsequently known as the International Cooperation Development Fund (ICDF) – with the objective of 'streamlining development loans and technical assistance to "developing nations," Taiwan's official development assistance (ODA) policy has slowly transformed to include both diplomatic partners and non-official allies, while also focusing increasingly on longer-term oriented projects'.[43] She emphasises that while the Taiwanese foreign ministry's 2009 white paper 'outlined broad goals on how Taiwan could play a larger role in the global foreign aid system', 'criticisms of Taiwan's ODA practices began to surface significantly, namely accusations of bribery, embezzlement, and ill-gotten funds', leading to the adoption of the International Cooperation and Development Act (ICDA) in 2010. The ICDA prescribed central goals of Taiwan's international development assistance policies, amongst which two are particularly noteworthy: 'to promote diplomatic relations' and 'to enhance friendly relations with countries that do not have diplomatic ties with the ROC'. Earlier ODA expenditures also 'funded [the] so-called "cheque book diplomacy" operations, including the case of former Guatemalan President Alfonso Portillo, who admitted to taking

[40] PL Hsiao-Pong, 'Planting Rice on the Roof of the UN Building: Analyzing Taiwan's "Chinese" Techniques in Africa, 1961–present' (2009) 198 *The China Quarterly* 381, 198.

[41] Lin and Lin (n 7) 469.

[42] Z Weaver-Lee, 'Building Bridges: An Overdue Update on Taiwan's ODA Policy' (2022) 7(13) *Global Taiwan Brief*.

[43] ibid.

US$2.5 million in bribes from Taiwan – earmarked originally for the construction of several libraries – in exchange for maintaining diplomatic ties'.[44] Taiwan has often been criticised for being too political in its foreign aid practice to the extent that 'Ministry of Foreign Affairs has been accused of exerting undue pressure on the IECDF in approving nearly half the loan applications without making proper assessment of their feasibility'.[45]

Notwithstanding its diplomatic isolation, since the 1970s Taiwan has emerged as an economic giant 'becoming one of the world's main exporters of manufactured products, and therefore accumulating large amounts of foreign currency reserves (the sixth in the world according to IMF, 2019)'.[46] This essentially 'enabled Taipei to use its economic advantages to pursue ambitious foreign aid programs', the primary goal is to 'retain diplomatic recognition, but also breaking its isolation and maintaining the possibility to participate in a variety of international forums and multilateral organizations'.[47]

The ODA-for-recognition is a publicly known model used by Taiwan and its allies. When Honduras severed diplomatic ties with Taiwan on 25 March 2023, the Honduran foreign minister claimed that its government received US$50 million ODA from Taiwan annually.[48] However, this amount of foreign aid is just a base price for all diplomatic allies as a reward for granting diplomatic recognition and does not include policy-oriented loans to allies. As such, the volume of this foreign aid does not reflect the actual costs. A reasonable assumption would be that this is essentially an unpaid debt in the disguise of policy-oriented loans, undertaken by Taiwan state-owned banks rather than the Taiwan foreign ministry. A practical estimation of Taiwan's policy-oriented loans based on revealed Honduran unpaid debt amounts to more than US$449.1 million.[49] Using this unpaid debt as a benchmark to calculate the amount of debt involving 12 of Taiwan's allies, the total debt amounts to US$5.389 billion. Given the clandestine nature of the deals, it is safe to assume that this figure is underestimated.

Between 2013 and 2023, Taiwan's diplomatic ties reduced from 22 countries to 13 countries. The erosion in diplomatic ties peaked during President Tsai Ing-Wen's administration (2016–2022), who, being ideologically pro-independence, constantly engaged in quarrels with China. Taiwan, under Tsai's administration, severed diplomatic ties with nine countries. Apart from the Vatican, the remaining 13 sovereign states which have retained their diplomatic relationship with Taiwan are mostly small and developing countries in the south.

[44] ibid.

[45] Chan (n 39) 53.

[46] L Maggiorelli, 'Taiwan's Development Aid to Latin America and the Caribbean and the One China Policy' (2018) 7 *Razón Crítica* 180, 180.

[47] ibid.

[48] K Everington, 'Honduras cut ties with Taiwan over refusal to double aid' *Taiwan News* (16 March 2023), www.taiwannews.com.tw/en/news/4836903, accessed 14 November 2023.

[49] R Yanes, 'Honduras aun le debe $449.1 milliones a Taiwan' *La Presnsa* (17 April 2023), www.laprensa.hn/premium/honduras-aun-debe-449-1-millones-taiwan-prestamos-china-rompimiento-relaciones-OL13093296, accessed 14 November 2023.

The decreasing diplomatic recognition is a sign that Taiwan may need to reconsider the effectiveness of the ODA. The severance of diplomatic relations with nine countries and the decrease in the number of diplomatic allies from 22 to 13 may serve as a wake-up call for Taiwan to articulate an alternative strategy for implementing its foreign aid. Considering that China is the second largest economy next to the USA, the Taiwan government has realised that competing with China in ODA is unrealistic and thus bound to fail. In recent years, the gap in ODA output between China and Taiwan has been widening. While Taiwan's ODA was US$ 502 million in 2020, China's ODA reached $4.8 billion in 2019.[50] If this trend continues, then China is likely to further squeeze Taiwan's diplomatic space. In retrospect, since 1987, the democratically elected government in Taiwan has consistently followed a policy and practice of providing bilateral grants and loans as the major forms of ODA to its diplomatic allies regardless of the change in ruling parties. There is an obvious path dependency on the ODA for Taiwan when it comes to competition with China.

Foreign aid is arguably the only and most effective diplomatic tool available to Taiwan to counterbalance China's repression of Taiwan's international manoeuvring space. Research reveals that diplomatic recognition is the direct issue which is pushing both states to compete over foreign aid.[51] While foreign aid is an indispensable policy tool, Taiwan is constantly facing three competing interests: the number of official diplomatic allies (in competition with China); the improvement of its international reputation; and the containing of aid spending.[52] The only relatively smooth period was between 2008 and 2016 when Taiwan President Ma Ing-Jeou advocated for a diplomatic truce with China. During his tenure, Taiwan lost only one diplomatic tie, which was with Gambia, although Taiwan's foreign aid policy and practice underwent no fundamental change during Ma's administration. The traditional school of thought in Taiwan considers that the ODA-for-recognition approach in the form of bilateral policy-oriented loans is a necessary evil to counterbalance China's diplomatic repression. As shown in this chapter, the efficacy of this approach is less and less workable in light of the decreasing number of diplomatic ties. Notwithstanding, a minimum number of diplomatic relations is required for Taiwan to be both a *de jure* sovereign state and to have an appropriate channel for its voice to be heard within the international community.

[50] R Fabbro and R Gramer, 'Taiwan Isn't Playing Dollar Diplomacy Anymore' (*Foreign Policy*, 24 April 2023), foreignpolicy.com/2023/04/24/taiwan-china-competition-dollar-diplomacy/, accessed 14 November 2023.

[51] See J Atkinson, 'Aid in Taiwan's foreign policy: putting Ma Ying-Jeou's aid reforms in historical perspective' (2014) 27(3) *The Pacific Review* 409; G Dobell, 'China and Taiwan in the South Pacific: Diplomatic Chess versus Pacific Political Rugby', CSCSD Occasional Paper 1, 2007, Lowy Institute for International Policy, Sydney, 1–19; C-W Tseng and others, 'An Empirical Evaluation of Taiwan's Foreign Aid Projects: Case Study of a Food Security Development Project in Haiti (2011–2013)' (2021) 60(3) *Issues and Studies* 115.

[52] ibid 409.

According to Wang,[53] to maintain the existing official relationships, the ODA-for-recognition pattern continues, within the government's annual budget. The only nuance is a decrease in the classified ODA budget compared with Ma's successor, President Tsai Ing-Wen. As tensions spread across the Taiwan Strait after President Tsai took office in 2016, Taiwan's foreign aid significantly increased in terms of both unclassified and classified ODA. The classified budget for 2018 soared from NT463 million to NT1.56 billion, which is almost quadruple the previous fiscal year; a reasonable speculation is that an increase in classified ODA would prevent a further breakdown in diplomatic relations.[54]

There is a dearth of information within the government and academia that clearly describes Taiwan's foreign aid. However, it may be deduced from the above observations that, Taiwan, regardless of the change in the ruling parties, consistently embraces the theory of sustaining the *de jure* sovereign state.

Accordingly, in its competition with China, Taiwan considers the ODA as the only leverage for maintaining diplomatic relations with small states. 'Alliances have often switched back and forth, as a product of domestic politics and in response to economic incentives.' In one instance, the St Lucia foreign ministry was reported to have said that one should 'support those who give you the most'.[55] On 18 May 2023, the Taiwan foreign ministry announced that its diplomatic allies who are UN members have urged the WHO to include Taiwan in the World Health Assembly (WHA) as an observer.[56] It should be noted that Taiwan has been consistently rejected, under China's pressure, from participating in the WHA since 2016 due to the rivalry across the Taiwan Straits. The support from Taiwan's diplomatic allies in advocating for Taiwan's inclusion in the WHA symbolises the marginal benefit of Taiwan's foreign aid, although the likelihood of Taiwan's presence at the WHA in the foreseeable future remains elusive.

VI. Taiwan's 'Policy-oriented Loans': A Unique Genre of Concessional Loans

According to the Organisation for Economic Co-operation and Development (OECD), the ODA must be 'concessional (i.e., grants and soft loans) and administered with the main objective of promoting economic development and welfare

[53] S Wang, 'Comments and Analysis on Taiwan ODA' (*National Policy Foundation*, 25 October 2017), www.npf.org.tw/3/17567, accessed 15 January 2024.

[54] SY Wang, 'Two Billion More Foreign Affairs Budget?' (*The News Lens*, 2 October 2017), www.thenewslens.com/article/80174, accessed 15 January 2024.

[55] K Ponniah, 'Taiwan: How China is poaching the island's diplomatic allies' (*BBC News*, 14 June 2017), www.bbc.co.uk/news/world-asia-40263581, accessed 20 October 2023.

[56] S Wu and Y Lee, 'Hoping for invitation to WHO meeting, Taiwan gathers more support' (*Reuters*, 18 May 2023), www.reuters.com/world/hoping-invitation-who-meeting-taiwan-gathers-more-support-2023-05-18/, accessed 20 October 2023.

of developing countries'.[57] The ODA is composed of grants, technical assistance and soft loans. The soft loan, also known as a concessional loan, is a common foreign aid practice which takes place in the form of loans with reduced interest rates as well as technical assistance.[58] The lender provides reduced interest rate and a sum of principal (cash) to the borrower for designated purposes. This affordable funding theoretically stimulates recipient countries' economies or addresses emergency needs. The Taiwan government implements the 'soft loan' discreetly and asymmetrically.

Figure 13.1 presents the uniqueness of Taiwan's concessional loan practice which has three distinct characteristics. First, they are given to borrowers, who diplomatically recognise Taiwan as a sovereign state, and who are poorly rated in the international credit market. Since the costs of borrowing are too high to sustain, they prefer to seek a cheaper, stable alternative.[59] The second interesting feature is that the borrowing countries are mostly found to rank at the lower bottom of the annual Corruption Perceptions Index (CPI) published by Transparency International in 2022.

Figure 13.1 Taiwan's unique model of policy-oriented loans

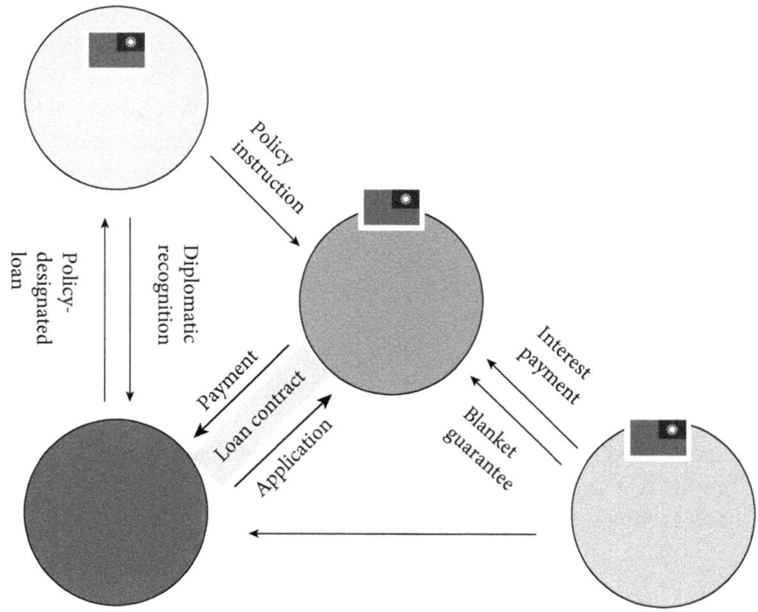

[57] See OECD, 'Official Development Assistance (ODA)' (OECD), www.oecd.org/dac/financing-sustainable-development/development-finance-standards/official-development-assistance.htm, accessed 10 October 2023.

[58] See JICA Official Development Assistance Loans, 2023, www.jica.go.jp/english/our_work/types_of_assistance/oda_loans/overseas/index.html, accessed 10 October 2023.

[59] Wang (n 53).

Third, Taiwan's concessional loans, termed as 'policy-oriented loans' by the Taiwan government, are mostly implemented in a bilateral approach. The rigid policy goal, if not the sole purpose, is to maintain diplomatic relations. It gives both state parties strong incentives to undertake under-table deals due to a lack of adequate audit and control.[60] According to the Budget Center of the Taiwan parliament, 93.51 per cent of the ODA for the budget year 2023 is designated for bilateral aid due to the request of recipient countries.[61]

These bilateral policy-oriented loans are made in the form of asymmetric contracts in favour of the borrowers, who are mostly Taiwan's diplomatic allies or democracy allies. In this arrangement, at the initiative of the Taiwan government, a specific public bank provides a significant amount of money at a reduced interest rate to the borrowing country. In other words, 'the Taiwan public bank serves as the lender, the Taiwanese government (officially the Ministry of Foreign Affairs) acts as the guarantor, and the recipient country, which typically has a low credit rating in international financial markets, is the borrower'.[62] The government-to-government interest rate is based on the London Interbank Offered Rate (LIBOR), which is a benchmark interest rate followed by major global banks when lending to one another in the international market for short-term loans,[63] at reduced rates. The fact that both the lender and the guarantor are in essence Taiwan gives the borrower strong incentives to default. To avoid the borrowers' default, the Taiwan Ministry of Foreign Affairs appropriates an annual budget to pay for the interest. These items are normally arranged in the classified budget, which renders congressional oversight weak and non-transparent.[64]

Taiwan seems to have adopted a dual-track approach comprising both project-oriented aid and policy-oriented aid on which to spend its ODA. The inception of the International Cooperation and Development Fund (ICDF) in 1996 is a milestone of project-oriented aid for Taiwan to catch up with developed countries, namely the World Bank and the OECD member states, in implementing foreign aid and humanitarian assistance.[65] The ICDF has systemically conducted various project-oriented evaluations to verify its aid effectiveness. For example, to tackle the serious malnutrition problem amongst Haitian families, Taiwan's food security programme for Haiti between 2011 and 2013 proved that an input of one US dollar can generate a 5.5 dollar reward for rice farmers and rice mills.[66] While the

[60] ibid.

[61] Legislative Yuan, 'Budget Assessment Report on Foreign Ministry Budget 2023', Budget Center (2022), www.ly.gov.tw/Pages/Detail.aspx?nodeid=45831&pid=223832, accessed 12 June 2023.

[62] Ko (n 15).

[63] Ko (n 7) 137; J Kagan, 'LIBOR: What the London Interbank Offered Rate Is and How It's Used' *Investopedia* (23 November 2003), www.investopedia.com/terms/l/libor.asp, accessed 1 September 2023.

[64] ibid 138; Wang (n 53).

[65] C Alexander, 'Development assistance and communication: The case of the Taiwan International Cooperation and Development Fund' (2015) 21 *Global Governance: A Review of Multilateralism and International Organizations* 119, 124–26.

[66] Tseng and others (n 51) 137.

ICDF plays a prudent and responsible role of aid provider on behalf of Taiwan, clandestine forms of waste and corruption in other branches of the government nonetheless exist, such as policy-oriented loans.

The aggregate amount of these policy-oriented loans has not been made public for years, as a business-as-usual practice.[67] In an interview over the telephone,[68] an anonymous government ethics officer maintained that all banks, including the ODA-related lending banks, are required to 'keep confidential all related information on deposits, loans or remittances of its customers' under section II, article 48 of the Bank Law. More importantly, these loans are counted as bank-customer business lending contracts rather than the foreign ministry's budget of the ODA. Sadly, congressional oversight is minimal and powerless and is largely unable to unveil the details of the loan terms and conditions. In an official response from the Export-Import Bank of the Republic of China (Eximbank) to a query by a legislator of Taiwan's Legislative Yuan on 17 July 2023, the Eximbank insisted that 'all loans are business loans according to international business practice of credit and audit procedures' and according to the Bank Law, it is obliged to not 'disclose the loan terms'. The Eximbank also referred to the press release by the foreign ministry on 18 January 2023, one of the few publicly available pieces of information confirming financing and investment from Taiwan to Lithuania but lacking in clear specification of the terms of the policy-oriented loan.[69]

VII. Corruption in Countries Receiving Taiwanese Foreign Aid: Selected Instances

In theory, foreign aid from donors in the north is supposed to contribute to the development of recipient countries in the south. In practice, however, such foreign aid has been problematic in many aspects, such as inefficiency, inequality and corruption. Scholars[70] Atkinson and Dobell conclude that Taiwan's ODA in the forms of grant and loans leads to the escalation of corruption in recipient countries but the staff and managers of the International Cooperation and Development Fund (ICDF), the official aid agency under the foreign ministry of Taiwan, argue that project-oriented aid from Taiwan contributes to economic growth as well as humanitarian energy needs.[71]

[67] Ko (n 7) 141; Wang (n 53).

[68] Conducted by co-author Ernie Ko.

[69] Taiwanese Representative Office in Lithuania, 'Representative Huang Congratulates Three Lithuanian Companies to Become Joint Partners on Taiwan Semiconductor, Central-Eastern European Investment, and Financing Fund Respectively' (18 January 2023), roc-taiwan.org/lt/post/624.html, accessed 7 July 2023.

[70] Atkinson (n 51) 409; Dobell (n 51) 10, 16–17.

[71] Tseng and others (n 51) 121; J-Y Wu and others, 'Taiwan's Pragmatic Approach in International Humanitarian Aid: A Case study on the ICDF' (2003) 11 *International Development and Aid Quarterly* 32, 36–38.

Interestingly, out of Taiwan's 13 diplomatic allies, all, except The Vatican, are either consistently ranked at the lower bottom of the list of Transparency International's Corruption Perception Index (CPI) – Haiti, Guatemala, Paraguay, Eswatini, St Lucia and St Vincent, or are missing from the ranking chart altogether, such as Marshall Islands, Nauru, Palau, Tuvalu, Belize, and St Kitts and Nevis.

A look at Guatemala's position ranking in the CPI shows a steady decline in scores, which indicates a high level of corruption (shown in a downward trend in scores) over the years. The average score is consistently lower than 30 out of 100. The Guatemalan government is perceived to be highly corrupt with a poor human rights track record.[72] Prosecutors and judges, who previously dealt with corruption cases, have been forced to resign, detained without due process, or forced to leave the country.[73]

The news media in Latin America published various articles, flagging the misuse of Taiwan's foreign aid in Guatemala. For example, a newly built hospital costing US$20 million saw at least three incidents of corruption in procurement.[74] Admitting to existing corruption, the Guatemalan president openly asked Taiwan President Tsai Ing-Wen to provide more aid to address the problem during her state visit to Guatemala in April 2023.[75] Taiwan's foreign aid is found to be used for driving domestic politics in Guatemala. Estimated Taiwan aid of US$450,000 was reportedly used to pay for Guatemalan lobbying activities in the USA.[76] While the Guatemalan government is happy with Taiwan's aid arrangement, members of its civil society harbour concerns over receiving aid from Taiwan. At least two independent comments from the opinion leaders of civil society in Latin America reveal how negatively they view Taiwan's bilateral aid to Guatemala.

> It's a shame for Taiwán to support the most corrupt government [Guatemala] of America after Venezuela and Nicaragua.[77]

[72] US State Department, '2022 Country Reports on Human Rights Practices: Guatemala', www.state.gov/reports/2022-country-reports-on-human-rights-practices/guatemala> accessed 11 July 2023, 1–2.

[73] ibid 17.

[74] 'Presidenta de Taiwán cierra viaje a Guatemala con visita a polémico hospital involucrado en un millonario caso de corrupción', Prensa Libre (2 April 2023), www.prensalibre.com/guatemala/politica/presidenta-de-taiwan-cierra-viaje-a-guatemala-con-visita-a-polemico-hospital-involucrado-en-un-millonario-caso-de-corrupcion/, accessed 12 June 2023.

[75] PD Rivera, 'Presidenta de Taiwán visita Hospital de Chimaltenango, involucrado en corrupción' (*Soy502*, 2 April 2023), www.soy502.com/articulo/presidenta-taiwan-visita-hospital-chimaltenango-101567-0, accessed 12 June 2023; HQ Tzok, 'Tras caso de corrupción, gobierno lleva a presidenta de Taiwán a Hospital de Chimaltenango' *La Hora* (2 April 2023), lahora.gt/nacionales/hquino/2023/04/02/tras-caso-de-corrupcion-gobierno-lleva-a-presidenta-de-taiwan-a-hospital-de-chimaltenango/, accessed 12 June 2023.

[76] J Garcia, 'A Taiwán le cuesta 450,000 dólares intentar mejorar la imagen de Guatemala en EE', (*UU*, 31 March 2023), www.plazapublica.com.gt/content/taiwan-le-cuesta-450000-dolares-intentar-mejorar-la-imagen-de-guatemala-en-ee-uu, accessed 12 June 2023.

[77] In conversation with a civil society leader in Honduras on 4 April 2023 (identity withheld on request).

> The problem, as you mention, is the decision to consider as allies, governments that abuse human rights, do not believe in democratic values and are corrupt. A diplomatic relation based exclusively on money is ethically wrong and fragile.[78]

It is alleged that Taiwan's foreign aid has been funnelling billions of dollars to recipient heads of state under the disguise of ODA.[79] A review in 2023 of multiple news and independent investigative reports reveals incidences of corruption in recipient countries involving Taiwan's foreign aid in the preceding decade. This article draws on five examples of grand corruption using Taiwan's foreign aid reported between the period 2018–2023 involving heads of states and dignitaries of countries receiving foreign aid from Taiwan.

In 2018, the former First Lady of Honduras, Porfirio Lobo Sosa, was detained for embezzling a quarter of a million dollars which was taken from Taiwan for providing medical and humanitarian assistance. In 2019 it was revealed that during Yahya Jammeh's dictatorship between 1996 and 2017, the West African state of Gambia suffered high inflation and low economic growth, while Jammeh's personal wealth grew phenomenally, mainly from stolen state coffers, illicit timber revenue, and foreign aid from Taiwan.[80] Gambia is not an isolated case, showcasing the abuse of foreign aid from Taiwan to the Global South.

There is a clear time gap between the occurrence of corruption and the media reports, primarily due to fear of reprisal from the incumbent power base. Most of the reported cases surfaced years after the presidents concerned stepped down from power, except in Guatemala. In 2022, ex-Guatemalan President Alfonso Portillo was found guilty of taking US$2.5 million as a bribe from the Taiwan government. In 2022 it was alleged that the former president of Panama, Mireya Moscoso, was involved in making bribes to win international favour in the face of dwindling 'diplomatic ties'. The money came from Taiwan's Democratic Progressive Party. In 2023, former President of Panama, Martinelli, and a few others were put on trial on charges of money laundering. Again in 2023, on the eve of the Taiwan President Tsai Ing-Wen's state visit to Guatemala, the local news reported that the Health Minister of Guatemala Gerardo Hernandez, a close friend of Guatemalan President Alejandro Eduardo Giammattei Falla, was involved in fraud and embezzlement in Chimaltenango Hospital, which was funded by Taiwan's foreign aid. President Giammattei has reportedly admitted to corruption in the procurement process in the said hospital. The commonality of these cases lies in three aspects: incumbent corruption with investigation delayed for a long time; bribery in the disguise of bilateral aid; and repeated patterns of corruption regardless of their predecessors' convictions for corruption.

[78] In conversation with a civil society leader in Peru on 26 April 2023 (identity withheld on request).

[79] M Anderson and others, 'Jammeh's Taiwanese Alliance and the Hezbollah Laundromat' (*OCCRP*, 27 March 2019), www.occrp.org/en/greatgambiaheist/the-alliance-and-the-laundromat, accessed 20 April 2023.

[80] ibid.

Needless to say, the misappropriation of Taiwan's foreign aid contributes to widening the gap between the North and the South further. For example, the Gambian dictator Yahya Jammeh's personal assets of 975 million dollars come from mostly stolen state assets and Taiwan's foreign aid, which caused half of Gambia's population to live below a dollar a day.[81] The Gambian case clearly illustrates the negative impact of Taiwan's foreign aid on the Global South. According to Anderson and others, the 'former president [Yahya Jammeh] played China and Taiwan against each other to obtain more than $100 million of bilateral aid that was dished out with few questions asked'.[82] Three members of the Organized Crime and Corruption Reporting Project (OCCRP), a transnational network of independent investigative journalists founded in 2006, coauthored an investigative report in 2019, linking Taiwan's foreign aid to Gambian former dictator and president Yahya Jammeh's personal wealth and possible contribution to Hezbollah in Lebanon.[83] Despite this breaking story, Taiwan officials were found to be dismissive about this matter.[84] Anderson and others describe how in 1995, Jammeh, who ruled this West African country between 1994 and 2016, defied Beijing's One-China policy, which insisted that Taiwan is part of China, in order to forge diplomatic relations with Taiwan. The scholars contend that the 'move was a clear-cut cheque book diplomacy' because the recognition was 'worth millions of dollars for Jammeh'.[85] They add that 'Taiwan gave Gambia more than $100 million in aid and soft loans between 1995 and 2015, becoming one of the country's largest bilateral donors'.[86] However, instead of using this aid to boost Gambia's economy, part of it was secretly spent on purchasing military weaponry and ammunition to suppress Gambian democratic movements and part of it was given to Jammeh's close business associates, who provided financial support to Hezbollah, a Lebanon-based militia group, which has been branded by the US State Department as a terrorist group.[87] In one clear piece of evidence obtained by the OCCRP, Richard Shih, the then Taiwanese ambassador to the Gambia, signed an official letter marked 'strictly confidential' and addressed to the Gambian presidential office regarding an annual grant from Taiwan in four instalments (US$900,000, US$800,000, US$800,000, and US$512,500 respectively) and the shipment of ammunition procurement worth US$3,012,500 from Taiwan.[88]

[81] MK Darboe, 'Gambia: Jammeh's Wealth to Go to His Victims' (*Justiceinfo.net*, 21 October 2019), www.justiceinfo.net/en/42679-gambia-jammeh-wealth-victims.html, accessed 12 June 2023.

[82] Anderson and others (n 79).

[83] ibid.

[84] During an official meeting hosted by the Agency Against Corruption (AAC) and the Ministry of Justice (MOJ) on Taiwan's implementation of the United Nations Convention Against Corruption (UNCAC), concerns in this regard raised by Ernie Ko, co-author of this article, were brushed aside by the foreign ministry representative who responded that 'it is no longer the practice of the current government'.

[85] Anderson and others (n 79).

[86] ibid.

[87] ibid.

[88] ibid.

Gambia unilaterally cut diplomatic ties with Taiwan on 14 November 2013. Due to the clandestine nature of Taiwan's ODA, there is no concrete information on exactly how much of Taiwan's foreign aid was abused by Gambia. Notwithstanding, it can be reasonably deduced that the amount was substantial and that Jammeh's grand corruption was not an isolated case given the publicly available information that indicates that several incumbent and ex-presidents of current and previous diplomatic allies were involved in various forms of corruption directly linked to Taiwan's foreign aid.

The Taiwanese experience demonstrates that foreign aid is often not utilised for the purpose it was granted in the first place. Instead, it is captured by powerful elites. The fact that many of the countries that received foreign aid from Taiwan have high levels of corruption reinforces the perception that, in the absence of transparency and accountability, the flow of aid ends up in the pockets of the ruling politicians and their cronies.[89] This experience serves as a lesson for both donors and recipient countries. Donors must implement due diligence in aid allocation and strengthen partnerships with recipients committed to enhancing their governance structures to prevent corrupt practices. The debate gains insights into the necessity of tailoring aid strategies to the specific contexts of recipient countries. Understanding local governance structures and adapting aid programmes accordingly can contribute to more effective and corruption-resistant interventions.

VIII. Impact of Corruption on Sustainable Development in Aid-recipient Countries

Corruption involving aid adversely affects various aspects of economic, social and environmental progress in recipient countries. It introduces distortions that reverberate through the entire development process of the country. One of the immediate impacts is the reduction in aid effectiveness. When funds are diverted or misused, the intended positive outcomes such as poverty reduction, infrastructure development, improved healthcare, enhanced education and other sustainable goals are compromised. Corruption introduces inefficiencies, leading to suboptimal resource allocation and implementation of development projects. When diverted for personal gain, resources that could catalyse sustainable economic development hinder the very progress aid seeks to foster. The cumulative effect of corruption leads to the unequal distribution of resources, reinforcing social inequalities. The perpetuation of inequality hampers social justice and undermines efforts to build inclusive and resilient societies. Seen from another perspective, persistent corruption weakens institutions responsible for governance, the rule of law, and public

[89] A Alesina and B Weder, 'Do Corrupt Governments Receive Less Foreign Aid?' (2002) 92(4) *American Economic Review* 1126, 1130–1131.

administration. Weak institutions struggle to gain public trust and provide the necessary frameworks for sustainable development, hindering progress in various sectors.

The perception of corruption in a country can affect its global reputation, potentially reducing collaboration with international partners. Corruption involving foreign aid has far-reaching implications for both the donor and recipient countries as both can suffer reputational damage due to corruption scandals involving foreign aid. It can impact the willingness of other countries or international organisations to engage in partnerships or provide assistance and deter foreign investors who may be concerned about the integrity of business environments. Limited collaboration may result in missed opportunities for knowledge transfer, technology exchange and collaborative solutions to sustainable development challenges. Reduced foreign direct investment limits the availability of capital for economic development and job creation. It distorts economic decision-making, thus hindering investment and economic growth. This can lead to reduced job creation, limited opportunities for entrepreneurship, and overall economic stagnation.

If aid is misused or does not effectively contribute to long-term development, recipient countries may become more dependent on continuous aid in-flows. This dependency can create a cycle where sustainable economic growth becomes elusive. The significance of corruption in foreign aid lies not only in its immediate fiscal implications but also in its systemic impact on the social fabric of recipient nations. The long-term consequences extend to the achievement of the SDGs, where corruption acts as a formidable barrier to realising inclusive, equitable and socially just outcomes. Addressing corruption is essential for unlocking the full potential of aid and ensuring that resources contribute effectively to long-term sustainable development goals. The erosion of trust in governance structures, the exacerbation of inequality, and the subversion of development goals collectively underscore the urgency of addressing corruption as a central challenge in the realm of foreign aid.

IX. Conclusion

The intricate relationship between foreign aid and corruption presents a complex web of challenges and opportunities for both donor and recipient countries. While foreign aid is provided to promote economic development, poverty reduction and improved living standards in recipient countries, the risk of corruption looms large, threatening to undermine these noble intentions. Corruption diverts resources away from their intended purposes, leading to a failure to achieve these development goals. This can perpetuate poverty and hinder sustainable development and erode trust between the donor and recipient countries.

It is clear from Taiwan's experience discussed above that corruption involving foreign aid tends to benefit a small elite at the expense of the broader population.

Besides, characterised by political interests, Taiwan's foreign aid behaviour appears unconcerned by the potential erosion of Taiwan's international image as a result of the corruption committed with its aid money in recipient countries. The traditional school of thought in Taiwan is that the ODA-for-recognition approach in the form of bilateral policy-oriented loans is a necessary evil to counterbalance China's diplomatic repression. However, the efficacy of this approach is increasingly less viable in light of Taiwan's decreasing diplomatic ties. Notwithstanding, a minimum number of diplomatic relations is required for Taiwan to remain a *de jure* sovereign state and to have a voice within the international community.

The prioritisation of good governance in foreign aid can help foster an environment where it can catalyse sustainable development, empower communities and improve lives. That good governance in foreign aid is significant for promoting development in aid-recipient countries is undeniable. Governments with strong institutions, capable leadership and lower levels of corruption tend to do better at managing foreign aid for economic growth and sustainable development of their countries.

Institutional efficiency and a robust governance framework within both donor and recipient countries are crucial in determining whether foreign aid serves as a catalyst for positive transformation or inadvertently fuels corruption and malfeasance. It is evident that successful outcomes of foreign aid hinge on a shared commitment to building resilient, accountable and transparent institutions, which necessitates a departure from traditional top-down approaches to aid delivery. It is imperative to recognise the nuanced relationship between the donor and the recipient and to adopt comprehensive strategies that go beyond merely providing and receiving financial assistance. Addressing corruption in foreign aid requires a multifaceted approach that includes promoting transparency, strengthening governance structures, and fostering accountability at both ends of the aid transaction. Donor countries must engage in responsible aid practices, ensuring that funds are used efficiently and effectively, while recipient countries must commit to implementing robust anti-corruption measures to safeguard the integrity of aid programmes. Otherwise, donor countries may become hesitant to provide aid if there are concerns that the funds would be misused or embezzled. Recipient countries, in turn, may become sceptical about the true intentions behind foreign aid, potentially straining diplomatic relations.

Despite the challenges, the potential positive impact of foreign aid remains significant, and efforts to combat corruption can enhance the efficacy of aid initiatives. By learning from past experiences, fostering collaboration, and prioritising ethical and accountable practices, the international community can strive to create a more resilient and equitable global landscape where foreign aid serves as a genuine catalyst for positive change. In doing so, we can move closer to realising the true potential of foreign aid as a force for sustainable development, poverty alleviation, and international cooperation.

14

Bridging the Capacity Gap in the Global South: Bangladesh's Path to SDG Attainment

JESMUL HASAN

I. Introduction

The quest for sustainable development has become a focal point in international relations, culminating in the adoption of the Sustainable Development Goals (SDGs) by the United Nations. However, the journey towards realising these goals is fraught with complexities, particularly for the Southern countries, which face multidimensional challenges.

This chapter focuses on four key aspects crucial to understanding the dynamics of SDG implementation in the Global South. First, it explores the genesis of the SDGs within the realm of international relations theories, shedding light on their emergence and significance in shaping global development discourse. Second, it offers a critical reflection on the enduring North–South divide, highlighting disparities in progress towards the SDGs between regions. Third, the chapter presents a hypothetical framework delineating the capacities of Southern countries in SDG attainment, providing insight into the multifaceted challenges that lead to the ultimate global development gap. Lastly, it focuses on Bangladesh and analyses its efforts, achievements and capacity constraints in SDG implementation.

Through this exploration, it becomes evident that while policies and institutions are in place, Southern countries grapple with deficiencies in public and private financing, exacerbated by unforeseen global events like the Covid-19 pandemic. Moreover, despite Bangladesh's commitment to the SDGs, capacity constraints persist, necessitating strategic investments in human resources, technology and governance structures. Furthermore, the chapter underscores the crucial role of Northern countries in supporting Southern counterparts, both financially and through collaborative partnerships. It calls for a reevaluation of global strategies and a stronger commitment to transnational cooperation to effectively address the shared challenges of sustainable development.

II. SDGs in International Relations

The SDGs are 17 interlinked objectives designed to serve as a 'shared blueprint for peace and prosperity for people and the planet, now and into the future'. The SDGs emphasise the interconnected environmental, social and economic aspects of sustainable development by putting sustainability at their centre. There are 169 targets in the five pillars of SDGs, namely, people, planet, prosperity, peace and partnership. To understand the paradigmatic origin of the SDGs, analysis of theories of international relations and global norms is essential.

In international relations, theories of transnationalism and structuralism evolved deviating from nationalist realism when economic crisis, emergence of new states, consolidation of international organisations, and welfare of humanity became prominent in the global agenda.[1] That is why the theoretical basics of transnationalism contain the initial indications of sustainable development in international relations. On the other hand, the structuralism of international relations reflects on causes that generate inequality and foster underdevelopment in parts of the international society. This centre-periphery asymmetry and its negative cause-effect relationship served as the forerunner of the embedding process of sustainable development in international relations. These two theories were the underpinnings behind the UN's Brundtland Commission's Report[2] 'Our Common Future', which challenged the long-standing assumption that economic goals must take precedence over environmental concerns. Its key message was that sustainable development pursues economic, technological and social progress without compromising the future generations, due to the negative impact these improvements may have on the environmental ecosystem. Recognising the centre-periphery asymmetry acknowledges the unequal distribution of power, resources and development across the international system. This conceptual framework underscores how certain regions or countries, often referred to as the 'centre', wield disproportionate influence and enjoy greater access to resources, while others, the 'periphery', are marginalised and struggle with limited access to resources and opportunities. This understanding is crucial in analysing various global phenomena, such as economic disparities, geopolitical dynamics and development challenges. By acknowledging the centre-periphery asymmetry, policymakers and scholars can better address issues of inequality, promote inclusive development, and strive for a more equitable global order. This perspective draws attention to the historical legacies of colonialism and the persistence of global inequalities.[3] Some critics argue, however, that centre-periphery models may oversimplify global dynamics by overlooking the agency of states and the impact of internal factors on development.

[1] K Waltz, *Theory of International Politics* (Addison-Wesley Publishing Company, 1979).

[2] GH Brundtland, 'Our common future – Call for action' (1987) 14(4) *Environmental Conservation* 291–94.

[3] I Wallerstein, *The Modern World-system: Capitalist Agriculture and the Origins of the European World-Economy in the Sixteenth Centenary* (Academic Press, 1974).

Besides, the world is dynamic, and power structures can shift over time. On the other hand, highlighting the negative cause-effect relationship between structural inequalities and underdevelopment sheds light on the persistent challenges faced by many countries in achieving sustainable development.[4] This perspective encourages addressing root causes rather than just symptoms. Summarising this report, it is found that the guiding principles for global development are based on three pillars: economic growth, social development, and environmental protection. More importantly, this was accepted by many international actors (states and organisations), thereby fostering transnationalism manifested by consensus through many multilateral events since the 1990s. Critics say that the challenge lies in operationalising and implementing sustainable development in a way that is equitable and effective. There may be tensions between the pursuit of economic growth and environmental sustainability, requiring careful policy navigation.[5] Some argue that the report has a human-centric or anthropocentric focus, giving priority to human needs and development over environmental concerns. Critics suggest that a more ecocentric approach, which emphasises the intrinsic value of ecosystems and non-human species, might be more appropriate for addressing environmental issues.[6]

The twenty-first century experienced poverty, inequality, and violence that generated human rights violations and wars; on the other hand, current threats which have acquired significant relevance in the global agenda include environmental degradation and the creeping effects of climate change.[7] These forced the international community to adopt global agendas such as the Millennium Development Goals (MDGs) and the Sustainable Development Goals (SDGs), establishing a global framework to achieve sustainable development, end poverty, protect the planet, and ensure prosperity for all people. The very formulation of the 2030 Agenda is carried out from a political perspective or what is known as 'soft law'.[8] They are a powerful source of legitimacy – the result of discussion among experts and imperative moral arguments. The SDGs integrate the principles of idealism into international relations, advocating for the adoption and adherence to international law, as well as the establishment of a multilateral global order.[9] Thus, the paradigm of sustainable development can be defined as construction of a new international order aimed at the fulfilment of the SDGs, through the

[4] S Fukuda Parr and D McNeill. 'Knowledge and Politics in Setting and Measuring the SDGs: Introduction to Special Issue' (2019) 10 *Global Policy* 5.

[5] N Kumar and others, 'Strategies for achieving the sustainable development goals (SDGs) in South Asia: lessons from policy simulations' (2016) 1601 South and South-West Asia Development Papers.

[6] H Washington and others, 'Why Ecocentrism is the Key Pathway to Sustainability' (2017) 1(1) *The Ecological Citizen* 35.

[7] S Morán Blanco, 'Sustainable Development in International Relations Theory: Its Presence or Absence: A Proposal for a New Paradigm' (2022) 11(2) *Iberoamerican Journal of Development Studies* 78.

[8] ibid.

[9] N Asadullah, A Savoia and K Sen, 'Will South Asia Achieve the Sustainable Development Goals by 2030? Learning from the MDGs Experience' (2020) 152 *Social Indicators Research* 165.

strength of cooperation, the increase of duly managed institutionalisation, and the progressive consolidation of a common global identity based on sustainability.[10] SDG 17 reflects this by stating that partnership for the goals requires to be built at global, regional, national and local levels based upon principles and values, and a shared vision and shared goals placing people and the planet at the centre.[11] In this way, the realism or state-centric paradigm has been overcome by the support and participation of each and every one of the actors, committed through strategies, integrated and interrelated actions, and strong global partnerships, as intended by transnationalism.

III. The Concept of the North–South Divide

The concept of transnationalism discussed above does not permit any grouping of countries of the world, but rather suggests a collective global approach towards development for all. On the contrary, the North–South model, developed largely by a Professor of Economics at Columbia University, Ronald Findlay, is a model in development economics that explains the growth of a less developed 'South' or 'periphery' economy that interacts through trade with a more developed 'North' or 'core' economy.[12] However, the world economy has been globalised with increasing interdependence of the countries due to increased movement of goods and services, labour migration and the expansion and exchange of information and technologies. Countries from the Northern Hemisphere are better off economically than the countries of the South because of historical colonialism, exploitative economic relations, unequal access to the global market, debt burden, weak institutions and the global economic system. This has inevitably created a North–South divide from a political economy viewpoint. However, the answer to the question of what is the global 'South' is not simple, as no easy definition is available. Due to the diversity in terms of ecology, geography, economic and political systems, a 'one size fits all' approach to sustainable development does not apply to the countries of the South.

Nations situated in the Northern regions are often characterised by greater wealth, reduced inequality and a perception of higher levels of democracy and development.[13] These countries typically specialise in exporting technologically

[10] J Wouters and M Hoornick, 'The Triangle of Human Rights, International Law, and Sustainable Development' in S McInerney-Lankford and R McCorquodale (eds), *The Roles of International Law in Development* (Oxford University Press, 2023).

[11] M Blicharska, C Teutschbein and RJ Smithers, 'SDG Partnerships may Perpetuate the Global North–South Divide' (2021) 11 *Scientific Reports* 22092.

[12] A Abdenur, 'Tilting The North-South Axis: The Legitimization of Southern Development Knowledge and its Implications for Comparative Education Research' (2002) 4(2) *Current Issues in Comparative Education* 57.

[13] S Mago, 'North–South Research Collaboration and the Sustainable Development Goals: Challenges and Opportunities for Academics' in H Tor and others (eds), *Knowledge for Justice: Critical Perspectives from Southern African-Nordic Research Partnerships* (African Minds, 2017).

advanced manufactured goods. In contrast, Southern states are frequently described as less affluent, undergoing development, and having fragile democracies. They depend on exports from the primary sector, often sharing a history of colonialism by Northern states.[14]

Some critics argue that the traditional North–South divide is becoming increasingly inconsistent with reality, because as countries progress economically, they may be classified as part of the 'North' irrespective of their geographical location. Notwithstanding, nations that do not meet the criteria for 'developed' status are effectively considered part of the 'South'.[15] Due to the so-called North–South divide, global development standards like the SDGs cannot be realised by the countries of the South on the same scale or by the same method as the countries in the North.

IV. A Hypothetical Framework of SDG-related Capacities in the Southern Countries

Traditionally, state capacity is defined from a power dimension for achieving its policy goals. The most popular framework of state capacity is the World Bank's 'institutional' one, which includes quality of public services, civil service, policy formulation and implementation, and the credibility of a government's commitment to improving or maintaining these aspects. Other elements include voice and accountability, political stability, regulatory quality, the rule of law, and control of corruption.[16]

In the case of a group of nations like the Southern countries, the common features of transnational capacity, as dissected from the global non-binding agreements and resolutions, are (a) collective (b) partnership (c) solution-centric (d) management-focused and (e) measurable. A reflection of these transnational characteristics of capacity is found in the UNGA Resolution 70/1 on SDGs,[17] which can be used as the basis for a hypothetical framework of SDG-related capacities. Paragraphs 40 and 43 include a list of global policies for implementation such as the Addis Ababa Action Agenda and the Istanbul Programme of Action. Paragraph 41 includes: (1) mobilisation of financial resources, capacity building and technology transfer; (2) public finance, both domestic and international; (3) private finance. Paragraph 45 emphasises the inclusion of the goals in domestic legislation for ensuring accountability and for determining the role of

[14] A Anghie and BS Chimni, 'Third World Approaches to International Law and Individual Responsibility in Internal Conflicts' (2003) 2(1) *Chinese Journal of International Law* 77.

[15] Finance Center for South-South Cooperation, www.fc-ssc.org/en/partnership_program/south_south_countries, accessed 20 August 2023.

[16] D Kaufmann and A Kraay, *Worldwide Governance Indicators* (May 2023).

[17] UNGA RES 70/1 (21 October 2015) UN Doc A/RES/70/1.

public institutions in implementation. Finally, para 46 recommends the role of an effective United Nations system in achieving the SDGs.

Analysing UNGA Resolution 70/1 and features of transnational capacity, Figure 14.1 illustrates a sequential process comprising five elements, which can be devised as a hypothetical framework.

Figure 14.1 Elements of SDG-related capacities

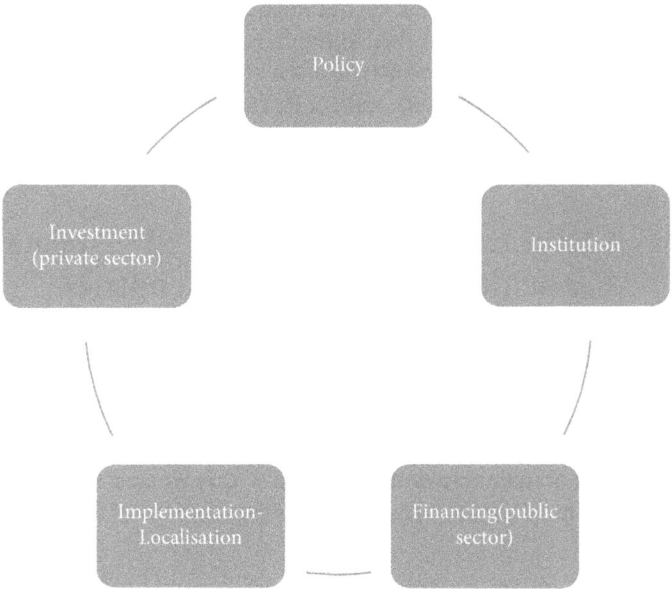

This hypothetical framework assumes that the SDG capacity cycle starts with the adoption of relevant policies followed by forming institutions. Public sector financing is undertaken to ensure localisation and implementation. Motivated by the policies, institutions and public sector financing, the private sector is expected to come forward with SDG-related investments. Lessons from all four elements can be translated into policy correction or new policy formulation. From a conceptual perspective, it can be seen that the different elements of the SDG capacity cycle are interconnected. For example, effective policies are essential for attracting investment and ensuring that it is aligned with the SDGs. Institutions play a vital role in implementing and enforcing policies, and funding is needed to support all of these activities. Examining both capacity and impact aspects allows for a nuanced evaluation, helping policymakers and practitioners make informed decisions to enhance the effectiveness of their SDG interventions.

SDG-related policies and guidelines are essential to govern decision-making. The policymakers require the requisite capacity to formulate, implement and adapt SDG-related policies, while the impact of policies can be assessed by examining their alignment with SDGs, inclusivity and responsiveness to changing circumstances.

SDG-related institutions include government agencies, non-governmental organisations (NGOs) and international bodies, which need to be able to govern, make decisions and deliver services. The impact of SDG-related institutions can be measured by assessing their ability to achieve intended outcomes and provide public goods and services.[18]

Public sector financing for SDGs involves the allocation and management of funds by governments to support public services, infrastructures and SDG-aligned development projects. However, the capacity for budgeting, revenue generation and debt management is essential for fiscal and financial management of public sector investments in SDGs. The impact of SDG financing is reflected in efficiency in the use of resources, provision of essential services, and overall economic development of the country.

Implementation of SDGs involves the actual execution of policies, projects or programmes on the ground while *localisation of SDGs* refers to adapting these initiatives to the specific needs and contexts of local communities. Implementation capacity involves the ability to carry out activities efficiently, monitor progress, and adapt strategies as needed. The success of implementation is measured by the achievement of project objectives, community engagement and the positive changes experienced by the target population.

Private sector investment refers to the financial support that businesses, investors and entrepreneurs provide for SDGs. Key challenges of the private sector are that they contribute indirectly to SDGs, if not directly, but it is difficult to measure their contributions to and impact on SDGs.[19]

Hypothetically, the SDG capacity cycle initiates with the adoption of relevant policies, establishment of institutions, and subsequent public sector financing for localisation and implementation. While the SDGs themselves are not legally binding, deriving their normative basis from global consensus, the ability to enforce or achieve these goals varies significantly across countries and regions. Notably, democratic practice and governance structures diverge between the North and South. While democratic governance is relatively stable and institutionalised in many Northern countries, numerous Southern countries face challenges due to weak democratic bases and governance structures. These deficiencies impede the efficient implementation of SDGs. Therefore, addressing these challenges necessitates strengthening democratic institutions, promoting transparency, enhancing public participation, and fortifying legal and institutional frameworks underpinning SDG implementation. Integrating these considerations into the hypothetical framework underscores the critical role of governance in facilitating effective SDG implementation efforts.

However, the issue of governance as a barrier is not adequately addressed. Good governance is crucial at every stage of the SDG capacity cycle. Effective policies

[18] F Rosati and LGD Faria, 'Addressing the SDGs in Sustainability Reports: The Relationship with Institutional Factors' (2019) 215 *Journal of Cleaner Production* 1312.

[19] A Breuer and others, 'Integrated Policymaking: Institutional Designs for Implementing the Sustainable Development Goals (SDGs)' (2023) 170 *World Development* 106317.

are essential for attracting investment and ensuring alignment with the SDGs, but without good governance, there is a risk of mismanagement or corruption hindering progress. Institutions, too, rely on good governance for their effectiveness in implementing and enforcing policies.[20] Additionally, transparent and accountable public sector financing is vital to ensure resources are allocated efficiently and effectively towards SDG initiatives.

This hypothetical framework will be tested in this chapter to see if it has been working or if it requires a new approach.

A. Policy Capacity

Countries of the Global South need to affiliate their national development policies with the SDG goals. Different countries have different national development priorities. Reflections on how countries have incorporated SDGs into their national development policies are discussed here.

The Sustainable Development Solutions Network of the United Nations[21] tracks public practices in support of the SDGs. Its Sustainable Development Report 2021 included a survey report[22] that found that

> most governments had by 2021 developed strategies and action plans to implement the goals. For many governments, this is a national sustainability strategy explicitly linked to the 2030 Agenda goals and targets. Some governments though have preferred to take a mainstreaming approach, whereby each government ministry implements the SDGs within the scope of its mandate (instead of via an overarching national action plan).

The report also revealed that most countries have designated a focal unit or office responsible for coordinating the implementation of the SDGs. The survey measured the SDG policy performance of the countries on voluntary national review, high-level statements, SDG strategy/sectoral plans, SDGs in the national budget, national SDG monitoring, designated lead unit, and SDG in national Covid-19 recovery plan.[23]

Among 60 countries which have SDG policies, of which only 26 countries are from the South, namely: Algeria, Argentina, Bangladesh, Benin, Brazil, Bolivia, Chile, China, Colombia, Democratic Republic of Congo, Egypt, Ethiopia, India, Indonesia, Jamaica, Kenya, Malaysia, Morocco, Nigeria, Pakistan, The Philippines, Senegal, South Africa, Thailand, Uganda and Vietnam. The report[24] has identified

[20] WD Towah, 'The Impact of Good Governance and Stability on Sustainable Development in Ghana' (PhD Thesis, Walden University 2019) 23–24.

[21] 'Sustainable Development Solutions Network', www.unsdsn.org/about-us, accessed 4 March 2023.

[22] JD Sachs and others, 'Policy Efforts and Commitments for the SDGs' in *Sustainable Development Report 2022* (Cambridge University Press, 2022).

[23] S Mejía-Dugand, S Croese and SA Reddy, 'SDG Implementation at the Local Level: Lessons from Responses to the Coronavirus Crisis in Three Cities in the Global South' (2020) 2 *Frontiers in Sustainable Cities* 598516.

[24] Wallerstein (n 3).

several reasons for this SDG policy gap in southern countries. First, internationally comparable policy trackers and measures (such as laws, regulations, investments and subsidies) are less available than international outcome data. Generally, more comparable policy trackers and measures are available for Organisation for Economic Co-operation and Development (OECD) countries than for others. Second, policy efforts need to be interpreted with an understanding of national challenges and contexts (for instance, the absence of an advanced cybersecurity policy matters less in a country with low internet access and poor digital infrastructure).[25] Third, with a few exceptions, government pledges and policies do not result in their effective implementation. For instance, Sweden's approach involves a broad societal consensus and collaboration with various stakeholders to achieve the goals, while Norway's policies aim to align domestic efforts with the principles outlined in the SDGs.[26] On the other hand, Bangladesh is yet to offer a comprehensive national budget on SDGs, but the ministries concerned are implementing projects for achieving the SDGs. The submission of voluntary national reviews is a domestic policy issue, which countries may or may not submit depending on national reporting capacities. High-level statements are part of diplomatic exercises, where some countries commit and others abstain, considering political dynamics and diplomatic relations. The inclusion of SDG indicators in national/sectoral plans is an easy exercise that does not entail any commitment. Given that most countries did not include SDGs in their budget or in their overarching narratives implies a lack of financial commitment towards SDGs. Most of the countries are monitoring SDGs but there is considerable variation in the number of indicators they monitor, pointing to variation in monitoring willingness or capacities.

B. Institutional Capacity

The United Nations Office for South-South Cooperation (UNOSSC) is a pivotal actor in fostering institutional capacity building to attain the SDGs in developing nations.[27] Its operations revolve around three strategic outcomes: (a) promoting policy decisions favouring South–South and triangular cooperation (SSC) and coordinated UN system support for such endeavours; (b) enhancing capacity through knowledge and experience sharing; and (c) forging strategic SSC partnerships to underpin demand-driven programmes. The recognition of the diversity of SSC approaches and their inherent principles were enshrined in the outcome document of the Buenos Aires Programme of Action (BAPA+40) in 2019.

[25] DV Malito and others, 'Measuring Governance to Achieve Sustainable Development: Promises and Challenges' in WL and others (eds), *Peace, Justice and Strong Institutions* (Springer, 2021).

[26] Government Offices of Sweden, *Report on the Implementation of the 2030 Agenda for Sustainable Development* (2021) 125–26.

[27] 'Transforming Our World: The 2030 Agenda for Sustainable Development' (Department of Economic and Social Affairs), sdgs.un.org/2030agenda, accessed 3 August 2023.

Over 80 United Nations Sustainable Development Frameworks at the country level explicitly highlighted the significance of South–South cooperation.[28]

The South-South Galaxy, an international knowledge-sharing and relationship-facilitating platform supported by UNOSSC, has established itself as a global repository of solutions and resources by connecting seekers and providers of solutions. The UNOSSC helped in the formulation of the South–South cooperation strategy and encouraged the international community to act upon the recommendations from the BAPA+40. It has formulated the 'South-South in Action Series', comprising 10 volumes, alongside other knowledge products. These publications disseminate policies, initiatives and activities that have contributed to the realisation of developmental objectives. The UNOSSC-managed funds have played a crucial role in supporting development projects across diverse regions, encompassing Africa, the Arab States, Asia and the Pacific, and Latin America.

Despite many good achievements, the UNOSSC has faced fund scarcity, inefficient staffing, unintegrated institutional structure and uncertain partnerships with stakeholders. This entity has the highest potential to act as an intermediary between the North and the South to ensure collaboration on funding and investments. However, it seems that the North is willing to support policy formulation in the South but not to fund its implementation.[29]

C. Financing Capacity

Financing the implementation of the SDGs is a tough challenge. There have been relentless efforts to marshal the resources needed to meet the SDG resource gap, which is now between US $5–7 trillion annually, as identified by the UN Alliance for SDG Finance.[30] The Addis Ababa Action Agenda, the outcome document from 2015, provides a new global framework for financing sustainable development that aligns all financing flows and policies with economic, social and environmental priorities. The specific action areas of the Addis Agenda are[31] domestic public resources; domestic and international private business and finance; international development cooperation; international trade as an engine for development; debt and debt sustainability; addressing systemic issues; science, technology, innovation and capacity building.

[28] J Sharma and SK Varshney, 'Role of India in South–South Cooperation to Achieve Sustainable Development Goals' in V Ittekkot and JK Baweja (eds), *Science, Technology and Innovation Diplomacy in Developing Countries: Perceptions and Practice* (Springer Nature, 2023).

[29] K Bäckstrand, F Koliev and A Mert, 'Governing SDG Partnerships: The Role of Institutional Capacity, Inclusion, and Transparency' in E Murphy, A Banerjee and PP Walsh (eds), *Partnerships and the Sustainable Development Goals* (Springer International Publishing, 2022).

[30] United Nations Global Compact, 'UN Alliance for SDG Finance' (United Nations, 2023), www.unglobalcompact.org/take-action/action/globalallianceforsdgfinance, accessed 3 October 2023.

[31] United Nations, 'Financing for Sustainable Development' (United Nations, 2023) www.un.org/sustainabledevelopment/financing-for-development/#:~:text=The%20Addis%20Agenda%20provides%20a,economic%2C%20social%20and%20environmental%20priorities, accessed 2 July 2023.

For the Southern countries, there are some key public sector financing challenges. First, the international community is falling behind in its commitment to support the Least Developed Countries (LDCs). Only six countries have met the target of contributing 0.7 per cent of Gross National Income as official development assistance to LDCs, and the average for OECD countries has never exceeded 0.4 per cent.[32]

Second, there is a concern that the SDGs might leave many developing countries with a high debt burden. There are signs that LDC debt has been rising fast, both in absolute terms and in relation to economic indicators such as Gross Domestic Product (GDP), export earnings and government revenue. The Deputy Managing Director of the International Monetary Fund (IMF) writes, '40 percent of low-income countries face high risk of debt distress or are unable to service their debt fully'.[33] Third, a report by the UN's Department of Economic and Social Affairs (DESA) identified low tax revenue and weak international support as potential hurdles in the path of SDG achievement.[34]

The new challenge that the southern countries face on SDG financing is the impact of the Covid-19 pandemic. Financing for Sustainable Development Report 2022 of the Inter-Agency Taskforce for Financing for Development[35] states that:

> COVID-19 has dramatically set back SDG progress, and affected all aspects of financing for development: the global economy has experienced the worst recession in 90 years, with the most vulnerable segments of societies disproportionately affected; around 120 million people have fallen back into extreme poverty; 114 million jobs have been lost; tax revenues, foreign direct investment, trade and remittances have decreased; and debt vulnerabilities increased along with the rise in debt levels.

The report proposes to (i) invest in people and a sustainable and risk-informed recovery; and (ii) reform the global financial and policy architecture, to ensure that it is supportive of recovery and is aligned with the 2030 Agenda.

At the centre of the Addis Ababa Agenda are national sustainable development plans and strategies supported by integrated national financing frameworks (INFFs). A country's sustainable development strategy lays out what needs to be financed. INFFs spell out how the national strategy will be financed and implemented, relying on the full range of public and private financing sources.

A multi-partnered trust fund, the Joint Sustainable Development Goals (SDG) Fund, aims to stimulate strategic investments required to meet the SDGs. To date,

[32] Factsheet, '0.7% Aid Target Factsheet' (*Development Initiatives*, 28 August 2013), devinit.org/resources/0-7-aid-target-2/#:~:text=The%20first%20countries%20met%20the,to%20meet%20the%200.7%25%20since, accessed 4 July 2023.

[33] T Zhang, 'Managing Debt Vulnerabilities in Low-Income and Developing Countries' (IMF, 22 March 2018) www.imf.org/en/Blogs/Articles/2018/03/22/managing-debt-vulnerabilities-in-low-income-and-developing-countries, accessed 4 July 2023.

[34] ibid.

[35] United Nations, *Inter-agency Task Force on Financing Development, Financing for Sustainable Report 2021* (United Nations, 2021) 130–31.

it has funded 200 joint programmes focused on SDG finance. It has stimulated over 1,000+ partnerships alongside the UN to support the SDGs and has tested over 300 innovative solutions to accelerate the 2030 Agenda.[36] The contributions it receives are not entity-specific but aim to support broader UN system-level functions. Consequently, it differs from restrictive earmarked funding which can fuel competition and hamper cooperation among UN entities. The pooling of multi-partner trust funds is widely considered 'multilateralism'-friendly – and is more suitable for integrated support at the scale essential for achieving the 2030 Agenda. With a total of US$250 million for three years, the Joint SDG Fund is still short of the annual US$290 million target envisioned by the UN Secretary-General and agreed at the Fund's Funding Compact.

Global development goals become meaningless without funding. The Joint SDG Funds and INFFs formulated for financing SDG frameworks have both failed to attract the required resources, necessitating reform of the global policy and financial architecture. Besides, if the debt burden of the Southern countries increases, they will prioritise repaying debt rather than achieving the development goals which may or may not be part of the debt financing.

D. Implementation and Localisation Capacity

The Global Taskforce of Local and Regional Governments and UNDP and UN-HABITAT developed a roadmap for localising the SDGs. The critical elements of the roadmap are awareness-raising, advocacy, implementation and monitoring. However, there were four first-generation challenges identified for the Southern countries.[37] Those were: aligning the SDGs with national planning processes; coordination, management and leadership of the SDG implementation process; adequacy of financing and other means of implementation; data-related issues and capacity of national statistical agencies; and partnership and stakeholder participation in SDG implementation. The data availability for tracking the SDGs in Bangladesh is summarised in Figure 14.2. All organisations that generate data were involved in the SDGs Data Gap Analysis effort, including the Bangladesh Bureau of Statistics. According to the GED study, 108 indicator-related data are only partially available, 63 indicators-related data are now unavailable, and 70 indicators-related data are easily accessible in the current system. This illustrates the challenges relating to lack of data availability faced by countries like Bangladesh.[38]

[36] 'Who We Are' (Who we are / Joint SDG Fund), jointsdgfund.org/who-we-are, accessed 3 March 2023.

[37] D Bhattacharya and S Jahan, *Initial Challenges of SDG Implementation: Regional Trends and Country Experiences* (Southern Voice, 2020).

[38] Bangladesh Bureau of Statistics, *Data Gap Analysis for Sustainable Development Goals* (General Economic Division (GED), 2017).

Figure 14.2 Data availability on SDGs in Bangladesh

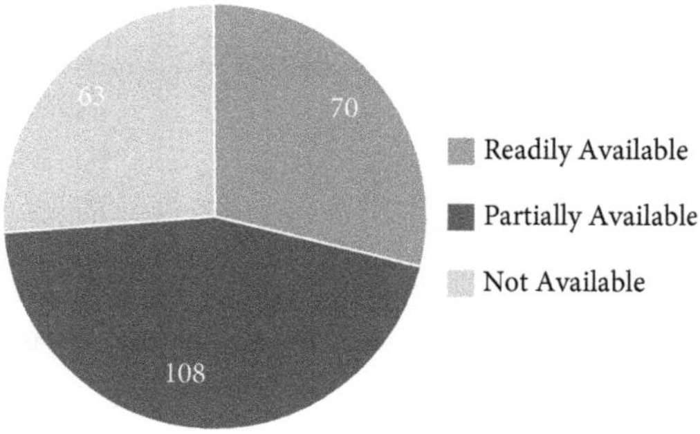

Source: Bangladesh Bureau of Statistics, 'Data Gap Analysis for Sustainable Development Goals' (General Economic Division, 2017) 22, figure 2.

Figure 14.3 displays the SDG status of the Southern countries in various regions as at 2022.

Figure 14.3 SDG index 2022

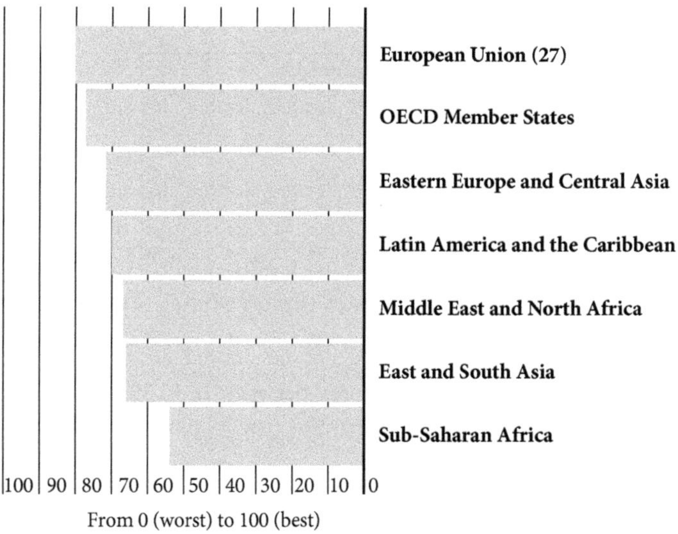

Source: J Sachs and others, *Sustainable Development Report 2022: From Crisis to Sustainable Development: The SDGs as Roadmap to 2030 and Beyond* (Cambridge University Press, 2022) ix.

The regional SDG progress index in Figure 14.3 indicates that most of the Southern countries are lagging behind in SDG progress on most of indicators. The EU, OECD member states, Eastern Europe and Central Asia have scored above 70 on all indicators. Governments of these regions belong to the North. Latin America, the Caribbean, Middle East, North Africa, East and South Africa and Sub-Saharan Africa are Southern countries and have scored below 70 in this index.

Figure 14.4 Country Progress Based on Ranking

Summary table	
Rank	**Number of countries**
0–50	7
51–100	41
101–150	49
151–163	13
Total	110

Source: Compiled from the Sustainable Development Report dashboard, see dashboards.sdgindex.org/rankings.

A review of the SDG ranking of 134 countries of the South reveals that seven countries are within the range of 0 to 7; 41 countries are in the range of 51 to 100; 49 countries fall in the zone of 101 to 150; and 13 countries are in between 151 to 163 (see Figure 14.4). Information from 24 countries is not available. So, most of the Southern countries are in the middle range of SDG ranking at various stages and require support for their progress.

Figure 14.5 Country Progress Based on SDG Score

Summary table	
SDG Score	Number of countries
0–25	0
26–50	7
51–75	99
76–100	4
Total	110

Source: Compiled from the Sustainable Development Report dashboard, see dashboards.sdgindex.org/rankings.

In the SDG scoring, seven countries scored between 26 to 50; 99 countries scored 51 to 75; and 4 countries scored 76 to 100 (see Figure 14.5). Information on 24 Southern countries is not available.

This analysis indicates a mixed performance of the Southern countries on SDG achievement. Some have done well, whereas others need to improve. The reasons why some of them performed well most likely include the following:[39]

- *Political will and governance:* Countries with strong political commitment and effective governance structures are often more successful in implementing and achieving SDGs.
- *Economic stability:* Nations with a stable and growing economy may find it easier to allocate resources toward SDG-related initiatives.

[39] United Nations, 'The Future We Want' (Department of Economic and Social Affairs), sdgs.un.org/future-we-want, accessed 1 March 2023.

- *Social investment:* Prioritising investments in education, healthcare and social welfare contributes to improved human development indices and progress on many SDGs.
- *International cooperation:* Countries actively engaging in international cooperation, partnerships and collaboration may benefit from shared knowledge, expertise and resources.
- *Innovation and technology:* Embracing technological advancements and fostering innovation can enhance a country's capacity to address SDGs efficiently.

The reasons for poor performance most likely include:

- *Economic challenges:* Countries facing economic downturns or having limited financial resources struggle to invest adequately in SDG-related projects.
- *Conflict and instability:* Nations dealing with internal conflicts, political instability or insecurity may find it challenging to focus on sustainable development efforts.
- *Lack of infrastructure:* Inadequate infrastructure can hinder progress on various SDGs, such as those related to clean water, sanitation and energy.
- *Environmental degradation:* Nations grappling with environmental issues, such as pollution and climate change impacts, face difficulties in achieving environmental sustainability goals.
- *Inequality:* Persistent social and economic inequalities within a country, especially in the LDCs, can impede progress on poverty reduction, education and health goals.

E. Investment Capacity of the Private Sector on SDGs

Private sector investment is based on underlying business motives and profit outlook, while SDGs are more development-oriented and people-centric. Private sector investors demand attractive rates of return based on levels of risk. For instance, private sector financing is exposed to risk factors such as demand and supply fluctuations, governmental policy changes, credit risk, market and liquidity risk, interest rate risk, and political and regulatory risks. Developing economies that require the bulk of the SDG financing perform poorly due to the risk factors associated with investing. This raises operational costs while increasing uncertainty and discouraging participation by private sector entities.

Since the adoption of the SDGs in 2015, the United Nations Commission on Trade and Development (UNCTAD) has been observing progress in sustainable development investment across several SDG sectors, including infrastructure, climate change mitigation, food and agriculture, health, telecommunications and ecosystems and biodiversity. However, international private sector investment flows to developing and transition economies, mostly located in the southern hemisphere, in sectors relevant to the SDGs fell by about one-third in 2020 because of the Covid-19 pandemic.[40] For instance, the credit growth was 10.7 per cent in September 2019 and later it was reduced to 7.55 per cent in May 2021 in Bangladesh.[41] This poses a risk to delivering on the 2030 Agenda for sustainable development.

According to UNCTAD,[42] although many national SDG strategies highlight the need for additional financial resources, very few contain concrete road maps for promoting private sector investment in the SDGs. Existing investment promotion instruments applicable to the SDGs are limited in number and follow a piecemeal approach, with less than half of UN member states maintaining specific tools for promoting investments in SDGs.

Sustainability funds have grown to invest in sustainable development, which, according to UNCTAD, has reached US$1.2–1.3 trillion. However, most of these funds are invested in developed countries (for example, in renewable energy, biodiversity conservation and sustainable agriculture). The private sector impact investors, that is, individuals, organisations or funds are also investing in developing countries to generate positive social or environmental impact alongside financial returns. Unlike traditional investors whose primary goal is financial profit, impact investors prioritise investments that contribute to sustainable development goals, such as poverty alleviation, environmental conservation, social equity and economic empowerment. For example, Finnfund, an impact investor, has invested in Guinea and Lebanon in energy-efficient telecommunications projects, sustainable teak and cocoa plantations in Nicaragua, and solar power solutions in Nigeria's banking sector.[43]

The challenge lies in combining growth with the channelling of funds to SDG-relevant investment projects in developing countries, especially the LDCs. This growth indicates a positive trend in addressing environmental and social challenges through financial investments. It is also about ensuring good environmental, social and governance (ESG) practices in business operations to ensure a positive investment impact. This reflects a growing awareness of the need for responsible and ethical business operations. More than half of stock exchanges worldwide have guided listed companies on sustainability reporting. The SDGs are increasingly becoming a focus of investor interest and company reporting for impact. A key challenge is the quality of disclosure and harmonisation of reporting standards.[44]

UNCTAD proposed a strategic framework for private investment in SDGs where public financing could catalyse private investment in sustainable development

[40] United Nations Conference on Trade and Development, *World Investment Report 2020* (30 years anniversary edn, United Nations 2020) xiv.

[41] JN Alo and S Prince, 'Private Sector Credit Growth Returns to Pre-Pandemic Level After Two Years' *The Business Standard* (29 December 2021), www.tbsnews.net/economy/banking/private-sector-credit-growth-returns-pre-pandemic-level-after-two-years-350179, accessed 2 July 2023.

[42] Sharma and Varshney (n 28).

[43] 'Climate Investments' (*Finnfund*, 2 March 2020), www.finnfund.fi/en/investing/finnfunds-climate-investments/, accessed 3 April 2023.

[44] R Boffo and R Patalano, 'ESG Investing: Practices, Progress and Challenges' (OECD, 2020).

projects. For example, Public-Private Partnerships (PPPs) can encourage private sector investment for public good. Since the adoption of the SDGs, some initiatives were taken to encourage investment in sustainable development. More than 150 investment measures have been adopted worldwide to specifically liberalise or promote investment, targeting mostly transportation, innovation, food and agriculture.[45] However, the inadequate reorientation of national investment regimes toward SDGs denotes that current measures may not be effectively addressing broader sustainability goals. This difficulty stems from the fact that a significant number of existing treaties pre-date the establishment of the SDGs. Updating these treaties to align with current sustainability goals poses a challenge due to legal complexities and the need for consensus among treaty signatories.[46] Recent treaties incorporate SDGs, and countries are seen to be reformulating their treaty models, which indicates a growing awareness of the need to align investment agreements with sustainable development objectives. It also suggests a willingness among countries to update their approaches to international investment in light of changing global priorities. However, the challenges in updating existing treaties and incorporating SDGs underscore the need for global collaboration.

Responding to the United Nations General Assembly resolution on 'Promoting investments for sustainable development' (A/RES/74/199), for 'concrete recommendations for the advancement of investment for the implementation of the 2030 Agenda', UNCTAD's new Action Plan combines policy instruments to provide an implementation framework for the UN Secretary-General's Strategy for Financing the 2030 Agenda for Sustainable Development. These six instruments are as follows.[47]

- Mainstreaming the SDGs in national investment policy frameworks and in the international investment treaty regime. This entails integrating SDGs both in national and international investment policy frameworks. This would present a significant opportunity for the Global South to attract investment that fosters sustainable development, addresses socioeconomic challenges, and promotes resilience in the face of global uncertainties.
- Re-orienting investment promotion and facilitation strategies toward SDG investment. This involves adjusting strategies employed by countries to attract foreign and domestic investments in sectors aligned with the SDGs. Emphasising SDG-aligned investments can enhance the attractiveness of countries in the Global South to responsible investors who prioritise sustainability and corporate social responsibility. This can result in increased investment flows that contribute to sustainable development outcomes while fostering partnerships between governments, businesses and civil society.

[45] United Nations Conference on Trade and Development (n 40).

[46] ibid.

[47] United Nations, *Roadmap for Financing the 2030 Agenda for Sustainable Development 2019–2021* (United Nations, 2021).

- Establishing regional SDG Investment Compacts. This requires the adoption of regional collaborative agreements to attract and channel SDG-related investments for various regional countries. For the Global South, these compacts hold significant implications. They offer a platform for fostering regional cooperation and integration, which is essential for maximising the impact of SDG-related investments. By coordinating investment promotion efforts and sharing best practices, countries can amplify their collective voice and attractiveness to investors, thereby increasing the flow of resources into critical sectors such as infrastructure, healthcare and education.
- Fostering new forms of partnerships for SDG investment, including collaborations among governments, the private sector, civil society and international organisations to leverage collective resources and expertise. Fostering partnerships for SDG investment can facilitate knowledge exchange and capacity-building initiatives, particularly in areas where expertise may be limited. By collaborating with international organisations and private sector partners, countries in the Global South can access technical know-how, innovative solutions and best practices to enhance their ability to implement effective and sustainable development projects.
- Deepening ESG integration in financial markets by establishing a global monitoring mechanism with a harmonised approach to disclosure. This has recognised the importance of environmental, social and governance factors in the investment decision-making process and a harmonised system to monitor and assess ESG performance. A harmonised approach to ESG disclosure can improve transparency and accountability in financial markets in the Global South. By standardising reporting requirements, investors can more easily assess the sustainability credentials of companies and projects, reducing information asymmetry and mitigating risks associated with unsustainable practices.
- Changing the global business mindset in the perspective and behaviour of businesses on a global scale that needs a responsible and sustainable approach to business operations. Adopting responsible business practices can help address pressing environmental and social challenges faced by countries in the Global South. By reducing carbon emissions, minimising waste and promoting fair labour practices, businesses can contribute to environmental conservation, social equity, and community development in these regions.

V. Status of Bangladesh on SDG Capacity Elements

Bangladesh, as a least developed country (LDC) of the Global South, will graduate out of LDC status by 2026. It needs to prepare itself to confront the obstacles that may arise following its graduation. The year 2030 represents another crucial landmark for Bangladesh in its pursuit of achieving the SDGs. Bangladesh is currently facing capacity constraints in determining suitable solutions to the difficulties it is confronted with. This section focuses on the capacity issues confronting Bangladesh to achieve the SDGs and underpins possible ways to overcome them using a stop-focus-narrow-deepen-decide (SFNDD) method.

A. Policy

Bangladesh has many policies and plans at the national and sectoral levels that can help implement the SDGs. Table 14.1, which is not exhaustive, highlights the policies which align with several SDGs.

Table 14.1 Bangladesh's SDG Law and Policy Alignment

SDG goals	Related Bangladeshi laws and policies
1. No poverty	The 8th Five-year plan; National Sustainable Development Strategy (NSDS) 2010–21; National Social Security Strategy (NSSS) of Bangladesh 2015; National Plan for Disaster Management (2016–29).
2. Zero hunger	National Food and Nutrition Security Policy, Plan of Action (2021–2030); National Nutrition Policy 2015.
3. Good health and well-being	Bangladesh National Health Policy 2011.
4. Quality education	National Education Policy 2010; National Skill Development Policy 2011.
5. Gender equality	National Women Development Policy 2011; Domestic Violence (Prevention and Protection) Act 2010; Prevention and Suppression of Human Trafficking Act 2012; National Acid Crime Prevention Act 2010; Pornography Control Act 2012; National Children Policy 2011; Child Marriage Restraint Act 2017; DNA Act 2014; Dowry Prohibition Act 2018.
6. Clean water and sanitation	National Strategy for Water and Sanitation in the Hard-to-Reach Areas of Bangladesh 2012; National Strategy for Water Supply and Sanitation 2014; Sector Development Plan (2011–2025).
7. Affordable and clean energy	Power System Master Plan 2016; National Solar Energy Action Plan 2021–2041; Energy Efficiency and Conservation Rules 2013.
8. Decent work and economic growth	Child Labor Elimination Policy 2010; Bangladesh Labor Act 2006 and its amendment 2018.
9. Industry, innovation and infrastructure	Industrial Policy 2016; Road Master Plan (2010–30); Bangladesh Public Private Partnership Act 2015; Revised Strategic Transport Plan 2016; 8th Five-year Plan.

(continued)

Table 14.1 ***(Continued)***

SDG goals	Related Bangladeshi laws and policies
10. Reduced inequality	National Social Security Strategy (NSSS) of Bangladesh, 2015; Disabled Persons Rights and Protection Act 2013; 'Expatriates' Welfare and Overseas Employment Policy 2016; Bangladesh Planning Commission, *Sustainable Development Goals: Bangladesh Progress Report 2020* (General Economic Divisions, 2020).
11. Sustainable cities and communities	Local Government (Municipalities) Act 2009; City Corporations Act 2009; Water Supplies and Sewerage Authorities Act 1996; Waste Management Rules 2021; National Road Safety Action Plan 2017–2022.
12. Responsible consumption and production	Consumer Rights Protection Act 2009; National Environment Policy 2018.
13. Climate action	Bangladesh Climate Change Strategy and Action Plan 2022; Nationally Determined Contribution 2021; Bangladesh Delta Plan 2100; Mujib Climate Prosperity Plan 2021; National Adaptation Plan 2022.
14. Life below water	The Marine Fisheries Act 2020; Blue Economy Initiative; National Shrimp Policy 2014; Bangladesh Oceanographic Research Institute Act 2015.
15. Life on land	National Sustainable Development Strategy (NSDS) 2010–21; Biodiversity Act 2017 and National Biodiversity Strategy and Action Plan; Forest (Amendment) Act 2000; Forest Policy 1994; Wildlife (Protection and Safety) Act 2012; Social Forestry (Amendment) Rules 2010; Forest Produce Transit (Control) Rules 2011; Brick Burning (Control) (Amendment) Act 2001; Saw-Mill (Licence) Rules 2012.
16. Peace, justice and strong institutions	Constitution of Bangladesh; Strategic Plan of Controller and Auditor General of Bangladesh (2013–18);
17. Partnership for the goals	Public Money and Budget Management Act 2009; Statistics Rule 2014; Bangladesh Planning Commission, *Sustainable Development Goals: Bangladesh Progress Report 2020* (General Economic Divisions, 2020) 224–30.

Source: Author's compilation based on data collected from multiple government ministries and divisions.

Largely led by politicians and bureaucrats, the policy planning process in Bangladesh follows a top-down approach. The government has introduced several measures to guarantee public involvement, specifically in local government decision-making. First, election-related participation: elections are held periodically at the Union Parishad and Upazila Parishad levels following a five-year interval.[48] Second, participation through meetings: the Local Government (Union Parishad) Act (2009) mandates open budget and ward-level meetings in which the public can participate. Research, however, claims that these public forums, largely a formality, do not provide the public with a meaningful voice in operation of local government operations.

B. Institutions

The Prime Minister's office has set up an Inter-ministerial SDG Implementation and Review Committee comprising Secretaries from 20 ministries. The committee includes a representative each from the Federation of Bangladesh Chamber of Commerce and Industries representing the private sector, a member from the NGO Affairs Bureau representing NGOs, two civil society platforms[49] and the UN Resident Coordinator's Office. A Principal Coordinator on SDG Affairs heads the committee. The Planning Commission acts as its Secretariat. An SDG Working Team provides recommendations to the Committee. Different ministries and departments have been tasked with attaining different SDG goals. In the case of multiple ministries tasked with one SDG goal, coordination becomes a challenge. and reports are periodically collected from the ministries on SDG progress and reviewed. Although established to fulfil international commitments, this machinery is not effective because the ministries focus more on implementing regular development works without trying to establish linkages with the SDGs. National level mechanisms can provide instructions and guidance, but implementation lies with the ministries and field administration and there is no accountability if the SDG-related performance of any ministry or department is unsatisfactory.

Bangladesh has been active in sharing its lessons and good practices with the other Southern countries through South-South Cooperation (SSC). It has produced a strategy document on South-South Cooperation for financing SDGs.[50] Its Access to Information (A2I) Programme spearheads three platforms that employ SSC methodologies to enhance the sharing of knowledge, experiences and best practices, while seeking inventive solutions. These platforms include the South-South Network for Public Service Innovation, the Alliance for Asian Apprenticeship, and the South Asia Civil Registration Network. The UN Global Publication on Best Practices has integrated five pioneering development solutions

[48] N Uddin, 'Empowerment through Participation in Local Governance: The Case of Union Parishad in Bangladesh' (2019) 22 *Public Administration and Policy* 40.

[49] 'Environment and Climate Change Unit' (Palli Karma-Sahayak Foundation (PKSF), 13 February 2019), pksf.org.bd/our-activities/core-programmes/environment-and-climate-change-unit/, accessed 2 June 2023.

[50] Economic Relations Division, 'South-South Cooperation for Financing SDGs' (Ministry of Finance, Government of the People's Republic of Bangladesh, 2017).

from Bangladesh into its framework. These solutions comprise the Union Digital Centre, SDG Tracker, Empathy Training, Service Innovation Fund, and the Time Cost Visit Model for public service delivery.[51] The above initiatives indicate that Bangladesh has been enthusiastic about in portraying its interventions. However, information is not available on whether such proactive sharing has entailed additional funding and investments for SDGs.

C. Public Sector Financing

According to the General Economics Division[52] of the Bangladesh Government, the total additional unsynchronised cost for the SDGs for financial year (FY) 2021 to FY2030 has been estimated at US$1294.69 billion at FY2021 prices and projected exchange rates. The investment rate was anticipated to increase from 32 per cent of GDP in FY2020 to 37 per cent of GDP in FY2025 to achieve the projected growth targets, with the private investment rate projected to grow from 23.6 per cent of GDP in FY2020 to 27.4 per cent of GDP by FY2025.[53] The private sector is expected to contribute 75 per cent of the total investment required for the plan (Tk 47.5 trillion) and the public sector, 25 per cent.[54] The report has identified five potential sources of SDG financing. These are (a) public financing; (b) private sector financing; (c) public-private partnership (PPP); (d) external sources including foreign direct investment (FDI) and foreign aid and grants; and (e) non-government organisations (NGOs). It is estimated that, on average, the private sector would account for 44 per cent of the financing needs while the public sector, external sources and NGOs would mobilise 34 per cent, 14 per cent and 6 per cent respectively during the periods of FY2021–FY2030.

Domestic public finance for SDGs: there are two constraints on this. First, with LDC graduation, the ODA grants are reducing and shifting towards non-concessional finance; and second, the need for changes in public investment in infrastructure, technology, high-end services, education, skills and health which are essential for improving productivity and attracting and enhancing private sector investment in line with Bangladesh's middle-income country aspirations. In 2019, the tax-to-GDP ratio was 8.9 per cent, and this had fallen to 7.9 per cent in FY2020–21.[55] This figure represents the lowest among South Asian countries.

[51] 'South-South Cooperation' (Permanent Mission of the People's Republic of Bangladesh to the United Nations, 24 April 2019), bdun.org/bangladesh-priorities-at-the-un/south-south-cooperation/, accessed 5 June 2023.

[52] General Economic Division, 'SDGs Financing Strategy: Bangladesh Perspective' (Planning Commission of Bangladesh, 2018) 39–40.

[53] Zhang (n 33) 11.

[54] General Economics Division, 'Development Finance Assessment for the 8th Five Year Plan and SDGs in Bangladesh (draft), Executive Summary' (unpublished) 9.

[55] CEICdata.com, 'Bangladesh Tax Revenue: % of GDP' (*CEICdata.com*, 12 July 2020), www.ceicdata.com/en/indicator/bangladesh/tax-revenue--of-gdp, accessed 2 March 2024.

Notably, the private sector is anticipated to contribute a larger share (44 per cent) compared to the public sector (34 per cent) in financing the SDGs. However, achieving this balance requires an equitable tax policy to increase the tax-to-GDP ratio. This, in turn, is expected to naturally boost the private sector's contribution to SDG financing through increased tax revenue. In a nation of 170 million people, there are only 8.5 million holders of Tax Identification Numbers (TIN) and only one-third of them submit tax returns annually.[56] This indicates a significant untapped potential for increasing domestic revenue by the public sector that can be invested in SDGs.

Domestic private finance and investment: despite the rise in the investment-GDP ratio in the past 30 years, private sector investment, in proportion to GDP, remained stagnant for years even before the Covid-19 pandemic. The private sector investment contributed substantially to Bangladesh's economic development in the 1990s and 2000s, elevating the investment-GDP ratio.[57] If Bangladesh wants to achieve an 8.5 per cent real GDP growth rate by 2025, the investment-GDP ratio must be increased annually by around one percentage point between 2020 and 2025. Contrarily, the recent increase in public sector borrowing and dwindling foreign currency reserve have reduced lending to the private sector which has slowed down the economy and does not contribute to the SDGs.[58]

Domestic philanthropy and non-governmental organisations (NGOs): NGOs have delivered a wide range of services including education, health, training, women's empowerment, microcredit, agriculture, climate change and social protection. Annually more than 1,000 projects receive foreign grants amounting to over half a billion dollars, but these funds are not reflected in the budget preparation process.[59] Most of the NGOs depend on foreign aid for their activities and in recent years, this has declined because of Bangladesh's LDC graduation.[60]

Public-private partnership: the PPP Authority was established as an autonomous office under the Prime Minister's Office to assist sector line ministries in identifying, developing and tendering PPP projects. A PPP Unit was established under the Ministry of Finance to ensure fiscal responsibility and sustainability in PPP projects. The government has also developed several additional measures, incentives and financial benefits for PPP investors. There are key challenges that will require attention for achieving the SDGs: (i) a national infrastructure

[56] R Hossain, 'Only One-Third of TIN Holders File Tax Returns' *Business Standard* (2 January 2023), www.tbsnews.net/economy/only-one-third-tin-holders-file-tax-returns-561994, accessed 3 March 2023.

[57] General Economics Division (n 54) 18.

[58] 'Private Sector Credit Growth Hits 23-Month Low in Sept' *Dhaka Tribune* (5 November 2023) www.dhakatribune.com/business/330164/private-sector-credit-growth-hits-23-month-low-in, accessed 21 May 2024.

[59] United Nations (n 47) 19.

[60] K Siddiqui, 'Foreign Funds for NGOs Hit 6-Year Low as Grants Diverted to War-Torn Ukraine' *Business Standard* (6 August 2023), www.tbsnews.net/bangladesh/foreign-funds-ngos-hit-6-year-low-grants-diverted-war-torn-ukraine-677598, accessed 3 April 2023.

development strategy for PPPs and improving the quality of infrastructure planning; (ii) a strategy to bring in banks and financing institutions for long-term financing to ensure adequate involvement of the local private sector in the PPP projects; (iii) many infrastructure projects with high social returns are not financially viable, and projected returns are typically insufficient to cover project costs.[61]

External finance for SDGs: the ODA that Bangladesh receives is not significant when compared to exports. The challenge of ODA is that a large amount of foreign aid remains in the pipeline, which the government cannot use fully and in a timely manner. The second challenge is inefficiency in disbursement and utilisation because of slow implementation of the Annual Development Programme each year caused by various procedural reasons.

Foreign direct investment: Bangladesh's FDI has remained modest when compared to regional comparators. Bangladesh has one of the lowest levels of FDI inflow in Asia, at roughly 1 per cent of GDP. Its stock of FDI stands at 6 per cent of GDP, which is also far below the low-income-country average of 25 per cent.[62] A high-level committee headed by the Cabinet Secretary to the government is working to improve Bangladesh's position in attracting foreign investment. The Bangladesh Investment Development Authority (BIDA) is a dedicated government agency providing a one-stop service for foreign investors. Several economic zones with efficient infrastructures as well as easy road and port connectivity are also being developed to encourage foreign investment. However, there is no mechanism to monitor how FDI is contributing to SDG implementation.

International public finance: Bangladesh is currently receiving most of the available vertical funds, which include the Global Environment Facility (GEF), and vertical funds in the health sector, including the Vaccine Alliance (GAVI) and the Global Fund to Fight AIDS, Tuberculosis and Malaria (GFATM). Although vertical funds are an effective source of resources, they inhibit prioritisation by the government and undermine its development agenda. Bangladesh has accessed bilateral channels of climate funding including the British Foreign, Commonwealth and Development Office, the United States Agency for International Development, the Swedish International Development Cooperation Agency, the Netherlands, the Swiss Agency for Development and Cooperation and the German Agency for International Cooperation. In addition, key international funding sources for Bangladesh include the Green Climate Fund (GCF), and the Adaptation Fund (AF). Like FDI, there is no mechanism to monitor how international public finance is contributing to SDG implementation.

[61] World Bank, 'Infrastructure Challenges and How PPPs Can Help' (World Bank, 23 June 2022), ppp.worldbank.org/public-private-partnership/infrastructure-challenges-and-how-ppps-can-help, accessed 23 January 2024.

[62] General Economics Division (n 54) 25.

D. Implementation-localisation

According to the Bangladesh Progress Report on SDGs 2023,[63] Bangladesh's SDG index is 65.9 and it ranks 101st out of 166 countries. It is confronting constraints on SDG 1 (No poverty), SDG 2 (Zero hunger), SDG 3 (Good health and wellbeing), SDG 6 (Clean water and sanitation), SDG 7 (Affordable and clean energy) and SDG 9 (Industry, innovation and infrastructure). There is reportedly no progress in SDG 5[64] (Gender equality), SDG 8 (Decent work and economic growth), SDG11 (Sustainable cities and communities) and SDG 13 (Climate action). SDGs 14, 15 and 16 have relapsed, with SDG 4 (Quality education) and SDG 12 (Responsible consumption and production) being on track. Among all SDG targets, 30.9 per cent are on track, 41.2 per cent have made partial progress and 27.9 per cent are deteriorating.

The Cabinet Division has formed three committees to better implement and coordinate SDG localisation works at the divisional, district and sub-district level. The government has included SDG targets in annual performance assessment of the ministries and departments.

As the SDG Progress Report mentions,[65] 10 per cent of the population of Bangladesh live under extreme poverty[66] and the top 10 per cent of the population hold around 38 per cent of the total income; and several regions are lagging behind. These aspects include access to basic services like education, healthcare, sanitation and infrastructure, as well as economic opportunities, employment rates, income levels and overall living standards. The lagging-behind regions may also face challenges related to environmental sustainability, gender equality, social inclusion and governance effectiveness.

The government of Bangladesh has identified action programmes including a fund for marginalised groups and region- and community-specific actions in the lagging-behind areas of the country. As part of the strategy, the government has implemented a district development plan for nine lagging-behind districts. It is found that there are significant sector-specific spatial disparities, a lack of accurate data, and a need for greater alignment between priorities and annual budget. Assessment of requirements, priority mapping and linking actions with SDG indicators are some of the major activities being implemented in those districts.

It is important to localise the SDGs for a bottom-up implementation considering local dynamics and adjusting policies accordingly. For instance, the needs of different areas vary – coastal areas are more prone to the impact of climate change and natural disasters; some areas may experience shortage of drinking

[63] 'Sustainable Development Report 2023', dashboards.sdgindex.org/profiles/, accessed 3 April 2024.

[64] V Malesa and S Vyas-Doorgapersad. 'Assessing the Implementation of SDG 5 in South African Public Service' (2023) 5 *Journal of Southwest Jiaotong University* 58.

[65] Bangladesh Planning Commission, *Sustainable Development Goals: Bangladesh Progress Report 2020* (General Economic Divisions, 2020) 41.

[66] Extreme poverty increased due to the Covid-19 pandemic.

water due to arsenic pollution and salinity intrusion; some areas might have a seasonal need for employment and food; and some areas have a below-average literacy rate. Localisation of SDGs through the Local Government Institutions (LGIs) can ensure inclusive development and strengthen the LGIs – leading to a win-win situation. Table 14.2 illustrates the relevant SDG goals and targets that need to be implemented through localisation. The targets have been shortlisted from the 40 priority indicators selected by the SDG Working Committee of the Prime Minister's Office.[67]

Table 14.2 SDG Goals and Targets that Need to be Implemented through Localisation

Sustainable Development Goals (SDGs)	Targets tailored for Bangladesh[a]	Role of Local Government Institutions (LGIs) in achieving SDGs[a]
Goal 1: No Poverty	Reducing the proportion of population living below extreme and national poverty line below 3% and 10%, respectively.	Given their experience of working directly with local communities and knowledge of local contexts, several LGIs' activities involve poverty alleviation of the local people through social safety net programmes.
Goal 2: Zero Hunger	Reducing the prevalence of stunning among children under 5 years of age to 12%.	Goal 2 is linked and somewhat similar to goal 1 (No Poverty). For example, allocation of allowance to lactating mothers can lead to achieving this goal.
Goal 3: Good Health and Wellbeing	Reducing neonatal mortality rate to 12 per 1,000 live births. Reducing under 5 mortality rates to 25 per 1,000 live births. Reducing maternal mortality ratio to 70 per 10,000 live births.	This goal is linked with the goals 1 (No Poverty) and 2 (Zero Hunger). Therefore, its success depends largely on the completion of the above two goals and engaging LGIs in it.

Note: [a] M Monem and A Zahid, *Effective Local Government System for Localization & Achievement of SDGs and Goals of the 8th Five Year Plan: Policy, Local Resource Mobilization, Women, Participation and Accountability Perspectives* (Wave Foundation, 2018) 15.

A survey on SDG localisation,[68] conducted by the Wave Foundation, a local NGO in Bangladesh working on local governance, reveals that financial constraints in conjunction with lack of people's trust on LGIs and the unhealthy competition over power at the local level (among various tiers, members of parliament and local administration) act as barriers to SDG localisation. For example, as a public

[67] SDG Tracker Bangladesh, sdg.gov.bd/resource/103/0#1, accessed 4 February 2024.

[68] M Monem and A Zahid, *Effective Local Government System for Localization & Achievement of SDGs and Goals of the 8th Five Year Plan: Policy, Local Resource Mobilization, Women, Participation and Accountability Perspectives* (Wave Foundation, 2018).

institution, LGIs invest in public goods with their scarce resources. They tend to take on small projects instead of big projects, but they are few in number and require a recurrent operation and maintenance budget. However, a lot of money from the already scarce financial resources of the LGIs gets wasted in the form of informal transaction costs.

E. Private Sector Investment in SDGs

In 2022, an SDG investor mapping was conducted by UNDP Bangladesh[69] to identify SDG-aligned investment opportunities for promoting investment as well as SDG progress. The 17 identified Investment Opportunity Areas (IOA) cover eight sectors, including e-Commerce, Education, Financials, Food and Beverage, Healthcare, Infrastructure, Renewable Resources and Alternative Energy, and Technology and Communications, each indicating investments in technology-driven startups, digital infrastructure projects, or innovations in areas such as artificial intelligence, blockchain, or cybersecurity; 10 IOAs promote inclusion involving investments in projects that target underrepresented groups, promote diversity, or enhance financial inclusion, and seven IOAs promote environmental action projects related to renewable energy, conservation efforts, sustainable agriculture or initiatives that address climate change and environmental challenges.[70]

The combined value of all the IOAs is more than US$13.3 billion. This represents the potential economic impact of these opportunities. The median rate of return for these investment opportunities is estimated to be in the range of 10–15 per cent, which is the expected profitability of the investments.[71] The median investment time frame for these opportunities is less than five years and the identified projects are expected to yield returns within a relatively short period. More than half of the IOAs have an investment ticket size between US$1 million and US$10 million. This indicates that these opportunities are accessible to a range of investors, including those with moderate capital-spanning digital technology, inclusion and environmental actions. This diversity aligns with a holistic investment approach, considering economic, social and environmental impact.[72]

Furthermore, the map development process helped identify three Business White Spaces (SDG-aligned business models with high impact potential, but limited investment due to adverse market conditions, despite policy support) and three high-level Policy White Spaces (policy intervention areas to facilitate

[69] 'SDG Investor Map to Identify Market-Specific Investment Opportunity Areas' (*LightCastle Partners*, November 2022), www.lightcastlebd.com/cases/developing-sdg-investor-map-to-identify-market-specific-investment-opportunity-areas-ioas/, accessed 3 April 2023.

[70] ibid.

[71] 'SDG Loan Fund Mobilizes USD 1.1 Billion of Investor Capital' (*Allianz.com*), www.allianz.com/en/press/news/commitment/environment/231201-allianz-sdg-loan-fund-mobilizes-over-usd-one-billion-of-investor-capital.html, accessed 3 March 2023.

[72] ibid.

SDG-aligned business models). The Policy White Spaces were meant to be: (1) creating an enabling environment; (2) incubating impact; and (3) empowering people and enterprises.

The biggest exclusion on the map is the Ready Made Garments (RMG) sector. This sector accounts for more than 80 per cent of the country's exports and contributes more than 15 per cent to the GDP. It employs around 4 million people of whom about 60 per cent are women. Nevertheless, the sector is one of the largest polluters due to inadequate effluent treatment. Simultaneously, labour conditions in the sector have been criticised. Conscientious investments in the RMG sector can improve sustainability and contribute to SDGs 5, 6, 8 and 9.

The aquaculture sector does not appear on the map either. Bangladesh is the world's fifth largest producer of aquaculture products; this sector has been growing steadily in recent years. Investments in the sector have the potential to boost SDG 1 (No Poverty), 2 (Zero Hunger) and 14 (Life below Water).

Lastly, the Blue Economy may also make effective contributions to SDG-aligned investments. The value of the Bangladesh's Blue Economy has been estimated to be US$6.2 billion annually.[73] SDG-aligned sectors such as maritime trade and shipping, oceanic renewable energy, tourism, aggregates mining, marine aquatic products and fishery have huge potential to produce SDG-related results. Apart from producing a feasibility report and establishing a cell in the Ministry of Energy and Mineral Resources, the government did not take any substantive investment initiative in this sector.

The implementation of SDGs in Bangladesh is intricately linked to the nation's capacity to address multifaceted challenges. As underscored by various national and sectoral policies, Bangladesh demonstrates a commitment to realising the SDGs, but capacity constraints remain a paramount concern. The capacity issues encompass challenges in data collection, policy coherence, governance and inter-agency coordination. The government must continue its efforts in building institutional capacity, fostering collaboration among diverse stakeholders, and ensuring that policies are not only comprehensive but are also effectively implemented. As Bangladesh endeavours to transform its developmental landscape in alignment with the SDGs, strategic investments in human resources, technology and governance structures will play a pivotal role in overcoming hurdles and steering the nation toward sustainable and inclusive growth.

VI. Conclusion

The discussion reveals that the Southern countries cannot fulfil the elements of capacity hypothetical model in SDG implementation. While policies and

[73] HM Irfanullah, 'Strengthening Our Blue Economy' *The Daily Star* (13 December 2023), www.thedailystar.net/opinion/views/news/strengthening-our-blue-economy-3493636, accessed 3 March 2023.

institutions are mostly in place, public and private financing fall short of expectations. The unforeseen shock and force majeure events, exemplified by the global Covid-19 pandemic, which were not initially considered during the adoption of the SDGs, have had a significant impact on the capacity of Southern countries to advance in SDG implementation. Although force majeure events did not influence the Agenda 2030 directly, they influenced the global policymakers to rethink the strategies.

SDGs are not legally binding on countries. These are aspirations of the global community and cannot be legally enforced or challenged in court if not achieved. SDGs derived its normative basis from the consensus of the nations of the world. The degree of power to enforce or achieve these goals at country or regional level varies. Particularly, the levels of democratic practice by countries of the North and the South are not the same. While democracy has been relatively stable and institutionalised in the countries of the North, it is not the same in many countries of the South. Weak democratic bases and governance challenges in many countries of the Global South impede the efficient implementation of the SDGs. Addressing these governance deficiencies is crucial for realising the full potential of SDG initiatives. Strengthening democratic institutions, promoting transparency, enhancing public participation, and fortifying legal and institutional frameworks are essential steps in overcoming these challenges.[74] Integrating governance considerations into SDG implementation efforts is imperative for fostering synergy and maximising impact. By prioritising governance reforms alongside policy formulation and institutional capacity building, countries can enhance their ability to effectively pursue sustainable development objectives.

The absence of anticipated support from the Northern countries, both in terms of public sector financing and private sector investment, exacerbates the North–South divide in SDG achievement. Despite the interconnectedness of the five SDG-related capacity elements, a strong partnership between the Northern and Southern countries is lacking. This deficiency contradicts the concept of transnationalism, emphasising the need for collaborative efforts to address global challenges collectively.

Notably, while SDG Goal 17 underlines partnership as a means of implementation and revitalisation of global collaboration for sustainable development, it is suggested that this element should constitute a separate element in the capacity framework. The partnership aspect is crucial for fostering cooperation between countries and the five essential elements for SDG achievement. The realisation of sustainable development goals necessitates a collective commitment from nations across the globe, transcending geographical, cultural and economic boundaries.

The adoption of global development goals like the SDGs is tantamount to the globalisation of development policies. This raises the question whether there was

[74] H Liu, C Lee and C Alden, 'The Dynamics of Governance and Sustainable Development Goals in the Global South' (2022) 15 *Global Policy* 5.

sufficient analysis of the readiness of the global system to implement the SDGs. Was it assumed that the SDGs would be achieved by the existing global system, which is not equal horizontally? The global development system is based on the voluntary suspension of national sovereignty. It cannot make authoritative and binding decisions when interrelated institutions and their respective activities fail to produce results. The SDGs were based on demands, but the corresponding supply of resources did not follow. The feedback process has been established but it has not elicited necessary course correction.

Proposing a comprehensive assessment of the global community's performance vis-à-vis the SDGs, with a particular emphasis on formulating alternatives rooted in responsive actions guided by rational choices, is warranted. This evaluative undertaking seeks to discern effective strategies while adapting to dynamic global challenges. Furthermore, an exploration of mitigation strategies for the persistent North–South divide emerges as an imperative, ensuring inclusivity and fostering global collaboration in the collective pursuit of sustainable development objectives. This academic discourse underscores the exigency for strategic recalibration and adaptive methodologies to navigate the intricate terrain of SDG implementation within the defined temporal constraints.

15

Feasible Governance Strategies for Sustainable Development Financing

MUSHTAQ H KHAN

I. Introduction

The sustainability of development financing requires that the money raised for financing development delivers the highest possible developmental returns. This is essential to ensure that any money borrowed or invested can provide returns deemed satisfactory by lenders and investors or taxpayers. If these conditions are not met, the sources of financing will dry up, particularly sources of international financing, and sustainable development may be severely challenged. If the financing is borrowed or invested by private investors, the sustainability of financing requires that the repayments of capital, and payments of profits and interest over time, are satisfactory. If the financing is raised through taxation, sustainability requires that the development outcomes provide value for money to taxpayers so that they remain willing to keep paying taxes. At the most general level, the sustainability of financing therefore requires several related governance conditions.

First, there must be a process for selecting the portfolio of investments and projects that maximise the collective benefit of society. This is a governance challenge because societies are complex organisms with multiple priorities. Different groups are likely to have different priorities. Sectors and projects are also interdependent so, for instance, investments in roads and bridges may only deliver returns if there are simultaneous investments in industrial clusters around these infrastructures, and in the health and education of workers. Without new businesses using the infrastructure and paying the tolls or taxes, the debt may be impossible to repay. Apart from different groups in society having different priorities, politicians and bureaucrats are likely to have their own objectives. Politicians may want to prioritise sectors and projects that give them the most votes or taxes. In countries with a weak rule of law, they may also prefer sectors and projects where kickbacks and collusion are easier to organise. Getting a balanced portfolio that delivers developmental outcomes, but which is also financially viable and can repay the investments made, requires political, technical and financial assessments based on discussions between state and society. This essential and initial condition is itself often missing in many developing countries.

A second governance requirement is that there should be effective processes for allocating the contracts or jobs for delivering these goods or services at the lowest cost. If the contracted costs are too high (the price per kilometre of roads, the cost of delivering specific healthcare outcomes per head, and so on) then once again the debt or investments may be difficult to repay. Even if the infrastructure or projects are entirely financed by tax, taxpayers may be unwilling to keep paying taxes if the returns (in terms of developmental benefits) are low as a result of projects being overpriced. These two governance problems are related. Sometimes the selection of particular projects such as roads and bridges may be deliberately pushed because these are easier to overprice for the extraction of collusive margins that are shared between businesses, bureaucrats and politicians.

Finally, a third requirement is the presence of sufficiently good monitoring and evaluation processes during implementation and throughout the life of the project or service delivery programme to ensure that quality is maintained. The development outcomes achieved (the quality of the roads, the quality of the healthcare outcomes, and so on) have to be good enough to justify the expenditures and should be comparable to outcomes achieved with similar expenditures in other countries. All three conditions are necessary to ensure that development financing remains sustainable. Poorly selected projects, or overpriced projects, or poorly implemented projects, and certainly projects that have all these characteristics, will not generate sufficient financial or developmental returns to service the debts or justify the taxes.

This chapter will focus on the flows of foreign financing that are critical for financing development in developing countries, though similar issues arise for domestic debt. The feasibility of servicing domestic debt also depends on the use made of the money, the pricing and the quality of implementation of projects and service delivery programmes. Nevertheless, governments have more flexibility in dealing with domestic debt. They can increase taxes, or in a crisis they can even print money to service domestic debt, but they cannot raise taxes or print money in foreign currency. Commitments to foreign debtors and investors therefore impose harder constraints on governments. Moreover, almost all development projects require more or less significant levels of imported inputs that have to be financed by the country's own reserves or fresh inflows of foreign funds.

As flows of aid have stagnated, new financing for developing and emerging countries have increasingly come from global private and public sector investors. These have been motivated by the search for commercial returns (for private investors) and a combination of commercial and strategic interests (for public investors). As investment flows have increased, many developing and emerging countries have made a rapid transition from aid to debt-financed development. As a result, the governance of finance has become even more important to ensure that the financing remains serviceable and therefore sustainable.

The data on international debt and financing illustrate these arguments in broad way. But the governance challenges discussed in this chapter require looking at country examples in greater detail. To illustrate these arguments, this chapter will refer to evidence from Bangladesh and Sri Lanka in the decade leading to their financial problems in the early 2020s. Both countries achieved rapid development driven by significant new investments in infrastructure, largely funded by foreign loans. In both countries, the political processes of project selection were not fully transparent and the relative benefits of different investments in terms of developmental or financial returns were not publicly debated and contested. For instance, the prioritisation of infrastructure rather than health or education was not discussed and deliberated. In both countries, there is evidence of substantial overpricing of many infrastructure projects. In both there is also evidence of at least some poorly implemented or incomplete projects. While both appeared for a time to achieve substantial development success, the sustainability of the financing, and therefore the sustainability of this development strategy, was much weaker. The weakness of governance in the selection, pricing and implementation of projects contributed to a reduced feasibility of servicing debts and a weakening of foreign currency reserves. A mismatch between foreign currency liabilities as debts became due and foreign currency earnings to pay these debts was gradually emerging but came to a head with the global slowdown following the Covid-19 pandemic and the war in Ukraine. Sri Lanka defaulted on its foreign debts in 2022. Bangladesh suffered declining foreign currency reserves in 2023 and negotiated pre-emptive loans from the International Monetary Fund (IMF) under the Extended Credit and Extended Fund Facilities.

The default in Sri Lanka and the pressure on repayments and reserves in Bangladesh in these years clearly had multiple causes, but the selection of projects with poor developmental or financial returns – overpricing many of these projects and poorly implementing others – contributed to a financial fragility that was exposed during a slowdown. Going forward, sustainable financing for sustainable development requires robust governance systems to ensure that occasional shocks do not result in financial meltdowns. The objective is not to assess the relative contribution of global shocks and domestic governance in the growing debt sustainability problems facing many developing countries. The sustainability of development financing has indeed been affected by factors that are outside the control of individual developing countries, but some problems are of their own making. To remove or reduce the adverse impact of external shocks, developing countries need to take strong steps to address the problems that are within their control. This will also give them much greater bargaining power with development finance institutions (DFIs) and the IMF if they occasionally need assistance to manage unexpected shocks.

The policy response to the types of governance problems referred to in this chapter has usually been to try and improve high-level governance characteristics like democratic accountability, the rule of law, or the reduction of corruption. These are desirable goals in themselves, but they simply cannot be improved fast enough to make a difference to the challenge of maintaining the sustainability of development financing. More targeted, feasible and effective steps need to be identified at critical sectoral and project levels to ensure that debt remains sustainable, and countries do not fall into debt distress or default followed by costly restructuring programmes. If these strategies can be identified, countries will sustain developmental progress and improve the distribution of power and capabilities that make improvements in high-level governance more feasible. Section II outlines some of the broad trends in how the financing of development has changed, creating both opportunities but also new risks for developing countries. It makes the distinction between long-term governance *objectives* and immediate governance *strategies* that are feasible to implement. The selection of a portfolio of projects that maximises social benefit is a particularly difficult task, even in a well-working democracy. Democratic accountability is a critical component of the broad 'good governance' reform approach, but it is one of the most difficult processes to deliver in many developing country contexts. Democratic institutions are weak in most developing countries and may take a long time to improve. In the interim, some social checks on rent-seeking politicians and bureaucrats may come from robust discussions of alternative priorities by think tanks and the media. Nevertheless, an inclusive identification of developmental priorities is one of the most difficult governance problems for any society, and particularly developing ones where democratic processes are weak.

Section III examines the governance challenge of discovering the lowest competitive prices at which projects should be contracted. This is not as easy as it may appear, because it is not possible to simply compare costs across countries. Costs can vary not only because of obvious economic reasons like differences in wages or differences in terrain that affect construction cost, but also because of differing levels of investor risk across countries. Investors face high risks in developing countries and justifiably demand a risk premium built into their prices. The challenge here is to discover the lowest risk premium, and therefore the lowest price at which the project or service can be delivered. This requires governance strategies that can enhance competition to discover the minimum risk premium. This is particularly important because there may be collusion between foreign and domestic investors and local politicians and bureaucrats to overstate the risk premium and therefore the price. The extra margins can then be shared between the parties to the contract, while the burden of repayment is passed on to the unsuspecting public and to future generations. This can rapidly make the financing of projects unsustainable and push countries into an eventual debt crisis. Feasible ways of reducing these risks of overpricing involve discovering implementable strategies that effectively improve competition in the granting of contracts.

Section IV discusses the related governance challenge of ensuring that important projects (however priced) are implemented efficiently, without significant delays or leakages due to corruption. Even a competitively priced project may fail if it is poorly implemented because of inefficiency, corruption or other reasons.

The resulting infrastructure or services will not generate sufficient financial or developmental returns to repay or justify the debt. Once again, feasible governance strategies must be discovered that can improve implementation outcomes. The governance strategies that can address these issues must themselves be implementable. In a context of a weak rule of law, this usually means the implementation must be supported by sufficiently powerful actors in their own interest. To identify such strategies requires an understanding of the distribution of power and capabilities in society, which is described here as its political settlement. Implementation is more likely if the policy design can mobilise competing power and interests who will check each other out of self-interest and thereby improve the governance of implementation. Gradual but effective improvements in these types of governance are critical for ensuring that development financing and sustainable development remain on track.

II. Financing Development: Risks and Opportunities

Over the last three decades, the relative importance of overseas development assistance (ODA) to developing countries has significantly declined relative to foreign direct investments (FDI) and other 'commercial' flows such as remittances and foreign borrowing. FDI flows include both public and private investments. A growing share of this is also coming from the Global South, from countries like India and China, driven by their own strategic and economic considerations. Second, the capacity of developing and emerging countries to finance their own development has also greatly increased with economic development. This includes the growing role of remittances earned by nationals in other countries. These flows of foreign currency can be used to convert domestic savings into investments requiring imported equipment or raw materials. Many of these remittances are also South–South, as workers from developing countries go to work in other developing countries.[1] A final element has been the growth of financing through international sovereign bonds.[2] This is still relatively small in aggregate compared to the other two flows but have been important in a number of countries, including Sri Lanka.

The concern with governance as an economic problem emerged partly out of the experiences of development aid. When developing countries achieved poor results with ODA financing or faced repayment problems, DFIs like the World Bank, the Asian Development Bank and other regional development banks

[1] OECD, *Development Cooperation Report* 2023 (OECD, 2023) 108. Between 2000 and 2020, the real value of ODA increased by a factor of 2.1, FDI by 2.6 and remittances by 4.7. By 2020, in absolute terms, FDI was 3.2 times greater than ODA while remittances were 3 times greater.

[2] AF Presbitero and others, 'Sovereign Bonds in Developing Countries: Drivers of Issuance and Spreads' (2016) 6 *Review of Development Finance* 1.

identified governance as a critical factor that determined how effectively financing was converted into development outputs.[3] The DFIs generally identified the right problems: there was often non-transparent selection of projects, contracts were often granted to companies that charged excessive prices resulting in high construction costs, there was wastage and corruption in implementation and operation, and so on. These types of problems doomed the financial viability of many investments from the outset and made it difficult to service debt liabilities even if DFI lending was on very concessionary terms. Unfortunately, the necessary economic and governance reforms that DFIs identified often proved to be unimplementable in the typical developing country context.

This failure to implement governance reforms was not dissimilar to the results of earlier attempts by DFIs to improve the efficiency of markets in developing countries using different types of structural adjustment strategies. In both structural adjustment and good governance reforms, DFIs sometimes made lending conditional on specific types of reform in order to reduce the chances of future default. While these reform attempts were generally not very successful, the rapid increase in alternative foreign flows to developing countries and the growing share of commercial and strategic investments and lending created new opportunities and challenges. On the one hand, the much greater volume of development finance available from new sources reduced the power of multilateral DFIs like the World Bank and other multilateral banks that were conduits for multilateral ODA. This was often welcomed in many developing countries where the power of DFIs and the IMF to impose conditions on countries was deeply resented.

The problem was that even though the conditions the DFIs imposed were often ineffective, and sometimes did more harm than good, the identification of governance weaknesses as a source of the sustainability problem was surely correct. The orthodox economic thinking that informed policies like structural adjustment and good governance reforms were often ineffective or not implementable in developing countries where markets and contracts operated very differently, and the rule of law was much weaker. The ways in which markets and institutions work depends critically on the underlying distribution of power and capabilities in a society, which is described in this chapter as the political settlement.[4] The operation of institutions and governance arrangements in practice depends on how actors respond to rules and whether they have the power and interest to subvert particular rules. If powerful actors can distort the implementation of rules and other powerful actors do not stop them, rule violations will persist. Reforms are more likely to work if they are designed so that some powerful actors have an

[3] World Bank, *World Development Report 2017: Governance and the Law* (World Bank Publications, 2017); Asian Development Bank, 'Promoting Good Governance: ADB's Medium-Term Agenda and Action Plan' (Asian Development Bank, 2000); AfDB, 'Knowledge and Economic Governance at the AFDB – A Roadmap' (Economic Governance and Knowledge Management Complex (ECVP), African Development Bank, 2017).

[4] MH Khan, 'Political Settlements and the Analysis of Institutions' (2018) 117 *African Affairs* 636.

incentive to want the policy to succeed and their self-interested activities suffice to block other actors who benefit by distorting the policy.[5] Otherwise, as Gunnar Myrdal pointed out a long time ago in his magisterial book, policies and institutions that attempt to create incentives for productive behaviour (for instance using changes in relative prices like interest rates or governance reforms that impose penalties for the violation of rules) often do not have the desired effect because these incentives are drowned out by stronger incentives and opportunities for rule violations or resource capture.[6]

This is one reason why the earlier structural adjustment programmes had poor results in developing countries. These programmes aimed to cut wasteful public spending financed by borrowing. In theory, if wasteful spending were cut, this would help reduce interest rates and enable more efficient private sector investments. Variants of these programmes were tried in many developing countries but the expected increases in private investments usually did not materialise, or when they did, the private investments were often as poor as the public ones.[7] Structural adjustment programmes achieved disappointing results because they ignored the actual distribution of power and capabilities in the target countries. The programmes assumed that freeing up resources from wasteful public investments would lead to productive private investments and would force the public sector to become more efficient. But the competitiveness of most firms in many developing countries was low to begin with and they could not become competitive simply because financing was available at slightly lower interest rates. Instead, politicians and bureaucrats colluded with private sector firms to continue sharing public resources in different ways rather than ensuring that structural adjustment led to greater efficiency.[8] Not surprisingly, the results of structural adjustment were much weaker than expected.

The limitations of these market reforms led international financial institutions to another round of reforms, where they now identified weak governance as the problem. Governments were not enforcing contracts properly, thereby allowing non-performing companies, banks, and government departments to continue to waste money, and politicians appeared to be immune to any political repercussions of poor economic performance. This was attributed to an absence of 'good governance'. Development partners began to support and indeed to insist upon policies to improve contract enforcement, reduce corruption, improve the rule of law and improve democratic accountability. These were all desirable reforms, but the reform strategy again ignored the distribution of power and capabilities

[5] MH Khan, 'Institutions and Development' in D Nayyar (ed), *Asian Transformations: An Inquiry into the Development of Nations* (Oxford University Press, 2019).

[6] G Myrdal, *Asian Drama: An Inquiry into the Poverty of Nations* 3rd edn (Pantheon, 1968).

[7] W Easterly, 'What did Structural Adjustment Adjust? The Association of Policies and Growth with Repeated IMF and World Bank Adjustment Loans' (2002) Working Paper No 11, ssrn.com/abstract=1106277, accessed 3 March 2023.

[8] S Haggard and R Kaufman, 'The Politics of Stabilization and Structural Adjustment' in J Sachs (ed), *Developing Country Debt and the World Economy* (University of Chicago Press, 1989).

(the political settlements of these countries). Reformers failed to ask whether there were enough actors with the power and interest to want to implement these reforms properly. The cross-country historical evidence shows that improvements in these types of high-level governance characteristics is not achieved simply through legislation. It requires an effective demand for enforcement from many high-capability and powerful organisations.[9] This is why the path to the rule of law is a slow and incremental one, and that path is based on many intermediate governance strategies.[10] The disappointing results of the good governance programme were due to a failure to identify intermediate or transitional strategies that could incrementally address critical governance problems. There was a confusion of the *objectives* of governance (democratic accountability, low corruption, rule of law and so on) with feasible transitional *strategies* that could take us towards these outcomes by working with the existing distributions of power and capabilities.

By the early 2000s, the balance of financial flows had begun to shift out of ODA and the DFIs towards FDI, and increasingly, towards FDI from the South. The role of China has been particularly important. This weakened the discourse on governance, which usually came from DFIs where developed OECD countries had a greater say. A greater proportion of development financing became dependent on the commercial and strategic calculations of new investors, often located in BRICS-type countries like China, Russia, India, Saudi Arabia and the United Arab Emirates. These new types of investors no longer pushed for the market and governance reforms that the DFIs had been promoting. Public and private investors from countries like China, Russia and India, which themselves did not satisfy many good governance conditions, even though they had achieved rapid growth in the recent past, did not demand general improvements in governance conditions in the countries they were investing in. Public and private investors from such jurisdictions are frequently alleged to have protected their interests by making opaque deals directly with recipient governments to create high returns for themselves and for the politicians and bureaucrats approving such deals.[11] The high prices contracted in such deals obviously reduced the risk for the investors in that project, but it increased the risk for the country, because the more that overpriced projects of this type emerged, the higher the chance of a default. Moreover, because many of these projects were unsolicited, without competitive scrutiny, many of the contractors selected were of poor quality, resulting in poor implementation as well.

[9] MH Khan, 'Governance and Growth: History, Ideology and Methods of Proof' in A Noman and others (eds), *Good Growth and Governance for Africa: Rethinking Development Strategies*, (Oxford University Press, 2012).

[10] DC North and others (eds), *In the Shadow of Violence: Politics, Economics and the Problems of Development* (Cambridge University Press, 2013).

[11] See for instance an in-depth analysis of Chinese investments in Sri Lanka: Verité Research, *The Lure of Chinese Loans: Sri Lanka's Experiment with a Special Framework to Finance its Infrastructure Investments* (Verité Research, 2022).

The problematic combination of high returns for selected international investors, high-priced project allocation to contractors, and poor implementation of some of these projects, raised the risk that many of these countries would go into debt stress when repayments became due, or if they faced any external shock. Investors and connected parties may have contracted returns far in excess of what could actually be generated by the investment, leaving the country with foreign currency debts that would not be financially serviceable in the future. Ironically, this exposed many countries to the very same harsh readjustment conditions that DFIs were often accused of imposing in the past. According to a 2023 report by the UN Global Crisis Response Group, entitled 'A World of Debt', a total of 52 countries – almost 40 per cent of the developing world – are already in 'serious debt trouble'.[12] In its International Debt Report for 2023, the World Bank reported 18 sovereign debt defaults in the past three years, more than in the previous three decades.[13] Countries under debt stress are likely to have to go back to DFIs or the IMF to borrow money with conditions so as not to default or to make adjustments after defaulting.

To respond to these governance failures, we first need to understand why they happen. Governance failures can be the result of quite different underlying drivers. Violations of rules also happen in 'rule of law' countries where most people follow rules most of the time. When a violation is detected in countries that have or are close to having a rule of law, social and political pressures rapidly emerge to ensure the violator is penalised and the violation corrected. The political settlements analysis says that this comes about because these countries have a distribution of power and capabilities where many powerful organisations want rules to be enforced in their own interest, because their businesses and transactions are too complex to operate without impartial rule enforcement. All organisations may also have incentives to cheat, for instance to not pay taxes or to violate contracts themselves, but when violations are detected in rule of law contexts, regardless of the power of the violator, other powerful organisations will insist on enforcement, and enforcement will therefore usually follow.[14] Violations in this context are mainly instances of free riding (cheating) by individuals and organisations who try to benefit by *hiding* their violations.

The earlier good governance reforms supported by international financial institutions implicitly assumed that developing countries were also close to a rule of law, and violations that were happening were essentially due to a few violators hiding information. A strengthening of transparency and accountability systems would improve governance in these contexts by making violations more difficult

[12] UN Global Crisis Response Group, *A World of Debt: A Growing Burden to Global Prosperity* (United Nations, 2023).

[13] World Bank, *International Debt Report 2023* (World Bank, 2023).

[14] MH Khan, 'Political Settlements and the Governance of Growth-Enhancing Institutions' Research Paper Series on Governance for Growth (SOAS, University of London, 2010), eprints.soas.ac.uk/9968, accessed 3 March 2023.

to hide (by improving transparency) and making corrective processes easier and more effective (by improving accountability). However, in developing countries, the political settlements are quite different. Large segments of society are informally organised, and actors in this sector typically have limited power and capabilities. Moreover, many large and powerful firms may also have low productive capabilities and engage in accumulation strategies based on violating formal rules because they are not globally competitive themselves. There are typically very few organisations that are competitive on the global stage and therefore want rules to be followed and enforced; and have the power to ensure this. In these political settlements, rule violations are usually not secret free-riding activities, but transparent violations carried out by powerful organisations acting with impunity. Other powerful organisations are engaged in similar activities, and do not react to the detection of violators by putting pressure on enforcers and governments to take action against the violators. Transparency and accountability reforms therefore fail on their own.

However, not all rules are violated in these contexts. Many rules are enforced in pockets of activities because some actors have the power and the interest to ensure that other actors follow rules. This is why we have the interesting phenomena in developing countries where people will stand in queues in some locations, but the same individuals will not stand in queues in other places. Behaviour in queues depends on subconscious assessments of the power and interests of other people in the queue and what they may do if someone breaks the rules. The implication is that we can improve governance in critical pockets if we can find feasible ways of incentivising or mobilising sufficiently powerful actors engaged in those activities to pursue monitoring and enforcement in their own interest to limit specific violations. Understanding the configurations of power and capabilities in countries and sectors is therefore a necessary starting point for identifying feasible transitional strategies and pathways of reform.[15]

A bottom-up approach to identifying and incentivising enforcement in specific areas is essential to complement 'good governance' reforms that improve transparency and accountability rules. In countries that are close to the rule of law, the latter may be sufficient. We do not usually need to worry about who will use information about violations to engage in enforcement. There are many powerful organisations all over society that are already enmeshed in rules-based trading, investment, research and innovation, and other activities that require complex contracts to be enforced. When information about violations is revealed in these rule of law contexts, these powerful organisations emerge and engage in 'horizontal' activities to ensure that enforcement against the violator is implemented. They may stop transacting with the violating organisation till it agrees to corrective

[15] MH Khan and P Roy, 'Making Anti-Corruption Real: Using a "Power Capabilities and Interest Approach" to Stop Wasting Money and Start Making Progress SOAS-ACE Synthesis Paper No 1' (SOAS, University of London, 2022), ace.soas.ac.uk/publication/making-anti-corruption-real/, accessed 3 March 2023.

action, and they may put effective pressure on enforcement agencies to operate sanctions from above, even if the enforcement agencies are not interested or are proceeding slowly.

But in contexts where the distribution of power and capabilities is narrower, simply focusing on transparency and accountability rules and processes is insufficient. The revelation of a violation by a powerful organisation often does not result in activity by other similarly powerful organisations insisting on enforcement. In these contexts, not only is there limited horizontal pressure for enforcement, enforcers like regulatory bodies or anti-corruption commissions may get into trouble if they try to enforce rules on powerful organisations. Instead of horizontal pressure from powerful organisations to enforce rules, enforcers may come under horizontal pressure from powerful organisations to *not* enforce. When this happens, we need to ask whether sufficient levels of horizontal pressure for enforcement can be generated. To do this we need to identify opportunities for using additional policies to create and strengthen incentives for actors to engage in horizontal monitoring and checking activity to enforce the rules we are interested in. This is the bottom-up component of a feasible governance strategy. Research in Bangladesh and other countries has shown that when policy design triggers effective horizontal checks, resource leakages due to corruption are effectively reduced even in contexts where there is a weak rule of law.[16] A package of reforms that *combines* vertical enforcement based on transparency and accountability *with* effective policies to strengthen horizontal checking based on the self-interest of powerful actors, is a transitional strategy that takes us towards the rule of law.[17]

From this perspective, effective improvements in democratic accountability are the most difficult of our three areas of governance affecting the sustainability of development financing. This is because the impartial operation of electoral institutions and laws requires effective checks and balances between competing political parties and their different constituencies of organised supporters. In developing countries, a broad distribution of productive interests does not yet exist and so there are weak pressures on politicians to uphold rules required for complex contracting. Instead, patron-client politics and the distribution of patronage can create informal coalitions and networks, often based on populist or nationalist ideologies. This can allow rule-violating coalitions to stay in power and allow persistent violations of rules of accountability.[18]

[16] See for instance MH Khan and others, 'Win-win: Designing Dual-use in Climate Projects for Effective Anti-corruption in Bangladesh' (2022) 14 *Climate and Development* 921; MH Khan, M Watkins and I Zahan, 'De-risking Private Power in Bangladesh: How Financing Design Can Stop Collusive Contracting' (2022) 168 *Energy Policy* 113146; P Roy, A Slota and MH Khan, *A New Approach to Anti-Corruption: When Rule-Breakers Rule* (SOAS, University of London, 2022).

[17] Khan and Roy (n 15).

[18] MH Khan, 'Markets, States and Democracy: Patron-Client Networks and the Case for Democracy in Developing Countries' (2005) 12 *Democratization* 705.

From 2010 onwards, there has been a global slide away from democracy and an increase in the number and strength of authoritarian regimes.[19] At the same time, flows of capital from countries like China and India have increased. As a result, governments in developing countries have been able to approve and fund large infrastructure and other development projects with even less scrutiny than in the past. In this global and regional context of democratic backsliding and of reduced opportunities of scrutinising government decisions, it may be difficult to achieve significantly improved scrutiny of government investment decisions and the holding of decision-makers to account. Nevertheless, popular movements and pressure are important, but to be effective, pressure has to be ongoing and not after the event. When Sri Lanka was about to default in 2022, a mass uprising, the Aragalaya movement, brought down the Rajapaksa government and family. The latter were widely perceived to be responsible for Sri Lanka's default that led to a deep financial crisis. Unfortunately, this uprising came too late to stop the piling up of unsustainable debt that Sri Lankans will now have to repay. Looking forward, developing countries have to achieve ongoing scrutiny and pressure to stop undesirable investments in a context where parliaments and the institutions of political accountability are not working well. Popular movements, think tanks and the media will have to create checks and balances until the global tide turns and democratic institutions start strengthening.

While significant improvements in democratic accountability will take time, sectoral improvements in governance to limit overpricing and improve implementation can begin to address the other two governance challenges referred to earlier. These transitional strategies will not immediately take us to the rule of law, but they may achieve incremental improvements in rule-following behaviour that constitutes the pathway towards a stronger adherence to the rule of law. A feasible governance strategy is therefore one that uses an analysis of the power, capabilities and interests of actors involved in that activity to design incentives for horizontal checking activities that constrain violations. By enabling more rapid and sustainable development, these strategies also help to widen the distribution of power and capabilities over time, in turn enabling further sequential strategies for strengthening the rule of law.

III. Pricing Projects and the Sustainability of Debt

Debt sustainability is usually understood in terms of macroeconomic flows: the growth rates of debt in domestic and foreign currency versus the projected growth

[19] International IDEA, *The Global State of Democracy 2023: The New Checks and Balances* (International Institute for Democracy and Electoral Assistance, 2023); '2021 Corruption Perceptions Index Reveals a Decade of Stagnating Corruption Levels amid Human Rights Abuses & Democratic Decline – Press' (*Transparency.org*, 25 January 2022), www.transparency.org/en/press/2021-corruption-perceptions-index-press-release, accessed 3 April 2024.

rates of incomes and foreign exchange earnings.[20] The IMF, for instance, projects the risks of countries becoming unable to pay their foreign exchange debt using available statistical trends in macroeconomic indicators. This process often fails to identify risks because the microeconomic contexts are always evolving and affect the macroeconomic flows. The macroeconomic indicators assume that what is happening at the project (microeconomic) level, or at the level of sectors and departments of government will all continue as before. In fact, leakages at these levels are subject to substantial variability. The projected growth of incomes and foreign exchange earnings depends on ongoing project choices, project pricing and the processes of project implementation and operation. A country that borrows one billion dollars and has a projected rate of growth of GDP and of foreign exchange earnings based on past performance may have very different prospects of repaying the interest and capital depending on where it allocates the new money and how carefully it manages the investment. Does it efficiently invest in a portfolio of education, health, and infrastructure that collectively creates jobs and exports that finance the lending, or does it build overpriced bridges and poorly implemented roads that do not create new jobs or exports to service the debt? Without effective governance, the country may rapidly slide towards default with dire consequences for sustaining its development path.

The lower-level governance processes through which projects are selected, contracted and implemented are usually not the focus of financial sustainability discussions. Yet financial sustainability clearly depends on these things. To attract flows of FDI from specific countries, developing countries often engage in government-to-government negotiations to make projects attractive to investors by offering high returns. The foreign financing may also be tied to buying machinery and inputs from that country, implementation by companies from those countries, and their selection of preferred partner companies in the recipient country, all of whom may collectively set high prices as a way of increasing their returns. In the absence of strong public scrutiny, the incentives for insiders may result in the choice of the wrong projects, at high prices, and with poor eventual implementation. This is particularly likely in big projects in infrastructure, power, energy, mining and other similar sectors.

Some evidence from Sri Lanka and Bangladesh can illustrate the problem. In a study of Sri Lanka, Verité Research showed how the presence of tied infrastructure loans from China created strong incentives to approve projects without proper discussion of alternatives, to appoint inferior contractors selected by the lender, and to overprice the contracts.[21] During 2010–16 China provided 37 per cent of all infrastructure loans to Sri Lanka. Other countries too provided tied loans linked to specific projects of their choice with their own selection of contractors. The

[20] IMF, 'Review of the Debt Sustainability Framework for Market Access Countries' IMF Policy Paper (International Monetary Fund, 2021).

[21] Verité Research, *The Lure of Chinese Loans: Sri Lanka's Experiment with a Special Framework to Finance its Infrastructure Investments* (Verité Research, 2022).

formal processes set up by the Sri Lanka government to vet these projects did not work well in the context of these incentives and weak democratic institutions. The overpricing problem is severe because a small element of overpricing in projects without competition can wipe out the concessional element of the loan. The concessional element in a loan is the difference in repayment conditions and interest rates relative to a commercial loan. In many Chinese and Indian infrastructure projects in Sri Lanka, it is estimated that a 5–30 per cent overpricing of the project will wipe out the concessional element of the loan. Overpricing higher than that makes these 'concessional loans' more costly than fully commercial borrowing. In many infrastructure projects in Sri Lanka the overpricing is higher than this. The problem is less severe in infrastructure loans to Sri Lanka from countries like Japan or from DFIs because those loans usually have a much higher concessional element.[22]

The overpricing of infrastructure and power projects funded by loans is also widely reported in Bangladesh and in other developing countries. In 2017, the World Bank revealed that the price of constructing a kilometre of road in Bangladesh is between two to 10 times higher than in India or China. Part of the reason may be the softer soil in Bangladesh, but according to the World Bank a major part of the reason has to do with a lack of competition, and collusion and corruption in the granting of infrastructure contracts.[23] Many power projects in Bangladesh are also overpriced. Price differences between identical power plants in Bangladesh are around 25 per cent, depending on the presence or absence of potential competition at the time of contracting.[24]

Some strategies of attracting foreign lenders and investors have therefore been very damaging for the sustainability of debt. Overpriced contracts clearly do attract new investors in higher-risk contexts, but when many such projects come on stream, the increased likelihood of future default obviously increases. As financial sustainability declines, this can drive out good investors who now perceive even higher country investment risks. In the next round, the country may have to offer even higher collusive overpricing to attract politically connected investors, that further reduces future sustainability, and so on till a default happens. Thus, while many developing countries have been successful in attracting very large investments in infrastructure, in sectors such as roads and bridges, the power sector and mining, where investments often come from other Southern countries like China and India, the financial risks have also significantly increased.

The policy question is what can be feasibly done to reduce the risks of investors in countries where the rule of law is not as strong as it should be. In these

[22] Verité Research, *Financing Infrastructure: The (Non) Concessionality of Concessional Loans* (Verité Research, 2020).

[23] 'Road Construction Cost Way Too High' *The Daily Star* (21 June 2017), www.thedailystar.net/frontpage/road-construction-cost-way-too-high-1423132, accessed 3 April 2024.

[24] Khan and others, 'De-risking Private Power' (n 16).

countries, transparency and accountability and formal procedures are not sufficient, as the studies referred to earlier on Sri Lanka show. An alternative route is to use innovative processes to enhance competition and bring down prices by discovering the lowest risk premium at which investors are willing to invest in specific sectors and countries. Investors do indeed face higher risks in countries with a weaker rule of law. For instance, new governments may question contracts made by earlier governments, and court rulings on contracts may be difficult to enforce. As a result, investors may justifiably want higher, risk-adjusted, returns in these contexts. From the perspective of the recipient country, the challenge is to discover the lowest feasible risk premium in specific types of projects.

There are feasible strategies for enhancing competition to discover the lowest risk premium. For instance, in the Bangladesh power sector, the underlying problem was that high contracting risks kept politically unconnected investors away from bidding in big power projects. Politically connected investors perceive lower levels of risk because they are likely to be prioritised for payments, at least during the tenure of their government. They can further reduce their risks by negotiating high prices for power so that they recover their investments faster. In the absence of competition, these closed-door negotiations can result in very high collusive prices being set. But the liabilities of the public power purchaser increases, as it will have to make inflated payments in the future, as does the overall risk that the government will not be able to meet its payment commitments in the future, even to these politically connected investors.

If the only bidders in a bid are politically connected companies, improved transparency and accountability cannot prevent collusion. The lowest bid from a political connected company may still be very high and the government can truthfully say that it accepted the lowest bid. The World Bank and other agencies have attempted to improve the pricing of power projects using transparency and procurement reforms, but these are not sufficient. Transparency and procurement reforms work if business risks are low and there are many players with sufficient competitive capabilities to bid in relevant projects. If that is the case, these competitors will be vigilant during the bidding process, and are likely to complain loudly if violations are detected or suspected. But if business risks are high, and politically unconnected investors stay away from bidding, no-one with sufficient power will take action if collusive prices emerge from this process.

To break this collusion, a broader range of investors must be attracted to bid. This is only possible if investor risk can be feasibly reduced without offering overpriced contracts. Fortunately, there may be feasible ways of doing this in some sectors and countries, and the increased competition that results can reduce prices significantly. In the Bangladesh power sector, some power projects are contracted at a much lower price than other projects that are otherwise identical. It turns out that the lower-priced projects had forms of preferential financing available that reduced risks for politically unconnected bidders. This was usually a line of credit from DFIs available for a specific power project at an interest rate slightly lower than the market interest rate.

While politically connected investors want the highest possible price they can negotiate with government (because they are sure they will be paid), politically unconnected investors paradoxically often perceive an even higher risk when charging high prices. This is because consumers cannot fully pay for very expensive power in developing countries and investors with expensive power contracts implicitly require a government subsidy to be paid on their contracts. The higher the contracted price, the more dependent the investor is on implicit government subsidies, and the higher the risk for investors with weak political connections. Lower-cost financing can reduce this risk for unconnected investors by allowing them to contract at a lower price. As risks reduce, a greater number of politically unconnected investors are potentially interested in that project. Their interest triggers horizontal checking during the bidding processes as these potential investors have the power and interest to complain to DFIs if they detect evidence of collusion. In the Bangladeshi case, projects which had financing with these characteristics achieved procurement prices that were a whopping 25 per cent lower compared to other identical projects, even though the direct contribution of the preferential financing was only to reduce investor costs by 2–3 per cent. This was sufficient to enhance potential competition by reducing the risks for unconnected parties to bid in those projects, achieving a significant reduction in contracted prices, by breaking up the collusion that would otherwise have happened.[25]

Countries clearly need to discover effective risk-reduction strategies in critical project areas to attract new investors. The ensuing competition is the only effective way of discovering the lowest risk premia that investors will accept in that country and sector. However, attracting politically unconnected investors may not be possible in every sector in every country. In some cases, political interference or even threats of violence may keep out politically unconnected investors. Creating the space for economic competition may require some level of openness and political competition (with or without multi-party rule) so that a small group of politicians cannot determine all the contracting. But provided there is some space for economic competition, a feasible strategy is to experiment with implementable risk-reduction strategies to attract new investors that can enhance the degree of competition in bids.

The achievement of 'good governance', a good rule of law, low corruption, public accountability and so on are, in theory, ways of reducing risks for investors and constraining political capture. But the configuration of power, capabilities and interests in developing country political settlements may not allow these governance characteristics to be rapidly achieved. A more feasible pathway is to deploy bottom-up sectoral approaches to create sufficient horizontal checks in critical areas to reduce collusion and keep debt sustainable. Using our earlier analogy, if policymakers cannot ensure that every queue in the country is orderly, they must ensure a few critical queues work properly. The specific mechanism that worked

[25] ibid.

in the Bangladesh power sector will not necessarily work in other sectors or countries. Nevertheless, it shows that feasible strategies may exist that can induce the actual or potential entry of politically unconnected investors and trigger horizontal checks that make transparency and accountability systems more effective. The challenge is to find risk-reduction strategies that are sufficiently effective in critical sectors in each country to enhance competition and reduce the contracted prices of major projects. This can significantly contribute to reducing the risk of unsustainable debt.

IV. Project and Programme Implementation

Closely related to the problem of project overpricing is the poor governance of implementation. This too can result in unsustainable debt if development financing is used to construct poor-quality projects or deliver poor services, or if the projects suffer from long delays and cost overruns. These investments may also not generate the returns required to justify or service the financing. The problem is obviously no less important if projects are financed with tax revenues or domestic debt. If tax-funded projects do not offer developmental returns for citizens, their willingness to pay tax can decline. With borrowed money, failures of implementation have more immediate adverse effects. In particular, if the projects fail to generate sufficient returns for foreign lenders, the country can rapidly slip into debt stress or default.

There are no universally accepted measures of project implementation failures. Data are usually compiled at a country and project level and may be difficult to compare across projects let alone across countries. But some indicative figures illustrate the seriousness of the problem and the need for better data and monitoring. In Sri Lanka, the Auditor General's office looks at the available data on government investments every year and compares the expenditure claimed each year with the reported construction or purchase of physical assets, financial assets, other non-financial assets, and other reported investments. Over the period 2006–2021, a massive 67.5 per cent of the total government investment expenditure claimed by projects could not be matched against any observable or reported physical, financial or other assets in those projects.[26]

Consolidated figures of this type do not exist in Bangladesh, but the overall implementation problem is well recognised. The World Bank's review of projects in Bangladesh in its Completion and Learning Review for 2016–21 identified project implementation as a significant constraint.[27] While some projects of strategic

[26] National Audit Office, *Annual Report of the Auditor General 2021* (National Audit Office of Sri Lanka, 2021) 114.

[27] World Bank, *Bangladesh: Country Partnership Framework for the Period FY2023 – FY2027* (World Bank Group, 2023) 12.

political importance, like the Padma Bridge, were reported to be reasonably well implemented at the construction phase, many other projects had severe cost overruns, long delays in completion, and in some cases, structures actually collapsed during construction.[28]

While the figures and evidence reported above may reflect several different types of problems, the governance problem here is that without effective checks and constraints, contractors and implementing companies, whether politically connected or not, may syphon resources out of the project, or contracts may be given to less qualified parties resulting in delays, cost overruns and poor-quality construction. Whatever the price at which the project was initially contracted, if the quality of the construction is poor, or there are cost overruns, or there are significant implementation delays, the project will not deliver sufficient direct or indirect returns to enable the repayment of the construction cost or justify the tax revenues allocated to it. The severe problems of project implementation in developing countries are well known. These involve the diversion of funds from the project, informal subcontracting where the initial contractor subcontracts parts of the project to others at lower prices and keeps the difference, corruption in buying overpriced or inferior quality materials, or allocating the contract to connected parties without considering their experience or qualifications. Poor implementation may also be combined with overpriced contracts, due to the lack of effective competition in the granting of contracts.

Conventional 'good governance' approaches of transparency and accountability, including the digitalisation of procurements, have not resulted in very significant reductions in these problems. Their limitations are closely related to the political settlements problem discussed earlier. If most contractors in a sector have low productive capabilities and are colluding with government agencies, or if some contractors are closely connected to political actors, the availability of evidence on the quality of implementation or even of actual corruption is not likely to lead to action by any party with the power to make a difference. Civil society organisations or the media occasionally raise these issues, but they usually do not have the power or the interest to engage in sustained actions that can impose costs on violators. As a result, their initiatives usually stop having an effect after a while. Effective checking requires incentivising sufficiently powerful actors who will, in their own interest, use information about violations to ensure that implementation quality is not poor.

These actors often exist, and that is why not all projects in developing countries are poorly constructed. There are many projects that are reasonably well constructed. Closer investigation usually reveals that these projects had some variants of horizontal checking by actors who had the power and the interest to

[28] 'Bangladesh's Tragic Project Implementation Record' *Daily Star* (12 October 2023), www.thedailystar.net/opinion/views/news/bangladeshs-tragic-project-implementation-record-3441156, accessed 10 February 2024.

monitor the project and to ensure that it was completed to reasonable specifications. Some projects may be well constructed because they are of strategic interest to the top political leadership. But usually there are too many projects for the top leadership to supervise and in the typical case, the quality of supervision at lower levels is much more important. Effective horizontal checking sometimes happens at lower levels if enough interested actors have the power and the interest to influence the outcome of implementation. Governance strategies should focus on identifying and incentivising these processes to reduce leakages across a wider range of investment projects.

Research on the construction of climate adaptation projects in Bangladesh shows that some flood protection embankments and cyclone shelters are much better constructed than others and have lower levels of leakages.[29] Surveys of the local populations and their engagement in monitoring shows that the better implemented climate adaptation projects happen to be ones where because of accidents of design, there were immediate benefits from the project for a wide range of actors in the local community, who were therefore induced to engage in monitoring and putting effective pressure on contractors. When individuals with sufficient power to credibly constrain corruption in a project become involved in checking activities out of self-interest, the governance of these projects improves. The community members whose monitoring was important in the climate adaptation projects were not very powerful people in an absolute sense, but they were sufficiently powerful in the local community, and relative to the contractors, to make a difference to the outcome. They were in fact rather poor people, but because they had small landholdings, or were small traders, they were *relatively* powerful in the local community, and could check the contractors who were implementing the projects.

The self-interested involvement of relatively powerful people in monitoring activities emerged in those adaptation projects where the infrastructure had dual uses that were of immediate benefit to the local community. Embankments can be used as roads, so when an embankment is built exactly where the road is of greatest value to the community, self-interested local involvement emerges to ensure its proper implementation. In particular, when the climate adaptation infrastructure has immediate dual-use benefits, this triggers the involvement of locally influential people, as they are more likely to have trading and other interests that benefit from this. Similarly, cyclone shelters have dual uses and can be used as community centres or schools. When their location and design ensure dual uses of high value for the local community, the latter get involved, and the involvement of more powerful community members increases. In general, when monitoring activities are more extensive and involve a larger number of influential local community members, effective horizontal checking leads to better implementation outcomes.[30]

[29] Khan and others, 'Win-win' (n 16).
[30] ibid.

These types of findings suggest that there are feasible ways of improving implementation quality. In societies where horizontal checks are weak, it is necessary to ensure there are sufficient real benefits for local communities to get involved in checking activities in their own interest. Governance improves if policy can be designed to incentivise this engagement, and particularly the engagement of those who have the power and capability to engage in monitoring and pursuing violations in their own interest. In the case of the climate adaptation projects, this involved local small landholders and traders coming out to observe and check construction activities and putting informal pressure on contractors and local political actors when construction quality was poor. The result was better construction quality and lower evidence of corruption leakages in these projects.

The challenge is to figure out how best to mobilise the relevant local interests to strengthen effective horizontal checking. In climate adaptation projects, a potentially effective method may be for the planning process to provide several alternative engineering designs and locations for an embankment or a cyclone shelter. The local community could then be invited to select the design and location that is of greatest value to them. Such a process would mobilise the local community, and in particular the individuals who stand to benefit the most from the better implementation of the selected projects. These are likely to be the very individuals whose checking activities are potentially most effective.

Every type of investment project may not immediately present such opportunities. In larger infrastructure projects, where large amounts of money are at stake, contractors are likely to be closely connected to higher political levels. The projects may also involve considerable technical complexity, and outside observers may not be able to easily assess quality of construction or leakages during construction. Community pressure may not be effective in reducing leakages in such projects. Other forms of internal monitoring and accountability must be devised, working on the self-interest of different parties involved in, or benefiting from, the project. But if attempts are made to incrementally identify opportunities that do exist, implementation effectiveness, and thereby the sustainability of development financing is likely to gradually improve.

V. Conclusion

Sustainable development clearly requires sustainable development financing. If a country defaults on its debt, or if flows of financing are volatile, or shrink or dry up entirely, they cannot support sustainable development. Some of the factors that can cause these problems are beyond the control of individual countries and have to do with how the international financial system and global economy operate, and on global shocks outside the control of individual countries. However, some causes of unsustainable financing are rooted in governance failures within countries. We looked at three of the most important variants of these governance failures. The first results in the selection of projects that are not the best options in terms of delivering developmental and financial returns. The second involves the process of contracting, which can result in the emergence of overpriced projects. Too much may be committed to projects that are worth less in terms of the revenues and developmental benefits that they can feasibly generate. Finally, there may be governance failures at the implementation level that result in poor implementation, or leakages of funds, so that the investments again generate insufficient welfare or financial returns to justify the resources dedicated to their construction and operation. All three may contribute to countries ending up with debt or other forms of financial liabilities that they are not able to service or sustain. As commercial investments become more important flows of financing, wasteful investments are no longer just wasted opportunities, they add to unsustainable debt that must be repaid to avoid the risk of default, often at great cost to the economy.

A rules-based economy, where the formal rules of democratic accountability and contract enforcement are sufficient to protect project selection, pricing and implementation, will take a long time to achieve. A rule of law requires the emergence of a broad base of capable and powerful organisations that provide the horizontal checks essential for its enforcement. In many developing countries this distribution of power and capabilities does not yet exist, and some developing countries are considerably further away from these conditions than others.

One of the goals of development must be to move towards broader distributions of power and capabilities that enable an impartial rule of law. In the meantime, intermediate governance strategies must be used to support development in these directions. The effective governance of financing is part of that process. Countries are likely to develop faster if they are more experimental and innovative in discovering ways of scrutinising and prioritising projects that generate broad-based development, and mobilising effective checks to keep a lid on prices and implementation leakages. These strategies will be effective if they take account of the existing distributions of power, capabilities and interests in that country. To the extent that these strategies are successful, they will ensure that the financing of development remains sustainable, and that will ensure the development path too will be more sustainable. This in turn will help move societies towards the broader distributions of power and capabilities that make democratic governance and the emergence of a rule of law more likely.

16

Monitoring and Evaluating SDG Progress in Developing Country Contexts

MUSTAFIZUR RAHMAN

I. Introduction

On 25 September 2015, 193 states of the United Nations unanimously adopted the Sustainable Development Goals (SDGs) with 17 goals and 169 targets.[1] The understanding was that SDGs were global aspirations and an integral part of the 'One World' vision. Para 79 of the adopted document referred to above also stated that over the next 15 years, implementation of goals and targets of the 2030 Agenda would be closely monitored. Monitoring and Evaluation (M and E) of SDG implementation progress was to take place with the help of institutional initiatives and frameworks in reference to nationally as well as globally determined parameters. The progress of implementation was to be tracked through periodic review and evaluation. As part of its follow-up and review mechanisms, the 2030 Agenda encouraged member states to conduct regular and inclusive reviews of progress at the national and sub-national levels, which are country-led and country-driven At the global level, countries were expected to report on SDG implementation progress periodically, based on national level M and E exercises. Progress was to be reported at the High Level Forums on a voluntary basis (Voluntary National Review (VNR) process).[2] Subsequently, indicators were developed to monitor and assess the implementation progress in terms of the various SDG targets; 248 such indicators were identified for this purpose.

[1] BX Lee and others, 'Transforming Our World: Implementing the 2030 Agenda Through Sustainable Development Goal Indicators' (2016) 37 *Journal of Public Health Policy* 13, link.springer.com/article/10.1057/s41271-016-0002-7, accessed 19 June 2024.

[2] The VNRs are held each year at the High-Level Policy Forums (HLPF) organised by the Economic and Social Council (ECOSOC) which review the progress of selected Goals periodically.

A number of national and global entities as well as many non-state actors (NSAs) have been carrying out a host of M and E activities to evaluate the progress being made in implementing the SDGs. Other than this, as part of the United Nations System, various programmes are being implemented to track SDG implementation progress under the aegis of, for example, the United Nations Development Programme (UNDP), the Economic and Social Council (ECOSOC), the United Nations Environment Programme (UNEP) and other organisations, which undertake periodic assessment of SDG progress.

As is widely known, what cannot be measured cannot be monitored and what cannot be monitored cannot be evaluated and assessed for capturing the progress being made. It is here that the discourse on monitoring and evaluating SDG progress assumes such heightened importance. While SDG progress was to be evaluated in terms of global achievements of the aspirations as envisaged in the 'One World' slogan of the SDGs, SDG implementation is primarily the task of individual countries. The spirit of SDG implementation was to be to 'Leave No One Behind' (LNOB). Also, localisation of SDG was seen to be crucial to SDG implementation. At the same time, SDG 17 talked of global partnerships to help attain the other SDGs. Accordingly, the leave no one behind spirit of the SDGs can also be interpreted as 'leave no country behind'. Thus, while there is an issue of national responsibility in implementing the SDG, implementation also entails a global commitment to help national governments to implement the SDGs through global support. M and E of SDG progress thus needs to be seen not just from the angle of attaining the goals at the national level but also from the perspectives of whether the promised global support has been delivered on the ground.

Indeed, the importance given to issues of M and E of the SDG progress, on an ongoing basis, is one of its distinctive features, and an important departure when juxtaposed to that of the Millennium Development Goals (MDGs).[3] In the context of the MDGs, M and E was primarily seen from the vantage point of outcomes. Indeed, many countries had failed to attain a number of critically important goals and targets of the MDGs precisely because assessment of achievement (or non-achievement) was made towards the end of the MDG timeline of 2015. In contrast, M and E in the context of the SDGs was embedded in the SDG framework itself, as an integral part of both process and delivery of outcomes. While M and E initiatives in the context of MDGs were back-loaded, in case of the SDGs this was frontloaded. Organisations such as the United Nations Development Programme (UNDP) and the International Development Evaluation Association (IDEAS) took the lead in this respect very early on. The Sustainable Development Solutions Network (SDSN) played a pioneering role in this context. In many developing countries, citizens' organisations also supported SDG implementation and monitoring of the SDG progress by pooling resources together.[4]

[3] The eight MDGs had 18 targets and 48 indicators.

[4] The Citizens Platform for SDGs, Bangladesh, is an example of such a grouping. The Platform has more than 130 non-state organisations working on SDG-related issues, and undertakes activities to

An attempt has been made in this chapter to capture the salient features of the efforts to monitor and evaluate SDG progress, in the context of developing countries, on the basis of extensive literature review, particularly drawing on the VNR reports submitted by several developing countries: Bangladesh (2020); India (2020); Pakistan (2022); Indonesia (2021); and others. SDG progress reports prepared by various international organisations and initiatives were also consulted: SDSN (2023); WB (2023); Southern Voice (2023); and others. In doing so, to keep the discussion more manageable, focus has been put mainly on the experiences of the developing countries in Asia in view of SDG-related M and E.

Following these introductory remarks, the rest of the discussion in this chapter is presented in three sections. Section II highlights why monitoring and evaluating SDG progress is so critical to attaining the SDGs, particularly since the world has already crossed the halfway line – the equator so to say – in moving towards the final year of 2030. Section III reviews and takes a critical look at the experience of M and E of SDGs in developing country contexts. Section IV offers a set of recommendations to strengthen SDG-related M and E in implementing the SDGs in developing country contexts. The chapter ends with some concluding remarks.

II. Growing Importance of M and E in the SDG Discourse

Since the adoption of the SDGs, the overriding consensus which has evolved is that the old distinction between 'developed' and 'developing' countries has given way to the new concept of 'developing towards a sustainable, equitable and inclusive future.[5] Sustainable development goals embrace the above vision under its concept of 'one world'. The moot question that haunts all concerned is, is the required progress towards attaining these lofty aspirations being actually made? At what pace? Is the speed adequate to attain the SDG goals and targets by 2030? Is the implementation inclusive? Are SDGs being implemented by leaving no one behind? Are the spatial dimensions of SDG implementation properly considered? Answers to these questions hinge on proper M and E of SDG progress, which would help identify the deficits and undertake mid-course corrections.

The Independent Evaluation Office of the UNDP and the International Development Evaluation Association (IDEAS) merit appreciation for their initiative, just a month after the SDGs were endorsed,[6] to initiate discussion on the role

advance the cause of SDG implementation in Bangladesh, monitors progress of implementation, works with various state entities, and prepares independent monitoring reports that focus on both overall progress and progress from an LNOB vantage point.

[5] RD van den Berg, I Naidoo and SD Tamondong, *Agenda Evaluation for 2030: Providing Evidence on Progress and Sustainability* (UNDP (United Nations Development Programme) and IDEAS, 2017), web.undp.org/evaluation/documents/Books/Evaluation_for_Agenda_2030.pdf, accessed 10 June 2024.

[6] ibid.

that M and E was expected to play in implementing the SDGs. This was followed by many other initiatives which have generated a wealth of information, knowledge and data relating to success and best practices, deficits and challenges concerning SDG implementation in developing country contexts.

The drafters of the SDGs had tried to learn from the MDG experience, as mentioned above. It was noted at the time of design of the SDGs that while the indicators were quantitative in nature, many of the attendant goals and targets concerned qualitative aspects. Progress with respect to these was to be captured through appropriate M and E exercise. For example, objective of Goal 4 of the SDGs was not just 100.0 per cent enrolment in primary education, but also quality of education; objective of Goal 8 was to create not just jobs, but decent jobs.[7] This newness of the SDGs called for proper design of appropriate metrics for evaluating the state of the qualitative aspects mentioned above. It was also felt that M and E of SDG implementation progress should be seen as an ongoing process in order that shortcomings and gaps could be addressed through timely interventions. The concept of *Data Revolution* was launched precisely in view of the need to measure SDG progress on a continuing basis. Accordingly, embedding of monitoring and evaluation was seen as an integral part of SDG implementation and its success.

The Voluntary National Review (VNR) process was expected to encourage countries to track and measure SDG progress at the national level and present progress reports covering selected SDG areas at the High-Level Policy Forums (HLPF) under the auspices of the UN ECOSOC. This was a novel initiative in view of the SDGs. By promoting data revolution and putting in place the VNR process countries were motivated to give due importance to issues of monitoring and assessing SDG implementation progress on an ongoing basis. As stipulated in para 84 of the 2030 Agenda, regular reviews by the HLPF are to be voluntary, state-led, undertaken by both developed and developing countries, and involve multiple stakeholders.[8] The VNRs had impacted positively on three fronts: first, the reviews incentivised members to carry out assessment of the progress being made in respective countries in attaining the various SDG goals and targets; second, countries perceived participation in the VNRs to be a symbol of national dignity and as an opportunity to report on what they were doing and what progress they had achieved in the context of the SDGs; and third, the reporting exercise created a healthy environment to check and compare SDG progress with other countries and induced the reporting countries to perform better and seek to excel. The VNR process was also perceived to be important from the perspective of mobilising resources to help bridge the financing gaps and mobilise global partnerships.

[7] United Nations, *Sustainable Development Goals Report* (United Nations, 2015), www.un.org/en/development/desa/publications/global-sustainable-development-report-2015-edition.html, accessed 10 June 2024.

[8] As of July 2023, seven VNR events had taken place in New York where 291 country reports had been presented up to that date: indeed, 38 countries submitted respective reports for the second time, and one for the third time. The next VNR is scheduled to take place in July 2024.

Indeed, this was the spirit of SDG Goal 17 which talked of collaboration and extending support to countries in need in the context of SDG implementation.

The SDG spirit of leave no one behind (LNOB) underscores the need for monitoring and evaluating the SDG progress from the perspectives of the marginalised and left-behind groups. The LNOB spirit embeds inclusivity, equity, distributive justice and fairness in the process of implementing the SDGs. This implies that special care has to be taken so that issues of concerns and interests to the disadvantaged and marginalised groups are given due priority while implementing the SDGs. Such a disaggregated approach ought to inform both the process of SDG implementation and the SDG results. M and E of SDG implementation needs to go beyond the average numbers and monitor how marginalised groups are faring in terms of various SDG indicators, If the MDGs primarily focused on average numbers in assessing progress and achievement, the SDGs, in contrast, were also concerned with issues of disaggregation – whether all concerned stakeholders, particularly the left behind and disadvantaged groups and communities, were benefiting from attaining the SDGs. SDGs, thus, went beyond and behind the averages, and talked of distributive fairness, and addressing the challenges of reaching the *last mile*. This meant that an M and E exercise was to be undertaken to also audit whether the aforesaid aspects of the SDGs were being ensured in the process of SDG implementation. This, no doubt, made M and E a daunting and difficult exercise in the context of the SDGs.

The importance of M and E of SDG implementation also arises from the fact that many SDGs are interconnected. Leveraging the implementation of different goals and drawing synergies from those were key to successful implementation of the different clusters of the SDGs. For example, No Poverty (SDG 1) and Zero Hunger (SDG 2) are closely linked; so are Decent Work (Goal 8) and Reduced Inequality (Goal 10). If there is no poverty, there should be no hunger because food security is an essential element, and consequent result, of eliminating poverty. Decent Work connotes productive, well-remunerative jobs which reduces poverty, raises the share of wages in gross domestic product (GDP) and should lead to better income distribution. Another example could be Gender Equality (Goal 5) which is a cross-cutting theme and can be achieved only if most other SDGs are attained. Thus, in implementing Goal 16 (Peace, Justice and Strong Institutions) it should be ensured that women's specific issues and vulnerabilities are considered and taken care of adequately. Attaining these goals and associated targets calls for interlinked interventions. If the interventions could be leveraged effectively, SDG implementation would gain from synergistic impacts. The M and E exercise associated with the SDG implementation, when informed by this interconnectedness and assessed accordingly, would help countries to attain the goals and targets in both an effective and cost-effective manner.

The SDGs, as is known, promote the *whole of society approach*, meaning that the goals and targets are to be achieved with participation and contribution from all involved stakeholders, through public-private (and broadly public NSAs) partnerships and collaboration. Such partnerships envisage involvement of concerned stakeholders not only in the process of SDG implementation, but also in activities that concern monitoring and assessing the progress of SDG implementation. This is yet another distinctive feature of the SDGs from the perspective of M and E.

An additional factor which makes the exercise of M and E of crucial importance in the current juncture is concerned with the adverse implications of the various shocks such as the impact of the Covid-19 pandemic of the recent past on SDG implementation progress. Some of the positive results of the first one-third of SDG implementation period (2025–2020) were significantly affected by the adverse impacts of the pandemic on many of the SDG-related areas, particularly if the LNOB angle is kept in perspective. This was particularly so in the context of the developing countries. SDG progress assessment was required to take into consideration of the ramifications of the pandemic as countries pursued policies of *building forward better.* Moreover, the ongoing Ukraine–Russia war, and the consequent inflation and macroeconomic-external balance-fiscal-monetary challenges have also meant that the M and E exercise needs be cognisant of these recent developments as the SDG implementation enters into the second and final phase.

For example, as the SDG progress report of the United Nations Economic and Social Commission for Asia and the Pacific (UN ESCAP)[9] indicates, at midpoint, countries in Asia-Pacific region have made impressive progress during 2015–2022 period, in case of some indicators. In Timor Leste health workers trained in emergency obstetric care and deployed in community health centres have helped bring down the infant mortality rate significantly through a higher percentage of births attended by skilled professionals. In Cambodia and Pakistan, skilled birth attendance reached 70 per cent and 98 per cent respectively thanks to education and training, resulting in lower infant and maternal mortality. In Cambodia, the childhood stunting rate has been reduced from 34 per cent to 22 per cent between 2014 and 2021.

However, as ESCAP 2022 report shows, disparities have increased because of the Covid-19 pandemic which left adverse footprints for SDG achievements.[10] The key message of the ESCAP (2023) report is that, only 15 per cent of the required progress has been made in the region at the midpoint of the agenda. The pace of progress has been rather slow (progress towards all 17 SDG in the Asia-Pacific region increased from 4.4 per cent in 2017 to 14.4 per cent 2022). According to ESCAP (2023), progress was very slow particularly in case of Goal 14 (Life below water), Goal 8 (Decent work and economic growth) and Goal 12 (Responsible consumption and production). Indeed, in case of Goal 13 (Climate action), there has actually been some regress. The report assesses SDG progress in terms of four indicators: (a) reverse trend; (b) accelerate progress; (c) on track indicators; and (d) can't be measured. A significantly large number of indicators could not be

[9] ESCAP, *Asia and the Pacific SDG Report: Championing sustainability despite adversities* (ESCAP, 2023), www.unescap.org/kp/2023/asia-and-pacific-sdg-progress-report-2023, accessed 10 June 2024.
[10] ESCAP, *Asia and the Pacific SDG Report: Widening disparities amid COVID-19* (ESCAP, 2022), https://www.unescap.org/kp/2022/asia-and-pacific-sdg-progress-report-2022, accessed 10 June 2024.

measured, and monitored because of lack of data (particularly, in case of Goal 5: Gender equality and Goal 16: Peace and justice, but also others to varying degrees). Data sufficiency for the various indicators was found to be as follows: Sufficient: 128; Insufficient: 80; No data: 23. The report underscored the importance of monitoring progress on a continuing basis as a key driver of SDG attainment. Thus, the experiences of a number of developing countries indicate that many of these are falling behind in achieving several key indicators of the SDG goals and targets. At this pace of progress, many targets and indicators are likely to remain unattained.

The VNR reports also testify that a major factor contributing to slow progress relates to lack of proper M and E of SDG implementation progress which is so crucial to undertaking corrective measures and additional steps to put the implementation process on course and on track. An M and E exercise is thus crucial to identify not only the required national tasks but also to signal the direction regarding the type of international support measures (ISMs) which are needed to address the gaps.

Thus, it is seen that evaluating SDGs brings with it added challenges when compared to traditional monitoring and evaluating tools that focus on SMART (specific, measurable, achievable, relevant and time-bound) metrics. The distinctive features of disaggregation, LNOB spirit and localisation were noted above in view of the SDG implementation. The SDGs also emphasise on climate change impacts, distributional and social justice and equity, human rights, gender sensitivity, empowerment and participation. This makes the task of M and E of SDG implementation, particularly in the context of developing countries, both important and challenging.

III. Cross-country Experience in M and E of SDG Implementation

At a time when SDG implementation timeline crosses the midway, it is important to take stock of the experience, and the knowledge generated, in monitoring the implementation of the SDGs in cross-developing country contexts. Such an exercise could provide valuable lessons about what has worked and what did not, what are the best practices, and what more needs to be done to make the M and E of SDG implementation progress more effective. The purpose here is not so much to go into specific country level experience but identify some of the general learnings that have informed the SDG implementation process to date, both positive experiences and also the areas that need particular attention (the framework issues); institutional mechanisms in place to monitor progress; alignment and synergies in monitoring and assessing progress; fiscal-financial space; localisation of the SDGs; LNOB perspectives; and regional cooperation and global support measures.

A review of cross-country experiences indicates that the emphasis on M and E was significantly higher in the context of the SDGs than was the case with the

MDGs. The MDGs were criticised for not being precise and lacking in quantitative targets; weak alignment between the various goals and targets; lack of data disaggregation to monitor progress involving vulnerable groups; and inadequate attention to qualitative dimensions of development such as environmental dimensions and issues of sustainable development. Lack of proper and ongoing M and E was specifically mentioned in this connection.[11] Against this backdrop, SDGs have taken lessons from MDG implementation experience. Developing countries understood that an ongoing assessment process was key to attaining the SDGs. As noted earlier, one of the lessons drawn by the developing countries from the experience of MDG implementation was that undertaking assessment of attaining goals and targets towards the end period, while providing a measure of the progress attained, was of rather limited value. Drawing on the MDG experience, developing countries felt that an embedded M and E system in the SDG implementation plan was the way to go forward to avoid the underlying reasons behind some of the lacunae in the context of MDG implementation.[12] It was felt that institutionalisation of the M and E exercise would help to identify gaps, undertake corrective actions, reprioritise what was required to be done and redirect resources to where it was most needed and would be most effective. Governments of many developing countries have set up new bodies mandated with the tasks of M and E of SDG implementation and recommending actions for addressing the attendant deficits (this point is elaborated in next section). An ongoing M and E was also expected to be helpful in mobilising global, financial, technical and institutional supports towards implementation of the SDGs.

The following sub-sections briefly capture the range of initiatives that were put in place, and country level experiences in connection with tracing, tracking, monitoring and assessing SDG implementation progress in the context of a number of developing countries in Asia.

A. Institutional Framework

By and large, all developing countries have recognised the task of monitoring and evaluating the SDG progress as important in the context of SDG implementation. Some have made an attempt to undertake this periodically, others as part of an ongoing tracking process. A review of relevant literature shows that many developing countries have put in place institutional frameworks for this purpose.

[11] United Nations, *Sustainable Development Goals Report* (United Nations, 2015). www.un.org/en/development/desa/publications/global-sustainable-development-report-2015-edition.html, accessed 19 June 2024.

[12] M Bangha and others, 'Monitoring the Millennium Development Goals: The Potential Role of the INDEPTH Network' (2010) 3 *Global Health Action*; A Ogunrotifa, 'Grand Developmentalism: A Critical Appraisal of Millennium Development Goals' (2015) 4(2) *Journal of Asian Development Studies* 43.

At the national level, keeping in the purview that the national governments were the signatories of the SDGs, the M and E of SDG progress is led by selected government organisations. Governments have either set up new bodies that are entrusted with the task of M and E, or have redesigned and reassigned existing bodies for this purpose. For example, the Government of Bangladesh has set up a high level SDG Monitoring and Implementation Committee. This was a new entity under the Prime Minister's Office (PMO) to monitor and assess SDG implementation progress and take steps to ensure that measures are taken to address where progress is relatively slow.[13] The rationale was that, monitoring SDG progress required significant coordination among various concerned entities and Ministries and it was beyond the remit of the Bangladesh Planning Commission to do this effectively. For this, a higher, more powerful body was needed to be created which would be mandated to monitor progress and ask Ministries and agencies to undertake M and E from an SDG lens, and report and take corrective measures where required. While the Committee is dominated by government high level officials, from various Ministries and government bodies, representatives from chambers of business and trade bodies and also from civil society groups have been included in this body. In India, the NITI Aayog[14] is entrusted with the task of coordinating implementation and monitoring of the SDG progress. The NITI Aayog has replaced the erstwhile Planning Commission of India with the mandate to monitor SDG progress. Nepal has constituted a National Steering Committee to oversee SDG implementation. The Maldives has set up SDG coordination and Implementation Committee. These bodies enjoy the backing of political leaders at the highest level. They perform the dual tasks of coordinating the work of various activities involved in SDG implementation, and monitoring progress of implementation of the different goals and targets. The bodies bring out periodic reports on SDG implementation progress. They organise national conferences and dialogues to assess the progress of SDG implementation, review who is doing what, and suggest what new measures are necessary to address the deficits. They also play a lead role in preparing the VNRs. These bodies work closely with non-state organisations (NSOs) to measure the progress being made, or lack thereof, in the context of SDG implementation. A review of developing country VNRs indicate that, in general, these are doing a commendable job. Some developing countries are found to coordinate SDG implementation with their respective medium-term plans (generally five-year plans) and align a large part of SDG monitoring with monitoring of implementation of five-year plans (eg Bangladesh).

A number of countries have put in place other mechanisms to help monitor SDG progress. Bangladesh has set up an All-party Parliamentary Caucus for SDGs; Surinam has initiated a Youth Ambassador Programme for SDGs; and Lao PDR

[13] The SDG Implementation Plan of Bangladesh includes a matrix with Ministries and other bodies that would be responsible for implementation and monitoring of progress in terms of the relevant SDG.

[14] NITI Aayog is the government agency in India that has replaced the erstwhile Indian Planning Commission.

has developed a SDG localisation framework to encourage partnership between government entities and NSAs.

B. Methods of Monitoring Progress

In view of the methods of the M and E of SDG implementation, it is found that in some countries existing programmes and policies have been tagged with a particular SDG target and the progress of that specific programme is interpreted from the perspective of SDG implementation in the concerned area. For example, in India, the National Rural Employment Guarantee Scheme (NREGS) has been aligned with SDG 1 and some of the related targets, and the National Health Mission has been aligned with SDG 3 (Government of India, 2017). In Bangladesh, the National Women's Development Policy 2011 has been aligned with SDG 5 and progress in terms of attaining the relevant SDG targets have been tagged with implementation of this policy. From the perspective of coordination of implementation and optimum use of scarce resources, this approach is not without its merit. However, M and E of distributional impacts, local level results and the LNOB aspirations has proved to be difficult in absence of disaggregated information. Nepal has introduced SDG-Based Public Expenditure Tracing Survey (PETS) which evaluates resource allocation and spending patterns for SDGs. In developing countries with federal system of government, SDG targets are often set both centrally and at the level of states. India is a good example of this.

A number of developing countries went for intensive monitoring of implementation of a select set of targets (out of the total 169 SDG targets). These were prioritised based on perceived national demands and needs. For example, in Bangladesh, 39 plus one (40) targets have been prioritised for purposes of implementation and assessment of SDG progress.[15] Arguably, this could result in neglect of non-prioritised targets. The rationale that informs such an approach is that in view of significant resource constraint, a number of targets were identified where resources are to be directed on a priority basis for attaining the relevant targets, at more disaggregated and localised levels, by leaving no one behind. This does not necessarily mean that other targets will remain neglected. However, one could argue that SDGs are integrated and preference for particular goals or targets could undermine achievement of others. Some countries have clustered the 17 goals into various groups for purposed of monitoring. For example, Malaysia has grouped SDGs into five clusters: Cluster 1: Inclusivity (Goal 1, Goal 2, Goal 4 and Goal 10); Cluster 2: Wellbeing (Goal 3, Goal 11 and Goal 16); Cluster 3: Human Capital (Goal 4); Cluster 4: Environment and Natural Resources (Goal 6, Goal 7 and Goal 12); Cluster 5: Economic Growth (Goal 8, Goal 9 and Goal 17).

[15] On the basis of perceived national priorities, 39 targets have been prioritised, while the additional one is to be determined at the local level, according to local priorities and needs.

The rationale here is to best leverage the implementation of clusters of goals and targets.[16] While some countries have centralised the tracking and monitoring of SDG implementation, others have followed a more decentralised approach. This often depends on the form of government – centralised, unitary (e.g. Bangladesh) and decentralised, Federal (eg India, Malaysia, Nepal). In India, for example, the NITI Aayog monitors both country-wise progress as also progress being made at the level of states (in terms of 16 goals, barring Goal 17). This allows the policy makers to oversee monitoring of SDG implementation at the country level and also promote competitive and comparative federalism among states.[17] However, in most cases the institutional framework is a blend of the two streams: while detailed SDG target-specific monitoring is entrusted with relevant government bodies and Ministries, the National Committees are tasked to pool data and information in a centralised format. In countries with a federal system of government, province and state level data are pooled for monitoring purposes at the central level. Many countries have established a dedicated SDG portal to trace and track SDG progress. The data in most cases are publicly accessible open source data (e.g. in the case of Bangladesh, India, Malaysia and Indonesia).

C. Cross-country Comparability of M and E Results

For many of the targets, cross-country comparisons of results of M and E exercises relating to SDG progress is to be difficult. It has been left to individual countries to set their own bars and reference points for measurement purposes and for monitoring the SDG implementation progress. For comparability purposes, in some cases global metrics have also been set; however, many SDG indicators are nationally determined. For example, progress in attaining Goal 1, zero poverty, is measured with reference to respective national poverty (and extreme poverty) lines, but also with respect to the global poverty line (per capita per day income of US$2.15). How the national poverty line is to be defined, and which quantitative measures are to be set, is for the national governments to decide. Nationally determined metrics for purposes of setting reference points and measurement of progress, though, have their limitation. When one reviews the VNRs, one cannot but fail to discern an attempt to put national achievements in terms of SDG progress in a better light and a tendency to interpret progress on a positive note. This is often so because the indicators, such as the national poverty line for Goal 1, are different in different countries. However, this is not to say that it is of lesser value. Apart from national M and E exercises, global trackers also monitor and report on the progress of implementation of the SDGs on a regular basis.

[16] Government of Malaysia, *SDG Roadmap for Malaysia: Phase 1: 2016–2020* (2016), www.ekonomi.gov.my/sites/default/files/2021-05/SDG_Roadmap_Phase_I_2016-2020.pdf, accessed 10 June 2024.

[17] NITI Aayog, 'NITI Aayog Releases SDG India Index and Dashboard 2020–21' (2021), www.pib.gov.in/PressReleasePage.aspx?PRID=1723952, accessed 10 June 2024.

For example, the Sustainable Development Report (SDR) prepared by Sustainable Development Network (SDSN) reviews SDG progress on an annual basis;[18] the World Bank's Atlas of Sustainable Development Goals presents visualisation and interactive story telling about the Goals where information on country level progress is periodically reported.[19] The UN ESCAP interactive portal allows to monitor SDG implementation progress in countries of Asia and Pacific. However, while in some cases, the progress reports draw on independently generated data, for most others the data is drawn from country official sources. Concerning the quality of data, it depends. For example, Target 1.1 talks of eradicating extreme poverty by 2030 defined as share of people living on less than \$1.90 a day. Target 1.2 talks of reducing poverty by 2030 by at least 50 per cent, with poverty being defined as people living below the national poverty line. However, these relate to two different reference points. Moreover, where the national poverty line is to be set depends also on the ambitions of countries. Thus, the data needs to be carefully examined to assess actual progress being made on the ground.

D. Conduct of M and E from LNOB Perspective

While M and E exercises are common in view of SDGs, there is a lack of disaggregation which make monitoring progress from the perspectives of LNOB challenging. The distributional aspects – sectional, marginalised group specific, gender dimensions, and so on – often tend to be missing in the M and E reports. Thus, while poverty measures generally indicate a secular fall in percentage of population below the poverty line (be it national or global), there is hardly any reporting on, for example, distributional aspects, income concentration and spatial dimensions. These often tend to remain hidden under the robust average achievements. Bangladesh, for example, is a country where tangible progress has been attained in terms of poverty reduction. However, at the same time income and wealth inequality in the country has been on the rise.[20,21] This is the case also for many other developing countries such as India, Pakistan and Sri Lanka in South Asia.[22] The progress in terms of multi-dimensional poverty (MPI), as envisaged under the SDGs, is not monitored and assessed on a regular basis by most developing countries. M and E exercises tend not to focus on the MPI, as is discernible from a review of the various VNR reports.

[18] SDSN, 'Sustainable Development Report 2023' (SDSN, 2023), resources.unsdsn.org/sdr-2023, accessed 10 June 2024.

[19] World Bank, 'ATLAS of Sustainable Development Goals 2023' (World Bank, 2023). datatopics.worldbank.org/sdgatlas/, accessed 10 June 2024.

[20] The gini-coefficient of income concentration has risen secularly over the past years: from 0.46 to almost 0.50 during the SDG implementation (2016 to 2022).

[21] Bangladesh Bureau of Statistics (BBS) (2023), www.bbs.gov.bd/.

[22] J Hasell, 'Is income inequality rising around the world? (2018), ourworldindata.org/income-inequality-since-1990, accessed 19 June 2024.

The other challenge facing the M and E of SDG progress in developing country settings relates to quantifying the targets themselves, against defined reference points, for purposes of measuring progress. One such example concerns the number of victims of intentional homicide per 100 thousand population, by sex and age and proportion of population that feel safe walking around the area they live (SDG 16.1). In preparing their M and E reports, many countries are found to be lacking data relating to, for example, the safety-related indicator. Monitoring the progress being made in view of this indicator is thus not possible. Another example is the proportion of persons who had at least one contact with a public official and who paid a bribe or were asked to pay a bribe (SDG 16.5). In most cases such data are not available – either not collected, or not reported. Many governments are also not very keen to generate this type of data and information which could show them in an unfavourable light. For example, SDG 4.1 talks of minimum proficiency, in reading and mathematics, of children in various grades. The assessment is to be made on the basis of international learning scale(s) or in view of nationally determined scores. Most developing countries choose to select a national reference point rather than an internationally recognised assessment measure such as the Programme for International Student Assessment (PISA).[23] In most cases PISA results are likely to be significantly below the results as per the national measure. However, such practices are likely to give misleading signals about SDG (Goal 4) progress and have medium to long-term adverse development implications for the concerned countries. Also, when some countries do generate this type of data, it is often not publicly available. Because of this approach, actual progress (or lack of it) can not be measured and reported and monitored in a timely way. Although civil society and rights-based organisations often generate this type of data, these are not accepted by national statistics authorities, either on grounds of lack of representativeness, or more often, on grounds of alleged bias on the part of concerned civil society organisations.

E. Monitoring of Localisation of SDGs

Localisation of the SDGs[24] and monitoring of the progress in this regard is also found to be weak in most developing country contexts. Local government institutions are often under-developed and under-resourced. These lack human, technical and financial resources to undertake M and E of SDG progress. Often the concerned central authority neither sets local level targets nor delegates local

[23] PISA (Programme for International Student Assessment) has been developed by OECD. The relevant score is generally accepted as a reliable measure of the student's competencies.

[24] There is a debate in the literature as to how localisation of SDGs is to be defined. However, localisation is interpreted here in terms of attaining SDGs at the local level, in a disaggregated manner, and by addressing local vulnerabilities and risks and by creating opportunities for taking advantage of the possibilities and opportunities of the local economy.

authorities to do so. This often demonstrates false progress or lack thereof at local levels as many of the SDG indicators remain uncaptured.

F. M and E at the Regional Level

It is to be noted that, in certain regions, respective regional bodies are also participating in M and E activities, by coordinating implementation of specific SDGs and also monitoring progress being made at the regional level. For example, the Association of Southeast Asian Nations (ASEAN) has integrated SDGs with the ASEAN Vision for Development.[25] Assessment of progress is being made based on the understanding that the Vision is aligned with SDG implementation progress. Regional banks such as the Asian Development Bank (ADB) have aligned their corporate results framework and strategy 2030 with the SDGs. Indeed, ADB's contribution to SDG implementation is being assessed in line with its contribution to the progress it is making in areas of SDG implementation.

G. Making Data Revolution Work for M and E

Generating disaggregated data, localising the SDGs and pursuing the LNOB spirit in SDG implementation call for generating reliable data and information that can then be deployed for purposes of monitoring and evaluating SDG progress.

H. Data Revolution in Practice

The SDG talks about Data Revolution, the objective of which is to take appropriate measures to generate reliable, disaggregated and trusted data to monitor SDG progress. Data revolution involves not only generating the needed data, but also data accessibility which is crucial for independent monitoring of SDG progress by NSAs. A number of developing countries have taken a diverse range of measures in view of the above. Some countries went for enhancing the sample size of national household surveys (to ensure that the results were representative at subnational and levels). Some conducted group-specific surveys to monitor the state of progress of left-behind and marginalised groups. It was understood by many developing countries that the vulnerabilities would vary depending on sectional and spatial dimensions (which needed to be identified and defined) and then tackled in the best way possible. For example, in case of Bangladesh, vulnerability was defined in one of the studies as taking 12 different forms.[26]

[25] 'ASEAN Community Vision 2025' (2015), www.asean.org/wp-content/uploads/images/2015/November/aec-page/ASEAN-Community-Vision-2025.pdf, accessed 10 June 2024.

[26] Vulnerabilities were defined in the study in the following terms: income, gender, geographic location, life cycle, civil identity, disability, education and skills, health, occupation, religion and ethnicity,

A number of countries have set up SDG websites and developed trackers which provide information on various SDG-related targets and indicators on a fairly regular basis. Many countries, including Bangladesh,[27] Nepal, India and Malaysia have set up SDG trackers/dash boards to track SDG progress. The degree of disaggregation, spatial and sectional, however, tend to vary. Some countries are also taking advantage of geo-spatial, night-time and satellite data to monitor SDG implementation. India could serve as a good example in this connection. Technology is proving to be particularly helpful in generating disaggregated and localised data and also helping to identify left-behind areas.[28] Many developing countries are paying increasingly more attention to the use of the new technology for M and E of SDG progress. With advancements in artificial intelligence (AI), the internet of things (IoT) and other technologies, there is significant potential for innovative methods of data collection and analysis. However, many developing countries will need targeted global support, technical assistance and technology transfer to help them take advantage of these.

Evidence suggests that many developing countries are investing in strengthening their NSOs. There is also a growing understanding that NSOs cannot do it alone. SDG implementation experience indicates a need for strengthening collaboration between NSOs and the academia, think tanks and other non-state sources of information and data. This may also be seen as a way to strengthen the 'whole of society approach' promoted by the SDGs. Some developing countries have indeed linked up with NSAs, particularly national and international NGOs working in the country, in implementing the various goals and targets of the SDGs. Governments have come to appreciate that public institutions do not have the required financial, technical and human resources to attain the SDGs on their own. This is equally applicable with respect to monitoring progress, particularly if these are to be attained by leaving no one behind and at the local levels. In a number of developing countries, non-governmental organisations (NGOs) and other NSAs working at the grass-roots levels are partnering with respective governments in a number of ways in both implementing and monitoring the SDGs. First, by delivering services to the most vulnerable people in some key SDG areas (health, education, nutrition). Second, by partnering with government programmes as

sexual orientation and shock induced vulnerability (D Bhattacharya and others, *Quest for Inclusive Transformation of Bangladesh: Who Not to Be Left Behind* (Centre for Policy Dialogue (CPD) and Citizen's Platform for SDGs, Bangladesh, 2017), www.researchgate.net/publication/334736152_Quest_for_Inclusive_Transformation_of_Bangladesh_Who_Not_to_Be_Left_Behind, accessed 10 June 2024).

[27] Relevant information is collected through the government administrative set up and aggregated centrally thanks to SDG tracker set up under the a2i (aspire to innovate) initiative of Bangladesh. The a2i is an entity set up at the PMO in Bangladesh which is entrusted to play a key role to realise the 'Digital Bangladesh' aspiration of the government of Bangladesh.

[28] For example, night-time satellite data clearly identifies areas without electricity. Since access to energy and power is a key driver of economic activities from the perspective of industrialisation and development in general, and is a major facilitator of SDG attainment, such data are very helpful in identifying LNOB groups and spatially deprived areas.

implementers, ie governments are spending the earmarked funds through service delivery NGOs. Bangladesh is a pertinent example where organisations such as the Bangladesh Rural Advancement Committee (BRAC) are implementing a number of government projects targeted at the ultra-poor and for health and nutritional improvements of the marginalised committees. It is, however, found that NSOs often tend not to recognise the information NSAs generate as reliable and having the required representativeness. Here, collaboration between NSOs and think tanks and other NSAs in the selection of samples and development of methodology could provide a cost-effective solution to the data problem.[29] Some NSOs and think tanks in developing countries are also actively collaborating with platforms such as the UN World Data Forum (WDF) which have developed rigorous protocols for *A World with Data We Trust*.[30] The Forum has appealed to the international community and national governments 'to work together in the data ecosystem to ensure that governments, policymakers, planners and decision takers invest in national data ecosystem to enable high-quality, timely, open, reliable and disaggregated data'. Since many national governments do not have the required human and financial resources to respond to this appeal, the international community needs to come forward to pool in resources to help reduce the capacity gaps in this regard.

I. National Institutional and Human Resource Capacities

It was noted earlier that many developing countries have set up institutional frameworks to monitor SDG implementation. Ministries and government agencies have set up SDG focal points who report to the National Apex Committees, if not on a regular basis, then at least when VNRs are being prepared. In the case of almost all developing countries training programmes are organised for SDG focal points on how to measure and monitor SDG progress. A major problem here is that the concerned officials get transferred to other Ministries/agencies where they are not necessarily the SDG focal points. Institutional memory gets lost in the process. Development of specialised human resources for SDG-related M and E is found to be absent in the majority of developing countries. Particularly at local levels, government officials lack the training to track and monitor SDG progress. Disaggregation aspects, spatial dimensions and LNOB angle in the M and E process are adversely affected because of this. In many countries, traditional methods are still in practice in the context of evaluating SDG progress

[29] M Rahman, *Tackling data scarcity in developing countries through public-private partnerships* (OECD Development Matters in collaboration with Southern Voice, 2022), southernvoice.org/tackling-data-scarcity-in-developing-countries-through-public-private-partnerships/, accessed 10 June 2024.

[30] United Nations World Data Forum, *Bern Data Compact for the Decade of Action on the Sustainable Development Goals* (2021).

(such as measuring poverty – Goal 1 – against the national poverty line and not using MPI as reference point, or measuring the quality of education – Goal 4 – against national exam scores rather than PISA, as noted earlier). There is thus a need to strengthen institutional and human capacities in the area of SDG-related M and E activities.

J. Growing Urgency of Mobilising Additional Resources

In many developing countries, financial constraints limit the extent to which M and E exercises could be carried out. As noted earlier, SDG implementation calls for significant amounts of additional financial resources. The financing gap to achieve the SDG in developing countries is estimated to be US$2.5–3.0 trillion per year.[31] For example, it has been estimated that Bangladesh would require an amount of about USD 70.0 billion additionally, each year, to implement the SDGS.[32] Many developing countries are not in a position to mobilise such a significant amount of new resources, although this is critical to attaining the SDGs in order to meet many of the targets and goals and to ensure gender parity in education and jobs and build resilient infrastructure, and to achieve the SDGs in general.

K. Importance of Avoiding Silo Approach in M and E

As noted earlier, SDGs are interconnected and implementation is more effective when done with a holistic approach. However, a review of country level experiences of SDG implementation shows that in most developing countries, M and E exercise are Ministry-specific, fails to draw on the synergies involved in SDGs implementation, and has not been able to leverage implementation of the various clusters of SDGs. For example, there was a lacking in terms of drawing on the synergies involved in implementing SDG targets relating to poverty (SDG 1), health (SDG 3), education (SDG 4) and decent jobs (SDG 8); similar is the case with leveraging the implementation of SDGs such as clean energy (SDG 7) and industry and innovation (SDG 9). The silo approach not only slows down SDG attainment but also leads to non cost-effective use of resources. The novelty of the SDGs and the new approach that was required to capture progress, identify gaps and suggest measures to improve the situation is found to be undermined because of the silo approach. The lesson is that M and E process should take into account the interfaces between related targets towards better SDG outcomes.

[31] UNCTAD, *World Investment Report. Investing in the SDGs: An Action Plan* (United Nations, 2014). unctad.org/system/files/official-document/wir2014_en.pdf, accessed 10 June 2024.

[32] Planning Commission, 'Sustainable Development Goals: Bangladesh Progress Report 2018' (2019), www.undp.org/bangladesh/publications/sustainable-development-goals-bangladesh-progress-report-2018, 10 June 2024.

L. Relevance of Cross-country and Regional Cooperation

Attainment of a number of SDGs, particularly those that relate to environment, water resources and forest resources, is dependent on collaboration in the use of regional public goods. Some SDG-related areas do not necessarily follow national boundaries, but align with eco-zones and eco-systems. Without regional cooperation, the relevant targets cannot be achieved on a sustainable basis. M and E of whether sustainable progress is being made in view of these targets and indicators can be appropriately carried out if done from the perspective of the region rather than at the country level. This, however, is found to remain a challenge since, because of cross-boundary tensions (eg India and Pakistan) or disputes over sharing of common resources (eg Bangladesh and India in case of rivers), regional coordination in SDG implementation is largely absent in many instances. Bilateral, trilateral and multilateral initiatives and coordination are required in this connection, both for SDG implementation and for purposes of M and E of SDG progress.

The upshot of the above discussion is six-fold:

- Developing countries, by and large, have taken M and E of SDG implementation progress seriously, and have put in place institutional frameworks for this purpose.
- Many developing countries have demonstrated a keenness on reporting progress through national SDG progress evaluation events which are organised periodically, and also through participation in the VNRs.
- While availability of data and information on progress of SDG implementation has improved over time, disaggregated, spatial and sectional disaggregated data for purposes of tracking, monitoring and evaluating SDG progress, particularly in the spirit of the LNOB, is lacking.
- The 'Data Revolution' that SDGs have promoted so strongly has seen only limited success and many developing countries have not been able to align national statistical systems (NSOs) in tune with the Data Revolution aspirations.
- Undertaking proper M and E requires significant financial resources and technical capacity, which many developing countries lack.
- Global support for SDG implementation, including for M and E of SDG implementation progress, has not been forthcoming in a way that meets the emerging needs. Implementation of SDG 17, which focuses on deepening of global partnerships and extension of financial and technical support to help implement the SDGs and monitor SDG progress, has remained weak.

Developing countries realise that attaining the SDGs is aligned with their national aspirations of an economically developed, socially inclusive and environmentally sustainable future. As the implementation timeline crosses the halfway line, it is also becoming increasingly evident that while most countries are committed to implementing and monitoring the SDG progress, lack of resources have emerged as a serious concern that seriously undermine their efforts on both counts.

Implementation of some of the SDG targets hinges on the efficacy of public-private partnership (eg poverty eradication), some on cross-boundary cooperation (eg combating climate and natural disasters), and others on global initiatives (eg doubling the share of least developed countries (LDCs) in global exports to by 2020). Equity-based, gender-responsive and disaggregated approach adds to the challenges in this complex setting. M and E capacities in place in many developing countries is not capable of addressing these challenges. Global assessment of SDGs progress by reputed organisations such as SDSN and the World Bank testify that if corrective measures are not taken, many of the SDG targets and indicators will remain unattained. Hence there is an urgent need for targeted global support to help strengthen M and E capacities in developing countries.

Based on the preceding discussion and SDG implementation experience across developing countries, the next section proposes a number of actions for improving the effectiveness of M and E of SDG implementation progress.

IV. Towards an Effective M and E in SDG Implementation

The preceding sections II and III have noted the importance of monitoring and evaluating progress from the perspective of attaining the SDG goals and targets in developing country contexts by 2030. The discussion has also identified some of the emergent deficits in this regard as well as some of the innovative and good practices to make the M and E exercise more effective and results-oriented. However, based on the global report on SDG progress (WB, 2023; SDSN, 2023 and Southern Voice, 2023) and observations made in sections II and III, it is clear that developing countries will need to do a lot more if SDGs are to be attained by the final year of 2030. The message is that M and E exercises will need to be carried out in a more rigorous manner, with a view to identifying the gaps, learning from cross-country experiences and drawing on the best practices. It was noted that both implementation and M and E require global support. Without this, it will not be possible to move towards achieving the goals, targets and indicators associated with the SDGs over the next seven years left to reach the finishing line. A number of actions for M and E of SDG progress are preposed in the following section, based on the preceding discussion on the experience of developing countries.

A. Prioritise M and E in SDG Implementation Plans

If the SDGs are to be achieved in developing countries by 2030, M and E of the progress ought to be seen as an integral part of the SDG implementation. Action will be required in a number of areas, some of which are the following: prioritisation of M and E as an action agenda in SDG implementation plans; human and technical capacity building of NSOs and other related entities to undertake M and E activities; investing in generation of data at disaggregated levels; harnessing M and E capacity of NSAs and think tanks. As has been noted, the deployment of the resources required to address these has been inadequate in case of many developing countries. Since SDGs are crossing the halfway mark, now is the time to put in place the hardware, software, human-ware and appropriate institutional mechanisms to monitor, evaluate and take corrective action to address the emerging deficits. Many developing countries have put in place SDG trackers, but these are not equipped to provide disaggregated data that meets the demands of the LNOB spirit of the SDGs and SDG localisation. For redirecting resources where these are most needed for meeting SDG-related areas (e.g. quality of education, reducing cost of migration, enhancing human rights, gender empowerment), there is a need to undertake comprehensive evaluation and assessment of the progress made to date from the vantage points of the LNOB and SDG localisation. There is still time to take mid-course corrective actions and initiate innovative and target-specific interventions to attain the SDG targets by 2030. Developing countries should revisit what changes need to be made in their respective statistical systems in view of the Data Revolution. They must do more to generate the required data, and deeply appropriate tools, so that M and Es can play a more meaningful role towards achieving the goals and targets.

B. Make the VNR Reports a Meaningful Exercise

As noted earlier, many developing countries are coming forward to report on the progress being made in view of specific goals, targets and indicators in the VNRs.[33] These reports will serve their purpose if and when M and E exercises are rigorous and reliable. However, in many instances these are not fully reflective of the actual progress and there is a tendency to showcase the country in a positive light through the VNR reports. Particularly, SDG reporting with respect to some of the Goals such as Goal 16 relating to human rights, independence of judiciary and good governance are often not adequately reflective of the real situation in many countries. Reports prepared by NSA actor groups at the VNRs often tend to differ significantly from the official version of the SDG progress. In view of this, the VNR exercise should ensure inclusion of NSA's views in the reports submitted by participating countries. To note, the VNR Handbook mentions about involving all stakeholders including all sectors and levels of government, civil society, private sector, trade unions, Members of Parliaments and national human rights institutions, both in implementation and in monitoring and evaluation systems concerning SDG implementation.[34] This needs to be ensured for reliable and

[33] The last VNR was held in July 2023 under the auspices of ECOSOC.

[34] United Nations, *Handbook for the Preparation of Voluntary National Reviews.* (United Nations, 2023). hlpf.un.org/sites/default/files/vnrs/handbook/VNR%20Handbook%202023%20EN_0.pdf.

meaningful M and E. This should inform not only the implementation but also the M and E of SDG progress. Developing countries may think of putting in place an institutional framework to include NSAs in preparing the VNRs to enhance their authenticity. The objective should be to take advantage of this volunteerism (Preparation of VNR report is a welcome move) to have a realistic picture of the progress in SDG implementation on the ground (through proper evaluation and monitoring of the results) which will enable developing countries to take mid-course corrective actions and mobilise global support.

C. Mobilise Global Support Towards Monitoring of SDG Progress

When SDGs were designed, it was recognised upfront that many developing countries do not have adequate resources to implement the lofty goals, neither do they have the necessary resources to undertake an ongoing monitoring and evaluation of the SDG progress. The estimated financial gap of US$2.5–3.0 trillion was noted in the preceding section. Indeed, the gap has increased by some estimates by about 56 per cent following the outbreak of Covid-19, totalling US$3.9 trillion in 2020.[35] Concrete actions were promised, on both counts, through financial and technical support and by supporting the capacity of the NSOs to meet the emergent tasks. However, a review of relevant literature indicates significant gaps in the resources required to address the attendant deficits. For example, there were some targets (e.g. SDG 17.2 relating to doubling the share of global exports of LDCs by 2020) for which concrete actions were promised by the global community (the target was to be attained through implementation of the WTO Doha Round Agendas and the WTO decision on duty-free, quota-free market access for all exports originating from all the LDCs).[36] The timeline for this was set for 2020. These targets have not been realised. A number of other such interim targets, mentioned in the SDGs, have continued to remain unrealised. These should be identified through proper M and E exercises and concrete actions of time-bound support must be drawn up.

In recognition of the critical importance of climate change issues for not only sustainable economic development, but for the sustainability of the planet itself, a number of global initiatives have been put in place in recent past years. Since addressing climate change impacts and climate-related vulnerabilities lie at the heart of SDG attainment, these initiatives are contributing to achieving the SDG Goals and Targets. For example, an Agreement to establish a Loss and Damage

[35] OECD, *Global Outlook on Financing for Sustainable Development 2023: No Sustainability Without Equity* (OECD, 2022), www.oecd.org/finance/global-outlook-on-financing-for-sustainable-development-2023-fcbe6ce9-en.htm, accessed 10 June 2024.

[36] The sixth Ministerial Meeting of the WTO (MC-6), held in Hong Kong on 13–18 March 2005 took a decision to provide duty-free, quota-free market access for products originating in the LDCs for 97.0 per cent of tariff lines.

Fund (LDF) was one of the most important deliverables of the COP 27 Summit of November 2022.[37] The Fund is geared to assist countries which are particularly vulnerable to the adverse impacts of climate change. In a similar vein, the 15th Convention on Biological Diversity (CBD 15) resulted in a number of commitments on biodiversity, including a promise to mobilise at least US$200 billion each year for biodiversity-related funding, by 2030.[38] However, negotiations on final details of COP 27 are yet to be worked out and the discussions which followed the CBD 15 have not delineated a roadmap to achieve the target.[39]

Also, there should be an alignment between the SDG targets and the decadal programme taken at the LDC5 Conference in Doha, Qatar, in March 2023, where the Doha programme of actions (DPOA) was endorsed at the highest political level. This decadal Programme of Actions promised a number of concrete steps towards domestic capacity building and strengthened global integration of the most vulnerable sub-strata among the developing countries – the least developed countries (LDCs). There is a need to establish concordance between the SDGs implementation, WTO negotiations and LDC5 decisions. Accordingly, monitoring and evaluation of SDG implementation progress and progress being made in view of the above must be coordinated to see if the promised deliverables are actually being delivered. Other initiatives should also be considered for generating funds for SDG implementation, including debt relief for the highly indebted developing countries. Such initiatives will release much-needed resources to implement the SDGs and also undertake M and E work more effectively.

D. Take Measures to Strengthen M and E at the Local Level

As noted in the previous section, localisation of SDGs remains a challenging task in developing country contexts. As often stated, *all development is local*. Where local governments are strong, they play an important role in implementing SDG targets and monitoring progress of implementation at the local level. However, in majority of developing countries, in view of weak (or in the absence of) strong local level government institutions, there is no mechanism to monitor the progress achieved at the local levels, outside of and in addition to those that are carried out under the purview of the general development plans. One key reason is weak local government institutions which lack the capacity to develop SDG implementation plan for the specific locality and monitor the progress being made in this regard. This is a broader policy issue that concerns whether the developing country is keen

[37] The 27th Conference of Parties to the UN Framework Convention on Climate Change (COP 27) Summit was held in Sharm-el-Sheikh, Egypt in November 2022.

[38] Convention on Biological Diversity (CBDs) are held every two years. The 15th Conference of Parties to Connection on Biodiversity (CBD 15) held in Montreal in December 2022 envisaged that this fund will be mobilised from public and private sources.

[39] CUTS, 'Unity, not division, could help evolve climate, biodiversity finance roadmap' (CUTS 2023), https://cuts-international.org/unity-not-division-could-help-evolve-climate-biodiversity-finance-roadmap/, accessed 7 July 2024.

to strengthen local government institutions or prefers a centralised administration. However, three measures, nonetheless, could be brought to play. First, local level administration should be sensitised about the SDGs and may be asked to identify those goals that are of priority interest in view of local demands. They may be asked to draw plans in view of the identified gaps, as has been the case in a few developing countries. Periodic M and E to assess SDG progress should inform the exercise. Second, governments should collaborate more effectively with NSAs such as grass-roots organisations and local NGOs and engage these in M and E activities. Third, elected local representatives including Members of Parliament should be sensitised about SDG needs in their respective areas and should be encouraged to take a more active interest in the progress being made in this regard. As noted, in some countries, a SDG caucus of Members of Parliament who are playing a lead role in monitoring implementation progress has been formed. These activities should be encouraged and supported by making the human resources required available, and by other means. A greater role of MPs is also crucial from the point of view of redirecting resources through budgetary attention to areas where SDG implementation progress is found to be slow.

E. Strengthen Regional Collaboration

Many SDG-related areas have cross-boundary spillover effects, and their impacts and implications are not confined to national boundaries. For example, in case of environment, water resource management, ecological sustainability and natural disaster management, the importance of cross-border cooperation cannot be denied. The need for this in areas of health and containment of spread of diseases was amply demonstrated during the recent past pandemic time. Neighbouring countries and countries in the same climate-ecological zones need to redouble efforts to deepen collaboration not only to implement the SDGs but also to undertake M and E activities to assess progress. However, there are also good examples to be emulated. As has been noted, the ASEAN grouping has taken an initiative to deepen coordination in both implementing the SDGs and monitoring implementation progress. This is of particular importance since spillover impacts concerning a number of goals and targets are very high (eg SDG 7: Affordable and Clean Energy; SDG 3: Climate Actions; SDG 14: Life Below Water; SDG 15: Life on Land).

V. Concluding Remarks

Drawing on review of relevant literature, VNR reports submitted by many developing countries, global monitoring reports and cross-country experiences involving M and E of SDG implementation progress, this chapter has attempted to capture the progress made in areas of SDG-related M and E, identify best practices, and point out some of the attendant weaknesses. The chapter has made a number of recommendations to improve M and E of SDGs in developing country contexts. The chapter has focused primarily on the experiences of developing countries in Asia. It observed that in most cases SDG implementation and monitoring frameworks have been put in place; important lessons were drawn from the experiences gained in the course of M and E of the implementation of the MDGs. The chapter has noted that ongoing monitoring of progress of implementation of SDGs goals and targets were embedded in the design of the SDGs, a distinctive departure from the MDGs. The chapter noted that countries are trying to generate the needed data to monitor and assess progress also because they are keen to participate in the VNRs and showcase their progress in terms of SDG implementation.

However, as the preceding discussion points out, a majority of countries are falling behind in attaining the SDG targets and in addressing the challenges of Data Revolution. The chapter notes that without disaggregated, micro-level, localised data, it is hardly possible to assess progress in line with the LNOB and localisation spirit of the SDGs, which requires an assessment of how SDG implementation is impacting on lives, livelihoods and wellbeing of marginalised groups and left-behind communities. The chapter in this connection proposed in favour of strengthening the NSO capacity to generate SDG-related data to enable the undertaking of proper M and E, particularly at the local levels and through the LNOB lens. The need for collaboration between NSO and think tanks was highlighted in this connection.

In light of the above, the chapter has identified a number of action areas, both drawing on the deficits identified, and in anticipation of the demands of meeting the goals, targets and indicators of the SDGs. The chapter has drawn attention to the adage that 'what cannot be measured, cannot be monitored, and what cannot be monitored cannot be assessed to capture progress'. It is from this vantage point that M and E exercise is so critical to successful implementation of the SDGs.

The chapter has stressed the need for local level initiatives, the importance of engaging NSAs in M and E activities and strengthening of capacity of local level institutions in this regard and has underscored the need for deepening public-private partnerships to promote a 'whole society' approach in SDG-related M and E and SDG implementation.

The chapter has drawn attention to the point that SDG-related M and E activities, replication and scaling up of best practices and deployment of new tools and frontier techniques of M and E will call for significant strengthening of oversight and monitoring institutions in developing countries. The chapter has identified a number of areas in this connection including human resource development, targeted training programmes to undertake SDG-related M and E, technology transfer to monitor SDG progress, and financial support to strengthen M and E activities, among others.

By any account, the real battleground in the context of SDG implementation will be the developing world. However, many countries are falling behind in terms of the goals and targets. The chapter has noted that global support and commitment towards implementation of the SDGs, and monitoring and evaluation of SDG progress has been, by and large, long on promises but short on delivery. There is a need for concrete actions on the part of global community in this backdrop. Targeted actions at country, regional and global levels will be needed if the aspirations that the global community set for itself back in 2015 are to be attained.

17

Public-Private Partnership and Alliance Building for the Implementation of Sustainable Development Goals

STELLINA JOLLY

I. Introduction

The Sustainable Development Goals (SDGs) encompass 17 aspirational goals with 169 specific targets to achieve by 2030 in an integrated, interdependent, indivisible and inclusive manner, balancing the economic, social and environmental dimensions of sustainable development.[1] SDGs which include environmental protection, labour issues, human rights, climate change, sustainable consumption and innovation under their ambit[2] set ambitious goals for humanity's pursuit of sustainable development.[3]

As aspirational political goals, SDGs are soft laws and do not impose binding obligations on states under international law.[4] Thus, the 2030 Agenda for sustainable development only establishes an 'obligation of conduct' upon states to strive

[1] UNGA, 'Transforming our World: the 2030 Agenda for Sustainable Development' (21 October 2015) UN GAOR 70th Session Supp No 1 UN Doc A/70/1.

[2] UNESCAP, 'Integrating the Three Dimensions of Sustainable Development: A Framework and Tools' (30 December 2015) ST/ESCAP/2737; M Kaltenborn, M Krajewski and H Kuhn, 'Introduction' in M Kaltenborn, M Krajewski and H Kuhn (eds), *Sustainable Development Goals and Human Rights* (Springer, 2019).

[3] VP Nanda, 'The Journey from the Millennium Development Goals to the Sustainable Development Goals' (2016) 44(3) *Denver Journal of International Law and Policy* 389; S Jolly and A Trivedi, 'Implementing the SDG-13 through the Adoption of Hybrid Law: Addressing Climate-Induced Displacement' (2020) 2(1) *Brill Open Law* 69, brill.com/view/journals/bol/2/1/article-p69_69.xml, accessed 27 October 2022.

[4] Å Persson, N Weitz and M Nilsson, 'Follow-up and Review of the Sustainable Development Goals: Alignment vs. Internalization' (2016) 25(1) *Review of European Community and International Environmental Law* 59; RE Kim, 'The Nexus between International Law and the Sustainable Development Goals' (2016) 25(1) *Review of European Community and International Environmental Law* 15; R Pavoni and D Piselli, 'The Sustainable Development Goals and International Environmental Law: Normative Value and Challenges for Implementation' (2016) 13(26) *Veredas Do Direito* 13.

to achieve those objectives.[5] Despite the nonbinding nature of SDGs, the Agenda focuses on the means of implementation and emphasises the importance of partnership between various stakeholders, including the private sector.[6] Paragraph 39 of the Agenda reads, 'the scale and ambition of the new Agenda requires a revitalized global partnership to ensure its implementation. … This partnership will work in a spirit of global solidarity, in particular solidarity with the poorest and people in vulnerable situations. It will facilitate an intensive global engagement in support of implementation of all the goals and targets, bringing together governments, the private sector, civil society, the United Nations system and other actors and mobilising all available resources.'[7] The Agenda also highlights the mobilisation of financial resources, capacity building and the transfer of environmentally sound technologies to developing countries on favourable terms, including concessional and preferential terms as mutually agreed upon, as crucial in effectively implementing SDGs.[8] It acknowledges the role of the diverse private sector, ranging from micro-enterprises to cooperatives to multinationals, and that of civil society organisations and philanthropic organisations in implementing the new Agenda.[9] The significance attached to the private sector needs no elaboration as the private sector has been a key factor in economic growth in developed and developing countries.

It should also be noted that the emphasis accorded to 'implementation' and 'partnership' has further been strengthened through adopting implementation means as a specific SDG. SDG Goal 17 depicts the seriousness attached by the international community to the implementation. It envisages a vision of partnership based on sharing responsibility at national, regional and global levels.[10] Target 17 of SDG 17 explicitly refers to Public-Private Partnerships (PPPs) as a means of building effective partnership to boost SDG investment.[11] It prescribes the states to 'encourage and promote effective public, public-private and civil society partnerships, building on the experience and resourcing strategies of Partnerships.'[12]

Against this background, where SDGs have lucidly stated the importance of public and private sector collaboration, the chapter analyses the role of PPP in implementing sustainable development goals. With this in mind, section II examines

[5] Kim (n 4) 17. See also S Morton, D Pencheon and N Squires, 'Sustainable Development Goals (SDGs), and their implementation: A National Global Framework for Health, Development and Equity needs a Systems Approach at Every Level' (2017) 124(1) *British Medical Bulletin* 81.

[6] UNGA (n 1).

[7] ibid para 39.

[8] ibid. See P Dumitriu, UN Joint Inspection Unit, 'The United Nations System – Private Sector Partnerships Arrangements in the Context of the 2030 Agenda for Sustainable Development' (2017) UN Doc JIU/REP/2017/8, 2.

[9] UNGA (n 1) para 41.

[10] M Bexell and K Jönsson, 'Responsibility and the United Nations' Sustainable Development Goals' (2017) 44(1) *Forum for Development Studies* 13.

[11] R Saner, 'The Need for a High-Quality SDG 17.17.1 Indicator' in R Saner and others (eds), *Making PPPs fit the 2030 Agenda* (Centre for Socio-Eco-Nomic Development (CSEND) and World Association of PPP Units & Professionals (WAPPP), 2021).

[12] UNGA (n 1) Goal 17.

the concept, origin, evolution and necessity of introducing PPP. Section III evaluates the integration of PPP under international conventions. This has been done to understand whether international law in its present state plays a facilitative role in regulating PPP. Section IV explores the incorporation of PPP under MDGs and its transition to being part of SDGs. Section V explores the legal initiatives undertaken by the international community in regulating PPP. The chapter focuses on how the UN Global Compact is relevant in ensuring accountability and transparency in PPP with a human face. Section VI examines the Guiding Principles on People-First Public-Private Partnerships for the UN SDG. The chapter examines how national and local governance can embrace these principles while envisaging PPP models to enhance the attainment of SDGs.

II. Concept, Origin and Necessity of Introducing the PPP

The PPP has evolved and expanded across the world as a durable component of governance. The idea and desire to engage the private sector in the development process have emerged out of the ever-expanding role of the welfare state and the inability of the state to fulfil the responsibility effectively.[13] For instance, in the sixteenth and seventeenth centuries many European countries undertook public works concessions in transportation, waste collection, etc.[14] It was argued that a PPP can combine the efficiency, technical innovation and financial resources of the private sector and the regulatory mechanisms of the public sector, thus bringing accountability to the process.[15] However, the two World Wars exposed the vulnerabilities of private investment, and the focus of the governments again shifted to raising public funds.[16]

In the 1970s, the private sector was again been brought in to overcome the failure of the governments to ensure essential services to the public in the wake of the increased public debt crisis.[17] UK initiated the first systematic government procurement policy through the Private Finance Initiative (PFI).[18] In the Global South, the move towards liberalisation and privatisation enunciated in the 1980s

[13] T Bovaird, 'A Brief Intellectual History of the Public–Private Partnership Movement' in GA Hodge, C Greve and AE Boardman (eds), *International Handbook on Public–Private Partnerships* (Edward Elgar Publishing, 2010).

[14] ibid.

[15] MJ Romero, 'What lies Beneath A Critical Assessment of PPPs and their Impact on Sustainable Development' (*Eurodad*, 9 July 2015) 14, www.eurodad.org/what_lies_beneath, accessed 9 November 2022.

[16] M Frilet, 'Evolution of PPP Concepts and Practice' in Saner and others (n 11).

[17] Jomo KS and others, 'Public-Private Partnerships and the 2030 Agenda for Sustainable Development: Fit for Purpose?' (February 2016) ST/ESA/2016/DWP/148, 1–28.

[18] M Spackman, 'Public–Private Partnerships: Lessons from the British Approach' (2002) 26(3) *Economic Systems* 283.

boosted and consolidated PPP models.[19] In India, the Burman committee appointed to look into solid waste management (SWM) highlighted the need to improve accountability and the level of service through private sector participation in SWM services ranging from the door-to-door collection of domestic waste and commercial waste to setting up compost plants and landfills.[20] Private sector participation or PPPs were suggested in areas where local administrative bodies were not providing services.[21] Many explanations have been offered for the desirability of fostering private sector participation in governance. It is reasoned that the private sector brings the needed efficiency with respect to management, which has generally been fraught with inefficiency in the public sector.[22] In addition, the private sector has had a bad reputation in the past for wreaking havoc on life-supporting ecological systems and contributing to social and political inequality.[23] Hence, it is logical to expect that the private sector, led by corporations, will play its share in addressing and ameliorating these developmental challenges.

PPPs can take various forms, and multifarious jurisdictions have adopted diverse models. Broadly, the PPPs can be categorised into two systems: contractual and institutional.

(1) Contractual PPPs are of two kinds.
   (a) *User pays PPP:* In user pays PPP, a private entity provides service to the public and charges users for the service. For instance, managing a road toll or operating an infrastructure. However, the user PPP brings in issues of equity as people experiencing poverty may be excluded from basic services due to unaffordable tariffs.[24]
   (b) *Government pays PPP:* Government pays PPP is founded on the idea that the government is the source of revenue for the private party. Government payments can depend on the asset or service available at a contractually-defined quality.[25]

[19] Frilet (n 16) 18–19.

[20] 'Solid Waste Management in Class 1 Cities in India', Report of the Committee constituted by the Hon Supreme Court of India (March 1999) 16, swachcoop.com/pdf/BarmanCommitteeReport.pdf, accessed 9 November 2022.

[21] ibid 16.

[22] E Farquharson, C Torres De Mästle and ER Yescombe, *How to Engage with the Private Sector in Public-Private Partnerships in Emerging Markets* (World Bank, 2011); MTJ Kok and HC de Coninck, 'Widening the Scope of Policies to Address Climate Change: Directions for Mainstreaming' (2007) 10(7–8) *Environmental Science & Policy* 587.

[23] See K Baylissm, G Mattioli and J Steinberger, 'Inequality, Poverty and the Privatization of Essential Services: A "Systems of Provision" Study of Water, Energy and Local Buses in the UK' (2020) 25(3–4) *Competition & Change* 478; R Prizzia, 'An International Perspective of Privatization and Women Workers' (2005) 7(1) *Journal of International Women's Studies* 55; Studies have found that 100 companies are responsible for 71% of greenhouse gas emissions, www.activesustainability.com/climate-change/100-companies-responsible-71-ghg-emissions/, accessed 19 November 2022.

[24] J Leigland, 'Public-Private Partnerships in Developing Countries: The Emerging Evidence-based Critique' (2018) 33(1) *The World Bank Research Observer* 103.

[25] 'PPP Reference Guide – PPP Basics' (World Bank, 2017) 8; see also ADB Business Center, *Public-Private Partnership Handbook* (Asian Development Bank, 2008) 29.

(2) Institutional PPP involves the establishment of a joint legal entity represented by public and private partners. The joint entity is mandated to manage the service or developmental activity for which it has been created.[26]

As noted, countries have adopted varied patterns and models of PPP in their governance process. The multiple models and patterns of PPP create ambiguity in developing a concrete understanding of its legal foundation and facets. There are challenges in the operationalisation of PPPs, ranging from poor enforcement mechanisms, inadequate policies, lack of transparency, poor oversight and unequal participation of people in decision-making processes.[27] PPP was adopted in the education sector in Uganda by outsourcing the education service delivery to the private sector. Due to the faulty selection of partners, most selected schools faced resource shortages, and the object of the PPP failed.[28] In many cases, the over-emphasis of the private sector on profit eventually impacted the affordability and accessibility of the poorest sections to basic services. For instance, private sector participation in education and the health sector has not always corresponded with significant quality of health care services for the marginalised.[29] A similar disjointed PPP approach is seen in the (Balochistan) Urban Girls' Fellowship, adopted in Balochistan, Pakistan, to increase the enrolment of girls from the poorest households in the province's districts. However, no coordination was made between the existing programme of the Basic Education Project to produce a better-targeted intervention for girls from the poorest households in the province.[30] Such a scenario points to the need for precise regulatory mechanisms to guide the conceptualisation and operationalisation of PPPs to ensure that PPPs contribute effectively to sustainable development goal implementation.

However, regulatory initiatives cannot be understood only in the domestic context, as many areas where PPPs have been sought are inherently global. Hence, it is important to explore international conventions that provide best practices to prevent instances that occurred in Uganda and Pakistan. The next section analyses how far PPPs have been made an integral part of international environmental conventions.

[26] ibid 41.

[27] 'Public-Private Partnerships in Developing Countries' (Ministry of Foreign Affairs, The Netherlands, April 2013), www.oecd.org/dac/evaluation/IOBstudy378publicprivatepartnershipsindevelopingcountries.pdf, accessed 9 November 2022; see also T Batjargal and M Zhang, 'Review of Key Challenges in Public-Private Partnership Implementation' (2021) 5(2) *Journal of Infrastructure Policy and Development* 1.

[28] Batjargal and Zhang (ibid); see also IK Twinomuhwezi and C Herman, 'Critical Success Factors for Public-Private Partnership in Universal Secondary Education: Perspectives and Policy Lessons from Uganda' (2020) 12(2) *International Journal of Educational Administration and Policy Studies* 133.

[29] AH De Wolf and B Toebes, 'Assessing Private Sector Involvement in Health Care and Universal Health Coverage in Light of the Right to Health' (2016) 18(2) *Health Human Rights* 79.

[30] S Fennell, 'Public-Private Partnerships in Education and the Pursuit of Gender Equality: A View from South Asia' (2014) 5(3) *International Development Policy / Revue internationale de politique de développement* [Online], journals.openedition.org/poldev/1798, accessed 3 July 2023.

III. PPP under International Conventions

The origin of modern international environmental law can be traced to the 1972 United Nations Conference on Human Environment (UNCHE)[31] held at Stockholm, which for the first time saw the international community focusing its concerted attention on environmental problems.[32] However, it should be noted that there was no consensus among the international community on the need to address environmental issues, with the Global South opposed to the idea of environmental protection as an agenda of focus.[33] Though the Stockholm Declaration lacks a comprehensive enunciation of environmental principles, the negotiation laid the foundation for a wide environmental agenda beyond the sphere of conservation to include issues such as development assistance, trade and development.[34] In 1972, most business entities did not consider environmental issues a serious matter of concern. The attitude of many of the companies had undergone a gradual transformation by the time the Earth Summit was convened in 1992.[35] The change in attitude has mainly been to create a brand image and influence consumer choices rather than a genuine interest in environmental protection.[36]

Along with these changes in the attitude of the corporates, the submission of the Bruntland Commission Report and its articulation of sustainable development gave a new fillip to environmental protection by broadening its ambit to include economic and social dimensions.[37] One of the core aspects of the Earth Summit[38] was the adoption of Agenda 21 as a blueprint for furthering sustainable development at all levels of governance.[39] Agenda 21 explicitly noted the inability of governments alone to address the environmental crisis and legitimised the

[31] Declaration of the United Nations Conference on the Human Environment (adopted 16 June 1972, entered into force 17 May 2004) UN Doc A/CONF.48/14 ('Stockholm Declaration').

[32] EB Weiss, 'The Evolution of International Environmental Law' (2011) 54 *Japanese Year Book of International Law* 1, 5; see generally P Birnie, A Boyle and C Redgwell, *International Law and the Environment* 4th edn (Oxford University Press, 2009).

[33] A Najam, 'Developing Countries and Global Environmental Governance: From Contestation to Participation to Engagement' (2005) 5(3) *International Environmental Agreements: Politics Law and Economics* 303, 307; DL Shelton and A Kiss, *Guide to International Environmental Law* (Martinus Nijhoff Publishers, 2007) 35.

[34] P Chasek, 'Stockholm and the Birth of Environmental Diplomacy' International Institute for Sustainable Development, Earth Negotiation Bulletin (September 2020) 1–8, www.iisd.org/system/files/2020-09/still-one-earth-stockholm-diplomacy_0.pdf, accessed 9 November 2022; AM Halvorssen, 'The Origin and Development of International Environmental Law' in S Alam and others (eds), *Routledge Handbook of International Environmental Law* (Routledge, 2014) 39.

[35] M Usui, 'The Private Business Sector in Global Environmental Diplomacy' in N Kanie and PM Haas (eds), *Emerging Forces in Environmental Governance* (United Nations University Press, 2009).

[36] L-G Engfeldt, 'The United Nations and the Human Environment – Some Experiences' (1973) 27(3) *International Organization* 393.

[37] UNGA (42nd Session) 'Report of the World Commission on Environment and Development on Our Common Future' (4 August 1987) UN Doc A/42/427.

[38] Rio Declaration on Environment and Development (adopted 14 June 1992) 31 ILM 874 ('Rio Declaration').

[39] UNCED, 'Agenda 21' (12 August 1992) UN Doc A/CONF. 151/26 (Vol II), 32.

role of private sectors in sustainable development.[40] Agenda 21 urged businesses and industries, including transnational corporations, to recognise environmental management as among the highest corporate priorities and a key determinant of sustainable development.[41] Agenda 21 went on to state that business entities should fully participate in implementing and evaluating activities related to Agenda 21.[42] It identified specific areas like efficient production processes, preventive strategies and cleaner production technologies where corporates can play a major role in reducing impacts on resource use and the environment.[43] It reiterated the rationale for private sector participation by noting that technological innovations, development and the more comprehensive aspects of partnership and cooperation are, to a very large extent, within the province of business and industry.[44] The emphasis on the role of the private sector was understandable; as noted in the previous section, this was also the period where many of the Global North and South jurisdictions increasingly sought the participation of the private sector in their developmental pursuits. In legal parlance, the 'public-private' partnership represented a deviation from the state-centric nature of international law.[45] The role and participation of the private sector became a key reference point for the subsequent UN-led environmental conferences and conventions including the Millennium Development Goals (MDG) in 2000, which enunciated a comprehensive agenda for development.[46] The next section explores the public-private coordination and alliance building integrated into the MDGs and SDQs.

IV. PPP in Development: Millennium Development Goals to Sustainable Development Goals

A. Millennium Development Goals to Sustainable Development Goals

In 2000, the MDGs targeting poverty reduction to the HIV crisis in the world's poorest countries were adopted.[47] The MDGs contain provisions explicitly exalting

[40] LK Caldwell, 'Rio de Janeiro and Agenda 21' in LK Caldwell and PS Weiland (eds), *International Environmental Policy: From the Twentieth to the Twenty-first century* (Duke University Press, 1996); J Dernbach and the Widener University Law School Seminar on Law and Sustainability, 'US Adherence to Its Agenda 21 Commitments: A Five-Year Review' (1997) 27 *Environmental Law Reporter* 1.

[41] UNCED, 'Agenda 21' (n 39) ch 30.3.

[42] ibid ch 30.1.

[43] ibid ch 30.4.

[44] ibid ch 30.2.

[45] S Deva, 'Global Compact: A Critique of The UN's "Public-Private" Partnership For Promoting Corporate Citizenship' (2014) 34(1) *Syracuse Journal of International Law and Commerce* 107.

[46] UNGA, 'United Nations Millennium Declaration' (18 September 2000) UN Doc A/RES/55/2 ('Millennium Declaration').

[47] ibid; See also J Castellino, 'The MDGs and International Human Rights Law: A View from the Perspective of Minorities and Vulnerable Groups' (2009) 13(1) *International Journal of Human Rights* 10.

the role of the private sector. Target 8.E provides that access to affordable essential drugs in developing countries should be provided in cooperation with pharmaceutical companies.[48] It should also be noted that, as a result, generic medicines were being made available to the vulnerable and marginalised sections of society in developing countries.[49] Similarly, Target 8.F focuses on the need to enhance the benefits of new technologies, especially information and communications, to the poorest sections with the cooperation of the private sector.[50] In the context of MDGs, PPP has been fruitful in forging partnerships in sectors like health.[51] Though the MDGs have stressed the importance of private sector participation, it was presented as a North–South cooperation mechanism, and the contours of PPP were driven majorly by companies from Global North by providing aid and assistance to the Global South.[52] This was understandable since the entire focus of MDGs itself was on developing countries.

In 2012, the international community renewed the global commitment to sustainable development at the United Nations Conference on Sustainable Development (Rio+20).[53] It was considered that understanding and integrating the complexity of development and widening the pillars of development could only help achieve the full MDG target.[54] The unprecedented global negotiations, which followed the UN summit, culminated in the adoption of focused SDGs for 2016–30 with an overarching objective of sustainable development.[55] Unlike the MDGs, whose primary focus was developing nations, the targets and goals of SDGs applied to all countries and all people.[56]

All SDGs are interdependent: the realisation of one SDG is contingent on the accomplishment of other SDGs, and achieving one SDG enables states to make strides towards the achievement of the other SDGs.[57] For instance, integrating climate change measures into national policies to achieve the objectives of SDG-13 can complement the availability and sustainable management of water and sanitation (SDG 6) ensure access to affordable, reliable, sustainable and modern energy for all (SDG 7).

[48] Goal 8: Develop a Global Partnership for Development, *UN Millennium Development Goals and beyond 2015*, www.un.org/millenniumgoals/global.shtml, accessed 9 November 2022.

[49] ibid.

[50] ibid.

[51] J Nelson and D Prescott, 'Business and the Millennium Development Goals: A Framework for Action' (UNDP, 2008) 19, gbsn.org/wp-content/uploads/2016/04/Business_and_MDGs2008.pdf, accessed 9 November 2022.

[52] S Kumar, N Kumar and S Vivekadhish, 'Millennium Development Goals (MDGs) to Sustainable Development Goals (SDGs): Addressing Unfinished Agenda and Strengthening Sustainable Development and Partnership' (2016) 41(1) *Indian Journal of Community Medicine* 1.

[53] UNGA Res 288 (11 September 2012) UN Doc A/RES/66/288.

[54] Nanda (n 3) 402.

[55] JD Sachs, 'Goal-based Development and the SDGs: Implications for Development Finance' (2015) 31(3–4) *Oxford Review of Economic Policy* 268.

[56] Nanda (n 3) 407.

[57] P Kumar and others, 'Determination of Hierarchical Relationships among Sustainable Development Goals using Interpretive Structural Modeling' (2018) 20(5) *Environment, Development and Sustainability* 2119.

The attainment of these ambitious, integrated and indivisible goals demands a new approach to implementation involving multistakeholder participation. Scholars have pointed to the interlinkage between the role of private sectors and specific SDGs. Tosun and Leininger have linked private sector competence to SDGs 2 (Zero Hunger), 6 (Clean Water and Sanitation), 8 (Decent Work and Economic Growth), 9 (Industry, Innovation, and Infrastructure) and 12 (Sustainable Consumption and Production).[58] The Agenda 2030 has aptly recognised the role of the private sector and has stressed the need for legal and policy measures to encourage private-public collaboration. However, designing models for private sector participation and collaboration can be challenging given the wide scope of SDGs; no single model of PPP can apply to the economic, environmental and social dimensions of SDGs.[59] As a first step, most jurisdictions have some experience in dealing with varied PPP models.[60] The same should be leveraged further in the context of SDGs. Following are some mechanisms through which private sector participation can be sought in implementing SDGs.

- *Corporate Social Responsibility (CSR):* The most straightforward way businesses can contribute to the SDGs is by respecting human rights, ensuring environmental protection, and facilitating transparency and accountability.[61] Many large companies have established policies of integrating sustainable practices as core business strategies.[62] Apple commits to be 100 per cent carbon neutral for its supply chain and products by 2030.[63] These developments suggest that CSR can be a key factor in promoting sustainability by addressing health, environment and gender issues.[64] However, exclusively relying on corporate responsibility will be leaving the discretion to the companies and will lack accountability.
- *Financing:* It is estimated that US$5–7 trillion a year is needed to realise the 2030 Agenda for sustainable development worldwide.[65] Given the constricted

[58] J Tosun and J Leininger, 'Governing the Interlinkages between the Sustainable Development Goals: Approaches to Attain Policy Integration' (2017) 1(9) *Global Challenges* 1.

[59] Saner and others (n 11).

[60] India is the front-runner in terms of the number of PPP projects and investments. Bangladesh, Pakistan and Sri Lanka have many successful PPPs. Afghanistan, Bhutan and Maldives have not seen much PPP investment.

[61] The Organisation for Economic Cooperation and Development (OECD), *Development Cooperation Report 2015: Making Partnerships Effective Coalitions for Action* (OECD Publishing, 2015) 15.

[62] 'Private Sector Collaboration in Sustainable Development: Experiences from Asia and the Pacific' (UNDP, 17 June 2015) 2.

[63] 'Apple commits to be 100 percent carbon neutral for its supply chain and products by 2030' (Apple, 21 July 2020), www.apple.com/in/newsroom/2020/07/apple-commits-to-be-100-percent-carbon-neutral-for-its-supply-chain-and-products-by-2030/, accessed 9 November 2022; Vishwa Mohan, '24 Companies, including Tata & RIL, Pledge to be "Carbon Neutral"' *Times of India* (6 November 2020), timesofindia.indiatimes.com/business/india-business/24-companies-including-tata-ril-pledge-to-be-carbon-neutral/articleshow/79072359.cms, accessed 9 November 2022.

[64] K Buhmann, J Jonsson and M Fisker, 'Do No Harm and Do More Good Too: Connecting the SDGs with Business and Human Rights and Political CSR Theory' (2019) 19(3) *Corporate Governance* 389.

[65] 'The Sustainable Development Agenda' (UN Sustainable Development Goals), www.un.org/sustainabledevelopment/development-agenda/, accessed 9 November 2022.

government resources, massive private financing will be needed to streamline the SDG process. PPPs are presented as an appropriate model to attract supplementary resources and increase access to capital and innovation. One example is the Sustainable Development Goals Fund (SDG Fund), established as an international multi-donor and multi-agency development mechanism in 2014 by the United Nations. The Fund supports sustainable development through integrated and multidimensional joint programmes.[66] The Green Climate Fund (GCF) has established a Private Sector Facility (PSF) to facilitate the engagement of private sectors at the local and global levels to support climate change mitigation and adaptation projects in developing countries.[67] As of October 2019, 25 private sector projects amounting to US$2.2 billion and mobilisation of an additional US$7 billion in co-financing have been approved. The associated mitigation portfolio is expected to reduce 1.1 gigaton of CO_2 equivalent, while the adaptation portfolio is expected to reach 47 million beneficiaries.[68]

B. PPPs in South Asia

It is also relevant to refer to South Asia as an illustration – South Asia accounts for one-third of the global poor figures, and is low in most socio-economic indexes and parameters.[69] Mobilising adequate financing is critical in South Asia, and the private sector can play a facilitating role in pursuing sustainable development goals in the following ways.

- *Inclusive partnerships:* Public-private coordination brings together diverse stakeholders, including governments; businesses, civil society and international organisations, creating inclusive partnerships that can address the multidimensional challenges of development. For instance, the Bhutan Health Trust Fund (BHTF), through the joint partnership of private and public organisations, financial institutions and individuals, attempts to generate funds to support sustainable and self-reliant primary health care services.[70] Similarly, NITI

[66] 'Who We Are' (Sustainable Development Goals Fund), www.sdgfund.org/who-we-are, accessed 9 November 2022.

[67] 'Private Sector Facility' (Green Climate Fund, 7 October 2019) 4–5, www.greenclimate.fund/sites/default/files/document/green-climate-fund-s-private-sector-facility_0.pdf> accessed 9 November 2022.

[68] 'Green Climate Fund's Private Sector Facility' (Green Climate Fund, 2019) 9, www.undp.org/sites/g/files/zskgke326/files/migration/az/UNDP-AZE-The-Green-Climate-Fund-s-Private-Sector-Facility.pdf, accessed 10 August 2023.

[69] 'Achieving the SDGs in South Asia: An Integrated Approach to Accelerate SDG Progress and COVID-19 Recovery' (United Nations Economic and Social Commission for Asia and the Pacific, 15 November 2021) i-ii, www.unescap.org/kp/2021/achieving-sdgs-south-asia-integrated-approach-accelerate-sdg-progress-and-covid-19-recovery#:~:text=Achieving%20the%20SDGs%20in%20South%20Asia%20calls%20for%20adopting%20an,to%20address%20the%20twin%20challenges, accessed 6 June 2024.

[70] ibid 53–54.

Aayog and the Ministry of Railways in India are spearheading reforms in passenger train operations through the PPP model aimed at better passenger experience.[71]

- *Joint investment and funding:* By collaborating, the public and private sectors can pool financial resources, making it possible to invest in large-scale sustainable development projects that might be otherwise unattainable. For instance, the Dhaka Bypass project supported by the Asian Development Bank, the Bangladesh Infrastructure Finance Fund Limited and the Dhaka Bypass Expressway Development Company, is the first PPP road project in Bangladesh.[72]
- *Knowledge exchange:* Alliance building facilitates the exchange of knowledge and best practices between the public and private sectors, leading to efficiency in management, which has generally been fraught with inefficiency in the public sector.[73] Gandhinagar in Gujarat, India, has successfully implemented rooftop solar panels in schools, hospitals and residential buildings to enhance energy access for urban households.[74] The project has since paved the way for large solar initiatives to connect solar rooftop panels through the grid. This is an example of alliance building facilitated knowledge exchange between the public and private sectors, leading to more effective and evidence-based approaches to achieving the SDGs.
- *Innovation and technology transfer:* The private sector's expertise in innovation and technology can be harnessed to support sustainable development efforts. For instance, CDM projects in India have aided the exchange of knowledge and best practices between the public and private sectors, leading to more effective and evidence-based approaches for mitigating climate change.
- *Policy alignment:* Public-private coordination helps align regulatory frameworks and policies with sustainable development objectives, enabling a conducive environment for businesses to invest in sustainable practices. A 750MW photovoltaic (PV) solar park located in the Rewa district of Madhya Pradesh, India, developed through PPP, is considered to be one of the biggest single-site solar power plants in India.[75] The Rewa Solar Park has been developed and operated by separate private companies on a build-own-operate-transfer (BOOT) basis for 25 years.[76] The experience gained from working of the Rewa Solar Park has helped PPP regulatory frameworks and policies with sustainable development objectives and enabled a conducive environment for businesses to invest in sustainable practices and contribute to the SDGs.

[71] N Ayog, Government of India, www.niti.gov.in/verticals/ppp#:~:text=NITI%20Aayog%2C%20along%20with%20the,experience%20is%20one%20such%20initiative> accessed 10 July 2023.
[72] Public Private Partnership Authority, Government of the People's Republic of Bangladesh, www.pppo.gov.bd/projects-dhaka-bypass.php, accessed 12 August 2023.
[73] Farquharson, Torres De Mästle and Yescombe (n 22); Kok and De Coninck (n 22).
[74] Roof Top Solar, *Public Private Partnerships Lesson from Gujarat* (World Bank, 2022) 1–2.
[75] 'Rewa Ultra Mega Solar Ltd', rumsl.mp.gov.in/, accessed 10 August 2023.
[76] ibid.

C. Challenges in the Implementation of PPPs in South Asia

Although many successful PPPs can be identified in South Asia, several challenges have been identified from the operationalisation of many of the PPPs. The first question is identifying when and where business interests align with development concerns. PPPs can be realised only if there are opportunities for gain by both public and private parties. This can only be achieved when the public sector collaborates with the private sector in risk allocation.[77] Second, it has been noted that many of the PPPs have resulted in serious social and environmental impacts, and the developmental benefits in terms of poverty reduction are far from automatic.[78] For example, the PPP employed in the thermal plant in Mundra, Gujarat has caused severe environmental and health impacts in the form of water quality, impacting the lives of women and girl children in particular.[79] However, rectifying these are possible only in an atmosphere with broad participation of multiple stakeholders.[80]

D. Regulating the Operationalisation of PPPs

India, Bangladesh and Pakistan have introduced legal initiatives to regulate the operationalisation of PPPs. In the Indian context, the Government of India has set up a Public Private Partnership Appraisal Committee to streamline the appraisal and approval of projects.[81] Bangladesh enacted its first Public-Private Partnership law in recent 2015.[82] At the institutional level, the Office for Public-Private Partnership was established in September 2010 as a catalyst to realise PPP projects proactively.[83] Similarly, the Pakistan government has enacted the Public-Private Partnership Authority Act 2016, aimed at promoting the effectiveness of PPP through expeditious project implementation, leveraging public investments, and augmenting transparency.[84] One of the major constraints observed in the

[77] 'Public–Private Partnerships in Developing Asian Countries: Practical Suggestions for Future Development Assistance' (Asian Development Bank, 2021) 7.

[78] *History RePPPeated – How Public Private Partnerships are Failing* (Heinrich Boll Stiftung, 2018): see also A Estache and MA A Rossi, 'Have Consumers Benefited from the Reforms in the Electricity Distribution Sector in Latin America?' (2004) Policy Research Working Paper No 3420.

[79] ibid 11.

[80] E Antonio and C Philippe, *The impact of private participation in infrastructure in developing countries: Taking stock of about 20 years of experience*. No ECARES 2012-043 (ULB – Universite Libre de Bruxelles, 2012).

[81] Public Private Partnership Appraisal Committee (PPPAC) Department of Economic Affairs, India, pppinindia.gov.in/pppac#:~:text=Government%20of%20India%20has%20streamlined,have%20uniformity%20in%20appraisal%20mechanisms, accessed 10 August 2023.

[82] B Anwar and others, 'Meta Review of Critical Risk Factors in PPP Projects of Emerging nations in South Asia' (2018) 52(1) *Journal of Developing Areas* 183. See the Bangladesh Public-Private Partnership Act 2015 (Act No 18 of 2015).

[83] 'Public Private Partnership Authority', www.pppo.gov.bd/ppp_office.php, accessed 10 August 2023.

[84] The Public-Private Partnership Authority Act, 2016, Pakistan, ppp.worldbank.org/public-private-partnership/sites/ppp.worldbank.org/files/2022-03/1462871623_498.pdf, accessed 10 August 2023.

implementation of PPP is the lack of capacity in public institutions,[85] public officials, the private sector, users and other stakeholders to manage the conceptualisation and operationalisation of the PPPs in a transparent manner. Capacity building in the form of training, manuals and tool kits for governments, local bodies and communities is essential so that an increased understanding of the benefits of PPPs can lead to a robust PPP project pipeline across diverse sectors.[86]

In addition, it has been observed that there is a weakness in government-enabling policies[87] and regulatory framework concerning stakeholder participation and transparency.[88] Many PPPs lacked transparency, failed to consult with affected communities, and undermined democratic accountability. As a result, many of the PPPs failed in the face of strong opposition from civil society, local media and other stakeholders. Feedback and consultations with citizens, labour unions, relevant government agencies, private investors, civil society organisations and the media will ensure public support for the project.[89] Hence, it is vital that adequate regulatory and policy reforms are undertaken at the government levels. Such regulatory and policy reforms should focus on technical, fiscal and socio-economic feasibility and environmental sustainability, and evaluate the performance and quality of services delivered at a reasonable cost to society.[90]

Hence, for South Asian countries, it is essential to align PPP services with a focus on the accessibility and affordability of services to the poor. Studies have identified numerous priority areas for the South Asian region where substantial gaps exist in education, health, gender and equality, along with the looming climate crisis.[91] In all these sectors, private sector participation can be encouraged, and many sectors, like education, agriculture and energy access, build on the existing private sector participation.[92] PPPs should also endorse gender equality and the empowerment of all women and girls while also recognising the pivotal role of women in achieving the SDGs.[93] This means private participation needs to be identified in those sectors where PPPs may be viable.[94] Such an approach can be instrumental in areas of human rights, gender issues, etc; hence, PPP needs

[85] The author's interaction with several experts revealed the capacity-building problem.

[86] Draft National Public Private Partnership Policy (Department of Economic Affairs Ministry of Finance Government of India, 2011) 20.

[87] E Eduardo, RD Fischer and A Galetovic, *The Economics of Public-Private Partnerships: A Basic Guide* (Cambridge University Press, 2014).

[88] G Nataraj, 'Infrastructure Challenges in South Asia: The Role of Public-Private Partnerships' ADB Institute Discussion Paper No 80 (2007) 30–31.

[89] 'Facilitating Public–Private Partnership for Accelerated Infrastructure Development in India, Regional Workshops of Chief Secretaries on Public–Private Partnership' Workshop Report (December 2006) 12, wr.indianrailways.gov.in/wr/award/1294730399017_05.pdf, accessed 10 September 2023.

[90] UNDP (n 62) 3.

[91] 'Achieving the SDGs in South Asia' (n 69) 10–38.

[92] ibid 44–47.

[93] 'Agenda 2030 & Public Private Partnership' (*Friends of Europe*, December 2018) 12, www.friendsofeurope.org/wp/wp-content/uploads/2019/04/2018_foe_dpf_pub_agenda-2030_web.pdf, accessed 9 September 2023.

[94] Jomo and others (n 17) 17–18.

to be broad-based in its scope and should consider the critical benefits to marginalised communities.[95] Most of the UNDP-backed PPP initiatives in Pakistan benefited women in the dairy and garment sectors.[96] Developing capacities for implementing PPPs can contribute to an effective pathway to sustainable development.[97]

In the context of SDGs, the successful implementation of goals and targets can be facilitated by a carefully conceived PPP. With their focus on inclusivity and integration, the SDGs require reinvigoration in the operationalisation of PPP, whose definition, modalities and contours have not been clearly understood in the policy and legal sphere. In this context, the challenge for developing nations that lack substantial experience in establishing PPP systems will be to envisage an adequate regulatory, policy and legal framework to ensure transparency accountability, and business practices beyond profit consideration. The international community has been taking earnest steps in that direction– vital among them is the UN Global Compact and Draft Guiding Principles on People-First Public-Private Partnerships (PPPs) for the United Nations Sustainable Development Goals (UN SDGs) by the United Nations Economic Commission for Europe (UNECE). The next section evaluates the UN Global Compact.

V. UN Global Compact

The Global Compact, which brings together corporates, is relevant in ensuring accountability and transparency in PPP with a human face.[98] Established in 1998, the Compact has attracted corporates representing diverse sectors and spanning more than 162 countries.[99] As noted earlier, the varied models of PPPs adopted in developing countries lack accountability mechanisms and face the challenge of ensuring adequate services to the local population. Adequate regulatory mechanisms are essential when private sectors are part of the governance process, and their activities have the potential to impact the rights and lives of people, ecosystems and society.

In this scenario, the Compact builds on the earlier attempts of the international community to strengthen the linkage between human rights and business practices.[100] It draws inspiration from the core principles of the Universal Declaration

[95] R Scheyvens, G Banks and E Hughes, 'The Private Sector and the SDGs: The Need to Move Beyond "Business as Usual"' (2016) 24(6) *Sustainable Development* 371.

[96] UNDP (n 62) 3.

[97] ibid.

[98] UN Global Compact, 'The Ten Principles' (2015), www.unglobalcompact.org/AboutTheGC/TheTenPrinciples/index.html, accessed 9 November 2022.

[99] UN Global Compact, 'Our Participants', unglobalcompact.org/what-is-gc/participants/search, accessed 9 November 2022.

[100] JG Ruggie, 'Business and Human Rights: The Evolving International Agenda' (2007) 101 *American Journal of International Law* 819; OF Williams, 'The UN Global Compact: The Challenge and the

of Human Rights, the Rio Declaration on Environment and Development and the United Nations Convention Against Corruption for the business to follow in four areas: human rights, labour, environment and anti-corruption.[101] The principles are:

- respect for the protection of human rights;
- eliminating all kinds of discrimination in employment;
- upholding freedom of association; and
- providing a space for collective bargaining.[102]

The working of the Compact shows that it has emerged as a forum to share and learn from each other's experience in enunciating better corporate practices.[103] Annual summits of the UN Private Sector Forum organised by the Compact encourage exchanges between government and private sectors and have focused on SDGs since 2015.[104] In addition, local-level networks are established to facilitate the dissemination of the ideals underpinning the Compact. For instance, Global Compact Network India (GCNI) attempts to provide a foundation for Indian business entities in responsible business practices.[105] Although participation in the Compact is voluntary and lacks legal backing, it has gained support from the corporates and increased awareness of their role in attaining SDGs.[106] To encourage further participation by companies, the national governments can prescribe compulsory membership in the Compact for all businesses that want to engage in PPP. Nevertheless, the Compact has not been prepared with the specific intention to operationalise and lay down guidelines on the functioning of PPP and SDGs. The basic objective of the Compact has been to promote doing business with a human face, which can be leveraged in the context of SDGs. However, with its focus on peer learning and sharing of experience, the Compact can highlight the specific issues and challenges faced by companies while engaged in PPP, which can be replicated by other companies in their operations. The Compact has been partnering with various agencies to effectively define and streamline the process of effective implementation of PPP projects.[107]

Promise' (2004) 14(4) *Business Ethics Quarterly* 755; See generally LC Curzi, *General Principles for Business and Human Rights in International Law* (Brill, 2020).

[101] LC Curzi and C Malafosse, 'A Public International Law Outlook on Business and Human Rights' (2022) 24(1–2) *International Community Law Review* 11.

[102] UN Global Compact, 'The Ten Principles' (n 98).

[103] MA Gonzalez-Perez and L Leonard, 'The Global Compact: Corporate Sustainability in the Post 2015 World' (2015) 17 *Sustainability and Environmental Justice* 1.

[104] AH Rashed and A Shah, 'The Role of Private Sector in the Implementation of Sustainable Development Goals' (2021) 23 *Environment, Development and Sustainability* 2931.

[105] Global Compact Network India (GCNI) (UN Global Compact), globalcompact.in/, accessed 9 November 2022; AD Gupta, 'Social Responsibility in India Towards Global Compact Approach' (2007) 34(9) *International Journal of Social Economics* 637.

[106] Deva (n 45) 122–25.

[107] Public Private Partnership Framework for Infrastructure Sector (Global Compact India Network 2017) (VMC Management Consulting, 2017), smartnet.niua.org/sites/default/files/resources/gnci_

In the context of PPP and SDGs, the Guiding Principles on People-First Public-Private Partnerships (PPPs) is the first focused attempt by the international community to infuse a direction and principles for its operation. The next section evaluates the Principles on People-First PPP for the SDGs.

VI. Guiding Principles on People-First Public-Private Partnerships (PPPs) for the United Nations Sustainable Development Goals

SDG 17 calls for a stronger commitment to partnership and identifies PPP as one of the mechanisms that can be used to mobilise investments and promote innovation.[108] However, it has not clarified the most appropriate PPP models and procedures that can contribute to achieving the SDGs across a wide spectrum of sectors like water and sanitation, health and renewable energy.[109] In order to provide direction regarding the way PPPs have to be developed in the context of the SDGs, the UNECE pioneered a 'people-first' approach that ensures PPP projects advance the SDGs by paying attention to the social and equity components and focusing on improving the quality of life of communities.[110] This approach is based on five core project outcomes and 10 guiding principles that deviate from the general notion of profit and the private sector and place the interest of the public at the core. The five outcomes include access and equity, economic effectiveness, replicability, environmental sustainability and resilience, and stakeholder engagement.[111] The outcomes are supported by a set of principles that act as guiding factors for project development.

- ensure people's needs are addressed;
- develop simpler people-first projects in collaboration with governments and facilitate cities and local bodies to develop projects themselves;
- increase skills in delivering people-first projects to empower women, and encourage the private sector to contribute to the necessary transfer of skills;
- greater participation of communities through inclusive policy and legal frameworks and focus on a zero-tolerance approach to corruption;

v360_ppp_infra_framework_detailed.pdf; 'Unilever, UNDP and UNGC Initiate Strategic PPP's Around 2030 Agenda', *Daily Mirror* (11 December 2017) www.dailymirror.lk/print/business-news/Unilever-UNDP-and-UNGC-Initiate-Strategic-PPP-s-Around-Agenda/273-141916, accessed 10 September 2023.

[108] UNGA (n 1) Goal 17.

[109] F Miraftab, 'Public-Private Partnerships: The Trojan Horse of Neoliberal Development?' (2004) 24(1) *Journal of Planning Education and Research* 89.

[110] 'Guiding Principles on People-First Public-Private Partnerships (PPPs) for the United Nations Sustainable Development Goals (UN SDGs), Part II' (UNECE, 3 May 2018), unece.org/fileadmin/DAM/ceci/documents/2018/PPP/Forum/Documents/The_8_Guiding_Principles_for_People-first_PPPs_in_support_of_the_UN_SDGs-Part_II.pdf, accessed 9 November 2022.

[111] ibid.

- place information about projects in the public domain;
- de-risk projects by providing more predictability in the enabling environment;
- use robust and clear selection criteria that can promote value for people;
- use environmental sustainability as a key component of evaluating, awarding and implementing people-first PPP projects;
- ensure that blended financing catalyses private partners to invest in people-first projects;
- avoid debt traps by ensuring the fiscal sustainability of people-first projects and the transparency of fiscal policies.[112]

These principles form the foundation for conceptualising and operationalising PPPs in the context of SDGs. It should be noted that the focus on people-first PPPs was achieved in 2015 alongside the discussions around the Addis Ababa Action Agenda (to stress the societal element of sustainable development).[113]

As a follow-up, UNECE launched an evaluation methodology for evaluating the PPP projects and their alignment with SDGs.[114] This methodology is founded on the following three elements:

- criteria and indicators to show achievement in the five people-first PPP outcomes;[115]
- a weighting system;
- a scoring system to help adjust projects to make them more compliant with people's first PPP outcomes and the SDGs.[116] The methodology is dynamic and will be reviewed based on the feedback emerging from its implementation.[117] The methodology, with its emphasis on access and equity, economic effectiveness and fiscal sustainability, environmental sustainability and resilience, replicability and stakeholder engagements, can be valuable for developing countries. For instance, the 'replicability' criteria specifically include indicators to evaluate the opportunity for technology transfer that contributes to inclusive growth and enhances the community capacity.[118] In addition, public participation and effective stakeholder feedback and grievance mechanisms are essential parts of the evaluation strategies.[119] The evaluation criteria have adequate inbuilt hooks to ensure lasting positive social and environmental

[112] ibid.

[113] J-C Barth-Coullaré, 'The Emergence of People-first PPP' in R Saner and others (eds) (n 11).

[114] UNECE, 'People-first Public-Private Partnerships Evaluation Methodology for the Sustainable Development Goals' (1 October 2021) UN Doc ECE/CECI/WP/PPP/2021/3.

[115] ibid 10.

[116] ibid 23.

[117] RJ Sánchez and J Lardé, 'Public-Private Partnerships under the "People-First" Approach' (*Facilitation of Transport and Trade in Latin America and the Caribbean*, 27 December 2020) 13, repositorio.cepal.org/bitstream/handle/11362/46538/1/S2000676_en.pdf, accessed 9 November 2022.

[118] UNECE, 'People-first' (n 114) 20.

[119] ibid 23.

impacts and address the challenges faced by developing countries while implementing PPP. It is too early to comment on its efficacy as the methodology has just been rolled out to governments in 2022. However, the idea of putting people first and framing a set of quantitative and qualitative evaluation criteria can support governments in identifying, designing and implementing projects aligned with SDGs. Creating awareness and encouraging adequate capacity building for developing nations can be instrumental in implementing these criteria effectively.

Thus, the PPPs originated as a means to complement the service delivery of the governments and have evolved to become a vital partner in the development process at the domestic and international levels. PPPs have been touted as a key player in the humanities pursuit to attain the SDGs. However, for that to happen, the biggest responsibility will be on the governments, who are the stewardess of the PPP. The effective implementation of the PPP and their impact on SDGs would depend on the enabling ecosystem and a system of good governance created by the government[120] which does not just let the windows open for corporations to influence UN processes and domestic governments' decision-making.[121]

VII. Conclusion

SDGs are ambitious goals for the holistic development of humanity. They are soft laws that do not impose any obligations on states but encourage voluntary and universal state participation. The 2030 Agenda focuses on the means of implementation, and partnership between various stakeholders (including the private sector) has emerged as the ideal way to foster SDGs. The private-public partnership is a mechanism where the private sector is engaged in the development process to support the states in fulfilling their responsibilities. On a global level, PPP plays a paramount role in bringing together governments, the private sector, civil society, the United Nations system and other actors to mobilise available resources to foster SDGs. The private sector brings the needed efficiency in management, and hence PPP can be used as a tool to further innovations and support sustainable development projects effectively. There are some challenges in the operationalisation of PPPs, such as poor enforcement mechanisms, corruption, lack of capacity, inadequate policies, lack of transparency, and unequal participation of people in decision-making processes. Designing models for private sector participation and collaboration can be difficult as no single model of PPP

[120] UNECE, 'Guidebook on Promoting Good Governance in Public-Private Partnerships' (2008) UN Doc ECE/CECI/4.

[121] S Deva, 'From Business or Human Rights to Business and Human Rights: What Next?' in S Deva and D Birchall (eds), *Research Handbook on Human Rights and Business* (Edward Elgar Publishing, 2020).

applies to the economic, environmental and social dimensions of SDGs. A challenge to implement SDGs, especially for developing nations that lack substantial experience in establishing PPP systems, has been formulating adequate regulatory, policy and legal frameworks to ensure transparency, accountability and a business practice beyond profit consideration. Keeping this in view, the Global Compact was introduced to strengthen the linkage between human rights and business practices. Although it did not lay down guidelines on the functioning of PPP and SDGs, it enumerated universal principles ensuring accountability and transparency in PPP with a human face. Eventually, these efforts led to the first focused attempt by the international community to draft principles for the operationalisation of PPPs in the form of the Guiding Principles on People-First Public-Private Partnerships. It propounded a 'people-first' approach to ensure that PPP projects advance the SDGs by paying attention to the social and equity components and focusing on improving communities' quality of life. With these international regulatory developments, PPP can be effectively utilised as a durable component of governance to foster SDGs. But in the end, the viability of PPP as a tool to achieve SDGs depends on the commitment of the states to provide an enabling ecosystem for effective implementation of the PPP.

18

Development Cooperation: Southern Voices for the South

ABDUL PALIWALA

I. Introduction

Historically development cooperation was seen as a North–South affair, with the 'developed' Northern countries 'assisting' 'developing countries' to reach their state of development. Development was apparently initiated by a famous statement of President Truman.[1] The true beginning of 'development' in fact lies in calls from President Sun Yat Sen in 1921 and Haile Selassie in 1945 for restructuring of global relationships ravaged by imperial adventures.[2] These Southern calls continued through the Bandung Conference and subsequent calls for a New International Economic Order, and have continued in recent times including demands for repatriation for imperial injustices.[3] This has resulted in the various avatars of development from economic growth to human, needs and sustainable development reflected in Sustainable Development Goal (SDG) 17's call to 'strengthen the means of implementation and revitalize the Global Partnership for Sustainable Development'.[4] I suggest that the current law, development and sustainable development constitute sticking plasters for the real struggles of Global South peoples against global social economic environmental, cultural and legal injustices.[5] There is need for a deconstruction of the terminology of law and

[1] H Truman, 'Inaugural Address' 20 January 1949, www.trumanlibrary.gov/library/public-papers/19/inaugural-address. He called for 'making the benefits of our scientific advances and industrial progress available for the improvement and growth of underdeveloped areas'; G Esteva, 'Development' in W Sachs (ed), *The Development Dictionary: A Guide to Knowledge as Power* (Zed Books, 2010) ch 1.

[2] A McVety, 'Wealth and Nations: The Origins of International Development Assistance' in S Macekura and E Manela (eds), *The Development Century: A Global History* (Cambridge University Press, 2018) 21, 25.

[3] See generally L Eslava, M Fakhri and V Nesiah (eds), *Bandung, Global History and International Law: A Collection* (Cambridge University Press, 2017); UNITAR, *Progressive Development of the Principles and Norms of International Law Relating to the New International Economic Order* (UN Institute for Training and Research, 1983).

[4] UN Sustainable Development Goals, Goal 17, sdgs.un.org/goals/goal17.

[5] S Adelman and A Paliwala (eds), *The Limits of Law and Development* (Routledge, 2021) and *Beyond Law and Development: Resistance, Empowerment and Social Injustice* (Routledge, 2022).

development, so as to strip it of colonial and post-colonial hegemonic meanings. North–South development cooperation requires understanding of the environment and real needs, wishes and desires of the peoples of the Global South and the effective ending of historic and contemporary injustices. This applies also to increasing South–South cooperation based on the growing economic power of some countries and the establishment of South-based institutions and development banks. South–South cooperation has also been dependent on North–South development ideologies.

Global South struggles against injustices find echoes in the reemergence of the voices of the Global South, especially in the relational epistemologies of Ubuntu, Buen Vivir, Sumak Kawshay, Maori Tē Atānoho and Kaitaki, ecological swaraj (*liberation*), and radical ecological democracy.[6] These are key to South–North and South–South cooperation for reconstruction of global social, economic, cultural, environmental and legal justice.

II. Sustainable Growth as Neoliberalism

The term sustainable development has become the latest avatar of developmentalism. On the positive side it appears to be a concession to those seeking social and environmental justice. However, there is an inherent anachronism in having a juxtaposition of the terms. Development has become so associated with the mantra of growth in neoliberal capitalism that it becomes impossible to give a real meaning to sustainability other than one involving a very subservient status. That is, sustainability becomes an appendage of growth and neoliberal capitalism. This can be seen in the examination of the UNs Sustainable Development Goals. The main criticism has been levelled at Goal 8 which demands the promotion of 'Sustained, Inclusive and Sustainable Economic Growth'. Critics such as Hickel, Ponte, Kotzé and Adelman question the notion of growth itself.[7] Apart from the failure of growth-based development to deliver for vast numbers of global peoples, it has condemned the world to a disastrous global climate crisis as well as a range of environmental crises. The idea of sustainable growth is based on the notion of green capitalism, when what is needed for planet survival is a questioning of the whole system of production and consumption – of the idea of growth itself. The non-questioning permits states and enterprises to pay lip service to the idea of sustainability.

[6] E Gudynas, 'Beyond Varieties of Development: Disputes and Alternatives' (2016) 37 *Third World Quarterly* 721; A Kothari, F Demaria and A Acosta, 'Buen Vivir, Degrowth and Ecological Swaraj: Alternatives to Sustainable Development and the Green Economy' (2014) 57 *Development* 362.

[7] J Hickel, 'Is Global Inequality Getting Better or Worse? A Critique of the World Bank's Convergence Narrative' (2017) 38 *Third World Quarterly* 2208; S Ponte, *Business, Power and Sustainability in a World of Global Value Chains* (Pluto, 2019); L Kotzé and S Adelman, 'Environmental Law and the Unsustainability of Sustainable Development: A Tale of Disenchantment and of Hope' (2022) *Law & Critique*.

III. Southern Voices: Relationality

The tinkering with sustainability is challenged by reassertion of indigenous ideologies of the Global South – of peoples who have suffered most from historic and contemporary depredations. Among the most significant have been the Latin American ideas of *Pachamama* and *Buen Vivir*, African *Ubuntu* and Maori *Kaitaki* or Five Wellbeings.[8] These relationality conceptions challenge the hierarchical relationship between humans and non-human environment. For example, Pachamama envisages that mother earth and all things within it have rights of reciprocity. World-renowned native American botanist Robin Wall Kimmerer uses berries to illustrate relationality among humans and between humans and the environment:

> The berries are always present at our ceremonies. They join us in a wooden bowl. One big bowl and one big spoon, which are passed around the circle, so that each person can taste the sweetness, remember the gifts, and say thank you. They carry the lesson, passed to us by our ancestors, that the generosity of the land comes to us as one bowl, one spoon. We are all fed from the same bowl that Mother Earth has filled for us. It's not just about the berries, but also about the bowl. The gifts of the earth are to be shared, but gifts are not limitless. The generosity of the earth is not an invitation to take it all. Every bowl has a bottom. When it's empty, it's empty. And there is but one spoon, the same size for everyone.
>
> How do we refill the empty bowl? Is gratitude alone enough? Berries teach us otherwise. When berries spread out their giveaway blanket, offering their sweetness to birds and bears and boys alike, the transaction does not end there. Something beyond gratitude is asked of us. The berries trust that we will uphold our end of the bargain and disperse their seeds to new places to grow, which is good for berries and for boys. They remind us that all flourishing is mutual. We need the berries and the berries need us. Their gifts multiply by our care for them, and dwindle from our neglect. We are bound in a covenant of reciprocity, a pact of mutual responsibility to sustain those who sustain us. And so the bowl is filled.[9]

Such relational voices echo Eastern philosophies of Buddhism, and the ancient Greeks. They are revived by feminist and community ethics of care to replace the failures of modernity.[10] Human beings are not self-founding, self-motivated autonomous subjects of classical liberalism, but are born in a state of helplessness,

[8] Kothari, Demaria and Acosta (n 6); E Gudynas, 'Buen Vivir: Today's Tomorrow' (2011) 54 *Development* 441; C Spiller and others, 'Relational Well-Being and Wealth: Māori Businesses and an Ethic of Care' (2011) 98 *Journal of Business Ethics* 153.

[9] RW Kimmerer, *Braiding Sweetgrass: Indigenous Wisdom, Scientific Knowledge and the Teachings of Plants* (Milkweed Editions, 2013).

[10] M Lupisella, *Cosmological Theories of Value: Science, Philosophy and Meaning in Cosmic Evolution* (Springer, 2020); C Rovelli, *Helgoland* (Allen Lane, 2021); D O'Neill and others, 'A Good Life for All Within Planetary Boundaries' (2018) 1(2) *Nature Sustainability* 88; O Onazi, *An African Path to Disability Justice: Community, Relationships and Obligations* (Springer Nature, 2020).

and from birth are dependent on others for care and continue to be connected with others throughout life for a variety of needs.[11] In other words, no one is born an independent and autonomous citizen; we require care and support from others. Yet relations of care are not to be read as subservience to exploitative systems of gender, indigenous or class injustices, but ones which enable forms of resistance to ensure balance in otherwise unbalanced relationships.[12] Remarkably these ideas also find an echo in scientific departures from the fixed certainties of Newtonian physics to post-Einsteinian affirmation of relationality in quantum theory.[13]

Thus a relational approach to sustainable development has to be located in the idea of 'just sustainability' where sustainability has to involve flexible practices which connect humans in non-dominant cultural, ecological, technological and economic relationships with their environment.[14] This idea of relational sustainable regulation can be illustrated by the 2020 initiative of the Union of Indigenous Communities of Lomerío (CICOL) which had obtained regulatory autonomy over its territory to develop a range of activities to control wild fire risks. These included 'a written burning protocol, a fire monitoring programme, water basin and forest conservation policies, participatory research conducted by indigenous researchers about the use of fire in Lomerío and cultural revitalization strategies'.[15] The communities resisted the threats and blandishments of the Bolivian Fire Prevention Agency in relation to their fire use practices. The difference between the two approaches was that indigenous holistic land and forest use policies were more protective of their natural resources than statist regulatory strategies which categorised indigenous fire practice as a primary fire risk rather than the responsibility of contemporary destructive farming, mining and forest logging techniques. A similar recent relational regulatory initiative involves the joint creation of the Nunatsiavut Conservation Area in the Arctic between the Canadian government and the Inuit as an exercise in just sustainable conservation of the Arctic.[16]

[11] J Butler, *Precarious Life: The Powers of Mourning and Violence* (Verso, 2006) 32; L Davy, 'Negotiating Between an Ethic of Care and an Ethic of Autonomy: Relational Autonomy, Disability, and Dependency' (2019) 24 (3) *ANGELAKI Journal of the Theoretical Humanities* 101.

[12] Davy (ibid).

[13] Lupisella (n 10); Rovelli (n 10) 44.

[14] R Datta, 'A Relational Theoretical Framework and Meanings of Land, Nature, and Sustainability for Research with Indigenous Communities' (2014) *Local Environment: The International Journal of Justice and Sustainability*; A Escobar, 'After Nature: Steps to an Antiessentialist Political Ecology' (1999) 40 (1) *Current Anthropology* 1.

[15] I Rodriguez and others, 'Decolonizing Wildfire Risk Management: Indigenous Responses to Fire Criminalization Policies and Increasingly Flammable Forest Landscapes in Lomerío, Bolivia' (2023) 147 *Environmental Science and Policy* 103.

[16] O Michelin, 'New Dawn for Arctic's First People: The Inuit Plan to Reclaim their Sea', *The Guardian* (27 August 2023).

IV. Failures of North–South Cooperation

The idea of cooperation is enshrined in SDG Goal 17 of 'revitalising the global partnership for sustainable development'. Instead, the ideology of developmentalism has enabled the North to ensure a post-imperial, post-colonial embrace of the South. 'Trickle-down' development has always been a contested ideology. The orthodoxy suggests that some of the gains of the 'development' of the North can be passed on to the Global South so that it can grow and develop through a modernisation of backward institutions.[17] More insidiously, 'trickle-down' is a device to strengthen the economic hold of the North over the South through powerful global corporations to capture valuable Southern resources.[18] Thus the post-colonial South is welcomed to join international organisations including the UN and its agencies such as the Office of the UN High Commissioner for Refugees (UNHCR) and the United Nations Development Programme (UNDP), and the Bretton Woods organisations – the International Monetary Fund (IMF), the World Bank and the World Trade Organization (WTO).[19] This embrace has been sought by South countries, yet they have long understood its unequal nature with power residing in the dominant countries of the North. 'At the heart of the hierarchy of states is the paradox of sovereignty where formal equality of states coexists with the institutionalisation of unequal relations of economic, political and ideological power between former colonial powers and colonised nations'.[20] Successive attempts by developing countries to redress the balance, through the Bandung Conference, a New International Economic Order, a Development Round of the WTO, debt forgiveness, reparations for imperial/colonial depredations, and for the principle of differential responsibility in relation to climate change, have met with rhetorical acceptance and effective denial.[21]

The apparent benefits for the South of developmentalism are recognition of their sovereignty and access to multilateral and bilateral aid. Sovereignty is an overdue recognition of the end of colonialism, thus countries of the South are apparently equal members of the UN and its agencies and also of the Bretton Woods organisations. Yet, effective power is retained by the powerful countries whether it be in membership of the UN Security Council as opposed to the

[17] G Rist, *The History of Development: From Western Origins to Global Faith* (Zed Books, 2008).

[18] A Escobar, *Encountering Development: The Making and Unmaking of the Third World* (Princeton University Press, 2012); HW Arndt, 'The "Trickle-down" Myth' (1983) 32 *Economic Development and Cultural Change* 1.

[19] J Faundez, 'Between Bandung and Doha: International Economic Law and Developing Countries' in Adelman and Paliwala, *The Limits of Law and Development* (n 5) 147.

[20] R D'Souza, 'International Law and Development: From "Company Raj" to Global Governance via Indirect Rule' in Adelman and Paliwala, *The Limits of Law and Development* (n 5) 167, 168.

[21] Faundez (n 19).

General Assembly, and quota based voting power in the IMF and World Bank.[22] Even at the consensus-based WTO, real decisions often happen in 'green rooms' historically dominated by the North. Alternatively, the WTO process is by-passed by unequal bilateral treaties.[23] Global corporations use unequal trade to transfer valuable resources to the North. The charters of the UN, WTO, World Bank and IMF enable the Northern embrace. The WTO's mantra of unrestricted free trade,[24] and World Bank and IMF conditionalities promote neoliberalism. The price for financial aid was economic liberalisation by opening up markets to global investment and trade – to accept a model of development which advanced Northern global interests at the expense of their own agency and autonomy.[25] The neoliberal global order generates the injustices of poverty, economic inequality and environmental costs that 'diminish the agency of the poor and render them more vulnerable to economic and political coercion'.[26] Protest and resistance ultimately led to apparent softening of conditionalities regimes through poverty relief strategies 'owned' by the supplicant states themselves. Yet, this apparent yielding led to a fundamental configuration of global governance through networks involving states, supranational bodies, private foundations and global corporations. The Foucauldian power embrace was retained through acceptance by supplicant countries of a self-imposition, or responsibilisation, of neoliberalism with sticking plaster obeisance to the idea of poverty relief.[27] International financial institutions reflect US strategies subtly by staff either consciously demonstrating their support for their largest financial backer's interests or unconsciously sharing their worldview.[28] Northern strategies respond to shifts in global geopolitics such as the rise of China, and the socio-economic as well as the political position of the donees.

At first glance, SDG 17's call to 'revitalize the Global Partnership' and emphasise 'multi-stakeholder partnerships' appears to involve a paradigm change by the Global North in acknowledging the need to ensure development which meets the interests of the Global South as well as environmentally sound strategies. A research study of SDG 17 found uncertainty among participants as to whether it represented a Western or Southern perspective on development.[29] History and

[22] JW McArthur and E Werker, 'Developing Countries and International Organizations: Introduction to the Special Issue' (2016) 11 *Review of International Organisations* 155.

[23] K Hopewell, *Breaking the WTO* (Stanford University Press, 2016) especially ch 3; T Soobramanien, B Vickers and H Enos-Edu, *WTO Reform: Reshaping Global Trade Governance for 21st Century Challenges* (Commonwealth Secretariat, 2019).

[24] Hopewell (ibid).

[25] D Ingram, *World Crisis and Underdevelopment: A Critical Theory of Poverty, Agency, and Coercion* (Cambridge University Press, 2017).

[26] ibid 190.

[27] H Thörn, 'Aid(s) Politics and Power: A Critique of Global Governance' (2011) 38 *Politikon* 433.

[28] R Clark and L Dolan, 'Pleasing the Principal: U.S. Influence in World Bank Policymaking' (2021) 65 *American Journal of Political Science* 36, 37.

[29] A Maltais, N Weiss and A Persson, *SDG 17 Partnership for the Goals: A Review of Research Needs* (Stockholm Environmental Research Institute, 2018).

current practice suggest that it represents a milder version of trickle-down: assistance is given provided it does not affect the dominant interests of the Global North. This is apparent, as shown below, in relation to a range of issues, whether it is aid transfers and debt forgiveness, intellectual property rights, AIDS and Covid medicines and refugee regimes. For Ingram, the antidote to domination and coercion is a global social contract involving a duty to improve the lives of fellow participants appended to a political duty to create just international relations.[30]

A. Aid: North to South or South to North?

Aid from the North to the South seems a vehicle for development. The aid flows are substantial, involving $125 billion in 1917 rising to $185 billion in 2021, an increase of 4.4 per cent on the previous year, although a significant amount of this aid was donations of Covid-19 vaccines.[31] The UN General Assembly Resolution 2625 of 24 October 1970[32] adopted a target of 0.7 per cent of Gross National Income for aid from developed to developing countries which was subsequently endorsed by the EU and other major economies although not the USA. Very few countries have adhered to this aid target. The UK which had adopted a 0.5 per cent principle has subsequently reneged even on this amount.[33] Under a Faustian pact, the cost of aid was the acceptance of 'Washington Consensus' and neoliberalism. Resistance and global protests led to amelioration of policies, resulting in a focus on country ownership and pro-poor growth. After the global financial crash of 2008, the Bretton Woods Institutions seemed to declare that the Washington Consensus was dead – according to the then IMF president: 'We do not do that anymore.'[34] In the post-Washington Consensus period, global institutions are paying greater regard to the role of the state and also to institutional development, income distribution and the social sector. However, these are in the main appended to policies which emphasise the private sector dominated by global corporations with an emphasis on growth and integration into the global economy.[35] A Cambridge University Study found that there has been little change.[36] Instead of promoting local industries through tariffs or other forms of state activism, the Bretton Woods Institutions continue to favour integration of South countries into the global economy.[37]

[30] Ingram (n 25).
[31] UN Sustainable Development Goals Website, Goal 17, sdgs.un.org/goals/goal17; Hickel (n 7). References to $ throughout are to US$.
[32] UNGA RES 2625 (XXV) (October 24, 1970) UN Doc A/RES/2625 (XXV).
[33] R Fenner and T Cernev, 'The implications of the Covid-19 pandemic for delivering the Sustainable Development Goals' (2021) 128 *Futures* 102276.
[34] Transcript of the International Monetary and Financial Committee (IMFC) Press Briefing, 12 April 2014, www.imf.org/en/News/Articles/2015/09/28/04/54/tr041214b.
[35] J Marangos, *International Development and the Washington Consensus* (Routledge, 2020) 202.
[36] AE Kentikelenis, TH Stubbs and LP King, 'IMF conditionality and development policy space, 1985–2014' (2016) *23 Review of International Political Economy* 543.
[37] Thörn (n 27).

At the same time, recent policies of states in the North, especially of the USA, seem to be abandoning the principle of free trade.[38] The underlying consideration is that donors primarily desire to advance their own interests whether political, economic or strategic, with the formal goals involved in the aid transaction being subordinate rather than irrelevant.[39] Much of the 'aid' funding may in fact be spent in paying international consultants or in the purchase of goods and services from the donor or other Northern country.[40]

Remarkably, flows towards the Global South are vastly offset by flows going in the opposite direction – from South to North! Thus South countries pay over $200 billion in interest payments to the North each year and $500 billion in repatriation of profits. In addition illicit financial flows amounted to $2 trillion in 2012, of which $1.6 trillion in 2018 were mis-invoiced trade-related flows, robbing countries of vitally needed capital and exacerbating global inequality.[41]

B. Refugees and Displaced Persons

As of 2022 there were nearly 90 million globally displaced people including refugees; asylum seekers suffering among other things from oppressive regimes and the effects of warfare, often involving and thus the responsibility of North and South countries, as in Afghanistan, Iraq, Syria and now Ukraine and the devastation in Gaza as well climate displacement. Remarkably 83 per cent were located in the regions of the Global South compounding the already serious social and economic problems in those countries.[42] According to the UN High Commissioner for Refugees: 'To effectively achieve the Sustainable Development Goals, it is imperative to improve the situation of refugees, internally displaced and stateless people and to implement sustainable solutions, particularly in conflict-affected regions'.[43] Underlying this is the idea of global solidarity, which according to Moreno-Lax denotes shared responsibility towards third countries as well as

[38] J Bacchus, 'Biden and Trade at Year One: The Reign of Polite Protectionism' (2022) *CATO Policy Analysis* 926.

[39] M Rahman and L Giessen, 'Formal and Informal Interests of Donors to Allocate Aid: Spending Patterns of USAID, GIZ, and EU Forest Development Policy in Bangladesh' (2017) 94 *World Development* 250; D MacNeill, *The Contradictions of Foreign Aid* (Routledge, 2019).

[40] MacNeill (ibid); J Bennett, 'Consultants earn £11bn in aid cash. Charity group reveals consultancy fees help flatter G7 aid donations by billions' (2005) *Accountancy Age* 9; B Whitty and others, 'Outsourcing the Business of Development: The Rise of For-profit Consultancies in the UK Aid Sector' (2023) *Development and Change*.

[41] Hickel (n 7); 'Trade-Related Illicit Financial Flows in 134 Developing Countries 2009–2018' (2021) *Global Financial Integrity*, gfintegrity.org/report/trade-related-illicit-financial-flows-in-134-developing-countries-2009-2018/.

[42] C Smith, 'Towards Genuine Responsibility-Sharing in the International Refugee Regime: Solidarity and Resettlement as a Response to Unequal Burdens and Democratic Spoilers' (2022) 70(6) *Canadian International Council*.

[43] 'Sustainable Development Goals' (UNHCR UK), www.unhcr.org/uk/sustainable-development-goals.html, accessed 3 April 2024.

to asylum seekers and refugees.[44] The global refugee regime is under threat.[45] Whereas the Global South largely bears the burden of responsibility, the rhetoric of a global sense of responsibility or solidarity, while propounded in various fora, has largely remained a rhetoric. The North countries have adopted policies to prevent migrants including displaced persons from entering their territories, including building walls or fences to create fortresses as part of election-winning strategies. Thus, while the Africa-EU Strategic Partnership grandly adopts the rhetoric of solidarity and burden-sharing, the reality has been limited subsidies for the countries to keep the displaced penned in.[46] The New York Declaration for Refugees and Migrants and the Comprehensive Refugee Response Framework 2016, have been largely unsuccessful.[47] Thus the Declaration's Global Compact on Responsibility Sharing for Refugees 'recognize[d] that international cooperation and solidarity in shouldering the burden are fundamental in assisting States faced with large-scale refugee displacement in hosting refugees', and 'commit[ted] to an equitable sharing of responsibility for hosting and supporting refugees, while taking account of differing capacities and resources among States'.[48] Yet, the final text of the non-binding New York Declaration removed reference to responsibility-sharing in the title and postponed implementation for two years.[49] The lack of progress is underlined in the UNHCR Indicator Report on the Compact for 2021 with an effective worsening of the burden of responsibilities between developed and developing country host states.[50]

C. Climate Crisis

SDG 13 calls for 'urgent action to combat climate change and its impacts'. Unfortunately, the global cooperation demanded suffers from hypocrisy. The UN Framework Convention on Climate Change of 1992 acknowledged the impact of 'increasing the atmospheric concentrations of greenhouse gases' on climate change and recognised that developed countries were overwhelmingly the largest emitters, in contrast with low emissions in developing countries.[51] All countries were to reduce greenhouse emissions but, significantly, under Article 2(3) and (4) developed countries should assist developing countries in their endeavours

[44] V Moreno-Lax, 'Solidarity's Reach: Meaning, Dimensions and Implications for EU (external) Asylum Policy' (2017) 24(5) *Maastricht Journal of European and Comparative Law* 740.
[45] *Geneva Convention Relating to the Status of Refugees*, UN 1951 and Protocol of 1967; D Stevens, 'Access to Justice for Refugees' in Adelman and Paliwala, *Beyond Law and Development* (n 5) 198.
[46] M Strange and B Oliveira Martins, 'Claiming Parity between Unequal Partners: How African Counterparts Are Framed in the Externalisation of EU Migration Governance' (2019) 5(3) *Global Affairs* 235.
[47] Stevens (n 45).
[48] UNGA RES A/73/12 (2018) UN Doc A/RES/73/151.
[49] Stevens (n 45).
[50] '2023 Global Compact on Refugees Indicator Report' (UNHCR – The UN Refugee Agency), www.unhcr.org/media/2023-global-compact-refugees-indicator-report.
[51] S Treaty Doc No 102–38, 1771 UNTS 107.

to reduce greenhouse emissions and minimise the adverse effects of climate change. The Kyoto Protocol of 1997 affirmed these principles and established an obligation to reduce emissions by 5 per cent below 1990 levels.[52] The Paris Agreement of 2015 obliged states to make commitments to avoid temperatures rising 2 degrees over preindustrial levels and to work towards net zero emissions after 1950.[53]

Northern hydrocarbon corporations and regimes, including the USA (in particular under former President Trump), Australia and Brazil until recently, have indulged in climate change denial, with corporations employing underhand practices.[54] These strategies have consistently helped to undermine, delay and/or minimise effective action. Although the obligations established involve significant progress at a legislative level, they are notable for their lack of fulfilment. Much damage has been done by the on/off attitude to the agreements from the USA, a major polluter. Frequently, this is on the basis that China and India had become major emitters and should take on greater obligations, but also because of the Trump administration's negativity on the climate crisis. While the Biden administration has ratified the Paris Convention, it has been prevented from taking effective action by Republican and some Democratic climate deniers. In 2009, countries had agreed that developed countries should provide $100 billion a year to developing countries by 2020 through to 2025. The understanding was that this would be 'new and additional' in addition to existing aid funding. Sadly, the reality has fallen short of the achievement of these targets. According to the Care International Report of 2022:

> Rich countries have admitted that they missed this target, but as we document in this research, they also failed to ensure that climate finance was 'new and additional' to their support for development. In fact, most of the public climate finance reported by rich countries is taken directly from development aid budgets. This means less support for health, education, women's rights, poverty alleviation, and progress towards the achievement of the Sustainable Development Goals. By assessing the most up-to-date data reported to the UNFCCC, only 6 per cent of the climate finance provided from 2011 to 2018 is seen to be new and additional to rich countries' official development assistance commitments.[55]

A Carbon Brief report indicates that in particular the USA, Australia and Canada had actually reduced funding, but the UK was also falling well short of its commitments to meet the target.[56] While COP28 achieved a remarkable fund for Loss

[52] 37 ILM 22 (1998); 2303 UNTS 148.

[53] TIAS No 16-1104.

[54] For the latest revelations see O Milman, 'Revealed: Exxon Made "Breathtakingly" Accurate Climate Predictions in 1970s and 80s' *The Guardian* (12 January 2023), www.theguardian.com/business/2023/jan/12/exxon-climate-change-global-warming-research, accessed 3 April 2024.

[55] A Hattle and others, *That's not New Money: Assessing how much Public Climate Finance has been 'New and Additional' to Support Development* (Care International Denmark, 2022).

[56] Carbon Brief Staff, 'Analysis: US Falling $32bn Short on "Fair Share" of $100bn Climate-Finance Goal' (*Carbon Brief*, 7 November 2022), www.carbonbrief.org/analysis-us-falling-32bn-short-on-fair-share-of-100bn-climate-finance-goal/, accessed 3 April 2024.

and Damage caused by climate change, the $700 million pledged so far is considered unrealistic in comparison with estimates of over $500 billion required.[57] In the meantime, global emissions continue to grow with catastrophic effects in all countries, but disproportionately in the South as witnessed by devastating floods in Pakistan in 2022.[58] Further disasters await, after 2023 proved to be the hottest year in history up to that point, and close to the 1.5C increase in global temperature limit envisaged under the Paris Convention.[59]

D. HIV/AIDS and Covid-19

SDG 3 seeks to 'Ensure healthy lives and promote well-being for all at all ages'. In similar fashion to climate change, HIV/AIDS, SARS and Covid-19 are aspects of globalisation of disease which impact more harshly on the impoverished populations especially in the South.[60] During the HIV/AIDS pandemic the impoverished suffered additionally because of substantial reductions in health and social services imposed by structural adjustment programmes of the International Financial Institutions in the preceding years.[61] Global pandemics have led to a realisation of the need for global solutions and some concern for social justice. At the same time, any desire to assist the South has been undermined by attitudes that ensure that health assistance for the South, while being significant, amounts to crumbs from the table. This has been the story of both the HIV/AIDS and Covid-19 pandemics.

Worldwide protests at the inadequacy of health provision in the Global South and especially unconscionably high costs charged by pharmaceutical corporations under intellectual property rights protection highlighted the links between disease and impoverishment.[62] This led to two very different responses each being transformative of global governance mechanisms. Urged by participants at two African conferences and Kofi Annan, then UN Secretary General, the G8 decided at its 2001 Genoa Meeting to establish the Global Fund to Fight Aids, Tuberculosis and Malaria.[63] The Fund, a Swiss law Foundation, is a co-operative

[57] Lukas Becker, 'COP28 – Results, Key Findings and Summary' (DFGE – Institute for Energy, Ecology and Economy, 18 December 2023), dfge.de/cop28-results-key-findings-and-summary/, accessed 3 April 2024.

[58] F Otto and others, 'Climate change likely increased extreme monsoon rainfall, flooding highly vulnerable communities in Pakistan' (2023) *World Weather Attribution*, www.worldweatherattribution.org/wp-content/uploads/Pakistan-floods-scientific-report.pdf.

[59] 'Copernicus: 2023 Is the Hottest Year on Record, with Global Temperatures Close to the 1.5°C Limit' (Copernicus), climate.copernicus.eu/copernicus-2023-hottest-year-record, accessed 3 April 2024.

[60] P Antràs, SJ Redding and E Rossi-Hansberg, 'Globalisation and Pandemics: Surprising Interactions' (2020) *Centrepiece – the Magazine for Economic Performance* 591.

[61] Ingram (n 25).

[62] M Kamal-Yanni, 'Should Covid-19 Vaccines and Drugs Be Not for Profit?' (2022) *British Medical Journal* 376: o755.

[63] 'Home' (The Global Fund to Fight AIDS, Tuberculosis and Malaria), www.theglobalfund.org/en/, accessed 3 April 2024.

network of states, global organisations, non-governmental organisations, private foundations and corporations. By 2022, it had invested $51.8 billion for the three diseases.[64] In 2020 it also took on responsibility for Covid-19 and has invested $4.4 billion.[65] These significant funds are an illustration of North and South being in it together. However, this humanitarian response cloaks some problematic phenomena. The Fund constitutes a new mode of networked global governance reflecting the ideas of 'global and multi-stakeholder partnerships' as envisaged by SDG 17. A network of donating public and private agencies interacts with a similar network of receiving agencies bypassing traditional mechanisms of state governance. Thus, each receiving country has to set up a Country Coordinating Mechanism (CCM), which is responsible for ensuring effective governance of the aid through complex auditing and reporting mechanisms.[66] Ultimately, the notion of country ownership is undermined through a Foucaultian embrace involving systems of intimate control where effective power resides in the globally powerful.

The US Bush administration separately provided apparently magnanimous aid for the HIV pandemic amounting to $15 billion over five years under the President's Emergency Plan for Aids Relief (PEPFAR).[67] Like the Global Fund it worked through a network of preferred non-governmental organisations (NGOs) in the countries it supported. However, the Fund came with heavy imperial strings as only those agencies which prohibited condom use and promoted AB or 'Abstinence' and 'Be Faithful' were supported. Aid involved new forms of control over sexuality of those being 'assisted'. Fundamentalist US-based evangelical Christian agencies became prominent in the administration of the aid with consequences for power relationships in the societies concerned.[68]

An even greater problem is that the 'we are all in it together' rhetoric is not matched by performance in dealing with pandemics. This came into stark prominence in the response to Covid-19. The existence of the Global Fund and the provision at cost price of the University of Oxford developed Astra-Zeneca vaccine opened up the tantalising possibility that for once a global pandemic would be resolved by a truly equitable global solution. Unfortunately, the fulfilment was much less than the promise. Whereas governments contributed substantial costs towards vaccine development, with the exception of Astra-Zeneca, the pharmaceutical giants insisted on maximum profits and intellectual property protection

[64] 'A Year in Review: 2022' (The Global Fund to Fight AIDS, Tuberculosis and Malaria), www.theglobalfund.org/en/stories/2022/2022-12-19-a-year-in-review-2022> accessed 3 April 2024.

[65] ibid.

[66] M Twesiime-Kirya and S Sekalala, 'Countering Corruption to Promote Social Justice in the Global Fund to Fight AIDS, Tuberculosis and Malaria: The Case of Uganda' in Adelman and Paliwala, *Beyond Law and Development* (n 5) 240.

[67] 'The United States President's Emergency Plan for AIDS Relief – United States Department of State' (United States Department of State, 20 February 2019), www.state.gov/pepfar/, accessed 3 April 2024.

[68] JS Santelli, I Speizer and Z Edelstein, 'Abstinence Promotion under PEPFAR: The Shifting Focus of HIV Prevention for Youth' (2013) 8 *Global Public Health* 1.

resulting in making egregious billions in profit.[69] The corporations, supported by Northern countries, proved reluctant to waive intellectual property rights to enable production of vaccines and other medicines in the South. A limited waiver under the TRIPS Agreement was only agreed in June 2022.[70] Furthermore, Global North countries bought up huge stocks of vaccines for their own populations, depriving developing countries. Consequently, while over 60 per cent of Northern populations have been vaccinated at least once and often on multiple occasions, only 20 per cent of the Global South populations have received the vaccine.[71] Just as with the climate crisis, North–South cooperation in global health is readily acknowledged in rhetoric, but ultimately limited to crumbs from the table.

V. South–South Cooperation (SSC)

As an alternative to domination by the Global North, South countries have long recognised the necessity for cooperation, but have consistently fallen short. In recent years, the rise of the so-called BRICS (Brazil, Russia, India, China and South Africa) countries seemed to signal a potential for dramatic changes in relationships. However, while the promise is there, the reality of performance is questionable.

The Bandung Conference of 1955 was the pivotal beginning of collaboration among Global South countries.[72] It focused on respect for independence and sovereignty and a collective demand for equity from the North. This was continued by a wider group of countries of the Non-Aligned Movement which was the basis for the formation of the Group of 77.[73] It culminated in the UN Resolution on the New International Economic Order (NIEO) which called for the right to economic and political sovereignty including permanent sovereignty over natural resources; equitable terms of trade; preferential treatment in trade and development including transfer of technology; equal participation in international fora; and assistance for development without political interference.[74] The NIEO led to the formation of the UN Centre on Trade and Development (UNCTAD) and the UN Centre on Transnational Corporations (UNCTC). However, the Global North, especially the USA, resisted the NIEO and ultimately defeated it through

[69] Pfizer received revenues of $36 billion from its Covid-19 vaccine in 2021; Pfizer and Moderna are expected to make $100 billion from vaccines in 2022.

[70] P Ranjan and P Gour, 'The TRIPS Waiver Decision at the World Trade Organization: Too Little Too Late!' (2022) *Asian Journal of International Law* 1; J Love, 'The June 17, 2022 WTO Ministerial Decision on the TRIPS Agreement' (Knowledge Ecology International, 17 June 2022), www.keionline.org/37830, accessed 3 April 2024.

[71] Kamal-Yanni (n 62).

[72] See generally L Eslava, M Fakhri and V Nesiah, *Bandung, Global History and International Law* (Cambridge University Press, 2017).

[73] Faundez (n 19).

[74] UN Resolution (n 32).

the global spread of Reaganomics.[75] The decline of Soviet power meant that Washington Consensus became the only game in town. It promoted a globalised free market ideology largely serving Northern and global corporate interests enforced by multilateral agencies such as the WTO and the International Financial Institutions. UNCTAD which had been a focus for struggles against unfair trade terms and for an international intellectual property regime favourable to Global South needs, decided at its Cartagena conference that the best vehicles for technology transfer were the neoliberal intellectual property regimes favoured by the North and promoted in the World Intellectual Property Organization and the General Agreement on Tariffs and Trade (GATT).[76] The Doha Round of negotiations adopted the Doha Development Agenda which aimed to:

> ensure that developing countries, and especially the least-developed among them, secure a share in the growth of world trade commensurate with the needs of their economic development. In this context, enhanced market access, balanced rules, and well targeted, sustainably financed technical assistance and capacity-building programmes have important roles to play.[77]

This and other attempts to revive the spirit of the NIEO have not had any success. The rich countries have fiercely resisted dilution of their subsidy systems, especially for agriculture. The newly emerging economies such as Brazil, India and China have dual purposes. On the one hand, they are interested in combating the rich country subsidy systems, yet at the same time they have developed the need to protect their own growing subsidy systems. In the circumstances, the poorest countries have seen the protection of their own limited interests in systems that give preferential access for their products into the rich countries.[78] Bilateral treaties between individual or collective Northern entities with individual South countries have continued to prevent effective collective global equity.[79]

Recently, there has been greater attention paid to South–South cooperation. This results from globalisation involving shifts in production with South countries including China, India, Brazil, South Africa and South East Asian countries becoming strong players. There is a consequent decline in the economic and political power of the North with the hegemony of the USA challenged by Russia and China in particular. In an optimistic scenario, the emerging Global South countries could promote non-imperialist South–South cooperation. More plausibly, the reduced hegemonic power of the North could operate to create greater independence for Southern non-aligned nations. A bleaker possibility is that the new power distribution merely results in more distributed substitute imperialisms with little benefit for the majority of the Global South.

[75] K Gray and BK Gills, 'South–South Cooperation and the Rise of the Global South' (2016) 37 *Third World Quarterly* 557.

[76] ibid 558.

[77] 'WTO' (The Doha Round), www.wto.org/english/tratop_e/dda_e/dda_e.htm, accessed 3 April 2024.

[78] Hopewell (n 23).

[79] Faundez (n 19).

A significant development in the reorganisation of global power has been the rise of cooperation among the BRICS countries (Brazil, Russia, India, China and South Africa). The 2023 BRICS summit agreed to expand to six more countries in 2024 including Argentina, Egypt, Ethiopia, Iran, Saudi Arabia and the United Arab Emirates as an attempt to move towards an alternative global economic order.[80] The BRICS countries are symbolised by the New Development Bank and the Contingent Reserve Fund.[81] Non-traditional currencies, especially Chinese and Russian currencies, are being used to bypass the dominant US$.[82] There has been strong growth in aid and investment especially from China but to a lesser extent from India, Brazil and South Africa to other Global South countries.[83] The BRICS countries have also pressurised for stronger representation on global institutions including permanent membership of the Security Council and the G20.[84]

Do these developments really represent the dawn of an optimistic new era for most of the Global South? The BRICS do not operate with a uniform position in global fora and divisions have emerged on the appointments to both the IMF and World Bank directorships with the result that candidates preferred by the USA have continued to be appointed.[85] On the one hand, the BRICS New Development Bank (NDB) and the Contingent Reserve Arrangement (CRA) each with a capital of $100 billion represent steps in the right direction and were a consequence of dissatisfaction with the Bretton Woods Institutions. Until recently all projects, worth over $8 billion, have been in the BRICS countries. Membership of the Bank was extended to Bangladesh, the United Arab Emirates and Uruguay in 2021. The Bank's objectives indicate that lending will be focused on socially, economically and environmentally sustainable projects, in principle promoting the SDGs. The Bank has entered into agreements with various Southern development banks and financial institutions including the Chinese Asian Infrastructure Investment Bank, the Asian Development Bank and the World Bank. The CRA is an alternative to the IMF-based funding facility with the potential to 'replace the IMF as the provider of resources for BRICS members and other poor societies when there are balance of payments difficulties'.[86]

The seemingly positive infusion of real Global South engagement into development banking and finance is not unproblematic. In an extensive study, Costa Vasquez and others suggest that while the Bank has prioritised environmentally

[80] Wikipedia, 'BRICS', en.wikipedia.org/wiki/BRICS.

[81] H Campbell, 'BRICS Bank Challenges the Exorbitant Privilege of the US Dollar' *Pambazuka News* (24 July 2014), www.pambazuka.org/global-south/brics-bank-challenges-exorbitant-privilege-us-dollar, accessed 3 April 2024.

[82] S Arslanalp, B Eichengreen and C Simpson-Bell, 'The Stealth Erosion of Dollar Dominance: Active Diversifiers and the Rise of Nontraditional Reserve Currencies' (2022) IMF Working Paper WP/22/58.

[83] Gray and Gills (n 75).

[84] Gray and Gills (n 75); D Nayyar, 'BRICS, developing countries and global governance' (2016) 37 *Third World Quarterly* 575.

[85] Nayyar (ibid).

[86] Campbell (n 81).

sustainable projects such as alternative energy development, it lacks a broader concept of sustainability such as impact of projects on local communities.[87] Bond suggests that the NDB and CRA have made strenuous attempts to fit into the currently dominant global structures. The NDB uses the US$ as its lending currency, and made agreements with the existing institutional frameworks and, in Southern Africa, has promoted projects benefiting extractivist corporations. The CRA subordinates itself to the IMF by insisting that borrowing countries first apply to the IMF including its conditionalities. The new institutions become subsidiary to the previously criticised institutional furniture.[88] Of course, this is an early period for both the NDB and the CRA, and perhaps greater independence will follow growing global power shifts, but current signs are not hopeful.

BRICS countries have a significant role in Global South development with a rise in aid and investment, especially from China, which profoundly wishes to reshape global links with the Belt and Road initiative.[89] In the worldwide race for resources, especially minerals critical for electronics and sustainable energy, most less well off Global South countries are mainly of interest to Chinese or Northern investors for their natural resources.[90] A win-win solution would promote global environmental sustainability including sustainable livelihoods and just governance in the Global South.

Is BRICS aid and investment genuine South–South cooperation or is it led by national interest and even new imperialism?[91] In a study of Chinese aid and other official flows, Herchaui and others suggest that China desires strong market positions whether for extraction of natural resources or as markets for Chinese exports.[92] They find that the Chinese consider the quality of institutions and good governance irrelevant where resource extraction is the primary goal, but important for official money flows where they seek export market expansion. While Chinese and other BRIC countries' extractive investment may show consequent gross domestic product (GDP) growth, GDP rates do not take into account losses from removal of precious resources from the country and the dispossession of local people.[93] While China constitutes a special example, other BRICS countries are also motivated by self-interest. Thus South Africa has become an African investment hub. However, its investors are involved in questionable resource

[87] K Costa Vazquez, S Roychoudhury and C Borges, 'Building Infrastructure for 21st Century Sustainable Development: Lessons and Opportunities for BRICS-Led New Development Bank' (OP Jindal Global University, 2017), pure.jgu.edu.in/id/eprint/2874/, P Bond, 'BRICS banking and the debate over sub-imperialism' (2016) *Third World Quarterly* 611.

[88] Bond (ibid).

[89] Nayyar (n 84); L Cheng, 'Three Questions on China's Belt and Road Initiative' (2016) 40 *China Economic Review* 309.

[90] S Kalantzakos 'The Race for Critical Minerals in an Era of Geopolitical Realignments' (2020) 55(3) *The International Spectator* 1.

[91] Gray and Gills (n 75).

[92] T Harchaoui, R Maseland and J Watkinson, 'Carving Out an Empire? How China Strategically Uses Aid to Facilitate Chinese Business Expansion in Africa' (2021) 30 *Journal of African Economies* 183.

[93] Bond (n 87).

extraction projects, as in the Democratic Republic of Congo, and are intimately linked to global institutional extractive strategies. Brazil's role in South–South cooperation also involves self-interest of its national corporations.[94]

VI. Beyond BRICS Cooperation

Cooperation among the Global South countries leading to just sustainable development thus suffers from a great number of problems. Perhaps the most significant has been colonialism and imperialism with the histories of warfare, enslavement and economic exploitation and its easy segue into contemporary, even if currently creaking, neoliberalism. While lip service has been paid to these responsibilities by the North, there is no acceptance of a duty of reparation by the North. This is compounded by a lack of political will in Southern states, as indicated by the differences over the Doha round. Endemic corruption and undemocratic governance whether by civilian or military rulers result too readily in compliance with the demands of the globally powerful, especially global corporations. While recent global economic and political power shifts have led to significant advances in South–South relationships, the major economic relationships of South countries currently remain with the North. This is a consequence of historic Northern political and economic domination, especially through global corporate capitalism. Changes taking place are mainly the result of South links with the BRICS countries. Tariffs of most countries in South–South trade remain high. Nevertheless, there are growing possibilities of regional trade agreements such as the Bolivarian alliance for the Peoples of Our America-Peoples' Trade agreement (alBa-TCP).[95] This initiative of Chavez of Venezuela and Castro of Cuba in 2004, aimed as an alternative to the non-completed Free Trade Area of the Americas, currently includes 10 Latin American and Caribbean nations. It has suffered various ups and downs including the withdrawal of Ecuador and withdrawal and re-accession of Bolivia. The Agreement has been greatly affected by global political currents. Oil-rich Venezuela, its effective funder, has been suffering an economic and political crisis.[96] Other South–South relationships are also growing, although some include BRICS countries which may be dominant influences. South–South economic cooperation agreements include Mercosur, the Andean Community, the Economic Community of West African States (ECOWAS), the East African Community, the Southern Africa Development Community, the Asia Pacific Trade Agreement and the South Asian Free Trade Area (SAFTA). However, none of these attempts at cooperation involve questioning the underlying concept of

[94] Gudynas (n 6); Gray and Gills (n 75).
[95] www.albatcp.org/en/.
[96] K Ciupa 'Shifting Tides, Regional Reverberations: A Class-Relational Analysis of the ALBA-TCP' (2022) 19 *Globalizations* 587.

development. As Gudynas insists 'SSC is more closely related to changes in power and representation in the global political arena, or to participation in flows of capital, goods and services among countries, but not to changes in the ideas of development'.[97] This type of SSC could replicate exploitative relations initiated by the colonial, imperial and post-colonial adventures.

VII. Voices of/from the South?

Nevertheless, as elaborated earlier, the Global South has continued to provide counterpoints to Northern developmentalism including the original social justice claims of Sun Yat Sen and Haile Selassie, followed by the Bandung Conference of non-aligned states, the NIEO, the Group of 77 initiatives, the WTO Doha Round, the South initiatives for compensation for mainly North-induced climate catastrophes under the COP climate initiatives, and the claims for reparation for colonial and imperial injustices such as slavery and genocidal extinction.[98] The global acceptance of the concept of Sustainable Development appears to signal a major change. This is undermined by Northern recalcitrance and insistence on economic structures which favour global corporate capitalism even, as we saw above, in the post-Washington Consensus environment. The rise of significant Global South countries, such as the BRICS, has opened up the possibilities of more even collaboration. Unfortunately, BRICS governments have tended to advance their own interests at the expense of effective collaboration in the interest of global social justice.

Instead, alternatives to developmentalism reside in new visions of relational sustainability which decolonises, de-imperialises and de-neoliberalises the imposed meanings. Radical intellectuals have a role in this process as is the case with the Organic Intellectuals Network in Africa.[99] Ideas linked to relationalism, such as Buen Vivir, Sumak Kawshay and Pacha Mama, also find a reflection in contemporary alternative critiques of Northern modernity such as that of relational feminism as well as in ancient Southern and Northern philosophies. There is a constant struggle between these ideas and their subjugation or colonisation of meaning by neoliberal modernity. The struggle by the Yasuni peoples against a devastating eco and human destructive oil exploration project, together with other indigenous struggles, assisted the electoral victory of Moreno and the 'Movement' in Ecuador. Buen Vivir and Pacha Mama were incorporated in Andean constitutions. The Moreno government promised to keep the oil in the ground in the interest of ecological sustainability of mother earth and indigenous peoples.

[97] Gudynas (n 6) 725.

[98] C Stahn, 'Reckoning with Colonial Injustice: International Law as Culprit and as Remedy?' (2020) 33 *Leiden Journal of International Law* 823.

[99] See, for example, N Maghanga and N Mwangi *Breaking the Silence on NGOs in Africa* (Daraja Press, 2023).

It asked the world community to pay for this, which the North declined. Moreno then resorted to an eco-destructive oil extraction agreement with China.[100]

Thus the effectiveness of Southern Voices is greatly dependent on Southern action which goes beyond governments. It is that dynamic popular resistance which led to the initially successful Andean constitutional incorporations and the Yasuni project, but sustaining the resistance is a matter of continuing activist struggle. Resistance and activist struggles take many forms, peaceful or violent, within or beyond the law. What forms of resistance are then appropriate? What about Islamist or white racist extremism? The decisive factor has to be whether the resistance is to support relationality or anti-humanity. There is a marked difference even in relational struggles between the attitudes of some of our greatest humanists. Thus Gandhi and Martin Luther King would not tolerate violent forms of resistance. Non-violent resistance has the underlying objective of changing the hearts and minds of the oppressors.[101] By contrast, Ambedkar and Mandela would support violence as long as its objective was to achieve justice.[102] The judgement of history suggests that it cannot be an either/or approach, but a complex interwoven dynamic. Often different forms of struggle coincide and have a cumulative effect. Thus in South Africa, the Umkhonto wa Sizwe liberation army was supported by Mandela but coincided with a largely peaceful South African and global anti-apartheid movement. State-based struggles for social, environmental and climate justice have both strengths and weaknesses. Calls by states for compensation from the North to the South for climate and environmental depredations and colonial wrongs involve an element of Global South unity. Yet, the rulers of these states are involved in perpetuating their own interests at the expense of South solidarity. States predate on their own peoples in unholy alliance with neoliberal agencies, as is the case with African land grabs,[103] obeisance to neoliberalism[104] and anti-indigenous destruction in Amazonia.[105] Movements against these injustices are not intentional political acts but often the oppressed peoples' action 'to survive and improve a dignified life'.[106] This has been the case for the Operation Dead Towns Movement in West Africa, the Bolivian Water and Gas Wars and the Soweto Water Wars, and many workers'

[100] Gudynas (n 6).

[101] M Gandhi, *Non-violent Resistance (Satyagraha)* (Dover, 2001); ML King Jr , 'Letter from Birmingham Jail' (1963), www.africa.upenn.edu/Articles_Gen/Letter_Birmingham.html.

[102] For Ambedkar see W Kuber, *Builders of Modern India: Dr B R Ambedkar* (Gov't of India, 2007); N Mandela, 'Nelson Mandela International Day' (20 April 1964), www.un.org./en/events/mandeladay/court_statement_1964.shtml, accessed 3 April 2024.

[103] J-C Ashukem, 'The SDGs and the Bio-economy: Fostering Land-grabbing in Africa' (2020) 47 *Review of African Political Economy* 275.

[104] In 1999, Dr Arigbede of the Nigerian Poverty Eradication Forum noted: 'We are on a mission to rescue the president [Obasanjo] who has been hijacked by the IMF and World Bank. This country belongs to Nigerians'. As cited by V Prashad, *The Poorer Nations: A Possible History of the Global South* (Verso, 2014) 234.

[105] M Kröger, Extractivisms, *Existences and Extinctions: Monoculture Plantations and Amazon Deforestation* (Taylor & Francis, 2022).

[106] Prashad (n 104) 273–74.

actions against oppression.[107] It is then appropriate that however fitful, there is an important role for solidarity alliances among protesting peoples South and North. Thus, Zapatista Marcos said of the Intergalactic (or Intercontinental) Encounter Against Neoliberalism and for Humanity that 'All the rebels around the world started it'.[108] The World Social Forum (WSF) involved the coming together of a wide range of movements, but inevitably faced contradictions of becoming dominated by NGOs and potential cooption by the very global financial institutions they opposed.[109]

The issue is not development, but the righting of injustices to Global South peoples and the earth. The North in the past and present remains unwilling to truly cooperate to right injustices except as trickle-down. The growing strength of Southern states such as the BRICS has potential for greater South–South cooperation, and pressure on the North, but this is undermined by self-interested politics. Southern states' resistance against injustices is undermined by collaboration with North-dominated neoliberalism, leading to oppression of their peoples and environment.

Nevertheless, we cannot end here! I write at a time when the world and all things within it including peoples are facing the greatest danger in history with thoughtless wars such as in Palestine, and climatic and environmental destruction coinciding with the rise of neo-fascism. At a time when solidarity based on relationality ought to be our focus, we are subsumed by cruel destructive wars and perversion of fitful climate and environment and even Covid-19 negotiations into instruments for cold warfare. And yet, global survival and flourishing is more dependent on cooperation than at any time in history. The bases for such cooperation are there. The post World War II settlement established an international rule of law system which provided for cooperation between sovereign states, rules against warfare, regimes for refugees and stateless persons, financial cooperation and international aid. The limitation of this regime was its power imbalances, emphasis on state sovereignty and individualism or rights discourse. An insidious colonisation of meaning has marred these unique achievements and disempowered Southern peoples. The notion of developmental modernity has been exposed as 'myth' by Fitzpatrick.[110] The potential of a Marshall plan for the Global South ended up instead with anodyne approaches to development and odes to neoliberalism which exacerbated existing injustices. The notion of sustainable development represents some progress. Yet, the UN's Sustainable Development Goals Report for 2023 confirms the dismal record of under and non-achievement of the goals.[111]

[107] ibid.

[108] EZLN (Zapatista Army of National Liberation): 'Closing Words of the EZLN at the Intercontinental Encounter: 2nd Declaration of La Realidad' (1997) Spain, library.uniteddiversity.coop/More_Books_and_Reports/Zapatista_2nd_Declaration_LaRealidad.pdf.

[109] Prashad (n 104) 246–47.

[110] P Fitzpatrick, *The Mythology of Modern Law* (Routledge, 1992).

[111] United Nations, 'The Sustainable Development Goals Report 2023: Special Edition' (United Nations Publications, 2023).

According to the UN Secretary General, 'Unless we act now, the 2030 Agenda will become an epitaph for a world that might have been'. This adds to the desultory record on the climate crisis with the Secretary General saying 'Humanity has "opened the gates to hell" by allowing the climate crisis to worsen'.[112] And he has termed the devastation of Gaza 'an ongoing nightmare'.[113] Ideas won through resistance, including 'just' sustainable development, are undermined, colonised, imperialised and neoliberalised right from their inception. There is therefore need to anti-colonise international law towards a greater acceptance of relational values and transformation of historical injustices into just relations not only in relation to reparations but also in a comprehensive reconfiguration of areas such as migration, global pandemics, economic law, the subjects of international law and the relationship between peoples and their environment. Colonial injustices are still felt as ongoing and real by individuals, peoples and communities.[114]

Santos suggests therefore the continuing need to use 'hegemonic tools in a counter-hegemonic way'.[115] For Baxi, ideas such as sustainable development have the quality of 'magic' because they are 'dreams of a human future that is truly emancipated from exploitation drudgery and power that some people and entities exercise over most others'.[116] Our hope/dream(?) lies in a cultural revolution – one based on relationality, and one involving struggles to build global solidarity.

[112] A Guterres, 'Secretary General's Opening Remarks at the Climate Ambition Summit' (United Nations 2023), www.un.org/sg/en/content/sg/statement/2023-09-20/secretary-generals-opening-remarks-the-climate-ambition-summit.

[113] 'Humanitarian Ceasefire Only Way to End Gaza "Nightmare": Guterres' (*UN News*, 22 December 2023), news.un.org/en/story/2023/12/1145067, accessed 3 April 2024.

[114] Stahn (n 98); S Adelman and A Paliwala, 'Beyond Law and Development' in S Adelman and A Paliwala (eds), *The Limits of Law and Development* (Routledge, 2021) 15.

[115] B de S Santos, 'Public Spheres and Epistemologies of the South' (2012) 37 *Africa Development* 43.

[116] U Baxi, 'Ameliorating Human Futures through Postdevelopment?' in Adelman and Paliwala, *The Limits of Law and Development* (n 5) 38, 39.

INDEX

www.ingramcontent.com/pod-product-compliance
Ingram Content Group UK Ltd.
Pitfield, Milton Keynes, MK11 3LW, UK
UKHW020229290926
15470UKWH00001B/433